# The Encyclopedia of Career Change and Work Issues

Edited by
## Lawrence K. Jones

Consulting Editors

Consuelo Arbona

Ellen Galinsky

Norman C. Gysbers

Douglas T. Hall

L. Sunny Hansen

Edwin L. Herr

Sylvia Ann Hewlett

Frederick T. L. Leong

Julianne M. Malveaux

Rafael Moure-Eraso

Nancy R. Russell

Kenneth Shearer

Thomas P. Slavens

Howard E. A. Tinsley

Oryx Press
1992

The rare Arabian Oryx is believed to have inspired the myth of the unicorn. This desert antelope became virtually extinct in the early 1960s. At that time several groups of international conservationists arranged to have 9 animals sent to the Phoenix Zoo to be the nucleus of a captive breeding herd. Today the Oryx population is nearly 800, and over 400 have been returned to reserves in the Middle East.

Copyright © 1992 by The Oryx Press
4041 North Central at Indian School Road
Phoenix, Arizona 85012-3397
"Ethical Dilemmas" © 1992 by Robert C. Solomon
"Sexual Harassment" © 1992 by Freada Klein

Published simultaneously in Canada

Printed and Bound in the United States of America

∞ The paper used in this publication meets the minimum requirements of American National Standard for Information Science—Permanence of Paper for Printed Library Materials, ANSI Z39.48, 1984.

**Library of Congress Cataloging-in-Publication Data**
The encyclopedia of career change and work issues / edited by Lawrence K.
   Jones.
      p. cm.
   Includes bibliographical references and index.
   ISBN 0-89774-610-4
   1. Vocational guidance—Encyclopedias.   2. Career changes–
–Encyclopedias.   3. Labor—Encyclopedias.   I. Jones, Lawrence K.
HF5381.E516   1992
650.1—dc20                                        91-33913
                                                    CIP

*To my parents,*
*Stanley Alvin Jones*
*Irene Galyen Jones*
*Juliette Laubinger Wehr*

# Contents

# Contents

# Acknowledgments

Many individuals contributed to the success of this book. Foremost among them were the contributors. They were generous in their time and effort, despite many other competing demands for their knowledge and expertise. They did so primarily because of their commitment to help others. It was inspiring to me to meet so many individuals who are working to improve the safety and success of people in their home and work lives.

This was also true for the consulting editors. In addition, they saw the potential for this book at the outset and were willing to commit their reputations and time to its success. Their support and advice over the length of the project was a great help.

It has been a pleasure working with The Oryx Press. It was Art Stickney, Director of Editorial Development, who saw the potential for the *Encyclopedia*, and John Wagner, my editor, who has seen it through—in a personable, professional manner.

Others have helped in special ways. Raymond L. Corsini got me off to a strong start by sharing with me his extensive experience as an editor and an "author's guidelines" booklet from which I borrowed liberally. Don C. Locke, my "boss," provided material and moral support throughout; it was most appreciated. Susan A. West and her colleagues at the campus computing center provided friendly and expert support in converting contributors' computer disks.

Special acknowledgment must go to my wife, Jeanine Wehr Jones. She provided the spark for the idea of the *Encyclopedia*—combining her love for reference books and my interest in career development. Her training as a librarian, practical judgment, and loving support were invaluable.

# Introduction

Whether you are 16 or 60, you are challenged by the problems and issues of work. Everyone is. Choosing an occupation . . . interviewing for a job . . . preparing a resume . . . coping with job insecurity . . . preparing for retirement—these are well-known problems of working life. There are many others. They may include coping with sexual harassment, genetic testing, mentoring, job sharing, or language discrimination. The question everyone is faced with is: How do I deal with these problems and issues effectively? This encyclopedia is written to help you answer this question.

*The Encyclopedia of Career Change & Work Issues* is a comprehensive source of information and practical advice on the problems and issues of work. Experts from all work-related fields were identified to serve as consulting editors, and they reviewed the topics to be included for completeness. With their help, article contributors who are experts in their respective fields were identified—151 in all; most are nationally known. Contributors were asked to provide up-to-date, objective, and practical information on their topic and to offer practical advice to the reader in language understandable to the general public. In the 159 articles included in the *Encyclopedia*, the contributors (a) present and discuss the most important facts and ideas about the topic, (b) offer practical suggestions for how this information can be used, and (c) recommend recent, well-written books that provide further information and instruction.

While the *Encyclopedia* is primarily written for the general public, it will also be helpful to professionals in work-related fields, such as career counseling, human resource management, law, career education, college career planning and placement, and industrial hygiene. Each article provides a current, objective synopsis of a problem area and gives the reader a list of the best sources for learning more about the topic. Many will find sharing the contents of articles with their clients to be helpful. The *Encyclopedia* will be especially helpful to those who want to learn about a problem or issue that is not closely connected to their area of expertise. The *Encyclopedia* is unique in bringing together in one volume the informed expertise of authorities in all work-related fields.

## TIPS ON USING THE *ENCYCLOPEDIA*

### Finding a Topic

The articles are listed in alphabetical order. Following this introduction are several aids to assist you in finding articles. The "Guide to Related Topics" groups articles together according to general topics and the "Alphabetical List of Articles" provides a complete listing of article titles and contributor names. If you cannot find what you are looking for in these listings, be sure to consult the index at the back of the book.

### Reading Articles on Related Topics

Most of the articles contain cross-references to other, related articles in the *Encyclopedia*, e.g., " (See **Mentoring**)." To be well informed, it is recommended that you read these suggested articles as well. All of the articles end with a *See also* section where related articles are noted. These articles will frequently provide additional useful information.

### Using the Bibliography

Each article concludes with a bibliography that contains two types of references: (a) publications that the contributor has mentioned in the article, and (b) additional ones that the contributor wants to recommend to the reader. *The contributors have written brief descriptions for those publications that they especially recommend to readers.* These are the ones that you will want to read to gain a more comprehensive and in-depth understanding of the topic.

### Getting Further Help

The editors and contributors have made every effort to provide information that is accurate and advice that is consistent with sound professional practice. However, the *Encyclopedia* is not intended to subsitute for the advice or other help offered by individuals professionally trained for this purpose. Solving a problem of work may well require the assistance of a professional, such as a trained career counselor, lawyer, physician, psychotherapist, or psychiatrist. Even if not required, these individuals can often provide invaluable help toward a satisfactory solution. You are encouraged to seek out their help.

## A FINAL WORD

The articles in the *Encyclopedia* offer you power and hope. Information is power, and these articles inform. It is not an exaggeration to say that the knowledge you will learn in the *Encyclopedia* has helped millions live more satisfying lives. It can help you as well.

*L. K. J.*

# Consulting Editor Profiles

**Consuelo Arbona** received her Ph.D. in Counseling Psychology from the University of Wisconsin-Madison in 1986. Currently she is an assistant professor of Counseling Psychology in the Educational Psychology Department, University of Houston. She specializes in cross-cultural psychology and career counseling. Her research interests include the identification of variables that predict academic achievement among minority students, the distribution of Hispanics in the workforce, and the role of acculturation in personality development.

**Ellen Galinsky** is co-president of the Families and Work Institute, a national clearinghouse on work and family life devoted to helping employees balance their job and family responsibilities. She is currently president of the National Association for the Education of Young Children and formerly a faculty member of Bank Street College of Education. She has published widely, recently coauthoring *The Preschool Years*. She has appeared extensively on television, including "The Today Show" and the "MacNeil/Lehrer News Hour."

**Norman C. Gysbers**, Ph.D., is professor of Educational and Counseling Psychology at the University of Missouri-Columbia. He was editor of the Vocational Guidance Quarterly and is currently editor of the *Journal of Career Development*. He has served as president of the National Career Development Association and the American Personnel and Guidance Association. He has served as director of numerous national and state projects on career development and counseling. He is author of 42 journal articles, 17 chapters, 12 monographs, and 6 books.

**Douglas T. Hall**, Ph.D., is professor of Organizational Behavior in the School of Management at Boston University. He received his academic degrees from Yale and MIT and is a Fellow of the American Psychological Association and the Academy of Management. He is the author of *Careers in Organizations* and coauthor of several books, including *The Two-Career Couple* and *Career Development in Organizations*. He has served as consultant to such organizations as Sears, AT&T, GE, Monsanto, Honeywell, and the World Bank.

**L. Sunny Hansen**, Ph.D., is professor of Counseling and Student Personnel Psychology in the Educational Psychology Department, University of Minnesota. She is an APA Fellow and past president of the National Career Development Association and the American Association for Counseling and Development. In 1971 she created BORN FREE, a program to expand life options and reduce stereotyping for women and men. She has authored more than 100 books, monographs, book chapters, and articles in professional journals.

**Edwin L. Herr** is professor and head, Division of Counseling and Educational Psychology and Career Studies, Pennsylvania State University. He is author of over 200 articles and 20 books, including *Career Guidance and Counseling Through the Life-Span: Systematic Approaches*. He has served as president of the American Association for Counseling and Development, the National Vocational Guidance Association, and the Association for Counselor Education and Supervision.

**Sylvia Ann Hewlett** is visiting professor of Public Policy at Sarah Lawrence College. Born in Great Britain and educated at Cambridge, Harvard, and London universities, she received her Ph.D. in Economics in 1973. She was assistant professor of Economics at Barnard College, Columbia University from 1974 to 1981 and executive director of the Economic Policy Council in New York City from 1981 to 1986. Her published works include *The Cruel Dilemmas of Development, A Lesser Life,* and *When the Bough Breaks.*

**Frederick T. L. Leong**, Ph.D., is assistant professor of Psychology at Ohio State University. He has a double specialty in Counseling Psychology and Industrial/Organizational Psychology and serves on the editorial board of the *Career Development Quarterly* and the *Journal of Vocational Behavior.*

**Julianne Malveaux**, Ph.D., is an economist, writer, and member of the visiting faculty in the African American Studies Department, University of California, Berkeley. Her research focuses on the labor market, public policy, and their impact on minorities and women. Her academic and popular writing appears in a number of national newspapers, magazines, and journals. Her weekly commentary on socio-political issues is syndicated by King Features. She is coeditor of *Slipping Through the Cracks.*

**Rafael Moure-Eraso**, Ph.D., is a certified industrial hygienist; associate professor in the Department of Work Environment, College of Engineering, University of Lowell; and Commissioner of the Michigan Occupational Health Standard Commission. As industrial hygienist for the United Automobile Workers, International Union, he provided technical consultation services on occupational health for 3,500 workplaces in the U.S. and Canada.

**Nancy R. Russell** is a free-lance writer. She is a former manager of Information Services for the American Society for Personnel Administration (now the Society for Human Resource Management) and is accredited as a professional in Human Resources. Ms. Russell was associate editor for the 1987–90 annual editions of the *The Human Resources Yearbook.*

**Kenneth Shearer** is professor of Library and Information Science North Carolina Central University in Durham. He edited *Public Libraries* for over 10 years, and has published over 30 articles on such topics as public librarianship, the political environment of libraries, the geography of information, and library collection development. He has been active in the Public Library Association and the Library Administration and Management Association.

**Thomas P. Slavens** is professor in the School of Information and Library Studies at the University of Michigan, where he has been on the faculty since receiving his Ph.D. in 1965. He was the first recipient of the Warner G. Rice Faculty Award in the Humanities at the University of Michigan. A past president of the Association for Library and Information Science, he has published 16 books and approximately 60 articles.

**Howard E. A. Tinsley,** Ph.D., is professor of Psychology and director of the graduate training program in counseling psychology at Southern Illinois University at Carbondale. He is a Diplomate of the American Board of Vocational Experts, has served on the editorial boards of seven prominent psychology journals, and is editor elect of the *Journal of Vocational Behavior.* He has authored more than 90 articles and 13 chapters dealing with counseling, psychological measurement, work, and leisure.

# Contributor Profiles

**Thom Alcoze** currently serves as director of The Division of Native Education at Northern Arizona University. He received both his B.A. and M.S. in Biology from the University of North Texas, and his Ph.D. in zoology from Michigan State. He has authored and coauthored publications and videos focused on understanding traditional Native influences and their relevance to Science, Education, Environmental Ethics, and other disciplines.

**Norman E. Amundson** is associate professor in the Department of Counseling Psychology, University of British Columbia. He is coauthor of *The Experiences of Unemployment* and *At the Controls: Charting Your Course Through Unemployment* and has written numerous articles on unemployment and other related topics. In 1988 he received the Ontario College Counsellors' Association Award for national contribution to career counseling.

**Robert T. Angarola** is a partner with Hyman, Phelps and McNamara, P.C., a Washington, DC law firm that advises clients on legal issues concerning food and drug law. He was legal advisor to the United Nations International Narcotics Control Board (Geneva) and General Counsel in the Office of Drug Abuse Policy, The White House. He coauthored *Urine Testing in the Workplace*, published by the American Council for Drug Education.

**Consuelo Arbona,** Ph.D., is assistant professor of Counseling Psychology in the Educational Psychology Department, University of Houston. She specializes in cross-cultural psychology and career counseling. Her research interests include the identification of variables that predict academic achievement among minority students, the distribution of Hispanics in the workforce, and the role of acculturation in personality development.

**Thomas J. Armstrong** is professor in the Department of Environmental and Industrial Health, University of Michigan. He has contributed numerous scientific papers and chapters on the causes of cumulative trauma disorders and the design of work equipment.

**Susan B. Asselin** is associate professor of Vocational Special Needs Education in the Division of Vocational and Technical Education at Virginia Polytechnic Institute and State University. She is author of a transition guide for vocational educators and has published in such journals as *Career Development for Exceptional Individuals, Journal of Vocational Education Research, and Journal of Vocational Special Needs Education.* Dr. Asselin directs a transition technical assistance center and conventional special needs graduate programs.

**Arnetha F. Ball** is a Ph.D. candidate in the Language, Literacy and Culture Program, School of Education, Stanford University. Her research concentrates on oral and written linguistic behavior of minority populations. Her professional career encompasses a broad range of experiences, including classroom teaching, administrative work, diagnostic and therapeutic work in Speech Pathology/Audiology, and consultant work. She has been awarded the Spencer Dissertation-Year Award to complete her studies this year.

**William J. Banis** is director of Career Development Services at Old Dominion University, and a consultant in private practice. He is coauthor of *High Impact Resumes and Letters* and *Moving Out of Education: The Educator's Guide to Career Management and Change* and author of several articles on career issues. He is a national certified counselor and a national certified career counselor.

**Jonathan Baron** is professor of Psychology at the University of Pennsylvania, Philadelphia. He is author of many articles on the psychology of thinking and decision making, author of *Rationality and Intelligence* and *Thinking and Deciding,* and coeditor (with Rex. V. Brown) of *Teaching Decision Making to Adolescents.*

**Richard W. Beatty** is professor of Industrial Relations and Human Resources in the Institute of Management and Labor Relations, Rutgers University. Dr. Beatty has authored *Personnel Administration: An Experiential Skill-Building Approach,* which won the American Society of Personnel Administration's 1978 book award; *Performance Appraisal: Assessing Human Behavior at Work*; and *The Productivity Sourcebook.*

**Franklin Becker,** Ph.D., is professor of Facility Planning and Management and Human-Environment Relations in the Department of Design and Environmental Analysis, Cornell University. Professor Becker has written over 70 academic and professional articles, and is the author of *Housing Messages, Workspace: Creating Environments in Organizations, The Successful Office,* and *The Total Workplace: Facilities Management and the Elastic Organization.*

**William A. Borgen** is professor and head of the Department of Counseling Psychology, University of British Columbia. He has conducted research in the area of career/employment counseling for over 10 years, and is coauthor of *The Experiences of Unemployment* and *At the Controls: Charting Your Course Through Unemployment.* He is also an editor of *Methodological Approaches to the Study of Career* and author of numerous articles regarding unemployment and other related topics. In 1988 he was given the Ontario College Counsellors' Association Award for his national contribution to career counseling/education.

**Paul E. Bracke,** Ph.D., is a licensed psychologist in private practice, with offices in Palo Alto and Oakland, California, specializing in problems involving chronic stress, self-esteem, Type A behavior, and relationships. As a consultant to the Meyer Friedman Institute in San Francisco, he trains group leaders and conducts groups designed to change Type A behavior.

**Loretta J. Bradley,** Ph.D., is associate professor of Educational Psychology at Texas Tech University. She is author of *Counseling Midlife Career Changers* and *Counselor and Supervisor: Principles, Process and Practice*, which won the American Association for Counselor Education and Supervisor Best Publication Award in 1990. She is coauthor of *Community Agency Counseling* and corecipient of the 1987 American Association for Counseling and Development Research Award. Her other publications cover such topics as career assessment, career counseling with ex-offenders, hi-tech and the workforce, and moral development.

**Susan Hatcher Bradshaw** is an attorney at law and practicing in Raleigh, North Carolina. For the past seven years she has been in private practice and limits her practice to social security claims. Previously she worked as a disability specialist and examiner for the state of North Carolina and a staff attorney for the Social Security Administration's Office of Hearings and Appeals, where she wrote the decisions of the administrative law judges.

**Ed Brandt** is special sections editor of *The Baltimore Sun*. He is the author of *Fifty and Fired, When Hell Was in Session, Last Voyage of the USS Pueblo,* and *A Cultural History of the Soviet Union.*

**Michael T. Brannick** is assistant professor of Psychology at the University of South Florida. He received his Ph.D. in Industrial and Organizational Psychology from Bowling Green State University in 1986. He has written articles on personnel assessment, decision making, and psychological methodology. He also consults for the U.S. Navy on team performance measurement issues.

**Joel Brockner** is professor of Management at Columbia University's Graduate School of Business. He earned his Ph.D. in Personality/Social Psychology at Tufts University in 1977. His research interests include the roles of employee self-esteem in the workplace, "sunk cost" decision making, and the effects of job layoffs on the employees who are *not* laid off. He has published extensively, and is a regular consultant to organizations on the management of human forces in the workplace.

**Nancy H. Brown,** Ph.D., is an educator whose experience includes classroom teaching, supervision, and administration in preschool, elementary, secondary, and higher education settings. Her knowledge of child and elder care has been complemented by serving as head of a state licensing agency for child care and participating in professional associations. She is currently director of the Early Childhood Information Exchange at North Carolina State University.

**Thomas G. Burish** is professor of Psychology and Medicine and associate provost for Academic Affairs at Vanderbilt University. He has coauthored or coedited four books, including *Behavior Therapy* and *Health Psychology*, and has written numerous articles and chapters in the areas of stress and coping, behavior change, and behavioral medicine. He is the winner of Vanderbilt's Madison Sarratt Award for Excellence in Classroom Teaching.

**John J. Burke** is president of Burke/Taylor Associates, Inc., a private provider of Employee Assistance Program services that serves employers throughout the Southeast. He is a frequent speaker and instructor on employee assistance programs, a designer of national standards for the profession and a contributing editor for *Employee Testing and the Law.* Mr. Burke is a member of and has held leadership positions in numerous professional organizations.

**Rene Cailliet,** M.D., is retired chairman and professor of the Department of Rehabilitation in the University of Southern California's School of Medicine. He is the author of nine medical books on musculoskeletal pain and numerous articles on physical medicine and rehabilitation.

**Arlene Rossen Cardozo** is an international authority on women and workplace issues, who has pioneered work on the ways women sequence careers and family lives. The author of four books and numerous articles, she teaches at the University of Minnesota, lectures extensively throughout the country, and consults in both the public and private sectors. Cardozo teaches at the University of Minnesota in both the School of Mass Communication and Split Rock Arts Program.

**Norma Carr-Ruffino** is professor of Management at San Francisco State University. She is the author of *The Promotable Woman, Business Student's Guide,* and *Writing Short Business Reports,* and of numerous articles. She has served as editor of the *California Business Education Journal* and as a referee of the California State Bar Court.

**Jim Case** is assistant vice president of Employer Relations and Career Services at the American Graduate School of International Management in Glendale, Arizona. He has developed various internship programs, and served as the president of the National Society for Internships and Experimental Education. He has served as a trainer, consultant, and evaluator for many internship, community service, and cooperative education programs, and has a B.A. and M.Ed. from Johns Hopkins University.

**Donna E. Cassell** is associate director for Student Services at the University Placement Services, Virginia Polytechnic Institute and State University. Dr. Cassell also serves as an adjunct professor for the Counselor Education and College Student Affairs Graduate Program. She is a board member of the Virginia College Placement Association and is on the New Professionals' Development Committee for the Middle Atlantic Placement Association.

**James Chelius** is professor of Industrial Relations and Human Resources at Rutgers University. He is the author of several books and numerous articles on workers' compensation and occupational safety and health. He served as an economist for the National Commission on State Workmen's Compensation Laws. His current research is on the impact of the accident liability system on railroad safety.

**M. Anne Corbishley** is a graduate faculty assistant in the Counselling Psychology Program at Simon Fraser University. She has published in the areas of depression and sleep disorders and is coauthor of *Career Counseling: A Psychological Approach.* Dr. Corbishley has taught career decision making at the University of Arizona, where she has also conducted individual career counseling with undergraduate students and mid-life career changers.

**Diana I. Cordova** is a Ph.D. candidate in Social Psychology at Stanford University. She has conducted research on the related topics of prejudice, discrimination, and racism.

**Stanley H. Cramer** is professor of Counseling Psychology at the State University of New York at Buffalo. He is coauthor of *Career Guidance and Counseling Through the Lifespan: Systematic Approaches,* along with 15 other books and over 60 articles. Professor Cramer is currently a member of the editorial board of the *Career Development Quarterly.*

**William L. Cron** is professor of Marketing at the Edwin L. Cox School of Business, Southern Methodist University. He is coauthor of *Sales Management: Concepts and Cases.* Professor Cron has published numerous articles on career issues and serves on the editorial review boards of the *Journal of Marketing, Journal of the Academy of Marketing Science*, and *Journal of Personal Selling and Sales Management*.

**Faye J. Crosby** is a social psychologist. After earning her Ph.D. in 1976, she taught at Rhode Island College and Yale University. In 1988 she joined the faculty at Smith College. She has done research on gender issues and justice.

**Truman W. Cummings** is a retired Pan American Airways captain who, in 1974, pioneered a program to help people overcome their fear of flying. Since then he has held seminars in major cities in the United States and in London. He has lectured at several annual conferences of the Phobia Society of America. Captain Cummings has contributed to several books, including *Phobia* and *Handbook of Phobia Therapy*. He is coauthor of *Freedom From Fear of Flying*.

**Lucille Cupples** is business and financial manager of The Impact Group in St. Louis, Missouri. She has over 30 years experience in human resources, personnel, and financial management in the private sector, and has worked in the field of relocation for several years.

**Jilliann Daly** is currently an intern at the University Counseling Services, University of Iowa. Her graduate research at Southern Illinois University examined such areas as romantic relationships of lesbians, occupational development of lesbians and gay men, and the measurement of people's attitudes toward lesbians and gay men.

**Rene V. Dawis** is professor of Psychology and adjunct professor of Industrial Relations at the University of Minnesota. He is author or coauthor of over 100 (articles, chapters, and books, including *A Psychological Theory of Work Adjustment* with L.H. Lofquist). He was director of the Counseling Psychology Training Program (1970–85), and is currently co-director of the Vocational Assessment Clinic and co-principal investigator of the Work Adjustment Project.

**Cecilia I. Delve** was formerly the director of the Volunteer and Public Service Center at Georgetown University and is now director of student activities at Willamette University. She is coauthor and coeditor of *Community Service as Values Education* and has written numerous articles on service-learning and its relationship to citizenship and community-building. Ms. Delve is a board member of the National Society for Internships and Experiential Education.

**Carolyn J. Dobbins** has a Ph.D. in Clinical Psychology and is currently research associate in the Department of Psychology at Vanderbilt University. Her areas of interest include health psychology, applied social psychology, and the training of health professionals.

**Donna Douglass** has a varied background in business and education. Both her degrees were earned from Indiana University. She is the author of *Time Tips for Today's Busy Woman*; *Choice and Compromise: A Woman's Guide To Balancing Family and Career*; and *Manage Your Time, Manage Your Work, Manage Yourself*, which was written with her husband.

**Merrill Douglass** has been writing and speaking on time management since 1970. He earned a Ph.D. in Management and Organizational Behavior from Indiana University. He is author of the cassette tape album, *The New Time Management*, and creator of the unique *Time Management Profile*.

**Roger L. M. Dunbar** is associate professor of management at the Leonard N. Stern School of Business, New York University. His numerous articles have appeared in such journals as *Administrative Science Quarterly, Academy of Management Journal, Academy of Management Review*, and *Organization Studies*. He designs and conducts executive training programs to develop managerial skills.

**Jean R. Eagleston**, Ph.D., is a licensed psychologist in private practice in Palo Alto, California; her major areas of expertise include stress management, modification of Type A behavior, and the management of chronic pain. She has conducted research and published articles on Type A behavior, chronic stress, and social support during her affiliations with Stanford University and SRI International.

**Helen Elkiss** associate professor of Labor and Industrial Relations and Coordinator of the Chicago Labor Education Program, Institute of Labor and Industrial Relations, University of Illinois at Urbana-Champaign. She works with labor organizations to provide occupational safety and health training for their members and has written journal articles on legal issues related to job safety.

**Albert Ellis** is president of the Institute for Rational-Emotive Therapy in New York City. He has published over 600 articles, over 100 cassettes and videotapes, and over 50 books, including *Reason and Emotion in Psychotherapy, A New Guide to Rational Living, The Practice of Rational-Emotive Therapy*, and *How to Stubbornly Refuse to Make Yourself Miserable About Anything—Yes, Anything!*

The **Employee Benefit Research Institute** is a nonprofit, nonpartisan, public policy research institute in Washington, DC. EBRI's goal is to facilitate the development of sound public and private policies on retirement income, health, and other benefit programs.

**Frank W. Erwin** is president of Richardson, Bellows, Henry & Co., Inc., Washington, DC, a consulting firm specializing in personnel management, including the design and validation of selection and performance measurement systems. With the Peace Corps he has served as director, recruiting operations and deputy director of selection. He is a member of the Advisory Committe, "Principles for the Validation and Use of Personnel Selection Procedures," Division 14, American Psychological Association. He was honored by inclusion in *Who's Who in America—Who's Who in Finance and Industry*.

**Charles H. Fay**, Ph.D., is associate professor of Industrial Relations and Human Resources at Rutgers University. His research on compensation and performance management has been published in many journals. He is the coauthor of several books, including *Compensation Theory and Practice* and *The Compensation Sourcebook*. He is a certified compensation professional and teaches in the American Compensation Association Certification Program.

**Alfred G. Feliu** is an employment attorney in the New York office of the national law firm of Paul, Hastings, Janotsky, and Walker. He represents management in all aspects of labor and employment law. Mr. Feliu coedited *Resolving Employment Disputes Without Litigation* with Dr. Alan F. Westin.

**Marianne A. Ferber** is professor of Economics at the University of Illinois at Urbana-Champaign. She was director of Women's Studies from 1980 to 1983. Her research has focused on the standing of women in academia, the interface of work and family, and international comparisons in the status of women. She has published in a variety of scholarly journals and is coauthor with Francine D. Blau of *The Economics of Women and Work*, as well as author of *Women and Work, Paid and Unpaid*.

**Charles L. Fine** is presently a senior member in the law firm of O'Connor, Cavanagh, Anderson, Westover, Killingsworth & Beshears in Phoenix, Arizona. He is a former associate professor of

Law at the University of Detroit School of Law. He is the author and contributor of over 25 articles and publications on labor and personnel relations and employment law.

**Jerald R. Forster** is director of the Clinical Service and Research Center in the University of Washington's College of Education. He is also an associate professor in Educational Psychology and the director of the Dependable Strengths Project. He has authored several instruments designed to facilitate the articulation of goals and other self-descriptors. He edited two seminal special issues on Counselor Credentialing in the *Personnel and Guidance Journal* and authored several chapters and articles.

**Nadya A. Fouad** is an associate professor in Educational Psychology (Counseling) at the University of Wisconsin-Milwaukee. She received her Ph.D. from the University of Minnesota (Counseling Psychology) in 1984. Her research interests include career development of women, cross-cultural vocational assessment, and minority career development. She also has a private practice in Milwaukee specializing in vocational counseling and women's issues.

**Geralyn McClure Franklin** is assistant professor of Management at Stephen F. Austin State University. She is author or coauthor of numerous articles related to AIDS in the workplace, as well as other employment law issues.

**Randy O. Frost** is associate professor of Psychology at Smith College. He has authored over 30 journal articles on topics in clinical psychology and psychopathology. His most recent works include "The Dimensions of Perfectionism" and "Perfectionism and Evaluative Threat," both of which will appear in *Cognitive Therapy and Research*.

**Dale R. Fuqua** is professor and head of the Department of Applied Behavioral Studies, Oklahoma State University. He received his Ph.D. from Indiana University in 1980 with majors in research methodology and counseling. Dr. Fuqua was previously a faculty member and department chairperson in the Department of Counseling at the University of North Dakota.

**John J. Gabarro** is the UPS Foundation Professor of Human Resources Management at the Harvard Business School. He has authored four books, including *The Dynamics of Taking Charge*, which won the 1988 Johnson, Smith and Knisely Prize for research on leadership. He is also author of "The Development of Working Relationships" in *The Handbook of Organizational Behavior* and coauthor with John Kitter of "Managing Your Boss," which won a 1980 McKinsey Foundation Best Article Prize.

**John P. Galassi** is professor and former coordinator of the Counseling Psychology and Counseling programs at the University of North Carolina at Chapel Hill. He is a Fellow (Division of Counseling Psychology) of the American Psychological Association and the author of over 70 publications. Dr. Galassi currently serves on the editorial boards of *Computers and Human Behavior, Journal of Behavior Therapy and Experimental Psychiatry, Journal of Counseling and Development*, and the *Journal of Counseling Psychology*.

**Merna Dee Galassi** is a counselor at Seawell Elementary School in Chapel Hill, North Carolina, and a Clinical Associate Professor of Education at the University of North Carolina. She is coauthor of *Assert Yourself! How to Be Your Own Person*, and has trained psychologists in North America and Europe in assertion techniques. She has also conducted assertion workshops for mental health professionals, school teachers and administrators, business executives, and members of women's organizations.

**Lucia A. Gilbert** is professor of Educational Psychology at the University of Texas at Austin. She is author of *Men in Dual-Career Families: Current Realities and Future Prospects, Sharing It All: The Rewards and Struggles of Two-Career Families*, and numerous chapters and articles on work and family. Professor Gilbert is associate editor of *Psychology of Women Quarterly* and a member of the editorial board of the *Journal of Family Issues*.

**Brian G. Gilmartin** is associate professor of Psychology/Sociology, Northern Montana College. He is the author of *The Gilmartin Report: Inside Swinging Families, Shyness and Love, The Shy Man Syndrome*, plus more than a score of articles on topics germane primarily to shyness or human sexuality.

**Katherine A. Grant** is the developer and coordinator of the state of North Carolina's preretirement planning program, PRE-PARE. She has written a number of preretirement planning workbooks for preretirees and leaders' manuals for organizing and conducting preretirement planning workshops. She has concentrated research in this field for the last seven years. She serves on a number of boards and work groups promoting prevention of dependency in older adults as well as providing productive opportunities for them throughout the lifespan.

**Denis O. Gray** is associate professor of Psychology at North Carolina State University in Raleigh. He is coordinator of the Human Resource Development Program. He has authored several articles on job clubs, including those on experimental social innovation and client-centered job-seeking programs in the *American Journal of Community Psychology*. He is currently conducting research on industry-university cooperation for the National Science Foundation and is coeditor of *Technological Innovation: Strategies for a New Partnership*.

**Gail Hackett** is professor of Counseling Psychology in the Division of Psychology in Education at Arizona State University. She is the author of numerous journal articles on social cognitive applications to career development and gender issues in counseling. She is a Fellow of Division 17 of the American Psychological Association and vice-president of the Counseling and Human Development Division of the American Educational Research Association.

**Bernard Haldane**, social inventor, was commended by the White House in 1947 for developmental work involving transferable skills of returning military officers, and again in 1961 for recruitment of exceptional personnel. He pioneered modern college placement systems at Harvard Business School (1948), career planning at the American Management Association (1958), and outplacement at Exxon (1961). He has authored numerous career planning articles and books, and presently chairs the Board of the University of Washington's Dependable Strengths Project.

**Douglas T. Hall**, Ph.D., is professor of Organizational Behavior in the School of Management at Boston University. He received his academic degrees from Yale and MIT and is a fellow of the American Psychological Association and the Academy of Management. He is the author of *Careers in Organizations* and coauthor of several books, including *The Two-Career Couple* and *Career Development in Organizations*. He has served as consultant to such organizations as Sears, AT&T, GE, Monsanto, Honeywell, and the World Bank.

**Stephen L. Hayford** is associate professor of Management in the Babcock School of Management, Wake Forest University. He is an active labor and commercial arbitrator and mediator and a member of the National Academy of Arbitrators and the Florida Bar. Dr. Hayford has published numerous articles in the labor relations and dispute resolution literature.

**Edwin L. Herr** is distinguished professor and head, Division of Counseling and Educational Psychology and Career Studies, Pennsylvania State University. He is the author of 28 books and monographs and more than 200 articles. His most recent books include *Counseling in a Dynamic Society, Opportunities and Challenges,* and *Career Guidance and Counseling Through the Life Span: Systematic Approaches.* Professor Herr has served as president of the American Association for Counseling and Development, the National Vocational Guidance Association, and the Association for Counselor Education and Supervision. He has taught, lectured, and done research in 14 nations.

**Laura Herring**, a psychologist and relocation specialist, is president of The Impact Group in St. Louis, Missouri. Fifteen years of working with relocating families and three years of intensive research and nationwide marketing to major corporations have made her an expert in the field of relocation. She is a nationally known speaker on relocation issues, and has authored numerous articles for magazines and relocation trade journals.

**J. Scott Hinkle** is assistance professor of Counselor Education at the University of North Carolina at Greensboro. He teaches the graduate course on computer applications in counseling, and researches the impact of computer technology on professional counseling.

**Paul M. Hirsch** is Distinguished James Allen Professor of Strategy and Organization Behavior at the Kellogg Graduate School of Management, Northwestern University.

**Sandra N. Hurd** is associate professor of Law & Public Policy in the School of Management, Syracuse University. She edited *Employment Testing: Testing Resource Manual,* and serves on the editorial board and is contributing editor to *Employment Testing,* a biweekly reporter on drug, polygraph, AIDS, and genetic testing. She has presented and published extensively in the area of employment testing.

**Ira L. Janowitz** is co-director of the Spine Center of the Eastbay in Oakland, California. Mr. Janowitz has degrees in Industrial Engineering, Management, and Physical Therapy. As a consultant to employers, unions, and insurance companies, he has participated in the development of training and injury prevention programs in industry for several years. He is the author of "Prevention of Low Back Pain in Industry" in Occupational Health and Safety (National Safety Council) and several other articles on the treatment and prevention of low back pain.

**Lawrence K. Jones** earned his Ph.D. in Counseling Psychology and is professor of Counselor Education at North Carolina State University. He has researched and written extensively on career counseling and development and is a member of the Select Panel of Reviewers for the *Career Development Quarterly.* He is the author of several career guidance instruments: *Occ-U-Sort, The Career Key,* and the *Career Decision Profile.* He serves as a vocational expert with the Bureau of Hearings & Appeals, Social Security Administration.

**Hilda Kahne** is professor of Economics at Wheaton College. Her publications span the areas of aging and social welfare, flexible work structure, and changing roles of women in relation to economic development. She is author of *Reconceiving Part-time Work: New Perspectives for Older Workers and Women.* Currently she is coeditor (with Janet Giele) of *Women's Lives and Women's Work: Common Themes and Contrasts in Modernizing and Industrial Countries.*

**Carole Kanchier**, president of Questers Career Development Services and University of Alberta instructor, has 20 years career counseling/consulting experience. She is the author of nu-

merous articles on career development, and of the award-winning and best-selling *Questers—Dare to Change Your Job—and Your Life* and *Open to Change.* She also gives presentations on career transitions to business, professional, and lay groups. Ms. Kanchier chairs the Career Change and Retirement Committee, National Career Development Association.

**Jerome T. Kapes** is professor of Vocational Education and Educational Psychology at Texas A & M University, where he teaches courses in vocational guidance, measurement, and evaluation and research. He is a nationally certified career counselor and is professionally active in the American Vocational Association, the American Educational Research Association, and the American Association for Counseling and Development. He is coeditor of *A Counselor's Guide to Career Assessment Instruments* and is author or coauthor of over 60 articles, books, and monographs.

**Beverly L. Kaye** is an organization consultant with a specialty in career development. For the past 15 years, she has been designing and conducting career development programs for business and industry. She has authored *Designing Career Development Systems* and *Up Is Not the Only Way.* She is also featured in the Barr film, *Up Is Not the Only Way.* She has received national awards from ASTD and University Associates, Inc., and speaks to professional groups nationwide.

**W. Monroe Keyserling** is associate professor in the Departments Industrial & Operations Engineering and Environmental & Industrial Health, University of Michigan. He is the author of over 50 articles and book chapters on ergonomic aspects of occupational health and safety and serves on the editorial board of the *International Journal of Industrial Ergonomics.*

**Freada Klein,** Ph.D., co-founded in 1976 the first organization in the U.S. to offer comprehensive services, training, and consultation on the topic of sexual harassment to both the private and public sectors. Dr. Klein has consulted with dozens of organizations to help them develop policies, grievance procedures, and training programs; in addition, she has conducted numerous surveys to assess the prevalence and impact of sexual harassment and other forms of discrimination. She also serves as an expert witness in sexual harassment litigation.

**Richard Klimoski** is professor of Psychology and vice chair of the Psychology Department at Ohio State University. He received his Ph.D. from Purdue University in Psychology and Management. Currently his teaching and research interests revolve around the areas of organizational control systems in the form of performance appraisal, assessment centers, and performance feedback programs. He is a fellow of the Society for Industrial Organization Psychology (division of the American Psychological Association) and of the American Psychological Society. He is coauthor of *Research Methods in Human Resource Management.*

**Ronit Kopelman** is a graduate student in the Organizational Program at the Leon Recanati Graduate School of Business Administration of Tel Aviv University. Her interest lies in the area of quality of work life and her research thesis deals with the relationship between the various domains of life that view the individual from a wholistic viewpoint. At present she is also employed in an industrial psychological institute dealing with the placement of academic professionals.

**David Kotelchuck**, Ph.D., M.P.H., C.I.H., is associate professor and director of the Environmental and Occupational Health Sciences Program at the Hunter College School of Health Sciences of the City University of New York. He is co-director of the Hunter-Montefiore Health and Safety Training Program, directs the Hunter

College component of the NJ/NY Hazardous Materials Workers Health and Safety Training Program, and is a faculty member in the NIOSH Educational Resource Center.

**Kathy E. Kram** is associate professor in the Department of Organizational Behavior, Boston University School of Management. She holds a B.S. and M.S. from the M.I.T. Sloan School of Management, and a Ph.D. from Yale University. She teaches courses in human behavior in organizations, leadership and group dynamics, self-assessment and careers, and organization development and change. She also consults with private and public sector organizations on a variety of human resource management concerns.

**Teresa D. LaFromboise**, a descendent of the Miami tribe, is associate professor of education at the University of Wisconsin. Her work as a counseling psychologist focuses on coping and stress-related problems of American Indians and other ethnic minorities. She teaches seminars on cross-cultural counseling, career and personal counseling in culturally diverse settings, and American Indian mental health. She is the author of *Circles of Women: Skills Training for American Indian Professionalization*, and many articles.

**Courtland C. Lee** is associate professor and director of counselor education at the University of Virginia. His research specializations include multicultural counseling and adolescent development. He has written numerous articles and book chapters on counseling across cultures and adolescent career development. He is editor of *Multicultural Issues in Counseling: New Approaches to Diversity* and former editor of the *Journal of Multicultural Counseling and Development*.

**Patricia Lee** is author of *The Complete Guide to Job Sharing*, as well as various articles, employee handbooks, market research studies, and training manuals. She divides her time between her home in Maine and her apartment in New York City, where she provides consulting services in flexible work-time programs as well as personal computer applications. She is a member of the Author's Guild.

**Michael P. Leiter** is professor and head of the Psychology Department, Acadia University. He has conducted research on career burnout, and on professional efficacy in human service settings in the U.S. and Canada. He has worked with colleagues at Dalhousie University to develop the region's first Ph.D. program in clinical psychology. He works as a consultant with people to enhance human services agencies' support for effective professional functioning.

**Frederick T. L. Leong**, Ph.D., is assistant professor of Psychology at Ohio State University. He has a double specialty in Counseling Psychology and Industrial/Organizational Psychology from the University of Maryland. He currently serves on the editorial board of the *Career Development Quarterly* and the *Journal of Vocational Behavior*.

**Tobi Mae Lippin** is a free-lance writer and trainer living in Durham, North Carolina. She is the former director of the North Carolina Occupational Safety and Health Project and has written extensively on workplace and occupational health issues.

**John J. Liptak** is coordinator of Career Development at Berea College. He is author of the *Career Exploration Inventory*, an instrument which measures developmental work and leisure interests. Dr. Liptak has written several journal articles on the interaction of work and leisure.

**Patricia W. Lunneborg** received her Ph.D. in Psychology from the University of Texas in Austin in 1962. She taught from 1967 to 1988 at the University of Washington, during which time she published over 100 professional publications, principally concerning women's career development. Most recently, she wrote *Women Police Officers: Current Career Profile* and *Women Changing Work*, concerning women in nontraditional occupations.

**Lisa A. Mainiero** is associate professor of Management at Fairfield University. She is the author of *Office Romance: Love, Power, and Sex in the Workplace*, and coauthor of *Developing Managerial Skills: Readings, Exercises and Cases in Organizational Behavior*. She has authored numerous journal articles on women in management, power and politics, and the career issues of technical professionals. Dr. Mainiero received her Ph.D. from Yale University in 1983.

**Betty Lou Marple** is assistant dean and director of special programs, including professional development, at the Harvard University Graduate School of Design. She has held administrative positions in numerous colleges and universities, including 10 years as director of continuing education at Wellesley College. Dr. Marple is author of *Zingers! A New Approach to Getting a Job, Changing Careers, Getting Ahead*, and of articles on many topics, including continuing education and adult learners.

**Marjorie M. Mastie** is supervisor of assessment services at Washtenaw Intermediate School District in Ann Arbor, Michigan. She is author or coauthor of numerous chapters and journal articles and of five books, including *A Counselor's Guide to Career Assessment Instruments*. She presents training workshops in career assessment nationwide. She has taught at the University of Michigan, Eastern Michigan University, and in public schools, and directed the assessment of career and occupational development at the National Assessment of Educational Progress.

**Donald Mayall** is institutional research analyst at Ohlone College. He is author of *Careers in Banking and Finance*, coauthor of *The Temporary Help Supply Service and the Temporary Labor Market*, and has written numerous research reports and articles on career information and the labor market. He was co-founder of EUREKA, the California Career Information System, and co-developer of several computer-based occupational search strategies, including SKILLS and RAVE.

**Christopher J. McCullough** is director of the Anxiety and Phobia Recovery Center in Cary, North Carolina. He is coauthor of *Managing Your Anxiety* and author of *Outgrowing Agoraphobia* and *Always At Ease*. Dr. McCullough has appeared widely in the media to educate the public about anxiety disorders: *Prevention Magazine*, *USA Today*, Oprah Winfrey's show, CNN, and hundreds of radio shows. He is currently the host of two radio talk shows in Raleigh, North Carolina, which deal with psychological issues.

**James M. Melius**, M.D., is director of the Division of Occupational Health and Environmental Epidemiology for the New York State Department of Health, and professor of Environmental Health and Toxicology, School of Public Health, State University of New York at Albany. He previously worked for the National Institute for Occupational Safety and Health. His current research involves occupational and environmental epidemiology.

**Philip H. Mirvis**, an organizational psychologist, is an independent researcher and consultant in Sandy Spring, Maryland. He is the author of four books, including *The Cynical Americans* (with Donald Kanter), and many articles on working people's attitudes and values in the changing American economy and society. He has also created a "map" and guidebook to *Work in the 20th Century*. His consulting work is concerned with the human aspects of mergers and acquisitions, technological change, and organizational development.

**Timothy H. Monk** is associate professor of Psychiatry at the University of Pittsburgh School of Medicine and director of their Human Chronobiology Research Program. Research interests include how the biological clock is affected by aging, depression, and abnormal routines. In addition to more than 80 articles and chapters, Dr. Monk has published two books on shift work. Since 1983 he has served on the Scientific Committee on Shiftwork of the International Commission on Occupational Health.

**Bruce A. Montville** is founder and president of the Hampton, New Hampshire, firm EXETER 2100, a contingency search firm specializing in computer professionals. He is vice president of a placement network, National Personnel Associates, and chairman of the contingency search group of the Employment Management Association. Mr. Montville is a founding sponsor of the Professional Employment Research Council. He holds a B.A. in Sociology from the University of New Hampshire and began his recruiting career in Boston in 1961.

**Jody L. Newman** is assistant professor and director of the Counseling Psychology Program at the University of Oklahoma. She received her Ph.D. in Counseling Psychology in 1985 from the University of North Dakota. Dr. Newman has previously served on the faculties at Iowa State University and Western Michigan University.

**Wendi M. Norris** is a graduate student in the University of North Carolina School of Social Work. Her specialization focus is on families and children. Ms. Norris is a member of the National Association of Social Workers.

**Ann M. Orzek,** Ph.D., is a licensed psychologist and coordinator of training at the Counseling and Testing Center, Southwest Missouri State University. She has numerous publications in such journals as *Women and Therapy, Journal of Counseling and Development,* and *Journal of College Student Development.* Dr. Orzek has presented regionally and nationally in the areas of women's issues, alternative lifestyles, victimization, and counselor development.

**Jonathan W. Palmer** is director of corporate relations, Peter F. Drucker Graduate Management Center, Claremont Graduate School. He directed career development activities at Claremont McKenna College and the Fletcher School of Law and Diplomacy at Tufts University, and directed the Career Resources Center at Harvard Business School. He is editor of *How to Find a Job in Southern California.*

**Jeanne Boland Patterson** is professor and coordinator of the Rehabilitation Counseling Program in the Department of Counseling and Human Development Services, University of Georgia. She is author of numerous articles on rehabilitation counseling, president of the National Council on Rehabilitation Education, chair of the Commission on Standards and Accreditation of the Council on Rehabilitation Education, and past-chair of the Commission on Rehabilitation Counselor Certification.

**Teresa Patty** began her career at Indiana University where she assisted in the implementation of several nationally recognized studies on special-needs children. She also played a critical role in developing a comprehensive Self-Employment Training System, which has guided the start-up of nearly 1,000 successful small businesses. As president of All Things Considered, Inc., a Tempe, Arizona, consulting firm, Ms. Patty regularly leads seminars and workshops on small business development and directs Self-Employment Training programs across North America.

**Patricia L. Pearce,** M.D., is a practicing, board-certified psychiatrist in Raleigh, North Carolina, with specialized instruction in cognitive therapy through the Rational Behavior Training Center at the University of Kentucky. Past clinical associations have included the VA Hospital in Lexington, Kentucky, and Kaiser Permanente in Raleigh, North Carolina. She is currently in the private practice of general adult psychiatry, with clinical interests that include cognitive and insight-oriented therapies in treatment of depressive and anxiety disorders.

**Roger R. Pearman** is president of the Association for Psychological Type. He is a career counselor in Winston-Salem, North Carolina, and a professional affiliate with the Center for Creative Leadership. He teaches as an adjunct faculty member for Wake Forest University and High Point College in the behavioral sciences.

**Juan F. Perea** is assistant professor of Law at the University of Florida College of Law. He is the author of "English-Only Rules and the Right to Speak One's Primary Language in the Workplace," published in the *University of Michigan Journal of Law Reform.* Before entering teaching, he practiced employment and labor law both as an attorney at Ropes and Gray, and later with the National Labor Relations Board.

**Nancy J. Piet-Pelon** has been living and working abroad as a consultant to governments and private organizations for more than 20 years. Her consulting in the field of population, family planning, and mother/child health has taken her to many countries in Asia and Africa. Ms. Piet-Pelon has also developed and conducted workshops for women on professional development and for families on expatriate living and cross-cultural adjustment. She has written extensively concerning expatriate issues.

**Mike Pilot** is manager, Occupational Outlook Program, Office of Employment Projections, Bureau of Labor Statistics, U.S. Department of Labor.

**Barbara A. Plog,** M.P.H., C.I.H., C.S.P., is associate director of technical services at the Labor Occupational Health Program, Center for Occupational and Environmental Health at the University of California, Berkeley, and teaches industrial hygiene in the graduate Biomedical and Environmental Health Sciences Program at UCB's School of Public Health. She has taught and developed numerous courses in various aspects of industrial hygiene and is editor and coauthor of the textbook, *Fundamentals of Industrial Hygiene.*

**Stacey J. Pomerantz** is research associate at Catalyst, a national, nonprofit organization that works with business to effect change for women. Her responsibilities include research on women in corporate management and corporate experiences with maternity leave. She has authored two reports: "A Feasibility Study: Emergency Child Care Service in New York City and the Metropolitan Area," and "The New York City Sick Child Care Study." She holds a B.A. from Brandeis University and a M.A. of Health Science in Maternal and Child Health from the Johns Hopkins School of Public Health.

**Samuel B. Pond, III** is associate professor of Psychology at North Carolina State University. His research and teaching interests focus on organizational behavior. His research has appeared in *Group and Organizational Studies, Journal of Applied Behavioral Science, Journal of Applied Psychology, Journal of Business and Psychology, Journal of Vocational Behavior,* and *Personnel Psychology.*

**Robert E. Rainey** is an industrial psychologist and president of OutPath, an Arlington, Texas, career counseling and outplacement firm. Previously, he held a succession of corporate positions with Fortune 500 companies such as Pepsico, International, American Can International. He was also a senior vice-president with the world's largest executive outplacement firm. He is listed in the current edition of *Who's Who in the South and Southwest.*

**Susan M. Robison** is a psychologist in private practice in Ellicott City, Maryland. She is also a professor of Psychology at the College of Notre Dame of Maryland. Dr. Robinson is the author of *Discovery and Sharing Your Gifts*, a leadership manual and program for the National Council of Catholic Women. She is coauthor of *Thinking and Writing in College*. She consults nationally on stress management, leadership, and executive stress, especially for women executives.

**Samia Nahir Rodriguez** is an associate with Hyman, Phelps and McNamara, P.C., a Washington, DC, law firm that advises clients on legal issues concerning food and drugs. She has published in the *Food, Drug, Cosmetic Law Journal*, and coauthored "State Legislation: Effects on Drug Programs in Industry," NIDA Research Monograph 91 (*Drugs in the Workplace: Research and Evaluation Data*) and "Drug Testing After Skinner and Von Raab," *Employment Testing*.

**Simcha Ronen** is professor of Organizational Psychology and Comparative Management at the Graduate School of Business Administration, Tel Aviv University, and is a fellow of the American Psychological Association. He published widely in the area of alteration work schedules (including two books) and is now concentrating on the application of organizational behavior in cross-cultural perspective. He recently authored *Comparative and Multinational Management*.

**Esther D. Rothblum** is associate professor of Psychology at the University of Vermont, and editor of the journal *Women and Therapy*. Her research and writing have focused on women's mental health, including procrastination and fear of failure, social skills and assertion, depression, and stigma of obesity. She has edited seven books, including *Treating Women's Fear of Failure: From Worry to Enlightenment*.

**Mark A. Rothstein** is professor of Law and director of the Health Law and Policy Institute at the University of Houston. He has concentrated his research on employment and occupational health law. He has written numerous articles on these subjects as well as four books: *Cases and Materials on Employment Law* (with Knapp and Liebman), *Medical Screening of Workers, Occupational Safety and Health Law*, and *Medical Screening and the Employee Health Cost Crisis*.

**Nancy R. Russell** is a free-lance writer. She was formerly manager of information services for the American Society for Personnel Administration (now the Society for Human Resource Management) and is accredited as a professional in human resources. Ms. Russell was associate editor for the 1987 through 1989 editions of the *Human Resources Yearbook*.

**Paul R. Salomone** is professor of Rehabilitation Counseling and of Counselor Education at Syracuse University. He is the editor of the *Career Development Quarterly*, and author of over 50 articles dealing with rehabilitation counseling and/or career counseling. He was awarded a Fulbright Senior Scholarship to research in Egypt in 1984.

**Mark L. Savickas** is professor and chair in the Department of Behavioral Sciences at the Northeastern Ohio Universities College of Medicine and an adjunct professor in the Department of Educational Psychology and Leadership Studies at Kent State University.

**Edgar H. Schein** is Sloan Fellows Professor of Management at the MIT Sloan School of Management, where he has taught since 1956. He received his Ph.D. in Social Psychology from Harvard University. He is the author of numerous books and articles, including *Organizational Psychology, Organizational Culture and Leadership, Career Dynamics*, and *Process Consultation Vol. 1 and Vol. 2*. He is a consultant to major organizations in the U.S. and overseas.

**Nancy K. Schlossberg** is Professor in the Counseling and Personnel Service Department at the University of Maryland. She is coauthor of *Improving Higher Educational Environments for Adults* and author of *Overwhelmed: Coping with Life's Ups and Downs*. Recent awards include Outstanding Contribution to Literature or Research from the National Association of Student Personnel Administrators, Contribution to Knowledge Award from American College Personnel Association, and Eminent Career Award from the National Career Development Association.

**Lee Schore**, M.S.W., L.C.S.W., is the executive director of the Center for Working Life in Oakland, California. Ms. Schore is a nationally recognized expert on the mental health effects of work on workers and their families, and pioneered the development of Occupational Stress Groups that deal with both the symptoms and the causes of stress. She currently serves on the National Association of Social Workers Commission on Employment and Economic Security.

**Barbara M. Seeger** received her M.Ed. in School Counseling from North Carolina State University. She is presently employed as Industry Education Coordinator for Enloe High School in Raleigh, North Carolina. She also writes the Career Choices User's Guide annually for the North Carolina State Occupational Information Coordinating Committee.

**Joel Shufro** is executive director of the New York Committee for Occupational Safety and Health, Inc.(NYCOSH). He is the vice-president of the Cornell University Adjunct Faculty Federation, Local 4228, American Federation of Teachers.

**John W. Slocum, Jr.** holds the O. Paul Corley Chair in Management at the Cox School of Business at Southern Methodist University. He teaches organizational behavior, organizational design, and management. He has written over 90 articles and 5 books on leadership motivation, career management, and how corporate strategy impacts human resources practices in organizations. He is a fellow in the Academy of Management and the Decision Science Institute, and has served as a consultant to numerous organizations in the areas of human resources management.

**Leslie E. Smith** is associate director of the National Association for Female Executives (NAFE), a 250,000-member organization which provides women with the tools and information they need to reach their career goals. Leslie writes the networking column for *Executive Female Magazine* and her book on networking, *Successful Connections*, will be published in the fall of 1991. Leslie is a graduate of Mount Holyoke College and holds a master's degree in women's studies from George Washington University.

**Robert C. Solomon** is Quincy Lee Centennial Professor at the University of Texas at Austin. He has held positions at several major universities. He is author of six books on ethics, including *Above the Bottom Line* and *It's Good Business*. He is also the author of *Passions, In the Spirit of Hegel*, and *About Love*. He is the recipient of the 1973 Standard Oil Outstanding Teaching Award and the University of Texas Presidential Associates' Teaching Award.

**Southern Regional Council**, the South's oldest interracial organization, works to attain equal opportunity for all. The Southern Labor Institute, a special project of the Southern Regional Council, conducts programs to improve southern workplace conditions through research, analysis, and community education. Ken Johnson, SLI director, supervised *The Climate for Workers in the United States: 1990*, which was written by Gretchen and Bruce Maclachian, with a case study by Nancy Peckingham.

**Cheryl L. Spinweber** is associate adjunct professor in the Department of Psychology at the University of California, San Diego. She is an internationally known researcher in the areas of sleep, human performance, jet lag, and psychopharmacology, and is also a sleep disorders specialist. Her curriculum vitae lists over 60 publications in these areas.

**Judith K. Sprankle** is a free-lance copywriter and author specializing in career issues. Her published titles include *Calling It Quits: Turning Career Setbacks to Success, Working It Out: The Domestic Double Standard*, and, with Henry Ebel, *The Workaholic Syndrome*.

**David J. Srebalus** is professor of Counseling Psychology at West Virginia University. He has authored several textbooks for counselor education programs, and consults regularly with business, mental health clinics, and government agencies. Professional interests include distressed psychologists, high performance work organizations, and psychotherapy.

**John E. Steele** is a consultant in the fields of Career Planning and College Recruiting. He taught and directed career programs at four major universities. A founder and past president of the MCPA and CPC professional societies, he also served as president of the ECPO regional association. He coauthored *Planning Your Career* and *Career Planning & Development for College Students and Recent Graduates,* and is the first person in his field in the national edition of *Who's Who in America*.

**Diane Stein** is safety and health specialist at the New York Committee for Occupational Safety and Health, Inc. (NYCOSH). NYCOSH is a coalition of labor unions and safety and health activists in the New York City metropolitan area. COSH groups around the country offer educational seminars and technical assistance to unions and worker activists on a variety of occupational safety and health issues, including video display terminals.

**Marian Stoltz-Loike**, Ph.D., is president of Stoltz-Loike Associates, a Queens, New York, company which presents corporate seminars focusing on practical approaches to balancing family and career demands and assists individual clients with their work and family concerns. She is also coordinator of career development and guidance at Touro College. She has written a variety of papers and presented many lectures on family and career concerns.

**Stephen A. Stumpf** is professor of Management and director, Management Simulation Projects Group, the Leonard N. Stern School of Business, New York University. He has written over 60 articles which have appeared in such journals as the *Academy of Management Journal* and *Journal of Vocational Behavior*. He has also authored several books, including *Managing Careers, Management Education*, and *Choosing a Career in Business*. He is currently coauthoring *Strategic Leadership in the Middle Game*.

**Donald E. Super** is professor emeritus of Psychology and Education at Columbia University. He now serves as international coordinator of the Work Importance Study, which examines the roles and values of high school and college students and adults in 12 countries as diverse as Australia, Portugal, Yugoslavia, Poland, Israel, Japan, South Africa, and the United States. He is author of many books and articles on careers, and of tests for the assessment of career maturity, role importance, and values.

**Edna Mora Szymanski** is associate professor in the Department of Rehabilitation Psychology and Special Education, University of Wisconsin-Madison. She has authored or coauthored many articles in rehabilitation counseling and has received research awards for her research on the relationship of rehabilitation counselor education to client outcome. Dr. Szymanski has served on the Commission for Rehabilitation Counselor Certification and the Commission for Standards and Accreditation of the Council on Rehabilitation Education.

**Bradford H. Taft** is vice-president in the Los Angeles office of Lee Hecht Harrison, Inc., an outplacement consulting firm. He is author of "Effective Selection and Utilization of Outplacement Services" in *The Employment Management Association Journal*, as well as numerous articles on employee transition and career planning. He has spent 14 years in human resources consulting, initially in executive recruitment prior to outplacement. He is on the board of directors of the Employment Management Association.

**Carol Tavris** earned her Ph.D. in social psychology, and has developed a career as a teacher, lecturer, and science writer. She is author of *Anger: The Misunderstood Emotion*; coauthor of *The Longest War: Sex Differences in Perspective* and *Psychology*, an introductory textbook; and editor of *EveryWoman's Emotional Well-Being*. She writes about psychological research for a variety of magazines, and currently teaches in the Department of Psychology at UCLA.

**Felix Toledo** obtained his J.D. from Georgetown University Law Center in Washington, DC, where he has been practicing immigration law since 1986 at AYUDA, Inc., a nonprofit legal services corporation. He began his studies at the University of Puerto Rico, where he majored in Literature and History. He studied Latin American history at the National Autonomous University in Mexico City. He has traveled widely through Mexico, the Caribbean, and the United States.

**Eileen Vollowitz** is president of Back Designs, Inc. in Oakland, California. She is a physical therapist with extensive training, both in the United States and Norway, in the prevention and treatment of musculoskeletal problems. Ms. Vollowitz is a consultant in ergonomics with a specialty in office and technical environments. She is author of "Furniture Prescription for the Conservative Management of Low Back Pain" in *Topics in Acute Care and Trauma Rehabilitation*.

**Thomas H. Vonk** is a doctoral student at the Kellogg Graduate School of Management, Northwestern University, studying strategic issues pertaining to the development and retention of the work force.

**Myer Waxler**, Ph.D., a human resource psychologist with over 25 years of experience in education and training, is co-founder and president of the Human Enterprise Development Group, Inc. in Bloomington, Indiana. He coauthored the nationally acclaimed book, *Goodbye Job, Hello Me*. His work has been featured on radio and television talk shows as well as in national publications, including *Entrepeneur Magazine*, *The Los Angeles Times*, *Woman Magazine*, and the Wall Street Journal's *National Employment Weekly*.

**William D. Weston** is director of cooperative education at North Carolina State University, with over 1,200 student job placements per year. He is author of several articles on cooperative education and its contribution to career identity, competence, autonomy, and purpose. Dr. Weston is a national certified counselor, a member of the editorial board of the *Journal of Cooperative Education*, and serves on the research committees of the Cooperative Education Association and the Cooperative Education Division of the American Society for Engineering Education.

**Susan C. Whiston** is assistant professor in the Department of Counseling and Educational Psychology and Foundations at the University of Nevada, Las Vegas. She has written numerous articles in the area of career counseling, including "Utilizing Family Systems Theory in Career Counseling." She has also done workshops to help parents enhance involvement in their children's career development.

**Elizabeth B. Yost** is associate professor in the Department of Psychology at the University of Arizona and research associate in the Department of Psychiatry, University of Arizona College of Medicine. She is coauthor of *Effective Personal and Career Decision-making, Career Counseling: A Psychological Approach*, and

numerous articles on career counseling. Dr. Yost has worked as staff psychologist at the Career Development and Placement Center, Pennsylvania State University.

**Donald G. Zytowski** is counseling psychologist and professor of Psychology at Iowa State University. Besides counseling students on their careers and other concerns for the past 30 years, he has researched and written extensively on career development and assisted Frederic Kuder in the development of the most recent editions of his interest inventories.

# Alphabetical List of Articles

# Guide to Related Topics

**CAREER CHOICE**

Career Changes at Midlife
Career Choices: Youth
Career Counseling
Career Indecision
Choosing a College
Choosing a Major
Choosing an Occupation
Decision Making
Job Changing
Military Career: Changing to a Civilian Career
Parent Involvement in Career Planning
Post High School Training

**CAREER CHOICE: THEORIES**

Career Development: Donald Super's Theory
Trait-Factor Approach to Career Choice
Vocational Choice: John Holland's Theory

**CAREER DEVELOPMENT**

Assessment Centers
Career Development System within the Organization
Career Identity
Career Planning
Continuing Education
Managerial Skills
Organizational Culture
Organizational Politics
Mentoring
Negotiating
Networking
Promotion/Raise
Women's Barriers and Opportunities

**CAREER EXPLORATION**

Career Exploration

*Occupational*

Career Tests and Inventories
Computerized-Assisted Career Guidance Systems
Continuing Education
Cooperative Education
Information Interviewing
Internships
Job Outlook: Major Trends
Occupational Information
Realistic Job Preview
Service-Learning
Volunteer Work

*Personal*

Abilities
Career Anchor
Career Identity
Career Roles
Interests
Skills
Work Values

*Matching Personal and Occupational Traits*

Choosing an Occupation
Myers-Briggs Type Indicator
Occupational Groups
Trait-Factor Approach to Career Choice

**CAREER TRANSITIONS**

Career Changes at Midlife
Fired/Laid Off
Job Changing
Managing Transitions
Military Career: Changing to a Civilian Career
Outplacement
Pre-Retirement Planning
Relocation
Retirement

**DISABILITY**

Disability: Adjustment to
Disability: Student's Transition from School to Work
Discrimination: People with Disabilities
Rehabilitation Counselors and Agencies
Social Security Disability Claim

**DISCRIMINATION AND HARASSMENT**

Discrimination: Age
Discrimination: Language
Discrimination: People with Disabilities
Discrimination: Race
Discrimination: Sex
Nonstandard English
Sex-Role Stereotyping
Sexual Harassment

**ETHNIC MINORITIES**

African Americans
American Indian Men
American Indian Women
Asian Americans

Testing
Testing: AIDS
Testing: Drugs
Testing: Genetic
Testing: Integrity

## WOMEN

Lesbian Women
Nontraditional Job for One's Sex
Parental Leave
Sequencing: A Career and Traditional Mothering
Sex-Role Stereotyping
Sexual Harassment
Women in the Workforce
Women: Reentry into the Workplace
Women's Barriers and Opportunities
Women Who Live/Work Overseas

## WORK-FAMILY

Child Care
Dual-Career Families
Elder Care
Parental Leave
Relocation
Sequencing: A Career and Traditional Mothering
Working Family Issues

## WORK OPTIONS

Career Path Possibilities within the Organization
Flextime
Job Changing
Job Hunting: International
Job Sharing
Nontraditional Job for One's Sex
Part-Time Work
Self-Employment
Temporary Employment
Women Who Live/Work Overseas

# A

## ABILITIES

Abilities are those special skills, talents, and aptitudes that allow a person to perform in some areas better than in others and perhaps to outperform many or most other people in those areas as well. As we will see later in this article, some abilities are in very specific areas, such as singing or sprinting, and others are broader, such as general academic learning ability.

At one time, it was commonly believed that people were born with a fixed amount of aptitude for different things: "I never was any good at math"; "My Susie is a born writer"; "He has no athletic ability." Now we know better. While people may begin with somewhat more ability in some areas and somewhat less in others, much of the difference in abilities in adults is actually the result of *different opportunities to develop these skills and talents*. Different opportunities to engage in widely diverse experiences, different training opportunities, different levels of support and encouragement, even differences in personal commitment and motivation, when added up throughout the developmental years, will yield adults with very different levels of abilities as they begin career planning. But *all people can improve their present level of functioning* if they are motivated to take additional training, get additional experience, or apply themselves more diligently in practicing the skill. People make choices for their lives based on the assessment of their own abilities: what hobbies to try, what friendships to cultivate, what purchases to make, what leisure activities to pursue, what classes to take, what jobs to apply for. For all of these decisions, people, to some degree, probably consider their level of ability to be a way of checking out the compatibility (or fit) between the situation and what they bring to it. As a result, it is important that people have both a clear view of their present abilities and a firm belief that they can improve them if they want to (see **Self-Efficacy**). Anything else is a way of "selling oneself short" and limiting the options one considers for oneself in approaching these decisions.

## Types of Abilities

Abilities come in almost as many varieties as people themselves do. In fact, our different abilities are part of what makes us different from each other, part of what comprises the richness of the human race. No list of human abilities can ever be complete, but the list which follows will serve to illustrate the wide variety of aptitudes, talents, skills, and abilities which exist.

| | |
|---|---|
| Acting/Dramatics | Organization |
| Artistic Talent | Persuading Others |
| Imagination | Physical Coordination |
| Integrating/Seeing | Physical Strength |
|   Connections | Planning Ahead |
| Leadership | Problem Solving |
| Logical Analysis | Putting Others at Ease |
| Making Decisions | Social Ease |
| Manual Dexterity | Spatial Perception |
| Mathematical Reasoning | Speaking |
| Mechanical Reasoning | Supervising Others |
| Negotiating Differences | Writing |
| Numerical Computation | |

Some of these abilities are depended upon heavily for success in school work—and directly rewarded there by grades and test scores—so that people may have a fairly good idea of their current level of skill in some areas. Other areas may be depended upon—and rewarded—in social, occupational, or leisure activities, giving people another good measure of their present ability levels. Still other abilities, however, may come so naturally that, without a sense that they are difficult for a person or valued by others, the person may not notice them in himself or herself and may fail to recognize special talents.

Sharpening the perception of one's own abilities is an essential step in beginning or refining one's career path. A fairly accurate picture of present abilities puts one in a position to decide whether to be content with those or to give oneself opportunities (training and experiences) to develop some of them further. The next section will address ways people can appraise their ability levels, on their own or with external help.

## Assessing Abilities

**Self-Assessment.** As noted above, self-assessment of abilities can be a good place to begin the process of sharpening perception of abilities. Each individual should ask: "What do I believe I do best? What would my friends say is one of my special talents? My boss? Coworkers? Former teachers? People I've just met?" Serious reflection on such questions will yield a good beginning sense of where a person's special strengths lie. Each individual should also consider past and recent successes, whether these are on the job, in school, in hobbies, in sports, in the home, in groups to which he or she belongs, or in any other avenue of life. When people are "hitting full stride" and experiencing a sense of "peak performance," that is evidence of aptitudes around which they can build future successes. Each person should think about those experiences and try to give a name to the special talent being displayed.

Next, the opposite approach may be taken. Each person should ask: "What do I think is presently an area where my skills need to be improved? What would my friends say? My boss? Coworkers? My former teachers? People I've just met?" Serious reflection on such questions will yield a beginning sense of areas in which the individual may wish to develop his or her abilities more in order to achieve certain goals. People must remember not to let this part of their self-assessment get them down! Finding areas where they are not as strong right now as they want to be doesn't mean they have to live with these shortcomings. These should be seen as goal areas, holes in a person's background to be filled with new learning, new experiences, and hard work. In this way, each person will be able to determine his or her own limits and opportunities.

**External Assessment.** Beyond self-assessment, there are several sources of information about a person's abilities. One source, of course, is other people who know the person well. They can be asked to discuss the findings from the self-evaluation and to add their reactions, or they can simply be asked for an honest appraisal of the person's special strengths and areas of need in order to assist in setting some goals. This can be an effective way to begin the process of confirming the self-assessment with external data. Next, a person may take any of a number of standardized tests which measure the present level of developed ability in certain areas and allow comparison with other people's ability levels. Some of these tests also allow comparison against required levels in certain training programs and jobs in order to assist in setting goals. Some examples of standardized ability tests are listed below:

1. *Differential Aptitude Tests, Form C* (The Psychological Corporation, 1990): The DAT is a multiple aptitude battery appropriate for use with students in grades 7-12 and adults. It measures levels of developed ability in Verbal Reasoning, Numerical Reasoning, Abstract Reasoning, Perceptual Speed and Accuracy, Mechanical Reasoning, Space Relations, Spelling, and Language Usage. It is given in schools, colleges, and employment/training programs, and is frequently used in career counseling and educational planning. Norms allow an individual's performance on the test to be compared with that of his or her peer group nationwide.

2. *Armed Services Vocational Aptitude Battery, Forms 18 & 19* (Department of Defense, 1991): The ASVAB is a multiple aptitude battery appropriate for use with students in grades 10-12 and young adults. It measures levels of developed ability in General Science, Arithmetic Reasoning, Word Knowledge, Paragraph Comprehension, Numerical Operations, Coding Speed, Auto & Shop Information, Mathematics Knowledge, Mechanical Comprehension, and Electronics Information. It is given in schools and in military recruiting stations and is used both to guide young people in their general vocational and educational planning and to help them consider military options. Norms allow an individual's performance to be compared with his or her peer group nationwide.

## Relationship to Occupational Choice and Work

A clear picture of one's abilities will greatly assist an individual in starting out on a career path that can be followed successfully throughout life.

During the initial career exploration and decision-making stages of adolescence and young adulthood, an essential step is to examine your abilities, through self-assessment alone or with external aid. Information about your abilities can then be added into the total picture you are assembling of your interests, values, preferred environments, training needs, and long-term goals for the purpose of identifying possible career paths for yourself.

It is essential to remember in this process, that your present level of ability does not limit your choices so much as it defines areas where you must do additional work (e.g., obtain more training, practice, or experience) in order to consider certain options.

Similarly, individuals already in the workforce will continue to experience choice points throughout their career when decisions must be made about advancement, retraining, specializing, and the like. The essential career decision-making process applies at all such times, and good planning will be done by individuals who take the time to assess their abilities and other factors and then select educational and occupational options for themselves in the light of this information. Once again, the best assurance of success along your lifetime career path is thoughtful decision-making which takes into consideration both the special abilities that you already have and those that you are willing to work to develop.

*See also* Career Tests and Inventories; Choosing an Occupation; Trait-Factor Approach to Career Choice.

## Bibliography

*Exploring careers: The ASVAB student workbook.* (1991). Washington, DC: U.S. Department of Defense. This hands-on workbook uses recurring cartoon characters to assist students with putting self-assessment and test information together in career exploration plans. Available free to anyone taking the ASVAB.

Figler, H. E. (1979). *PATH: A career workbook for liberal arts students.* Cranston, RI: Carroll. This hands-on workbook for students includes an exceptionally complete listing of different abilities and aptitudes for student self-assessment.

Herr, E.L., & Cramer, S.H. (1988). *Career guidance through the life span: Systematic approaches.* 3rd ed. New York: Scott, Foresman. Excellent basic text for career counselors. The chapter on assessment in career guidance is especially helpful for noting instruments and describing appropriate and inappropriate interpretations from the data.

Kapes, J.T., & Mastie, M.M. (1988). *A counselor's guide to career assessment instruments.* Alexandria, VA: The National Career Development Association. This definitive reference book provides full descriptions and critical reviews of all important tests and assessments for career development, and includes appended materials on selecting tests, interpreting data, etc.

—MARJORIE M. MASTIE

# AFRICAN AMERICANS

African Americans are members of the ethnic group in the United States which ultimately traces its cultural roots to Africa. The African American work experience can be traced to 1619, when a boatload of Africans was deposited in Jamestown, Virginia, as indentured servants. Shortly thereafter, large numbers of African people were brought to the United States as slaves. Until its abolition in 1863, slavery characterized much of the African American work experience. Since then however, African Americans have established important traditions in a variety of areas in the world of work.

## Labor Market Experience

African Americans make up 12% of the U. S. population and approximately 11% of the workforce (U.S. Bureau of the Census, 1990). In 1988, 64% of the African American population 16 years of age and older participated in the civilian labor force (U.S. Bureau of Labor Statistics, 1989). However, the world of work for African Americans can be landscaped with social and economic struggle. Despite important gains made by African Americans in the past several decades, labor force participation data from the 1980s generally present a bleak picture of African American occupational involvement. For example, the unemployment rate for African American high school graduates is generally three times the rate for whites (American Council on Education, 1988); 25% of all young adult African American males have never held a job (National Alliance of Business, 1987); and African Americans are overrepresented in the slow-growing or declining occupations but underrepresented in the fastest growing occupations (Kutscher, 1987).

The reasons for these data may be traced, to a large extent, to the traditions of social and economic disadvantage that have often served to impede the life progress of many African Americans. This disadvantage, which may be partly accounted for by the legacy of the slavery experience, is complicated by the presence of racism in the American workplace. Racism has been and continues to be a major barrier to occupational opportunity for scores of African Americans. Racism is a relatively constant pattern of prejudice and discrimination between one group of people that is favored and another group that is devalued, solely on the basis of race, in a common relationship (Pinderhughes, 1973). African Americans, because of their race, have had to constantly deal with long-standing prejudicial traditions and preconceived negative notions about their abilities in the workplace. These racist traditions and notions have often been barriers to workplace equity for African Americans. In addition, they have served to limit many African American occupational aspirations and expectations.

## Career Development

Despite social and economic barriers to full workforce participation, the value of hard work is highly prized in African American culture. Similarly, education is an important value. For African Americans education is seen as having a positive impact on success in the world of work.

The experience with racism and discrimination in society has impacted the career development of African Americans. Often African Americans have lower expectations of reaching their occupational aspirations. Additionally, African American career interests and choices have generally been geared toward people-oriented, rather than thing- or data-oriented jobs. Smith (1980) notes that this may be indicative of the general reaction of many African Americans to the often dehumanizing factors that they must cope with in American society.

## Application

The following are guidelines for African Americans or those interested in promoting the career development of African Americans from childhood through adulthood:

1. *Childhood.* Begin the process of occupational decision making with career education in childhood. In elementary school, for example, provide African American children with comprehensive career education that insures they begin to develop both self-awareness and career awareness. Make concerted efforts to insure that children develop a positive self-identity as African Americans.

It is also important that African American children become aware of a wide range of career opportunities. Expose them to a variety of African American occupational role models and assist them in understanding the scope of career options available in the world of work.

2. *Adolescence.* In adolescence, career education efforts should take the form of comprehensive life planning (Lee & Simmons, 1988). Promote long-range career goal setting, including the development of occupational, educational, and marriage and family plans, among African American adolescents in four important ways: (a) by promoting self-awareness of abilities, interests, and values; (b) by promoting an expansion of educational and occupational options; (c) by encouraging educational and occupational decision making based on knowledge and experience; and (d) by encouraging young people to anticipate future events.

Coordinate African American educational, community, and business resources with the life-planning processes of adolescents. For example, have positive African American community role models, from both traditional and nontraditional occupational fields, develop mentor relationships with young people to expose them to significant others who represent occupational success in a variety of fields and have made crucial life decisions.

3. *Adulthood.* Promoting career development among African American adults has several important aspects. First, when necessary, raise the personal expectations that African American adults hold about opportunities and success in the world of work. This may be important if they have a narrow view of the range of job options, limited educational background, or lack of job training. This can be

done by identifying and reinforcing perceptions of their unique abilities and resources, helping them develop positive attitudes toward the workplace through interaction with role models, learning self-assertion skills, and acquiring relevant career information.

Second, it may be necessary to help African American adults improve the quality of their working life through personal strategies that reduce stress and improve factors that may negatively influence their interactions within the workplace.

Third, African American adults may need to channel energy and skill into breaking down institutional and social barriers that impede full workforce participation. They may need to actively challenge discriminatory traditions and preconceived racist notions that stand in the way of equity in the workplace. Likewise, it may be important to push for continuing legislation that abolishes discriminatory employment practices.

*See also* Discrimination: Race; Nonstandard English.

## Bibliography

American Council on Education. (1988). *Minorities in higher education.* Washington, DC: American Council on Education.

*Black enterprise.* New York: Earl G. Graves Publishing Co. A monthly magazine devoted to African American business and career issues. There are features on African Americans in corporate American and African American entrepreneurship. Each January, the magazine publishes an economic outlook for African Americans.

Davis, G., & Watson, G. (1982). *Black life in corporate America: Swimming in the mainstream.* Garden City, NY: Anchor Press/ Doubleday. A comprehensive look at the challenges confronting African Americans in executive positions in business and industry. Includes an extensive bibliography.

Foner, P. S., & Lewis, R. L. (Eds.) (1989). *Black workers: A documentary history from colonial times to the present.* Philadelphia: Temple University Press. A comprehensive history of the African American work experience in the United States. Includes an extensive bibliography.

Franklin, J. H. (1980). *From slavery to freedom.* 5th ed. New York: Knopf. The classic comprehensive social, political, and economic history of African Americans. The book examines the occupational history and traditions of African Americans. Includes an extensive bibliography.

Johnson, J. H., & Bennett, L. (1989). *Succeeding against the odds.* New York: Warner Books. A detailed autobiography of John H. Johnson, founder of the largest African American publishing company in the United States, Johnson Publications of Chicago.

Kutscher, R. (September, 1987). Projections 2000: Overview and implications of the projections to 2000. *Monthly Labor Review,* U. S. Department of Labor.

Lee, C. C. (in press). Counseling blacks: From theory to practice. In R. L. Jones (Ed.), *Black psychology.* 3rd ed. New York: Harper & Row. A through review of developmental counseling techniques for African Americans. This chapter contains a section on promoting the career development of African Americans across the life span.

Lee, C. C., & Simmons, S. (1988). A comprehensive life-planning model for black adolescents. *The School Counselor*, 36: 5-10.

National Alliance of Business (September 30, 1987). A critical message for every American who plans to work or do business in the 21st century. *New York Times Magazine*.

Pinderhughes, C. A. (1973). Racism and psychotherapy. In C. V. Willie, B. M. Kramer, & B. S. Brown (Eds.), *Racism and mental health*. Pittsburgh: University of *Pittsburgh Press*.

Smith, E. J. (1980). The profile of the black individual in vocational literature. In R. L. Jones (Ed.), *Black psychology*. 2nd ed. New York: Harper & Row.

U. S. Bureau of Labor Statistics. (1989). *Monthly Labor Review*. Washington, DC: Department of Labor.

U.S. Bureau of the Census. (1990) *Statistical abstract of the United States.* Washington, DC: U.S. Department of Commerce.

— COURTLAND C. LEE

## AMERICAN INDIAN MEN

The work ethic of American Indian people differs in many ways from that of mainstream American society. One area where Native values impact the work environment concerns the relationship between Native people, their home and community, and their values. In general, Native people are more rooted to their home communities and exhibit a strong reluctance to relocate geographically to take advantage of job opportunities. From a Native man's perspective, a good job must fulfill a number of criteria, with the most critical factor being the relationship between the job and the home community.

The community and family have expectations and requirements which the Indian man must consider very carefully. American Indian men are considered an extension of the immediate nuclear family and community. From a traditional perspective, these men are recognized essentially as the primary provider for their families. This role as the primary provider is an expression of the strong distinction existing within Native American communities between male and female roles.

The original American Indian nations can be separated into two distinct groups with regard to the role of men in the family. Some of the original nations of the Great Plains consider children to be of the same clan as their father, so the lineage and responsibility of the father are of great importance for child rearing. Other American Indian peoples consider the mother's clan relationship to be the most important for kinship ties. Among these communities, the father is more of an advisor to his wife's children who are members of their mother's clan. His primary responsibility is to his sister's children, who are members of his own clan. The man is respectfully recognized as the biological father, but the mother, with the assistance of her family, is the driving force in child rearing. The Indian man's paternal role becomes apparent and is recognized through the guidance, coaching, and directing of his sister's children.

Viewed from within Native culture, these role distinctions establish a reciprocal process based on the principles of sharing, respect, and unity. Definition of sex roles are expressed as a way to achieve balance, equality, and respect for all members. Besides establishing the boundaries of responsibilities, without diminishing respect for the parent without prime child-rearing responsibility, these traditional values serve as the basis of a model critical to preserving Native American culture.

While some of these relationships have certainly begun to change with modern interpretations of sex roles in contemporary mainstream society, the Indian man's role of primary provider remains intact. On the other hand, the roles of Native American women have expanded to include nontraditional functions which are widely recognized and accepted. Pressure to function as an American Indian man is based on expectations originating from family (both nuclear and extended) and other relationships, relevant to, yet external to the family.

A reality of the reservation system is that very few wage-oriented jobs are available within or near the home and community. To meet his needs and responsibilities the Native American man usually has no choice but to take whatever work is available locally. And such work consists of highly competitive low paying labor positions. Higher wages often require the man to commute or relocate, hindering his desire to remain among family. The American Indian man is thus faced with a paradox: to remain close to home, he either does not work or works at minimum wage. To meet his financial responsibilities, he reluctantly moves away from community and family to obtain employment with higher wages and potential.

The commitment to family and community often manifests itself in ways that can develop conflicts between the Native man as employee, and his employer. Besides financial responsibilities to the nuclear family, the Native man is also responsible to extended family members. When relatives experience difficulties associated with death, health, or other personal crises, it is customary for family members to show their support by banding together and sharing their burdens. The Native Indian man is obligated to be available for family matters that demand immediate attention. Family emergencies require all family members to work conscientiously toward a consensus on the matter. Depending on the nature of the situation, these decisions can sometimes take long periods of time to resolve, thus, prolonging the Native man's time off work. This usually results in tension at work because non-Native employers usually view lost time for these reasons as unjustifiable. The issue is further compounded if the Native man is employed and temporarily residing off the reservation.

Another area of potential conflict involves different perceptions and the importance of "clocking timecards." Native values in regards to work expectations are often goal or product oriented rather than time centered. This results in the Native man prioritizing quality of work over the time allowed to complete a task. This could further be expressed by a willingness to work overtime without additional compensation, or if arriving late for work, an expected willingness to work late to compensate. Where employers have expressed a willingness to deal with this openly, work schedules have been modified to allow a greater degree of flexibility. Such flexibility allows the employee time to address specific family needs and benefits the employer with the high quality of work produced.

The traditional work ethic of Native men is not necessarily in conflict with the work ethic of the wage conscience economy. It is, however, important to recognize the cultural orientation of the two entities. What is involved and how to approach the needs of both demonstrate the degree of flexibility and compassionate understanding required in order to achieve a balance between the two differing views of work, job, and purpose of employment. From a Native viewpoint this purpose is to sustain the family and thus provide an environment for the individual to positively express his traditional values and successfully achieve his goals.

## Application

There are many things to consider when we, as Native men, become part of the work environment of mainstream American society. For the survival and preservation of our own heritage, culture, and tradition, it is becoming very important to re-examine the importance of our original teachings within the context of modern society.

We, as American Indians, represent the original nation of this continent. It is becoming evident that success in the future requires us to reclaim our culture and heritage. For some, it will be a beginning process; for others it will be a continuation of the process to restore the long neglected principles and teachings of our heritage. A word that has emerged to describe this idea is "empowerment." We, as American Indian men, the leaders of our family and people, can begin to rely on our own history, language, government, education, and traditions to determine how we can best reclaim our place in the world as a first nations people. While this may not be a simple or easy task, it is a goal which we can achieve. In fact, there are many people throughout the country and among Native peoples throughout the world who have begun to "empower" themselves as

the original people of their lands. In practical terms, "empowerment" means that we take the initiative and do this ourselves. We cannot rely on others to fulfill this need; it is up to our own individual and collective will to regain our place as the powerful, sophisticated, and great people we have always been.

We can begin the process of finding this knowledge and strength at home. The culture which some people consider lost, is, in fact, only hidden, and needs to be revived, nurtured, and emphasized. Through our elders, the old people in our communities, we need to ask for guidance and assistance. They are the key to our success as American Indian peoples. They can teach us the ways, the myths, and the values associated with our heritage and culture. Indian men must uncover and reclaim these teachings so our children may learn and live this knowledge as proud, confident, and secure individuals. However, so we may be successful examples to our children, we must positively incorporate these teachings into our own lives and practice them daily. Besides instilling a sense of pride in who we are into our young children, this attitude will further enhance the success of our children through high self-esteem and confidence.

As we begin to understand our own traditions once again, it is vital and critical that we also understand the values, culture, and behavior of mainstream society. This will be instrumental in enabling our children to bring together the knowledge and expertise gained from both worlds to benefit our people. They will then have an advantage over "us," for they will be better prepared to approach those issues which may involve or require knowledge and wisdom from each.

As Native American men we represent the generation that must be creative and discover how to live our American Indian traditions within the context of mainstream society. This can be achieved through positive interaction in all areas between Native culture and mainstream society. Emphasizing the importance of what both have to offer and how we can best influence the needs and issues addressing us as American Indians depends on the attitude and approach we take. Foremost, it is our responsibility to achieve a balanced lifestyle where American Indian families are healthy, happy, secure, and a part of American Indian traditions once again.

*See also* American Indian Women.

## Bibliography

Knox, R.H. (1980). *Indian conditions: A survey.* Ottawa, Canada: Department of Indian Affairs and Northern Development. This government report outlines the principle developments and trends in the social, economic, and political conditions of Indians in Canada and, by extension, the United States.

Nicholes, Roger L. (1986). *The American Indian past and present.* New York: Alfred Knopf. This collection of essays represent many of the important factors which have led up to the contemporary American Indian experience. It outlines some of the historical issues which have resulted in the development of American Indian policy in the United States.

Tedlock, Denise, & Tedlock, Barbara. (1975). *Teachings from the American Earth.* New York: Liveright. This anthology contains a well-written and accurate representation of American Indian religious experiences and philosophical beliefs largely from the Native American point of view.

Weatherford, J. (1988). *Indian givers: How the Indians of the Americas transformed the world.* New York: Crown Publishers. This exciting text presents the history and contemporary position of Native people in a world context. Issues examined center around the important contributions Native nations of the Americas have made to modern society.

—THOM ALCOZE

## AMERICAN INDIAN WOMEN

American Indian women are consistently reported as the lowest paid, lowest ranked, and most unemployed segment of the national work force. Like 80% of all employed women, Indian women are primarily employed in "women's jobs,"—which, according to one researcher, can easily be defined as "any jobs that pay less than what a man will do them for."

Although these women hold a slightly higher percentage of managerial or professional jobs than their male counterparts, according to a 1983 Census, only 2% of all American Indian women are managers or administrators, and only 11% are employed in professional or technical fields. Of the 5,804 American Indian engineers and natural scientists, only 854 are women and only 150 Indian women (compared with 713 Indian men) are in health-diagnosing occupations, according to the same Census.

The majority of American Indian women, like their non-Indian counterparts, are employed in two of the lowest status, lowest skilled occupation groups—clerical and service occupations. Some have suggested that American Indian women enter these occupations because they believe they can best serve Indian people in them, or because many Indians are simply not impressed by affluence, material gain, or job prestige as ends in themselves. Whatever the reason, a 1983 analysis by the Ohoya Resource Center indicates that the income for nearly a quarter of American Indian households headed by women is $9,320—well below the poverty line. On many reservations, as many as three-fourths of the households are headed by women alone.

Indian women have been classified as "culturally disadvantaged" job applicants. They tend to be passive and unassertive, fail to talk about themselves easily, and apparently fail to understand the rationale behind interview questions, which causes them to be viewed as unskilled, unresponsive, and unsuitable for employment. As a result, the National Institute of Education identified career planning as the most important educational need.

So far, this need has been largely unmet, because of Indian women's lack of educational and employment opportunities, bicultural conflicts, sexism, and racism. Today, however, more and more of these women are challenging these barriers.

In the majority culture, a professional achieves status by striving for individual success in some specialized occupation or field. For the American Indian woman, however, the professionalization process generally involves something much broader; her goals include concerns relevant to her family and people as well as to herself as an individual. Her striving for excellence in any occupation is in many ways an extension or reflection of the deeply rooted traditional concern in Indian culture for quality and pride in all circles of life.

Consequently, many Indian women first become interested in the professionalization process as they examine their communities and see the need for their contributions as professionals. They see the need to preserve and disseminate Indian cultural values and ways of living. They see the need for more commercial radio and television programs of interest to Indians, as well as for the accurate portrayal of contemporary and historic American Indians. They are concerned about the difficulties their sisters face in gaining a foothold in state politics and tribal leadership, and they carefully scrutinize the appointment of Indian women to advisory positions in the federal government. They are also concerned about their incarcerated brothers and sisters, many of whom are denied access to traditional spiritual counseling despite the Native American Religious Freedom Act of 1978. They see the need for more Indian women to become business owners, and the need to encourage tribes to offer incentives to private industries to increase employment opportunities for Indians through the growth of industries on reservations. They have called for improved access to health care for Indian people, who remain the poorest of any ethnic group; they emphasize the need for Indian health professionals to serve Indian people and help deal with rising rates of alcoholism. They are concerned that nearly one-third of their sisters live in rural areas and are isolated from social services. They read the statistics on school and college completion and dropout rates, and insist that data be collected by sex and race to combat the lack of clear, uniform data on Indian women and children. They want to provide basic education about child abuse and the need for affordable child-care services to tribes and Indian organizations nationwide. At the same time, the American Indian woman must combat race and sex bias to meet her career potential, and that discrimination comes not only from the non-Indian community, but from American Indian men as well. For example, Indian women face unrealistic peer and family pressures to date and marry American Indian men, even though many of their male counterparts date or marry non-Indian females while castigating Indian women who do likewise. Further, Indian women have a realistic fear that Indian men with less formal schooling will not marry an educated Indian woman.

Many Indian women experience difficult career decisions because they have been historically channeled into careers in teaching or social services. Nevertheless, many Indian women are increasingly visible in professional roles such as social workers, psychologists, writers, artists, and political leaders serving their communities and tribes. Some noteworthy examples of Indian women leaders include: LaDonna Harris (Comanche), president and director of American Indians for Opportunity; Wilma Mankiller, chief of the Cherokee Nation; Jo Ann Sarracino (Laguna), developer of the Native American Mineral Engineering and Science Program; and Nancy Wallace (Comanche/Creek), manager of the Industrial Engineering Department at Digital, the third largest computer company in the world. These American Indian women have achieved success by exhibiting independence, leadership, confidence, competitiveness, and emotional control. Without ignoring their cultural heritage, losing acceptance among their people, or forfeiting the ability to behave appropriately within Indian cultures, Indian women leaders have increased respect and status for Indian people and gained professional recognition for themselves.

Women's political power in a substantial number of tribes is significant and on the rise. Their interest and position in the policy making arena has stemmed from traditional concerns for the community and has often found a foundation in existing or vestigial female networks and power bases within the tribe. In a study of 10 tribal councils on Nevada reservations, a researcher reported that women constituted the vast majority of local committees and service clubs and that only one tribal council did not have women members.

For many Indian women, positions of authority and prominence are natural evolutions of their caretaking role and they see their actions as personal rather than organizational. Their goal is to be productive yet humble leaders by virtue, not position. It is important to recognize that retraditionalization efforts ("retraditionalization," as its name implies, attempts to revitalize the culture, language, and religion of American Indians) on the part of Indian women are often inconsistent with some goals of the current majority culture women's movement. Non-Indian feminists emphasize middle-class themes of independence and androgyny, whereas Indian women often see their work in the context of their families, their nations, and "Sacred Mother Earth." Preservation and restoration of their race and culture is at least as important to Indian women as are their individual goals for professional achievement and success, although many Indian women clearly have made important professional commitments and value the role of work in their lives.

## Application

Your successful entry into a professional area may depend on the following:

1. *Meeting Indian women you consider to be professional role models*—their shared experience can enable you to make a realistic assessment of the qualities necessary to achieve success in the field.
2. *Learning how Indian professional women achieve power within the Indian community*—many credit traditional family skills, kinship connections, and advancing social and community goals to their rise to power within the public sphere.
3. *Exploring unwritten "rules" and bicultural sex role expectations*—majority culture espouses a work ethic centered around individual achievement, competitiveness, and the accumulation of property and titles. These values conflict with the primary caretaking ethic of women in the Indian community. Often multiple and opposing role conflicts arise and you may try harder to meet role demands (rather than relinquish roles or redefine expectations associated with roles) thus compounding stress.
4. *Attending a course on assertiveness training*—finding one that focuses on the situational appropriateness of assertive behavior in both the majority culture and Indian environments is necessary for career success. The same assertive behavior that would be appropriate for an Anglo woman may exacerbate the problem for an Indian woman given cultural norms or stereotypical notions of Indian behavior.
5. *Professional networking for jobs*—to find the people in different areas who can let you know of positions as they become available, coaching you as to the specific qualities desired in these positions, and mentoring you for career advancement once the job is acquired (see **Networking**).

*See also* American Indian Men; Assertion; Discrimination: Sex; Job Interviewing; Job Search; Networking.

## Bibliography

LaFromboise, T. D. (1989). *Circles of women: Skills training for American Indian professionalization.* Newton, MA: Women's Educational Equity Act Press. A manual for counselors, teachers, workshop leaders, and trainers.

Ohoyo Resource Center. (1981). *Words of today's American Indian women: Ohoyo Makachi.* Wichita Falls, TX: Ohoyo Resource Center. A collection of oratory by American Indian/Alaska Native women participating in the 1981 OHOYO Resource Conference in Educational Equity Awareness. Topics include networking in Indian country, assessing education, leadership development, role modeling, and the changing and diverse roles of contemporary Indian women.

*Windy Boy, B. (1987).* Women's job search strategy or . . . How to keep the wolf away from the door. *Denver: Arrowstar Publishing.* A practical, positive, and energetic 90-page book with down to earth information and examples of Indian women who have achieved career success. Contains lists to set goals and resources for personal growth and job search support.

—TERESA D. LaFROMBOISE

# ANGER

Anger at work is very different from anger in the family. Most people are motivated to keep the lid on at work, either because anger with colleagues has the potential to provoke unsolvable conflicts, or because anger at a boss has the potential to get a person fired. So we alternate between bottling up our feelings of resentment (or maybe displacing them on friends and other captive audiences) and blowing up when things get too bad.

Many people spend a lot of energy talking to friends and worrying about whether they should "suppress" or "express" their anger, and how. This is a common reaction. But when anger at work becomes a chronic emotional state instead of a momentary irritation, it is time to solve the problem that has caused the feeling in the first place.

Expressing anger, a popular solution, is not always the best one. The question to ask is why you want to express anger. Most people usually have one of two reasons: they want to change the other person (this is the expressed motive) or they want to make the other person feel as bad as they do (this is often the real, hidden motive). These motives (one to improve matters, the other to wound the offender) are often incompatible. Many people end up attacking and hurting one another in the name of making "constructive changes."

## Application

The solutions to anger in the workplace have more to do with solving problems than simply with "managing" emotions or freely ventilating them (Tavris, 1989). Research today provides some new solutions:

*First, know why you are angry—and verify your reasons.* Anger is not an inevitable response to an "annoying" situation, but a response stemming from our perceptions of the situation (Burns, 1980, 1989). This is why two people often have entirely different emotional reactions to the same event. One might say of a co-worker's behavior, "she's intentionally lazy," and feel angry. The other might say, "poor thing; she's got trouble at home," and feel sad. Anger vanishes the moment misperceptions are corrected, for instance, when you learn that a coworker didn't intentionally snub you, but had just lost a contact lens and couldn't see you (see **Rational Thinking**).

Therefore, the first step to managing anger is to know whether your beliefs and expectations about the other person are accurate. Many people work themselves into a state of righteous indignation while failing to check out their assumptions. For example, you might become angry if your employer doesn't even comment on a project you slaved over. You might think, "How rude; what arrogance." But if you barge into your employer's office complaining of this, chances are you will provoke an explosive confrontation. What you can do instead is simply ask your employer for an evaluation of your work. Many employers assume their staff knows when they do good work and don't need the feedback.

Talking about anger or "ventilating" it is helpful if it leads you to a new understanding of the situation ("I see now that he really isn't out to get me"). Another way to verify your beliefs is to talk to yourself—not by storming around your office, but by writing down your arguments and perceptions. Try to specify exactly why you believe you are angry: what is the other person's specific offense? Are your expectations about that person reasonable or inflated? What other explanations of that person's bad behavior are possible? What other explanations of your own anger are possible—for instance, are you fatigued, worried about family problems, hot and bothered, under unusual pressure?

*Second, decide what you hope to accomplish by expressing anger.* Do you want to feel better? Get the other person to change? Wound the other person to compensate for your misery? Improve your relationship? These goals call for different ways of expressing anger.

Suppose that you have accumulated your grievances against a coworker whom you feel is taking advantage of you. You could burst into his office and yell, "Look, I've had enough. You've been lazy and thoughtless and I'm sick of covering for you." Now, he might suddenly see the error of his ways, apologize for his behavior, and vow to change. It is more likely, though, that he will counterattack: "I thought you were my friend! You know what a rough time I'm having—how could you let me down?" You might feel momentarily better that you ventilated your feelings and hurt your coworker's, but you will not have solved the problem between you and your coworker.

*Third, focus on solving the problem.* The idea is to collaborate with the other person on fixing the problem between you. If you're working with someone, you'll make better headway than if you're confronting them. Keep your eye on solving the problem, not on "expressing your feelings," getting revenge, or making the other person feel bad.

Suppose you are working with a secretary who becomes defensive and insecure every time you offer constructive (and necessary) criticism. Because defensive, angry people are often frightened, insecure, or troubled, empathy goes a long way; it helps you ignore their surface emotional response and concentrate instead on how best to reach them. Perhaps the secretary is afraid of being fired or thought incompetent. If these fears are unjustified, you can address them directly and reassure the person that her competence is not in question.

Next, you can give the secretary constructive feedback by creating a collaborative bond: "I know you have a lot of work and conflicting demands here, which you manage brilliantly. But I'm unhappy about the number of errors in these weekly reports. What do you suggest we do about this?" Now the problem is framed in terms of time and task management, not in terms of the other person's personality, and you give her responsibility for solving the problem.

The emphasis on solving problems bypasses the "what-do-I-do-about-my-anger" question entirely. Specify the goal, and stick with it: "I want fewer errors in these reports"; "I want credit for my work"; "I deserve a raise"; "I want this sexual harassment to stop." Speak calmly but assertively, without being apologetic or defensive. You don't have to be cold or hostile toward the other person, but neither should you let tears or belligerence deflect you from your goal. You might say: "I understand that you're unhappy about this [or, I'm sorry my point of view makes you angry]. It's not my intention to hurt your feelings. Now, what are we going to do next? What ideas do you have to solve this difference of opinion?"

*Fourth, understand your role in perpetuating the anger-generating pattern.* New approaches to understanding anger in relationships, at work as in the family, invoke trying to break away from everyone's usual habit of accusing the other person of "starting it" and getting the other person to change. In the systems view, everyone started it,

and if one person changes, all other members of the system will have to change as well (see Lerner, 1985). This means that instead of saying, "How should I express my anger to get Harold to straighten out and fly right?," the angry person can say "How can I change my part in encouraging Harold's screwy actions?" You might say to a colleague whom you have been protecting: "You know, I'm enormously sympathetic to your problems at home and wanted to help you. But now I think I'm adding to them, because I can't cover up indefinitely for you, and sooner or later it's bound to come out that you aren't doing your share. I feel it would be best for us both if I stop protecting you." You then specify exactly what you will and will not do for your colleague in the future, so both of you know the new ground rules. Then follow them.

Once you get into the habit of generating many possible solutions to an infuriating or depressing problem, you can break out of the narrow choices that most of us set for ourselves: "Stay here and suffer" versus "leave here and die." Suppose you are the victim of a bullying boss. What are the possibilities? You can:

- Yell back at your boss—some bullies only back down that way. (Be careful about this one.)
- Talk to him or her calmly when you are both in a good mood, stating clearly that these tirades upset you and what does he or she suggest that you do?
- Set yourself a bottom line of behavior you will not tolerate, and warn your boss that if the abusiveness continues, you will quit. (And if it does, you must; false threats are useless.)
- Say nothing and look for another job. If the problem is that you feel trapped in the one you have, you can investigate ways to get out of the trap: perhaps by going to night school to learn new skills, transferring within your company, contacting employment agencies . . . .
- Change your usual pattern of responding to your boss: instead of taking it personally and becoming upset, you might bypass his or her words entirely with sympathetic remarks designed to reach the boss's own unhappiness ("Gosh, Fred, I didn't realize you're having such a tough time with that Cassidy account; I don't blame you for being upset. I'll get back on it right away").
- See if there are other employees in the company who feel the way you do about the boss or who have experienced the same problem (e.g., harassment, discrimination). One person may not be able to do much, but an organized group can.
- Remember that humor is an excellent antidote to anger. Try to put things in perspective and see whether the situation really is as serious later as it seems to be now.

What all these strategies have in common is the recognition that anger is not a mysterious force over which we have no control. We may not be able to control the momentary irritations and larger furies of life, but we can decide what to do about them.

*See also* Bosses: Managing Relationships with Superiors; Rational Thinking; Self-Managed Change; Self-Talk; Stress; Type A Behavior Pattern.

## Bibliography

Burns, David. (1980). *Feeling good: The new mood therapy.* New York: Bantam. This book is the "godfather" of the cognitive-behavioral approach to emotion management, and still the best explanation of how we generate our own emotions.

Burns, David. (1989). *The feeling good workbook.* New York: New American Library. A practical guide to living with, and getting beyond, negative emotions.

Lerner, Harriet G. (1985). *The dance of anger.* New York: Harper & Row. An excellent description of the systems approach to anger in relationships, with many useful case studies.

Tavris, Carol. (1989). *Anger: The misunderstood emotion.* 2nd ed. New York: Touchstone. A review of the uses and abuses of anger in modern life, and a critique of common assumptions (e.g., that anger is a "natural instinct," that anger must always be expressed or it will fester). New concluding chapter offers practical solutions to anger with difficult people, chronic anger, anger after divorce or disaster, and anger at injustice.

—CAROL TAVRIS

# ANXIETY

Anxiety is experienced as a complex of physical and emotional responses to the anticipation of a future event which is perceived as potentially overwhelming. Since anxiety is a response to what might happen, it differs from fear, which is a response to what is happening. Anxiety symptoms can include the following: warmth throughout the body, shakiness, hyperventilation, sweating palms, light-headedness, nausea, choking, blurred vision, and mental disorientation.

## Relationship to Work

Anxiety or panic attacks commonly occur when one or more stress factors exist in a person's life (Handly, 1985). Job stresses may include one or more of the following: too much work, low pay, coworker friction, low performance confidence, decreasing promotional opportunities, and low job interest. These and other stresses can decrease the worker's sense of control over his or her situation and lead to a sudden panic attack. The powerlessness that stems naturally from unresolved conflicts and chronic feelings of being trapped precipitates the onset of work-related anxiety. Work-related anxiety includes two levels of stressful concern: evaluation and internal conflict.

**Evaluation by Others.** Concern over possible negative evaluation is one of the major sources of job stress:

1. *Job Interviews.* Anxiety indicates that something is important to us. The more we want something that we anticipate not getting, the more anxious we become. Going into a job interview with the attitude that we must have that job and no opportunities will ever come this way again is to fuel the fires of anxiety.

2. *Criticism.* When self-esteem is low, we are all especially vulnerable to the criticisms of others. This may lead to feeling uneasy in the presence of both coworkers and superiors, since we may anticipate a rejecting response from them.

3. *Performance Anxiety.* When we base our whole self-worth as a person on how we perform, we may create an attitude which constantly anticipates failure. Any mistake represents a potential discrediting of our entire being. Anxiety is the natural consequence of a perfectionistic expectation of one's performance.

**Internal Conflict.** Anxiety is generated by chronic unresolved conflicts which lead to feelings of being trapped and out of control.

1. *Home-Career Conflict.* One patient who loved her job also wanted desperately to be the perfect mother and stay home with her newborn child. Suddenly, she developed a driving phobia and could no longer commute to work. As distressing as the phobia was, it served to resolve an overwhelming and anxiety-producing conflict.

2. *Dream Job Versus Practical Need.* Much stress can be generated when we feel that we *must* stay with the job we have. We may dream of being able to do what we've always wanted to do, but fear that it would not put food on the table. Persons like this may start resenting their families and subconsciously blame them for keeping the family from doing the work they want. They feel trapped, and that will eventually lead to anxiety.

3. *Anticipating Retirement.* If our identity has been excessively defined by our employment, we may experience a great deal of anxiety due to inadequate new sources of self-definition. Even if we have not been happy with our job for a very long time, it is better than having no identity.

## Application

There are two levels of treatment for work-related anxiety: symptomatic and attitudinal.

**Symptomatic.** This first level addresses the physical experience of anxiety which includes various behavioral techniques to reduce the bodily sensations of anxiety. This symptomatic level of treatment may include the following:

1. *Breathing.* When you are chronically stressed, you tend to breathe in a shallow manner, which in turn can lead to lightheadedness or dizziness. Slow, diaphragmatic breaths can go a long way in helping your body feel more relaxed.
2. *Exercise and Diet.* Adhering to basic principles of good eating and exercise is a major way to reduce stress and anxiety. Exercise is not only an effective way to burn off anxiety-producing adrenaline, but has a positive effect on your self-esteem.
3. *Acceptance.* Fighting anxiety makes it worse. Accepting anxiety often allows it to pass naturally.
4. *Focusing.* When you direct your attention onto some external object, you are not dwelling on the fears and conflicts which breed anxiety.

**Attitudinal.** The second level of treatment addresses the attitudinal or cognitive dimension. How we think affects how we feel; our perceptions influence our emotions. When assessing and changing our anxiety-producing thoughts and perceptions, we can, as a consequence, assert some control over our feelings. Below are some attitudinal treatments which have anxiety-reducing potential:

1. *Freedom.* You may feel trapped because you are not aware that everything you do is a choice. Saying "should," "ought," or "have to" usually indicates feelings of helplessness and the belief that life (and your job) is something that happens to you, not something that you make happen. Not liking your job doesn't make you anxious; your illusion that you have no choices makes you anxious. You are trapped by your attitude that you have no freedom. You may not have every choice, but you do always have the potential to choose between or among the choices.
2. *Assertiveness.* Whenever you have an important feeling that you do not give permission to yourself to own and express, you are setting up the conditions for anxiety. If you are in a job situation which creates feelings of frustration and resentment, but you do not give yourself permission to process them, you are creating an emotional trap to which anxiety naturally responds.
3. *Self-Esteem.* It is fine to strive for excellence, but it is not healthy to feel that your worth as a person depends on being perfect. There is more to you than

your work. Work can be an important source of confidence, but it does not have to represent all of who you are.

*See also* Assertion; Job Interviewing; Job Search; Perfectionism: Overcoming; Rational Thinking.

## Bibliography

Freudenberger, H.J., & North, G. (1982). *Situational anxiety.* New York: Carroll and Graf. Explores specific anxiety-producing situations and how to deal with them more effectively. Chapter 8 discusses "new job anxiety."

Goodwin, D. W. (1986). *Anxiety.* New York: Ballantine Books. Clarifies the difference between fear and anxiety and reviews the whole range of anxiety disorders, including research into biochemical treatments.

Handly, R. (1985). *Anxiety and panic attacks: Their causes and cure.* New York: Rawson. Written by a former anxiety sufferer, this book outlines a five-point recovery program which the author calls "life-plus." Emphasizes how the subconscious can control our life.

May, R. (1977). *The meaning of anxiety.* New York: W.W. Norton. A classic that explores anxiety from a biological, psychological, cultural, and philosophical perspective.

McCullough, C. J., & Mann, R.W. (1985). *Managing your anxiety.* Los Angeles: Jeremy P. Tarcher. A comprehensive treatment program from a holistic perspective.

Wilson, R. (1986). Panic: *Taking control of anxiety attacks.* New York: Harper and Row.

—CHRISTOPHER J. MCCULLOUGH

# ASIAN AMERICANS

According to the 1980 U.S. Census, there are 3.7 million Asian Americans and Pacific Islanders in the United States. The largest subgroups are Chinese (812,178), Filipinos (781,894), Japanese (716,331), Asian Indians (387,223), and Koreans (357,393). While it is not possible in this brief overview to provide a history of the various Asian American subgroups, a complete understanding of Asian Americans requires an appreciation of the historical context of their early immigration and adaptation in this country. This history, while unique for each subgroup, was generally characterized by the provision of cheap labor, social isolation, benign neglect, and discrimination (e.g., the Chinese Exclusion Act of 1882).

More recently, Asian Americans have been subjected to a paradoxical form of prejudice. In the past, they have often been referred to as the "invisible minority" or the "forgotten minority." The latest stereotype has labeled them the "successful minority." This label has perpetuated the neglect of this minority group by the government, policy makers, and social scientists. A "successful" minority group must have no need of assistance or attention.

## Relationship to Work

Research studies of Asian Americans' vocational needs and characteristics are limited. The results of these studies and more recent observations are summarized here. First, some studies suggest that Asian Americans have personality traits that are clustered into three dimensions which are relevant to their career development: personal control, interpersonal orientation, and tolerance of ambiguity.

**Personal Control.** Asian Americans tend to be more dependent and obedient to authority than whites. Personal autonomy also seems to be less important for Asian Americans. This high level of conformity may be due to the traditional values of respect for authority and submergence of individuality so common among Asian cultures.

**Interpersonal Orientation.** Research has found that Asian Americans tend to be more emotionally withdrawn, socially isolated, and verbally inhibited than whites. The Asian subgroups also tend to be less expressive and less aggressive. Researchers have concluded that the social discomfort experienced by these Asian American students may be caused by conflict between the informal nature of social relationships in American culture and their own more formal and traditional cultural values and minority status.

**Tolerance of Ambiguity.** Asian Americans also seem to dislike uncertainty, ambiguity, and novel-experimental situations. This low tolerance of ambiguity among Asian Americans may be why they tend to choose highly technical and scientific fields.

Besides personality differences, Leong's (1985) review of the literature on Asian Americans also identified cultural differences in work values. Unlike white Americans, Asian Americans may have more extrinsic and pragmatic work values (e.g., money, security). To the extent that work values may guide career choices and career plans, Asian Americans may make choices that are consistent with their values but that may be misperceived by other Americans. In general, white Americans tend to have a preference or bias for more intrinsic and self-fulfillment-type work values.

## Application

**Asian American Workers.** In planning your own career development, you need to be aware of your personality styles and how these styles may be perceived by other Americans. To the extent that you may possess personality styles that are not congruent with white majority culture, these styles may serve as barriers or impediments to your career advancement. Such barriers may be based on either stereotypes or actual cultural differences in personality styles and problem-solving behaviors. The same applies for work values.

If you are likely to be overly dependent on authorities for direction and support, it could affect not only your career decision-making style, but also the nature and scope of your career choices. White Americans, as managers and supervisors, may perceive this external and nonindividualistic orientation as evidence of a lack of self-initiative, achievement drive, and assertiveness. In general, highly group-oriented and conforming individuals are seen as lacking leadership abilities. Such stereotypical perceptions often lead to barriers to the career aspirations and advancement of Asian Americans. These cultural stereotypes, similar to sex role stereotypes, operate to limit the career options of Asian Americans. Many Asian Americans, like women, are perceived as lacking the requisite traits to be a good manager or a good lawyer.

Their interpersonal orientation may also explain why Asian Americans tend to segregate into a few occupational groups. The tendency of Asian Americans to choose occupations in computer science, engineering, physical sciences, and technical trades may be due to this social anxiety, discomfort, and inhibition. In other words, Asian Americans are underrepresented in the social sciences and similar vocations because these occupations require verbal-persuasive skills and high levels of social interactions (e.g., lawyers and psychologists) which is counter to their personality style and interpersonal orientations. This would also explain why there is a general lack of movement into managerial and executive positions among Asian Americans. There are, of course, individual differences among Asian Americans in their levels of social anxiety. Such social difficulties may be due to personality differences or cultural differences between Asian Americans and white Americans. Regardless of the causes, social inhibition among Asian Americans can serve as a career barrier, especially in careers which require a high level of social interaction (e.g., management).

You will have to decide for yourself how you will handle these cultural, personality, and value differences. For example, some Asian Americans have taken assertiveness workshops to help advance their careers, while others have chosen to stay in careers dominated by Asian Americans. Regardless of the type of strategy, you need to recognize the potential problems created by these cultural/personality differences and strive to minimize them. One common approach has been to learn about white American work behaviors and to use those behaviors at work without giving up one's cultural value system. E. C. Stewart's *American Cultural Patterns* provides an excellent introduction to mainstream American cultural patterns.

**Non-Asian Americans.** If you are not an Asian American, but work with them, you need to counter some of the stereotypes associated with Asian Americans while at the same time recognizing important cultural differences in personality styles. It cannot be overemphasized that many occupations can be successfully performed by individuals with different personality styles. Recognizing the important cultural differences outlined above allows us to identify the strengths of this minority group which can be optimally used in appropriate career or job placements. Just as many organizational consultants are using the Myers-Briggs Type Indicator (MBTI) to educate organizational leaders to the fact that it takes different types of individuals to make up an efficient organization, it should be recognized that the unique cultural and personality traits of Asian Americans can be an asset in many different occupations. Research on organizations has found that increasing the homogeneity of the workforce in an organization may lead to stagnation, whereas increasing diversity may lead to innovation and synergism.

*See also* Culturally Different: Working with; Discrimination: Language; Discrimination: Race; Law in the Workplace.

## Bibliography

Daniels, Roger. (1988). *Asian American: Chinese and Japanese in the United States since l850.* Seattle: University of Washington Press. A contemporary book on the various dimensions of Asian American experience.

Leong, F.T.L. (1985). Career development in Asian Americans. *Journal of College Student Personnel,* 26: 539-46. A scholarly review of personality and vocational studies related to the career choice and behavior of Asian Americans.

Stewart, E.C. (1971). *American cultural patterns: A cross-cultural perspective.* Pittsburgh: Regional Council for International Understanding. An excellent introduction to mainstream American cultural values and patterns of behaviors.

Tachiki, A. et al. (1971). *Roots: An Asian American reader.* Los Angeles: UCLA Asian American Study Center. Another excellent collection of articles on the Asian American experience.

—FREDERICK T. L. LEONG

# ASSERTION

Assertion is the appropriate expression of one's ideas, opinions, feelings, or preferences to another person in a direct and honest manner. It involves the ability to stand up for one's rights without infringing upon the rights of others. An appropriate assertion should be neither threatening nor punishing toward another person. In addition, assertion does not involve an undue or an excessive amount of anxiety. The goal is to be able to say how one feels about something if one chooses to do so. There will be some situations in which individuals will wisely choose not to express themselves, not because they can not handle the interchange, but because they believe it is not in their best interest to speak out.

## Relationship to Work

In the work setting, there are many situations in which it is in one's best interest to be able to appropriately assert or express oneself. There are the everyday situations of just initiating or maintaining a conversation with people at work, asking for assistance or clarification on a job-related task, or complimenting another colleague on a job well done. There are also less common but very important situations, such as requesting a promotion or a salary increase, asking a supervisor or boss for a special favor, or expressing annoyance or anger toward someone who has not done what they were supposed to do.

Work situations constantly require people to assert themselves. Some of these situations will be easy to handle, while others will be very difficult. The difficulty of the situation for each person varies based on a number of factors. A major factor for most people is whether or not they have had to deal with that type of interaction previously. Assertion, like most communication skills are learned behavior. If a person has not had to learn how to interact in such a situation he or she will likely lack the skill to do so. Mastery of any skill requires practice, whether one is learning to jump rope, swim, or communicate effectively. In addition, if the person has previously been punished or received an unfavorable comment or reaction for trying to assert him or herself in a situation, the person is likely to feel anxious and be less willing to try expressing him or herself again. Thus the individual has, in a sense, learned not to speak up. Fortunately, for any particular type of situation that one cannot handle, the individual can always learn or relearn how to express him or herself in such a situation if given enough instruction and practice.

The ease or difficulty of the situation varies for each individual depending on the person with whom he or she must interact and with the type of behavior called for in the situation. In the workplace, an individual may have to deal with six categories of people:

1. Supervisors/superiors/ bosses
2. Colleagues/coworkers
3. Subordinates—people whom one supervises
4. Consumers
5. General public
6. Good friends or family members at the same workplace

The importance of dealing with each type of people will vary depending on a person's occupation. For instance, a foreman's ability to relate to his crew (subordinates) is critical. A nurse's ability to relate to patients (consumers) and doctors (colleagues or superiors) is also critical. Each person's ability to handle these different types of people will vary considerably. Some people have an easier time dealing with superiors and others find it easier to deal with the general public. Each person has his or her own hierarchy of which people are easier or more difficult to interact with.

Similarly, the type of behavior needed in the interaction will influence the ease of handling the situation. The type of behaviors include expressing positive feelings, self-affirmations, or negative feelings. These feelings may include the following:

*Expressing Positive Feelings*
1. Giving positive feedback
2. Complimenting someone
3. Asking for help or clarification on a task
4. Initiating, maintaining, or terminating a conversation
5. Presenting a report
6. Asking for personal assistance

*Self-Affirmation*
1. Standing up for legitimate rights
   a. Asking for promotion
   b. Asking for raise
   c. Asking for time off
   d. Asking someone to cover for you
2. Refusing requests
   a. Extra duties/assignments
   b. Overtime work
   c. Personal favors
3. Expressing personal opinions including disagreements

*Expressing Negative Feelings*
1. Providing constructive criticism
2. Expressing justified annoyance or disappointment
   a. Repeated tardiness
   b. Incomplete assignments
   c. Sloppy workmanship
   d. Poor performance
   e. Failure to comply with regulations
3. Expressing justified anger after annoyance has been expressed and suggestions for improvement have been offered (see also **Anger; Employee Assistance Programs**).
   a. Continued tardiness
   b. Continued incomplete assignments
   c. Continued sloppy workmanship
   d. Continued poor performance
   e. Continued failure to comply with regulations

People find that different types of assertion are more or less difficult for them. Some will have no trouble standing up for rights but immeasurable difficulty expressing justified annoyance or anger toward others. Other people will have a different pattern of behaviors that are difficult for them. Difficulty level may also be affected by the combination of the particular behavior to be expressed and the person to whom it is being directed. Again, with instruction and practice most people can learn to handle almost any situation they might encounter in the workplace.

## Application

Learning how to assert yourself will take a certain amount of work and practice. However, there are a number of things that you can do to help yourself.
1. First, you need to look at the areas in which you have difficulty. Which behaviors and people at work are difficult for you to deal with?
2. Do you feel anxious in these situations or just lack the verbal skills of knowing what to say and how to say it?
   a. If you are too anxious to deal with the situation you may need to learn some relaxation techniques (see **Relaxation: Progressive Muscle**)
   b. If you aren't sure of what and how to say your response, consider the following guidelines.
      1) Think about what you really want to say
      2) Look the person in the eyes when you speak
      3) Make your message brief, concise, and to the point
      4) Be clear and include necessary details
      5) Do not give long-winded explanations
      6) Try to use appropriate loudness, tone, and inflection
      7) Avoid whining, pleading, and sarcasm
3. Once you have decided what you need to say and how to say it, you will want to practice or rehearse the situation. You can do this in a variety of ways. You can write out a script and read over it a number of times. You can close your eyes and imagine delivering your message to the other person. You can practice with an audio- or videorecorder. Probably the best way to practice is to have another person rehearse the situation with you. Let the other person play the person you need to deal with at work. Repeatedly practice what you want to say. Practice until you feel relatively comfortable in the situation(not too much anxiety) and until you can make fairly good eye contact.

4. Sometimes you may know what you want to say and basically how to say it, but are still having difficulty making yourself deliver the message. In such cases, it is likely that you have some counterproductive beliefs that are inhibiting you from speaking (see **Rational Thinking**). If you identify that you have a counterproductive belief that is interfering with your message, you will have to work on changing that belief to a more productive one. Your counterproductive beliefs may fit into one of the following categories (Galassi & Galassi, 1977):

a. Counterproductive beliefs about rights and responsibilities: I don't have the right to inconvenience other people; I don't have the right to question authority.

b. Counterproductive beliefs about how to behave or appear to others: If I ask for assistance at work, I'll appear incompetent.

c. Counterproductive beliefs about probable consequences: If I say what I think, I might get fired.

It is important, as you learn to express yourself in the workplace, that you consider the rights of others and the appropriateness of your assertion. Do not become overzealous and just blurt out inappropriately. This behavior will not work in your best interest. On the other hand, if you learn to express yourself appropriately, you will reap many everyday rewards and feel better about yourself.

*See also* Anger; Anxiety; Employee Assistance Programs; Rational Thinking; Relaxation: Progressive Muscle; Self-Talk; Shyness.

## Bibliography

Alberti, R. E., & Emmons, M. L. (1986). *Your perfect right: A guide to assertive living.* 5th ed. San Luis Obispo, CA: Impact Publishers. An introduction to assertive behavior with a number of examples and a discussion of the differences between assertive, aggressive, and nonassertive behavior.

Galassi, J. P., & Bruch, M. A. (in press). Counseling with social interaction problems: Assertion and social anxiety. In S. D. Brown & R. W. Lent (Eds.), *Handbook of counseling psychology.* 2nd ed. New York: John Wiley. A comprehensive review of describing and treating social interaction problems.

Galassi, J. P., Galassi, M. D., & Fulkerson, K. (1984). Assertion training in theory and practice: An update. In C. M. Franks (Ed.), *New developments in practical behavior therapy: From research to clinical application* (pp. 319-76). New York: The Haworth Press. A scholarly review of the empirical literature on the assessment, conceptualization, and treatment of assertion.

Galassi, M. D., & Galassi, J. P. (1977). *Assert yourself! How to be your own person.* New York: Human Sciences Press. A systematic and easy-to-understand book for increasing self-expression. The book has discussions and exercises on a variety of topics, including assertion with authority figures and assertion at work.

Kelley, C. (1979). *Assertion training: A facilitator's guide.* LaJolla, CA: University Associates, Inc.

—MERNA DEE GALASSI

# ASSESSMENT CENTERS

Assessment Centers involve a program and set of procedures developed and used by an organization to systematically describe and evaluate individuals (usually employees) for purposes of personnel decisions. The term assessment center may also refer to a program or set of activities which take place over a period of time ranging from one to five days.

Although the U.S. military used elements of the assessment center method in the Second World War, the method's first industrial application was in 1956 by AT&T (Bray & Grant, 1966). Gaugler, Rosenthal, Thornton, and Bentson (1987) estimate that more than 2,000 organizations (both private and public) are currently involved in some type of an assessment center program. Centers are used for such diverse purposes as selection, placement, early identification of management potential, promotion, employee development, career management, and training program design. Although assessment centers are most often used for evaluating current or potential managers, they have also been used with college students, engineers, salespersons, military personnel, rehabilitation counselors, school administrators, and blue collar workers (Gaugler et al., 1987, p. 493).

While there is a great deal of variability in the design of assessment centers (usually linked to their specific purpose), the following elements are typically involved:

1. *Assessment Center Dimensions.* At the heart of most assessment centers is the task of evaluating individuals on a set of job relevant knowledge and skill dimensions. In the classical application of the method, first-level supervisors would be assessed as potential candidates for promotion to middle management. Thus, the knowledge, skills, abilities, and behavior patterns required for a middle manager's job would first be established. Candidates being reviewed for promotion are then evaluated against these factors.

Common assessment center dimensions for managerial jobs include oral and written communications, personal impact, planning, decision making, interpersonal relations, and problem solving. Most centers make use of eight or more skill domains or dimensions.

2. *Multiple Assessment Techniques.* Assessment centers make use of a variety of techniques to measure the extent to which a person possesses each of the critical

worker requirements. Techniques include psychological tests (most often ability and interest inventories); the in-depth, structured interview; work samples (e.g., composing work-relevant correspondence, performing job relevant computations); and behavioral simulations. Gaugler et al. (1987) found that over three-quarters of the assessment centers in their study made use of an intelligence test. They also report that, on average, the centers used over seven different devices to evaluate candidates.

3. *Reliance on Behavioral Evidence.* A distinguishing feature of the assessment center method is the reliance on an individual's behavior as exhibited at the center as a basis for inferring level of functioning vis-a-vis the critical job dimensions. Thus, much of the time spent in the typical center is in groups of from six to eight similar individuals who are performing in behavioral simulations. For example, such groups may be asked to perform a planning or a budget allocation task. Such tasks are designed to promote certain interpersonal dynamics and behaviors. Staff members observe and record incidents of behavior which serve as the basis of inferring skills.

4. *Multiple Points of View.* The typical assessment center makes use of several staff members. Often these are company employees (either managers or personnel specialists). However, it is not uncommon to use outside experts as well. For example, according to one review, approximately 12% of the centers used a psychologist as a member of the assessment center staff (Gaugler et al., 1987).

5. *Careful Integration of Information.* In most assessment centers, staff meet immediately after the last session involving candidates to review the information that was gathered. Each candidate is carefully and thoroughly discussed.

The outcome of this discussion is an assessment (usually reached by consensus) of the candidate's strengths and weaknesses. Often this takes the form of both a quantitative profile (ratings on the skill dimensions) and qualitative report. Where the center is intended to aid in some personnel decision (e.g., who to promote), the staff are asked to provide recommendations. The recommendation is then placed in the candidate's personnel file or passed on to the appropriate decision maker.

6. *Feedback to Candidates.* Most organizations provide information to each candidate with regard to the assessments (and recommendations) made by the center staff. This often takes the form of a written report that is sent to the candidate directly. However, centers set up for purposes of employee development or career planning may make use of a face-to-face meeting with each candidate. Here a center staff member delivers the feedback personally to the candidate at his or her workplace. At the discretion of the candidate, the candidate's manager may or

may not attend such a session. One study found that only 26% of the companies provided feedback directly to the immediate supervisor of a candidate (Gaugler et al., 1987).

## Relationship to Work

An individual might encounter an assessment center under a variety of circumstances. These include being involved in one or more of the following roles:

1. *As a Candidate for Promotion.* In this context the individual is being assessed for possible promotion to a higher level.
2. *As a Candidate for Development.* Here, the individual would be participating in the center to obtain insight regarding job-related strengths and weaknesses. This might be with regard to either the qualities needed for a current job or those required for future assignments in the company. Presumably, any deficiencies identified would then be addressed with a developmental action plan.
3. *As a Center Staff Member.* Under these circumstances the individual would be trained in the skills needed to assess candidates and then be assigned in a center in the future.

## Application

Because assessment centers are used for many aspects of personnel work in organizations, you may wish to take advantage of one to further your career goals.

1. *Picking a Company to Work For.* When considering a company for a potential job, inquire about its use of assessment centers. Progressive organizations are more likely to use them.

2. *Learning About Your Developmental Needs.* If your organization uses an assessment center for developmental purposes, arrange to go through one. This would be to your advantage because usually such programs and resulting assessments are linked to a personalized plan for development. Your involvement also conveys to your supervisor and the company that you are serious about your career and motivated to take the initiative.

3. *Getting a Promotion.* Even when assessment centers are used for promotion, other factors (e.g., current job performance) are typically considered. However, it is usually to your advantage to seek out opportunities to go through an assessment center so that your availability and (hopefully) your suitability for promotion will be noticed by the company.

4. *Developing Your Assessment/Managerial Skills.* Assessment skills are important for managers. Thus, to the extent that this fits your career plans, take or create an opportunity to be trained as a center staff person. Your training will help you in many contexts. For example, Lorenzo (1984) found that managers trained as staff came away with better interviewing, oral presentation, oral defence, and written communication skills.

5. *Networking.* If you are trained as a center staff person, you will have the opportunity to meet with individuals (as other staff or as candidates) from all parts of the company. This can provide you with a wide perspective on the organization. It can also give you a large number of company-based contacts that will enhance your ability to do your current job or to obtain future jobs.

6. *Employment.* On-going assessment center programs make use of a number of individuals as personnel specialists. Thus, if your interests are in the personnel area, you might seek a job working in a center as a support or staff person.

*See also* Career Anchor; Career Development System within the Organization; Career Exploration; Career Path Possibilities within the Organization; Job Changing; Job Search; Managerial Skills; Networking; Promotion/ Raise; Testing.

## Bibliography

Bray, D., and Grant, D.L. (1966). The assessment center in the measurement of potential for business management. *Psychological Monographs.* 80, (17, WHOLE #625).

Gaugler, B.B., Rosenthall, D.B., Thornton, G.C. III, and Bentson. (1987). Meta analysis of assessment center validity. *Journal of Applied Psychology,* 72, 493-511. A somewhat technical summary of the evidence for the usefulness of assessment centers in personnel work.

Klimoski, R.J., & Brickner, M. (1987). Why do assessment centers work? The puzzle of assessment center validity. *Personnel Psychology,* 40, 243-60. A critical review of what we don't know about assessment centers with an emphasis on explaining their apparent usefulness.

Lorenzo, R.V. (1984). Effects of assessorship on managers' proficiency in acquiring, evaluation, and communicating information about people. *Personnel Psychology,* 37, 617-34.

Moses, J., & Byham. W.C. (eds.) (1977). *Applying the assessment center method.* New York: Pergamon Press. A series of original chapters covering most practical aspects of center design and operation (e.g., feeding back results).

Thornton, G.C. III, & Byham, W.C. (1982). *Assessment center and managerial performance.* New York: Academic press. Takes a theoretical and analytic view of assessment centers, covering research on assessment center features.

—RICHARD KLIMOSKI

# B

## BENEFITS

Employee benefits promote economic security by insuring against unpredictable events and raise living standards by providing access to important services. Employee benefits are any form of compensation paid for in whole or in part by the employer and not in the form of direct wages. Employee benefits also include services made available to the employee at no cost to the employer, such as information concerning health and fitness or local child care centers.

Social Security, unemployment insurance, and workers' compensation are legally required benefits. Other benefits, including pensions, health coverage, long-term disability insurance, and life insurance, are voluntarily provided by employers.

Employee benefit programs are not limited to income security and health insurance. As a result of demographic changes in the workforce, access to vital services such as child care and long-term care have become increasingly important employee benefit issues. Other specialized benefit programs include employer-provided education, training, and legal assistance. Some employee benefits, such as free parking, product discounts, and relocation-expense reimbursement, provide convenient and cost-saving services. Employee benefits also include paid sick leave, holidays, vacations, and parental leave.

An extensive (although not exhaustive) list of employment-based benefits is presented in Figure 1. As shown, a wide variety of mandatory and voluntary benefits serve a broad range of goals. Many voluntary benefits are encouraged by the federal government through favorable tax treatment.

## Relationship to Work

**Social Security.** Social Security Old-Age, Survivors, and Disability Insurance (OASDI) provides nearly all Americans a portion of covered earnings that are lost as a result of a person's old age, disability, or death. Workers' compensation and unemployment insurance also provide income security in case of unexpected events. The benefits provided under OASDI include:

1. Monthly benefits to those who are at least 62 years old (Although reduced benefits will continue to be paid at age 62, the age for full benefits, now 65, will be increased in the future) and retired or partially retired, along with monthly benefits to their eligible spouses and dependents
2. Monthly benefits to disabled workers and their eligible spouses and dependents
3. Lump-sum payment and monthly benefits to eligible survivors of deceased workers

Monthly benefit amounts are related to average earnings on which a worker pays Social Security taxes throughout his or her career years. The spouse's benefit adds an extra 50% to the primary retiree's benefit if the spouse is aged 65 or over, but somewhat less if the spouse is between ages 62 and 65. Once benefits begin, they are generally adjusted automatically to take into account consumer price index changes.

Since Social Security was not designed to meet all the financial needs that arise from a person's old age, disability, or death, particularly for persons earning higher than average incomes, employer-sponsored retirement, health, disability, and group life insurance plans were created to supplement Social Security benefits.

**Retirement Plans.** The two primary types of employer-sponsored pension plans are defined benefit plans and defined contribution plans. A defined benefit plan pays a predetermined benefit based on one of three formula types. The first type is the flat-benefit formula, which pays a specific dollar amount for each year of service recognized under the plan. The second is a career-average formula, which most often covers salaried workers. The third and most prevalent formula is the final-pay formula, which bases the benefit on earnings during the final years of the participant's career, when earnings are likely to be highest. This formula provides the greatest protection to the participant, but also represents the greatest cost to employers. According to the Bureau of Labor Statistics (BLS), 63% of

**Figure 1: Employment-Based Benefits in the United States**

## Types of Employee Benefits by Tax Treatment:

**Mandatory**
- Social Security retirement (OASI)
- Social Security disability (DI)
- Medicare Part A (Social Security HI)
- Workers'compensation
- Unemployment insurance
- Medicaid[a]
- Supplemental Security Income[a]
- Public assistance[a]

**Voluntary**

*Fully Taxable*
- Vacations
- Paid lunch
- Rest periods
- Severance pay
- Cash bonuses and awards

*Tax Exempt*
- Employee and dependent health insurance
- Retiree health insurance
- Dental insurance
- Vision insurance
- Employer-paid Medicare Part B (Social Security SMI) premiums
- Medicare Part B (Social Security SMI)[b]
- Education
- Legal assistance
- Child care
- Discounts
- Flexible spending accounts
- Parking
- Cafeteria facilities
- Meals

*Tax Deferred*
- Defined benefit pension plans
- Money-purchase retirement
- Deferred profit-sharing
- 401(k) salary reduction
- Thrift savings plans
- Employee stock ownershp plans
- Stock bonus plans
- Simplified employee pension plans
- IRA and Keogh plans

*Other Tax Preferred[c]*
- Life insurance
- Long-term disability insurance
- Sick leave or sickness and accident insurance
- Other leave (maternity, funeral, jury, etc.)

## Types of Employee Benefits by Function:

**Retirement Income Benfits**
- Social Security retirement (OASI)
- Defined benefit pension plans
- Money-purchase retirement
- Deferred profit-sharing
- 401(k) salary reduction
- Thrift savings plans
- Employee stock ownership plans
- Stock bonus plans
- Simplified employee pension plans
- IRA and Keogh plans
- Supplemental Security income

**Health Care**
- Employee and dependent health insurance
- Retiree health insurance
- Dental insurance
- Vision insurance
- Medicare (Social Security HI, SMI)
- Medicaid

**Other Benefits**
- Social Security disability (DI)
- Long-term disability insurance
- Life insurance
- Workers' compensation
- Unemployment insurance
- Public assistance
- Severance pay
- Child care
- Vacations
- Sick leave or sickness and accident insurance
- Other leave (maternity, funeral, jury, etc.)
- Paid lunch
- Rest periods
- Legal assistance
- Education
- Flexible spending accounts
- Bonuses and awards
- Parking
- Cafeteria facilities
- Meals
- Discounts

aFinanced from federal and state revenues.
bPremimums may be includable in itemized deductions or may be paid from after-tax income. Financed largely from federal general revenues.
cValue of insurance and leave availability are not taxed; insurance benefits and leave pay generally are taxed when paid.

**Source**: Joseph S. Piacentini and Timothy J. Cerino, *EBRI Databook on Employee Benefits,* Washington, DC: Employee Benefit Research Institute, 1990. Reprinted by permission.

full-time workers in medium-sized and large establishments participated in a defined benefit pension plan in 1989.

Under a defined contribution plan, an employer pays a certain amount into an individual account for each participant. Unlike a defined benefit plan, the benefit amount in retirement is not fixed. The contributions may follow a fixed formula, but the benefits vary in accordance with high or low investment returns and market values. The amount of the retirement benefit is determined by the amount in the account at retirement, and therefore cannot be calculated in advance. Employee contributions can be voluntary or mandatory. Employer contributions can be a percentage of salary or of profits. If a participant leaves the plan before he or she is fully vested, than the balance of the employer's contributions to that employee's account goes to increase other participants' accounts or to reduce future employer contributions. Benefits from a defined contribution plan are paid in the form of a lump sum, a series of installments, or annuities for the lifetime of the participant. Types of defined contribution plans include money purchase plans, profit sharing plans, and thrift plans, and may include 401(k) cash or deferred arrangements. In 1989, 48% of full-time workers in medium-sized and large establishments were covered by defined contribution plans, according to BLS (see **Pre-Retirement Planning; Retirement**).

**Health Insurance.** Employee benefits also provide American workers and their families access to important services, such as health care. Given the high cost of medical care, health insurance itself provides an important form of income security. Employers offer a wide range of health plans that cover other services in addition to basic health care, including dental, vision, mental health and substance abuse treatment, health promotion programs, and long-term care. Dependents of employees are generally covered under employer-provided health plans, and many plans continue coverage for workers who retire. In 1989, 94% of full-time employees in medium-sized and large establishments received medical care benefits fully or partially financed by their employer, according to BLS.

The traditional fee-for-service plan is the most prevalent employer-sponsored health plan. BLS reports that 74% of full-time employees in medium-sized and large establishments with health care coverage in 1989 participated in fee-for-service plans. Employer health plans can consist of basic health insurance, supplemental major medical insurance, or comprehensive insurance. Basic health insurance usually covers hospital expenses such as room and board, physician care in the hospital, and surgical procedures. Basic services usually are covered on a first-dollar basis with no deductibles or copayments. Supplemental major medical expenses cover medically necessary services not covered or fully covered under the basic plan. These services include inpatient and outpatient hospital care,

special nursing care, prescription drugs, and outpatient psychiatric care. Major medical coverage is usually subject to deductibles, copayments, and maximum benefit features. Insurance companies and employers are increasingly offering comprehensive plans that cover services typically found in both basic and supplemental plans. Most comprehensive plans require some type of employee cost sharing, such as deductibles and copayments.

As a result of soaring health care cost inflation, employers are adding managed care approaches, such as utilization review, and alternative health care systems, such as health maintenance organizations (HMOs) and preferred provider organizations (PPOs), to their fee-for-service plans in an attempt to control costs while maintaining high-quality medical care. Managed care approaches include design features whereby medical services personnel evaluate the type of care an employee receives and help the patient review health care options. They may employ panels of physicians and/or hospitals that use managed care approaches and provide group health care services at a discounted or flat rate.

An HMO delivers health services for a fixed prepayment and bears the financial risk if the cost of care exceeds the payment. As a result, HMOs have a strong incentive to control costs. HMO doctors have no motives for performing unnecessary services. In fact, most HMOs provide health promotion services such as drug counseling and nutrition workshops to reduce employee need for health care, thereby reducing expenses. HMOs can be classified as group/staff models and independent practice association (IPA) models. In a group/staff model HMO, there are limited treatment sites and the physicians work primarily for the HMO. In most cases, the employee is unable to choose a physician outside the HMO staff without incurring substantial out-of-pocket expenses. In an IPA model HMO, the HMO contracts with a network of physicians who see HMO patients in their private offices. The IPA model HMO may have higher premiums than the group/staff model, but the IPA model, which has many locations and providers, offers more choice for the employee. In 1989, 17% of employees in the BLS survey with employer-provided health insurance participated in HMO plans.

Unlike HMOs, PPOs do not accept a fixed payment for all services and often do not assume any financial risk for excessive use by employees. PPO physicians offer members individual health services at a discounted fee and agree to comply with utilization review. In return, PPO management channels patients to these providers. PPO patients are free to choose any provider; however, if they utilize providers in the PPO, they will generally face lower copayments than if they choose a provider who is not a member of the PPO. Ten percent of full-time workers in the BLS survey who were covered by employer-sponsored medical plans in 1989 used PPOs.

**Disability Insurance.** The two primary types of employer-provided disability insurance plans are short-term disability plans and long-term disability plans. Short-term disability protection includes paid sick leave, which is often available without a waiting period and pays 100% of the worker's normal earnings. Sickness and accident insurance has a waiting period of at least one week and pays 50% to 67% of normal earnings. A worker generally receives compensation under a long-term disability plan when short-term benefits expire and when the worker qualifies to receive Social Security disability benefits. In 1989, 89% of employees in the BLS survey had short-term disability coverage, while 45% had long-term coverage (see **Social Security Disability Claim; Workers' Compensation**).

**Group Life Insurance.** The major types of group life insurance coverage include paid-up, ordinary life, and term life insurance. The most commonly used type is group term life insurance which is coverage bought for a specific period (usually one year). Term insurance only pays a benefit upon death. There are no savings features or buildup of cash value. The amount of coverage is most often expressed as a flat-dollar amount or a percentage of salary. Since life insurance is intended to replace a portion of the deceased employee's income, coverage may differ depending on individual earnings. Some employers offer supplemental life insurance plans and dependent life insurance plans. Ninety-four percent of workers in the BLS survey received employer-sponsored life insurance coverage in 1989.

**Flexible Benefit Plans.** Some employers offer a flexible benefit plan, also known as a cafeteria plan because the employee is permitted to choose among benefit options. Flexible benefit plans provide employees with a minimum level of basic coverage. Additional coverage or additional benefits in a variety of areas may be purchased through nontaxable salary reductions.

## Application

Employee benefits make up a sizable portion of total compensation and it is important not to overlook their worth. If you accept a higher paying job and pay more out-of-pocket expenses to duplicate benefits at a prior job, you may gain nothing at all. Only by understanding your own personal and family situation and knowing which benefits are provided and how each works can you utilize the full value of a benefit package. Knowledge of your own needs and how each benefit works is especially important under a flexible benefit plan because of the degree of choice permitted. Don't choose solely based on your immediate need. Think long-term.

All private-sector employers that sponsor benefit programs must automatically provide a summary description of their benefit plan. Read it. If you have questions, most plan administrators will provide more information upon request.

When evaluating a benefit package, get answers to the following questions:

1. How is the value of the benefit enhanced by tax treatment?
2. What are the vesting requirements for the pension plan?
3. What type of health insurance coverage will your dependents receive?
4. How does your spouse's employer's health plan cover you?
5. What are your health insurance premium, deductible, and copayment costs?
6. What type of services does the health plan cover, and to what extent?
7. What is the plan's definition of disability and how long are you covered?

If you take the time to learn about your benefits, ask questions, and understand your own immediate and long-term needs, you will get the most value out of your employer's benefit plan.

*See also* Law in the Workplace; Pay; Pre-Retirement Planning; Retirement; Social Security Disability Claim; Workers' Compensation.

## Bibliography

Bernstein, M. C., & Bernstein, J. B. (1988). *Social Security: The system that works.* New York: Basic Books.

Employee Benefit Research Institute. (1990). *Fundamentals of employee benefit programs.* 4th ed. Washington, DC: Employee Benefit Research Institute. Basic primer on the entire field of private- and public-sector employee benefits. Reviews the history of each type of benefit, and outlines its design and structure. Also reviews related legislation and regulations.

Friedland, R. B. (1990). *Facing the costs of long-term care.* Washington, DC: Employee Benefit Research Institute.

Piacentini, J. S., & Cerino, T. J. (1990). *EBRI databook on employee benefits.* Washington, DC: Employee Benefit Research Institute. Provides extensive information in tabular form on the entire range of employee benefit programs and workforce-related issues.

Saltford, N. C., & Heck, R. K. Z. (1990). *An overview of employee benefits supportive of families.* Washington, DC: Employee Benefit Research Institute.

U. S. Department of Health and Human Services. (1988). *Social Security handbook.* Washington, DC: U. S. Government Printing Office.

—EMPLOYEE BENEFIT RESEARCH INSTITUTE
(WITH SPECIAL THANKS TO HEATHER KENNEDY FOR ASSISTANCE IN DEVELOPING THIS ARTICLE)

# BIODATA

The autobiographical questionnaire is the most complete and sophisticated form of what is commonly called "biodata." Biodata is information gathered in a standardized and scoreable manner by one of various data collection methods: paper and pencil, multiple-choice instrument that solicits answers on much of the personal characteristics and competency information obtained in application blanks, interviews, reference checks, and other sources. Everyone gets asked the same questions in exactly the same way, and no answer is scored unless it has been shown through research to be related to job performance in a statistically significant and rationally understandable way.

## Relationship to Work

The first use of biodata in the American industrial setting is reported to have been in 1892 in Georgia by insurance company managers seeking to improve agent selection. Today, 100 years later, the use of biodata to select agents is conducted nationwide under the aegis of the Life Insurance Marketing and Research Association. Biodata are now used for making selection and promotion decisions with a range of workers, including managers, firstline supervisors, power plant operators, office clerks, and police officers. Validity levels (which measure job-relatedness, the extent to which the data are related to actual job performance) for these uses are consistently as good as and usually better than those observed for the traditional general aptitude and related types of tests. There is also a very important "extra." In these days of civil rights concern about job-relatedness and the difference between how minorities and whites, and males and females, score on tests, the autobiographical questionnaire usually has 30% to 40% less minority-majority score difference than that produced by general aptitude and related tests. This very often is also accompanied by little or no male-female difference.

The logic of the autobiographical questionnaire measurement is (a) that past behavior is predictive of future behavior, and (b) that present values, judgments, and attitudes will be the same. What persons report, such as highest education level reached, grades achieved, prior absentee and lateness levels, and work dismissals typically, is related to job performance. Also typically related are answers to questions covering such present elements as (a) work preferences (e.g., working with varying numbers of others versus working alone, or working on a number of things at a time versus one) and (b) self-estimates of the performance ratings given by previous supervisors.

Several sample questions used to collect biodata are listed below:

1.  The grades I received in high school mathematics courses were:
    a. mostly A's
    b. mostly A's and B's
    c. mostly B's and C's
    d. mostly C's and D's or below
    e. I didn't go to high school
2.  In the last six months, the number of times I have been late for work is:
    a. none
    b. 1
    c. 2
    d. 3
    e. 4 or more
3.  My work habits are such that I prefer:
    a. to work on one thing at a time
    b. to work on several things at a time
    c. to work on many things at a time
    d. to work on a great many things at a time

While autobiographical questionnaires potentially may be used in many job situations, they aren't to be found on every street corner or shelf. Developing one is a very specialized process. First, an experimental instrument is developed and administered to a large group of workers, for example, police officers. Then, performance data are collected for these workers. Second, the answers to each question are analyzed to identify those responses which are significantly and rationally related to job performance. And, finally, a scoring system is developed by giving weights to those responses that are related to job performance. An acceptable questionnaire, then, must have been built on an exceptionally large group of workers and/or have clear "cross-validation" evidence (evidence on a second, independent sample which shows that the job-relatedness of the autobiographical system "holds up" when applied to new and different groups).

When compared with traditional general aptitude tests, well-developed autobiographical questionnaires are a fuller measure of a person's characteristics and competencies. They are less threatening and simpler; they have no time limit. Most important, they do their job with equal or greater validity and with less adverse impact.

*See also* Testing.

—FRANK W. ERWIN

# BOSSES: MANAGING RELATIONSHIPS WITH SUPERIORS

Managing relationships with superiors refers to the process of consciously working with one's superiors to secure the best results for oneself, one's boss, and one's organization. Studies suggest that effective employees make an intentional effort to manage their relationships not only with subordinates but also with their bosses (e.g., Gabarro, 1978, 1987; Gabarro & Kotter, 1980; Kotter, 1986). An employee's immediate boss can play a critical role in obtaining needed resources, ensuring that priorities are consistent with organizational objectives, and linking an employee's efforts to the rest of the organization (see also **Mentoring; Promotion/Raise**).

Superior-subordinate relationships often suffer from several recurrent problems: conflicts in working styles; failure to work out agreed-upon goals and priorities; and unrealistic expectations on the part of one or both parties (Gabarro, 1987). These problems can be minimized if subordinates recognize that boss-subordinate relationships involve mutual dependence between two fallible human beings. Some people fail to realize the extent to which their bosses are dependent on them for cooperation, effort, and dependability. Others fail to see the extent to which they are dependent on their bosses for critical information and resources. Still others assume that their boss should magically know what information or support they need. A more reasonable assumption is that bosses, like everyone else, are only human. They have strengths and weaknesses, limited time and resources, and stylistic preferences about working that may not match those of their subordinates.

Effectively managing this mutual dependence requires that subordinates (a) develop a good understanding of their boss as well as of themselves, especially in terms of each person's priorities, preferences, strengths, and limitations; and (b) that they use this knowledge to develop a set of mutually shared expectations and a working relationship which accommodates both parties' needs and work styles (Gabarro & Kotter, 1980).

## Application

**Knowing and Understanding Your Boss.** To manage your boss effectively, you must first appreciate your boss's world from his or her frame of reference.

1.  What are your boss's goals and objectives? How does this affect what he or she needs from you in terms of performance?

2.  What organizational and personal pressures is your boss under that can affect his or her priorities? Pressures from his or her boss? From other parts of the organization?

3.  How does your boss best process information? For example, does he or she prefer to get information through formal means such as memos or reports; or more informally, through phone calls or face-to-face interactions? Some bosses are readers. They prefer to get important information in written form before they are ready to discuss it. Others prefer to be orally briefed on a topic before delving into a report.

4.  What is your boss's preferred management style? Does he or she tend to be hands-on or delegatory? Hands-on managers need to be in touch with the details and will get anxious (and controlling) if you don't keep them informed on an ongoing basis. In contrast, delegatory managers don't want to be involved in details unless they are critical. They believe that is your job.

5.  What are your boss's strengths and limitations? Is he or she strong conceptually but poor at implementation? Does he or she thrive on conflict or handle it badly? In what ways can your strengths complement your boss's weaknesses (or vice versa) so you can enhance each other's performances?

**Knowing and Understanding Yourself.** Your boss is only one part of a superior-subordinate relationship; you are the other part and the one over which you have most control. To develop an effective working relationship you must understand your own needs, goals, strengths, and weaknesses, and how they interact with your boss's. For example:

1.  What are your own goals and priorities? How can you align them with those of your boss?

2.  What are your own work style and information handling preferences? Are they different from your boss's? Can you manage your interactions so both of you get what you need to be effective?

3.  At a more psychological level, how do you handle dependence on authority figures? Are your reactions counterdependent so that you are constantly challenging and rebelling against every decision your boss makes, escalating even small conflicts into major ones? Or are you passive-dependent, swallowing your anger and complying with what you know are poor decisions, even when your boss would welcome disagreement and discussion? Most people fall somewhere between these two extremes. If you fall toward either end of this continuum, you can understand and even predict what your reac-

tions are likely to be. With this knowledge you can conciously work to make your responses more realistic and productive.

**Developing and Managing the Relationship.** With a sufficient understanding of both yourself and your boss you can usually manage the relationship so that it becomes more effective for both of you. This means developing a set of mutual expectations and a working relationship which accommodates the needs and styles of both parties.

1. *Mutual Expectations.* Some superiors state their expectations and priorities explicitly and in detail. However, most do not. As a practical matter, the burden falls on the subordinate to take the initiative in getting expectations clarified on an ongoing basis. For example, what are your boss's top priorities in terms of problems and activities? What kind of information does he or she need and how often? What does the boss see as your role? His/her role? This is tougher to do with vague or nonexplicit bosses. This type of boss may require drafting a memo which can serve as a basis of discussion or initiating an informal series of discussions about priorities and goals. A workable set of expectations also requires that you communicate and negotiate your own expectations.

2. *Compatible Work Styles.* If you understand your boss's and your own stylistic needs and preferences you can make adjustments. Hands-on managers prefer to be involved in decisions and problems as they arise. Usually their needs and goals will be better met if you take the initiative to touch base with them frequently. This will minimize their "end-running." Other bosses prefer to delegate and they become impatient if you involve them too much. They need to be informed periodically, with only major problems being brought to their attention on an ad hoc basis. A final factor to consider is that most bosses, like yourself, have a limited amount of time and resources. Whatever their work style or need for information, common sense suggests that you draw on these resources selectively.

3. *Honesty and Dependability.* Nothing is more damaging to a relationship with a boss than being undependable or dishonest. Although it is unlikely that you would intentionally lie to a boss, you need to be careful not to shade the truth when there is bad news to deliver, or to make unrealistic commitments which you cannot meet.

*See also* Mentoring; Performance Appraisal; Promotion/Raise.

## Bibliography

Gabarro, J. J. (1978). The development of trust, influence and expectations. In A. G. Athos & J. J. Gabarro, (Eds.), *Interpersonal behavior* (pp. 290-303). Englewood Cliffs, NJ: Prentice-Hall.

Gabarro, J. J. (1987). The development of working relationships. In J. W. Lorsch (Ed.), *The handbook of organizational behavior* (pp. 172-89). Englewood Cliffs, NJ: Prentice-Hall. A scholarly but readable review of current research on the development of working relationships in organizations, including superior-subordinate relationships.

Gabarro, J.J., & Kotter, J.P. (1980). Managing your boss. *Harvard Business Review*, 58: 1, 92-100. A concise and very readable discussion of how to manage your boss and the factors to consider. Uses many case examples. Available in reprint.

Kotter, J.P. (1986). *Power and influence.* New York: Free Press. A very readable discussion of influence processes in organizations, including lateral as well as vertical relationships.

—JOHN J. GABARRO

## BURNOUT

Burnout is an experience of exhaustion and discouragement focused on one's career. Most writings and research on burnout have focused on human service professionals (e.g., health professionals, teachers) among whom the syndrome is associated with depersonalization—a cold, callous attitude toward service recipients. Among people in other career areas, depletion of creativity is a more central aspect of the syndrome than is depersonalization. The experience of burnout may be an acute crisis in an individual's career, or it may lead to leaving the career entirely.

### Relationship to Work

Burnout is a work-related problem, although aspects of it may spill over into personal or family domains. Human service workers experiencing burnout are more emotionally restrained with family, and often bring home tension from work.

A primary focus of research through the 1980s has been identifying aspects of organizational structures or procedures which predict the severity of burnout. Leiter's model of burnout (see Leiter, 1988, 1991) integrates the influence of organizational stressors and resources for professional performance in predicting burnout levels. It also takes into consideration personal coping styles of human service workers in the development of the three aspects of the burnout syndrome (emotional exhaustion, depersonalization, and diminished personal accomplishment).

The emotional exhaustion of burnout is a reaction to two classes of stressors: work overload and conflict with colleagues. Exhaustion, in turn, leads to higher levels of depersonalization as people attempt to disengage from the emotional demands of the job.

Burnout and its consequences (absenteeism, psychosomatic symptoms, low commitment, etc.) are more likely to develop when the setting provides insufficient support for effective professional performance (e.g., collegial support, autonomy, and skill utilization). An insufficient level of these professional resources also contributes to diminished feelings of personal accomplishment. That is, exhaustion does not invariably lead to diminished accomplishment; in fact, people may feel exhilarated while overextending their resources. The full burnout syndrome is most likely to develop when emotional exhaustion occurs in a worksetting that is both demanding and nonsupportive.

## Application

Burnout presents a real risk to professionals in a variety of fields, especially to those in the early phases of their career or confronting major transitions. The prevention or treatment of burnout may involve interventions on the individual, workgroup, or organizational level, as well as changes in professional training programs.

**Individual.** One step in your burnout prevention program may be re-evaluating the role of work in your life. If work is your whole life, its crises loom much larger. You also have fewer outside resources to call on. While a professional career does require a genuine commitment to providing first-rate service, all work and no play may make you dull to the point of burnout. Excessive commitment may be perpetuated through internalizing an idealistic, even romantic, view of profession dedication. Anxiety about the adequacy of your performance may also drive you into a workaholic phase of excessive commitment ( see **Career Roles**).

Another personal factor to consider is your general approach to coping with problems at work. While Lazarus and Folkman (1984) acknowledge that escape may be the best way to deal with some stressful situations, it appears to be unsuited to the problems encountered in a professional career. Leiter (1991) demonstrated that people who responded to problems at work by attempting to take control of the situation (e.g., talking with their supervisors, attempting to change policies and procedures) experienced less burnout, while those who consistently tried to escape from work problems were more burned out.

**Workgroup.** The people with whom you work every day play a central role in determining burnout levels. Persistent, unresolved conflict with colleagues aggravates emotional exhaustion, while supportive relationships with coworkers help to minimize the impact of exhaustion. People in leadership positions may have a particularly strong influence on the burnout level of a group by promoting a cynical attitude toward work. They may also model through their own behavior ways of striking a balance between intense professional involvement and a separate personal life. People who live exclusively for their work are particularly vulnerable to burnout. You can enhance the quality of your workgroup through promoting group problem solving and decision-making approaches which provide opportunities for genuine involvement. In some workgroups this may require a major team building intervention. Team building is a process through which members of workgroups clarify their roles and mutual expectations with one another. It permits group members to sharpen their communication skills and conflict resolution processes.

**Organizational.** Many factors which contribute to burnout are beyond the control of a single person. Changing the size of your caseload or the manner in which it is assigned requires modifications to an organization's procedures, or even to its stated mission. To enhance the material or human resources available to you at work requires a level of control over budgetary decisions possessed by few individuals. Interventions at this level generally require you to enter into cooperative efforts with professional, union, or management groups dedicated toward building work environments characterized by decentralized authority, opportunities for people to use and enhance their skills, and the integration of work into personal and family life (see **Dual-Career Families; Working Family Issues**).

**Professional Training.** In what remains one of the most substantial works on burnout, Cherniss (1980) identified unrealistic expectations which the public has about professionals (and professionals often have for themselves) as increasing the vulnerability of new professionals to burnout. Your training can paint a rosy picture of a professional service career. The reality of your first job can be quite different. Instead of providing you with an opportunity to use your creative skills to help solve the problems of clients, you may be constantly fighting deadlines while dealing with a large caseload of frustrated and angry people. Budgetary cutbacks may induce similar crises later in your career, as diminishing resources necessitate changes to established aspects of professional performance (see **Career Changes at Midlife**).

## Overcoming Burnout

While preventing burnout requires you to reflect on your approach to professional work and to devote energies to enhancing your work environment, overcoming burnout necessitates stepping back from your career. Burnout perpetuates itself. Emotional exhaustion makes you too tired to undertake ambitious interventions on any level, and diminished personal accomplishment undermines your self-confidence as well. As Golembiewski and Munzenrider (1988) have pointed out, a highly demanding burnout intervention could just make matters worse.

In general, your program for recovering from burnout should include disengagement (ideally, an extended vacation or sabbatical from work), social support (either a professionally managed or self-help group for people with similar problems), and re-evaluation (changing the way you manage your work time or integrate it into the rest of your life). Such interventions may constitute drastic steps for you, but unmanaged burnout can undermine your career.

*See also* Career Changes at Midlife; Career Plateauing; Career Roles; Dual-Career Families; Job Changing; Job Satisfaction; Mental Health and Work; Stress; Type-A Behavior Pattern; Work Hazards: Psychosocial; Workaholism; Working Family Issues.

## Bibliography

Cherniss, C. (1980). *Professional burnout in human service organizations*. New York: Praeger. A definitive work on the burnout syndrome which articulated many of the conceptual and research approaches to the syndrome.

Golembiewski, R. T., & Munzenrider, R. (1988). *Phases of burnout: Developments in concepts and applications*. New York: Praeger.

Lazarus, R., & Folkman, S. (1984). *Stress, appraisal, and coping*. New York: Springer Publishing.

Leiter, M. P. (1988). Commitment as a function of stress reactions among nurses: A model of psychological evaluations of work settings. *Canadian Journal of Community Mental Health*, 7: 117-34.

Leiter, M. P. (1991). Coping patterns as predictors of burnout: The function of control and escapist coping patterns. *Journal of Organizational Behavior,* 12: 123-44. This article provides the most up-to-date investigation of the integrated model of burnout described above.

Maslach, C. (1982). *Burnout, the cost of caring*. Englewood Cliffs, NJ: Prentice-Hall. A thoughtful consideration of burnout and its consequences written for the general reader.

Maslach, C., & Jackson, S. E. (1986). *Maslach burnout inventory manual*. 2nd ed. Palo Alto, CA: Consulting Psychologists Press. The scale primarily used to measure burnout in clinical and research settings, the Maslach Burnout Inventory (Maslach & Jackson, 1986), comprises a series of statements which describe feelings of emotional exhaustion, impersonal attitudes toward clients, and personal accomplishment.

—MICHAEL P. LEITER

# C

## CAREER ANCHOR

Career anchor is a self-concept that gives continuity and stability to a person's inner work life. It is those talents and skills, motives and needs, and personal values that a person has learned through work experience to be the thing he or she would not give up if forced to make a choice. It is what makes us feel who we really are, what we really care about, and what we really need.

All of us start our careers or work lives with a broad set of self-perceptions of what we are good at, what we want, and what we value. With accumulated work experience we refine those perceptions and gradually evolve a self-concept that is more realistic and that functions to guide and constrain career or work choices. Hence the concept of "anchor," in the sense that this self-concept keeps us "in our own safe harbor." Though we may have the basic elements of the anchor from early childhood on, it is only through work experience that we can learn what we are really good at, want, and value. Most people do not have a career anchor, therefore, until they are at least five to ten years into their work lives.

The career anchor concept differs from other career constructs in that it emphasizes the *self-concept* which emerges from actual work experience. We cannot really know what we can do, what we want, and what we value until we have had sufficient experiences in the real world to figure out "what is me" and "what is not me." When we are younger and in school we have ambitions and aspirations but we do not yet have realistic self-concepts.

### Relationship to Work

As a person develops the self-concept that becomes the career anchor, he or she becomes more vulnerable to making work and career choices not in line with the anchor. If that happens, the person becomes less effective and more dissatisfied. It is therefore important for each of us to become conscious of what our career anchor is so that if we are confronted with work-related choices, we can make them in our best interests.

It is especially important to identify one's career anchor if one is in a large organization that tends to manage the careers of its employees. No matter how carefully an organization attempts to lay out career paths for its people, there is a substantial chance that the person will be mismanaged at some point, in the sense of being given a transfer or promotion that is not in line with the career anchor.

It becomes more and more critical, therefore, for people in organizations to manage their own careers by becoming familiar with their career anchor and learning to negotiate with their employer to insure that future assignments are in line with the career anchor. This process of self-management and negotiation goes on throughout the career and may become especially important in the later stages of the career to avoid the Peter Principle of being eventually promoted to one's level of incompetence.

### Types of Career Anchors

Based on longitudinal studies of career occupants and life history interviews at various career stages and in various occupations, we have so far identified eight different career anchors (Derr, 1980; Schein, 1978, 1990):

1. *Security/Stability.* If this is your anchor, it means that you are primarily and always concerned about jobs and work that will make you feel economically secure and stable. You will worry less about the content of the work you do and more about the degree to which your employer offers you "tenure," good benefits, generous retirement, and so on. The so-called "golden handcuffs" are exactly what you are looking for. You may have a variety of talents and values, but none of these are more important to you than feeling secure and stable.

2. *Autonomy/Independence.* This anchor means that above all else you want your work life to be under your own control. You resist organizational routines, rules, uniforms or dress codes, hours of work, and all other forms of regimentation. You probably would prefer to work as a teacher, consultant, or independent businessperson, but some kinds of organizational jobs might suit you, such as field sales or professional staff jobs in research and develop-

ment. But you would become unhappy if promoted into headquarters where you lost your autonomy even if that was a "bigger" and better paying job.

3. *Technical or Functional Competence.* If this is your anchor it means that your self-concept is built around your particular talents or skills, and that the exercise of those talents and skills at ever higher levels is your primary means of "being yourself." You will seek higher levels of challenge within your skill area, and may go into administration or management in that skill area, but you will resist general management because that would require you to drop the exercise of your skill. You seek recognition primarily from others who can appreciate your skill and you will quit jobs that do not challenge you (unless for economic reasons you must keep the job, in which case you would endeavor to exercise your skill off the job by moonlighting or developing a hobby in that area). The biggest danger for you in most organizations is that your skill will lead you to being promoted into general management which you will not like and will not be good at.

4. *General Management Competence.* This anchor means that you want to rise to a high level in an organization where you can measure your own competence by the performance of the organization that you manage. You view technical or functional skills to be necessary to climbing the ladder, but you will not feel you have made it until you are a general manager integrating the other functions. You will have learned that to succeed as a general manager you will need some combination of high motivation, skills in analyzing and synthesizing information, interpersonal skills, and emotional skills in the sense of being able to make tough decisions day after day without becoming debilitated by them. Your basic identity and sense of success will come through the success of the organization you work for.

5. *Entrepreneurial Creativity* If this is your anchor, you have always wanted to create a business or product or service of your own, where your success was entirely due to your own creative effort. You probably already started up enterprises when you were in school and you think about such enterprises all the time, even while you might be employed in a more traditional kind of job. You want to make a lot of money eventually but the money is not the goal in itself; rather it is a measure of how successful you are in creating something new. The new enterprise is an extension of yourself so you will often give it your own name.

6. *Service/Dedication to a Cause.* If this is your anchor, you see your career entirely in terms of some core values that you are trying to achieve through the kind of work you do. Those values could be such things as "making the world a better place to live," "creating a more humane workplace for people in organizations," and so on. You will only remain in a job or organization if it allows you to fulfill the values you hold.

7. *Pure Challenge.* If this is your anchor, you require the kind of work that will always permit you to feel that you are overcoming "impossible" barriers, meeting very difficult challenges, or winning over tough competitors. The kind of work you do is less important to you than the fact that it allows you to win out over opponents or problems. You tend to define situations in terms of winning and losing, and you only get true satisfaction when you win.

8. *Life Style.* If this is your anchor, you feel that your work life and career must be integrated with other aspects of your total life—your family situation and your personal growth needs. You will therefore seek situations that allow you to make that integration even if that means some sacrifices in relation to the career. This situation comes up most clearly for you if you have a career-involved spouse and the two of you need to make joint life style decisions.

Other kinds of anchors may be found in future research, but so far all the cases we have looked at fit into one of the eight categories above.

## Application

In order for you to make good work and career decisions you should become familiar with your career anchor. To do this you must carefully examine the life choices and decisions you have made so far, and to identify the reasons why you made the choices that you made. This process works best if someone interviews you systematically and helps you to identify the main choices and the reasons for them. The pattern of reasons then helps you to see what your implicit self-concept is.

This process can be aided with a training exercise that identifies the types of anchors more carefully and structures the interview questions that your interviewer should ask you (Schein, 1990). It is important to work with another person on this task because if one attempts to decipher one's own anchor one is likely to think in terms of an "ideal self" rather than in terms of the reality of what we have done and why we have done it. Talking it out with a sympathetic listener corrects for this bias. The interviewer does not have to be a trained career counselor, however. It only requires someone who is interested enough to spend an hour or two helping you identify the main themes in your own career history.

You will find that to some degree you care about all of the things mentioned as career anchors. But you must try to imagine hypothetical situations where you could not have all of the them and figure out which is the one you would not give up if forced to make a choice.

*See also* Career Counseling; Career Identity; Career Roles; Skills; Work Values.

## Bibliography

Derr, C. B. (Ed.) (1980). *Work, family, and the career*. New York: Praeger. An excellent collection of papers reporting research on work, career, and career anchors.

Schein, E. H. (1978). *Career dynamics*. Reading, MA: Addison-Wesley. This overview reviews the stages of the career and the problem of integrating the needs of the organization with the needs of the individual. The original research leading to the career anchor concept is reported.

Schein, E. H. (1990). *Career anchors*. San Diego: University Associates. This booklet is designed as a self-administering exercise to help a person figure out what his or her career anchor is. It contains complete instructions and text describing the career anchors in detail.

—EDGAR H. SCHEIN

# CAREER CHANGES AT MIDLIFE

A career is a sequence of positions occupied by a person during the course of a lifetime (Super, 1980). Career change is defined as an occupational shift not merely from one job to another but a change in the actual career the worker is performing. Examples of career change are a painter becoming an electrician, a pharmacist becoming a teacher, a secretary becoming a lawyer. Since the term midlife refers to the years between 35 and 55, career change at midlife is defined as the career shifts that an individual makes during those years. There is little data on the actual numbers of persons at midlife electing to change careers. A recent publication (Bradley, 1990) indicates that at least 9% of the total workforce changes jobs each year. Sixteen percent of the adults between the ages of 30 and 49 years are in some form of career transition, with 12% of males between the ages of 35 and 45 actually changing careers. Information on the growing numbers of women entering the workforce in

recent years has resulted in large numbers of women entering the paid workforce at midlife as well as large numbers of women changing careers at midlife.

## Relationship to Career Change

There is no single factor that motivates individuals to change careers at midlife, although researchers have identified several factors influencing the change (Henton, Russell, & Koval, 1983). The factors include:

1. *Financial Support.* Having available financial support enhances the opportunities for making a career change at midlife.
2. *Self-Concept.* Having a high self-concept has been identified as a variable that increases the likelihood of career change (Bradley, 1990).
3. *Personal Meaning.* A desire to find more personally meaningful work enhances the likelihood of a career change at midlife
4. *Interests.* Incompatible interests with current career often lead to dissatisfaction in the workplace and eventually to career change.
5. *Beliefs.* The individual's personal beliefs about the ability to and the need for controlling his/her work life is a factor that motivates career change. Individuals who have a strong desire to control their lives are more likely to make a career change at midlife.

In contrast, other factors such as having less family responsibility, salary considerations, community role change, and family and friend's reactions have not significantly affected the individual's decision to make a midlife career change (Henton, Russell, & Koval, 1983).

Thomas (1979) studied men who were between the ages of 34 and 54 and who had changed from high-status careers. In response to a question about why they had decided to begin a new career, 76% of the midlife career changers said they wanted to find more meaningful work and 69% said they wanted a better fit between their values and their work.

It is important to look at midlife career change across two broad dimensions: (a) voluntary vs. involuntary change and (b) anticipated vs. unanticipated career change. Not all individuals are given a choice about making a career change at midlife. Being discharged by an employer, a plant shutdown, company reorganization, divorce, death, and retirement can force the individual to make a career change. Further career change can be anticipated or unanticipated. With anticipated career change, the individual often has time to plan for the new career. In contrast, an unanticipated change is often characterized by less time for planning, more stress, and more intense feelings of shock and helplessness.

## Application

In considering a career change at midlife, research and practice suggest these guidelines:

1.  Since career change at midlife may be voluntary or involuntary, anticipated or unanticipated, or externally or internally precipitated, you might clarify your thoughts on three basic questions: (a) Is your career change a voluntary or involuntary decision? That is, do you have a choice about whether you change careers, or are you forced to make a career change? (b) Did you anticipate, or were you surprised by the need to make a career change? (c) Did you make the decision (internal decision) to change careers, or did someone make the decision (external decision) for you?

2.  You may want to seek the assistance of a career counselor in helping you decide about your midlife career change. A counselor should be chosen carefully. Some considerations: (a) Select a counselor with a good reputation in career counseling. (b) Check to see if the counselor is licensed or board certified. Some certifications and/or licenses to consider include licensed professional counselor (licensed by your state), National Board Certified Counselor (NBCC), and National Certified Career Counselor (NCC). (c) Talk with former clients of the counselor to obtain their recommendations on the counseling services received (see **Career Counseling**).

3.  You might want to read some books about career change. Some suggested books include Bolles (1990), Bradley (1990), and Michelozzi (1984). Additional readings are listed at the end of this article.

4.  You need to begin your career search cautiously and realistically. Problems may include: (a) finding a job immediately, (b) finding the job that you want in a specific town, (c) finding a balance between available jobs, your wants, and your qualifications, (d) support (or lack of support) from family and friends, (e) sufficient time to devote to a thorough job search, (f) the possibility that your present employer will learn that you are looking for another job, and (g) the fear that you cannot find another job as well as the fear that you cannot succeed at the new job.

5.  In describing the process of launching a search for a new job, Bolles (1990) cautions that the usual approach of answering job advertisements and sending out resumes to various companies are not the most successful techniques. Instead, he says that you need to research the company for which you want to work, know who has the power to hire in that company, and obtain an interview with the person having the power to hire you (see **Job Interviewing; Job Search**).

6.  You should have more than one job search plan.

7.  The following eight questions may help you focus on your career change more realistically: (a) My career change fantasy is (describe in detail) _____. (b) What appeals to me most about the change is _____. (c) What I would gain most from the change is _____. (d) What is frightening about the change is _____. (e) What keeps me from making the change is _____. (f) The worst thing that could happen if I make the change is _____. (g) If the worst thing happened, then I could do _____. (h) If I were really serious about pursuing the career fantasy, my first step would be _____; my second step would be _____; my third step would be _____.

8.  For many individuals, the loss of a job at midlife is very stressful and devastating. Job loss, like loss of a loved one, can go through five stages of grief—denial, anger, bargaining, depression, and acceptance (Bradley, 1990). Having a counselor can be beneficial in understanding your job loss.

*See also* Career Counseling; Career Exploration; Career Identity; Career Plateauing; Climate for Workers; Job Changing; Job Interviewing; Job Outlook: Major Trends; Job Satisfaction; Job Search.

## Bibliography

Bolles, R.N. (1990). *What color is your parachute?* Berkeley, CA: Ten Speed Press. An enthusiastic self-help book on how to look for a job. Numerous exercises are provided throughout the book. The book contains excellent material on interviewing, hiring practices, assessing interests, and understanding the total job search. Anyone planning to or in the process of changing jobs should read this book.

Bradley, L. J. (1990). *Counseling midlife career changers*. Garrett Park, MD: Garrett Park Press. A thorough, scholarly, and very practical review of problems and situations involving midlife career changes. Numerous case examples and exercises are provided throughout the book. A readable book for career changers and counselors.

Henton, J., Russell, R., & Koval, J. (1983). Spousal perceptions of midlife career change. *Personnel & Guidance Journal*, 61: 287-91.

Michelozzi, B. (1984). *Coming alive from nine to five*. Palo Alto, CA: Mayfield. A popular book that contains numerous exercises for helping the potential career changer to realistically and thoroughly look at self in relations to actual and desired career options. An easy-to-read book with practical examples.

Super, D.E. (1980). A life-span, life-approach to career development. *Journal of Vocational Behavior*, 16: 282-99.

Thomas, L.R. (1979). Causes of mid-life change from high-status careers. *Vocational Guidance Quarterly*, 27: 20-28.

—LORETTA J. BRADLEY

## CAREER CHOICES: YOUTH

In our society, you are required to make vocationally related choices throughout your schooling. Whenever you decide on a course to take or a curriculum to pursue, for example, you are making a career decision. In the process of making these mini decisions during the time that you are in school, you are expected to experience and to deal with many factors that will shape your ultimate career choices. The way you deal with these choices—how you cope with the enormous volume of career information to which you will be exposed, how you sort out competing value systems related to your work choices, and how accurately you learn about your personal characteristics, for example—will eventually determine how satisfied and happy you will be in your work and how well you will perform the tasks of your occupation. Further, when you choose a career, you also choose a life style, so, in effect, the choices you make now will shape your entire life.

It is very important to realize that career choices do not happen by osmosis or spring as though from the head of Medusa or come as a result of a lightning bolt from the blue. Career choice is not a passive activity. You cannot sit back and expect inspiration suddenly to grip you and show you the path to career happiness. Rather, the career choice process is an active, assertive collection of experiences over the course of your years in school. The more you take control of the process, the better the likely result. The more you postpone or ignore the process, the greater the chance that your career choices will be marked by frustration, a lack of joy, and false starts. The career choices you make should be characterized by systematic, structured inquiry into appropriate aspects of yourself and the world of work and by good decision making, not by a hit-or-miss, helter-skelter, chaotic journey that will, in the end, leave you dissatisfied and unhappy. The seeds sown and the nurturance of career buds during the school years will ripen to career maturity in adult life.

There are some who say that youth are too young to make career choices, arguing that they have not been exposed to enough of the "real world" and have not ac- quired sufficient knowledge about themselves to make such important decisions. Indeed, there are very few people who have a career "passion." These are persons who know from a very early age what they want to do in life, and their career development is straight-line toward achieving that goal. Most of us do not have such a passion. Instead, we learn from our courses, from our out-of-school experiences, from our extra curricular activities, and from our school guidance activities what we like and do not like, what we value and do not value, what kind of people we are and what sorts of occupations might fit all these character-istics. Then we make some tentative, broad choices along the way. Youth are quite able to make these broader choices—these explorations—even if they may not be fully equipped to make more narrow choices. For example, many junior high school and most high school students are capable of accurately describing a generalized occupa-tional area in which they will eventually work. Looking back, they may not have been able to accurately identify whether they would be a doctor, historian, actress, and so on, but they could reasonably predict a career in the physical sciences, the social sciences, or the arts. It is clear, then, that the foundation for adult career choices is forged while you are in school.

It is extremely important that youth realize that they *do* have a choice. A recent Gallup Poll indicated that only 41% of American adults felt that they really had a career choice. Some students may have more to overcome than others in terms of the boundaries imposed on them by birth or circumstances, but all students have within themselves the capacity to transcend chance factors that may seem to constrain their choices. More effort may need to be exerted to leap over barricades of socioeconomic status, race or ethnic origin, and so on, but the barriers are not insurmount-able if youth are willing to make sustained, planned efforts over time to achieve realistic career goals.

### Application

What are the types of knowledge, skills, attitudes, and so on that you need in order to make good career decisions? Most experts are agreed that you need to address three different areas that we might call knowledge of self, knowl-edge of the world of work and education, and decision-making skills (see Figure 1). Each of these is discussed separately.

### *Learning about Yourself*

*Knowledge of self* refers to all those aspects of your-self that make a difference in vocational choice. They describe the kind of person you are. Presumably, if you know the kind of person you are, you will be able to choose an occupation and a career that will permit you to continue

**Figure 1. Strategies for Making Good Career Choices**

---

Be active and assertive in:

1. Learning about yourself—your,
   - Aptitudes and abilities;
   - Vocational interests;
   - Work values;
   - Personality characteristics;
   - Environmental or physical constraints; and
   - Attitude toward work.

2. Learning about the worlds of work and education by,
   - Exploring the fields of occupations that appeal to you;
   - Understanding the educational requirements of jobs that interest you and how much time you are willing to invest in education;
   - Understanding the economic system of this country; and
   - Getting a sense of the future of the occupations that interest you. Will they grow? Decline?

3. Making a good decision by,
   - Defining the problem;
   - Acquiring the necessary information;
   - Generating alternatives;
   - Choosing among the alternatives;
   - Implementing your choice; and
   - Evaluating your choice.

---

to be that kind of person and to flourish. Some say that you get an accurate picture of yourself (or a self-concept) and then you choose an occupation that will allow you to implement that concept in the world of work. Others put it in slightly different terms. They say that each of us has a dominant personality type, that occupations require a certain personality type, and that you simply need to match your personality type to any of many occupations that dovetail with it. In any case, both approaches start with the assumption that you need to know who you are.

To describe yourself in vocationally important terms requires several types of knowledge. First, you need an accurate understanding of your *aptitudes and abilities* (see **Abilities**). Most of us have one or two or a few dominant talents or abilities. There are people, however, who are multi-talented, who have abilities in many diverse areas. For example, there are students who get A's in all their courses, play a musical instrument well, are good athletes in several different sports, and are good artists too! You need not envy such students for they may have just as much conflict about career choice as any of us. Whether you have one or a few dominant aptitudes or many, it is crucial to recognize what they are—and what they are *not*.

How can you determine your abilities? The most obvious way is to look to your course work and other achievements. In what subjects do you excel and in which do you do less well? What subjects come easiest for you? In what subjects do you have to work extra hard, to strain just to keep up? Asking yourself these questions will help you to decide if verbal ability, numerical or quantitative ability, mechanical aptitude, clerical speed and accuracy, spatial visualization, artistic or musical ability, and so on are likely contributors to your success or lack of it.

A second way to figure your aptitudes is to look at what you do in your spare time—your hobbies and other out-of-school or in-school extra curricular activities. Most of us spend our leisure time doing things that we do well. If, for instance, you spend a lot of time working on engines, you might assume that you have some mechanical aptitude.

A third and final method of learning about your aptitudes is by means of special aptitude test batteries that measure many different (or differential) abilities. Many junior high schools and high schools give such aptitude batteries as part of their guidance program and then interpret the results to students in order to give them this type of self-knowledge. If your school does not, you can still take the Armed Services Vocational Aptitude Battery (ASVAB), a free assessment of your abilities. Ask your counselor.

Many career planning instruments, such as the Self-Directed Search, ask you to estimate your aptitudes in many areas as a prelude to decision making. It is essential, therefore, that you have some clear notion about and acceptance of your abilities. There are other abilities that you must gauge that are not so easily measured. For example, you may find it easy to understand yourself and your motives while other students may be slower to grasp this knowledge about themselves. You may be good at interpersonal relationships, at understanding people and working with them. You may be good physically. Whatever your abilities, they need to be catalogued and their occupational and career implications need to be explored (see also **Skills**).

A second type of self-knowledge necessary for good career decision making is for you to know your vocational interests (see **Interests**). Your interests tell you what you like or prefer in terms of work and leisure activities, occupations, and so on and enable you to compare your interests to those of successful people in various occupations. There are basically three ways to determine your interests. One is for you simply to express them. In what are you interested? Another way is to look at what you do that you do not have to do and assume that you do it because of some interest. Finally, you can take an interest inventory, an instrument that surveys your reaction to an array of activities and occupations and then you can compare your preferences to those of people in various occupational groups. In junior high school, it is not a good idea to take an interest inventory except in the most general sense, since vocational interests do not tend to be stable enough to be useful in planning until about age 16. In high school, interest inventories are very widely employed, and using the results is considered part of good career planning.

It is important, then, to know what occupational groups you most resemble in terms of interests. While different interest inventories have their own methods of classifying the types of interests that exist, it is common for measurement to include wide areas of interests such as business, scientific, artistic, mechanical, social service, outdoor, technology, and so on as well as to relate interests to specific occupations.

A third domain of self-knowledge for career planning is *work values* (see **Work Values**). Of all the values that you hold, which are the most important for you in terms of a career? Is the amount of money you can earn the primary value in choosing an occupation? How about the opportunity to be creative, or to receive a great deal of prestige, or to work in a pleasant environment? Maybe it is most important that you can have variety in your work, or that you have work that is secure so that you are never in danger of being unemployed. Maybe you would sacrifice all of these values in order to live a way of life that is important to you—to be your own boss, perhaps, or to get close to nature. Some people are oriented more to working with data (like manipulating figures), others to working with things (e.g., machines), others to working with people, and still others to working with ideas. Which of these is prominent in your mind? Other people want to have authority over others, to do something of great moral worth, or to avoid responsibility. These are but a few examples of the types of work values that need to be considered in the career planning process. Before you can consider them, however, you must identify them either through formal assessment (i.e., take a work values inventory or survey) and/or through speaking with your parents, friends, relatives, teachers, or a counselor. What is important to you in work?

A fourth kind of self-knowledge necessary for making career decisions is an understanding of your *personality characteristics*. When psychologists talk about "personality," they mean something different from your friend who wants to fix you up with a date because he or she "has a great personality." Psychologists refer to the psychological traits or characteristics that you possess. For example, are you a persevering sort of person, someone with a lot of stick-to-it-iveness, or are you impatient? Are you generally calm? Do you handle stress well? Are you easily upset? Are you introverted or extroverted? Are you oriented toward persons or away from persons? Do you go along with the crowd, or do you march to your own drummer? How assertive are you or how submissive? Are you hostile to or

tolerant of authority? These are examples of the types of traits or characteristics that you need to consider in developing career-relevant self-knowledge.

A fifth and final type of self-knowledge that needs to be addressed in career planning is to take stock of any *environmental or physical constraints* (see **Discrimination: People with Disabilities; Discrimination: Race; Sex-Role Stereotyping**) that may hinder your career development. We have already discussed the fact that accidents of birth or geography or gender or ethnicity make for an unevenness in career experiences. These may translate into some people who are advantaged as a result of chance factors and have a "leg up" in career planning, although socioeconomic advantage does not automatically lead to career advantage if a person does not seize the opportunity.

Those who are less advantaged may need to engage in compensatory experiences to become career-competitive. Do you have impeding factors—physical disabilities, socioeconomic hardship, minority group membership—that might prevent you from being all that you want to be or that you see as not giving you as much freedom to pursue certain occupational goals as other people? If so, you will need to devise a strategy to overcome these perceived deficits. Luckily, a lot of people are willing to help in this regard. Your counselor is a good person to talk to about these matters.

We have described five types of self-knowledge important to youth in career planning—aptitudes or abilities, interests, work values, personality, and environmental or physical constraints—and we have suggested ways of assessing these factors. Remember that the process for each person is active and assertive. *You* must make it happen.

## Learning about the Worlds of Work and Education

A second major type of knowledge area necessary in career decision making is *knowledge of the worlds of work and education*. There are literally thousands of different occupations that comprise the world of work. It is impossible for you to get even the most superficial knowledge of all of these. Consequently, the world of work is organized into more manageable structures so that career planning can be enhanced. What people have done is to sort all of these occupations into various wide fields and within these fields to describe occupations according to the education or training required and the complexity and responsibility of the work.

Let's take an example. One of the areas in which you might have an interest is scientific. Within that broad area, occupations run the gamut from unskilled to semi-skilled to professional and managerial and have corresponding educational or training requirements. It is clearly impossible for you to explore the entire world of work, but it is realistic for you, with adequate self-knowledge, to investigate one or two fields of work and the appropriate level of occupations within them.

One occupational scheme has six categories of work: realistic, investigative, artistic, social, enterprising, and conventional. Another category system presents eight fields: outdoor-physical, social-personal, business contact, administration- control, math-physical sciences, biological sciences, humanistic, and arts. Still another offers 15 clusters of occupations: business and office, marketing and distribution, communications and media, construction, manufacturing, transportation, agri-business and natural resources, marine science, environment, public services, health, recreation and hospitality, personal services, fine arts and humanities, and consumer and homemaking education. Knowing yourself will direct you to one or another of these fields or clusters (see **Occupational Groups**).

Once you identify a field in which to explore its relationship with your aptitudes, interests, values, and personality characteristics, you will want to engage in investigations of various types. Your counselor and/or your library will have all sorts of written occupational information as well as information available through other types of media—filmstrips, films, videotapes, and so on..A number of different interactive computer systems (such as DIS-COVER, Guidance Information System, and so on; see **Computer-Assisted Career Guidance Systems**) permit you to sort through occupations according to self-characteristics that you input.

There are other good ways to get information about the world of work. One is for you to interview people in occupations of interest to you and perhaps even get their permission to "shadow" them at work for a day or so to observe them at work. These people might be relatives, friends of your parents, or individuals to whom your counselor refers you (see **Information Interviewing**). Of course, the best way to get the feel of an occupation is by direct experience working in the field. Many schools have internship programs that will allow you to get a sense of what work is like in a field. For instance, if you are interested in exploring the hospitality industry, you might be placed in a hotel or restaurant, in an amusement park, or in a travel agency to observe and to perform some of the work tasks of the field. Part-time work while you are in school provides the same type of valuable exploratory experiences (see **Cooperative Education; Internships; Service-Learning; Volunteer Work**).

Another important aspect of understanding the world of work is to recognize *the relationship between education or training and work*. We have previously indicated that the higher you go in terms of level of occupation (from unskilled to professional), the more likely it is that you will

need to have extended education. While education will not guarantee you a good job, it is unlikely that you can get a good job without appropriate education (rock stars and professional athletes being notable exceptions). You must judge, therefore, how much time you are willing to invest in education prior to entering an occupation. Some feel that they have all the skills they need (or are capable of obtaining) in high school, while others feel that a two-year college degree is appropriate. Some think that a baccalaureate degree will be sufficient, while others opt for the MBA or other first graduate degree. Still others pursue the Ph.D. or a professional degree (M.D., D.D.S., J.D., D.O., etc.). Many do not feel that the formal educational system is appropriate for them, so they choose apprenticeship training, training in the military, on-the-job training, proprietary business schools or trade schools, or a job training program in the community. By whatever means, it is clear that your chances of entry into desirable occupations and your progress in that occupation will be increased by proper education and training.

That preparation, incidentally, is not a onetime event. Throughout your life you will be expected to keep current with your skills and knowledge. The half-life of knowledge (the amount of time it takes for what you learned in preoccupational preparation to become dated) is decreasing remarkably in almost every occupation. It is not uncommon for knowledge in many fields to double itself every few years. Keeping occupationally alive in terms of your skills and knowledge—whatever your field—will be a life-long endeavor. It is difficult to conceive of an occupational decision that does not also entail an educational consequence or an educational decision that does not have career implications. And it is still harder to think of any career or educational decision that is not made with some personal psychological or emotional investment.

A third part of the world of work knowledge that you will need in career planning is an *understanding of the economic system of this country*. Recognizing factors in a relatively free market economy that affect supply and demand characteristics are very important in your understanding of why some occupations undergo expansion and contraction of numbers while other occupations remain steadily in demand. Who gets rewarded for work and how are determined by the American economic system. In other countries that are not capitalistic, different reward systems exist.

A fourth type of necessary information in understanding the world of work is for you to try to get a sense of not only the present occupational structure but also the future occupational structure. Career choice decisions usually require you to project yourself into the future and to try to determine what occupational demands will be as many as a dozen years ahead. Our forecasting methods are relatively imprecise, but they do allow you some reasonable prediction of what will be "hot" and what will be less in demand for a period of up to a decade. The United States Department of Labor supplies us with this type of information and publishes it in the *Occupational Outlook Handbook*. Your guidance office will no doubt have a copy of this volume, and your counselor will be able to assist you with other data that will help you map out the contours of the future occupational world (see **Job Outlook: Major Trends**).

This is not to say that you should let supply and demand factors determine the occupation that you will enter. A few short years ago there was a glut of engineers and teachers; now shortages are present or anticipated. Things turn around occupationally. Further, there are those who argue that if you are good at your work, you will always do well no matter how crowded an occupational field might be. Nevertheless, it is useful to have some sense of the occupational world of the future as you engage in career decision making.

A final type of variable affecting your reaction to the world of work relates not so much to understanding as it does to *attitudes toward work*. Clearly, it is better for you to have attitudes toward work that are positive and healthful. A vanity license plate spotted recently read I H8 WRK. This person clearly is unhappy! Some work is not very desirable, because it is unclean, because it is repetitive, or for some other reason. Nevertheless, people bring to all work a worth and a dignity. Since you will spend, on average, 40-50 years of your life working at least one-third of each day, it would surely be better for you to regard work as a positive experience rather than as some negative drudgery to be endured. People obviously work for many reasons other than pay. The psychological rewards of work are equally important. Work will structure your time, in large measure determine your friends, provide you with psychological payment for a job well done. If money is your only motivation to work, you will end up with a vanity license plate of your own (if you can afford it).

All of these factors—an understanding of the occupational structure now and in the future, the relationship between education/training and work, the economic system of the United States, and attitudes toward work—contribute to an understanding of the worlds of work and education and are factored into career decision making. Again, this type of knowledge does not just happen; you must make it happen by actively pursuing these types of information.

## *Making a Good Decision*

Once you have acquired this self-knowledge and this knowledge of the world of work, you must process the information in ways that will lead to good vocational decision making. There are many self-help books on the market that try to help people do just that. There are also computer programs (e.g., DISCOVER) and paper and pencil instruments (e.g., the Self-Directed Search, Harrington-O'Shea Decision-Making System, etc.) that simulate a decision-making process in career choice. Almost all of them are based on a decision-making model that assumes that choices are logical; unfortunately, they are frequently more psychological than logical. Consequently, it is always a good idea for you to process your knowledge in the two domains with your counselor. If a counselor is not available to you, try a knowledgeable adult or a friend who can remain reasonably objective.

Most decision-making programs take you through a series of step-by-step, rational, by-the-numbers procedures. They require you to be active in determining what input is provided at certain times and to judge how that input will be weighted in the decision. Although the steps vary from program to program, they usually include:

1. *Defining the Problem*. In this case, the focus is on vocational choice. You must be motivated to grapple with this problem and to take the necessary actions to solve it.
2. *Acquiring Necessary Information*. This step refers to getting the knowledge of self and the knowledge of work and education previously described.
3. *Generating Alternatives*. On the basis of the knowledge that you acquired, you evolve several possible occupations to explore. You look into each of these thoroughly, using many of the techniques that were delineated earlier. You consider the educational and/or training implications of each; how they conform to your values, interests, and personality; how they dovetail with your aptitudes and achievements; and so on.
4. *Choosing from among the Alternatives*. Here you process all the information that you have generated. You choose the alternative that seems best for you and make a plan for achieving it. You also get a "Plan B" that will be an alternative for you if your original choice proves, for one reason or another, to be unworkable.
5. *Effecting Your Choice*. You implement your choice, carrying out all the necessary tasks along the way.
6. *Evaluating Your Choice*. After the fact, and frequently along the way, you evaluate to see if your choice still makes sense. How are you progressing toward your goal? What, if anything, is standing in the way of achieving that goal? Can the barrier be overcome? How? Are you satisfied? If not, what is contributing to your dissatisfaction? What can be done about it?

These steps apply not only to the mega-decision of career choice, but also to the micro-decisions inherent in the career choice process (e.g., choosing a curriculum, or a college, or a major, or a trade school, etc.; see also **Decision Making**).

As you go through school, you should get yourself in a frame of mind in which you constantly are asking yourself about the relationship between everything that you do and career preferences. Mainly, you need to assume responsibility for career planning. Career choice is too important for you to be buffeted by the winds of chance or accident. It is an area in which you indeed should be a person in control.

If you go on to further education, you will find your career planning intensified. Perhaps you have delayed serious consideration of a career choice; perhaps a choice made earlier has been re-evaluated in light of your performance in course work needed as preparation for entry into a chosen occupation; or perhaps your values have changed. Whatever the reason, college is a time when reality considerations are closer, and there is more of a press for decision making. In *Gone with the Wind*, Scarlett O'Hara consoled herself in times of distress by avoidance, saying "I'll think about it tomorrow." Students in college realize that their tomorrows are nearer and nearer and that they soon must go out into the "cold, cruel world" to be independent citizens. It is not surprising that just about every needs assessment conducted with college students places career planning as the primary need.

In junior and senior high school, you can acquire the necessary self-knowledge, knowledge of the world of work, and decision-making skills over a period of years. In college, if you have not already acquired these necessities, the imminence of reality dictates that you do so in an accelerated manner. Consequently, you can avail yourself of a number of relatively short-term workshops, courses, or seminars that will deal with such topics as choice of a major, selecting a graduate school, understanding yourself, career choices for liberal arts majors, interviewing techniques, and so on. Individual counseling through an office of career planning and placement is also available to you.

Whether in junior high school, high school, or college, you must bear the responsibility for your own career decision making. Who am I? What do I want in life? How do I get what I want? These are among the most profound questions that you will ever confront. How good the answers will be depends on the vigor and persistence of your own efforts at career planning.

*See also* Abilities; Career Counseling; Career Exploration; Career Indecision; Career Planning; Career Tests and Inventories; Computer-Assisted Career Guidance Systems; Cooperative Education; Decision Making; Discrimination: People with Disabilities; Discrimination: Race; Information Interviewing; Interests; Internships; Parent Involvement in Career Planning; Service-Learning; Sex-Role Stereotyping; Skills; Volunteer Work.

## Bibliography

Bolles, R. N. (revised periodically). *What color is your parachute? A practical manual for job hunters and career changes.* Berkeley: Ten Speed Press. The "grand-daddy" of self-help career books. Although meant for an older audience than secondary school students, there is much in this book that a younger population will find instructive.

Hecklinger, F. J., & Curtain, B. M. (1987). *Training for life: A practical guide to career and life planning.* 3rd ed. Dubuque, IA: Kendall/Hunt. Very comprehensive discussion of all aspects of career awareness, exploration, and decision making. Includes sections on job-finding techniques and strong segments on adult career concerns.

Herr, E. L., & Cramer, S. H. (1988). *Career guidance and counseling through the lifespan: Systematic approaches.* 3rd ed. New York: Scott, Foresman. This book is a standard reference in the field of career counseling. Although intended for graduate students who are studying in the field of vocational psychology, secondary school students and their parents will find many parts of the volume to be helpful.

Schwartz, L., & Brechner, I. (1985). *Career tracks.* New York: Ballantine Books. A "how to" book regarding career exploration and decision making that is applicable to adolescents as well as adults. This book is based on sound career development theory and is written in a clear, concise manner. Contains many useful suggestions.

Shields, C. J. (1988). *How to help your teenager find the right career.* New York: The College Board. "This book will tell you how to encourage your child to increase his or her options for finding challenging and rewarding career directions. The emphasis is on leading children to self-understanding in the area of career goals through education and experience" (p. xii). A "jargonless," comprehensive resource.

Sowell, T. (1989). *Chooosing a college: A guide for parents and students.* New York: Harper & Row. A down-to-earth, frank discussion of the high school-to-college transition that illustrates the relationship between education or training and work. Especially strong chapter on minority students.

— STANLEY H. CRAMER

## CAREER COUNSELING

Career counseling can be defined narrowly as a set of procedures used by counselors in helping clients choose an occupation. More broadly, career counseling is viewed as a process which focuses on issues related to the world of work, issues that vary according to the client's age and stage of career development. For example, high school and college students may explore a full range of career options in preparation for selecting a college major and, later, a first career. Young and midlife adults may be interested in making a career change, handling dual-career problems, resuming or beginning a career after the family has grown, dealing with stress and relationship difficulties at work, or balancing career and nonwork areas of life. Older adults may consult a career counselor in order to explore post-retirement part-time or volunteer work activities. Although career counseling may result in the client obtaining a new job, the main purpose is not job placement, but rather decision making, self-exploration, or problem solving around issues related to work. Despite this emphasis on work, career counselors understand that work cannot be entirely separated from the rest of life, and therefore help clients make work-related choices and changes in the context of their life environment and of their future goals.

During career counseling, clients typically explore their work and leisure preferences, their values and attitudes, their life-style goals, and family and cultural expectations. Career counseling may also involve exploration of such psychological factors as self-esteem, personality traits, moods and thinking patterns, in so far as they relate to how the person functions, or wishes to function, in the work world. Sometimes clients have problems that affect work, but originate outside the job and are unlikely to be resolved by changing the work situation. These problems can often be dealt with at the same time that work continues on career issues. However, in the case of problems that greatly disturb the client's functioning, (e.g., severe depression or serious substance abuse) the psychological difficulties may need to be resolved before career counseling can begin. If the solution to the client's career problem will have a strong impact on spouse or family members, the career counselor may request that they, too, attend one or more sessions, in order to include them in decisions that will affect their lives.

In its methods, career counseling tends to be more practical, more structured, and more goal- and task-oriented than many other forms of counseling. This organized approach is necessary because certain steps (e.g., choosing a career) cannot be taken until other steps have been completed (e.g., gathering information about several careers). Career counselors use face-to-face sessions, career interest inventories, perhaps psychological tests, and sometimes a computerized assessment battery to help clients understand themselves and their work needs and preferences. In addition, clients are expected to take an active part in counseling by working on specific tasks between sessions, for example, writing a personal job history or a resume, researching information about jobs by such methods as job-shadowing, interviewing prospective employers in the community, and practicing new behaviors at work. Since it is impossible for a counselor to keep up with all the available career information because it is too voluminous and becomes too quickly outdated, one of the counselor's main tasks is to know where such information can be found, and to act as a guide to the client who will then do the research pertinent to his or her own needs (see **Career Exploration**). It should also be noted that the career counselor does not tell clients which careers to pursue or make decisions for clients. In all, career counseling is a complex process for which counselors require an understanding of the world of work, and specialized ability in assessing career needs, in addition to basic counseling skills and a background in psychological knowledge. If counseling is conducted in groups or with family members, the counselor also needs some expertise in group and family counseling.

Career counselors work in a variety of locations: educational establishments, private and funded community agencies, vocational rehabilitation centers, health-care and correctional institutions, business and industry settings. Many of the career services provided at these sites are quite narrow in focus or are directed at a specific population. For example, the Department of Labor, Department of Economic Security, Veterans Administration, United Way, and many religious organizations fund job search classes or career counseling for diverse groups: disabled veterans, impoverished unemployed youths, displaced homemakers, etc. Programs and services vary in depth, from a one-day workshop to several months of individual weekly sessions, and also in price. It is important, therefore, for clients to act as consumers and shop carefully before expending time and money on counseling services that do not meet their needs, or on a counselor with whom they feel uncomfortable.

## Guidelines for Selecting a Career Counselor

1. Before contacting any career counseling agency or individual, decide on your own goals for counseling. Do you want to choose a career, change careers, make changes within your present job? The clearer you are about what you want, the better you can explain your needs and discover a fit with a counselor.

2. Contact several sources until you have several names. Begin with the following: your local college or university placement office, counseling center, departments of counseling and psychology, the personnel or human resource office in your work place, mental health and counseling agencies. Your local information and referral service may be able to direct you to specialized counselors and programs, for example, if you have a disability that places some restrictions on your career opportunities. Ask each contact for ideas about where else you can call.

3. When you have a short list of possibilities, call each one and conduct a brief interview over the phone, or even better, arrange to meet the person, with no commitment on your part, to get an overview of how they work. You need to ask about their training and their experience.

Many states require that counselors be certified, which means meeting certain minimum requirements, usually a Master's degree in a counseling-related field and one to two years experience. Ask your prospective counselor if he or she is certified by The National Board for Certified Counselors (see discussion at the end of this article), the National Academy of Certified Clinical Mental Health Counselors, or the Commission on Rehabilitation Counselor Certification. Some counselors and most psychologists will have a Ph.D. and will also be state licensed. You can call the relevant agency of your state government to find out the requirements for your area.

Because of the variety in types of training, ask what specific education the person has had in the field of career counseling. Perhaps more important, ask about experience, including what settings he or she has worked in and for how long. Ask how the person conducts career counseling; as explained, a certain amount of structure is essential to the process, and a counselor's description of his or her methods should reflect an understanding of the organization necessary to this type of counseling. In this preliminary contact, ask also about the cost of counseling. Counselors should be willing and able to provide all of the above information without hesitation or annoyance.

4. During your first session with a career counselor, look for the following: Do you feel that the person is paying attention to you, really listening and understanding your situation? Does the person use language that you understand? Do you and the counselor seem to have similar goals? Do you feel at ease with the person? Does the person explain in the first session how career counseling is conducted and what your respective roles and activities will be? Do you leave the session feeling encouraged and respected?

5. Do not make a commitment to continue counseling if you have any hesitation. Take time to decide, and perhaps even attend a first session with one or two other counselors before making a final choice.

## National Certified Career Counselor

Obtaining this certification is a two-step process. First, the candidate must have a Master's degree in professional counseling or in a related field (social work, psychology, etc.) and become a National Certified Counselor by examination. The person thus qualified must then obtain two years post-Master's experience in career counseling, present professional references, and pass a written examination covering the following topic areas: career development, career information and resources, individual and group assessment, program management and evaluation. The credential must be maintained by re-examination or continuing education every few years. Further information can be obtained from: The National Board for Certified

Counselors, 5999 Stevenson Avenue, Suite 402, Alexandria, VA 22304; (703) 823-9800, ext. 369. This organization provides referrals to specific credentialled career counselors and also a packet of consumer-oriented information about career counselors and their services.

*See also* Career Choices: Youth; Career Exploration; Choosing an Occupation.

### Bibliography

Yost, E.B., & Corbishley, M.A. (1987). *Career counseling: A psychological approach*. San Francisco: Jossey-Bass. Although this book is written primarily for the professional career counselor, the general reader can obtain a clear overview of the career counseling process and of psychological issues that need to be considered, and thus can develop realistic expectations both of the counselor and of the potential outcome of counseling.

— ELIZABETH B. YOST AND M. ANNE CORBISHLEY

## CAREER DEVELOPMENT: DONALD SUPER'S THEORY

Donald Super's theory describes and seeks to explain work-related situations and demands that people encounter as they progress from childhood through retirement. Super called these vocational situations and demands career development tasks. Mastery of a task advances a career toward greater success and satisfaction and prepares the person to meet later developmental tasks. Failure at a task delays or impairs career development and may cause a person to flounder in securing a job, drift aimlessly from job to job, or stagnate in a dead-end job.

Based on studies of life histories, Super ordered career development tasks along a time line that represented the life span from birth to death. He sequenced the tasks in the order in which people typically encounter them. Then, Super divided the life line of career development tasks into five segments that correspond to the life stages of childhood, adolescence, early adulthood, middle adulthood, and late adulthood. Super viewed each segment as a career stage during which people experience similar vocational situations, demands, and concerns. He called the five career stages Growth, Exploration, Establishment, Maintenance, and Disengagement.

### The Relationship of Career Stages to Work

**Growth Stage.** During elementary and junior high school, children grow in their capacity to work. To get ready for productive work lives, children need to learn positive work attitudes and responsible work habits. They must also develop self-confidence in their ability to do a job well. To complement confidence in their ability to compete, children also need the courage to cooperate. Career success requires that an individual "get along" as well as "get ahead." In fact, the most common reason for job loss is conflict with coworkers. When young people value work and have self-esteem, they usually start to think about their futures and daydream about working in different occupations.

**Exploration Stage.** During the decade from 15 to 24 years of age, optimal career development requires that people explore their communities and themselves. They should explore the world of work to learn about occupations and they should explore their interests, abilities, and goals to form vocational aspirations. The best way to explore self and environment is to participate in a wide range of activities. People with more life experiences are better prepared to engage in the three phases of the career choice process in Super's model. During the first phase, an individual broadly explores types of work to crystallize a preference for a particular field of interest. In the second phase, the individual investigates possible occupations within that field to make the general preference more specific. When a specific occupation suits the individual and the individual has viable opportunities to pursue that occupation, the individual specifies it as his or her occupational choice. During the third phase of the career choice process, the individual tentatively implements an occupational choice by preparing for and obtaining a job in that occupation (see **Career Exploration**).

**Establishment Stage.** During the period from about 25 to 44 years of age, people typically establish their careers. After settling on an appropriate occupation, an individual seeks to secure a permanent place in it. The 20-year period called the establishment stage can be thought of as having three phases. The first phase consists of stabilizing one's occupational position. New workers make their jobs secure by performing their assigned duties well and by adapting gracefully to their company's way of doing things (see **Organizational Culture**). Having stabilized in their position, workers must then consolidate that position in phase two of the establishment stage. To consolidate a position, a worker must be friendly and responsible. Friendly workers get along with coworkers and deal effectively with interpersonal problems at work. Responsible employees show good work habits and attitudes by being productive, dependable, enthusiastic, and responsive to supervision. Workers who have consolidated their positions may have opportunities for advancement to higher level positions in their own organization or another organization. Workers who want to advance should set goals for the future and identify career paths that lead to goal attainment.

**Maintenance Stage.** During the period from about 45 to 65 years of age, many people maintain positions that they have achieved while some people re-establish themselves in new positions. This is, therefore, one of several transitions often found in careers. Before deciding to maintain or re-establish, people typically spend several years considering their future direction and goals. They may ask themselves, "Do I want to do this for the next 25 years?" Some people say no to this question. Rather than maintain a position, they explore and establish themselves in a new position or occupation. Many people say yes to this question and then maintain their positions by holding on to what they have attained, updating their knowledge and skills, or innovating new ways of doing old work tasks. Occasionally workers who are maintaining a position modify their routines by shifting the focus of their jobs or expanding their job responsibilities.

**Disengagement Stage.** At about the age of 60, people begin to decelerate. People slow down their careers by reducing their work load, contemplating early retirement, planning for retirement living, training a successor, and turning some tasks over to other people. Eventually, when they do retire, people face the developmental tasks of organizing a new lifestyle and structuring free time.

## Application

The previous section described the career development tasks that should concern you if you want long-term satisfaction and success at work. This section explains how you can deal with these tasks. First, identify your career stage from the descriptions given above. Second, read the following action list for your career stage. Third, gather information on the action items listed for your career stage by reading relevant entries in this *Encyclopedia*. Fourth, use this information to make a plan that specifies exactly how and when you will perform each career action in your stage. Fifth, review and revise your plan to make sure that each step is achievable (you can do it), believable (you want to do it), controllable (you do not have to rely on others for help to do it), concrete (you can objectively prove that you did it), and dated (deadline for completion). And finally, carry out your plan.

**Growth Stage Career Action List:** perform regular household chores, get part-time jobs, achieve potential in schoolwork, participate in extracurricular activities, visit interesting places, join group activities, demonstrate adaptability by making the best of bad situations, think about the future, and imagine yourself in different occupations.

**Exploration Stage Career Action List:** participate in a wide range of activities, get to know yourself better, learn about types of work and specific occupations, narrow preferences to a few fields of interest and identify a group of occupations in each field, explore the occupational groups, choose an occupation that fits your abilities and interests, learn what preparation your preferred occupation requires, prepare to enter that occupation, and obtain a job in that occupation.

**Establishment Stage Career Action List:** settle down in a regular job, learn how things get done in your company, find better ways to do your job tasks, keep a positive attitude, be a dependable and productive worker, get along with coworkers, learn how people in your organization achieve stability or get promoted, and think about what you would like to be doing in ten years and what to do to make that possible.

**Maintenance Stage Career Action List:** weigh pros and cons of changing your occupation at mid-career, hold your own in competition with younger workers, learn about new opportunities, find ways to remain enthusiastic, keep abreast of new developments in your field, enroll in continuing education for job or personal growth, seek expanded responsibilities or shift focus of your work, and devise new ways of doing things.

**Disengagement Stage Career Action List:** reduce pace or load of work, devise easier ways to do your work, try new hobbies, participate in community activities, plan retirement income, talk to retired friends for tips on retiring, develop a circle of friends outside of work, and do things you have always wanted to do.

*See also* Career Choices: Youth; Career Exploration; Career Identity; Career Roles; Organizational Culture.

## Bibliography

Blocher, D. H. (1989). *Career actualization and life planning.* Denver: Love Publishing. Workbook for adults concerned about career development issues.

Campbell, R. E., & Cellini, J. V. (1980). Adult career development. *Counseling and Human Development,* 12: 1-14. Available from Love Publishing, 1777 South Bellaire Street, Denver, CO 80222. Discusses theories of adult career development, common career challenges, and career counseling for adults.

Super, D. E. (1957). *The psychology of careers.* New York: Harper and Row. Classic statement of Super's theory of career development.

Super, D. E., & Bohn, M. J., Jr. (1970). *Occupational psychology.* Belmont, CA: Wadsworth Publishing.

—MARK L. SAVICKAS

# CAREER DEVELOPMENT SYSTEM WITHIN THE ORGANIZATION

Career development is not just the concern of the individual any more. Increasingly, organizations are coming to see career development as a responsibility they share with the employee (Hall & Associates, 1986). They are implementing this concern through career development systems, which are programs and procedures to assist the employee in maximizing the utilization of his or her career potential.

## Definitions

A *career development system* is "an organized, formalized, planned effort to achieve a balance between the individual's career needs and the organization's workforce requirements" (Leibowitz, Farren, & Kaye, 1986, p. 4). The key word here is "balance"—organizations with effective career systems tend to have progressive, enlightened senior managements who recognize that the best way for the organization to maximize its effectiveness is to provide for the best utilization and growth of its employees. Two key aspects of the career development process were identified years ago by the late Walter Storey, who did pioneering career work at General Electric. The first element is *career planning*, which is the work of the individual employee who is attempting to chart a satisfying and productive direction for his or her career. Career planning consists of (a) becoming aware of self, opportunities, constraints, choices, and consequences, (b) identifying career-related goals, and (c) programming work, education, and related developmental experiences to provide the direction, timing, and sequence of steps to attain a specific career goal (Storey, 1976).

The second component is *career management*, which is an ongoing process of preparing, implementing, and monitoring career plans undertaken by the employee alone or in connection with the organization's career systems (Storey, 1976). Thus, the individual's utilization of career development systems can be viewed as the simultaneous enactment of career planning and career management. Elsewhere (Hall & Associates, 1986), this writer has shown how career planning and career management represent end points of a spectrum of career development activities (see Figure 1). At the extreme individual career planning end of the spectrum might be activities such as self-directed work books or tape cassettes. At this end of the spectrum the individual has high control and receives a lot of information, but he or she has little impact on the organization's activities.

**Figure 1. The Spectrum of Career Development Activities**

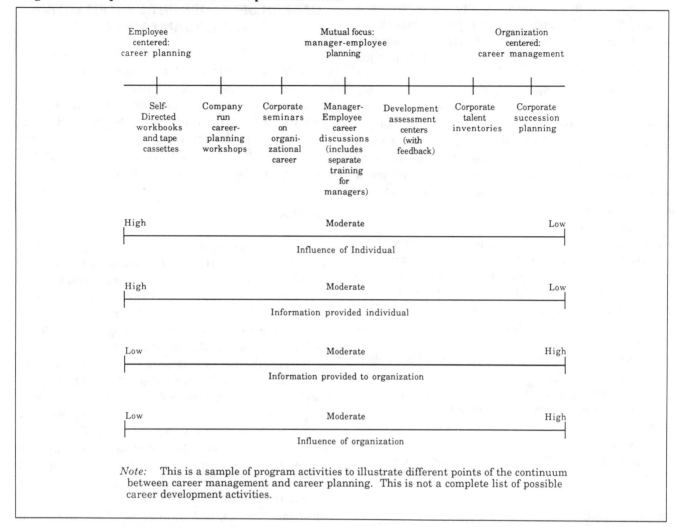

*Note:* This is a sample of program activities to illustrate different points of the continuum between career management and career planning. This is not a complete list of possible career development activities.

**Source**: D.T. Hall & Associates, *Career Development in Organizations,* San Francisco: Jossey-Bass, 1986, p. 4. Reprinted by permission.

At the career management end would be corporate activities with little employee input, such as succession planning. Here the organization has high control. Usually there is secrecy and little information communicated to the individual.

In the middle of the spectrum there are activities with more opportunity for equal involvement by the employee and the organization (usually represented by the employee's manager or a human resource professional). Career coaching and counseling between boss and employee would be good examples of this mutual focus. Here the focus would be on developing career plans for the employee, with the boss providing reality information on how the employee's strengths and weaknesses are viewed, as well as on organizational opportunities and constraints regarding future career moves.

## Application

**Becoming Aware of Career Development Systems.** You and your organization are more effective when you both have high information and influence. How can you as the employee or a potential employee increase your access to these activities? The first step is to learn what is already available in the organization.

The primary source of information on career systems is the human resource (or personnel) department. Often there is a brochure which describes the organization's career development programs. In many cases, there is also a specialized unit within the human resource organization with a name such as "Career Planning Department [or Office]," "Personnel Planning," "Employee Development," or "Organizational and Employee Development." (Sometimes the career planning function is combined with an organizational development function.)

Generally, more career resources are provided in the corporate human resource department, as opposed to the human resource unit within an operating company, region, or function. However, the corporate H. R. (Human Resource) department may not be easily accessible to you, so you could check with your local H. R. representative for information about how to proceed.

Another important source of information and access is your line manager. Often a manager will not be as aware of what career systems are available as will an H. R. person, but if your manager is familiar with them, that is the "acid test" of a good company career system.

Peers and informal mentors can be another good source of information about available career systems. This is probably the best source of information about how well these activities actually perform. Developing your own network of contacts and sources of help is very useful. And be sure that this help is mutual; you should be sure to provide as much help as you receive (see **Mentoring; Networking**).

If you are not now an employee but are considering employment in a particular organization, looking for information about the firm's career systems can be a good way to help evaluate that employer. Generally, there is a strong relationship between the quality of an organization's career development systems and the overall quality of the organization. So, the more the organization provides for career development, the more rewarding employment there would be for you.

So, specifically, what should you look for? A department or unit that specializes in career development work would be one good tangible indicator of career services, as would be a career resource center or library. Career planning workshops and training programs for managers in the skills of career coaching and counseling are also indicators of a good career system. Assessment centers, computerized resume systems or talent inventories, and formal succession planning processes are all indicators of good career management processes. It would also be useful to look for specific individuals who have taken advantage of these activities and ask them how useful the system has been for them (see **Assessment Centers**).

**Using Organizational Career Systems to Your Advantage.** In using a career system, the first thing to do is have an informal conversation with your boss about your desire to engage in a career development process. If you have had a recent performance appraisal, you might want to refer back to that as a point of departure. Get information about available career development activities from the boss and decide with him or her what activities you will pursue. And agree that you will check back after you have gone through these activities so that you and he or she can agree on action steps.

A next step would be to use whatever services are available to help you do a thorough self-assessment. These might be tests, exercises, inventories, and other instruments to help you identify your important values, skills, interests, experiences, past performance, and future potential. A second step would be to identify opportunities in the organization, perhaps from a job posting system, perhaps from a computerized career information system, or perhaps from counseling or informational interviews (see **Career Exploration**).

Combining the self-assessment and opportunity information, you would want to identify some sort of future direction, perhaps some specific goals. The next step would be to meet with either your boss, a mentor, or a human resource professional to work out a plan of action for working on those goals.

You would also want to inform the people in your organizations career management system as to what these goals and direction are, to increase the chances that you would be given the necessary job assignments, training, and other opportunities necessary to implement your plan.

In all of this, it is important to be proactive and to be constantly aware of opportunities to learn new skills, to demonstrate excellent performance, and to be visible to key people in the organization. And remember that the starting point to any kind of career development process is excellent performance in the current job. You will never be offered the next step in your career until you have done quality work in your current role.

*See also* Assertion; Assessment Centers; Career Counseling; Career Development: Donald Super's Theory; Career Exploration; Career Identity; Career Path Possibilities within the Organization; Career Tests and Inventories; Information Interviewing; Mentoring; Networking; Promotion/Raise; Self-Managed Change.

## Bibliography

Hall, D.T. & Associates (1986). *Career development in organizations.* San Francisco: Jossey-Bass. This volume contains chapters by leading scholars and practitioners in the careers field. In particular, the chapter by Gutteridge is an excellent overview of the state of career systems, and chapters by London and Stumpf and by Minor have good detail on how such systems can be utilized by employees.

Leibowitz, Z.B., Farren, C., & Kaye, B.L. (1986). *Designing career development systems.* San Francisco: Jossey-Bass. This "classic" on career development systems was written by leading career development practitioners. It is written more for the organization than the individual, with sections on assessing needs, creating a vision and plan, implementation, and maintaining results. Examples of model plans from leading companies are included.

Storey, W. D. (1976). *Career dimensions I, II, III, and IV.* Croton-on-Hudson, NY: General Electric Company.

—Douglas T. Hall

# CAREER EXPLORATION

Career Exploration refers to the actions taken by individuals to learn about occupations, work roles, or organizations, and their thoughts about these matters. The purpose of career exploration is to collect and analyze career-related information in order to enhance the individual's career management process. One can gather career information from a variety of sources, but the two major sources are the work environment and oneself. By gaining awareness of oneself and the work environment, one is able to develop career goals, career strategies for attaining those goals, and career actions to execute these strategies (Greenhaus, 1987; Stumpf, 1984).

Such behaviors as where one explores, how one explores, how much one explores, and what topics one explores define the process of exploration. The information obtained, or sought but not obtained, influences one's feelings about and reactions to the exploration process. Beliefs about the value of career exploration affect one's motivation to explore. These beliefs are influenced by the success of previous efforts at career exploration, the levels of stress experienced, and individual differences (Stumpf, Colarelli, & Hartman, 1983).

## Relationship to Work

Career exploration has been found to be an important factor in the psychological and organizational success of most workers throughout their career life cycle. It helps individuals to develop an occupational self-image, assess alternative occupations, and pursue the necessary education during their preparation for work (e.g., through age 25). Prior to an individual's first job, it provides information on organizations and jobs to facilitate making a meaningful choice. Thorough career exploration at this stage has increased the likelihood of obtaining job offers, helped individuals to develop realistic expectations regarding different work possibilities, and increased the likelihood that the work selected would be congruent with their personal traits (e.g., abilities, interests, values, personality, skills). Immediately following job entry, continued career exploration within the organization often helps individuals to become motivated to perform well, to evolve a sense of personal competence, and to develop commitment to the organization (Stumpf & Hartman, 1984).

Career exploration during early, mid, and late career stages often leads individuals to seek specific work or educational experiences, request a job change, change occupations, and/or leave an employer. In the early career stage (e.g., ages 25 to 40), individuals can learn more about their workroles, organizational rules and norms, and their personal competency for the tasks assigned through exploratory behaviors. Mid-career exploration involves the reappraisal of one's personal traits, values, and earlier career activities in light of the work knowledge acquired, reflection on how one's workroles have contributed to or impeded self-development, and reaffirmation or renewal of one's career goals and development plans. Career exploration during the late career stage (e.g., age 55+) tends to focus on finding ways to remain valued, satisfied, and productive in work; maintain self-esteem; and prepare for effective retirement (Greenhaus, 1987; see **Career Anchor; Career Identity**).

## Application

In exploring yourself and the work environment, you should consider the goals you want to accomplish, various techniques for effective exploration, and any obstacles that are likely to inhibit your progress.

**Goals.** If you are already job hunting, your most important initial goal is to learn enough about the job duties and work environment of potential occupations. Additional goals are: (a) to develop greater insight into what work roles are consistent with your personal traits and values, (b) to develop expertise in an area so as to improve your performance on the job, and (c) to identify opportunities for employment that are likely to lead to job satisfaction. Accomplishing the first goal without consideration of the latter three often leads to low job satisfaction and intentions to quit.

**Techniques.** You should use several techniques to conduct an extensive self-assessment as part of your career exploration. The objective of self-assessment is to understand the key themes that make up your distinct identity. Methods that have proved useful to many others include: (a) writing an autobiography or written interview which is your personal life story focusing on educational experiences, hobbies, work events, significant people in your life, changes, key decisions, and beliefs about the future; (b) completing self-assessment tests and inventories such as the Myers-Briggs Type Indicator, Holland's *Self-Directed Search,* the *Strong Interest Inventory,* a job skills inventory, a values inventory, and computerized career guidance activities; (c) keeping a diary, both general and hour-by-hour for a few days; and (d) envisioning your preferred lifestyle five, ten, and twenty years from now. After collecting this information you need to synthesize it into 20 to 30 themes that capture the essence of your being. By identifying the implications of these themes, you will be able to better understand your preferred work environment (see **Career Tests and Inventories**).

The aim of environment exploration is to learn enough about occupations, work organizations, positions, and social relations to make personally effective career choices. A variety of techniques have proved useful:

1. *Library Research*—or more broadly, read anything that relates to the occupations and organizations that appear to be viable alternatives (see **Occupational Groups; Occupational Information**).
2. *Networking*—talk with friends, acquaintances, your dentist, etc. to get names of referrals who are people that currently work in the occupation or organizations of interest (see **Networking**).
3. *Informational Interviews*—meet people employed in areas of interest to discuss what they do, what a typical day is like, what skills they use most often on the job, etc. (see **Information Interviewing**).
4. *Job Sampling*—find ways to do what it is you intend to do for a career—consider volunteer activities, internships, apprenticeships, work shadowing, cooperative educational programs, and participating in an assessment center. Use the themes developed in the self-assessment to guide the questions you ask and the methods you use to explore the environment (see **Assessment Centers; Internships; Realistic Job Preview; Service-Learning; Volunteer Work**).

**Obstacles.** Each effort at career exploration may not lead to the acquisition of adequate or useful information. To reduce this possibility, you need to overcome any complacency, sense of hopelessness, and fear you have about exploring. Such feelings are self-fulfilling in that they reduce your motivation to explore. A second obstacle is random or diffused exploration. There are too many possibilities to explore them all; deny yourself those areas that are inconsistent with your self-assessment themes. A final obstacle is to assume that career exploration is a defined, systematic process. It is not. It is fluid, nonlinear, and heuristic. Start where it is easiest for you, change your mind if you like, and keep learning as you go (Stumpf, 1989).

*See also* Assessment Centers; Career Anchor; Career Counseling; Career Development System within the Organization; Career Identity; Career Path Possibilities within the Organization; Career Roles; Career Tests and Inventories; Choosing an Occupation; Information Interviewing; Networking; Occupational Groups; Occupational Information; Realistic Job Preview; Service-Learning; Volunteer Work.

## Bibliography

Greenhaus, J.H. (1987). *Career management*. Hinsdale, IL: The Dryden Press. A thorough, scholarly book which summarizes major research findings on career management.

Stumpf, S.A. (1984). *Choosing a career in business*. New York: Simon & Schuster. A self-directed guide and resource on conducting a self-assessment, developing goals, and exploring business opportunities.

Stumpf, S.A. (1989). Towards a heuristic model of career management. *International Journal of Career Management*, 1: 11-20. An easily understood and applied framework for exploring oneself and one's environment which can greatly contribute to making more effective career choices.

Stumpf, S.A., Colarelli, S.M, & Hartman, K. (1983). Development of the Career Exploration Survey (CES). *Journal of Vocational Behavior*, 22: 191-226. Details use of a career exploration survey for research and counseling. The instrument is contained in the article and is available for use without charge.

Stumpf, S.A., & Hartman, K. (1984). Individual exploration to organizational commitment or withdrawal. *Academy of Management Journal*, 27: 308-29.

—STEPHEN A. STUMPF

# CAREER IDENTITY

Career identity, the extent to which a person views him or herself in the career role, is an important energizer for the process of career development. Let us start with the assumption that individuals generally strive to maintain or increase their self-esteem, since feeling good about oneself and taking pride in one's accomplishments are such intrinsically rewarding psychological states. From this assumption we will discuss how career identity serves both as cause and effect in career dynamics: it is a powerful influence on career choices, and it is a valued outcome of career behaviors and performance.

## Definitions

The main entity in the person's "self system" is the identity, the person's image of him or herself in relation to the environment. *Identity* will be used here synonymously with related terms such as self-concept, self-image, and sense of self. The distinction between identity and self-esteem is that identity is descriptive, indicating the person's perceptions of one's personal qualities, while self-esteem is evaluative, indicating the value one attaches to one's personal qualities.

One's sense of identity is made up of multiple subidentities. Each subidentity is the person's view of self in a particular social role (e.g., worker, mother, father, friend). The role represents the expectations held by significant others in the role set, while the *subidentity* represents the person's perceptions of him or herself as the person responds to these role expectations (Hall, 1976).

Other career concepts can be derived from these identity notions as well. *Career adjustment* may be viewed as the degree of fit between the career role and the career subidentity. *Career satisfaction* is the extent to which the person values his career adjustment. Adjustment and satisfaction do not necessarily mean the same thing. For example, a person could be in a career role which demands high intelligence, aggressiveness, and impersonal relationships, and the person could see him or herself as possessing those qualities, which would constitute good adjustment or fit. However, if the person attached more value to qualities such as cooperation and personal relationships, she or he could be dissatisfied with this career fit.

A final concept to be considered here is *career involvement,* which is a measure of the importance of the career subidentity in relation to the person's other subidentities. This concept has become especially salient in contemporary organizations in relation to work/life balance and the juggling of career and family involvements by working parents and two-career couples. To illustrate career involvement, sample subidentities of two hypothetical people, with high and low career involvement, are shown in Figure 1.

## Relationship to Work: Career Development

Career development or growth occurs as the career subidentity becomes larger and more differentiated (i.e., as it comes to incorporate perceptions of more skills, knowledge, abilities, values, experiences, and motivations). Thus, career development is literally the *creation of new aspects of the self* in relation to the career. In this way career growth is one type of self-actualization or self-fulfillment.

Career development occurs in a self-reinforcing spiral of success experiences (Hall, 1976; Hall, 1985). This cycle is illustrated in Figure 2. It starts with the person working toward some work goal or objective. (And this work may not be as proactive or intentional as the previous sentence might imply; it could be some chance event which leads the person to be working on a particular task.) If the task goal is one which the person values to some extent, and if the person is responsible for independent achievement of that goal (so that any success is one's own), and if the goal is attained, then the person will experience *psychological success* as a result of that achievement.

Psychological success is the feeling of pride and personal accomplishment which comes from knowing that one has done one's "personal best." Setting a personal record (PR) in sports would be a good example of a time when psychological success often occurs. The PR notion also illustrates the importance of a personal standard. A world class sprinter trying for a national record may be

**Figure 1. Career Involvement**

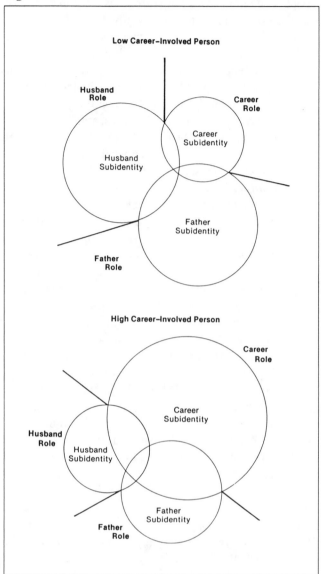

Source: D.T. Hall, *Careers in Organizations,* Glenview, IL: Scott, Foresman, 1976, p. 30. Reprinted with permission.

**Figure 2. The Psychological Success Cycle of Career Development**

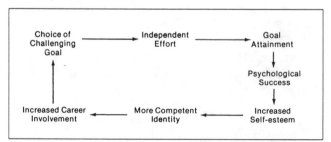

Source: D.T. Hall, *Careers in Organizations,* Glenview, IL: Scott, Foresman, 1976, p. 32. Reprinted with permission.

dissatisfied with running 11 seconds in the 100 meter dash, while a youngster who has never broken 12 seconds would be ecstatic over an 11.9.

The result of achieving psychological success on a career task is that the person experiences increased self-esteem and a more competent career subidentity. Since these are such rewarding experiences, the person's career involvement is increased, and the person is motivated to choose a more challenging goal for the future. The cycle is repeated, and "success breeds success." Thus, self-esteem is both an outcome of psychological success and a cause or motivator of future career task activity (Hall, 1976; Hall, 1985).

Extensive longitudinal research at AT&T, starting in the 1950s, has shown the operation of this career success cycle in the early career development of managers (Berlew & Hall, 1966; Bray, Campbell, & Grant, 1974; Howard & Bray, 1988). Using carefully collected assessment center data, as well as situational data describing job assignments and supervisors' expectations, this research has shown the interaction of challenging job goals and personal qualities such as self-esteem as determinants of career success (see **Self-Esteem**).

## Identity and Career Choice

Another way that identity can be a cause of career performance is by affecting the choice of career goals on which one will work. A person with a clear sense of identity and a high level of self-esteem is more likely to set challenging goals (i.e., those with about a 50% chance of success or failure), as opposed to goals which are very easy or nearly impossible. For the positive-identity person, success on a task has personal meaning only if there is a significant chance of failure; only then is the task a true test of the self. A person with lower self-esteem might either set an easy target (to insure success) or a near-impossible one (so that any failure could be attributed to the tough task rather than to the self).

Still another effect of career identity on career behavior is its impact on the operation of the psychological success cycle. The cycle is more likely to be self-reinforcing for the person with a positive career identity (Hall & Schneider, 1973). People with lower self-confidence would be more likely to stop after an initial success, to quit while they were ahead (see **Self-Efficacy**).

## Application

What can you do to facilitate this process of psychological success and career identity development? While the first answer that many experts might give is career counsel-

ing, this writer would argue that *learning from work experience* is the most promising (Hall & Associates, 1985). (Of course, learning from experience can be profitably combined with career counseling, but if you had to choose just one approach, you would do well to choose the learning-by-working route.) The following steps might be taken.

1. *Self-Reflection and Feedback from Work Experience.* To find a good career fit, you need good information about one's identity and about the world of work. The best way to obtain both is to get information about your identity as you operate in a work role. This kind of reality-based information is far more powerful than information obtained from career information manuals or from other people. Ways of getting such information might be summer jobs, internships, independent study field projects, and part-time jobs. Next best might be computer simulations, role playing and laboratory simulations, career games, and so forth.

To make this work experience most relevant to identity development, there should be a *conscious process of self-reflection* built in to it. One of the best approaches would be keeping a journal, with daily observations. Periodically, you could look over the journal and analyze the data, drawing inferences about personal themes, issues, and learnings which seem to emerge. Discussions with other people (peers, family, teachers, etc.) can also promote self-reflection. And this is where career counseling could play a strong role as well.

2. *Stimulate Initial Challenge in the Career.* The more opportunity you have to be stretched, especially early in the career, the more likely you are to experience psychological success. This means that job challenge should be a major factor in making job choice decisions; challenge is much more important than initial pay, for example. Also, the nature of the organization and its employee development processes should be given weight, since these will determine opportunities for *future* job challenge.

Once you are in an organization, it is important to be proactive in career management. This means looking for challenging next steps in the career assignment and enlisting the aid of the boss, the human resource department, and mentors in providing good information about opportunities and in helping you move into those assignments.

3. *Stimulate Task Success.* Once you are in a challenging work role, the key to future career development is good performance in the current role. You should aggressively seek feedback from the boss, from peers, from subordinates, from customers or clients (if present), and from mentors. Mistakes and setbacks should be examined carefully as *learning opportunities.* This is not just a euphemism, as research at the Center for Creative Leadership has shown that a major difference between successful and unsuccessful executives is not in the number of mistakes

they make but in their ability to learn from those mistakes (McCall, Lombardo, & Morrison, 1988). Success is learning, so that you don't make the same mistake twice!

4. *Deal with Different Issues in Different Career Stages.* It is important to diagnose what career stage you are in and then to develop success strategies appropriate to that stage. For someone in the exploratory stage, it may be most important simply to sample a variety of work experiences. The 1950s song, "Get a Job!" may be the best advice here. In the trial stage, when you have made a tentative commitment, it is more important that the job be the result of a strong attempt to match identity and work role; the main psychological task is to experience the work and to reflect upon your reactions to it. In the advancement and establishment stage, the key task is to be successful; factors which we just described relative to getting feedback and career support are most critical here. In the midcareer maintenance stage, you may have established a career routine as a result of early psychological success, and it may be important to stimulate a new round of career exploration to break out of that routine (Hall, 1985). In late career, during disengagement, you may want to test for success and satisfaction on a variety of second-career or retirement activities.

*See also* Career Anchor; Career Choices: Youth; Career Development: Donald Super's Theory; Career Exploration; Career Roles; Managing Transitions; Self-Efficacy; Self-Esteem; Self-Managed Change; Skills.

## Bibliography

Berlew, D. E., & Hall, D. T. (1966). The socialization of managers: Effects of expectations on performance. *Administrative Science Quarterly*, 11: 207-23.

Bray, D. W., Campbell, R. J., & Grant, D. L. (1974). *Formative years in business.* New York: Wiley. This is an early statement of the longitudinal research on managerial career development conducted at AT&T. For a later statement, see Howard & Bray (1988) listed below.

Hall, D. T. (1976). *Careers in organizations.* Glenview, IL: Scott, Foresman.

Hall, D. T. (1985). Breaking career routines: Midcareer choice and identity development. In D. T. Hall & Associates, *Career development in organizations* (pp. 120-59). San Francisco: Jossey-Bass.

Hall, D. T. & Associates, (1986). *Career development in organizations.* San Francisco: Jossey-Bass. This useful set of chapters by leading career scholars (e.g., Donald Super, Thomas Gutteridge, Kathy Kram) deals with both theoretical/empirical issues and practical career program topics.

Hall, D. T., & Schneider, B. (1973). *Organizational climates and careers: The work lives of priests.* New York: Academic Press.

Howard, A., & Bray, D. W. (1988). *Managerial lives in transition: Advancing age and changing times.* New York: The Guilford Press. This is an excellent summary of the highly important longitudinal research on managerial career development started in the 1950s at AT&T.

McCall, M. W., Jr., Lombardo, M. M., & Morrison, A. M. (1988). *Lessons of experience: How successful executives develop on the job.* Lexington, MA: Lexington Books. This is a "classic" empirical study of managerial learning from experience. The concepts are fresh and extremely practical, and the lessons described have had major impact on corporate management development programs.

—DOUGLAS T. HALL

# CAREER INDECISION

When an individual is unable to select and commit to a vocational or career choice, he or she is experiencing career indecision. Career indecision is often a natural part of career development during adolescence and early adulthood when individuals are seeking information about themselves and possible occupations/careers. Most adolescents and young adults are able to resolve career indecision independently as they mature. Career indecision can become a more serious problem when the individual is unable to make a career choice, despite adequate information and maturity. In such cases, career indecision may persist for a complex set of reasons.

## Relationship to Career Choice

Career indecision may be divided into three basic types:

- *Developmental Career Indecision.* Most persons experience some career indecision as a part of normal development. Career decision making is closely related to personal development, which means a young person's knowledge about self (e.g., their interests, values, and abilities) and occupations develops over a period of time. Later in life, career indecision may occur as a consequence of other developmental experiences, such as "midlife crisis." Since the career development process continues across the life-span, career indecision can occur at any stage of development. For example, individuals can experience career indecision when changing careers at midlife or when seeking a second career following retirement from the first. Individuals experiencing developmental career indecision need not be unduly concerned. People develop "normally" at different rates, and vary considerably in their experience and resolution of developmental issues, such as career indecision.
- *Situational Career Indecision.* Even when an individual is developmentally prepared to make an effec-

tive, satisfying career choice, situational barriers may prevent implementation of the choice. A college senior who has been accepted to medical school may lack the necessary financial resources for tuition and housing, and will, consequently, experience career indecision. The two major elements of this problem are the obvious situational barrier and the individual's ability to solve the problem. When situational barriers create career indecision, effective problem-solving and/or decision-making skills are essential for resolving the problem. Situational career indecision may also occur with changes in personal circumstances, e.g., women re-entering the work world after divorce or child-rearing and workers displaced as a result of plant closings or reorganizations.

• *Career Indecisiveness.* Career indecisiveness refers to a more severe type of career indecision involving more serious emotional and psychological problems. In this case, the inability to make a career decision is a symptom of these other difficulties. The inability to make decisions usually extends beyond just career choice to other decision-making situations as well. The career-indecisive individual typically requires more intensive personal counseling or psychotherapy to resolve emotional and psychological problems before career counseling can be undertaken.

These descriptions of various types of career indecision demonstrate that career indecision may occur for a variety of reasons. The most common reason is that the individual lacks adequate information about self and occupations/careers. Situational barriers and changes in personal circumstances may also contribute to career indecision. An individual may experience career indecision due to a lack of self-confidence in decision-making ability or due to an inability to choose between two or more equally attractive alternatives. Finally, career indecision may result from conflict when a person's expressed choice is not supported by significant others, such as parents or spouse.

Career development cannot be separated from broader personal and social development. Therefore, several personal and social factors may interfere with career decision-making ability. Career indecision may be accompanied and complicated by anxiety, difficulties in organizing and processing information, distorted self-perceptions, identity confusion, and interpersonal difficulties. Career indecision, then, may range from a normal developmental state that may be resolved personally without assistance to a more complex problem involving a range of social and psychological factors requiring intensive counseling or psychotherapy. In the latter case, counseling which addresses both personal/social concerns and career indecision is recommended.

## Application

Some level of uncertainty and/or indecision is quite common for people confronted by the need to make a career choice, and the majority of individuals resolve career indecision independently as they mature, gain information about themselves and the world of work, and gain additional exposure to specific educational and occupational fields. However, when such resolution of career indecision is not forthcoming, individuals may benefit substantially from more structured assistance through career counseling. The process of career counseling can often prove useful in aiding individuals in identifying specific factors inhibiting their ability to make a career decision and in generating strategies for resolving decisional conflicts. Career counseling can even be useful to decided individuals who have made a career choice, but are experiencing doubt regarding their particular decision.

The potential benefits of career counseling are numerous. A career counselor can provide a supportive environment for career and self-exploration and can provide objectivity not always available with family, friends, and peers. A career counselor typically possesses a variety of facilitative "tools" that may aid in decision making (see **Choosing an Occupation**). Perhaps the most important benefit of career counseling is in helping the individual identify the specific reasons for his or her indecision. A career counselor can guide exploration of the broad range of factors that are relevant to career decision making. Additionally, a career counselor can serve as a referral person to direct an individual to appropriate and beneficial resources in the environment that may prove helpful in career decision making.

You should seek career counseling if you become significantly uncomfortable in trying to make an occupational choice, if you have doubts or questions regarding a tentative choice, or, if for any reason, you are unable to resolve the indecision independently. However, there are many ways to deal with career indecision prior to or in addition to seeking career counseling. Teachers, parents, and friends can be excellent sources of information about careers. Seeking information about specific careers from people currently employed in particular careers of interest is highly advisable. Most libraries contain a wealth of information about careers in such resources as the *Occupational Outlook Handbook* and the *Dictionary of Occupational Titles*.

*See also* Anxiety; Career Counseling; Career Exploration; Choosing an Occupation; Decision Making.

## Bibliography

Bolles, R.N. (1981). *What color is your parachute?* Berkeley, CA: Ten Speed Press. The author provides a practical guide to career planning and job-seeking.

Borchard, D.C., Kelly, J.J., & Weaver, N.P.K. (1984). *Your career: Choices, chances, changes.* Dubuque, IA: Kendall/Hunt. The authors provide helpful suggestions for examining potential career alternatives and for pursuing choices.

Rettig, J.L. (1986). *Careers: Exploration and decision.* Belmont, CA: Davis S. Lake Publishers. The author provides assistance for exploring and integrating information about self with information about the world of work.

—DALE R. FUQUA AND JODY L. NEWMAN

# CAREER PATH POSSIBILITIES WITHIN THE ORGANIZATION

Career path possibilities within the organization refers to the alternative options and choices available to an individual in an organization. The old proverb "Don't put all your eggs in one basket" is particularly true in today's job market. Mandatory retirement no longer makes room at the top, and futurists tell us that over half the jobs people will hold in the next 20 years do not even exist today. Today's economic and technological situation makes it imperative for today's worker to keep as many career options open as possible.

Setting multiple career goals is now a necessity. Ideally, employees should not only select and name multiple career goals, they also should work toward more than one of them. There are six career options people can consider:

- Vertical Mobility
- Lateral Mobility
- Realignment (Downward) in the System
- Exploratory Research
- Job Enrichment
- Relocation Out of the System

## Relationship to Work

Individuals should be encouraged to look at these options in lieu of and as alternatives to vertical movement. Supervisors or counselors should coach employees in the selection of multiple and simultaneous career goals. This allows the employee to remain ready for and open to any change which may occur within the system, whether new opportunities or the foreclosure of existing ones. The positive psychological impact of doing so is significant.

Multiple goals encourage flexibility; individuals perceive themselves as being much less at the mercy of outside forces. Should the desired direction become blocked, they at least have begun to think about other options.

## Application

The following career path possibilities can be considered:

- *Moving Up:* You might be interested in moving up if you are unaware of the opportunities offered by the other possibilities. Also, upward mobility is often considered the only acceptable and rewarding way to develop a career. Upward mobility adds additional status, responsibility, compensation, and weight of title to a professional reputation. For many, movement "up" equals success; all other movement either does not count or counts against.

  You can begin this particular exploration process by discussing positions at the next higher level with your manager, or by organizing resource material about vertical moves to help you make specific plans. Key contact people within the organization can act as information resources. Using data available in the system, such as job posting bulletins, can also help you determine what the job requirements are for positions in other parts of the organization.

- *Moving Across:* Moving across involves a change in function and/or title without necessarily undergoing a change in status or salary. Although such moves were once considered a way of "dealing away" with employees, they are fast becoming a way of demonstrating adaptive abilities and broadening skills, learning about other areas of an organization, and developing new talents. Lateral movement is one way that organizations with limited advancement opportunities can continue to challenge their highly motivated employees. You might consider this kind of exposure as becoming a grooming mechanism for positions in higher management since it is bound to broaden your base of knowledge and is an opportunity to demonstrate management skills.

  Internal job rotation programs designed to rotate people on a temporary basis can be used as an avenue to help you experiment with transferring your present skills to similar level jobs in other departments.

- *Moving Down:* Moving down is another option that our changing value system has made more feasible during the last few years. Of course, this type of move is not an easy one to make personally. There are, however, many positive aspects of the move. For instance, you many be unhappy in your position, and the solution may be to move back to a former job where you performed successfully. Most people will agree that it is better to do what they do well than to struggle along in a job or location that is not suited to them.

If you desire a downward move, you must prepare for strong reactions from colleagues. Coworkers need to know that the move was voluntary and designed to accomplish a positive expectation. If the move was made for health reasons, coworkers may be wary of putting any added burden on you and you will have to learn to cope with this attitude. This move requires a particularly strong self-image and an inner dedication to your own personal career goals.

- *Exploring:* Exploratory goals encourage employees to consider other areas of the organization without committing to an actual move in another direction. Acting on exploratory goals replaces fantasizing about greener pastures with planning for action. Exploratory goals require effort, but they can easily be pursued in tandem with other goals.

Exploring involves researching, interviewing, and testing out ideas and opportunities so that a decision about another field of interest eventually can be made. One way to stimulate exploratory goal selection is to ask yourself: "If you were given a six-month paid sabbatical from your present job to explore any other area within this organization, what would it be?" Interviewing or talking informally with individuals in other areas of your organization about their jobs and the accompanying "satisfactions" and "headaches" that go with them is a crucial step in the exploration option.

- *Staying Put:* Staying put suggests opportunity begins at home. In fact, when employees recognize the advantages open to them in their present assignments, it is not unusual for them to decide to remain in their current jobs a little longer. This option calls for taking another look at your present job and viewing it as a potential launching pad for future opportunities.

You might compile a list of job duties and then consider how each one could be modified to increase the challenge, interest, and responsibility of your job. A next step would be to rank the possibilities on your list in order of importance and ease of attainability. From there, another step would be to decide how these changes would be implemented. Setting up an appointment with your manager and bringing in a detailed action plan is a smart last step in this planning process.

- *Moving Out:* While career planning and development discussions are usually aimed at keeping the employee satisfied and challenged within the organization, it is naive to assume that this will always be possible. After serious introspection, you may find that your present occupation, industry, profession, or firm does not meet your needs and you may opt to move out. Employees who may be better suited elsewhere should actively consider what kind of other positions in other organizations might best utilize their skills and abilities

## Conclusion

Flexibility is one vital key to success. Flexibility is required of employees who must look at more options, and flexibility is also required of organizations, since they cannot promise an upward trek to all. The encouragement of multiple career goals is a positive process with a positive outcome. It is a necessity and it pays in increased efficiency, morale, and productivity for both the individual and the organization.

*See also* Career Development System within the Organization; Career Planning.

## Bibliography

Kaye, B. L. (1985). *A guide for career development practitioners: Up is not the only way.* San Diego: University Associates.Significant portions of this article were drawn from this book.

## For Further Information

Also readers should be advised of the following tools:

*Career Leverage Inventory,* developed by Beverly Kaye and Nancy Kaye, for Career Systems, Inc., 1010 Wayne Ave., Suite 1420, Silver Spring, MD 20910, (301) 589-1862.
The eight-page inventory helps managers and employees explore and assess their preference for the six career options. Information pages detail the meaning of each option. Users also answer additional questions to examine whether their top-rated options are realistic.

*Up Is Not The Only Way,* video/film, 1988, Barr Films, P.O. Box 7878, Irwindale, CA 91706, (818) 338-7878.
This 24-minute film outlines the six career options and provides managers and employees with tips for career conversations.

—BEVERLY L. KAYE

## CAREER PLANNING

Career planning involves activities designed to enhance the likelihood of being successful and satisfied in one's work. These activities include identifying skills, preparing a report based on those skills, using the report to gain recognition of one's potential, and developing support groups.

Career planning, self-identity, and work are connected, because people strive to implement their self-concepts through their work. Consequently, career planning is more effective when it focuses on self-concepts. By exploring self-perceptions, career planners can gain greater awareness of their strengths and goals. Their increased self-understanding enables them to communicate their strengths and goals to others in more effective ways. Improved communication increases their ability to enlist support and mutual cooperation in their search for meaningful work that fits their strengths and goals. Effective career planning results in enhanced self-understanding, a greater sense of self-empowerment, and the implementation of self-identity through one's work.

## Application

The following guidelines for career planning emphasize self-identity and self-empowerment:

1. You should base your career planning on an awareness of your best self and your potential. See **Skills** for a description of steps to identify your best self.
2. As you gain a thorough understanding of your skills and strengths, you need to organize your thoughts and present yourself in a way that illuminates what you want and what you can do. This can be done in a brief report designed for use in your career planning. A format for such a report can be found in *Jobs Power Now*, a job-finding guide for young people

## Figure 1. Guidelines for Writing a Report

```
         Your report is a value statement. It reveals your worth at
the present moment and what you have learned from your
experiences.  It also reveals what an employer can expect from you
as a developing person.  It is designed to stimulate interview
questions for which you have positive answers.
         A report has several sections and it should fit on one page.
The titles of the sections and brief descriptions of each section
are described below:

1. REPORT on the capabilities of ....NAME, address, telephone.
   Other words such as talents, competence, etc. may be used in
   place of capabilities in the title for your report.

2. DESCRIPTION.  This section describes your focus, the direction
   and the effectiveness of your capabilities.  These descriptions
   are recognized when studying your past achievements and the
   motivated skills that were revealed by the process.  The first
   statement comes from your strongest-supported skill activity.
   Subsequent statements come from complementing and supporting
   skills in an order that gives a descriptive statement of you
   operating at your best. Remember, when you work with your
   motivated skills "your best" is sustainable with little stress.

3. SUMMARY OF BACKGROUND.  This paragraph pulls out of your total
   experience those events which strongly support the DESCRIPTION
   paragraph.  The first line should indicate how long you have
   been developing your capabilities. For instance, "More than
   five (any real number up to 15 - never more than that) years of
   human resource experience, which includes ....."  Here you
   indicate briefly three-to-five of your significant
   contributions during those years.

4. WORK HISTORY or EMPLOYERS INCLUDE. In this section you should
   give your title, a few words on your responsibilities, name of
   your employer, and years you were there.  Use two lines for
   each job, or run them together with a number of
   dots.....separating the different jobs.  If you did similar
   work for two or more employers, you may group them together,
   even if the employment dates are not in sequence.  In these
   cases, you state "employers include.." and give the names of
   two or more.  You do not have to go back more than 10 or 15
   years.

5. EDUCATION,  PERSONAL.  Try to end on a strong note.  Avoid
   terms that may have mixed impact, such as "divorced."  Where it
   would make a special impression, some of your personal or
   education data might be included in your DESCRIPTION.
```

listed in the bibliography to this article. Your report can be used for job finding or for career development where you are already employed. It should be organized to show your present level of skills development and your direction(s) of growth. Guidelines for writing a report are shown in Figure 1 (on previous page) and an example of a report is shown in Figure 2.

3. Your report can be used to locate new career possibilities by showing it to selected individuals during brief interviews. During these interviews you can ask that person if she or he will look over your report and suggest how you might improve the way it is organized or written. You can also ask the reader to suggest other people who might be interested in knowing about your particular pattern of skills. This approach may help you develop a network of acquaintances who value your strengths and interests.

4. Within your employment setting, your report can be used with your supervisor and others who might be colleagues and potential supervisors. When used with a current supervisor, your report can be presented as a description of your key strengths and accomplishments so you can see which skills you need to develop. You might also mention that you are working on an inventory of the ways you have contributed to the organization and you would like to check your list with the perceptions of others. Ask your supervisor to read it and question you about those events which seem unfamiliar or unsupported. Discuss the ways you have depicted your contributions and explore disagreements in perceptions. These interactions may cause your supervisor to become more aware of what you are doing and more supportive of your efforts for promotion, lateral moves, or even a pay raise.

5. Another valuable activity in career planning is to establish and maintain a support group focused around common goals. These common goals include mutual support as each participant develops and practices further articulation and application of skills. Regularly scheduled sessions with a support group provide opportunities to increase awareness of personal assets and exchange information about new opportunities. Many support groups are made up of people from different employment settings,

**Figure 2.  An Example of a Report**

```
            REPORT on the capabilities of.........  John Doe
                                                     2530 West Capitol St.
                                                     Seattle, WA  98122
                                                     (206) 528-3478


            description          Effective human resources manager, accustomed to
                                 creating and implementing policies that attract,
                                 develop and hold productive scientists,
                                 engineers, related employees. Budget-minded, good
                                 listener and negotiator, perceptive, practical,
                                 persevering, bi-lingual.  Good communicator,
                                 resourceful.

            summary of           Engineer with more than 12 years of human
            background           resource experience in electronics,
                                 transportation, rubber industries.  Directed the
                                 rapid tripling of 200-person workforce involving
                                 recruitment, training, and selective
                                 outplacement;  also negotiating health and other
                                 insurance contracts.  Strong experience in
                                 problem solving, including those related to the
                                 introduction of robots and computers.

            work                 Human Resources Director, major electronics
            experience           mfg. company, 5 years to present.  Developed and
                                 managed staff of more than 16;  reported to
                                 President and Board of Directors..... Senior
                                 Director of Personnel, Blueright, Inc. in
                                 Portland.  Responsible for training programs to
                                 reduce medical, accident and food costs.
                                 Developed monthly employee newspaper.
                                 Represented management at weekly grivance
                                 committee meeting with union for 3
                                 years.....Increasingly responsible personnel
                                 positions with companies in transportation and
                                 rubber industries - 5 years.

            education,           B.S.E.E., Indiana U.  High energy, excellent
            personal             health, 6'1" - 180 lbs.; activities include
                                 sports, church, community service, professional
                                 association leadership.
```

others involve people who are currently unemployed, and some have both. It is also useful to establish support groups within employment settings. While these groups can provide a place to express frustrations about current situations, they are more effective for career planning if they are focused on individuals' skills and development of one's strengths.

*See also* Assertion; Career Development System within the Organization; Career Exploration; Career Identity; Networking; Skills.

## Bibliography

Bolles, R.N. (1990). *What color is your parachute?* Berkeley, CA: Ten Speed Press. This best-selling practical manual has been regularly revised since 1970. It is for people who want to change their careers or find new jobs. The manual includes a major section on identifying transferable skills and suggests many ways to enhance your career possibilities.

Haldane, B. (1988). *Career satisfaction and success: How to know and manage your strengths.* Seattle: Wellness Behavior (Northwest). First published in 1974, this book provides a rationale and specific guidelines for assessing your motivated skills and using them in productive ways. Also included are several chapters on career planning and a foreword by Peter Drucker.

Haldane, B., Haldane, J., & Martin, L. (1980) *Job power now! The young people's job finding guide.* Washington, DC: Acropolis Books Ltd. This book provides a simplified description of career planning methods, with special attention to issues facing the younger person. The chapters on the job power tool and interviews provide practical and effective guidelines.

Irish, R.K. (1987). *Go hire yourself an employer.* 3rd ed. New York: Anchor Press; Doubleday. This book's title indicates the primary message of taking control of your own career and being assertive in your career planning.

Lathrop, R. (1989). *Who's hiring who.* Berkeley, CA: Ten Speed Press. Although some information is dated, the book still presents a well-developed rationale for a self-empowered approach to career search and planning, along with methods and guidelines that work. The book's description of how to write qualifications briefs is very useful to the career changer.

—BERNARD HALDANE AND JERALD R. FORSTER

## CAREER PLATEAUING

When an individual receives no further significant increases in responsibilities or rewards, the individual's career is said to have reached a plateau. When there is nothing new to learn, people frequently become bored with the lack of challenge. At the same time, highly motivated and aggressive people will respond to the possibility of greater recognition and rewards that accompany high performance. The traditional means of obtaining greater responsibilities and achieving significant increases in rewards is through hierarchical promotion up the corporate ladder. Unfortunately, a number of demographic and organizational factors limit the opportunity for promotion to fulfill these needs.

### Factors Influencing Career Plateauing

The baby boom generation (those born between 1946 and 1961) is of an age to compete for middle and top management positions. Between 1986 and 2000, the number of persons aged 35 to 47 will increase by 38%, the number between 48 and 53 will jump 67%, while the overall U.S. population will grow only 15%. This tremendous expansion in the number of middle-aged individuals will mean increased competition for scarce high-level organizational jobs. In 1987, one person in 20 was promoted into top management; in 2001, that ratio is expected to be one in 50.

Just as the workforce is changing, so too are organizations. First, organizations are restructuring along flatter, leaner lines, with fewer layers of management and fewer people at the top. Whereas downsizing once was undertaken only in the presence of dire economic pressures, more and more organizations are now using this practice to gain a competitive advantage. With over 15,000 firms involved in mergers in the 1980s, corporation mergers and acquisitions are frequently the driving force behind these downsizing efforts. More than 50% of top managers in an acquired company leave within one year after the merger and almost 75% leave within three years. The number of permanent white-collar staff cuts in 1990 are projected to be in excess of 225,000 in the U.S. Second, the focus of today's organizations has shifted from manufacturing to service. The service sector now accounts for more than 68% of the nation's GNP. Service organizations are typically smaller and require different techniques to plan, organize, develop, and deliver a product that promotes superior consumer satisfaction. Third, organizations are experimenting with alternative formats to the traditional office. An estimated 16 million employees now work in their homes at least part of the time, with about 30% having formal arrangements with their employers. These so-called "cottage" arrangements are possible because employees are linked together through computer technology which negates the need for face-to-face interaction.

The demographic and organizational forces outlined in the preceding section have led to a changing face and place of work. We have the largest population of educated and qualified people competing for management positions in the history of the country, but the number of positions is not expanding nearly as rapidly as the number of candidates. One major implication is that people will become plateaued earlier in life and for a longer period of time.

Despite these macro-environmental forces, not all people will face early career plateauing. How likely are you to become plateaued early with your present company? Research (Slocum, Cron, Hansen, & Rawlings, 1985) has shown that plateauing is more likely to occur within companies competing in low- growth, commodity type markets. Here the emphasis is on efficiency through high employee productivity and low direct costs. By comparison, the incidence of plateauing is significantly less within companies competing in growing markets and seeking new product or new market opportunities. Apparently, the development of new products leads to new opportunities for upward mobility. Differences in top management's attitudes between high-efficiency and high-growth companies were also found. Senior management in high-efficiency firms ranked "improving the quality of working life" tenth out of 10 goals. High-growth firms ranked quality of work life second in importance. Also, more than 52% of the plateaued people in high-efficiency firms were considered below average performers by their immediate supervisor, while only 26% of the plateaued people in high-growth firms were so considered.

The characteristics of the job are also associated with plateauing. Jobs with less of an opportunity to show performance improvement are more likely to lead to plateauing. Slocum, Cron, and Yows (1987) found that compared to plateaued employees, nonpleateaued salespeople were three times as likely to be in high growth territories in which the company has a high share of the total business. On the other hand, 76% of plateaued employees were placed in low-growth territories in which the company was at a competitive disadvantage.

## Application

How do people react to plateauing? The answer appears to be "not too well." In a longitudinal study of 122 people over a three-year period, Stout, Slocum, and Cron (1988) found that people who were plateaued became:

- Less interested in getting ahead in the organization
- Less interested in adapting to changes
- Less interested in identifying new problems to work on
- Less interested in developing new skills to cope with new opportunities
- Less committed to the organization

In order to address the problems created by plateauing, you should be aware of the different forms that it takes. There are three types of plateauing: structural, content, and life plateauing. *Structural plateauing* refers to the end of hierarchical promotions; it is the most visible type of plateauing. *Content plateauing* occurs when people know their job too well and there is not enough to learn. Most people need to feel the challenge and the associated risk of having something unfamiliar in a task and the satisfaction of learning something new. Content plateauing often results from structural plateauing. *Life plateauing* refers to feeling that there is little fulfillment in any area of life. While being plateaued in life follows from the other types of plateauing, it is more profound, more total, and frequently causes managers more of a problem than structural and/or content plateauing because its roots are more deep-seated and difficult to identify. People who make work the dominant aspect of their lives are especially vulnerable to life plateauing and susceptible to extreme negative reactions to structural plateauing at *work*.

Plateauing is a natural and inevitable phenomenon. The critical issue is how it is handled. Judith Bardwick (1986) has recommended some general changes people and organizations need to make to minimize the negative and destructive consequences of plateauing:

- Organizations must change their culture so that the structurally plateaued people can continue to grow and earn respect and experience success.
- Managers must honestly let people know where they stand so that they can continue to feel valued and motivated.
- Individuals must face the fact of plateauing so that old aspirations do not become frustrations and so that new ambitions can be created.

**Organizations.** Following are some specific steps that we recommend managers take to help eliminate the negative effects of structural plateauing:

1. *Provide honest performance appraisals.* Overall, most people get a performance appraisal that is too good. People want positive feedback. They also want negative feedback, but not criticism. Criticism refers to the person and creates resentment and resistance. Negative feedback focuses on what people do and includes explicit suggestions for doing better.

2. *Encourage retraining both in-house and from other institutions.* This may include providing tuition benefits, including personal development as part of the performance evaluation process, and developing a variety of in-house seminars available to a wide range of employees.

3. *Restructure the organization to provide more opportunity to increase responsibilities and impact the organization.* For example, people at multiple levels of the organization would be included as decision makers on specific issues, especially those which require in-depth studies.

4. *Create the opportunity and legitimacy of lateral transfers.* This will help to alleviate the stress of content plateauing, and will assure the individual that the organization is confident they can handle the new responsibilities. People will feel good about the transfer if there is a challenge and if they feel the new responsibilities are important to the success of the organization.

5. *Create new rewards other than promotion and money.* Anything can become a reward if it is something that people will compete for, value, and earn. Alternatives to money and promotion include vacation time, opportunity to do different work, attend outside conferences, sabbaticals, and the opportunity to lead. Some of the best rewards are symbolic: an expensive attache case, public ceremonies, etc. Top management must encourage creativity in constructing rewards, so that people are frequently reminded that their contributions are valued.

**Individuals.** The facts tell us that plateauing is normal and happens to almost everyone. While knowing this may be somewhat comforting, it doesn't diminish the importance of the problem or the crucial need to do something about it. Following are some recommendations for coping with personal plateauing:

1. *You must take the initiative to cope with plateauing.* No one thinks about you as much as you do, so you must do as much initiating for yourself as you can. You must accept responsibility for your future.

2. *Continuous learning is critical in a plateaued situation.* It is all right to be structurally plateaued, but there is rarely a reason to be content plateaued. The pace of change in work is continuously accelerating. Take advantage of continuous education opportunities.

3. *Broaden your set of important personal objectives.* Promotion should not continue to be your most important career objective. Many people who are successful at coping with plateauing adjust their activities to involve a larger purpose than increasing their own welfare. Individuals need mentors, for example, and organizations also need them.

4. *Adjust your time commitments to fit your new objectives.* This requires first thinking about how you would like to spend your time each week. Perhaps the most important change in terms of priorities is creating a balance between your personal and professional lives.

*See also* Burnout; Career Changes at Midlife; Career Development System within the Organization; Career Identity; Career Path Possibilities within the Organization; Job Changing; Managing Transitions; Performance Appraisal; Self-Employment; Self-Esteem.

## Bibliography

Bardwick, J.M. (1986). *The plateauing trap.* New York: AMACOM. A thorough discussion of plateauing, its causes, and the personal consequences. Practical advice is given for both what organizations and individuals can do about career plateauing.

Slocum, J.W., Cron, W.L., Hansen, R.W., & Rawlings, S. (1985). Business strategy and the management of plateaued employees. *Academy of Management Journal,* 28: 133-54.

Slocum, J.W., Cron, W.L., & Yows, L.C. (1987, March-April). Whose career is likely to plateau? *Business Horizons,* 30: 31-38.

Stout, S.K., Slocum, J.W., & Cron, W.L. (1988). Dynamics of career plateauing process. *Journal of Vocational Behavior,* 32: 74-91.

—WILLIAM L. CRON AND JOHN W. SLOCUM, JR.

## CAREER ROLES

During the course of a lifetime everyone plays a number of roles. One starts out with just one major role, that of child. At age 5 or 6 one adds another major role, that of student. Other minor roles may be played in the meantime, such as playmate and mother's helper. As one grows older, additional roles are played, for example, pursuer of leisure, worker, spouse, and homemaker. Later in life some roles are dropped; retirement usually means giving up the role of worker, and the completion of an educational program may mean giving up the role of student, at least temporarily, for that role is often resumed when changing occupational demands or avocational interests lead one to seek new understandings or skills.

### Relationship to Work

Viewed from the perspective of a lifetime, there is a logical sequence in the roles that people play. They move from the status of child to that of student to that of worker, adding on the role of homemaker (spouse, parent, maintainer

**Figure 1. The Life-Career Rainbow: Six Life Roles in Schematic Life Space**

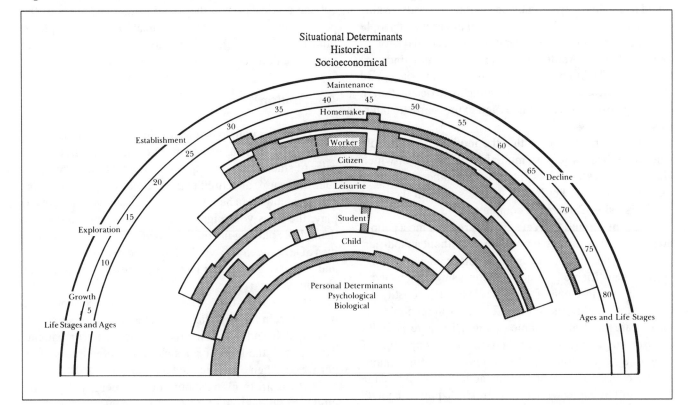

Source: D.E. Super, "A Life-Span, Life-Space Approach to Career Development." In D. Brown, L. Brooks, and Associates, *Career Choice and Development: Applying Contemporary Theories to Practice* 2nd ed., San Francisco: Jossey-Bass, 1990, p. 212. Reprinted by permission.

of a household), then dropping these one by one or perhaps several at a time. This may be called the maxicycle of life or a career, sometimes portrayed as a rainbow with each major role shown as one arc of the rainbow (Figure 1). Work is one aspect of a career. This analogy has the advantage of depicting the life span, of helping one see career development as a complex developmental process rather than a onetime, one issue, one-decision event. It also portrays the amount of time and interest given to each. The shading of each role shows the time devoted to it; making it darker or lighter shows the personal involvement in each role.

**Role and Style**. Use of the term "role" brings to mind the theatre, in which each actor plays a role. What the actor (role-player) does, what the actor says, and how he or she says it depend upon the role being portrayed. So it is with occupations, hobbies, and other life-career roles. Certain actions and certain kinds of statements are expected of people in certain roles, whether they are doing a certain kind of work or are at a certain stage in a courtship or marriage. These are known as *role expectations*. Some role expectations (occupational roles or a marriage contract) are part of a job description or contract, others are unverbalized expectations arising from needs ascertained as work

progresses, and still others are simply part of the folklore of an occupation or other role (see also **Sex-Role Stereotyping**).

Continuing the dramatic analogy, even though roles are socially defined and require certain kinds of behavior or actions, there is often some freedom for the actor (worker, in this context) to play the role his or her own way. Thus two equally effective teachers of the same subject, in the same school, play the same role. But they do it with different styles. One may communicate in a dramatic way, holding the attention of students and thus making learning easier for them. The other may organize subject matter well, use audiovisual aids effectively, and structure lessons to make learning attractive and easy. In some occupations, particularly the professions, there is great freedom to play the role one's own way; in other occupations, procedures have to be followed closely or the work of others is upset and chaos may result.

**Multi-Role Careers**. In everday language the word "career" has come to mean "occupation." But keeping its broader meaning in mind is important in career exploration, planning, and decision making, for what people want from life is rarely provided by any one or even two roles. For example, economic security and companionship may be found in a paid clerical job by one person, who also wants an outlet for musical ability and finds it in a group of people who form an amateur chamber orchestra that plays for its own satisfaction. Another person, however, may find economic security in an inherited estate or in marriage, and choose landscape and portrait painting as an occupation in order to realize aesthetic values and express artistic interests.

Research has shown that the most satisfied people tend to be those who play multiple roles, some of which allow the expression of one interest, while others are outlets for other interests. Putting all of one's eggs in the same basket is risky. Careers are complex.

**Occupational Careers.** These are what most people mean when they use the term "career" without a modifier. Since most people depend upon income from work, this is perhaps a justifiable if sometimes confusing usage. Occupation is therefore one of the two roles which constitute a career; homemaking is the other. These are the central roles in the careers of most people (homemaker here includes spouse and parent). Each of these roles takes up some of everyone's time, consumes some energy, and is a major source of satisfaction or dissatisfaction. The old adage "You can't be happy with it, you can't be happy without it" is a bit of folk wisdom that, in its overstatement, highlights the widespread concern with these two life-career roles.

**Dual Careers.** Another way of looking at roles is to view those played by one spouse in the light of their interaction with those of the other. Thus the roles of the working wife affect those of the working husband, for she has less time for the homemaker role, while her husband often finds that her employment leaves him less time for work. He is now expected to take on some of the domestic work that she handled prior to entry or re-entry into the labor force. Such couples are known as dual-career couples, meaning that each is pursuing an occupational career.

Today many dual-career couples share the homemaking role more fully than their parents did, thus giving each spouse more nearly equal opportunity for self-fulfillment in a combination of complementary roles. But at the same time they create more opportunities for role conflicts, both between each other as a couple and within themselves. The husband may feel that his wife is not as supportive (literally and figuratively) of him as she should be, and the wife may feel guilty because she is not doing as much for him as she might do or as she thinks social norms require a wife to do. The husband might also feel guilt over not doing all he could to facilitate her working career. Both may feel that they are imposing on the other by expecting more domestic support than either can afford to give (see **Dual-Career Families; Working Family Issues**).

Such dual-career problems are more common among college graduates than they are in other segments of the population, perhaps because education leads people to think more of self-fulfillment. Those who are less fortunate tend to be preoccupied with economic security.

## Application

Whether you do it consciously or not, you can imagine yourself playing one or more of the major life-career roles of student, worker, spouse, parent, homemaker, pursuer of leisure, or retired person. Coloring your own life-career rainbow can help you to think about the roles you do play, the roles you might play, and how you might play them. Role playing in your imagination can give you some idea of how much you would like to occupy such a position, and you may get a better idea of the impact you may have on others.

If you are a high school student, for example, you might play, in fantasy, the role of sales clerk (or surgeon), then switch and play the role of customer (or patient) dealing with the kind of sales clerk (or surgeon) that you portrayed. Then examine the feelings generated.

If you are thinking about a dual-career marriage, you might try on the role of husband in a dual-career couple, your "wife" having recently taken a job for the first time since your marriage. What would you do, on coming home from work and finding that she isn't home yet? Start fixing dinner? Sit down with the evening paper and wait for her to come home and fix dinner? Now change roles, and pretend that you are the wife coming home to find your husband engaged first in one, then, in another, of these activities. Think about how you would feel in each little scene.

Just how important are the roles you now play, the roles you might play, how you play them, and why? You may be able to figure the answers out for yourself, or you might want to talk over, with a trained career counselor, which roles appeal to you most and how you might better equip yourself to play them. A counselor might ask you to complete a few questionnaires or inventories of your values and of the roles you play. These may help you see yourself more clearly than you now do! Try drawing your own life-career rainbow as it now is, and again as you would like it to be a few years from now. Think about which things that you value most might be attained in each salient role.

*See also* Career Counseling; Dual-Career Families; Interests; Leisure; Mentoring; Sex-Role Stereotyping; Work Values; Working Family Issues.

## Bibliography

Biddle, B.J. (1979). *Role theory: Expectations and behaviors.* New York: Academic Press. Good coverage of the topic, dealing with basic theory while giving attention to specific roles such as the occupational (pp. 312-21), while slighting sex roles.

Brown, D., & Brooks, L. (Eds.) (1990). *Career choice and development.* San Francisco: Jossey-Bass. Deals with theory and applications, focusing on occupational careers of both females and males. Illustrative case studies.

Brown, S.D., & Lent, R.W. (Eds.)(1984). *Handbook of counseling psychology.* New York: Wiley. Deals with occupational and sex roles, role modeling, etc.

Goldsmith, E.B. (Ed.) (1989). *Work and family: Theory, research, and applications.* Newberry Park, CA: Sage.Up-to-date and generally good coverage in both scope and depth of studies of the family, but neglects almost entirely industrial/organizational/career psychology. Coverage of the worker role therefore leaves much to be desired.

Hall, D.T. (Ed.) (1986). *Career development in organizations.* San Francisco: Jossey-Bass. Focuses serendipitously on work (career) and the employing organization, thus providing a balanced view if read in conjunction with Goldsmith (above). Deals with mentoring (hence with role models) and with leisure (thus taking in another role).

Nieva, V.F., & Gutek, B.A. (1981). *Women and work.* New York: Praeger. Written by two organizational psychologists, this book deals directly with roles, focusing on those of worker, spouse, parent, and homemaker, and on topics such as role conflict, role demands, and role modeling.

Sekaran, U. (1986). *Dual-career families.* San Francisco: Jossey-Bass. Written by a professor of management (born and raised in India, now living in the U. S.) on work, organization, family, and sex roles, but not on ethnicity.

—DONALD E. SUPER

## CAREER TESTS AND INVENTORIES

Career tests and inventories are standardized commercially available assessment instruments used by career counselors to assess skills, knowledge, aptitude, judgments, attitudes, traits, and interests possessed by individuals. These instruments typically yield scores on one or more scales and provide both the counselor and the counselee with insight into the characteristics of the individual that are important for making a career (educational or occupational) decision.

## Relationship to Career Choice

Career assessment, using tests and inventories, is most often employed by those trying to decide on an initial educational or occupational choice. For those starting to think about these choices, the purpose is to facilitate and stimulate career exploration. Later in the process, an individual may use test results to narrow down a choice based on the likelihood of success or the similarity of characteristics to others who are satisfactorily engaged in the education or work under consideration.

When prediction of success is desired, instruments that measure ability, aptitude, or achievement are most useful (see **Abilities**). On the other hand, when the probability of liking an educational or occupational activity is most important, instruments that measure interest or values will likely provide the most relevant information (see **Interests; Work Values**). Even later in the career development process, it may be useful for some individuals to reassess their educational and occupational decisions because they are experiencing dissatisfaction. For this purpose one may want to use job satisfaction or personality measures (see **Job Satisfaction**), although all of the previously described instruments may be useful here.

Although a career counselor must often administer, score, and interpret the more complex instruments, it is ultimately the test taker who must make sense out of the results for him or herself. Furthermore, assessment is but one ingredient in the career counseling process (see **Choosing an Occupation**).

## Application

Many different tests and inventories are available for use in career counseling. The bibliography to this article lists several primary sources of information you may want to examine. Best known among these sources are the *Mental Measurements Yearbooks* published by the Buros Institute. Each yearbook contains the reviews of all published tests in the United States and other English-speaking countries. A second major source of test information and reviews is *Test Critiques*, which has published six volumes of reviews since its inception.

The above described sources cover all kinds of tests, not just those used in career counseling, and the information can be somewhat technical. An alternative source designed exclusively for those interested in career assessment is *A Counselor's Guide to Career Assessment Instruments.* This book, published by the National Career Development Association (NCDA), provides a practical description and critique of over 40 of the most used career assessment instruments. The most recent edition (1988) also provides lead articles on career assessment, instrument selection and interpretation, and testing competencies and responsibilities for counselors. In addition, over 125 less well-known career tests and inventories are briefly described. An annotated bibliography of other sources of information relevant to the topic and the names and addresses of publishers who sell career assessment instruments are also provided. All of these sources can be obtained from most university libraries.

Several surveys have been conducted over the past 10 years to determine which career assessment instruments are most used. These studies confirmed the popularity of the most used instruments. In the aptitude area, the *Differential Aptitude Test* (DAT), *Armed Services Vocational Aptitude Battery* (ASVAB), and the *General Aptitude Test Battery* (GATB) were the most popular, although only the DAT is commercially available to any qualified user. In the interests area, the most used instruments were the *Strong Interest Inventory* (SII), the *Kuder Occupational Interest Survey* (KOIS), and the *Self Directed Search* (SDS). In addition to measures of aptitude and interests, there are a great variety of other instruments which are used in career assessment. They include measures of work values, career maturity, career decision making, and personality. Some assessment systems combine an aptitude and interest measure such as the *ACT Career Planning Program*. Many of the most popular career assessment instruments are also available on computer, including the DAT, SII, and SDS.

Some of the more unique career assessment instruments are those designed for special populations such as handicapped and disadvantaged individuals. These instruments utilize pictorial nonreading approaches or hands-on work samples to assess interest and aptitude. Examples of these are the *Reading-Free Vocational Interest Inventory* and the *Valpar Component Work Sample System*.

Other unique approaches to assessing interest and work values use card sorts. With this approach, you are asked to sort cards that represent occupational activities or values into piles and arrange your preferences from high to low. Card sorts, such as the *Occ-U-Sort* (see bibliography), are usually designed to allow for self-administration. Their primary purpose is to help stimulate career exploration and self-exploration to broaden career options and to provide a framework for understanding the world of work.

Given that most career assessment instruments require a counselor to administer, score, or interpret them, they are not readily available to the general public. If you believe you would be helped by the results of a test or inventory, you could seek out a counselor in the public schools, a community college, a rehabilitation center, or private practice. You may want to ask about the counselor's certification or license.

Although it is possible to self-administer some of the instruments normally used in career counseling, it is not recommended that you undertake the entire career counseling process without the assistance of a professional. For example, the SDS is designed to be self-administered and scored, but reviewers of that instrument point out that people often attribute the wrong scores to themselves. An even greater problem is the interpretation of scores that result from any of these instruments.

Because many career tests and inventories yield scores that are based on some fairly sophisticated norming process, they require a trained professional to interpret. In other cases, misinterpretation of the meaning of terms used on the scales could have a damaging effect on your aspirations or self-concept. Common examples of these misinterpretations include confusing percentage with percentile scores or aptitude with interest.

Before you decide that you want to take a career test or inventory, you need to ask yourself what you hope to find out. Talking to a counselor about this will help him or her decide which instrument(s) to select. Also, when completing an instrument, be sure to follow the instructions and be truthful and candid. Remember, a career assessment instrument can not tell you what to do with your life, but it can help you expand and explore your options, make you more aware of your own strengths and weaknesses, and give you confidence in the decisions you do make.

***See also*** Abilities; Assessment Centers; Career Choices: Youth; Career Counseling; Career Exploration; Choosing an Occupation; Decision Making; Interests; Job Satisfaction; Skills; Work Values.

## Bibliography

Conoley, J.C., & Kramer, J. J. (Eds.) (1989). *The tenth mental measurements yearbook.* Lincoln, NE: Buros Institute of Mental Measurements.

Jones, L. K. (1981). *Occ-U-Sort.* Monterey, CA: CTB/Macmillan/McGraw-Hill.

Kapes, J.T., & Mastie, M.M. (Eds.) (1988). *A counselor's guide to career assessment instruments.* 2nd ed. Alexandria, VA: National Career Development Association.

The reader may also want to consult the first edition of this work, published in 1982, which contains reviews of 40 instruments, half of which do not appear in the second edition.

Keyser, D.J., & Sweetland, R.C. (Eds.) (1984-87). *Test critiques.* Vols. 1-6. Kansas City, MO: Test Corporation of America.

Six volumes have been published to date, each of which contains original reviews of the most frequently used tests in psychology, education, and business. The publisher has recently changed to Pro-Ed, Austin, TX.

Mitchell, J.V. (Ed.) (1983). *Tests in print III: An index to tests, test reviews, and the literature of specific tests.* Lincoln, NE: Buros Institute of Mental Measurements.

Sweetland, R.C., & Keyser, D.J. (Eds.) (1986). *Tests: A comprehensive reference for assessments in psychology, education and business.* 2nd ed. Kansas City, MO: Test Corporation of America.

Zunker, V.G. (1990). *Using assessment results in career development.* Monterey, CA: Brooks Cole.

This text provides some introductory material as well as a description of some of the most used career assessment instruments. Case studies illustrating interpretations of test scores are included for some tests.

—JEROME T. KAPES

# CHILD CARE

Child care is the provision of supplemental care for young children, usually while parents are working. The four basic types of care are: (a) in-home care provided in the child's own home by a nanny, au pair, or babysitter; (b) family day care for six or fewer children provided in the caregiver's home; (c) group day care homes for 6 to 12 children cared for by two adults, usually in the home of one of the caregivers; and (d) centers providing care for more than 12 children including half-day preschools, before- and after-school programs, and full-day programs.

## Relationship to Work and Family Life

Several studies have found that employees, both men and women, report a high degree of conflict between the demands of work and family, and that child care is one of their most frequently cited problems (Galinsky & David, 1988; Galinsky & Friedman, 1988; Galinski & Hughes, 1988).

The conflict caused by child care is twofold. First, parents worry about their children: whether the decision to work and place the child in a child care arrangement will be detrimental to the child, whether the arrangement they have selected will be reliable, and whether it provides a healthy environment for their children. Second, parents worry about their jobs: whether absence from work to care for a sick child or to attend a conference at school will hurt their relationships at work or their performance evaluation.

When working parents are worried about their children, they are likely to experience stress and to be less productive at work. Likewise, family life may be negatively affected by the stress of worrying about job performance or the consequences of missing work when a child is ill. On the other hand, when personnel policies of employers are supportive of family responsibilities, and when employed parents are able to place their children in high-quality child care, children are likely to prosper and their parents are likely to be productive at work and able to cope well with the challenges of parenting. The relationship of child care to work and families is significant, and it is clear that parents must approach the task of selecting child care with great prudence.

**The Effect of Child Care on Development.** Understanding that the most important consideration is the quality of the child care, parents should not be afraid that the decision to work and place children in child care will harm their children. Galinsky and David (1988) identify three additional variables which determine the impact of child care on the child and family:

1. *The Mother's and/or Family's Attitude toward Employment.* When either parent believes that the mother should not be employed, family stress results and affects the child. Conversely, when her employment is viewed positively, the child is able to develop pride in the family and its functioning.
2. *The Mother's and/or Father's Job.* Employment stresses can be carried home and affect the child.
3. *Other Stressful Events within the Family.* Stress tends to be cumulative and the effects on the child are relative to the way parents perceive and cope with problems.

**Quality in Child Care.** The most important variable is the quality of the child care selected. For parents to select high-quality child care for their children, they need to know that:

1. Development begins at birth, and young children need consistent and stable care in a warm and encouraging environment. Whether provided solely by parents or supplemented by child care, the child's needs remain the same. Custodial child care meeting physical needs alone does not respond adequately to the child's total developmental needs.

2. A high-quality early childhood program has been defined as one which meets the needs of and promotes the physical, social, emotional, and cognitive development of the children and adults who are involved in the program; involved adults are parents, staff, and administrators (Bredekamp, 1986). This definition is also applicable to in-home care, family day care, and care for school-age children.

3. The child's experience in a high-quality program is characterized by the consistent application of developmentally appropriate practice. This occurs when staff interact positively with children and provide activities which are both age appropriate and individually appropriate.

4. The significant variables which influence the potential for developmentally appropriate practice center around the staff. They include staff qualifications (education and experience), staff to child ratios, group size, and the continuity and stability of the staff.

5. The relationships between parents and staff are critical to the quality of an early childhood program. When parents are intimately involved with the program and collaborate with other parents and the staff to enrich the lives of the children and adults, all benefit. Child care can become a community nurturing children in which parents value the role of staff as significant to the lives of their children.

6. The most reliable predictor of high quality is accreditation. Licensing does not ensure high quality. Regulations establish a minimal level of quality below which a

facility is barred from providing care. Accreditation is voluntary and requires adherence to high standards designed and monitored by experts in the field. The National Academy of Early Childhood Programs administers the accreditation system for early childhood programs. The National Association of Family Day Care Providers administers the accreditation system for family day care.

## Application

In order to experience the best of both worlds—family and work—the following guidelines are suggested:

1. You need to discuss the pros and cons of employment and its effect on your personal needs and family responsibilities. If this means that two of you will be employed outside the home, you must both support the decision and avoid second guessing the decision. When circumstances change, you may wish to reconsider the decision, but it must always be a joint decision. If you are a single parent, you must avoid feelings of self-pity or anger and recognize that children in high-quality child care prosper and that all parents need assistance with child rearing.

2. Because there is a shortage of high-quality child care, you should begin the search for child care several months before it will be needed. For assistance in locating child care providers in the community, you may seek information and selection guidelines from local child care resource and referral agencies. If your community is not served by such an agency, you may contact the National Association for Child Care Resource and Referral Agencies or the National Association for the Education of Young Children for guidance.

3. You should read about child development, parenting, and child care. Attending parent workshops and support groups in your community is also helpful. Even well educated parents need help with parenting and establishing positive relationships with teachers.

4. You are responsible for selecting the most appropriate child care arrangement for your child. This will involve considering all types of child care in terms of feasibility for your family. You should visit providers, observe, and ask questions. Remember that your needs must also be met and that you are seeking a partner, not someone to assume responsibility for your child.

5. Recognize that high-quality child care is expensive and avoid unrealistic expectations. Unless you have a relative or friend to assist you, remember that the child care provider is also working to support her or his family and deserves a reasonable salary. If you have questions about the cost of care, share your concerns with the provider. Those who provide the best care are not offended by such questions and will share budgets.

*See also* Dual-Career Families; Working Family Issues.

## Bibliography

Bredekamp, S. (Ed.) (1986). *Developmentally appropriate practice.* Washington, DC: National Association for the Education of Young Children.

Galinsky, E., & David, J. (1988). *The preschool years: Family strategies that work—from experts and parents.* New York: Times Books. A comprehensive review of the major issues confronting parents of young children, this work reports actual questions and solutions to immediate problems based on hundreds of seminars with parents. Chapters 7 and 8 are particularly relevant to child care.

Galinsky, E., & Friedman, D.E. (1988). Investing in quality child care: A report for AT & T. In F. E. Winfield (Ed.), *The work and family sourcebook* (pp. 125-42). Greenvale, NY: Panel Publishers, Inc.

Galinsky, E., & Hughes, D. (1988). The Fortune Magazine child care study. In F. E. Winfield (Ed.), *The work and family sourcebook* (pp. 119-24). Greenvale, NY: Panel Publishers, Inc.

Powell, D.R. (1989) *Families and early childhood programs.* Washington, DC: National Association for the Education of Young Children. In this research monograph, Powell discusses the changing social context affecting families, needs and responsibilities of parents and early childhood professionals, and developmental issues for children. The writing style for reporting research and applying it to real families and early childhood programs is appealing to parents as well as professionals in the field.

Winfield, F. E. (Ed.) (1988). *The work and family sourcebook.* Greenvale, NY: Panel Publishers, Inc. This collection of scholarly papers addresses child care in the context of work and family issues and confirms the growing recognition that work and family are not separate and unrelated. In addition to the papers cited above, there are papers about child care for school-age children, care for sick children, and corporate responses to child care problems of employees.

## For Further Information

**National Association for Family Day Care Providers**
Suite 505
725 15th Street, NW
Washington, DC 20005
(202) 347-3356

**National Association for the Education of Young Children**
1834 Connecticut Avenue, NW
Washington, DC 20009
(202) 232-8777 or (800) 424-2460

**National Association of Child Care Resource and Referral Agencies**
2116 Campus Drive SE
Rochester, MN 55904
(507) 287-2220

—NANCY H. BROWN

# CHOOSING A COLLEGE

Choosing to continue one's education beyond high school is a positive career decision. College graduates typically earn more money, and have more challenging, secure, and prestigious jobs than those with less education. College also offers many opportunities to grow as a person—intellectually and culturally, as well as to become more articulate and adaptable—qualities that empower a person to better meet the challenges of life.

When choosing a college, high school seniors are frequently asked, "What are you going to major in?" "What are your career plans?" Questions like these can put pressure on students to make a decision about a career before they are ready, to choose a college based on a *premature* career choice. For example, for a student to declare, "I'm going to be a nurse," will lead that person to consider only those colleges having schools of nursing. This may lead to disappointment later when this individual has a clearer sense of self and discovers that nursing does not fit him or her at all well.

Most students who enter college are uncertain as to their career direction. This is not surprising since vocational interests tend to crystallize in the late teens, early 20's. Once in college, it is not unusual for students to change their major several times. Many students who enter college with a specific occupation in mind change later, although this is less true of those with scientific and technical interests.

In contrast to looking at a person's career choice, it is helpful to view college as a place where *a person can grow and develop,* to become an individual who can better meet the challenges of life. Today's workplace is dynamic, complex, and ever changing. It is a work world where occupations change, new ones are created, and workers frequently change jobs, get additional training, and are laid off. Workers are also challenged to balance work and other life roles, like parent and spouse. Succeeding in a career today requires individuals who are flexible, resilient, assertive, objective, sensitive, skilled, and self-directed. These qualities are vital. They are developed over time as a person interacts with his or her environment. A crucial environment is college. You are faced with the question, then, "Which college will help me grow as a person, to become a more mature, self-confident, and skilled individual?"

College environments affect the growth of students. And, because college environments differ, they affect students differently. Take size. A major study found that (Astin, 1977) students at large universities are less likely to participate in such areas as leadership and athletics, less involved in student government, less likely to interact with faculty, and less satisfied with classroom teaching than students in smaller colleges. This does not mean large universities are necessarily bad for students. For example, there are ways that large universities can compensate for this. Some have created small residential colleges on campus where students eat, live, and attend social and cultural events together. Another factor to consider is the student. How does he or she respond in this situation? Some will reach out, make friends, and join clubs, while other students may become isolated. In choosing a college, it is smart for students to ask themselves, "Is this an environment where I will feel challenged but not overwhelmed? Where I can become independent and self-reliant, but know that support from faculty and other students is there when I need it?"

How are college environments compared? One way (Moos, 1979) is to compare them with respect to student body composition, physical setting, organizational factors, and social climate.

**Student Body Composition.** Who attends the college? A college environment is primarily created by the people in it. To take advantage of this, colleges often encourage students with particular characteristic(s) to choose their school, in order to create a particular environment; more dramatic examples include women's colleges, military academies, and colleges associated with a particular religion. Student characteristics, such as age, ability level, proportion from out of state or who commute, male/female ratio, and socioeconomic level can play a major role in determining the environment. A college with a high proportion of commuters will create a far different environment from one where the students live on campus. The environment in a Ivy League school with students having high SAT scores, diplomas from prestigious private high schools, and affluent parents will obviously differ from one found at a state university.

Another factor: What do the students do? To what extent do they spend their time: partying, studying, dating, reading for pleasure, attending athletic events, etc.?

**Physical Setting.** Generally, a school that is spread out requires a significant amount of time traveling between places on campus, like the residence hall and between classes. Feelings of community and togetherness are less likely to develop in colleges like this, than a campus that is compact. College dormitories can affect the environment. Studies have found that college students often view low-rise dormitories as more cheerful, friendly, and relaxing than high-rise dorms. Furthermore, students generally help each other more in low-rise dorms. Dorms with a large percentage of single rooms can create an environment of competition, independence, intellectuality and inhibit a feeling of friendship, a concern for others in the dorm, and open and honest communication.

**Organizational Factors.** These characteristics include faculty-student ratio, size, private vs. public, and average salary level of faculty. It also includes whether the school is oriented toward the liberal arts, sciences, undergraduate or graduate education. Each of these factors can make a significant difference.

Another factor to consider: Does the school have an active and well supported group of college student development professionals who organize such activities as residence hall learning programs, career planning workshops, cooperative education, cultural and recreational events, student learning centers, and special programs for women and minorities? If so, this is a positive sign.

**Social Climate.** This factor is related to the other three. What do students emphasize: independence, competition, intellectuality, academic achievement, or helping each other. Also, what is valued by the college? There can be dramatic differences between colleges in these areas.

## Application

Choosing a college is one of the first steps in directing your career and personal development. Just as in choosing a career, you want to choose a college *that fits you*—your interests, abilities, and values. And, just as in choosing which company to work for, you want to choose one *where you have an opportunity to grow and develop*—one that offers reasonable challenges while providing you with the support you need.

For example, if you want to increase your ability to communicate and understand people of different cultural backgrounds (a very important ability in today's world), what opportunities does each college offer? Obviously, "College A" having a culturally diverse student body, campus clubs that welcome students having different backgrounds, and courses and activities where you can learn languages and cultures, will offer you more than "College B" that does not have these opportunities.

You will want to ask yourself, "What is important in my development?" Several areas of development are listed below (cf. Winston et al., 1988) with tips on what to look for:

**Physical.** What does the college offer in the areas of wellness and recreational sports? Activities regarding nutrition, weight control, aerobics, stress management, etc.? What is there in the way of intramural and club sports? To what extent is there an emphasis on being a sports participant versus spectator?

**Social and Emotional.** Are there good opportunities to work with others through clubs and other social activities? To work with the culturally different (e.g., minority or international students)? Opportunities for service-learning? Is there a climate on campus of tolerance and respect for others? A mutual respect for men and women? Does the climate foster cooperation and competition? Independence or conformity? Are there student development workshops dealing with topics like assertion, time management, date rape, leadership, negotiation, and intimacy?

**Academic.** Is the curriculum flexible so that you can explore several academic areas during the first year or two? Or are you tracked into a narrow band of courses? Does it have the academic majors in which you are presently interested? What is their reputation? What help is available to support you? Learning labs? Tutoring? How much interaction is there between students and faculty? How large are classes? Is there a spirit of students helping each other? What is their academic caliber (i.e., SAT range of entering freshman)? Are there opportunities for undergraduate research or independent study? Study abroad? What proportion of the graduates go on to professional or graduate education?

**Career.** Are there services and activities that will help you in developing a career direction, such as workshops, career fairs, work shadowing, and career counseling? Are there opportunities to do internships? How strong is the cooperative education program? What help is available in job placement and related areas like learning about networking, job interviewing, and resume writing?

**Esthetic.** What opportunities are available on campus for you to develop a capacity to create, critique, and appreciate the different art forms, like music, literature, drama, painting, architecture, and sculpture. Is there a climate of interest and activity in the arts?

**Intellectual and Moral.** Is the campus climate one that will stimulate and challenge your thinking with new ideas, concepts, and theories? Are there programs and courses dealing with ethical issues?

This article has focused on how a college choice relates to career success. In addition to those factors already mentioned, there are other considerations in choosing a college, including: cost and availability of financial aid; proportion of applicants who are accepted; and proportion of students who return after their freshman year, graduate in five years, or continue on to professional or graduate schools.

Like any other important decision, you will want to systematically consider all of your alternatives, evaluate the pros and cons of each, seek out additional information from books and others who are knowledgeable, and make plans (see **Decision Making**). Important sources of information include the traditional college day or night program in your area, college catalogs or viewbooks, videos, and reference books, like *The College Handbook,* the school's newspaper, college representatives, campus visits, students who are enrolled there, recent graduates, high school counselors and teachers, parents, and friends.

*See also* Choosing a Major; Cooperative Education; Internships; Liberal Arts and Career Choice; Service-Learning.

## Bibliography

Astin, A.W. (1977). *Four critical years: Effects of college on beliefs, attitudes and knowledge.* San Francisco: Jossey-Bass.

College Entrance Examination Board. (1990). *The College Handbook.* New York: Author. Provides extensive information on more than 3,000 postsecondary institutions. Indexes are provided for identifying schools based on such categories as the size of the school, specialized colleges, and colleges with services for the learning disabled. The sections on "Choosing a College" and "Paying for College" are helpful.

Lockerbie, D.B., & Fonseca, D.R. (1990). *College, getting in and staying in.* Grand Rapids, MI: William B. Eerdmans. The first three chapters discuss the pros and cons of going to college, factors to consider in choosing a college, and the changes that students can expect in their lives when entering college. A good source for dealing with the high school to college transition.

Miller, G.P. (1990) *Choosing a college.* New York: College Entrance Examination Board. Provides a step by step approach to deciding on a college.

Moos, R.H. (1979). *Evaluating educational environments.* San Francisco: Jossey-Bass.

Winston, R.B., Jr., Bonney, W.D., Miller, T.K., & Dagley, J.C. (1988). *Promoting student development through intentionally structured groups.* San Francisco: Jossey-Bass.

—LAWRENCE K. JONES

## CHOOSING A MAJOR

Choosing a major is a topic generally associated with students and others who wish to obtain a degree from a college or university. For young adults it represents one of the early important decisions in their lives. For adults who want to change their field of work, for students who are dissatisfied with their initial choice, choosing or changing a major opens up new options and opportunities.

In some schools the *major* is called a *concentration*. Either term refers to the number and sequence of courses in a particular field, and the related courses or work assignments that are needed to fulfill the degree requirements.

### Relationship to Work and/or Careers

Choosing a major can be directly or indirectly related to what a person wants to do with his or her life after graduation.

The greatest number of students in this country select majors in the Liberal Arts area. This gives them an opportunity to explore many areas of knowledge for personal satisfaction, and to learn more about themselves and the world in which they live. Courses in the "core curriculum" plus elective courses enable students to get acquainted with many subject areas. Selecting a major enables students to study one subject area in depth.

All the major subjects in the broad Humanities and Social Sciences areas help students develop their speaking, writing, and thinking abilities. By acquiring skills in research, analytical methods, and problem solving, students make better decisions, and acquire skills that will be useful in any type of activity. Choosing a major in a subject area of interest usually results in better grades, and motivates students to put more energy into their studies, thus getting more out of them.

Some individuals choose a major to obtain what is called "credentialing"—a term often used to indicate that a person has obtained the necessary training and fulfilled other requirements to be considered as "qualified" to practice or work in a field as a professional. Majors in teaching and nursing are typical examples of the need for credentialing.

For some students a major determines the type of work they want or expect to do after obtaining their degree. Thus, the major in college begins their career, as evidenced in the engineering and accounting fields.

A number of students declare majors which will help prepare or qualify them for a graduate school so they will have additional options for professional or other careers. Examples include majors in economics and computer science which would be especially beneficial to students planning to go to graduate school for a MBA degree. A major in Liberal Arts, plus some courses in accounting, economics, and communications would provide a foundation for students planning a corporate legal career.

### Application

For all readers, choosing a major that is best for you is similar to choosing a career, and involves several steps.

Begin with a "personal self-assessment." Here are some suggestions:

1. List the subjects and activities that appeal or interest you. Such a listing will help define your interests and clarify what is important to you (your value system)—the key factors in determining which major will be best for you.

2. Use one of the computer-assistance programs available in your college's career planning and placement office. Programs such as DISCOVER, CAREER NAVIGATOR, and SIGI (System of Interactive Guidance and Information) will help you analyze, study, and prioritize your interests, skills, and values. Such computer programs also generate ca-

reer options which fit the pattern of answers you put in, thus facilitating the process of determining the best choice of a major in college.

3. Take advantage of interest inventories and other tests available to you. Although test results will not make decisions for you, they can provide objective information to support your own thinking, or to provide alternatives which may be unknown to you (see **Abilities; Career Tests and Inventories; Interests; Work Values**).

Combine your self-appraisal with an exploration of the possible majors and career options:

1. Peruse your college's bulletin and its schedule of courses to ascertain what is offered, thus getting an overall view of the major fields of study.

2. Talk to knowledgable people in the fields that may be of interest to you. Ask questions, discuss your interests and concerns, and get advice and additional references from your faculty, counselors, family, and friends. (Persons seeking to change their fields of work can talk to family and friends, fellow employees, supervisors, and personnel counselors in their organization). Such conversations can help you get other viewpoints on your strengths, weaknesses, interests, and other qualifications. They may reassure your own thinking, or give you reasons for looking at other options (see **Information Interviewing**).

3. Read through a number of reference publications. Most libraries have books and periodicals similar to those listed in the bibliography of this article. Studying such data can be an important factor to help you choose the right major, broaden your intellectual horizons, and help make your college experience both educational and fulfilling.

4. Take advantage of all the resources on your campus. Speakers who come to the campus to talk about various fields of work can provide practical advice on majors and other courses that would be most beneficial for personal study or careers (see **Occupational Information**). Your campus career and placement service will likely offer many programs and services, such as, workshops to help students learn and make decisions regarding majors and career fields, career library, computer-assisted career guidance, and career couseling.

5. Continuing education students should obtain a transcript of courses taken to date, then talk to the Admissions Office to ascertain what credits can be transferred. Ask who should be contacted to determine the additional courses and other requirements for a major, needed for a degree.

## General Comments

Explore as many areas of knowledge as possible, then choose a major that will satisfy your curiosity and stimulate you. If you are interested in the field you will get better grades and be motivated to get the most out of that major. Don't lock yourself into a particular field too early, and don't worry about preparing for jobs—internships and on-the-job training programs will take care of this. After each year in college, appraise your progress; if dissatisfied, don't be afraid to change majors and take other corrective action.

*See also* Career Exploration; Choosing an Occupation; Liberal Arts and Career Choice.

## Bibliography

Hopke, W.E. (Ed.) (1990). *The encyclopedia of careers and vocational guidance.* Chicago: Ferguson.

*Lovejoy's college guide.* (1987). New York: Monarch Press. See especially the section on "Professional Curricula: Majors Special Programs Where to Find Them." This section covers 500 career fields and 45 special interest programs, and institutions where they are taught.

Powell, C.R. (1990). *Career planning today: Hire me* (2nd ed.). Dubuque, IA: Kendall-Hunt. This book is designed to serve students as a guide for planning and implementing a systematic approach to the direction they want their working lives to take. It provides action suggestions to help students develop a strategical plan for their lives, beginning with their major in college, and how to be continually in charge of their careers.

*Profiles of American colleges: Index of college majors.* (1990). Hauppauge, NY: Barron's Educational Series.

Steele, J.E., & Morgan, M.S. (1991). *Career planning & development for college students and recent graduates.* Lincolnwood, IL: NTC Publishing Group. See especially Chapter 3, "Career Resources on College Campuses," and Chapter 4, "Career Blueprint for College." These chapters will help you get the most out of your college experience, and provide specific information to facilitate choosing a major, other courses, and extracurricular activities that will fulfill your interests and lay a foundation for a lifelong career.

U.S. Department of Labor (1990). *The occupational outlook handbook,* 1990–91 Edition. Washington, D.C.: Author.

—JOHN E. STEELE

## CHOOSING AN OCCUPATION

Choosing an occupation is, at its simplest, selecting the occupation that best suits you from among several occupations. This is true whether you are choosing your first occupation, changing positions within an organization, re-entering the workforce, or changing careers. In order to make such a choice, however, you need to know the answers to a number of important and complex questions: What are my options? Which occupations should I consider? What do I know about them? How can I learn more? What do I know about myself that's important to consider?

Choosing an occupation may be further complicated by barriers to free choice, such as family responsibilities, lack of finances, the economic situation, and various forms of discrimination (e.g., age, race, sex, disability). Less obvious are the barriers like sex-role stereotyping, socio-economic deprivation, low self-confidence, and irrational thinking.

Fortunately, social scientists and practicing counselors have created a body of knowledge that makes choosing an occupation easier. Their work is presented in this *Encyclopedia*. This article will help you in choosing an occupation by giving you an overview of their work, and will direct you to articles in the *Encyclopedia* where you can learn more from these authorities.

## Job Satisfaction

The basic goal in choosing an occupation is the good feeling of getting what you hoped for from your job. But what do you expect or require from a job? What do other workers expect? According to the article, **Job Satisfaction,** workers rank most highly the "type of work"—a job that makes the best use of one's abilities and gives one a feeling of accomplishment. Other highly ranked expectations include job security, pay, and opportunity for advancement. Of course, job requirements differ from person to person, so you will need to consider what is important to you. The job satisfaction article summarizes what is known and will give you helpful ideas for thinking about this issue.

## Matching Your Requirements to Occupations

Two approaches for identifying occupations likely to fit you are trait-factor and motivated skills.

**Trait-Factor Approach.** In this approach, you first identify your traits—abilities, interests, work values, and skills—usually by taking tests or inventories, and then identify occupations having workers with traits similar to your own. For example, a person takes an interest inventory and the results show that his or her interests are similar to those of social workers and teachers. Various tests have been designed to assess a person's traits and relate the results to different occupations (see **Trait-Factor Approach to Career Choice;** see also **Career Tests and Inventories; Myers-Briggs Type Indicator; Occupational Groups; Occupational Information).**

One trait-factor approach that is widely used by career counselors is based on the work of John Holland (see **Vocational Choice: John Holland's Theory).** Holland describes six personality types: Realistic, Investigative, Artistic, Social, Enterprising, and Conventional. Each person can be described in terms of his or her resemblance to these six types. A brief description of each type taken from the *Occ-U-Sort* occupational card sort (see bibliography) is reprinted in Figure 1. Which types do you most closely resemble?

According to Holland's theory, *work environments* can also be described according to these six types. Work environments are determined by the personalities of the workers in them. For example, the work environment for musicians is Artistic because most of the workers in that work have personalities that strongly resemble the Artistic type.

According to the theory and supporting research, you are more likely to be satisfied in an occupation where the work environment is similar to your personality type. This is explained in an instrument called *The Career Key* (see bibliography) and illustrated by Figure 2.

A number of career guidance instruments use this approach. Typically, they assess your resemblance to the six types and then suggest occupations based on your scores. For example, a person who closely resembles the Artistic and Social types is directed to occupations having an Artistic-Social work environment, like Actor/Actress, Drama Teacher, Reporter, Writer, and Musician (see **Occupational Groups).**

**Motivated Skills Approach.** The principle of this approach is that you will do your best and be most satisfied by implementing your self-concept—doing work that allows you to use the skills that you most enjoy using. As described in the articles **Career Planning** and **Skills,** you first identify your skills, especially your *motivated skills,* which are transferable, personally valued, and enjoyable for you to use. Once you identify these skills, you organize them in a brief written report. A frequent by-product of this process is greater self-clarity and a feeling of empowerment. This report and clearer picture of self are then used to locate new career possibilities, often through information interviewing (see **Information Interviewing).** This approach was popularized by Richard Bolles' book, *What Color Is Your Parachute?*

The trait factor and motivated skills approaches differ primarily in emphasis. The trait-factor approach focuses more attention on "matching" persons with jobs, through information obtained from tests and media containing occupational information. The motivated skills approach emphasizes self-exploration, skills, and self-empowerment.

**Figure 1. Holland Personality Types**

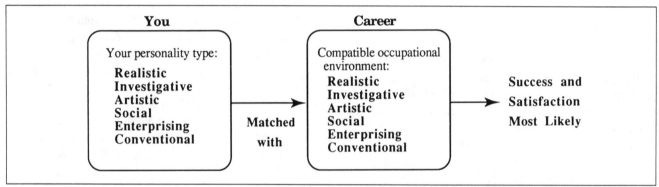

 Realistic: prefers working with tools, objects, machines, or animals and tends to avoid social activities

 Investigative: prefers observing and studying scientific objects and tends to avoid selling or social activities

Artistic: prefers working freely and creatively, expressing ideas or feelings through dance, drama, music, writing, craft arts, or other art fields and tends to avoid highly-ordered or repetitive activities

 Social: prefers helping or teaching people and tends to avoid working with tools or machines

 Enterprising: prefers selling or persuading people and tends to avoid activities that require careful observation or study

 Conventional: prefers activities involving numbers, records, or clerical materials and tends to avoid those that are not well ordered or that demand creative abilities

**Source:** Lawrence K. Jones, *Occ-U-Sort*, copyright © 1981, published by CTB/Macmillan/McGraw-Hill, 2500 Garden Rd., Monterey, CA 93940. All rights reserved. Reprinted by permission.

**Figure 2. Choosing Compatible Occupations**

**You**

Your personality type:

**Realistic**
**Investigative**
**Artistic**
**Social**
**Enterprising**
**Conventional**

**Matched with**

**Career**

Compatible occupational environment:

**Realistic**
**Investigative**
**Artistic**
**Social**
**Enterprising**
**Conventional**

**Success and Satisfaction Most Likely**

**Source:** Lawrence K. Jones, *The Career Key*, copyright © 1991, published by Careers, Inc., P.O. Box 135, Largo, FL 34649-0135. All rights reserved. Reprinted by permission.

## Career Exploration

Career exploration is vitally important in career choice and career development. Studies have shown that it is a major factor in the success of most workers.

Career exploration involves gathering information on yourself and on potential occupations. It is done throughout a person's working life. For *self*, it means examining such areas as your abilities, skills, and work values. For *occupations*, it involves such areas as skill requirements, pay, and opportunities for advancement. Information in these two areas can be gathered in a variety of ways, such as taking career tests and inventories, doing volunteer work, information interviewing, talking with your supervisor or other employees, or reading specialized books (see **Career Exploration** and also **Career Choices: Youth**).

For learning about "self," the following articles are recommended: **Abilities; Assessment Centers; Career Anchor; Career Planning; Career Roles; Career Tests and Inventories; Interests; Skills;** and **Work Values.** To learn about "occupations," see the following articles: **Ben-**efits; Climate for Workers; Information Interviewing; Job Outlook: Major Trends; Military Career: Changing to a Civilian Career; Occupational Information; and Pay.

## Making a Decision

**Considering the Consequences.** A common error in making a career decision is not seriously considering both the positive *and* negative consequences of the options from which you are choosing. This is one of the pitfalls described in **Decision Making**. The "decisional balance sheet" described in this article can help you overcome this problem.

**Considering All of Your Options.** Another potential pitfall is not considering all of your possible options. With respect to this, several articles are particularly recommended: **Career Development System within the Organization; Career Path Possibilities within the Organization; Job Sharing; Part-Time Work; Self-Employment; Sequencing: A Career and Traditional Mothering;** and **Temporary Employment.**

**Understanding the Effects of Feelings.** Making decisions about one's life always evokes feelings. Anxiety, self-doubt, excitement, confusion, and frustration are commonly experienced. This is a part of being human, and it is a natural part of making career decisions. It is important, therefore, for you to be aware of these feelings and to accept them.

Emotions can interfere with making an informed decision. For example, the pitfalls described above—not considering all of your options and their consequences—are often a casualty of emotions. These might involve the *excitement* of being recruited by another company; *fear* of disappointing someone; *anxiety* of not knowing which option to choose; or *frustration* with the current situation. Emotions can cause people to overlook other options, or to make a decision based on faulty information.

Therefore, be aware of your emotions and understand them. Ask yourself: How am I feeling? Why do I feel this way? What am I saying to myself? Often a good listener or a support group can play a vital role in helping you express your feelings and giving you support. Also ask yourself: How is what I am *thinking* making me feel this way? Is my thinking rational? Helpful? With respect to these questions, everyone should read the articles on **Rational Thinking** and **Self-Talk**.

The following articles may also be helpful: **Anger; Anxiety; Career Counseling; Career Indecision; Depression; Self-Efficacy; Self-Esteem;** and **Stress.**

## Understanding Your Situation

Often an important step in choosing an occupation is understanding the factors that affect your choice at that particular time and in that particular situation. For help with career and life development issues, see the following articles: **Career Changes at Midlife; Career Choices: Youth; Career Development: Donald Super's Theory;** and **Women: Reentry into the Workplace.** For issues surrounding termination from one's job, see the following articles: **Fired/Laid Off; Job Security; Job Security: The Free Agent Manager; Outplacement;** and **Unemployment.** For dealing with job satisfaction, the following articles are helpful: **Burnout; Career Identity; Career Plateauing; Job Changing; Self-Employment; Underemployment; Work Hazards: Psychosocial; Workaholism.** The following articles discuss career barriers: **Articles on discrimination (i.e., age, language, race, sex, disability);** Articles on different ethnic groups; Dual-Career Families; Sex-Role Stereotyping; Women in the Workforce; Women's Barriers and Opportunities.

## Bibliography

Bolles, R.N. (1990). *What color is your parachute?* Berkeley, CA: Ten Speed Press.
Jones, L.K. (1981). *Occ-U-Sort.* Monterey, CA: CTB/Macmillan/McGraw-Hill. *Occ-U-Sort* is a set of 60 cards, each of which has the name of an occupation, the *Dictionary of Occupational Titles* (DOT) code, the educational level, the Holland code (RIASEC), and a description of the occupation. These codes are sorted and resorted in a prescribed way by the individual to identify and clarify his or her thoughts about occupations. It was originally developed to be used by counselors in individual counseling, but another option is to use the *Self-Guided Booklet* which takes the individual through the various steps without supervision. The *Guide to Occupations* lists 555 occupations that are organized according to the six Holland types and the worker trait groups of the *Guide for Exploration* (see **Occupational Groups**). This is an excellent tool for helping the person sort out what's important to him or her in making an occupational choice.
Jones, L. K. (1991). *The career key.* Largo, FL: Careers Inc. A self-directed career guidance instrument designed to assess individuals' personality type, direct them to compatible occupations, teach the basics of Holland's theory, and guide career exploration.

—LAWRENCE K. JONES

## CLIMATE FOR WORKERS

Climate for workers refers to the quality of a state or region's environment for workers. Is the area characterized by such factors as stable employment? Adequate pay checks? Fair and safe workplaces? Good places to live? Protection for workers in need? These and many other factors are analyzed biennially by the Southern Labor Institute of the Southern Regional Council for the purpose of improving conditions of the workplace. These data are distributed to leaders in government, businesses, labor, and other groups concerned with social policy making. This article is based on the 1990 report, *The Climate for Workers in the United States.*

Thirty-five indicators were examined to determine an overall worker climate indicator for each state, the District of Columbia, and nine geographic regions. In addition, the indicators were divided into the following five categories:

- *Labor Market Opportunity,* which includes employment growth over the past 12 years as well as unemployment data;
- *Earnings and Income,* which includes earnings indicators for three sectors of employment, income changes, and median family income;

- *Workplace Conditions,* including employment opportunity for blacks and women, unionization, health insurance coverage, and workplace safety;
- *State Protection of Workers,* including wage, disability, and unemployment legislation and the extensiveness of unemployment insurance coverage; and
- *Quality of Life,* including environmental quality, health, education, cost-of-living, taxes, and crime.

## Overall Worker Climate

The national averages of rankings by region indicate that the Mideast and New England are the best regions in which to live and work, while the Southeast is the worst. The nine regions were ranked as follows, starting with the best: Mideast, New England, Pacific, Far West, Great Lakes, Plains, Rocky Mountains, Southwest, and Southeast.

Figure 1 shows the national rankings by state for overall worker climate. The best state for workers is Massachusetts, in spite of declining employment in 1989. The other top 10 states, in order, are: New Jersey, Connecticut, Maryland, New York, California, Rhode Island, Minnesota, New Hampshire, District of Columbia.

## Labor Market Opportunity

Where are the employment opportunities best? This category used seven different indices in the areas of job growth, unemployment rates, and the ratio of employment to total population. A composite score for each state was

**Figure 1. Overall Averages of Ranks**

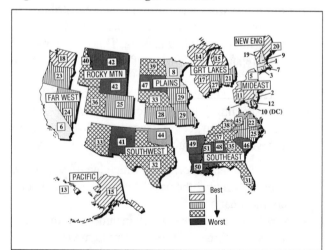

**Source**: Southern Regional Council/Southern Labor Institute. Reprinted by permission.

computed, and then the states were rank-ordered. The results are seen in Figure 2. The 10 best states are: North Carolina, Maryland, New Jersey, Virginia, Wisconsin, Indiana, Minnesota, California, Delaware, and Massachusetts.

## Earnings and Income

In which states do people receive the highest income? Income here is broadly defined. It includes earnings from work as well as income from capital assets, government

**Figure 2. Labor Market Opportunities**

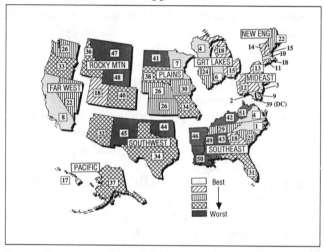

**Source**: Southern Regional Council/Southern Labor Institute. Reprinted by permission.

transfer income, and all other sources. The composite indicator is based on nine indices, including average weekly wages and annual earnings, per capita personal income, and median income for a family of four persons. The rankings are shown in Figure 3. The 10 best states are: Connecticut, New Jersey, Massachusetts, the District of Columbia, New York, Maryland, California, Illinois, New Hampshire, and Delaware.

When considering income, it is important to keep in mind that income is unequally distributed. In fact, it has become more unequally distributed in the past decade. The wealthiest one-fifth of the population received 43.5% of the income in the United States.

It is also important to note that this composite index of earnings and income tends to overstate the income people receive because of the presence of a very few high-income individuals in the population. For this reason, the median income figures for families of four is shown in Table 1, below. The median income figure exactly divides families into two groups—one-half with incomes above the median figure and one-half with incomes below. In other

**Figure 3. Earnings and Income**

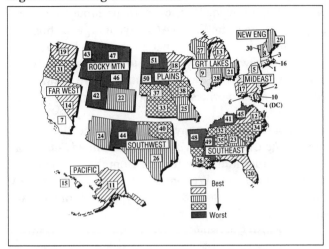

**Source**: Southern Regional Council/Southern Labor Institute. Reprinted by permission.

words, looking at the top ranked state—New Jersey—one-half the families of four have an income above $52,305 and one-half have an income below that figure.

## Workplace Conditions

This includes the following factors: employer-provided health insurance, occupation-related traumatic death rates and disease risk, labor union membership, occupational opportunities for African Americans and women. The composite rankings are shown in Figure 4. The 10 best performers are: Maryland, New York, Massachusetts, the District of Columbia, New Jersey, Hawaii, Connecticut, Washington, Michigan, and Ohio.

The index of occupational opportunity for African Americans contains important information and is presented here. The percentages of blacks employed in what tradi-

**Figure 4. Workplace Conditions**

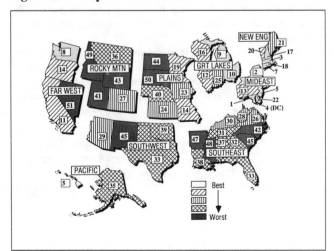

**Source**: Southern Regional Council/Southern Labor Institute. Reprinted by permission.

tionally have been predominantly white-male occupations were compared (see Table 2, below). These occupations are generally better paid, require higher skill levels, and carry higher status than other occupations. They include executive, managerial, and professional occupations, as well as technical and technical support, precision, craft, and repair occupations. Currently, 42% of white workers are in these occupations; 27.6% of black workers are also in them. Thirty-five states have significant numbers of black workers; the ranking of the states is shown in Table 2. The Mideast region has four states in the top group and clearly is the leading region on this measure.

Table 3 also shows how the states compare in opportunities for women. Using the same occupations—those traditionally dominated by white men—the percentage of women employed in them in 1989 were compared. The District of Columbia is way out in front on this measure.

## State Protection of Workers

How well does the state protect workers? This includes protecting the physical safety and the basic rights of workers; the effectiveness and benefits of unemployment insurance; minimum wage laws; amount of worker's compensation benefits paid to workers who become disabled due to injury on the job; and the right to a healthy workplace environment. As seen in Figure 5, the New England states protect their workers best; the Southeastern and Southwestern states the least. The 10 best states are: Rhode Island, Alaska, Massachusetts, Maine, Connecticut, Pennsylvania, New Jersey, New York, Minnesota, and Washington.

**Figure 5. State Worker Protection**

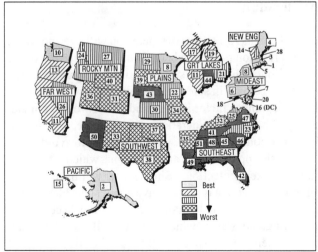

**Source**: Southern Regional Council/Southern Labor Institute. Reprinted by permission.

## Quality of Life

How will the quality of life of the state affect the worker and his or her family? This composite includes such factors as infant mortality rate; personal taxes as a percentage of all state taxes; state and local expenditures per public school pupil; crime rate; and Cost-of-Living Index. The results are shown in Figure 6.

The New England region is well ahead of other regions on these quality-of-life measures. Five of the six New England states are ranked in the top 10 and the sixth ranks eleventh nationally. The top 10 states are: Wyoming, Massachusetts, Vermont, Rhode Island, North Dakota, Connecticut, New Hampshire, Wisconsin, New Jersey, and Minnesota.

**Figure 6. Quality of Life**

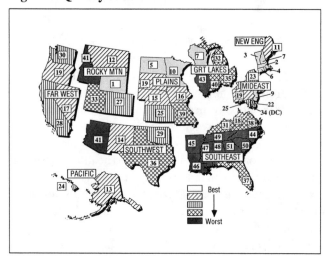

**Source**: Southern Regional Council/Southern Labor Institute. Reprinted by permission.

## Application

If you have a choice of where you will live and work, the information presented here should be of interest to you (even though the report's main audience is public policy makers). To help in selecting a satisfactory work location you will want to factor in these indices of worker climate along with other considerations. For example, if you work in a hazardous occupation, you might want to avoid states like Mississippi, Arizona, and Louisiana, which rate low in "state worker protection." Similarly, if you have school-age children, you may want to give greater consideration to those states that rank high on "quality of life," such as the New England states, which scored well on health and environment measures, support for public education, and generally had low crime rates.

You can refer to specific indicators as a ready reference for information such as the average annual earnings of workers in a particular state or the cost of living for a particular city. And if you are involved in efforts to improve workers' rights in your locale—perhaps through membership in a union or in the NAACP—your organization can use or disseminate this information as a basis for comparison of what now exists in your state (or your plant) and what could exist and does exist in states where people are concerned about workers' rights, job security, and working conditions.

Your local library may have, or order, the SRC's 1990 report: *The Climate for Workers in the United States.* Or, you may order it directly for $22 from the Southern Regional Council, 60 Walton Street, N.W., Atlanta, GA 30303-2199. Other sources of this type of information are given in the bibliography below.

*See also* Choosing an Occupation; Work Hazards.

## Bibliography

Institute for Southern Studies. (1990). *1990 Green Index: A state-by-state report card on the nation's environment.* Durham, N.C.: Institute for Southern Studies. Compares state ratings on a wide variety of environmental concerns, some of them workplace-centered, some community-wide.

Maclachlan, G., & Maclachlan, B. (1988). *The climate for workers in the United States: 1988.* Atlanta: The Southern Labor Institute of the Southern Regional Council. SLI's 1988 biennial report contains 33 indicators of working climate indexed by state and region. Analysis of findings is accompanied by 22 statistical tables, charts, and maps.

Maclachlan, G., & Maclachlan, B. (1991). *The climate for workers in the United States: 1990.* Atlanta: The Southern Labor Institute of the Southern Regional Council. The most recent in a biennial series of reports identifying the best and worst states in which to work by means of comparative indexes to opportunities, earnings and income, workplace conditions, worker protection measures, and quality of life. Includes a case study of working life in Arkansas by N. Peckingham.

Nelson, R. R. (1990, January). State labor legislation enacted in 1989. *Monthly Labor Review,* U. S. Department of Labor, pp. 35–55. Discussion of major state statutes enacted during the preceding year on a variety of labor related-subjects. This regular feature appears annually in the January issue of the *Monthly Labor Review.*

U.S. Department of Labor Bureau of Labor Statistics. *Employment and earnings.* Washington, DC, monthly. Each year's May issue contains the latest annual averages state by state on the total number of persons employed, unemployment rates, and hourly and weekly wages.

—SOUTHERN REGIONAL COUNCIL/
SOUTHERN LABOR INSTITUTE
(DIGEST AND SUPPLEMENTARY MATERIAL BY
LAWRENCE K. JONES)

**Table 1. Median Family Income: 1988**

**Table 2. Blacks in Traditional White Male Jobs: 1989**

**Table 3. Women in Traditional White Male Jobs: 1989**

| State | Dollars | Rank |
|---|---|---|
| New Jersey | 52305 | 1 |
| Connecticut | 50720 | 2 |
| Maryland | 49105 | 3 |
| Massachusetts | 48296 | 4 |
| Alaska | 47247 | 5 |
| New Hampshire | 45619 | 6 |
| Virginia | 42587 | 7 |
| Hawaii | 42353 | 8 |
| Delaware | 41742 | 9 |
| New York | 41700 | 10 |
| Illinois | 41635 | 11 |
| California | 41425 | 12 |
| Rhode Island | 41377 | 13 |
| Minnesota | 41076 | 14 |
| Michigan | 41044 | 15 |
| Washington | 39327 | 16 |
| Nevada | 39148 | 17 |
| Colorado | 39095 | 18 |
| Wisconsin | 38662 | 19 |
| Dst of Columbia | 38562 | 20 |
| Georgia | 38208 | 21 |
| Ohio | 38145 | 22 |
| Indiana | 37939 | 23 |
| Pennsylvania | 37855 | 24 |
| Florida | 37280 | 25 |
| Missouri | 37187 | 26 |
| Arizona | 36892 | 27 |
| Oregon | 36623 | 28 |
| Vermont | 36467 | 29 |
| Kansas | 35796 | 30 |
| North Carolina | 35678 | 31 |
| Maine | 35385 | 32 |
| Texas | 35280 | 33 |
| South Carolina | 34915 | 34 |
| Iowa | 34804 | 35 |
| Utah | 34410 | 36 |
| Nebraska | 34287 | 37 |
| Tennessee | 34160 | 38 |
| Wyoming | 33667 | 39 |
| Alabama | 33022 | 40 |
| Louisiana | 32514 | 41 |
| Montana | 32333 | 42 |
| Kentucky | 32088 | 43 |
| Oklahoma | 31905 | 44 |
| Idaho | 31454 | 45 |
| North Dakota | 31346 | 46 |
| South Dakota | 30503 | 47 |
| West Virginia | 29743 | 48 |
| Mississippi | 29624 | 49 |
| New Mexico | 29350 | 50 |
| Arkansas | 28665 | 51 |
| U.S. | 39051 | |

| State | % B Jobs | Rank |
|---|---|---|
| California | 36.1 | 1 |
| Maryland | 34.6 | 2 |
| ADJUSTED | | |
| New York | 31.5 | 4 |
| Massachusetts | 31.4 | 5 |
| ADJUSTED | | |
| Dst of Columbia | 30.3 | 7 |
| Tennessee | 30.3 | 7 |
| ADJUSTED | | |
| Colorado | 29.9 | 10 |
| Virginia | 29.7 | 11 |
| ADJUSTED | | |
| Kansas | 28.6 | 13 |
| New Jersey | 28.5 | 14 |
| ADJUSTED | | |
| Connecticut | 27.9 | 16 |
| West Virginia | 27.5 | 17 |
| ADJUSTED | | |
| Alaska | 27.5 | 17 |
| Michigan | 27.3 | 20 |
| ADJUSTED | | |
| Ohio | 27.2 | 22 |
| Texas | 26.8 | 23 |
| ADJUSTED | | |
| Rhode Island | 26.7 | 25 |
| Pennsylvania | 26.5 | 26 |
| ADJUSTED | | |
| Florida | 26.2 | 28 |
| Illinois | 26.1 | 29 |
| Georgia | 25.8 | 30 |
| ADJUSTED | | |
| Missouri | 25.1 | 32 |
| Louisiana | 25.0 | 33 |
| ADJUSTED | | |
| Delaware | 24.5 | 35 |
| Mississippi | 24.0 | 36 |
| ADJUSTED | | |
| Oklahoma | 23.9 | 38 |
| Kentucky | 23.9 | 38 |
| ADJUSTED | | |
| Alabama | 23.6 | 41 |
| Nevada | 23.1 | 42 |
| ADJUSTED | | |
| North Carolina | 23.0 | 44 |
| Wisconsin | 22.9 | 45 |
| ADJUSTED | | |
| South Carolina | 22.0 | 47 |
| Indiana | 21.3 | 48 |
| ADJUSTED | | |
| Nebraska | 20.4 | 50 |
| Arkansas | 20.4 | 50 |

| State | % F Jobs | Rank |
|---|---|---|
| Dst of Columbia | 49.5 | 1 |
| Massachusetts | 37.9 | 2 |
| Alaska | 36.8 | 3 |
| Maryland | 36.7 | 4 |
| Connecticut | 35.8 | 5 |
| Vermont | 35.0 | 6 |
| New Jersey | 34.7 | 7 |
| California | 34.7 | 7 |
| New York | 34.5 | 9 |
| Colorado | 33.8 | 10 |
| New Hampshire | 33.6 | 11 |
| Virginia | 33.1 | 12 |
| Washington | 32.3 | 13 |
| Texas | 32.3 | 13 |
| Arizona | 31.8 | 15 |
| Kansas | 31.7 | 16 |
| Hawaii | 31.7 | 16 |
| Oregon | 31.6 | 18 |
| Utah | 31.4 | 19 |
| New Mexico | 31.3 | 20 |
| Delaware | 31.3 | 20 |
| Rhode Island | 31.1 | 22 |
| Georgia | 30.9 | 23 |
| Maine | 30.7 | 24 |
| Ohio | 30.6 | 25 |
| North Dakota | 30.6 | 25 |
| Illinois | 30.4 | 27 |
| Florida | 30.3 | 28 |
| Kentucky | 30.2 | 29 |
| Minnesota | 30.0 | 30 |
| South Dakota | 29.9 | 31 |
| Missouri | 29.9 | 31 |
| Louisiana | 29.7 | 33 |
| North Carolina | 29.4 | 34 |
| Iowa | 29.2 | 35 |
| Montana | 29.1 | 36 |
| Mississippi | 29.0 | 37 |
| Nebraska | 28.8 | 38 |
| Oklahoma | 28.7 | 39 |
| Alabama | 28.7 | 39 |
| South Carolina | 28.6 | 41 |
| Pennsylvania | 28.3 | 42 |
| Michigan | 28.3 | 42 |
| Wisconsin | 27.4 | 44 |
| Wyoming | 27.3 | 45 |
| West Virginia | 27.2 | 46 |
| Idaho | 26.7 | 47 |
| Tennessee | 26.5 | 48 |
| Arkansas | 26.0 | 49 |
| Indiana | 25.5 | 50 |
| Nevada | 25.4 | 51 |

**Source**: Southern Regional Council/Southern Labor Institute. Reprinted by permission.

# COMPUTER-ASSISTED CAREER GUIDANCE SYSTEMS

CACG systems provide users with useful information and guidance in making educational and career choices. Most systems help users by providing extensive occupational and educational information, generating work and educational alternatives, and assessing their values, interests and other related factors. The work information component provides users with occupational data, such as the types of skills required for particular occupations, training requirements, salaries, and predictions about the number of jobs available in the future. Many systems provide information concerning different types of universities and technical colleges, available scholarships and financial aid, and costs for tuition and fees.

This extensive educational and occupational information can be easily manipulated by the person using the computer system. The user scans a menu and makes choices by pressing specific keys. Once all the choices have been made, the computer gives the user specialized educational and occupational information. For example, if a user wanted to attend no more than two years of training or college and wanted to work out-of-doors, this information would be keyed into the computer and only jobs requiring two years or less training and took place outside would be made available for consideration.

The computer's extensive database assists users in identifying occupations that meet the personal requirements set by the user, and also explores information about occupations that the user has not directly identified. Computers are also helpful in instructing individuals about the process of making career decisions and formulating career plans. Personal assessment of values and interests are possible when applying the various programs available from CACG systems.

## CACG Systems

The major CACG systems in use today include DISCOVER, ACTP, SIGI, and CHOICES (see bibliography). DISCOVER includes four modules: (a) self-assessment, which assists users in finding out more about their personalities, values, and habits and how they relate to work, (b) a structured search of occupational alternatives, (c) occupational information, and (d) a structured search of educational options information. These modules assist a user in enhancing decision-making skills, career plans, knowledge of occupations and educational opportunities, and knowledge of self focusing on personal interests, abilities, and values.

SIGI is comprised of five components: values, locate, compare, planning, and strategy. This CACG system assists a user in exploring values and career options, and provides occupational information and strategies for making effective decisions.

CHOICES allows users to explore occupations and obtain specific information about jobs. They can compare occupations as well as retrieve information about postsecondary institutions and junior colleges.

There are a number of other, inexpensive microcomputer programs available. Among these are CAREER FINDER, CAREER PASSPORT, VALUESEARCH, and TIPS. Each of these systems has its own advantages. For example, various programs help individuals develop job plans, survey life skill requirements for particular occupations, summarize salaries, and analyze related job components such as prestige, stress level, and potential for leadership. Reviews of these programs, as well as numerous others, can be found in the *Counseling Software Guide* listed in the bibliography. In addition, many states have computer-assisted occupational networks at regional locations.

While these programs may be used alone, they tend to be more helpful when used with a professional counselor. On the other hand, the major advantage of using a CACG system alone includes flexibility in scheduling and less cost.

When purchasing CACG software, it is important that the functions the program must perform be a priority. A common mistake is the purchase of hardware or computers before the purchase of software. Buying computers before a decision is made concerning the function of the software can leave the user quite frustrated. A classic example is the purchase of a computer for its "bells and whistles" only to subsequently find that it does not have enough "memory" to run the selected software program. The best way to protect oneself from such misfortune is to select a program that meets a particular need, and then find a computer that will effectively run it.

## Application

As a CACG user, you will want to seek an appointment with a career counselor who utilizes this technology in career counseling. These computer programs may also be available in many public libraries, continuing education centers, and high schools. Numerous programs are available. Like DISCOVER, SIGI, or CHOICES, a good program is not complicated, includes a manual that is easy to understand, and provides you with needed information. Other CACG programs (listed in the *Counseling Software Guide*) may be good adjuncts as you learn more about your career path and potential career choice. It is a good idea to review your CACG information with a career counselor since many of the programs are related to existing career theories of which counselors are knowledgeable.

Applying CACG systems in your career decision process can help you assess your unique skills and interests and learn how they are related to various occupations. A CACG system can also provide a structured format to assist you with planning and coming to a conclusion about a particular occupational choice.

*See also* Career Counseling; Career Exploration; Decision Making.

## Bibliography

American College Testing Program (ACTP). (1988). *Counselor manual: A complete training program for professionals using DISCOVER.* Hunt Valley, MD: American College Testing Program.

*Counseling software guide.* (1989). Alexandria, VA: American Association for Counseling and Development. Contains extensive information on counseling software, including CACG. Topics include trends and developments in computer-assisted career counseling and specific software descriptions and reviews of CACG software programs.

Harris-Bowlsbey, J. (1984). The computer and career development. *Journal of Counseling and Development,* 63: 145–48. Identifies and explains functions in career development that are best performed by computers. Interactive dialogue, storage and searching data files, assessment and interpretation, and individualization of treatment are presented. The relationship between major career development theories and computer applications in career guidance are discussed.

Jarvis, P. S. (1988). *CHOICES professional manual.* Ogdensburg, NY: CSG Careerware.

Katz, M. R. (1980). SIGI: An interactive aid to career decision-making. *Journal of College Student Personnel,* 21: 34–40.

Maze, M., & Cummings, R. (1982). Analysis of DISCOVER. In M. Maze, & R. Cummings (Eds.), *How to select a computer-assisted guidance system* (pp. 97–107). Madison, WI: University of Wisconsin, Vocational Studies Center. Provides information regarding the selection of CACG systems. Important parameters involved in making a choice that meets particular needs are presented.

—J. Scott Hinkle

# CONTINUING EDUCATION

Continuing education normally means education beyond the level of an undergraduate degree, although sometimes it refers specifically to professional training in a particular work area. Usually continuing education refers to academic work not for credit, sometimes specifically required by state law or a professional organization for keeping up to date in a profession, such as the medical fields. Occasionally, continuing education for credit may lead to a baccalaureate or, more usually, an advanced degree.

Continuing education may take place in any academic environment and may also be sponsored by not-for-profit, noneducational centers such as churches or YMCA's/ YWCA's. Professional organizations, universities, undergraduate colleges, high schools, trade and technical schools, occasional correspondence courses, and some government job training courses all are possible continuing education sources.

The Continuing Education Unit, or CEU, is used in some professions to document the amount of credit possible for a course or series of courses. Nurses, for example, may be required to complete a certain number of CEUs per year to maintain registration. Most continuing education programs geared toward professions requiring CEUs list the number of units per course in their brochure or catalog course listings. Continuing education may be a full- or part-time program, may extend over many years if not an entire work life, or may be intensive and short-term, such as the many evening courses or those held for partial or full days on weekends in a specific technical area. Degree programs, also full- or part-time, may last for one to three or more years.

## Relationship to Work

Continuing education is a growing reality in the U.S. work world. In 1972, only 28% of college students were over 24 years old. By 1988, the percentage had risen to almost 40%, and projections indicate that adult enrollments will continue to be an increasingly important factor in college enrollments in the twenty-first century. Of the courses taken in 1988, almost two-thirds were designed to help get a new job or advance in a present job.

In many fields continuing education is a standard employee benefit in union contracts and at staff and managerial levels. Many companies, industries, and professions encourage or require workers to keep up to date by taking courses related to their work. Some companies pay for all or part of continuing education courses, subject to certain terms and conditions, up to and including long-term graduate programs. Under specific circumstances, some expenses of continuing education may be tax deductible as well.

## Application

Continuing education can benefit you in your current job, prepare you for promotion or alternate opportunities in your current organization, or help you redirect your energies and interests into a related or entirely new field.

There are a number of ways to find out about opportunities for continuing education. These include the human resources office of your employer, your public library, local schools and colleges, and professional organizations. For instance, the American Banking Continuing Education Association has traditionally offered both courses in major cities as well as at-home study materials. The obvious variables to consider include relevance of course and program to your needs and desires, any educational or skills prerequisites for entering a course or program, location, cost, and timing.

**Caveat Emptor.** Continuing education is no guarantee that promotions or more interesting opportunities will come your way. Your income will not necessarily rise in the short- or long-term, nor will you necessarily be recognized as being wiser or more effective on the job.

In addition, there are personal factors to consider in undertaking continuing education. The expense, if not being borne by an employer, may be considerable and make a real dent on a household budget with no assurance of immediate return. The psychological factor of being a student again after formal education is supposedly over is bothersome to some people, even in the age of fairly common employee training programs. It is also a problem to some people to sit in a classroom, especially with much younger students or an instructor half the students' age, when they are accustomed to being in charge, sometimes supervising many people in the workplace.

On the other hand, you will by definition be better educated after participating in any further learning or training experience, and at the very least you will also have a more interesting and therefore better resume when you list continuing education courses or programs which you have taken. By knowing more than you did before, and having learned more than others, you will assure that your improved credentials must be regarded with greater interest in the job marketplace.

Above all, continuing education, like all education, becomes part of your life and can only be a help to you. No one can take it from you. Even if there is not an immediate effect on your work life, as there often will be, it will mean that you are better prepared to meet the world and what it brings, and therein lies its real value.

*See also* Benefits; Skills.

## Bibliography

Haponski, W. C., & McCabe, C.E. (1985). *New horizons: The education and career planning guide for adults.* Princeton: Peterson's Guides. A complete guide for those planning to re-enter the academic world. Includes specific names, addresses, and suggestions.

Menges, R. J. (1985). *Teaching-learning experiences for college students and other adults: A selected annotated bibliography.* Evanston, IL: Center for the Teaching Professions, Northwestern University. Organized by topics to assist the teacher, learner, and researcher investigate adult learning. A helpful author index is included.

Titmus, C. J., (Ed.) (1989). *Lifelong education for adults: An international handbook.* Oxford/New York: Pergamon. Written primarily for educators, this excellent reference contains articles by international educators and includes helpful sections on purposes of adult education and regional and international organizations.

—BETTY LOU MARPLE

# COOPERATIVE EDUCATION

A formal type of experiential learning, cooperative education is a college-level educational method that integrates classroom instruction with periods of employment related to students' majors. Agreements between higher education institutions and employing agencies provide for paid work opportunities monitored by a college coordinator and supervised by an employer.

## Relationship to Career and Work

Cooperative education (co-op) unites one's education with the beginning of one's career. This type of program was initiated at the University of Cincinnati in 1906 when Herman Schneider, a professor of engineering, realized that students took on part-time jobs to help cover their college costs. He reasoned that the work experience would be far more valuable if it related to the engineering courses the students were taking.

The interrelationship between education, career preparation, and work within the cooperative education framework can be better understood through a description of specific components.

1. *Optional and Required Co-op.* Most two- and four-year co-op colleges and universities offer optional co-op programs. Several major co-op institutions require students to participate in cooperative education, usually as part of a five-year curriculum, and a few institutions offer both optional and required co-op programs depending upon the curriculum. The type of college, its curricular offerings, its educational philosophy, and the needs of its students determine the nature of the co-op program, which can range from the traditional plan to a more flexible alternative.

2. *The Alternating Work Plan.* The traditional cooperative education program involves the alternating of full-time study semesters or quarters with full-time work semesters or quarters. Students are usually expected to obtain at least 12 months of full-time work experience to complete the program.

3. *The Parallel Work Plan.* Some colleges, primarily community colleges, allow students to work part-time on co-op jobs while carrying reduced course loads.

4. *Compensation.* With a few exceptions, cooperative education work experiences are paid at the going rate for employees with similar education and experience.

5. *Faculty Involvement.* College faculty advise students on designing study and work plans that will allow them to progress toward degree requirements, and often monitor work experiences.

6. *Academic Credit.* A cooperative education program may or may not award course credit for the work experience. Programs which award credit normally involve faculty and are found more often in liberal arts colleges and community colleges.

7. *Responsibility of the Employing Company or Agency.* Typically the company or agency makes a top-level commitment to establishing a well-defined cooperative education program. The company co-op coordinator participates in the interviewing and hiring process, orientation of new co-op students, and, with the manager, ongoing supervision of the students.

8. *Responsibility of the College or University.* Cooperative education programs typically have professional coordinators and/or faculty who develop jobs, recruit students, facilitate placements, monitor work experiences, and provide career counseling.

9. *Nontraditional Cooperative Education Programs.* Many colleges and universities provide flexible co-op programs to meet special student and curricular needs, often with a shorter work requirement.

10. *Difference between Cooperative Education and Internships.* Cooperative education differs from internships in that (a) the work period generally is longer, (b) students are paid by the company or agency, and (c) students assume responsibility for activities that might otherwise be accomplished by regular employees.

Presently there are over 1,000 colleges and universities in the United States and Canada that offer cooperative education programs. Nationwide, more than 250,000 students participate in cooperative education programs each year (National Commission for Cooperative Education, 1990).

## Application

As a student, you can use a cooperative education experience:

1. To reaffirm or test your choice of a major.
2. To discover what your academic program prepares you for.
3. To explore career fields when you are undecided.

In the process of preparing yourself for the cooperative education work experience, you will be assisted by the college or university co-op coordinator in evaluating your aptitudes and career options and in developing your resume writing and interviewing skills.

If you are an adult returning to college, cooperative education can be especially valuable. Likely, you are more focused on why you are in college and feel the pressure to move rapidly toward the degree. However, you need some assurance that you have made the best career decision. By participating in a co-op work experience, you will have the opportunity to try out your new career as part of your degree program.

Other benefits you can gain from participating in a cooperative education program include:

1. *Access to Facilities.* You have the opportunity to work with state-of-the-art equipment in industry that might not be available on campus.
2. *Access to Professionals.* You will be able to work side-by-side with professional adults in your chosen field and observe how they handle routine as well as unique job situations.
3. *Corporate Awareness.* You will be able to experience various corporate cultures in business, industry, and government and have the opportunity to try out your "fit" in those environments.
4. *Interpersonal Communication Skills.* You will be provided the latitude to develop your interpersonal communication skills and to discover how important they are in the world of work.
5. *Competence-Based Confidence.* You will have the opportunity to cultivate a sense of genuine confidence based on successful job experiences and newly developed competencies.
6. *Earnings.* You will earn money to meet college expenses. Many students have found that their earnings during one term on the co-op job will cover another term's expenses while in courses.
7. *Enhanced Career Opportunities.* With the cooperative education experience, you will become more marketable when you graduate. Companies prefer to hire individuals with relevant work experience who have proven they can do the work. With co-op work experience, you can expect to have a distinct

advantage when interviewing for a permanent job. And when hired, your chances for promotions and salary increases will be greatly enhanced.

In summary, the cooperative education experience will most likely contribute to your career development, career progress, and personal growth (Fletcher, 1989). You will be prepared to make better decisions about your life, and your chances of having a successful, meaningful career will be more assured.

As an employer, you could benefit from participation in a co-op program in several ways. Cooperative education offers your company or agency:

1. A cost-effective means of recruiting and training qualified future employees by providing the opportunity to select and test talented personnel in advance of a permanent commitment.
2. A good source of entry level workers.
3. The chance to participate in the career preparation of students through closer ties with educational institutions.
4. A means for improving the retention of good employees (Ryder, Wilson, & Associates, 1987).

Each cooperative education partnership of institution, students, and employers promotes the integration of education and work for the benefit of all the parties involved.

*See also* Career Exploration; Internships.

## Bibliography

Fletcher, J. K. (1989). Student outcomes: What do we know and how do we know it? *Journal of Cooperative Education,* 26 (1): 26–33.

National Commission for Cooperative Education. (1990). Cooperative education undergraduate program directory. 4th ed. Boston: National Commission for Cooperative Education. This directory is available in high schools and provides a brief description of cooperative education and its benefits, a listing by state of colleges and universities which offer cooperative education programs, and a sampling of employing organizations.

Ryder, K. G., Wilson, J. W., & Associates. (1987). *Cooperative education in a new era.* San Francisco: Jossey-Bass. Many experts in cooperative education describe programs, practices, and policies in educational institutions as well as in work environments. They explain in detail the benefits which accrue to students, higher education institutions, and employing organizations from their participation in cooperative education programs.

## For Further Information

**Canadian Association for Cooperative Education**
Suite 203, 1209 King Street West
Toronto, Ontario M6K 1G2.

**National Commission for Cooperative Education**
360 Huntington Avenue
Boston, Massachusetts 02115.

—WILLIAM D. WESTON

# COSH GROUPS

Committees (also known as Councils) for Occupational Safety and Health (COSH groups) are coalitions of local labor unions, health, medical, and legal professionals, and safety and health activists who provide training and technical assistance about workplace safety and health hazards. COSH groups also function to monitor city, state, and federal government government legislatures and agencies responsible for enacting and enforcing safety and health laws and regulations.

## Relationship to Work

COSH groups were founded in the mid-1970s by health professionals and rank-and-file safety and health activists to develop educational programs which would empower workers to fight for safer and healthier workplaces through union activity. The COSH movement grew during the Carter administration when several COSH organizations across the country received funding through OSHA's New Directions program. Despite the Reagan administration attack on OSHA's educational program, COSH groups were able to survive as a result of their strong connections to local labor unions which value the training and education services provided by the COSH groups. By 1990, 23 COSH groups had developed in 16 states. Though not formally affiliated with each other, COSH groups meet annually and maintain a national information network throughout the year. And while most COSH organizations currently employ at least one staff member, the COSH movement remains dependent upon the activity of volunteers.

Because of their diverse constituency, COSH groups have served as a bridge between the labor, health professional, medical, and legal communities. Through their contacts with workers on the shop floor, COSH organizations have been able to bring occupational safety and health concerns to the attention of the medical, health, and legal communities. At the same time, they have successfully conveyed to workers the findings of medical research about hazards posed by toxics in the workplace, as well as information about legal and regulatory developments. Through educational programs and materials developed by the COSH groups, news about workplace hazards and preventative strategies has reached hundreds of thousands of workers and their unions.

The COSH movement has also played a central role in safety and health political campaigns, both on the national and state levels. COSH groups help build broad-based coalitions to fight for legislative and regulatory reform, uniting labor unions with other professional, environmental, and community organizations. In 1980, COSH organizations also successfully mobilized rank and file opposition to the attempt of Senator Richard Schweiker to introduce crippling amendments to the Occupational Safety and Health Law of 1970. COSH organizations also played an important leadership role in the passage of state "Right to Know" laws during the early 1980s. These landmark laws provided workers with the right to information and training about toxic substances to which they were exposed. Currently, COSH groups are urging enactment of legislation which would give workers the "Right to Act"—giving them the power to eliminate hazards in the workplace.

## Application

COSH groups provide you with the following services:

1. Technical assistance about occupational health and safety hazards you may face and information about government safety and health laws and regulations;
2. Educational forums and training sessions about specific hazards and government regulations;
3. Assistance with the development of strategies to make your workplace safer and healthier; and
4. Help with the building of coalitions to campaign for enactment of new safety and health legislation or regulations.

## Directory of COSH Groups

**Alaska**
Alaska Health Project
431 W. 7th Avenue, #101
Anchorage, Alaska 99501
907-276-2864

**California**
LACOSH (Los Angeles COSH)
2501 S. Hill Street
Los Angeles, CA 90007
213-749-6161

SA-COSH (Sacramento COSH)
c/o Fire Fighters, Local 522
3101 Stockton Blvd
Sacramento, CA 95820
916-444-8134 or 924-8060

SCCOSH (Santa Clara COSH)
760 N. 1st Street
San Jose, CA 95112
408-998-4050

**Connecticut**

ConnectiCOSH (Connecticut COST)
P.O. Box 31107
Hartford, CT 06103
203-549-1877

**District of Columbia**

Alice Hamilton Occupational Health Center
410 Seventh Street, S.E.
Washington, D.C. 20003
202-543-0005
Illinois

CACOST (Chicago Area COSH)
37 South Ashland
Chicago, IL 60607
312-666-1611

**Maine**
Maine Labor Group on Health
Box V
Augusta, Maine 04330
207-622-7823

**Massachusetts**
MassCOSH (Massachusetts COSH)
555 Amory Street
Boston, MA 02130
617-524-COSH

Western MassCOSH
458 Bridge Street
Springfield, MA 01103
413-247-9413

**Michigan**
SEMCOSH (Southeast Michigan COST)
2727 Second Street
Detroit, MI 48206
313-961-3345

**New York**
ALCOSH (Alleghany COST)
100 East Second Street
Jamestown, NY 14701
716-488-0720

CNYCOSH (Central NY COSH)
615 W. Genessee Street
Syracuse, NY 13204
315-471-6187

ENYCOSH (Eastern NY COSH)
c/o Larry Rafferty
121 Erie Blvd
Schenectady, NY 12305
518-393-1386

MYCOSH (New York COSH)
275 Seventh Avenue, 25 Floor
New York, NY 10001
212-627-3900
ROCOSH (Rochester COSH)
797 Elmwood Avenue
Rochester, NY 14620
716-244-0420

WNYCOSH (Western NY COSH)
450 Grider Street
Buffalo, NY 14215
716-897-2110

**North Carolina**
NCOSH (North Carolina COSH)
P.O. Box 2514
Durham, NC 27705
919-286-9249

**Pennsylvania**
PhilaPOSH (Philadelphia POSH)
3001 Walnut Street, 5th Fl.
Philadelpha, PA 19104
215-386-7000

**Rhode Island**
RICOSH (Rhode Island COSH)
340 Lockwood Street
Procidence, RI 02907
401-751-2015

**Tennessee**
TNCOSH (Tennessee COSH)
1515 East Magnolia, Suite 406
Knoxville, TN 37917
615-525-3147

**Texas**
TexCOSH
c/o Karyl Dunson
5735 Regina
Beaumont, TX 77706
409-898-1427

**Wisconsin**
WisCOSH (Wisconsin COSH)
1334 S. 11th Street
Milwaukee, WI 53204
414-643-0928

**CANADA**

Ontario
WOSH (Windsor COSH)
1731 Wyandotte Street, East
Windsor, Ontario N8Y1C9
519-254-4192

**COSH-RELATED GROUPS**

**District of Columbia**
Workers Institute for Occupational Safety and Health
1126 16th Street, N.W. Rm. 403
Washington, D.C. 20036
202-887-1980

**Louisiana**
Labor Studies Program
Institute of Human Relations
Loyola University, Box 12
New Orleans, LA 70117
504-861-5830

**New Jersey**
New Jersey Work Environment Council
452 East Third Street
Moorestown, NY 08057
609-866-9405

**Ohio**
Greater Cincinnati Occup. Health Ctr 2450
Kipling Avenue, Suite 203
Cincinnati, OH 45239
513-541-0561

**West Virginia**
Institute of Labor Studies
710 Knapp Hall
West Virginia University
Morgantown, WV 26506
304-293-3323

*See also* Appendix I: OSHA Regional Offices; Work Hazards.

## Bibliography

National Safety Council. (1983). *Protecting workers' lives, a safety and health guide for unions.* Chicago: National Safety Council.
Polakoff, P. L. (1984). *Work and health, it's your life.* Washington, DC: Press Associates.
Stellman, J,. & Daum, S. (1973). *Work is dangerous to your health, a handbook of health hazards in the workplace and what you can do about them.* New York: Vintage.

—JOEL SHUFRO

## CULTURALLY DIFFERENT: WORKING WITH

Working with people from different cultural backgrounds requires sensitivity, knowledge, and skills. If workers are going to work together in a productive and harmonious way, they need to understand and appreciate the cultural backgrounds of their fellow workers. Also, skills can be learned to make this easier.

## Relationship to Work

The United States workforce is rapidly becoming more culturally diverse (Johnson, 1987). From 1986 to the year 2000, the number of black, Hispanic, Asian, and other minority workers entering the workforce will increase significantly. In addition, there will be approximately 20% more immigrants. Given this major change in the U.S. workforce, it is essential that all workers increase their awareness, knowledge, and skills in working with their culturally different coworkers.

## Frameworks for Cultural Understanding

The purpose of this article is to describe two frameworks for understanding cultural differences. You can use them as tools for learning and thinking about the cultural backgrounds of your coworkers. They will also help you understand how cultural conflicts occur and how to avoid them.

**Pedersen and Pedersen's Cultural Grid.** According to the Grid (Pedersen & Pedersen, 1985), behaviors, expectations, and values are the most important dimensions for understanding cultural differences. Cross-cultural con-

flicts occur when there are differences in behaviors, expectations, or values which are not understood by either party (Hines & Pedersen, undated, p. 12).

Knowing the categories of the Cultural Grid will help you understand your coworkers' cultural orientation and thereby avoid cultural conflicts. The categories of the Grid are shown at the top of Figure 1: Role Behaviors, Expectations, and Value Meanings. The categories running down the left side complete the Grid and consist of social system variables such as Race, Age, Sex, Ethnicity, Nationality, Language, Socioeconomic Status, etc. Figure 1 presents an example of a blank Cultural Grid.

The use of the Grid will be illustrated with a famous cross-cultural example (see Figure 2). In an interpersonal interaction, an Arab businessman keeps moving closer (Role Behavior) to the white American businessman in order to attain an optimal interpersonal distance (Expectations) according to his cultural value system (Value Meanings). If the white American businessman is not aware of this cultural difference in interpersonal space (Value Meanings), he may become offended at the Arab businessman's constant intrusions into his personal space (Behavior). Conversely, given his lack of knowledge of the Arab's cultural orientation with regards to interpersonal space, the

**Figure 1. Blank Cultural Grid**

| Social System Variable | Role Behavior | Expectation | Value Meaning |
|---|---|---|---|
| Demographic | | | |
| Race | | | |
| Gender | | | |
| Age | | | |
| Other | | | |
| Ethnographic | | | |
| Ethnicity | | | |
| Nationality | | | |
| Language | | | |
| Status Level | | | |
| Economic | | | |
| Social | | | |
| Educational | | | |
| Affiliation | | | |
| Formal | | | |
| Non-Formal | | | |
| Informal | | | |

**Figure 2. Example of Cultural Grid Illustrating the Effects of Differences in Optimal Interpersonal Distance between Arabs and Americans**

| Social System Variable | Role Behaviors | Expectations | Value Meanings |
|---|---|---|---|
| | | Time: When they first meet each other. | |
| Race: A = Arab | Moves closer | To establish optimal interpersonal distance. | Close distance = friendliness. |
| B = Caucasian | Moves back | To establish optimal interpersonal distance. | Close distance = intimacy. |
| | | Time: As they continue to talk. | |
| A = Arab | Moves closer again | To regain optimal interpersonal distance. | Views B's behavior as an offense. |
| B = Caucasian | Moves back again | To regain optimal interpersonal distance. | View's A's behavior as presumptutious or intrusive. |

white American businessman may attempt to attain his own cultural system's level of comfortable interpersonal space by consistently moving backwards (Role Behavior) as the Arab moves forward. Consequently, the Arab counterpart may become offended (Expectations and Value Meanings). The Cultural Grid provides a framework for conducting analyses of such cultural differences and how they are manifested in behaviors, expectations, and values. A more detailed exposition of the Cultural Grid and its applications is provided in Pedersen and Pedersen (1985).

**Hofstede's Value Dimensions.** This framework comes from Hofstede's (1980) international study of work-related value differences among many cultural groups (Hofstede, 1980). While Pedersen and Pedersen's Cultural Grid provides a structure or "shell" for examining cultural differences, Hofstede's study provides the content or "ingredients." Hofstede, in his analyses of the work value differences across many cultural groups, was able to identify several factors believed to represent major cultural orientation dimensions. Hofstede's model has the advantage of providing quantitative indices of where different cultural groups were located on each of these important cultural dimensions.

The first dimension is labeled "Power Distance (PD)." It is concerned with how power is distributed in institutions. Cultures with low PD tend to give equal power to all members. For example, in white American culture, which is low on PD, a college student can call a professor by his or her first name. On some occasions, students may also challenge the professor's authority. In cultures with high

PD, members do not have equal power and students being lower on the power hierarchy would never challenge professors in such cultures.

The second dimension is labeled "Uncertainty Avoidance (UA)." It is concerned with tolerance of ambiguity. Cultures with high Uncertainty Avoidance try to minimize ambiguity by using a great deal of structure, planning, and coordination in their approach to problem solving. Individuals from cultures with high UA will prefer to book a tour of a foreign country with a fully planned and detailed itinerary (i.e., every minute is scheduled and planned). Members of cultures with low UA would prefer to book their own flights and travel through the foreign country with a spontaneous, open-ended approach to sight-seeing. This dimension can be thought of as unstructured versus structured approach to problem solving.

The third dimension is labeled "Individualism versus Collectivism." The one pole, Individualism, is defined as "a situation in which people are supposed to look after themselves and their immediate family only," whereas its opposite pole, Collectivism, is defined as "a situation in which people belong to in-groups or collectivities which are supposed to look after them in exchange for loyalty" (p. 419). American society is very individualistic since the primary value of Americans is in self-fulfillment and taking care of one's immediate family. Japanese society, on the other hand, is very collectivistic. The group's primary value is in promoting compliance with socially determined goals which apply to all members. There is a famous Japanese saying that illustrates this well: "The nail that sticks out will be hammered down."

The fourth dimension is labeled "Masculinity versus Femininity." Masculinity is defined as "a situation in which the dominant values in society are success, money, and things," whereas its opposite pole, Femininity, is defined as "a situation in which the dominant values in society are caring for others and the quality of life" (p. 420). The masculine orientation is best illustrated by J. R. Ewing's behavior on the T.V. show "Dallas." He is always concerned with competition and winning at all cost. On the other hand, the feminine orientation is well illustrated by Mother Teresa of Calcutta who has devoted her whole life to helping the unfortunate.

The specific scores of the 40 countries on the four dimensions are presented in Hofstede's text (Hofstede, 1980, p. 315). The levels of the four dimensions for some selected countries are presented in Table 1.

## Application

In terms of the implications for interactions, white Americans interacting with individuals from different cultural groups would be most effective if they took into consideration their own levels on the four dimensions as well as the other person's level on those dimensions. For example, a white American who is low on PD may invite cultural conflicts if he or she treated his or her Chinese employer from Hong Kong (higher status) as an "equal" given that culture's high level of PD. Similarly, a white

American's open-ended, unstructured, problem-solving style (low UA) may be viewed as ineffective or evidence of low motivation by his or her coworkers from Singapore (high UA). Hofstede's data provide guidelines for examining and understanding cultural differences along several dimensions with empirically based scores.

Both the Cultural Grid and the Hofstede value dimensions can serve as valuable frameworks for coworkers to explore and think through cultural differences that may otherwise produce unproductive interpersonal conflicts. Both frameworks are excellent for improving intercultural communications because they emphasize the fact that there are no "right" or "wrong" ways of behaving. The frameworks encourage the exploration of cultural differences and hopefully the valuing of diversity.

## Bibliography

Hines, A., & Pedersen, P. (undated). The Cultural Grid: Management guideline to personal cultural orientation. *East-West Center Culture Learning Institute Report:* 12.

Hofstede, G. (1980). *Culture's consequences: International differences in work-related values.* Beverly Hills, CA: Sage. A report of the scholarly study identifying four major value dimensions for 40 countries.

Johnson, W. B. (1987). *Workforce 2000.* Indianapolis: Hudson Institute.

Pedersen, A., & Pedersen, P. (1985). The Cultural Grid: A personal cultural orientation. In L. Samovar & R. Porter (Eds.), *Intercultural communications: A reader* (pp. 50-62). Belmont, CA: Wadsworth. A description of the Cultural Grid approach to improving intercultural communication.

—FREDERICK T. L. LEONG

**Table 1. Position of Selected Countries on All Four Value Dimensions**

| Country | Power Distance | Uncertainty Avoidance | Individualism | Masculinity |
|---------|----------------|-----------------------|---------------|-------------|
| Canada | Low | Low | High | Medium |
| Hong Kong | High | Low | Low | Medium |
| India | High | Low | Medium | Medium |
| Japan | Medium | High | Medium | High |
| Korea | Medium | Medium | Low | Low |
| Mexico | High | High | Low | High |
| Pakistan | Medium | Medium | Low | Medium |
| Peru | Medium | High | Low | Low |
| Phillipines | High | Low | Low | High |
| Singapore | High | High | Low | Medium |
| Taiwan | Medium | Medium | Low | Medium |
| Venezuela | High | Medium | Low | High |
| U.S.A. | Low | Low | High | High |

# D

## DECISION MAKING

Decision making is a thought process that leads to the choice of a course of action (or inaction) from a set of alternative *options*. Each option has *outcomes* or consequences, which can be evaluated with respect to the decision maker's *goals*. Most decisions are made under *uncertainty*, without full knowledge of future outcomes.

### Relationship to Work

Many careers involve repeated decisions: treatment decisions for physicians; grading decisions for teachers; decisions to buy and sell for businesspeople; and decisions about whether and how to undertake a job or project. Other decisions are unique, made only once: deciding on an entry-level job; deciding on a career or job change; deciding on education to qualify for a kind of job; and making other life decisions that affect work (e.g., having children). Often, these unique decisions involve reflection on the importance of personal goals. In some cases, the outcome of decisions is fairly clear and the problem is to trade off different costs and benefits (e.g., which of two computers to buy). In other cases, decisions are characterized by uncertainty (e.g., investment decisions). All careers involve decisions with moral components, for example, decisions in which each option hurts different people or decisions in which one option is to violate a rule for the sake of some other beneficial outcome.

### How Decision Making Is Analyzed

The study of decision making is carried out by scholars from several disciplines, including psychology, philosophy, and economics. These scholars generally discuss three kinds of accounts or "models" of decision making:

*Normative* models are philosophical and mathematical theories about how decisions should ideally be made. The main theory of this type is that decisions should maximize expected *utility*. Utility is a measure of the extent to which the decision-maker's goals are achieved. By this theory, then, decisions should be made so as to achieve our goals as well as we can, based on what we know at the time of the decision. When an outcome is uncertain, we multiply its utility by its judged probability. When outcomes affect several people, we can try to maximize the total utility of the whole group.

*Descriptive* accounts tell us how we make decisions. Many psychological findings suggest that we sometimes depart systematically from the normative models. In this sense, our decisions are sometimes *irrational*, failing to achieve our goals as well as they might. To take a simple example, people often stick with a failing project because they have "sunk" money and time into it, even though switching to a new course of action would clearly have better future consequences.

*Prescriptive* accounts are practical suggestions about how to improve our decision making, bringing it closer to normative models and to achieving our goals more fully. In the case of sunk costs, a prescriptive rule might be "think about the future, because you cannot control the past." (The time and money cannot be retrieved.) Prescriptive accounts are needed because it is not usually practical to try to apply the normative model directly. However, the applied field of *decision analysis* tries to find ways of modifying normative models so as to make them more practical. Decision analysts often work for government agencies and businesses, and decision analysis is being used increasingly in medical decision making.

### Examples

Descriptive and prescriptive theories generally focus on common errors and ways of correcting them. For example, the *conflict theory*, developed by Irving Janis and Leon Mann, points to four common errors: complacency (thoughtless adherence to a course of action); unconflicted change (e.g., "Do whatever is recommended by an available advisor); "defensive avoidance" (procrastination, shifting responsibility onto others, wishful thinking, or rationalization); and panic (unsystematic search for alternative options and for evidence). By contrast, "vigilant" decision making involves reasonably thorough search for possible options, sufficient search for evidence, and open-minded interpretation of the evidence. The tendency to make various errors is affected by stress and time pressure. Too much stress can lead to panic, and too little can lead to complacency or unconflicted change. When time is available, one way to avoid these errors is to make a *decisional balance sheet,* listing the pros and cons of each option. Figure 1 illustrates this for a college student who is considering joining the Peace Corps after graduation.

Even when time is short, a brief but systematic search for options and evidence can be better than panic. Other common errors are the following:

- *Myside Bias.* Even under the best conditions, we sometimes act as lawyers for our own prior commitments. We seek reasons why we were right, not reasons why we were wrong. As a result, we achieve high levels of confidence that are not warranted. By failing to look for flaws in our plans, we prevent ourselves from improving them.

- *Single-Mindedness.* When we make decisions, we need to search for goals as well as for *options* and for *evidence* about what their consequences will be. Sometimes we act as though we had only a single goal, making the most money, getting a promotion, or whatever. When we reflect, we often find that we have other goals, such as doing the right thing, and that we can often find ways of achieving these other goals much better with only a small sacrifice of the goal we think is most important.

- *Shortsightedness.* We tend to neglect the future too much. We put off doing something painful now, such as reprimanding a subordinate, only to discover that we must do something much more painful later, such as fire the person. The same mechanism works for such habits as smoking, eating unhealthy food, and failing to exercise. Shortsightedness must be overcome by self-control strategies, such as making and following reasonable personal rules of behavior.

**Figure 1. Decisional Balance Sheet for Graduating College Student**

Option: ___Join the Peace Corps_____

|  | **Gains** | **Losses** |
|---|---|---|
| **Self:** | • Challenging work.<br>• Live in another country and culture.<br>• Opportunity to travel.<br>• Opportunity to teach and learn.<br>• Chance to test myself and grow as a person. | • Low earnings.<br>• Away from friends and family.<br>• May have trouble adjusting. |
| **Others:** | • They will learn some of my skills and knowledge so they can better themselves and their country. | • Family/friends will miss me. |

|  | **Approval** | **Disapproval** |
|---|---|---|
| **Self:** | • Helping others.<br>• I will help make this a better world.<br>• I can share with others, in a small way, the advantages I have had by birth. | • Will not be able to pay off college loans as soon as I said I would, and I may feel disappointment in myself because of this. |
| **Others:** | • Parents proud of me.<br>• My minister pleased. | • College advisor wants me to go to to graduate school at his alma mater.<br>• Brother who says I just want to be a do-gooder, that I should think about my future. |

- *Neglect of Others.* A common ideology holds that everyone is out for himself or herself. Much evidence shows that this is false. We are all motivated by fairness, sympathy for others, and concern for doing the right thing. When we neglect the effect of actions on others, we subvert a goal that is important to us. This applies especially to our choice of careers. We should ask about whether the career we choose is the best way we can use our talents to help others. Still, morality cannot always be relied on when high rates of cooperation are required, and we must also be willing to accept rules and constraints, such as those embodied in laws or professional codes of ethics, for the common good.
- *Omission Bias.* We think that inaction does not have outcomes. But it does. If we fail to act to solve a problem, then we are a cause of the persistence of the problem because we had a chance to solve it. A truly responsible worker takes thoughtful action to solve problems and does not simply wait for someone else to do it.

Most of these errors can be avoided by vigilant, *actively open-minded* thinking that tries to look for reasons for the other side, for new and better alternatives, and for evidence about future and distant consequences. Such thinking is the best way to discover errors before they are made. People do not always think this way naturally, and some people even believe that an effort to see the other side is wishy-washy or indecisive. Such a "macho" view of good decision making is one of the causes of poor, thoughtless decisions. Happily, good decision making can be taught.

*See also* Career Indecision; Choosing an Occupation; Rational Thinking.

## Bibliography

Arkes, H. R., & Hammond, K. R. (1986). *Judgment and decision making: An interdisciplinary reader.* Cambridge University Press. An excellent anthology of articles about decision making in life, the professions, and public policy.

Baron, J. (1988). *Thinking and deciding.* New York: Cambridge University Press. An introductory college-level textbook that reviews the literature on thinking and decision making from the point of view summarized in this article.

Baron, J., & Brown, R. V. (Eds.) (1990). *Teaching decision making to adolescents.* Hillsdale, NJ: Erlbaum. A collection of papers on various attempts to teach people to make better decisions. Some of these are based on the conflict theory.

Behn, R. D., & Vaupel, J. W. (1982). *Quick analysis for busy decision makers.* New York: Basic Books. A good introduction to decision analysis.

Dawes, R. (1988). *Rational choice in an uncertain world.* New York: Harcourt Brace Jovanovich. Another brief text that provides an interesting approach.

Dowie, J., & Elstein, A. (1988). *Professional judgment: A reader in clinical decision making.* New York: Cambridge University Press. Excellent collection of articles about decision making in the professions, especially medicine. Includes discussion of decision analysis.

Janis, I. L. (1982). *Groupthink: Psychological studies of policy decisions and fiascoes.* (Revised edition of *Victims of groupthink: A psychological study of foreign-policy decisions and fiascoes*, 1972). Boston: Houghton-Mifflin. A classic and highly readable account of good and poor decisions made by several presidents of the United States and their advisors.

Janis, I. L. (1989). *Crucial decisions: Leadership in policymaking and crisis management.* New York: Free Press. Errors and successes of executives and officials. This includes a readable account of the conflict model.

Kahneman, D., & Tversky, A. (1984). Choices, values, and frames. *American Psychologist,* 39: 341–50. A classic and highly readable paper on some errors in decision making.

Singer, P. (1979). *Practical ethics.* Cambridge University Press. An excellent introduction to moral issues, although the examples are mostly from big, controversial issues such as abortion and euthanasia.

Thaler, R. (1985). *Mental accounting and consumer choice. Marketing Science,* 4: 199–214. Another classic paper about errors in decision making, similar to Kahneman and Tversky (1984).

—JONATHAN BARON

## DEPRESSION

Depression is experienced by most people at some point in their lives. What serves to distinguish a passing, minor problem from a major category of mental illness is the severity and duration of the depression. While one person might handle the breakup of an intimate relationship, job stress, or loss of a loved one with a minimum of difficulty, another person might react to the same stressor much more dramatically by going into a clinical depression.

Depression becomes clinically significant when one is personally or occupationally impaired. Common signs and symptoms include change in overall mood and coping abilities, thinking abilities, eating patterns, and sleeping habits. For example, a person might find it difficult to fall (or stay) asleep, or might sleep much more than usual; one person might lose appetite and weight, while another person experiences appetite increase and weight gain. In some people, decision making becomes noticeably more difficult. There may be thoughts of death or suicide, even if there is no intention of acting on these thoughts. Some people may experience crying spells for no obvious reason, loss of interest in activities that used to be enjoyed, or a withdrawal from family and friends. Headaches, stomach upset, or other physical symptoms may be signs of depression. In short, the key word is change. Not all people with depression will have all the symptoms, and they will express the symptoms they do have differently.

Stress plays a major part in depression for most people, either as a primary cause following some kind of loss or as a contributing factor in a person who may be more vulnerable to depression biologically. A third kind of depression develops essentially independently of any situational problems or stressors; frequently these people seem to be at genetic risk with a positive family history for depression or other related mental illnesses, such as anxiety disorders or drug and alcohol abuse. Along this continuum ranging from the purely situational (or stress-associated) depression to the purely biological (or so-called "chemical imbalance") depression, clinical depression may fall at any point. The majority of depressions fall somewhere in the middle, with both situational and biological components, although all types of depression can lead to a final common pathway of symptoms as previously described. (There is no objective test to distinguish situational from biological depression, with treatment determined more by individual responsiveness to psychotherapy and/or antidepressant medications than by type of depression.) It is not uncommon for depression in those who are biologically vulnerable to begin with fairly trivial stressors, with symptoms virtually taking on a life of their own over time even after the stressors have been relieved. There is also emerging evidence to suggest that major depressions which go untreated make one increasingly vulnerable to further similar episodes later on.

## Relationship to Work

Work can impact on the development of depression in several ways. Our sense of personal identity is largely derived from our work, along with other social and family roles. If there are ongoing difficulties in the workplace, this can easily affect one's sense of wellbeing and emotional stability. Interpersonal difficulties with coworkers or authority figures may reawaken traumatic relationships from earlier in life, while stresses particular to various types of work take their own toll. Work stress may be especially inherent to jobs characterized by erratic hours, requirements of after-hours availability (as by pager), relative lack of structure or concrete feedback, unrealistic production schedules or job expectations, responsibility without commensurate authority, and little sense of control over one's work or work policies (see **Stress; Work Hazards: Psychosocial**).

Additional life stressors will magnify existing work pressures, as in the case of the parent tending to a newborn who does not yet sleep through the night after only a brief maternity/paternity leave, the single parent trying to juggle childcare demands with work responsbilities, or the near-retiree who feels powerless to complain lest retirement be at stake.

For many people, third shift work may cause inadequate daytime sleep, excessive use of caffeine to stay awake on the job, and headaches (probably aggravated by sleep loss and caffeine withdrawal) (see **Shift Work**).

Addressing such practical problems as listed above is the obvious first step where possible; after that, stress management techniques are probably the most effective means of addressing work stress. These are usually modeled after cognitive therapy approaches, and will include learning to set personal limits, defining one's personal expectations (as opposed to what may be unrealistic job expectations), depersonalizing conflicts with others, and retaining one's perspective on work in general (see **Anger; Anxiety; Rational Thinking**).

Conversely, the presence of depression can also have an impact on one's work. While the majority of people under treatment for depression will remain fully functional, potential impairment in the work setting is dependent on the severity of the depression. Cognitive symptoms which may affect one's job performance include difficulties in concentrating or remembering things, remaining attentive, and making decisions or coping with even minor conflicts at work. Such symptoms may be subtle enough to have little practical import, or severe enough to warrant temporary leave on medical grounds. Gross inability to function at work may be one of several criteria in favor of hospitalization; certainly if there is such a question, professional help should be sought.

Treatment of depression ultimately costs far less compared to the missed worktime and medical costs of untreated depression. There are an array of specific antidepressant medications on the market, and many newer ones cause minimal if any side effects. (None of these medications are addictive, so this should not be a concern when seeking treatment.)

## Application

Assessing the stresses inherent in a career field or particular job prior to entering it is advisable where possible. If you can find out ahead of time what stresses are likely, perhaps steps can be taken to make dealing with them easier when the time comes. Such preparation can also better prepare a family for what to expect, and perhaps even allow them to take part in the decision making. You should also take special notice of things that you may have had a bad experience with in the past, such as vague job expectations, odd hours, too much or too little responsibility over others, and, at the least, seek to clarify these prior to hiring on. While no job is completely stress-free, you have ultimate control over the degree of stress which you are willing to tolerate before speaking up about it or seeking a job change.

Should you find yourself weighed down under seemingly unmanageable problems, get a second opinion from someone you trust, a family member, friend, or mental health professional (part of their job is to help clarify the situation and provide the objectivity for you to put things back in perspective). Be gentle with yourself, and try to set your priorities so that you focus on only the most important things. Make time for activities that have been helpful to you in the past, such as taking yourself out to a movie, resuming an exercise program, or hiring household help. If it works for you, do it. By following that advice, most people can recognize and handle occasional depression on their own.

If, however, symptoms progress to the point where you no longer feel in control (such as regular insomnia, thoughts of death or suicide, frequent or unpredictable crying spells), professional help should be sought. Depression is a treatable illness for most people, with a variety of medical treatments and psychotherapy approaches available according to your needs. Many larger companies have confidential Employee Assistance Programs for evaluations and short-term treatment if depression or other mental health concerns should develop. Stress management programs may be available through your company; community hospitals or health organizations frequently also have similar outpatient, educationally based programs at minimal expense.

*See also* Anger; Anxiety; Burnout; Mental Health and Work; Rational Thinking; Self-Esteem; Self-Talk; Shift Work; Stress; Work Hazards: Psychosocial

## Bibliography

All books listed are available in paperback.

Burns, D.D. (1980). *Feeling good.* New York: NAL Penguin Inc. This is essentially a handbook of cognitive therapy, directed primarily at those dealing with depression. Much of its contents are also applicable to job stress.

Charlesworth, D.A., & Nathan, R.G. (1984). *Stress management: A comprehensive guide to wellness.* New York: Ballantine Books. All you ever wanted to know about the causes and management of stress. This book expounds in particular detail on the behavioral "how-to's" of specific relaxation techniques and the basics of a cognitive approach to stress management, it also includes sections on assertiveness, time management, and a host of other approaches to managing stress, from dietary and exercise advice to positive thinking. It is probably best approached as a reference book.

Ellis, A., & Harper, R.A. (1975). *A new guide to rational living.* Hollywood, CA: Wilshire Book Company. A primary work of cognitive therapy by masters in the field. It is very readable and provides a wealth of anecdotal illustrations of how distorted thinking can create and maintain a depression.

Hanson, P.G. (1986). *The joy of stress.* Kansas City, MO: Andrews and McMeel. Practical information on the physiological effects of stress by this physician-author. The often humorous style models the author's prescription to not take things too seriously.

—Patricia L. Pearce

## DISABILITY: ADJUSTMENT TO

Disability is a medical condition that has substantial impact on a person's ability to function normally at work, at home, or in other facets of life. Such medical conditions are due to (a) specific disease processes, such as diabetes, multiple sclerosis, cancer; (b) traumatic events, such as an automobile, farm, or industrial accident causing loss of limbs or sight, or confinement to a wheelchair; (c) severe chemical addictions to alcohol, prescribed drugs, or street drugs; and (d) congenital (at birth) conditions, such as cerebral palsy, mental retardation, or learning disabilities.

In 1980, the U.S. Commissioner of the Rehabilitation Services Administration, Robert Humphreys, indicated that the number of people with disabilities in the United States is far beyond common appreciation. He noted that 24 million Americans have arthritis (of which 5 million are severely impaired), almost a half million have multiple sclerosis, 13 million are hard of hearing (including 1.5 million with severe impairment), over 5.5 million have mental retardation, 4 million have epilepsy, and at least 2 million adults have severe, persistent psychiatric disabilities (Humphreys, 1980, p.2). Thus, it would not be an exaggeration, to estimate that *at least* 10 to 15% of the U.S. population has serious and disabling medical conditions.

A person *with* a disability (*not* a disabled person) is, in every way but one, like every other citizen of this country. Acquiring a disability is an event that can threaten one's sense of status and belonging. Although positive gains have been made in our society to reduce the barriers experienced by people with disabilities, many such persons perceive attitudes of rejection or devaluation by others. National legislation was enacted in 1990 to assure people with disabilities the same rights of accessibility and opportunity as all Americans.

Sometimes a disability prevents a person from performing certain types of work. A visually impaired person, for example, can not fly commercial airplanes. But keep in mind that we all are limited in certain ways that may affect our work potential. For example, short people do not work as professional basketball players and someone who is not handy with tools or machines usually does not become an office machine or automobile repairer. Over time, as all of us do, people with disabilities learn to adjust to their situation, their environment, and their limitations. They learn to maximize their strengths and to develop new coping skills and new vocational and life goals.

## Personal Reaction to Disability

Depending upon the way in which the disability occurred (a sudden injury or a gradual recognition of reduced capacity) and the individual's general ability to adjust to life events, the reaction to a serious medical condition can range from total shock to denial of medical findings to cautious acceptance of diminished physical capacities. Therefore, the reactions of different people to disabling conditions will vary substantially, since individuals, circumstances, and medical situations will vary widely.

Livneh and Evans (1984, pp. 363–64) wrote a concise but comprehensive article which described professional intervention strategies for assisting a person with a disability to accept and adjust to a disabling condition. They enumerated 12 phases of adjustment to disability that have been shown in numerous research studies to be typical, especially with persons who experience a traumatic injury or medical emergency. Of course, the 12 phases are *not* experienced by all people or, necessarily, in the sequence listed below:

1. *Shock:* psychic numbness resulting from an overwhelming physical trauma.
2. *Anxiety:* panic-stricken reaction upon initial recognition of traumatic event.
3. *Bargaining:* expectancy of recovery from disabling condition through protest and deal making.
4. *Denial:* defensive retreat from painful realization of disabled condition implications.
5. *Mourning:* relatively short-term grief response upon realization of personal implications stemming from disability.
6. *Depression:* relatively extended and generalized bereavement of lost body part or function.
7. *Withdrawal:* resignation from social-interpersonal interactions.
8. *Internalized Anger:* self-directed bitterness and resentment often associated with guilt feelings.
9. *Externalized Aggression:* hostility projected toward people, objects, and environmental conditions.
10. *Acknowledgment:* intellectual recognition of future implications stemming from disability and their integration into one's changing self-concept.
11. *Acceptance:* affective, in addition to intellectual internalization of future implications from disability and their integration into one's changing self-concept.
12. *Adjustment-Adaptation:* the final phase in the coping process. Behavioral adaptation and social integration into a newly perceived world.

## Psychological and Social Implications of Disability

A disability impacts upon people in all realms of life. While we will discuss separately the implications of disability upon the person's self-concept, career plans and family, and societal reactions to disability, this division is done only to facilitate discussion. For, clearly, a disabling condition affects people in *all* of parts of their lives and the impact in one facet of life (e.g., relationship with family) certainly carries over to other areas of life.

Beatrice Wright (1983), a leader in studying and describing the psycho-social impact of disability, noted that "what is regarded as a disability . . . . depends upon the requirements and expectations in the situation often culturally determined" (p.11). Our society, for example, by ignoring such architectural barriers as long flights of stairs or broken sidewalks, contributes to the mobility problems experienced by people who use crutches or wheelchairs. General societal attitudes that focus on self-sufficiency and neglect the physical or intellectual limitations of other people have "a negative impact on the lives of people with disabilities" and cause them to be "devalued both by themselves and by others" (Grealish & Salomone, 1986, p.147). "This contrast of value between able-bodied people and people with disabilities gnaws at the spirit. The constant frustration experienced by the person with a disability in attempting to bridge the equality gap has a corrosive effect on feelings of self-worth" (p.148).

Wright (1983) listed a number of principles for guiding our interactions with people who are different from us, including persons with disabilities.

1. Every individual needs respect and encouragement.
2. The severity of a (disability) can be increased or diminished by environmental conditions.
3. The significance of a disability is affected by the person's feeling about the self and his or her situation (pp. xi-xii).

Disability always involves an experience of loss, not only of some mobility, dexterity, or sense, but also a loss of our expected or usual relationships. If your disability impacts upon your vision or mobility, for example, then it will be difficult to continue with the bowling league or softball team. Lives are changed by the advent of severe medical conditions and, therefore, so are self-perceptions of competency, reliance, and, sometimes, esteem.

Our relationships may change substantially and, because unexpected change often produces anxiety, the person with a disability may be uncertain about the constancy of relationships with others. In addition, because people who are unfamiliar with epilepsy, multiple sclerosis, or spinal cord injury may be uneasy when interacting with persons having such medical conditions, a subtle message of diminished value is communicated. If you use a wheelchair, for example, and go to your local polling place to discover that it is inaccessible to you, the impact to your self-esteem of this (and many similar events) may perpetuate the notion that you are not as valuable as other people in our society (Grealish & Salomone, 1986).

## Vocational Implications of Disability

A serious medical condition may or may not have an impact upon a person's worklife. If two right-handed people, a college professor and a concert pianist, each lose their right hand in a woodshop accident, only the pianist's career is likely to be affected dramatically. In this instance, the medical condition (disability) becomes a vocational handicap. In the instance of a person who is born with a form of cerebral palsy that makes extended walking difficult or impossible, we can appreciate that work requiring much standing or walking would be problematic.

The residual functional capacity of a person with a disability (that is, the ability to function physically, intellectually, and emotionally after the advent of a disease or trauma-induced disability) is a critical factor in considering vocational possibilities. Much specific information about the individual's capacities is needed. Not only is physical capacity (lifting, bending, sitting, standing, climbing stairs, walking, etc.) important but intellectual or mental assets are significant. Can the person read, write, calculate, reason, analyze, etc.? With some disabilities (e.g., certain types of epilepsy or mental health problems) the influence of medications is critical. What are the side effects of the various medications the person is taking? Do one or more medications interact with each other to cause an unwanted physical condition? People with disabilities will wish to understand the medical condition as it applies to the world of work. Depending upon the person's skills, aptitudes, interests, values, and needs, certain types of work may be impossible.

But, more often than not, people with severe medical conditions can and do return to their work, sometimes to a job that has been slightly modified to meet their needs (e.g., a drafting desk raised three inches to accommodate a wheelchair).

## Adjustment to Disability

Adjusting to one's disability is a difficult process that could take many years. Often the assistance of a rehabilitation counselor (a career counselor especially trained to work with people with disabilities) can be helpful (see **Rehabilitation Counselors and Agencies**).

The process requires that you examine yourself carefully—your feelings and attitudes about the disease, the accident, or the event that produced the disabling condition. Then, you need to examine the consequences of the disability, those conditions of life that have changed or didn't change. What personal strengths, vocational or educational assets do you still retain? How can you build upon strengths rather than focus on limitations?

As with the loss of a parent, spouse, or child, the loss of a limb, sight, or mobility will require an extended period (often three or more years) for adjustment. And, new events and life situations will arise that can cause an "adjusted person" to lose perspective or emotional balance for a while. Sometimes, questions like "Why me, God?" crop up again and again. Adjustment to disability, like all phases of life, is dynamic not static. We must continue to grow in coping ability, self-confidence, and maturity by successfully dealing with difficult life situations, or we will stagnate and become bitter. A disability is another life challenge and, as you grow older, the chances increase substantially that you will live to face that challenge.

*See also* Anger; Depression; Discrimination: People with Disabilities; Managing Transitions; Rehabilitation Counselors and Agencies; Self-Efficacy; Social Security Disability Claim; Workers' Compensation.

## Bibliography

Grealish, C.A., & Salomone, P.R. (1986). Devaluing those with disability: Take responsibility, take action. *Career Development Quarterly,* 34: 147–50.

Humphreys, R.R. (1980). Disability in America: 1980 and beyond. In E.L. Pan, T.E. Backer, & C.L. Vash (Eds.) *Annual review of rehabilitation:* Vol. 1 (pp. 1–12). New York: Springer.

Livneh, H., & Evans, J. (1984). Adjusting to disability: Behavioral correlates and intervention strategies. *Personnel & Guidance Journal,* 62: 363–65.

Wright, B.A. (1983). *Physical disability—A psychosocial approach.* New York: Harper & Row.

—PAUL R. SALOMONE

# DISABILITY: STUDENT'S TRANSITION FROM SCHOOL TO WORK

This article discusses the process of moving from the security of high school to college or work for individuals with disabilities. The transition goal for all individuals with disabilities is to live independently in the community as a worker and citizen.

While in high school, teachers, counselors, parents, adult services, and the individual with a disability work together. This team will find out what the career interests and needs are, and then plan for high school courses, such as vocational education, employability skills, work experience, or family living. At the same time, community agencies such as rehabilitation services, employment commissions, and mental health services offer assistance that leads to employment or independence into adulthood. You will need to be informed about these support services.

## Relationship to Work

A disabled student's successful transition from high school to work, college, or community living depends upon the planning and preparation done in high school. When provided with vocational skills and experiences that are relevant to the world of work, and instructional programs suited to learning needs, one's chances for success are greatly enhanced.

There are numerous ways to get work experiences that reinforce vocational, social, and basic skills from the high school setting. Based upon the individual learning needs, ability levels, and level of supervision, options include:

1. Cooperative education in vocational area (e.g., business, health)
2. Summer youth employment programs (e.g., JTPA, Job Corp, Youth Tryout)
3. Community-based work experience (paid or unpaid)
4. Mobile work crew
5. Supported employment with a job coach
6. Sheltered workshop

## Application

As a student with disabilities, you are entitled to receive transition planning and services from your school. The following steps can be taken to get these services:

1. Talk to your parents about your career interests. Your parents need to know your interests so they can help you in selecting high school courses and work experiences.

There are also many community services, such as recreation, health, employment and rehabilitation, that you and your parents will need to learn about. While in high school you have a right to a free education that meets your needs. You and your parents have a responsibility to find out what your options are and participate in the decision-making process.

2. Talk to your special education teacher about your career interests and the programs and support services open to you. Services include such things as counseling, vocational evaluation, occupational therapy, aides, or vocational programs. You are guaranteed services if your individualized education program (IEP) indicates that you need them. The goals, objectives, and services are reviewed each year by the school, your parents, and yourself. You are also entitled to know about all available vocational programs in your school system no later than the ninth grade to help you select those that interest you and meet your needs. For instance, if the results of your vocational evaluation indicate you need an electronics program, your school must provide that training or pay to send you to the closest program.

3. Talk to your guidance counselor. Guidance counselors can give you career interest and aptitude tests. If you are interested in college, they can provide information about colleges, financial aid, and help you with a college application. If you don't know what you want to do, just start exploring different areas by visiting your career center, or just observing people at work. Most of us change careers several times in a lifetime, so a variety of experiences can be helpful to you.

4. Contact the student services counselor at the college you want to attend. Most colleges have persons who are responsible for making sure that students with disabilities are successful. Ask who that person is and find out what types of support services are available. Typical services include testing, study skills training, tutors, interpreters, adapted instructional materials, alternative testing, and individualized instruction.

5. Be an active member of the transition planning meetings with your teacher, parents, and community service persons. Transition planning should start around the age of 15 or sooner. Most schools do transition planning at the same time as the IEPs are developed for the coming school year. In transition planning, the team needs to talk about your school curriculum, employment, vocational training and work experience, transportation, independent living, and leisure/recreation goals.

6. Be persistent. The squeaky wheel gets the grease. You have to be your own advocate and use help that is available to get employment, training, and independent living services that you are entitled to or eligible for. Often, the support services you used while in high school will continue as you enter work or college.

*See also* Assertion; Career Counseling; Disability: Adjustment to; Discrimination: People with Disabilities; Job Search; Rehabilitation Counselors and Agencies.

## Bibliography

Gillet, F. (1983) *Preparing for the world of work.* Merrill, WI: F.R. Publications. Text and workbook provide skill building information on work-related topics such as seeking and keeping skills.

Gollay, E., & Bennett, A. *The college guide for students with disabilities.* Cambridge, MA: Abt Books. A directory of U.S. higher education services, programs, and facilities available to disabled students. Information is provided on enrollment statistics, accessibility, and services.

Izzo, M.V., Liming, R., & Kopp, K. (1986). *Corridors to careers: A guide for parents and disabled youth.* Omro, WI: Conover Company. Assists parents by providing activities and case studies for parents to use with adolescents who are disabled.

Mitchell, J.S. (1980). *See me more clearly.* New York: Harcourt Brace Jovanovich. Provides advice to adolescents with physical disabilities on development of positive self-concept to make educational, financial, emotional, and career decisions.

Mohr, J. (1983). *Whatever you decide.* Minneapolis, MN: Advocating Change Together. Provides information to young people who are mentally retarded to help them assert themselves and make life choices.

*A national directory of four year colleges and post-high school training programs for young people with learning disabilities.* (1984). Tulsa, OK: Partners in Publishing. Lists educational facilities providing special services to assist students with perceptual learning problems.

Phelps, L.A., Chaplin, C., & Kelly, A. (1987). *A parent's guide to vocational education.* No. 8. Washington, DC: National Information Center for Children and Youth with Handicaps. Describes stages of career development, how to work with school personnel, the transition process, and how parents can access services.

Summers, J. A. *The right to grow up.* Baltimore: Paul H. Brookes Publishing Co. Examines changing emotional and physical needs of maturing developmental adults with disabilities. In addition, focuses on self-determination, peer interaction, vocational activity, and spiritual development.

U.S. Department of Labor, Bureau of Labor Statistics. (1988). *Occupational outlook handbook, 1988–1989 edition.* Lists occupations by career clusters summarizing the type of work, education/training requirements, advancement opportunities, earnings, job outlook, and future job market.

—SUSAN B. ASSELIN

# DISCRIMINATION: AGE

Age discrimination occurs at all levels of employment, from the lowest clerical position to the highest management position. It refers to mistreatment of the older worker by the organization for which he or she works. This mistreatment takes many, often subtle forms, but it comes down to management by double standard. That is, the younger worker is judged and treated in a more favorable manner than is the older worker. This double standard is often an obvious and provable factor for the worker who believes he or she is being discriminated against because of age.

## Nature of the Problem

In 1967, the U.S. Congress recognized the severity of the problem of age discrimination by passing the Age Discrimination in Employment Act (ADEA), which protects citizens 40 years of age and over. Laws in some states protect workers at any age.

Age discrimination in the workplace is widespread. Some officials of the Equal Employment Opportunity Commission (EEOC) have described discrimination against the older worker as "rampant."

The EEOC was created by the Civil Rights Act of 1964 to investigate claims of discrimination, then negotiate the matter between the complainant and the company. If negotiation fails, the EEOC can take the company to court, or issue a "right to sue" letter to the complainant. Complainants have 60 days to file suit on their own, at their own expense. The local EEOC office, or the state's human rights commission, will furnish a list of lawyers skilled in handling age discrimination suits.

Age discrimination comes from a number of factors. Some employers say the older worker can't handle, or doesn't want to deal with new technology, but age discrimination arose long before the rapid growth of technology. Other reasons given for discrimination are:

1. The alleged inability or unwillingness of the older worker to change his or her ways of doing things.
2. A natural lessening of drive and aggressiveness due to the aging process.
3. The assumption that the older worker has long since reached his or her peak and is now on the downslope.
4. Pension considerations.
5. Health insurance considerations.
6. An attraction to the style and drive of the younger worker.
7. None of the above specifically, but a general feeling that a company is better served by the younger worker. Companies used to boast in their annual reports to stockholders that they had a "young, aggressive management team." It is a statement that is no longer found in any company annual report because of the chance that a complainant might cite the company statement in a courtroom as evidence of age discrimination. Also gone are ads specifying youth as a requirement for a job.

Dismissal is the most painful form of discrimination. If a person is dismissed from a job and replaced by a younger person, that is discrimination on its face, and therefore actionable. The displaced worker must then prove that his or her dismissal was based on age discrimination in order to recover damages.

A person passed over for promotion may cite age discrimination as the reason, and go to court. Some have, and have won their case. In another form of discrimination, some companies may simply isolate the older worker by placing him or her in a menial job at undesirable hours. The employee's history and tenure with the company may make the discrimination obvious. As an example, a 60-year-old sportswriter with 30 years of honorable service on a metropolitan newspaper was removed from his beat and placed on an 11 p.m to 7 a.m. desk shift in an effort to get him to retire. The sportswriter filed a complaint with his state's Human Resources Commission, and the commission negotiated the writer's return to his former beat.

## How to Protect Yourself

The older but wiser employee will always be on guard and paying attention. A newspaper editor, through a mixup, once ran the same story twice in his section. He admitted the mistake and accepted responsibility, but when his employer threatened him with dismissal, he pulled out another section in which a similar mistake had been made by a much younger editor. "If you dismiss me," he said, "you have to dismiss him." The matter was dropped.

Many older employees actually keep private files on mistakes by others as a protection. Similar mistakes must get similar punishment, regardless of the age of the miscreant.

Some employers, through ignorance, create a pattern of age discrimination, and this pattern is one of the easiest to prove in court. If older employees in your firm begin disappearing, keep records, and talk to those who have been dismissed. Precise records and crisp testimony are invaluable in court. If your turn to go arrives, your preparedness could save your job. Employers fear a court challenge. Frequently, the simple filing of a complaint can settle the matter.

The unwary are most at risk. Employees should be aware of their company's attitude toward the older worker. They should be aware of the laws that protect them. And they should know about and understand the functions of the various government agencies that have been created to protect them.

## Application

The EEOC and state human resources commissions are on parallel tracks, up to a point. If you file a complaint with the state, it will cross-file with the EEOC and you have a choice of which agency will pursue your case.

If you choose the EEOC, it will notify your employer of your complaint and assign a caseworker, who will investigate your claim of discrimination. The employer is forbidden by law to take action against you as a result of your complaint. The caseworker will try to resolve the differences between you and your employer by negotiation. If this fails, and the caseworker finds merit in your complaint, the EEOC will issue a "right to sue" letter to you. You can then hire a lawyer and file suit in federal court under the Age Discrimination in Employment Act.

Congress, when it passed the ADEA, recognized that the law had to have sharp teeth to make it work. It supplied the teeth in the form of "liquidated damages." If the jury finds in the complainant's favor and after it sets the amount of financial damage, the sum is doubled. The law also requires a jury trial. There is a downside, of course. Court action is at your expense, and it could take years.

The state human resources commission will also try to negotiate your complaint with your employer. Failing that, it will support you through a series of hearings held to determine the facts of the case and reach a resolution. Generally, these hearings incur no personal expense. The downside is that there are no double damages.

The EEOC has offices in all major cities. All states have a human resources commission or its equivalent, with offices in the major cities in the state.

*See also* Assertion; Law in the Workplace.

## Bibliography

Brandt, E., & Cowen, L. (1987). *Fifty and fired.* Lexington, MA: Mills & Sanderson. Advises the older worker on how to protect him or herself against age discrimination, what his or her rights are by law, and what steps to take if one is damaged by a discriminatory act.

Drucker, P. F. (1973). *Management.* New York: Harper & Row. An instructive analysis of management style, by the master of management studies.

Goodman, E. B. (1983). *All the justice I could afford.* New York: Harcourt, Brace, Jovanovich. The story of a man passed over for promotion because of his age, and the battle he eventually won in the courts.

—ED BRANDT

## DISCRIMINATION: LANGUAGE

Language discrimination refers to employment discrimination against persons whose primary language is not English, persons who speak English with a foreign accent, or persons with limited fluency in English. The issue of language discrimination arises under Title VII of the Civil Rights Act of 1964, which prohibits employment discrimination because of national origin.

The legality of restrictions on languages other than English in the workplace currently is not settled. Although one court concluded that language restrictions do not constitute national origin discrimination, another court and the United States Equal Employment Opportunity Commission (EEOC) have recognized that restrictions on the ability to speak languages other than English in the workplace, where such restrictions are not necessary for the employer's business, may constitute a form of national origin discrimination. Several courts have recognized that discrimination on the basis of foreign accent, where accent is not related to job performance, constitutes prohibited national origin discrimination. In jobs in which the ability to speak and to understand English is actually necessary, employers may properly require such ability as a prerequisite for employment.

### Relationship to Work

Employees whose primary language is not English may feel most comfortable, and most able to express themselves, in their primary languages to fellow employees who share the same primary language. This may happen very naturally and spontaneously. Some employers and supervisors, however, may not understand languages other than English and may attempt to restrict the use of these other languages. Employers may implement English-only rules, which may require that conversations in the workplace be in English, at least at certain times and in certain areas of the workplace. When this happens, the employee's desire to speak his or her primary language will conflict with the employer's desire to restrict usage of languages other than English. If an employee does not conform to the employer's rules, the employee may risk discipline from the employer and possible termination. Furthermore, employers may take adverse action against employees because of their accents or fluency in English.

### Application

Employers are entitled to expect good job performance from all of their employees. Job performance determines whether English-only rules or other restrictions on language or accent are permissible or not. The right to speak a language other than English in the workplace depends on the actual requirements of the job and the business in question.

In certain situations, use of a language other than English in the workplace may constitute poor job performance. For example, in a typical store, if a bilingual, Spanish-speaking salesperson insisted on speaking in Spanish to a prospective customer who spoke only English, leading to a lost transaction, an employer could properly discipline this salesperson for failing to do the job. In this example, using Spanish while dealing with someone who speaks only English is equivalent to an English-speaking salesperson ignoring or treating rudely the same customer, which would also be grounds for disciplining the salesperson.

But in situations in which the use of a primary language other than English does not interfere with job performance, especially in private conversations between employees, then English-only rules deny employees whose primary language is not English a privilege of employment enjoyed by English-speaking employees: the ability to express themselves in the language in which they can express themselves most comfortably and freely.

Similar principles apply when an employer takes action against an employee because of the employee's foreign accent or lack of fluency in English. When an employee's foreign accent does not interfere with the performance of a job, then the accent is not a legitimate justification for an adverse employment decision. On the other hand, if an employee's foreign accent actually interferes or probably will interfere with job performance, then an employer can justifiably refuse to hire or promote such an employee. Similarly, employer requirements of fluency in English will probably be invalid if they are not related to actual job requirements and valid if they are actually related to job requirements.

The United States Equal Employment Opportunity Commission (EEOC) is the federal agency responsible for enforcing Title VII of the Civil Rights Act of 1964. The EEOC has issued regulations regarding the legality of restrictions on languages other than English, discrimination because of foreign accent, and English fluency requirements (29 Code of Federal Regulations Part 1606, 1990).

If you are concerned that your employer has treated you unfairly in your employment because of your language or accent, in situations in which neither your primary language, your accent, nor your fluency in English, respectively, interfere with your job performance, you may be able to address these concerns. Depending on the nature of your workplace and its receptiveness to employee concerns, you might consider discussing these concerns with an appropriate person in your workplace, possibly your supervisor, your personnel office, or an employer or employee representative who deals with employee concerns, if available. If these alternatives are unsatisfactory or you are unable to get a satisfactory explanation of the reasons for the employer's actions or a satisfactory resolution of your concerns, then you may want to consult an attorney or the appropriate regional office of the EEOC promptly regarding the feasibility of further measures under your circumstances. In many instances, restrictions on employees' use of languages other than English may not be justified by an employer's business (Perea, 1990).

*See also* African Americans; Asian Americans; Assertion; Culturally Different: Working with; Discrimination: Race; Hispanic Americans.

## Bibliography

Code of Federal Regulations, Vol.29, Part 1606 (U.S. Equal Employment Opportunity Commission's Guidelines on Discrimination Because of National Origin).

Perea, J. (1990, Winter). English-only rules and the right to speak one's primary language in the workplace. *University of Michigan Journal of Law Reform,* 23: 265–318. Discusses legality of English-only rules under Title VII and analyzes justifications asserted by employers in support of such rules.

Piatt, B. (1990). *Only English? Law and language policy in the United States.* Albuquerque, NM: University of New Mexico Press. Discusses law and cases regarding language discrimination in the workplace.

—JUAN F. PEREA

## DISCRIMINATION: PEOPLE WITH DISABILITIES

Treating people with disabilities in a different, usually negative, manner solely on the basis of their disability is discrimination. Discrimination may be overt, as in the case of not hiring a qualified applicant because of a disability, or subtle, as in requiring a timed entrance test that does not take into consideration the extent to which a functional limitation may influence test results or requiring physical capabilities of job applicants that are not job-related.

A number of barriers can result in discrimination in all areas of life, home, school, and work. Architectural and environmental barriers frequently limit the access people with disabilities have to public transportation, health services, recreational activities, public services and accommodations, communication, and voting. Attitudinal barriers result in "outright intentional exclusion . . . , overprotective rules and policies, failure to make modifications to existing facilities and practices, exclusionary qualification standards and criteria, segregation, and relegation to lesser services, programs, activities, benefits, jobs, or other opportunities" (House of Representatives, July 12, 1990, p. 3).

## Extent of Discrimination

The extent of discrimination toward people with disabilities can never accurately be measured, because people with disabilities frequently lack legal recourse, are unaware of how to file a grievance, or, in some instances, may not recognize that discrimination has occurred. There are, however, approximately 43 million people with physical and/or mental impairments in the United States (Waldrop, 1990) and the Conference Report of the Americans with Disabilities Act (ADA) of 1990 noted that discrimination toward people with disabilities "continues to be a serious and pervasive social problem" and people with disabilities "continually encounter various forms of discrimination" (p. 3).

## Causes of Discrimination

Most discrimination toward people with disabilities results from lack of information and negative attitudes (Vash, 1981). The myths that nondisabled people hold about people with disabilities are extensive and undoubtedly contribute toward negative attitudes, which in turn, result in discrimination. Two major types of myths exist: those related to general knowledge about people with disabilities and those related to misinformation on specific disabling conditions (Patterson & Witten, 1987). Examples of myths of general knowledge include: (a) disability is a constantly frustrating tragedy; (b) the more severe the disability, the greater the psychological impact on the person; (c) persons with disabilities do not recognize their limitations or abilities; (d) if a person with a disability has a problem with employment, it is almost always the result of the disability; and (e) people with disabilities have "special" personalities or "special" abilities. Misconceptions about specific disabling conditions include: (a) all people with hearing impairments can read lips; (b) people with visual impairments can hear and feel things no one else can; (c) mental retardation can not be prevented; (d) people with epilepsy are likely to have seizures at any time; and (e) people who are mentally retarded are also mentally ill. Other kinds of myths relate to the cause of the disability (e.g., sin or lack of willpower, as in the case of alcoholism).

Employment discrimination results from these and other myths. For example, many employers mistakenly believe that (a) their health insurance rates or workers' compensation rates will increase if they hire people with disabilities; (b) people with disabilities have more absenteeism; (c) people with disabilities are substandard workers or are not highly motivated; (d) job modifications and accommodations are always expensive; and (e) their turn-over rates and/or accidents will increase.

Employers often erroneously believe that all people with disabilities need light duty jobs, or all people with disabilities have emotional problems, or that it would not be fair to subject a person with a disability to the hazards of a specific job. They may also believe that they could not fire a person with a disability, that the job is too complicated, or that other employees might perceive that special treatment is given to a person with a disability. Sometimes employers believe that customers would object if people with disabilities were hired or that OSHA prohibits hiring persons with a disability.

## When You Experience Discrimination

Although legal recourse is not always available, a number of laws have been promulgated to prevent discrimination. For example, Section 503 of Public Law 93-112 (the Rehabilitation Act of 1973, as amended) requires affirmative action by organizations with annual federal contracts in excess of $2,500 and Section 504 of the Act prohibits discrimination against "qualified" individuals with disabilities, solely on the basis of their disability, by any programs or activities receiving federal assistance. Public Law 94-142 (the Education of All Handicapped Children Act of 1975, as amended) requires a free and appropriate public education for all children with disabilities, provided in the least restrictive environment, and includes due process rights for students with disabilities and their families. The Fair Housing Amendments of 1988 (PL 100-430) prohibit discrimination on the basis of handicap in the sale, rental, or other provision of housing.

The Americans with Disabilities Act, signed by President Bush on July 26, 1990, addresses employment, public services, public accommodations, and telecommunications. Although the Regulations have not yet been written, ADA prohibits discrimination by employers against qualified individuals with disabilities "in regard to job application procedures, the hiring, advancement, or discharge of employees, employee compensation, job training, and other terms, conditions, and privileges of employment" (104 STAT.332). Employers with 25 or more employees are covered when the provisions take effect in two years and, four years after that, employers with 15 employees will be covered by the law.

ADA also requires all public entities that operate a fixed route transit system to purchase new buses or rail vehicles that are accessible to people with disabilities. Public accommodations (e.g., restaurants, theaters, offices, libraries, golf courses) must also be accessible and accommodate people with disabilities in an integrated setting, unless an undue burden results. They must also remove architectural and communication barriers, if removal is readily achievable. ADA also ensures the availability of telecommunications relay services for people with hearing or speech impairments.

If an individual believes that discrimination has occurred, there are numerous courses of action, including consulting an attorney who is knowledgeable about disability laws/employment relations or contacting the appropriate federal or state agency. For example, the Equal Employment Opportunity Commission (EEOC), with both regional and district offices, will be handling employment issues related to ADA. The Office of Civil Rights (OCR) also has regional offices and presently handles complaints related to employment and program access for educational services that are the recipients of federal funding. Both of these agencies typically provide referral service for complaints made to their offices, which should be addressed by another office. Federal employees experiencing discrimination related to disability should consult their Equal Employment Officer.

Many states also have agencies that are charged with enforcing anti-discrimination laws, including those that protect people with disabilities (e.g., Florida Commission on Human Relations). Most importantly, individuals who believe they have experienced disability-related discrimination should remember that the time to file claims is usually extremely short (depending on the agency, 30–180 days), therefore they need to take immediate action.

*See also* Law in the Workplace.

## Bibliography

House of Representatives. (July 12, 1990). *Conference report: Americans with Disabilities Act of 1990,* 101st Congress, 2nd session, report 101-596. Washington, DC: Author.

Goldman, C.D. (1987). *Disability rights guide: Practical solutions to problems affecting people with disabilities.* Oil City, PA: Park Avenue Press. Provides an overview of federal and state laws regarding employment, architectural accessibility, housing, education, and transportation. Appendices include laws and contacts for each state and major federal agencies that are involved with various anti-discrimination laws.

McCarthy, H. (Ed.) (1985). *Complete guide to employing persons with disabilities.* Albertson, NY: National Center on Employment of the Handicapped, Human Resources Center. Written as a practical reference for managers implementing equal opportunity programs for people with disabilities, this book includes the issues affecting affirmative action, strategies for accomplishing affirmative action, as well as resources for the development of affirmative action programs.

Patterson, J. B., & Witten, B. J. (1987). Myths concerning persons with disabilities. *Journal of Applied Rehabilitation Counseling,* 18(3): 42–44.

President's Committee on Employment of People with Disabilities. (1990). *Worklife: A publication on employment and people with disabilities,* 3(3–4). Volume 3 includes the full ADA legislation and Volume 4 provides background on ADA, as well as additional comments. Available from the President's Committee, 1111 20th Street, N.W., Room 636, Washington, DC. 20036.

Vash, C. L. (1981). *The psychology of disability*. Springer Series on Rehabilitation, Vol. 1. New York: Springer.

Waldrop, J. (1990). From handicap to advantage. *American Demographics*, 12(4): 33–35, 54.

—JEANNE BOLAND PATTERSON

## DISCRIMINATION: RACE

Racial discrimination in the workplace denotes unfair employment policies or practices of racial prejudice and of racism. For example, racial discrimination exists whenever people receive unequal compensation for equal work or whenever individuals have unequal access to job opportunities solely because of their racial background. This phenomenon generally occurs when a group that is in the racial majority discriminates against those groups in the racial minority in the workplace. Racial discrimination in the workplace is a part of the overall racism that has often been pervasive in American society (for a definition of racism, see **African Americans**).

In recent years legislative and social initiatives have helped to open the doors of opportunity and decrease somewhat the level of racial discrimination in the workplace. Affirmative Action is one of the most important of these initiatives. The term "affirmative action" was first used by President John F. Kennedy to refer to a duty placed on employers to take steps to remedy past discrimination (McCarthy, 1983). In spite of initiatives such as this, racial prejudice is still pervasive in many aspects of employment practices. As American society becomes more ethnically and racially diverse, it is incumbent upon people entering the workforce to understand the extent and causes of racial discrimination.

### Extent of Racial Discrimination

The extent of racial discrimination is often reflected in the differences in unemployment rates for racial groups. For example, members of racial minority groups (e.g., African Americans and Latino Americans) have higher unemployment rates than do whites (Bureau of the Census, 1990). When members of racial minority groups do enter the world of work, they tend to be overrepresented in slow-growing or declining occupations, but underrepresented in the fastest growing occupations (Kutscher, 1987).

Racial discrimination may also be seen in unfair hiring and promotion practices. Often discriminatory hiring practices have kept people from certain racial groups from applying for certain employment opportunities. Concomitantly, such practices have often overtly or covertly steered members of certain racial groups into lower status and lower paying jobs, while members of another group are encouraged to fill higher level positions with greater financial reward (Reich, 1981).

### The Causes of Unequal Treatment

The causes of racial discrimination in the world of work are varied and complex. However, two are worthy of particular attention. First, in many instances there are prejudicial assumptions regarding the intelligence, work habits, or educational preparation of members of certain racial groups which may influence discriminatory employment practices toward them. Such assumptions may work to prevent members of these racial groups from gaining equal access to the world of work.

Another cause of unequal treatment relates to competition for jobs. This is particularly the case in troubled economic times when employment opportunities become limited. Often members of the majority racial group perceive individuals from racial minority groups as competition for scarce jobs. This fear of economic competition for limited employment opportunities from individuals from different racial backgrounds can be the impetus for many discriminatory employment practices (Shulman & Darity, 1989).

### Application

Equal employment opportunity is mandated by federal, state, and local laws and polices. Taken together these constitute a ban on racial discrimination in the workplace. If you feel that you have been discriminated against because of your racial background, there are several steps you may take:

1. You can report the incidence of racial discrimination to the proper authorities (e.g., Affirmative Action officer) at your place of employment.
2. You may file a complaint with the National Labor Relations Board or Equal Employment Opportunities Commission. These agencies are designed to investigate and act upon incidents of racial discrimination in the workplace.

There are also some things you may do to prevent racial discrimination in the workplace and promote greater understanding among workers from different racial backgrounds:

1. You should be familiar with Affirmative Action and Equal Employment Opportunity Commission guidelines for your work setting.

2. You, your coworkers, and supervisors should attend workshops and seminars on improving intergroup and minority relations in the workplace.

*See also* African Americans; Law in the Workplace.

## Bibliography

Bureau of the Census. (1990). *Statistical abstract of the United States, 1990.* Washington, DC: U.S. Department of Commerce.

Equal Employment Opportunity Commission. (1988). *EEOC and the laws it enforces: A reference manual.* Washington, DC: U.S. Government Printing Office. A U.S. government publication that is a good resource on anti-discrimination laws. Includes a bibliography.

Ford, D. L. (Ed.) (1976). *Readings in minority-group relations.* La Jolla, CA: University Associates. A collection of selected material that offers useful explanations of basic concepts, examples of practical research applications, and new trends and techniques in minority group relations in work settings. Designed for people who are interested in managing the interaction between different groups of people in the workplace.

Fromkin, H. L., & Sherwood, J.J. (Eds.) (1976). *Intergroup and minority relations: An experiential handbook.* La Jolla, CA: University Associates. This book presents creative procedures to help members of different racial groups expand their perceptions of themselves and other people. A good resource for planning intergroup relations workshops in the work setting.

Kutscher, R. (1987, September) Projections 2000: Overview and implications of the projections to 2000. Washington, DC: *Monthly Labor Review,* U.S. Department of Labor.

McCarthy, M. M. (1983). Discrimination in public employment: The evolving law. Topeka, KS: National Organization on Legal Problems of Education.

McCarthy, M. M. (1987). Legal forum: Recent developments pertaining to affirmative action. *Journal of Educational Equity and Leadership,* 7: 60–67. Provides an overview of three significant Supreme Court decisions involving challenges to affirmative action plans. Considers their implications for affirmative action in public employment.

Reich, M. (1981). *Racial inequality: A political-economic analysis.* Princeton, N.J.: Princeton University Press.

Shulman, S., & Darity, W. (Eds.) (1989). *The question of discrimination: Racial inequality in the U.S. labor market.* Middletown, CT: Wesleyan University Press.

—COURTLAND C. LEE

---

# DISCRIMINATION: SEX

Sex discrimination exists whenever women and men receive unequal compensation for equal work or whenever women and men have unequal access to opportunities despite equal qualifications. Sex discrimination can occur in the absence of prejudice. It would be a misconception to imagine that discrimination necessarily involves hostility or even sex-role stereotyping (Kahn & Crosby, 1985).

## Relationship to Work

Although blatant forms of anti-female prejudice have diminished over the course of the past two decades, sex discrimination still exists in the workplace. Discrimination is pervasive and insidious; but with some care and thought, people can decrease the extent of sex discrimination. The first step toward creating a fairer world is to acknowledge the extent of current problems.

**Extent of Sex Discrimination.** Sex discrimination is manifested in rates of employment, occupational segregation, and unequal compensation.

A fundamental issue regarding sex discrimination concerns the wide gap in the unemployment rates of men and women. Women continue to have substantially higher unemployment and underemployment rates than men. The gender difference is documented by economists even when they control statistically for factors such as occupational distribution, job search time, and geographic mobility (Blau & Ferber, 1986). Moreover, women and men do not find new jobs of comparable levels after being laid off from work, even if they had occupied jobs of similar prestige before the lay-off (Ruhm, 1989).

When women do manage to obtain work, they are often shunted into occupations that are low in prestige and pay and have little chance for advancement. Some employers have preconceived notions about what men and women can and can not do, and these beliefs can, in turn, influence hiring decisions (see **Sex-Role Stereotyping**). Some employers resist innovations such as flex-time or deny parental leaves to their employees and in this way limit the options of mothers in the work-force. For a variety of reasons, women tend to be heavily concentrated in the administrative support (including clerical) and service occupations. In contrast, men are overrepresented in administrative, managerial, and executive positions (Bergmann, 1986).

The third major feature of sex discrimination is the difference in male and female earnings. A woman with a college degree who works full-time takes home little more pay, on average, than a man with comparable years of experience who failed to graduate from high school (Bergmann, 1986). Why? One reason is that the higher status "male" occupations typically command more financial benefits than the lower status "female" occupations. A physician, for example, earns more than a nurse. Another reason is that many institutions pay women less than men even when women and men perform the same work and have the same qualifications (Kuhn, 1987; Treiman & Roos, 1983).

**The Causes of Unequal Treatment.** Sometimes employers dislike women and knowingly refuse to give talented women the same opportunities and rewards that they give equally talented (or less talented) men. Sometimes coworkers harass women on the job (Swerdlow, 1989). Such treatment is called overt prejudice. More often, the prejudice has gone underground. Covert prejudice occurs, for example, when people assume that a highly accomplished woman has succeeded due to her good luck or good looks.

Even without any prejudice—overt or covert—sex discrimination can occur in today's organizations because of yesterday's injustices. Consider the union official who insists on an unvarying application of seniority rules. He or she may not stop to think how such apparently fair rules can perpetuate unequal outcomes simply because 10 or 20 years ago women never had a chance to join the queue.

## Application

To break the stranglehold of sex discrimination in the American labor market, we need first and foremost to recognize that discrimination is a systemic or institutional problem and not a matter of individual malice. What appears on the face of things to be fair and neutral may, in reality, be stacked against women. Having a pure heart and good intentions are not sufficient. We must also actively take steps to make sure that "equal opportunity" exists in fact as well as in word.

A concrete example may clarify the point. Imagine that your institution weighs heavily letters of recommendation in the granting of promotions. Imagine, further, that the organization has a health center and that people from all levels of the company "work out" at lunch time. Top executives might meet junior people on the squash courts or in the locker room. Friendships may develop, and when they do, it would be appropriate for the senior person to write a letter on behalf of a junior person who is coming up for promotion. If all or almost all of the senior people are men, junior men will stand a better chance than junior women of obtaining helpful letters. Neither prejudice nor anti-female hostility plays a role in the little drama; yet, gender asymmetries persist.

Organizations might become more thoughtful about how seemingly fair practices are, in fact, unfair if the women in the organization spoke up frequently (and dispassionately) about sex discrimination. Unfortunately, there is a well documented tendency on the part of most Americans to deny the extent to which they are personally disadvantaged by circumstances. Even when people recognize the true extent of unfairness that affects their membership group, they tend to imagine themselves as the lucky exception to disadvantage.

Such was the finding of a survey conducted a decade ago of women and men living in the Boston area (Crosby, 1982). The employed women in the sample, even more than the men, showed a lively awareness and a strong disapproval of sex discrimination as a society-wide problem. When asked about their own jobs, the women showed no recognition that discrimination affected their own situations. They claimed to be very satisfied, on average, with all aspects of employment, including pay; and, indeed, on eight separate measures of job satisfaction, the women were indistinguishable from the men. Yet, the women in the survey earned $8,000 a year less than the men, even though the women and men *matched perfectly* in terms of occupational prestige, years of education and training, experience, hours on the job per week, and age. Seeing themselves as exempt from sex discrimination, the women in the survey were, in fact, grossly mistaken.

*See also* Nontraditional Job for One's Sex; Pay; Sex-Role Stereotyping; Sexual Harassment; Women in the Workforce; Women's Barriers and Opportunities; Working Family Issues.

## Bibliography

Bergmann, B.R. (1986). *The economic emergence of women.* New York: Basic Books. A thorough economic analysis of women's inclusion in the labor market. Provides the reader with useful statistics on women's labor force participation, as well as salary comparisons between the sexes.

Blau, F.D., & Ferber, M.A. (1986). *The economics of women, men, and work.* Englewood Cliffs, NJ: Prentice Hall.

Crosby, F.J. (1982). *Relative deprivation and working women.* New York: Oxford University Press. Social psychologist Faye Crosby presents the results of a three-year, intensive study of more than 400 working women, working men, and housewives living in the Boston area. Among the most striking findings is that the women in Crosby's sample were not aware of being discriminated against in terms of salary. Written for the general public and scholars alike, this book is a must for those interested in gender issues.

Kahn, W., & Crosby, F.J. (1985). Discriminating between attitudes and discriminatory behaviors: Change and stasis. In L. Larwood, A. Stromberg, & B. Gutek (Eds.), *Women and work: An annual review* (pp. 215–38). Beverly Hills, CA: Sage Publications.

Kuhn, P. (1987). Sex discrimination in labor markets: The role of statistical evidence. *American Economic Review, 77*: 567–83.

Ruhm, C.J. (1989). Labor market discrimination in the United States. In F.A. Blanchard & F.J. Crosby (Eds.), *Affirmative action in perspective* (pp. 149–58). New York: Springer-Verlag. Scholars from various disciplines discuss the pros and cons inherent in the policy of affirmative action. Although it is a policy that elicits very strong reactions—both positive and negative—the authors in this volume conclude that if well-implemented, it can be an effective means of redressing past racial and sexual injustices.

Swerdlow, M. (1989). Men's accommodations to women entering a nontraditional occupation: A case of rapid transit operatives. *Gender and Society, 3:* 373–87.

Treiman, D.J., & Roos, P.A. (1983). Sex and earnings for industrial society: A nine-nation comparison. *American Journal of Sociology,* 89: 612–50.

—DIANA I. CORDOVA AND FAYE J. CROSBY

# DUAL-CAREER FAMILIES

Dual-career families are distinct in that *both* spouses are committed to occupational work and to a family life together and support each other's desire to combine roles that traditionally were viewed as incompatible. In contrast to the larger category of dual-wage families, in which the female spouse often must work out of economic necessity, both spouses in dual-career families consider employment essential to their life goals and sense of self.

Two high-power careers in the same family is not representative of dual-career families. Many combinations are possible, from two family-oriented spouses to two career-oriented spouses. Moreover, spouses do not assume that the woman will do her occupational work and all the work at home too and the man only his occupational work, helping out at home when he can. The kind of balance partners achieve depends on what seems fair to the two individuals involved, based on their own preferences and the reality of their situation.

Men's and women's lives are very much linked. Women have always worked, but historically it was with the understanding that any occupational work was secondary to the needs of husband and children. Male supremacy and dominance over women was not questioned. Women earned much less than men, were limited in their occupational choices, and, like their husbands, viewed the man as the main provider for women and children.

The situation today is quite different. Increasing numbers of women are entering the professional labor force. The large majority of these women are married and most have children (see **Women in the Workforce**). Women who prepare for occupational work and who marry do not "need" men the way that men (and women) were traditionally brought up to believe they did. Women who can support themselves, and want to, can afford to have expectations for their marriage beyond financial security. Such women expect men to be partners, not protectors.

These changes in the conduct of women's and, hence, men's lives—both within the marital relationship and occupationally—bring with them sources of stress tied to assumptions about gender. They also pose unique choices and dilemmas for partners. Not only is change difficult under

the best of conditions, but also society in many ways remains rigid in its assumptions of male prerogative and female accommodation.

## Sources of Stress Related to Gender Role Socialization

1. *Male Entitlement, Prerogative, and Assumed Superiority.* Many men advocate equality as an ideal. In reality, they may view a woman's career as secondary, and the emotional support they provide to their spouses and their level of involvement in family work may reflect this view. Male prerogative demands that what men do or want to do should take precedence; and for many men, a successful husband should not have to do housework. Needless to say, being a supportive husband or involved father is difficult when so doing is experienced as infringing on a husband's needs to maintain his own dominance or as interfering with his own ambition. For example, he may be unable to get excited about his spouse's career success, when he views his advances and salary as lagging behind.

2. *Female "Dependency" and Nurturance.* Women, on the one hand, have been encouraged to be more dependent than they really are. That is, they are encouraged to strengthen men by hiding their own strength and then to protect men from the knowledge that they can take care of themselves. This is commonly known as "protecting the male ego." Men, on the other hand, are encouraged to deny any feelings of dependence and to assume that women are dependent on them. Traditional male socialization asks that they hide any dependent feelings and instead assume they have power and dominance over women. Thus, men's normal dependency on women becomes manifest as a need for power over women rather than a need for connectedness between equals (Pleck, 1981).

Men's difficulty in recognizing their own dependency can be especially problematic because a core ingredient in a successful dual-career marriage is spouse support. Spouse support not only involves valuing a wife's or husband's abilities and ambitions, it also involves emotional support, empathic listening, and the ability to nurture. It requires putting aside one's own needs to be nurtured and doing so for another. It requires drawing out the emotions and feelings of the other person, something men have typically depended on women to do for them.

A typical motivation of men who choose the dual-career life style is the desire to nurture—particularly their children. Close emotional relationships have increasingly become a core part of these individuals' sense of self as a man. In my study of men in dual-career families, for example, 14% were judged by raters to be more involved than the female spouse in parenting, 32% as involved, and 54% less involved (Gilbert, 1985).

## Unique Choices and Dilemmas Typical in Dual-Career Marriages

Certain realities come with this life style. Partners need to be prepared for the kinds of choices they may need to make and the dilemmas they may face. Stress is synonymous with living and in itself is neither good nor bad. Eustress, or good stress, invigorates. Distress, or bad stress, debilitates. Stress, when it arises in these areas, typically centers around gender socialization and the constraints of an occupational world that assumes families adjust to work demands.

**Whether, When, and How to Parent.** When dual-career couples consider whether to have children, they also face the additional question of who will care for them. Parenting in our culture is typically equated with mothering. Moreover, given current employment benefits and policies, women are better able than men to ask for and receive the accommodations necessary for combining work and family responsibilities (e.g., maternity leaves, flexible schedules). As Congresswoman Pat Schroeder (1985) notes, "If the father would want to take off [to stay home with a newborn infant], if he even mentions it, it's like he has lace on his jockey shorts. You don't do that in America" (p. 16).

Perhaps most crucial to stress in this area is the importance of a child, and a close emotional relationship with a child, to each spouse's self-concept and life goals. Should this importance differ markedly between the spouses, the stress associated with a decision to remain childless could be considerable, depending on which spouse wanted a child more. The decision to have a child is also made more stressful when one spouse feels she (or he) will have to do all the accommodating. The psychological cost involved in deciding to have a child is lowered by limiting the number of children to one or two (contrary to popular beliefs, only children are normal, happy, and well adjusted), by a commitment on the husband's part to be involved in parenting, and by redefining traditional ideas that a child should be reared full-time by the mother.

Identifying quality day care is the next task. Although some corporations and communities provide some assistance in this area, the identification of suitable day care is by and large left to the individual family. In the vast majority of dual-career families some outside help is necessary to supplement the parents' care of children. The type of child care generally used depends on the age of the child. Most parents prefer group care for children older than three years, but they show no clear preference for individual or small-group care for children under three years of age (see **Benefits; Child Care; Parental Leave**).

Role conflict of varying degrees occurs with meeting the demands of both parenting and occupations. Often these relate to gender role socialization and the conflicts involved in developing more androgynous, varied roles. For a woman,

conflicts may involve not spending enough time with her child, or acting in ways that challenge the primacy of her husband's career. For a man, the conflicts may center around wanting to support his wife's aspirations or be an involved father but finding he puts his own career aspirations first (see **Sex-Role Stereotyping**).

**Combining Work and Family.** Basically there are three dual-career family patterns: traditional, ambivalent, and role-sharing. Couples who agree to one or another of these patterns generally do not differ in marital happiness. Where they differ is in what they bring to and want from the relationship.

In the first or *traditional dual-career family,* the responsibility for family work is retained by the woman, who adds the work role to her traditionally held family role. The husband believes that work within the home is women's work. The wife in these families generally accepts and acts upon the same premise. Far more professionally ambitious than their wives, the husbands in these families typically earn significantly more than their wives and see their wives as highly successful in combining their careers with family life.

At the other extreme is the *role-sharing dual-career family* in which both spouses are actively involved in both household duties and parenting. This type is the most egalitarian of the three and best represents the pattern many couples strive for. Spouses' salaries tend to be comparable and so is their involvement in childrearing and household chores.

The *ambivalent dual-career family* may be a transitional one. Here the parenting is shared by the spouses, but the woman retains responsibility for household duties. The husbands in these families want to be very involved with their children. But for them, housework is another story.

The pattern characteristic of a couple depends on personal, relationship, and environmental factors. These are summarized below:

## Personal Factors

- *Personality*: How important is a person's need to dominate, have an intimate relationship, be emotionally close with children, be number one in her or his field?
- *Attitudes and Values*: What are a person's beliefs about who should rear a child, who should be breadwinners?
- *Interests, Abilities, Stage in Careers*: How committed are partners to their work; how satisfying are their careers; how successful are they at what they do; is one spouse peaking career-wise and the other thinking about retirement?

## Relationship Factors

- *Equity and Power*: How are decisions made; what seems fair; how do spouses come to agreement; who does what?
- *Spouse Support*: Can spouses count on one another?
- *Shared Values and Expectations*: Do spouses share life goals?

## Environmental Factors

- *The Work Situation*: Are work hours flexible; any discrimination on the basis of sex; sexual harassment?
- *Employers' Views*: If a parent leaves at five to pick up a child, will she or he be viewed as not ambitious enough?
- *Societal Norms and Attitudes*: Is quality child care readily available; do employers offer paternity leave?
- *Support Systems*: Can friends or relatives help out with parenting; are colleagues supportive?

**Occupational Placement and Mobility.** Finding a position of choice or moving from a current position may very well be the most difficult issue for members of dual-career families. Couples often wish to give equal weight to the interests of both partners. In reality, locations or relocations based on the husbands' needs are still the norm. Husbands are usually older than wives and have more years in their profession. Also, men still generally command higher salaries than women. Those reporting high stress for either spouse receiving a job offer want to stay in their present situation because of the climate, their children, their family roots, or their positions. Those reporting low stress really have no conflict—they "would not consider moving" (see **Relocation**).

## Application

**Sources of Satisfaction and Fulfillment.** Many benefits have been reported by spouses and their children. These include:

1. For the female partner, the opportunity to develop yourself professionally and to establish a sense of self separate from a man and children, economic independence, and greater intellectual companionship and contentment.
2. For the male partner, freedom from the burden of total economic responsibility for your spouse and family (e.g., your wife's income allowing you to change careers or go back to school) and emotional involvement and bonding with your child(ren).

3. For your children, greater contact and involvement with both parents, exposure to less sex-role stereotypic behavior in the home, including the likelihood of seeing women treated as equals with men, and learning that they too are responsible for doing work around the house.

**Strategies for Effectively Managing the Demands and Stressors.** A satisfying, fulfilling dual-career marriage depends on many things. Most important is the willingness of both spouses to struggle with the difficulties of integrating career and family despite societal pressures to conform to sex-typed roles and behaviors. The resources needed to effectively weather these difficulties, dilemmas, and stresses are conceptually similar to the factors shown in the second table.

**Personal Resources.** These include you and your spouse's material or financial assets, education, physical health, beliefs and attitudes about love, work, and how men and women should live their lives, and strategies for coping. When individuals in my studies are asked, "Why is your marriage making it?," the most frequently noted reasons are personalities, values, and coping strategies that reflect redefinition, compromise, realistic expectations, and commitment (Gilbert 1985, 1988). Coping strategies are important for both short-term (e.g., whether to take a different job) and on-going conflicts (e.g., providing quality care for an infant).

Three types of coping strategies are generally used:

1. *Understanding*: understanding the sources of the stress
2. *Management*: managing the stress
3. *Change*: acting to change the source of the stress.

*Type 1* strategies require changes in attitudes, which in turn change the meaning given to the conflict situation. When using this strategy to deal with conflicts between your professional and parental roles, you might think, "It could be a lot worse" or "This is a natural feeling/reaction for working parents." You use *Type 2* strategies when you meet existing demands by working more efficiently, planning time more carefully, and so on. The danger in using only Type 2 strategies is trying to do it all and thus falling into the trap of striving to be the "superwoman" or "superman" who meets all the traditional demands of work and family roles.

You would use *Type 3* strategies to change the source of stress, say by negotiating a different work schedule with an employer to allow time for certain parenting responsibilities, negotiating schedules with your spouse, or arranging for child care certain evenings a week even though you will be at home. Other examples involve changes in definitions of your life roles, such as viewing family or career as coming first, altering career or parenting aspirations temporarily, or changing personal standards for home or work-related activities.

Type 1 and 2 strategies occur more often in the early stages of career and family and Type 3 strategies, which require change, when individuals feel more established and secure as a parent, spouse, and employee. How effective a particular strategy is for you also depends on the other resources available at the time and your life stage. If you and your spouse have a child when both partners are just developing careers, you typically will experience more stress than couples who wait until both partners feel more established in their careers.

**Family Resources.** The most essential family resource is spouse support—support by the husband for the wife's occupational work and support by the wife for the husband's involvement in parenting and housework. Stress is at a minimum when the husband has positive attitudes toward the wife's career and involves himself in housework and parenting. The husband is more involved in family work when the wife contributes more financially, and greater meaning and importance are attributed to her work by the family. The sense of fairness or equity about the balance of family and occupational roles achieved by you and your spouse is crucial. Equality of power is not the issue, but rather whether each of you feels that the other is doing his or her fair share when all aspects of the relationship are considered.

**Societal Resources.** This is the category of resource over which you have the least control and which is most unavailable for dual-career couples generally. The long-term acceptance of the dual-career family as a feasible option for men and women requires support from society as a whole. Flexible work hours, provision for adequate child care, rethinking of transfer and relocation policies, and increased career opportunities for women are all social policy innovations that would make it significantly easier for dual-career families to thrive (see **Benefits; Discrimination: Sex; Sex-Role Stereotyping; Sexual Harassment**).

Talk about conflicts. Without question there will be conflicts associated with you and your spouse's views of what women and men should do and how they should be. These conflicts are inevitable. And they must be talked about—not just once, but time and again as they come up. The handling of household responsibilities and parenting is one example of an area frequently associated with relationship difficulties. Oftentimes men wish that they felt differently than they do. Women get tired of "policing" things to be sure their husbands do their fair share. You need to talk about what does not feel right. You may need to examine the implicit and explicit expectations of your marital contract and how they may relate to traditional views of marriage. Open, honest discussions of what is preferred, what is needed, and what is workable are then possible.

Successfully undertaking and maintaining a dual-career family needs to proceed out of an understanding of the issues, and a measure of flexibility, compassion, and patience.

*See also* Benefits; Child Care; Discrimination: Sex; Parental Leave; Relocation; Sex-Role Stereotyping; Sexual Harassment; Stress; Women in the Workforce; Working Family Issues.

## Bibliography

Baruch, G., Barnett, R., & Ribers, C. (1983). *Life prints: New patterns of love and work for today's women.* New York: McGraw Hill. A well-written and heartening book that provides much needed facts about women's lives from a large-scale study using a diverse sample of women.

Gerson, K. (1985). *Hard choices: How women decide about work, career, and motherhood.* Berkeley, CA: University of California Press. A thoughtful and informative book that will assist individuals in their own decision making.

Gilbert, L. A. (1985). *Men in dual-career families: Current realities and future prospects.* Hillsdale, NJ: Lawrence Erlbaum. The first and to date only in-depth study of the male experience, this book reports on career paths, occupational aspirations, marital relationships, fathering styles, and ways of combining work and family roles.

Gilbert, L. A. (Ed.) (1987). Dual-career families in perspective. *The Counseling Psychologist,* 15(1): whole issue. A detailed review of the mental health and psychological functioning of dual-career families, their career transitions and normative dilemmas, and needed social policy.

Gilbert, L. A. (1988). *Sharing it all: The rewards and struggles of two-career families.* New York: Plenum. Written to be helpful to the women and men considering dual-career marriages, this book provides a comprehensive and highly readable view of what's involved.

Pleck, J. H. (1981). Men's power with women, other men, and society: A men's movement analysis. In R. A. Lewis (Ed.), *Men in difficult times: Masculinity today and tomorrow* (pp. 234–44). New York: Prentice Hall.

Pleck, J. H. (1985). *Working wives/Working husbands.* Beverly Hills, CA: Sage. Based on several large studies, the author concludes that men are changing.

Schroeder, P. (1985, December 29). Should leaves for new parents be mandatory? *The New York Times,* p. 16E.

—Lucia A. Gilbert

# E

## ELDER CARE

Elder care refers to the care of elderly people who have become dependent upon family members or society for varying levels of support in routine living. In many cases, the need for care reflects a change from self-sufficiency and provision for others to a role of dependency and inability to manage alone. Two major categories of elder care are care at home and care in a residential facility.

### Relationship to Work and Family Life

The needs of an aging population and the increasing role of women in the American labor force are changing the dynamics of the family and the workplace. The U. S. Bureau of the Census has predicted that the percentage of Americans who are elderly will double by the early twenty-first century, while the percentage of children will decline. Indeed the probability that workers will be faced with the dilemma of caring for aging parents or other relatives while also maintaining employment to support their immediate families is increasing. Unlike child care, which is expected and may be planned, the need for elder care may strike suddenly and the extent of the need is far more difficult to assess. This is particularly true when the aging person has led an independent and self-directed life. Role reversal of parent and child is emotionally painful, often physically exhausting, and frequently disruptive to work performance and family functioning. Sudden onset of the need for care or need extended over a long period of time may require absence from work and/or home and interfere with responsibilities in both places.

### Application

Considering current population statistics, you should assess your personal situation to determine the likelihood that you may be faced with the responsibility of caring for an elderly relative. Many problems can be avoided by thinking ahead and making hypothetical decisions. Questions which may be helpful include:

1. Who are the older adults who would need your assistance in the event of sudden disablement, and what is your relationship and level of responsibility in view of other resources and other individuals who may share the responsibility? Other resources may include assets owned or controlled by the disabled person or that person's independent access to medical care or assistance.

2. What physical, financial, and emotional barriers would constrain your ability to assist? Your own health or geographical proximity may create physical barriers. Balancing this responsibility with other responsibilities, particularly that of providing for your own family or fulfilling your work responsibilities and/or tolerating the behaviors of others who share the responsibility may create emotional stress.

3. What resources are available to help you respond appropriately? Federally required area agencies on aging ensure that support services will be available in all states and communities. Senior centers, meals-on-wheels, adult day care, chore services, and respite care are services available in most communities in addition to medical care assistance for low income families. Increasing numbers of employers are also providing assistance to employees who care for dependent older adults which may make the critical difference in balancing the responsibilities of work and family when an employee is responsible for a dependent adult.

The important points to remember are that help is available, that caring for an elderly relative may be physically and emotionally challenging but also fulfilling, and that failing to seek support would deny both you and the dependent adult the ability to capitalize on the merits of long life.

*See also* Benefits.

## Bibliography

Beck, M., et al. (1990, July 16) Trading places. *Newsweek,* pp. 48–54.

Winfield, F. E. (Ed.) (1988). *The work and family sourcebook.* Greenvale, NY: Panel Publishers, Inc. Chapter 6, "Options for Elder Care," presents an excellent collection of scholarly papers exploring issues faced by the worker caring for an elderly relative, the perceptions and feelings of the dependent elder, and types of employer responses.

## For Further Information

**National Association of Retired Persons**
1909 K Street, NW
Washington, DC 20049
(202) 872-4700

**National Council on the Aging**
600 Maryland Avenue, SW
Washington, D.C. 20024
(202) 479-1200

> The NCOA has produced numerous publications helpful to family caregivers of the elderly and offers information about resources relevant to a particular problem or geographic area

—Nancy H. Brown

---

# EMPLOYEE ASSISTANCE PROGRAMS

Employee assistance programs (EAP) are confidential services provided and endorsed by the employer or union for employees and their dependents to receive assistance for substance abuse and family, emotional, legal, financial, medical, and other personal problems. EAPs often provide a variety of services, such as assessment and referral services, short-term counseling, aftercare/follow-up, and management consultation.

Unlike community counseling services, Employee Assistance Programs are designed as an integral part of an employment setting. EAPs can be used as a supervisory tool to confront employees about decreases in the quality or quantity of work being produced, absenteeism, or accidents on the job. The goal of the EAP is to reduce the causes for decreased productivity and to enhance employee emotional and physical health. It is not the supervisor's job to understand or diagnose what is producing the lack of performance; instead, it is his or her job to suggest or strongly recommend that an employee participate in the EAP, so as to avoid any disciplinary action and/or termination. Thus, the EAP is used by management to maintain job productivity. It can also be used voluntarily by employees and their dependents for help with personal problems. The most common reasons people voluntarily use the EAP are for marital, relationship, and family problems.

The traditional EAP service model is called "assessment and referral." Employees meet with an EAP professional and discuss the problem(s) they are currently facing, or why their supervisor suggested they use the EAP. This professional is usually a trained counselor or social worker who is able to suggest various ways the employee may obtain help. Most often this help is provided by a community resource, not the EAP. Discussing together possible treatments or solutions for the problem(s) is called "arriving at a treatment plan." Employees always have the right to accept or reject the treatment plan recommended by the EAP professional. Depending on the employee's problem, the EAP professional will periodically check with the employee for a period of time to see that all needed services are being provided. All of the contacts between the EAP professional and the employee are confidential.

## Application

The EAP might be used in the following ways:

1. A peer or subordinate may have a problem about which you are aware. The EAP is an excellent resource to suggest to that individual.
2. EAP services are designed as a benefit to provide services at no cost to you and/or family members.
3. As an employee or manager/supervisor, the EAP can be used as an effective tool in turning around performance problems or containing health care costs and saving the company considerable expense.
4. As an employee or manager, the EAP can be used as a resource in the disciplinary process by providing professional help in dealing with problems that are beyond your ability to resolve.

*See also* Depression; Job Satisfaction; Stress; Working Family Issues.

## Bibliography

Shain, Martin, & Groeneveld, Judith. (1980). *Employee assistance programs.* Lexington, MA: Lexington Books. A comprehensive discussion of EAP philosophy, theory, application, and special topics and groups commonly dealt with through EAP services.

Spicer, Jerry. (1987). EAP program models and philosophies. In J. Spicer (Ed.), *The EAP solution: Current trends & future issues* (pp. 3–17). Hazelden. A thorough and readable book about the current trends, models, and issues facing EAPs and employers. Included case studies show how EAPs were developed in the recent past, how services are currently managed, and how EAPs will develop in the future.

Wrich, James T. (1980). *The employee assistance program: Updated for the 1980's*. Hazelden. Wrich covers many topics addressed by EAPs. He includes chapters about the history of EAPs; the elements and implementation of an EAP; cost factors, insurance, evaluation; and legislation, licensure, and standards.

—John J. Burke and Wendi M. Norris

---

## EMPLOYEE INFORMATION AND VERIFICATION

Every person who solicits employment after November 6, 1986 must comply with the employment verification requirements of the Immigration Reform and Control Act of 1986 and its implementing regulations codified in 8 C.F.R. Immigration Part 274a. These provide that "An individual who is hired or is recruited or referred for a fee for employment must: [A] Complete Sec. 1-'Employee Information and Verification' on the Form I-9 at the time of hiring . . . and [B]Present to the employer or the recruiter or the referrer for a fee documentation as set forth in Sec.(b)(1)(b) establishing his or her identity and employment eligibility."

The employer is required to physically examine the documentation you produce and complete Sec. 2 of Form I-9. The employer is required to keep in a file Form I-9 and may make a copy of your documents to keep in that file.

Documents that are acceptable evidence of both identity and employment eligibility are: (a) United States Passport; (b) Certificate of United States Citizenship; (c) Certificate of Naturalization; (d) an unexpired foreign passport that contains an unexpired stamp which reads "Processed for I-551," (or, alternatively, temporary evidence of lawful admission for permanent residence or has attached a Form I-94 bearing the same name as the passport and contains an unexpired employment authorization stamp); (e) an Alien Registration Receipt Card, Form I-151 or Resident Alien INS Form I-551 (the green card); (f) Temporary Resident Alien Card, INS Form I-688; and (g) Employment Authorization Card INS Form I-688A.

The following documents are acceptable to establish Immigration identity only: (a) state issued driver's license or state issued ID card; (b) school ID card with photograph; (c) voter's registration card; (d) U.S. military card or draft record; (e) ID issued by a U.S. government agency or entity. A minor (under 16 years of age) may also prove identity by a school record or report card or a clinic, doctor, or hospital record.

The following documents are acceptable to establish employment authorization only: (a) a Social Security number card, only if it does not have "Not Valid for Employ-

ment Purposes" printed on it; (b) a certificate establishing U.S. citizenship issued by the State Department; (c) an employment authorization document issued by the INS. This listing of documents is not exhaustive and only mentions the most commonly used documents. The complete list is in 8 C.F.R. Sec. 274a.2 (b)(v)(A)(1) through (C)(10).

*See also* Immigration.

### Bibliography

Clark Boardman Company, Ltd. (1987). *Immigration procedures handbook*.

Gordon, Charles, & Mailman, Stanley. (1989). Employment authorization. *Immigration law and procedure,* 6.19.

The Lawyers Cooperative Publishing Co. (1990), Immigration Reform and Control Act, Employment of Aliens, *Immigration law service*, Sec. 24:40.

United States Department of Justice, Office of the Special Counsel for Immigration-Related Unfair Employment Practices. (1989). *Immigration Reform and Control Act of 1986 (IRCA). Your employment and your rights*, Publication M-279.

—Felix Toledo

---

## ETHICAL DILEMMAS

In virtually every job, career, and profession there is the very real possibility of finding oneself confronting an ethical dilemma. An ethical dilemma is a practical conflict of more or less equally compelling obligations. For example, an employee may find him or herself torn between a promise to a subordinate and a new demand from the boss, or the employee might encounter a conflict between the responsibilities of the job and obligations to friends, family, or community. A manager may have promised a bonus to an assistant when the administration sends down an order to cut back on expenses, or a boss might land in the awkward position of having to fire the favorite cousin of a best friend. Some ethical dilemmas emerge when two more or less equally established rules contradict one another in a particular case. Some of the most painful dilemmas occur when there is a conflict of loyalties, to two different organizations, to two friendly colleagues, to one's co-worker and to one's company. An ethical dilemma can best be contrasted to ordinary, nonethical dilemmas: a conflict of two desires ("I love the chicken cacciatore, but I really would like the steak tonight") or between a desire and an obligation ("I know I promised I would study with him tonight, but then I'll miss the movie.")

## Ethical Dilemmas at Work

Responsibilities often involve obligations, and obligations sometimes conflict. Ideally, an organization will try to minimize such conflicts, either by structuring the organization so as to make priorities clear or by providing a set of procedures to resolve these conflicts. In an organization that is not so structured or that is rife with politics, such conflicts are far more common. There may be no established priorities between conflicting rules. There may be no possibility of consensus or no single authority who will accept ultimate responsibility for resolution of conflicts. Most serious of all (but not at all uncommon), there may be pressures from the top to perform—solve this problem, meet this deadline, or meet this financial goal—but no guidelines or court of appeal should these pressures prove unreasonable. Knowing how to handle ethical dilemmas is therefore essential to everyone's job, career, or profession.

## Recognizing and Resolving an Ethical Dilemma

To properly handle an ethical dilemma, one must first recognize it as an ethical dilemma. This sounds more self-evident than it often appears in practice. By their very nature, ethical dilemmas are typically painful affairs in which there may be no satisfactory solution (either hurt x or hurt y, disappoint p or let down q). It is all too tempting, therefore, to misread an ethical dilemma as something else. For example, in business situations people often try to translate an ethical dilemma into a straightforward business decision, perhaps by way of "cost/benefit analysis" in which only dollar amounts are weighed into the decision. The results are often disastrous. The engineers and senior vice presidents of one of the most successful automobile companies once decided to save a few dollars per car in return for an expected several hundred violent but avoidable deaths, calculating that the total cost of anticipated law suits and settlements would be less than the engineering costs of repairs. On a more personal level, people often try to make ethical dilemmas "easy" by removing the ethics and looking simply at dollars and cents. People sometimes re-interpret ethical dilemmas as nothing more than "personal differences," or they refuse responsibility by blaming the institution or system in which such dilemmas occur. But conflicts of obligation or loyalties, while undeniably "personal," are always much more. And while institutions and systems may well be blameworthy for fostering ethical dilemmas or making their resolution more difficult, recognizing and resolving ethical dilemmas is an inescapable part of one's job, even in the best organization.

How does one recognize such a dilemma? Ethical dilemmas are not all of a single kind, and so there are a number of different ingredients that should give us fair warning. The first is the conflicted and seemingly irresolvable nature of the situation. Whatever one decides, there are compelling arguments on the other side as well. Second, an ethical dilemma involves more than one's own wishes, desires, or ambitions. Other people are involved, or larger principles, or perhaps even the wellbeing of the entire community.

Ethics is often signified by such words as "ought" and "should," and ethical dilemmas are typically indicated by a conflict of oughts and shoulds: "on the one hand I should do x (because it is part of my new job description), but on the other hand I ought to do y (because I promised that I would do so before I was promoted)." Conflicts of loyalties are among the most common ethical dilemmas on the job, and these are not to be construed as merely "personal" issues. Which loyalty takes priority? What are the sources of these loyalties and are the loyalties justified? What are the consequences of following one loyalty rather than the other? Conflicts of duties on the job are also common, particularly if the job is complex, or if it was created as an amalgam of two (or more) different jobs, or if the duties involved shifting circumstances or changing personnel. Again, one must determine the priority of these conflicting duties and trace and evaluate their origins, continuing significance, and the consequences of one breach of duty rather than the other.

The most important feature in the resolution of an ethical dilemma is the thoroughness with which it is pursued. By its very nature, an ethical dilemma always leaves loose ends, leaves something undone or someone unsatisfied. It is therefore the conscientiousness of the resolution, rather than the resolution itself, that may be the test by which a person is measured. To have considered two (or more) difficult options and their consequences and chosen with difficulty between them is almost always the best that one can do. To have chosen a single conclusion without considering the alternatives, without considering the plight of the various people involved, without considering the various possible consequences, may be unforgivable, even if one were to choose (by chance) the best of the alternatives.

Under pressure, the temptation is to make as speedy a decision as possible, to get the whole matter out of the way. But the test of one's handling of an ethical dilemma typically comes afterwards, sometimes long afterwards (in a year-end review or lawsuit), and it is the detail and explicitness of one's considerations that makes the difference between a wise and well-considered decision and an irresponsible "cover-up." One should take the time, therefore, to make sure that one has considered all the options and all of those involved and evaluated all of the probable consequences. Living through an ethical dilemma is never a pleasant part of one's work, but it is often the ultimate proof that one is suited to the career that one has chosen.

*See also* Decision Making.

## Bibliography

Bowie, N. (1982). *Business ethics*. Englewood Cliffs, NJ: Prentice-Hall. A short, very readable introduction to questions of responsibilities on the job and the nature of business ethics.

Callahan, J. (1988). *Ethical issues in professional life*. New York: Oxford University Press. A thorough treatment of the various ethical dilemmas one encounters in all professions, with specific chapters on more particular questions in particular fields.

Englehardt, T. (1979). *Bioethics*. Englewood Cliffs, NJ: Prentice-Hall. An introduction to the major questions and dilemmas in the health care field. Essential for doctors, nurses, social workers, and bioscientists.

Solomon, R. (with K. Hanson). (1983). *Above the bottom line*. San Diego: Harcourt Brace Jovanovich.

Velasquez, M. (1982). *Business ethics*. Englewood Cliffs, NJ: Prentice-Hall.

—ROBERT C. SOLOMON

# F

## FEAR OF FLYING

A 1985 CBS News poll found that 20% of the persons it surveyed were afraid to fly and that an additional 24% were "slightly bothered by flying." A 1979 survey by the Boeing Airline Company found that 25 million adults in the United States are fearful about flying.

For those who have not flown, some fear of flying might be expected, especially if they have read sensational accounts in the press of a crash or hijacking. But it is important to distinguish those who have "first-time jitters" from those persons who have a disabling fear of flying, a phobia.

Common fear is experienced by everyone, and that is healthy. When there is a realistic risk to ourselves, it helps us to avoid danger and injury. When we are uncertain of the risks in a new situation, it makes us cautious. Persons who experience this fear when flying for the first time will often ask a lot of questions about flying and be calmed by the answers. They realize that there is no danger in boarding an airplane, and that the risks in flying are far lower than driving. Flying a U.S. airline to your destination is 60 times safer than driving. A recent study released by the Massachusetts Institute of Technology (MIT) reported that, for 1977–86, the death risk on a domestic nonstop jet flight operated by an established carrier was roughly one in 11 million. At that rate, a person who took one domestic jet flight every single day could expect to go more than 29,000 years before succumbing to a fatal crash!

A phobia is an irrational, disabling fear. The symptoms of a phobia of flying may include anxiety, nausea, diarrhea, sleeplessness, panic, avoidance of going to an airport, and other unpleasant reactions. Many people who experience this phobia say, "I know that flying is safe, but I'm still scared." It is usually not a problem of being uninformed; most people know the statistics. Instead, fear of flying is a set of feelings that are acquired and learned over time—a habit that can be broken. These "fear habits" can be replaced by habits of confidence and security. Phobias are treatable.

## Relationship to Work

The effect of fear of flying on work is predictable. People with this phobia may avoid occupations that require flying even though these occupations may best fit their talents and offer the greatest satisfaction. Similarly, people may turn down promotions or other career opportunities to avoid flying. They may not fly when their work requires it, and their job performance suffers. They may fly, but it upsets them to the extent that they have difficulty performing their job once they have landed. They are already worrying about the return flight. And, of course, it may lower their self-esteem.

## Application

If you have a phobia, you are not alone. A six-year survey by the National Institute of Mental Health indicates that more than 13 million Americans suffer from anxiety disorders, including phobias. And, according to Dr. Robert L. DuPont, "As a group, phobic people are intelligent, perfectionistic, eager to please, sensitive to feelings, and successful in school, work, and interpersonal relations." So, you are among a group of individuals having many positive characteristics.

Fortunately, most phobias are curable. To get better though, you have to face your fear and choose to go through the trouble to help yourself. Choosing to make that commitment to change is essential for success. Once you have made that decision, you will find that it is really not that difficult.

**Basic Principles of Overcoming Fear of Flying.** The basic problem is one of learning. You have unconsciously learned a fear or avoidance response to thoughts of flying. For some it may take this form:

Thought: "I will call the travel agent to make reservations." —> Response: Dry throat, feeling of anxiety. Thought: "When they close the plane door, I will panic." —> Response: Avoid making the reservations.

The problem, then, is this thought —> response link that you have learned. You have to break this link and learn a new response.

1. Relaxation will help break this link. Have you noticed that fear and relaxation are incompatible? You cannot experience the fear of flying if you are relaxed. If the thought "I will call the travel agent to make reservations" is linked with a *relaxation response,* then you will not experience fear. This can be accomplished by learning what is called "progressive muscle relaxation" and doing certain breathing exercises. With practice, you can learn to relax during stressful times. You can also replace those fear responses with relaxed ones!

2. You can also use this relaxation response to *desensitize* yourself to thoughts and images that cause you fear. If you imagine situations that have evoked fear before when you are in a relaxed state, this will diminish your fear response. For example, if you imagine the journey of driving to the airport when you are totally relaxed, this will help rid you of the fear associated with this trip. Of course, this procedure must be practiced and done systematically.

3. Since your thoughts about flying are linked with fear responses, if you don't think those thoughts, you won't experience those fears. The trick then is to keep those thoughts out of your mind. You do it with movement and breathing. If you concentrate on wiggling your toes, you won't have "bad" thoughts! Nor those feelings of fear! The same is true if you concentrate on your breathing.

**TRIPLE A/BM.** This is a formula for overcoming your fear of flying. It may sound like gimmickry, but it is based on sound psychological practice. It works. Memorize what it means: Triple A stands for *acknowledgment, acceptance,* and *action;* BM for the kind of action you take: *breathing* and *movement.*

1. *Acknowledgment.* Begin by acknowledging that your feelings of fear are the problem. You cannot change the airplane or the pilot, but you can change your reactions to flying. Acknowledge that you will have to change the way you think. Shakespeare wrote, "There's nothing good or bad but thinking makes it so." Become aware of how you feed your fear with negative thoughts. You have to change your way of thinking and what you say to yourself.

2. *Acceptance.* Don't try to squash your fears, accept them. Don't be embarrassed. Having fears is a part of being human. Fear of flying just happens to be a handicap you are burdened with, and you can overcome it.

3. *Action.* Here you learn to break the thought —> response link discussed earlier. First, you learn to relax. Look under **Relaxation: Progressive Muscle** and learn how to do it. Practice it until you feel confident in using it. Next, work on desensitizing yourself to fear-evoking thoughts. This is done by imagining feared situations while being completely relaxed, starting with the least feared, working up to the most. Let's take a look at one way this can be done: (a) Make a list of at least 15–20 thoughts and images that make you feel fearful of flying. For example: making the reservations, driving to the airport, the closing of the airplane's cabin door, taking off. (b) Rank order these thoughts from most feared to least. (c) Find a partner who will help you. This person should *not* be fearful of flying. He or she should be a caring individual with a good sense of humor, and one who is prepared to spend a couple of hours with you three times a week for several weeks and then join you on a flight. (d) Each session starts with you relaxing by using the progressive muscle relaxation technique. (e) Once relaxed, with your eyes closed, your partner reads off the least feared thought. For example, "Imagine that you are making your plane reservations." You imagine going through the whole procedure. When finished, you say, "OK", and your partner reads the next thought and you imagine it. Gradually, you work up the list. At any point that you feel yourself becoming tense, raise your finger. That is the signal for your partner to encourage you to relax and to not proceed further up the list. Instead, you return to a previous thought and gradually work back up the list.

As alternatives to doing this "Action" step, there are taped versions of it that you can purchase. There is also a book Captain Cummings has coauthored that explains this procedure in detail and includes a script that your partner can record on tape.

4. *Breathing and Movement.* Breathing can also help relax you. Escalating anxiety can be interrupted by breathing deeply and gently three times. It provides a way to *act,* rather than *react.* And you don't have to believe it will work; just do it. This should be done several times during the previous "action" step. It is also very helpful whenever you feel tension while actually preparing for a flight.

Movement involves *concentrating* on a physical exercise that you have memorized. One is done while standing: slowly and gently rotating your head in a circle a couple of times; then raising your shoulders high and releasing them; extending your arms outward and then bringing them back to your body; and then moving your feet up and down as if walking in place.

Another exercise is wiggling your toes when seated. For example, you may want to do this as your plane is taking off. Try this when you are doing the previous "action" step.

Breathing and movement makes you more relaxed and keeps your mind occupied. Practice them in your daily life along with the relaxation response. You will find them well worth it.

If you find the procedures we have described persistently frustrating or upsetting, seek the help of a psychologist trained in treating phobias. Treatment is usually short-term and successful.

## Tips for the Fearful Flyer

Here are 11 ideas to try if you are afraid of flying:
1. If you are a perfectionist, work on overcoming it. This is a common characteristic of fearful flyers, and it contributes to the problem (see **Perfectionism: Overcoming**).
2. Learn more about airplanes, flight, and safety of flight (see bibliography).
3. Review and practice what you have learned several times before flying.
4. Call the passenger service managers of several airlines to find out what services or programs they have for fearful flyers. Several airlines, like American, USAir, and Pan American offer programs. Ask for permission to board a parked aircraft for a few minutes. Sit down and relax. Walk around and ask questions. Just visiting the airport is often a helpful step.
5. Make your reservations early, and arrive an hour early. Reserve a seat near the front where it is quieter and smoother.
6. Consider bringing someone with you who is familiar with your problem and is caring and understanding.
7. Expect to be nervous, excited, and uneasy.
8. Do your deep breathing. Move, stand, stretch, bend, wiggle.
9. Bring a magazine or book that will hold your attention.
10. After liftoff, listen for the sound of the landing gear being raised then, later, the flaps being retracted.
11. As soon as permitted, stand up and move about.

*See also* Anxiety; Jet Lag; Perfectionism: Overcoming; Rational Thinking; Relaxation: Progressive Muscle; Self-Efficacy; Self-Manager Change; Self-Talk.

## Bibliography

Cummings, T.W. (1982). *Help for the fearful flyer.* (Cassette Recording). Captain T.W. Cummings, Freedom From Fear of Flying, Inc., 2021 Country Club Prado, Coral Gables, FL 33134. Two very helpful tapes explain how fear of flying originates and how to overcome it. The tapes lead the person through the relaxation, breathing, and desensitization exercises. There is an accompanying booklet that answers 75 common questions about flight and fear.

Cummings, T.W., & White, R. (1987). *Freedom from fear of flying.* New York: Pocket Books. This explains in greater depth the nature of the fear of flying and how to overcome it. The book is based on the nationally known Program for the Fearful Flyer, first developed in 1974 by Captain Cummings in cooperation with Pan American Airlines. It also includes informative chapters on such topics as "The Process of Flight" and "An Ocean Crossing."

Greist, J. H., & Greist, G. L. (1981). *Fearless flying.* Chicago: Nelson-Hall. The authors give specific instructions for using "exposure therapy," an approach similar to the one described in this article. This book also provides helpful information on potential medical problems in flight, such as air sickness or ear pain, as well as jet lag.

Stauffer, C., & Petee, F. (1988). *Fly without fear.* New York: Dodd, Mead. A well-written self-help book on the topic.

—TRUMAN W. CUMMINGS AND LAWRENCE K. JONES

# FIRED/LAID OFF

Being fired or laid off refers to losing a job as a result of actions taken by an employer. Being fired usually has an implication that the employer judged the employee's performance to be in some way inadequate and terminated the work relationship. Laid off is most often used in situations where the employer is unable to keep employees as a result of loss of business. In some cases, termination of employment comes with little or no warning. In other cases, worker-labor agreements demand a fixed period of notice prior to termination of employment. The method used to fire or lay off a worker can dramatically influence the nature and extent of the psychological reactions of the person affected.

## Relationship to Work

Being fired or laid off is most often seen as a threat to work involvement and career progression, which can precipitate several negative psychological reactions (Borgen & Amundson, 1987; Warr, Jackson, & Banks, 1982). Given the major changes in the competencies required in several occupations and the internationalization of the labor market (Freeman & Perez, 1988; Feather, 1987), it is likely that an increased portion of workers will be laid off or fired through the course of their working lives (Parum & Ploughman, 1988). The implication is that the opportunity to work without interruption may not be available as technology changes the nature of jobs, and as international competition forces some companies out of business.

## Application

If you are fired or laid off it is important to know your rights in the situation, that is, any contract protection you may have, as well as severance pay which may be coming to you (see **Law in the Workplace**). It is also important to anticipate some emotional reactions and to be prepared to employ some effective coping strategies.

*Emotional reactions* may vary according to your situation. Many people have gone through a process described as an emotional roller coaster which involved the following:

1. If job loss was without much notice, you may experience a sense of disbelief, shock, and anger. On the other hand, if you had a long period of notice about your job loss, you may have had the feelings described above before losing your job, and a sense of relief when it actually happened.
2. You may approach job search with some sense of optimism and pride in your marketable skills. You may also have an attitude of using the opportunity to get a better job.
3. If your initial job search is unsuccessful, you may experience some worry, discouragement, and pressure as financial and other pressures increase.
4. Prolonged job search may result in a questioning of your capabilities, as well as increased mood swings and feelings of desperation.
5. These feelings often result in a need to re-evaluate career options and may result in having to consider radical job changes or longer range educational/career planning.

The process just described is characterized by emotional turmoil and a perceived loss of personal control which can threaten your sense of vocational competence and psychological well-being.

*Coping strategies* are essential in maintaining a sense of dignity and optimism after being fired or laid off. The first things to consider are the ways that you can meet the basic needs that you may have taken for granted when you were working. These needs have been described by other unemployed people as follows:

1. *Money*. Working usually provides enough money for food, clothing, transportation, and housing. Being fired or laid off can quickly change your ability to meet your financial obligations.
2. *People*. Work is often a place where you make friends and develop a sense of belonging. When you are not working you lose this network and can feel lonely and isolated.
3. *Purpose*. Work helps to give you a sense of worth, of being useful to others, of making a contribution. Being out of work can lead to a loss of meaning and result in a loss of self-confidence and self-worth.
4. *Routine*. Work provides you with a daily routine. Being fired or laid off can lead to a period of time when you feel lost, with not enough to do to constructively spend your time.

Obviously, it is important following being fired or laid off to maintain your self-confidence and sense of well-being. To do this, of course, you must be able to meet your financial, people, purpose, and routine needs while out of work. The following strategies can be helpful:

1. *Support from Family*. It is important to discuss your situation with members of your family to let them know how you feel and to find out how they feel. In addition, you need to anticipate and discuss the fact that you will be home more of the time and may need some emotional support. Finally, your family may be of great assistance in your job search.
2. *Support from Friends*. Being laid off or fired can quickly alter friendship patterns, since you no longer see the people that you worked with each day. Also, you may lack the money often needed to engage in activities with friends. It is vital to keep contact with your friends; do not worry that they may think less of you because you are out of work. Also, develop new friends through hobbies, sports, or other activities. Some people have found it useful to make contact with other unemployed people, who may be having similar experiences.
3. *Job Search/Support Groups*. These groups can enhance your job search skills and provide ongoing emotional support. When surveyed, unemployed people said that these groups offered some of the best strategies for maintaining a sense of purpose, control, and optimism through a period of unemployment. Groups are usually available through government or private employment agencies, colleges and universities, and social service agencies (see **Job Clubs**).
4. *Positive Thinking*. What you say to yourself every day about your competence has a large impact on the way you view your situation. It is important to set achievable goals over which you have control. You do not have control over getting a job; the employer has that control. You do have control over the way you conduct your job search. It is important to give yourself positive messages about the job interview that went well, or the well-written resume—things over which you have control. This will help keep up

your energy for job search and help avoid resorting to "I can't do anything" or "Nobody will hire me" (see **Self-Talk; Self-Managed Change**).

5. *Career Changes/Retraining.* A very difficult thing to consider when you have been fired or laid off is the possible need for changing your job direction. However, it is important to do this, even as an alternative plan. This gives you options to exercise and forces you to examine your transferable skills, your need for further training, and labor market trends. It also opens up a whole range of jobs that you may not have thought possible (see **Job Changing; Skills**).

6. *Job Contacts.* It is important to set up a network of people who can help you gain access to the hidden job market, jobs that are never advertised. You need to contact the people you know, tell them about the kinds of jobs that you would like, leave them your resume, and keep in touch with them. It also can be very useful to contact employers directly in person or by telephone to gain more information about a company, perhaps through an information interview (see **Information Interviewing; Job Search; Networking; Resume**).

7. *Survival Jobs.* Getting a survival job can have several advantages. It can give you something to do while you continue to look for work. Also, getting a job part-time can help you get into an organization so that you are in a good position if a full-time job becomes open. Perhaps most of all, a survival job can help ease financial problems, get you out with people, and give you something useful to do each day (see **Part-Time Work; Temporary Employment**).

8. *Volunteer Work.* Volunteering in an area of interest can have the same benefits as taking a survival job (see **Volunteer Work**).

9. *Exercise.* Having a routine is very important to your mental health. For many people, an important part of this routine is physical exercise. It can be of great assistance in relieving stress and keeping a positive attitude towards yourself and your job prospects.

10. *Reducing Financial Pressures.* The shift from wages to unemployment benefits can cause a lot of financial pressures. It is important to anticipate the problem as soon as you have lost your job. Talk with your family, bank, and creditors to come up with a plan to balance your budget with less income. This will allow you to focus more of your energies on getting back into the labor market.

*See also* Depression; Information Interviewing; Job Changing; Job Clubs; Job Interviewing; Job Search; Law in the Workplace; Networking; Part-Time Work; Resume; Self-Employment; Self-Managed Change; Self-Talk; Skills; Stress; Temporary Employment; Volunteer Work.

## Bibliography

Amundson, N.E., & Borgen, W.A. (1987). *At the controls: Charting your course through unemployment.* Scarborough, Ontario: Nelson Canada. This 56-page booklet is based on research data collected from over 300 unemployed people. It describes their experiences and passes on their suggestions about how to develop effective job search strategies and cope with unemployment.

Amundson, N.E., & Borgen, W.A. (1987). Coping with unemployment: What helps and hinders. *Journal of Employment Counselling,* 24: 92–106.

Borgen, W.A., & Amundson, N.E. The dynamics of unemployment. *Journal for Counseling and Development,* 66: 180–84.

Hen, E., Amundson, N.E., & Borgen, W.A. (1990, in press). Shifting economic boundaries in North America: Implications for counselling. *International Journal for the Advancement of Counselling.*

Parum, E., & Ploughness, P. (1988). *Structural change and politics in the U.S.A. in the 80's.* Proceedings of the Conference on Structural Change and Labour Market Policy. Stockholm, Sweden: The Swedish Centre for Working Life (ALC).

Warr, P.B., Jackson, P.R., & Banks, M.H. (1982). Duration of unemployment and psychological well being in young men and women. *Current Psychological Research,* 2: 207–14.

—WILLIAM A. BORGEN AND NORMAN E. AMUNDSON

## FLEXTIME

An alternative work schedule that gives the employee some freedom in choosing the times of his or her coming to and leaving the workplace is called flextime. It assumes that the employees have individual needs and allows them to arrange their schedules accordingly. The simplest variation of flextime allows employees to decide starting and finishing times for the work day within a certain time range set by the organization, provided they work all the required daily hours.

The degree of flexibility is typically determined by the total number of hours the company works during the day, the hours the employee must be present, and the level of interdependence between jobs, departments, customers, and outside suppliers. The flexibility accorded the employees is the ability to choose the times of arrival and departure and the distribution of working hours. There is no choice in the number of hours; this is determined by the company or by law.

Flextime was first proposed in 1967 as a solution to peak-hour traffic congestion problems for employees of the German Messerschmitt Bolkow Blohm Aerospace Company. It soon became apparent, however, that the system also had other benefits.

Some common terms associated with flextime are defined as follows:

1. *Core Time*. A block of time established by the organization during which all employees must be present on the job; it does not apply to those who are ill, on vacation, or away on company business. The primary purpose of core time is to make sure there are some hours during the day when normal channels of communication are known to be open. Core hours also provide times for receiving, for communicating with suppliers and customers, and for dealing with the public.

2. *Flexband*. This refers to the periods of the day during which employees can choose to be present or absent, provided they meet the organization's requirements for total hours on the job. The flexbands occur at the beginning and at the end of the day or before and after the main meal break.

3. *Settlement Period*. This is the period during which the employee must work all the hours required by the company. It may vary from one working day to a week, a month, or even longer.

4. *Banking*. The employee can carry over credit or debit hours from one settlement period to another.

## Relationship to Work

Flextime can improve the quality of work life. The ability to choose working hours can affect the worker's autonomy through increased participation in decision making and the responsibility for maintaining coverage. Because employees must cooperate to maintain work processes, flextime may also result in enhanced group cohesiveness and orientation towards attaining the organization's objectives. In addition, flextime can help improve the fit between the work and nonwork domains. Flextime addresses issues of both organizational effectiveness and individual satisfaction.

## Application

As noted above, flextime can improve the fit between working life and individual life. Because flexible working hours give individuals a measure of control over their working hours, the range of benefits spreads far beyond the workplace. Given the option of deciding about your working and leisure hours, you can do many things you would be unable to do with fixed working schedules. People can and do use the time for taking advantage of educational opportunities, spending more time with the family, taking part in more social and recreational activities, shopping, and accommodating daily child-care routines.

1. *Family/Social Recreation*. Flextime can bring about a significant change in your family and social life by increasing your amount of leisure time during the hours that you choose. Traditionally, the husband would leave home early in the morning for work, and was gone all day, while the wife would take care of the children. By using flextime, both of you can start and finish the working day earlier to spend more time with the family, or you can have a longer midday break and have lunch at home. You can even have breakfast in the morning with the children and then drive them off to school and start the working day later.

In dual-career families, you can both adjust your schedules to each other or to the children's school times. You can also coordinate nonwork time to maximize efficiency in performing household chores. This innovation is also very helpful if you are a single parent and have to deal with the additional stresses of balancing work and family obligations by yourself.

The implications for leisure time are great. You can create large blocks of time for sports, hobbies, or community activities.

2. *Education*. This alternative work schedule can also create the opportunity for taking part in different kinds of educational activities. You can attend classes early in the morning, in the late afternoon, or even during lunch breaks if the conditions at your organization allow it.

3. *Transportation*. Flextime can make traveling to and from the workplace easier in several ways. You can avoid heavy traffic by traveling at off-peak hours. Traveling is safer during those times and you can save a lot of time, as well as relieving yourself of much pressure and stress. If you use public transportation, you can also take advantage of off-peak ticket prices. Cost saving can be substantial if your family can now function with one car instead of two. Finally, you can avoid traveling to work during extreme and dangerous weather conditions.

Cohen and Gadon (1978) deal with life stages for which flexible working hours are best suited. They suggest that if you are a working mother, flextime can be very helpful in arranging child care, enabling you to stay home in the morning to send the children off or be there for them in the afternoon when they come back home. If you are single, you can go out late at night and sleep late in the morning. You can also use your lunch break for meeting friends, going shopping, or even engaging in sports. And if you are near retirement, you may use the flextime for hobbies or community activities that will carry you into retirement.

*See also* Work Hazards: Psychosocial.

## Bibliography

Cohen, A.R., & Gadon, H. (1978). *Alternative work schedules: Integrating individual and organizational needs.* Addison-Wesley.

Ronen, S. (1981). *Flexible working hours.* New York: McGraw-Hill.

Ronen, S. (1984). *Alternative work schedules: Selecting, implementing and evaluating.* Homewood, IL: Dow Jones-Irwin.

—SIMCHA RONEN AND RONIT KOPELMAN

# G

## GAY MEN

Living as a gay man in our society often means experiencing prejudice and discrimination. This homophobia exists at the external or societal level of society's stereotypes and discrimination against gay men, and at an internal or personal level when these negative beliefs are accepted and internalized by gay men. Homophobia can have a serious impact on the career decision making process of gay men.

Coming out refers to a process gay men and lesbians go through in becoming aware of and accepting their sexual orientation. There are many different proposed models of the coming out process (e.g., Cass, 1979), but most start with stages of awareness and confusion, then tolerance and acceptance, and then some kind of integration or synthesis of this new identity. People can move through this process at different speeds, or stop at any point in the process.

### Relationship to Work

Deciding on a career is also a process. Career choice can be seen as an expression of one's interests, abilities, values, and self-concept. All these variables are likely to change over time, so vocational choice can be seen as a life-long process.

With gay men, the coming out process and the career decision-making process may occur at the same time. It is important to look at both of these processes and their interaction. For example, the initial stages of coming out can be chaotic, and this may interfere with career planning. At times, the coming out process may take precedence over the career decision-making process (Botkin & Daly, 1987).

In most parts of the country, gay men are not recognized as a legitimate minority and often have no legal protection from discrimination. Anticipation of both overt and covert discrimination can limit exploration of career options for some gay men. Conversely, occupations with a history of acceptance for gays may become more attractive to some men as they begin the coming out process; this may result in artificially limiting career exploration.

Both coming out and living as a gay man in our society can be a cause of internal and external stress (Hillerbrand, Hetherington, & Etringer, 1986). Potential internal stressors include: (a) internalizing society's homophobia, which can interfere with the development of a positive self-image, (b) resolving conflicts between sexual orientation and religious beliefs, and (c) complications involved with needing to hide identity from others. Potential external stressors include: (a) experiencing discrimination from society, (b) finding a niche and feeling comfortable in the gay community, (c) dealing with reactions from heterosexual friends and family members, and (d) living in a society that is predominantly heterosexual.

### Application

In addition to the typical concerns many people encounter when trying to decide on a career, gay men may face a number of additional concerns (Hillerbrand, Hetherington, & Etringer, 1986). Initially, you need to decide how disclosive you want to be on resume and job interviews; some employment is restrictive to openly gay men (e.g., military, FBI). Some possible geographic restrictions may also exist if living in a large gay community is important. HIV testing may be required for some jobs. Once hired, you need to decide whether or not you want to be open about your sexual orientation at work. If a you decide to be open, you may experience discrimination from both co-workers and from employers; you may want to decide ahead of time how you want to react to possible discrimination.

In addressing these concerns, it may be helpful for gay men to consider the following questions:

- Ideally, how open would you like to be at work and is this possible with the careers you are interested in?
- If you decide on being open, how can you handle possible discrimination?

- If you don't plan on being open, how can you deal with the contradictions?
- If you're interested in fields that are typically closed to gay men (e.g., elementary school teaching, military service), how can you work this out?
- How can you find out which occupations and professions will tolerate/accept gay men?
- How will you handle work-related social events (i.e., will you bring your partner, will you bring a female friend, will you not attend)?
- How will your level of disclosure at work affect your partner and his career?

In finding answers to these questions, it can be helpful to talk with other men active in the local gay community. If you are new to the area, or if you don't know many other gay men, it is possible to get information from the National Gay and Lesbian Task Force. Local colleges and universities often have gay and lesbian student groups which also have information about the gay community. Talking with a counselor or therapist can be helpful in finding answers to these questions. If you're having trouble dealing with stress, a counselor can also be a good person to talk with. If you decide you are interested in counseling, it's a good idea to set up appointments with several counselors and then see who you feel most comfortable with. Making a career choice is a complex decision, so it's important to gather as much information as you can, and allow yourself the time you need to make your decision.

*See also* Testing: AIDS.

## Bibliography

Botkin, M., & Daly, J. (1987, March). *Occupational development of lesbians and gays.* Paper presented at the annual meeting of the American College Student Personnel Association, Chicago.

Cass, V.C. (1979). Homosexual identity formation: A theoretical model. *Journal of Homosexuality,* 4: 219–35.

Hetherington, C., & Orzek, A. (1989). Career counseling and life planning with lesbian women. *Journal of Counseling and Development,* 68: 52–57.

Hillerbrand, E., Hetherington, C., & Etringer, B. (1986, April). *Career counseling with gay and lesbian students.*
Paper presented at the annual meeting of the American College Student Personnel Association, New Orleans.

McNaught, B. (1988). *On being gay: Thoughts on family, faith, and love.* New York: St. Martin's Press. Contains a collection of articles written over a 13-year period, including topics such as coming out, internal homophobia, religion, family, fitting into the gay community, AIDS, and friendship.

Muchmore, W., & Hanson, W. (1982). *Coming out right: A handbook for the gay male.* Boston: Alyson Publications. Practical information for men in the coming out process; outlines important aspects of life for gay men. Also contains a short chapter on employment.

## For Further Information

**Lambda Legal Defense**
666 Broadway
New York, NY 10012

**National Gay and Lesbian Task Force**
1517 U Street, NW
Washington, DC 20009

—JILLIANN DALY

# H

## HISPANIC AMERICANS

Hispanic Americans are a very diverse group of people who share a history of Spanish colonialism in the Americas. This group includes persons of Mexican, Puerto Rican, Cuban, and other Central and South American origin who have come to the United States at different times and for different reasons. Mexican Americans and Puerto Ricans, the two largest sub-groups (63% and 12% of the Hispanic population, respectively), have migrated mainly for economic reasons and tend to be young. The Mexican settlement in the U.S. dates back two centuries, when Mexicans inhabited what today is the southwestern U.S., lost to the United States in colonial wars. Even though Puerto Ricans have been U.S. citizens since 1917, their largest migration to the mainland took place during the 1950s, when approximately 20% of the island's population relocated (via New York) to work in industry and agriculture. The Cuban migration of the 1960s, on the other hand, consisted mainly of older, well-established people who left their country for political reasons. During the last decade, people from Central and South America have immigrated to the United States primarily because of political and economic unrest in their countries of origin.

Hispanics represent close to 8% of the United States population (approximately 20 million people). They are one of the fastest growing minority groups, as well as the nation's youngest sub-population (the median age for Hispanics is 25 years, as compared to 32 for the general population). Hispanics are geographically concentrated in a few states, with 88% living in urban areas. Approximately half of all Hispanics (51.5%) live in California and Texas. Mexicans are most concentrated in these two states, while Puerto Ricans are found mainly in New York, Cubans in Florida, and other Hispanics in California and New York.

The various Hispanic sub-groups differ in terms of their socioeconomic background, educational attainment, immigration status, and race (Hispanics share European, Indian, and black racial heritage). Information on the Hispanic population as a whole provides a useful overview; however, it also serves to mask the different experiences and problems faced by the individual sub-groups.

## Labor Market Experience

Compared to the majority population, Hispanics are disadvantaged in terms of educational and occupational attainment. This section will briefly discuss Hispanics' experiences in the labor market, including the barriers they face:

1. Hispanics presently account for 6.7% of the labor force and are projected to account for 8% to 10% by 1995. Hispanics are over-represented in the occupational categories of operators, fabricators, laborers, and farming and domestic service, while they are strikingly under-represented in managerial, technical, and professional occupations.

2. Hispanics tend to have lower unemployment rates than blacks (but higher than whites); however, they earn the lowest wages in the labor market.

3. The three most important barriers faced by Hispanics in the job market are lack of proficiency in English, low levels of formal schooling, and discrimination. These factors seem to be more important than age, work experience, and immigration status in determining Hispanics' ability to obtain good jobs (National Commission for Employment Policy, 1982).

4. Approximately 40% of the Hispanic population has difficulty communicating in English. The lack of fluency in English directly affects Hispanics' prospects for good jobs, impedes their educational attainment, and operates as a vehicle for discrimination.

5. The lack of educational attainment among Hispanics has been related to two major factors: (a) many U.S. school systems have systematically channeled Hispanic children into programs that virtually guaranteed that they would pursue low-status occupa-

tions (Stein, 1985), and (b) approximately 50% of Mexican-American and Puerto Rican students do not graduate from high school.

6. Discrimination against Hispanics in the labor market has manifested itself in three ways. First, Hispanics who are not fluent in English make lower wages than white non-Hispanics with an equivalent lack of language fluency. Second, after taking into account language proficiency, Hispanics are still in lower-paying jobs than non-Hispanics. And third, Hispanics receive a lower pay-off than whites or blacks for an additional year of schooling and for past work experience.

7. Hispanic groups suffer in different ways and to different degrees in the labor market, reflecting the varieties of location, education, and immigration/settlement histories of the various sub-groups. Mexican and Puerto Rican adults have less educational attainments than Cuban and Central or South Americans. Puerto Rican men and women have higher unemployment rates than any other Hispanic sub-group, partly due to the slow growth of the economies where they live. Mexican-American men have the lowest wage rates and the smallest proportion employed in white-collar jobs, while Cubans and Central and South Americans have the highest proportion of professional workers. Cubans also tend to have greater employment stability and less unemployment than Mexicans or Puerto Ricans. These differences in educational and occupational attainment have been attributed to the preponderance of the middle class among early Cuban refugees and recent legal immigrants from Central and South America.

## Career Development

The lack of educational attainment and upward mobility among Hispanics often has been explained in terms of cultural and ethnic factors. For example, it has been said that through socialization to traditional values (i.e., familism, fatalism, orientation toward the present), Hispanic families fail to motivate children to pursue long-term educational goals. Research in the area clearly contradicts these cultural explanations. Specifically, it has been found that:

1. Mexican-American and Puerto Rican youth generally express high occupational and educational aspirations, but they tend to be less optimistic than their Anglo peers about making their aspirations come true.

2. Parental values and the degree of identification with their own culture are not detrimental to the occupational aspirations of Mexican-American students.

3. The differences in educational attainment between Hispanics and Anglos can be explained better by family background characteristics (parents' education and occupation and family income) than by ethnic or cultural characteristics.

4. Ability to speak Spanish is not detrimental to the career development of Hispanics. For example, among Hispanic high school and college students, Cuban Americans are the most likely to be Spanish dominant and middle class. Also, they tend to have higher educational attainments than the other groups.

5. Hispanic students who complete high school are as likely as black and white students to attend college. Hispanic students who attend integrated high schools and complete college preparatory curricula (versus a vocational curriculum) have the best chances of attending college.

6. Mexican-American women who attend college tend to be assertive, bi-cultural, and have received support from their families to continue their education.

## Application

Research and experience suggest the following guidelines for Hispanics in the process of making career decisions:

1. In order to get better jobs, it is important that you become proficient in English and get as much education and training as possible.

2. Lack of finances is one of the major obstacles Hispanic students face in seeking higher education; therefore it will be important to plan ahead and seek sources of financial help (see list of resources at the end of this article).

3. Identification with your own culture will not constitute a disadvantage in achieving your educational and occupational goals. A preference to speak Spanish with family and friends and to interact socially with Hispanics will not hamper your ability to get a good job.

4. Ethnic identity is a dynamic, complex process. People are able to ascribe to different cultural patterns and rules of behaviors in the different roles they play. For this reason it is possible for a Hispanic person to function effectively in mainstream American society (acculturate) without losing his or her sense of ethnic identity and pride. That is, you may choose to speak Spanish at home and to identify strongly with your ethnic group and, at the same time, be able to speak fluent English and operate successfully in academic and work settings.

5. Seriously consider seeking career counseling to help you make your career decisions. Career counseling may be of help as you explore yourself, your

interests, and the world of work. Research has shown that the career interest inventories based on Holland's hexagonal model are appropriate for assessing the career interests of Hispanic students (see **Vocational Choice: John Holland's Theory**).

6. In the process of career decision making, it is important to spend time exploring the world of work. Seek information about many different occupations and their prospects for the future before making a final choice. Just relying on the occupations you are familiar with, through the people you know, may result in a very limited range of possibilities to choose from.

*See also* Discrimination: Language; Discrimination: Race; Immigration; Nonstandard English; Vocational Choice: John Holland's Theory.

## Bibliography

National Commission for Employment Policy. (1982). *Hispanics and jobs: Barriers to progress.* Washington, DC: National Commission for Employment Policy.

Stein, C.B. (1985). Hispanic students in the swim or sink era. *Urban Education,* 20: 189–98.

## For Further Information

This section includes a list of programs (at the national and state levels) and publications that may be of help to Hispanics in the pursuit of their educational and career goals:

**Aspira of America, Inc.** Primarily oriented toward young Puerto Ricans, Aspira's six field centers offer a variety of educational services, including college counseling and financial aid assistance. Field centers are in Miami (FL), Chicago (IL), Newark (NJ), Bronx (NY), Philadelphia (PA), and Carolina (PR). For more information contact: Aspira of America, Inc., 114 East 28th Street, New York, NY 10016.

**Inroads.** Its purpose is to prepare high school seniors and college youth, at the national level, for positions of leadership in corporate America. This is achieved, partly, through summer internships, during the college years, in participating corporations. For more information contact: Lorenzo Tovar, Vice President, Inroads Denver, Inc., P.O. Box 13439, Denver, CO 80201, (303) 292-2080.

**LULAC National Educational Service Centers (LNESC).** The 12 LNESC centers across the country provide students with college and career counseling, job training, and financial aid assistance. The national office coordinates the LULAC National Scholarship Fund. Field centers are in Pomona/East Los Angeles and San Francisco (CA), Miami (FL), Chicago (IL), Topeka (KS), Albuquerque (NM), Philadelphia (PA), Corpus Christi and Houston (TX), and Seattle (WA). For more information contact: LNESC National Headquarters, 400 First St., N.W., Suite 716, Washington, DC 20001, (202) 347-1652.

**MESA.** Based in California, MESA helps minority high school and college students prepare for math and science careers. For more information contact: Statewide Director MESA, Lawrence Hall of Science, University of California-Berkeley, Berkeley, CA 94720, (415) 642-5064.

**National Hispanic Scholarship Fund.** This fund provides financial assistance to help young Hispanics pursue their educational goals. For more information contact: Ernest Robles, Executive Director, National Hispanic Scholarship Fund, P.O. Box 748, San Francisco, CA 94101, (415) 892-9971.

**National Puerto Rican Forum.** Its purpose is to help unskilled young Hispanic women acquire English-language and clerical skills. The Forum also offers job placement assistance and helps entry-level employees acquire the skills needed for promotion. For more information contact: Rosaida Rosario, Vice President, Puerto Rican Forum, 159 Washington Street, Hartford, CT 06106, (203) 247-3227.

**The Arizona Hispanic Women's Corporation.** The corporation provides leadership training and professional development skills for working Hispanic women. It organizes an annual conference and is responsible for two additional projects. The Hispanic Scholars Project awards scholarships to Arizona students attending in-state universities and community colleges. The Leadership Institute focuses on facilitating the development of managerial skills among Hispanic women. For more information contact: Sylvia Arellano, President, Arizona Hispanic Women's Corp., 640 North First Avenue, Phoenix, AZ 85003, (602) 223-4285.

Additional information on Hispanic organizations may be found in these two sources: *Guidebook to Hispanic Organizations and Information* (1983), published by the ERIC Clearinghouse on Urban Education; and *Guide to Hispanic Organizations* (1980), published by the Phillip Morris Company (100 Park Avenue, New York, NY).

In 1987, the Garrett Park Press (P.O. Box 109B, Garrett Park, MD 20896) published a series of directories of financial aid sources for minorities interested in pursuing a college education. The titles in this series include: *Financial Aid for Minorities: Awards Open to Students with Any Major; Financial Aid for Minorities in Journalism/Mass Communication; Financial Aid for Minorities in Health Fields; Financial Aid for Minorities in Business and Law;* and *Financial Aid for Minorities in Engineering and Science.*

—CONSUELO ARBONA

# I

## IMMIGRATION

This is a nation of immigrants. The vast majority of its inhabitants are either foreign born or the descendants of people who came from other countries. During most of our history there were no controls over who entered the United States. Laws limiting and controlling immigration were first passed around 1850, at about the time the country reached the Pacific Ocean.

Historically, the immigration laws of the United States have had three principal objectives: the unification of families, the supply of workers who possess needed skills to the national labor market, and the protection of wage levels and standard of living of American workers. Unification of families refers to the families of immigrants and the foreign-born relatives of U.S. citizens. Immigration has often taken place gradually and involved not only the principal immigrant but his or her family as well. The law provides for the regulation of the issuance of immigrant visas or permits to the immediate relatives of immigrants to allow families to be reunited. The other two historical objectives are interrelated: to provide workers whose skills are needed in the country and to protect the wage levels of American workers by preventing an uncontrolled influx of alien workers with the same skills of American workers that would result in lower wages because there would be many more workers applying for the same jobs.

## Immigration Reform and Control Act of 1986 (IRCA)

The IRCA is the most recent and most comprehensive piece of legislation affecting the immigration laws of this country. It has changed the law in ways that affect not only aliens but U.S. citizens and lawful permanent residents as well. IRCA's provisions fall into three different categories: Employer Sanctions, Control of Employment of Aliens, and Anti-Discrimination.

**Employer Sanctions.** Employers who knowingly hire undocumented workers are subject to penalties that include fines and imprisonment. All employers are required to ask *all* job applicants for papers proving that they are entitled to work in this country. In the next section we will discuss what kinds of papers may be used to prove entitlement to work.

**Control of Employment of Aliens.** This category defines exactly which aliens may accept employment in the United States. An alien is any person who is not an American citizen. There are three categories of aliens authorized to accept employment:

1. *Aliens authorized employment incident to status.* This category includes lawful permanent residents, refugees, aliens who have been granted political asylum, parolees, and persons who are granted extended voluntary departure. These persons do not need to request employment authorization and there are no restrictions as to the location or the type of employment they can accept.

2. *Aliens authorized employment with a specific employer incident to status.* The persons included in this category may be employed in the United States by a specific employer, subject to certain restrictions on the type, length, and duration of their employment. The Immigration and Naturalization Service (INS) will not issue an employment authorization document to these persons. Instead, their passports bear appropriate notations describing the limits of their authorization. This group includes diplomats and representatives of international organizations, and their domestic servants; students with F-1 visas; temporary workers; and exchange trainees. The aliens in this group may be employed with the government, institution, or persons, through which they obtained their status and for the duration of their status. Any extension beyond that time requires a request for employment authorization to the INS.

3. *Aliens who must apply for employment authorization*. This group of persons includes the immediate relatives of non-immigrant students, any aliens who have filed non-frivolous requests for asylum, applicants for adjustment of status and for suspension of deportation, and deportable aliens who have been granted voluntary departure or deferred action status, if they can establish economic necessity.

**Anti-Discrimination.** These provisions of IRCA respond to a concern of the Congress that the employer sanctions and the verification requirements of the law could have the effect of encouraging employers to deny employment to individuals who look or sound foreign. To prevent this type of discrimination, Congress made it illegal for an employer to discriminate against a U.S. citizen or a work-authorized alien who is an intending citizen on the basis of citizenship status, with respect to hiring, firing, recruitment, or referral for a fee. An intending citizen is a permanent resident, temporary resident under the amnesty program, refugee, or asilee who intends to become a citizen.

It is also illegal to discriminate against all work authorized aliens with respect to hiring, firing, recruitment, and referral for a fee on the basis of national origin. These prohibitions apply to all employers of four or more employees. It is illegal for employers to establish "U.S. Citizens Only" employment policies. It is also illegal for employers to prefer one kind of document over others as proof of authorization for employment. For example, it is illegal for an employer of four or more employees to demand a "green card" as the only acceptable proof of employment.

To enforce the anti-discrimination provisions IRCA established the Office of the Special Counsel for Immigration Related Unfair Employment Practices. To file complaints and request investigations of employers who may be using such illegal practices, a person only needs to write the facts relating to the complaint or make an inquiry to: The Office of the Special Counsel for Immigration Related Unfair Employment Practices, P.O. Box 65490, Washington, DC 20035-5490, or call: 1-800-255-7688 (toll free) or (202) 653-8121.

## Relationship to Work

The employment verification requirements of IRCA apply to all employers and to all persons in search of employment. Every time you apply for employment you must be ready to comply with the documentary requirements of the law. This section will help you prepare to comply with the law by informing you of the kinds of documents you should be ready to present to your prospective employer upon your hiring. The lack of proper documentation may result in your not being hired or in a delay of your starting date.

## Application

Every person who solicits employment after November 6, 1986 must comply with the employment verification requirements of the Immigration Reform and Control Act of 1986 and its implementing regulations codified in 8 C.F.R. Part 274a. These provide that "An individual who is hired or is recruited or referred for a fee for employment must: [A] *Complete Sec. 1-'Employee Information and Verification' on the Form I-9 at the time of hiring . . . and [B]Present to the employer or the recruiter or the referrer for a fee documentation as set forth in Sec.(b)(1)(b) establishing his or her identity and employment eligibility.* "

The employer is required to physically examine the documentation you produce and complete Sec. 2 of Form I-9. He or she is required to keep in a file Form I-9 and he or she may make a copy of your documents to keep in that file.

Some kinds of documents are acceptable evidence of both identity and employment eligibility. These are: (a) United States Passport; (b) Certificate of United States Citizenship; (c) Certificate of Naturalization; (d) an unexpired foreign passport that contains an unexpired stamp which reads "Processed for I-551" (or, alternatively, temporary evidence of lawful admission for permanent residence or has attached a Form I-94 bearing the same name as the passport and contains an unexpired employment authorization stamp); (e) an Alien Registration Receipt Card, Form I-151 or Resident Alien INS Form I-551 (the green card); (f) Temporary Resident Alien Card, INS Form I-688; and (g) Employment Authorization Card INS Form I-688A.

The following documents are acceptable to establish identity only: (a) state issued driver's license or state issued ID card; (b) school ID card with photograph; (c) voter's registration card; (d) U.S. military card or draft record; (e) ID issued by a U.S. government agency or entity. A minor (under 16 years of age) may also prove identity by a school record or report card or a clinic, doctor, or hospital record.

The following documents are acceptable to establish employment authorization only: (a) a Social Security number card, only if it does not have "Not Valid for Employment Purposes" printed on it; (b) a certificate establishing U.S. citizenship issued by the State Department; (c) an employment authorization document issued by the INS. This listing of documents is not exhaustive and only mentions the most commonly used documents. The complete list is in 8 C.F.R. Sec. 274a.2 (b)(v)(A)(1) through (C)(10).

*See also* Discrimination: Language; Discrimination: Race; Law in the Workplace; Nonstandard English.

## Bibliography

Clark Boardman Company, Ltd. (1987). *Immigration procedures handbook.*

Gordon, Charles, & Mailman, Stanley. (1989). Employment authorization. *Immigration law and procedure,* 6.19.

The Lawyers Cooperative Publishing Co. (1990), Immigration Reform and Control Act, Employment of Aliens, *Immigration law service,* Sec. 24:40.

United States Department of Justice, Office of the Special Counsel for Immigration-Related Unfair Employment Practices. (1989). *Immigration Reform and Control Act of 1986 (IRCA). Your employment and your rights,* Publication M-279.

—Felix Toledo

# INFORMATION INTERVIEWING

An information interview is a face-to-face meeting with knowledgeable people to obtain career-related information to assist you in making career decisions and in developing job leads. If handled properly, information interviewing provides high-quality, in-depth information to help you understand jobs and occupations, and to improve the soundness of your career decisions. While you can acquire a basic understanding of occupations from written sources, information interviewing makes occupations come alive by allowing you to ask specific questions and to probe deeply into the details of the work. As part of a job search campaign, informational interviewing enables you to penetrate the job market to uncover job leads more effectively than any other method.

## How to Conduct Information Interviews

Six steps for conducting information interviews are presented below. Each step leads to the next. Taking short cuts in the process tends to undermine its effectiveness.

1. Conduct basic research to gain a general understanding of your targeted occupation or job. At a public library or college career center, read a description of the job in the Occupational Outlook Handbook published by the U. S. Department of Labor. Seek to gain a basic understanding of the nature of the work, working conditions, training, education, qualifications required, earnings, and employment outlook.

2. Develop a list of possible contact persons. A contact is either a person with first-hand knowledge of your targeted job or occupation, like a job incumbent, job supervisor, or hiring official, or someone who might be able to refer you to one of these people. In developing your contact list, think of all the people you know. Make a list of possible contacts with the help of family or friends. Then, decide which contacts might provide you with the type of information you need.

3. Send a short, personalized letter to your contact to request an appointment. Write your letter as follows:
   a. Begin with a cordial, personal statement that connects you to your contact. For example, you might begin with: "Since we are both alumni of ABC school and you work in an occupation I am exploring, I thought you would be a good person to approach for some assistance."
   b. Do not pressure your contact by asking for a job or by making time-consuming requests.
   c. Get to the point and set clear expectations. Indicate that you are requesting assistance to learn more about an occupation or organization and to get advice on your career plans or job search.
   d. Close your letter by requesting an appointment and indicating that you will call to see if a convenient time can be arranged. Do not include your resume; take it with you to the meeting.

4. Make the follow-up call to your contact and restate your request for information. Ask for an appointment.

5. Prepare for your meeting by learning about the organization and its industry and by developing a list of specific questions you want to ask. Your questions might focus on an overview of the work, key qualifications required, typical work setting, industry trends, employment outlook, new developments in the field, how to find employment, where the work is done locally, which employers are hiring, and additional sources of information to aid you.

6. Conduct the information interview. Arrive on time, dress appropriately, introduce yourself to the receptionist and state your purpose. In conducting information interviews, be organized, respect the person's time, and seek to accomplish these objectives:
   a. Establish rapport with your contact to enhance communication. Thank your contact for meeting with you and restate your purpose. Give a brief overview of your current career situation and indicate the kind of information you seek.
   b. Ask open-ended questions to obtain current and specific information on occupation(s), the employment

outlook, and potential job leads. Listen carefully and take brief notes on important points.

   c. Ask for advice on your career plans, your job search strategy, and your resume to help refine your approach.

   d. At the end of the meeting, request referrals to others who can assist you much like your contact person did.

   e. If job hunting, politely ask to be remembered for future reference by leaving a copy of your resume and by requesting that your contact person inform others of your availability if appropriate.

7. Send your contact person a thank you note to show appreciation for his or her assistance. This is an often overlooked courtesy. Thanking your contact persons for their time and information will help them think favorably of you and remember you should they learn of an appropriate opportunity.

8. Follow-up on all job leads which interest you and all referrals to other contact persons.

9. Keep your contacts informed of your progress periodically and be sure to let them know the outcome of your career plans and/or job search.

If you follow these steps and repeat the informational interviewing process consistently, you will obtain high-quality information to aid your career planning and, when using this approach as part of a job search campaign, you will generate leads to job opportunities.

## Summary Points

Informational interviewing works because it is a practical application of the concept of social networks—that entire societies are loosely linked and woven together by relationships based on families, friendships, occupations, and mutual interests. While you might hesitate to contact persons you know only vaguely or not at all, research suggests that you may achieve better results by contacting acquaintances and strangers because these persons have access to information and other people not known in your immediate network of family and friends. As it has become more widely known and practiced, information interviewing has been misused by some job seekers. As a result, you may find some contacts reluctant to meet with you. For informational interviewing to be an effective career planning and job finding method for you, keep these points in mind:

1. Be sincerely interested in meeting your contact person and in hearing his or her advice.

2. Always be honest and ethical in how you use this skill.

3. Remember that your contact person is doing you a favor. Be considerate of his or her time and comments.

*See also* Job Search; Mentoring; Networking.

## Bibliography

Krannich, R., & Krannich, C. (1989). *Network your way to job and career success: Your complete guide to creating new opportunities*. Manassas, VA: Impact Publications.

—WILLIAM J. BANIS

# INTERESTS

Interests have been defined (Kuder, 1977) as one's preferences among various activities. The activities may be school subjects, leisure activities, or occupations, almost anything that people do. Preferences may be expressed as whether one likes, is indifferent to, or dislikes any activity, or whether any activity is more or less desirable than another. Interests are also expressed as occupational choices. Holland (1985) and others believe that interests are part of, and correspond to, the attitudes and behaviors that constitute personality.

Interests tend to develop into patterns. That is, people's preferences usually crystallize around activities that are similar. In this way, instead of saying that a person likes reading science books, performing chemistry experiments, and trying out different designs of model airplane wings, it is possible to say that the person has scientific interests.

How patterns of interests develop is not fully understood. There is evidence that interests are in part inherited; twins tend to have more similar interest patterns than unrelated people. However, experiments have shown that people tend to like tasks and activities that they do successfully more than those at which they fail. There are gender differences in interests, which cannot be attributed reliably to either genetics or early socialization. Women tend to have stronger interests in the arts, helping others, and business detail, while men tend to be more strongly attracted to outdoor and mechanical activities, science, and business administration.

**The Structure of Interests.** How many kinds of interests are there? Psychologists have clustered similar interests together in order to reduce them to a structure that may be more easily measured and grasped by the lay person. Holland's (1985) work suggests that there are six types of interests: Realistic, Investigative, Artistic, Social, Enterprising, and Conventional. Kuder (1977) identifies 10 which break down Holland's types into finer groups: Outdoor, Mechanical, Computational, Scientific, Social Service, Persuasive, Literary, Art, Music, and Clerical (see **Occupational Groups**).

## Relationship to Work

Interests are generally assumed to determine, at least in part, a person's satisfaction with his or her occupation or job. Most individuals say that they want work that satisfies their interests. Yet, people whose interests are congruent with those of their occupations do not consistently report higher satisfaction. This is probably because other factors, such as working conditions, pay level, and quality of supervision influence reported job satisfaction too. Interests may also be thought of as motivating factors. Dawis & Lofquist (1984) have shown that interests contribute to job performance and success, although not as much as do knowledge, skills, and abilities.

## Application

You may believe that you have a good grasp of your interests and preferences. However, an unexpected success or failure in some task may suggest that you re-evaluate your beliefs about your interests. Usually this is best done by taking an interest inventory—that is, by responding with your likes and dislikes or preferences to a carefully selected list of activities. An interest inventory can tell you which interest areas are stronger and which are weaker. Often these inventories are accompanied by books listing occupations, college majors, or leisure activities that potentially satisfy different interest patterns. Some inventories will tell you what occupations have interest patterns that are similar to yours. These inventories usually have been given to several hundred people in a number of occupations, and their interests recorded in a computer memory for comparison with your preferences. It is very useful to know that you have interests typical of people in certain occupations.

Campbell (1971) suggests that your interests attain a stable pattern around age 21. Occupational choices made at that age are more stable than those made in the teen-aged years. And, it is known that many people keep their occupational interests an entire lifetime. Nevertheless, you may realize that your interests are changing, possibly because you have had exposure to activities that you never had previously, or simply because you have grown tired of certain activities.

There are interest areas, outdoor and arts especially, in which there tend to be more people interested than there are jobs. You may choose to pursue such interests as avocations and hobbies rather than as a career. Similarly,

clerical jobs, of which there are plenty, tend to be low paid, and you may decide to find your career in another field, reserving your clerical interests for keeping careful personal financial records or making collections of things.

How can you know your interests more certainly? There are a number of well-made interest inventories you may take: *The Kuder Occupational Interest Survey, The Strong Interest Inventory,* and *The Vocational Preference Inventory* are a few. These cannot be bought in a bookstore or from a mail-order catalog; you will need to find a vocational counselor or a college or university counseling center, where you will be able to have your results explained to you. Short interest "quizzes" that appear in popular books on job finding are generally less reliable, and should not be depended upon.

After completing an inventory, you will receive a report of scores, or an interest profile. Many profiles will suggest how much you may depend on your results, give the relative strengths of your interests in different fields, and then show which occupations have interests most similar to yours. Because of gender differences in interest patterns, the profile may give results compared to both males and females. Workbooks made to accompany many interest inventories, such as Brew's (1989), may help you integrate your interest inventory results into your future plans.

You may also have your interests assessed by the use of a card sort. One constructed by Jones (1981), *Occ-U-Sort,* is a good example. In this method, you sort a deck of cards representing a wide range of activities into "like," "indifferent," and "dislike" categories. You then may be asked to separate each category into groups of related activities, which can reveal how you personally organize your interests and suggest underlying reasons for your preferences.

Interests are important in making plans for occupations and other choices, but you should also be sure to consider your skills and abilities, values or personality style, and situational factors, such as family considerations.

*See also* Abilities; Career Counseling; Career Tests and Inventories; Choosing an Occupation; Occupational Groups; Skills; Work Values.

## Bibliography

Brew, S. (1989). *Career development guide for use with the Strong Interest Inventory.* Stanford, CA: Consulting Psychologists Press.
Campbell, D. P. (1971). *Handbook for the Strong Vocational Interest Blank.* Stanford, CA: Stanford University Press.
Dawis, R., & Lofquist, L. (1984). *A psychological theory of work adjustment.* Minneapolis: University of Minnesota Press.
Holland, J. L. (1985). *Making vocational choices: A theory of vocational personalities and work environments.* 2nd ed. Englewood Cliffs, NJ: Prentice-Hall. Holland explains his theory

of vocational behavior, including his six vocational personalities, which many psychologists consider to be six major interest areas.

Jones, L.K. (1981). *Occ-U-Sort*. Monterey, CA: CTB/Macmillan/McGraw-Hill.

Kuder, F. (1977). *Activity interests and occupational choice*. Chicago: Science Research Associates. A fundamental book for understanding how the 10-area interest structure was developed.

Strong, E. K. (1943). *The vocational interests of men and women*. Stanford, CA: Stanford University Press. This classic reports Strong's many years of investigation of interests, research which provides the basis of our present understanding of interests and their measurement.

—DONALD G. ZYTOWSKI

# INTERNSHIPS

Internships are work-related experiences which allow the intern to learn about a job or career by making a productive contribution to a sponsoring organization. Internships can be paid or nonpaid, part-time or full-time, and long or short in duration. Many internships are a formal part of an educational program, while others are completely independent of schools or colleges. Internship sponsors may be businesses, government agencies, or nonprofit organizations.

Internships are different from other work experiences since there is a shared understanding between an intern sponsor and the intern about the importance of learning as well as productivity through the experience.

## Relationship to Work

Internships provide exceptional career exploration opportunities. Through an internship a person can compare the demands of a profession with his or her own skills, values, and interests. People often describe their careers as a series of experiments with a variety of work responsibilities and organizations. When someone experiences satisfaction and is effective in a job, he or she tends to seek additional, related opportunities in the future. When less success is encountered, he or she will often avoid similar tasks in the future. Internships provide the opportunity to develop the skills and knowledge needed to be effective in a specific profession. Interns experience the relationship between theory and practice. They also build an understanding of what other experiences might add to their professional capabilities. Further, they can help one develop invaluable contacts for a job search.

Internships are very important to employers as they evaluate candidates in the hiring process for permanent employment. Prospective employers have had an opportunity to observe candidates "at work" and such experiences can provide impressive evidence of one's capabilities. In a recent survey of the graduates from the University of Rochester, work-related experience was cited most often as an important factor in an employer's hiring decision. It was cited twice as often as the next most frequently mentioned factor, written communication.

## Application

As you plan your internship, you must clearly define your expectations. Do you expect to work full-time or part-time? How important is earning money? Will the internship be part of a formal educational program? When would you like the internship?

An internship provides both a learning experience and an opportunity to serve a particular community, customer, or need. Four questions are important in organizing your search:

1. *What do I want to learn through this experience*? Before you investigate a work site, take a moment to decide what skills you might use in the internship (see **Skills**). Are there others you would like to develop? You may find it helpful to write down your answers so you can refer to them later. Once you begin thinking about who you are and what you have to offer, you are beginning to develop the criteria for selecting a work site.

   Work experiences also provide an excellent opportunity for you to apply theory to solving actual problems. Developing an understanding of both the relevance and the limitations of formal education is often a major dimension of what you learn in an internship. Carefully consider the connections between your school experience and possible work sites as you organize your search.

2. *What do I want to do*? Before you contact potential sponsors, develop a summary of the tasks, responsibilities, and types of projects that interest you. Record your expectations so you can refer to them later. Keep in mind that they should be broad and flexible and relate to the learning objectives you have defined.

3. *Do I want to connect the internship with a formal educational program*? Many schools encourage students to include one or more internships in their curriculum enabling them to learn more from the experience(s) they select. If you are enrolled in a school, you may want to explore how an internship might be included in your educational program.

4. *Do I want to be paid*? Sponsors are sometimes able to pay an intern, and you should explore what pay is available if earning money is important to you. Excellent learning experiences are often available in nonprofit organizations and through part-time internships. You may find, however, that pay is limited for such internships.

Applying for any work experience is similar to a search for a permanent job (see **Job Search**). You should develop a targeted resume which will represent your strengths and sell you appropriately. You should also prepare a summary of your learning objectives for the internship. Contact potential sponsors by letter, telephone, or mail to explore the availability of internship experiences in their organization.

Some internship sponsors have well-developed programs. You will find a variety of opportunities in one or more of the many published internship directories. Other sponsors may be open to creating an internship in response to your interest. Remember to use the full range of contacts and services available to you as you organize your search. Don't forget to ask your friends, parents, relatives, and others for help in identifying and contacting potential internship sponsors (see **Networking**). Take the initiative whenever possible in following through on correspondence or other aspects of the search process. Planning is critical since negotiating the right experience may consume several months from the initial contact.

While there is nothing easy about a well-organized search for a good internship, you can be assured that your hard work will pay off as you work your way to a career.

**See also** Career Choices: Youth; Career Exploration; Cooperative Education; Job Search; Networking; Service-Learning; Skills; Volunteer Work.

## Bibliography

Migliore, Sally A.(Ed.) (1989). *The national directory of internships.* Raleigh, NC: The National Society for Internships and Experiential Education. This comprehensive directory includes detailed descriptions of over 26,000 internship opportunities suitable for all ages and levels of experience. This resource includes indexes for particular areas of career interest, for specific types of organizations, as well as for geographic area. The cost is $22 plus $2 shipping and handling.

Stanton, Timothy K., & Ali, Kami. (1987). *The experienced hand: A student manual for making the most of an internship.* Raleigh, NC: The National Society for Internships and Experiential Education. This companion to the *National Directory* outlines 10 steps for arranging a satisfactory internship, and provides advice on how to make an internship the most satisfying experience possible. The cost is $12.95 plus $2 shipping and handling.

## For Further Information

Many public libraries and career counseling centers have copies of the above publications available for your use. You may get one for yourself by contacting the National Society for Internships and Experiential Education, 3509 Haworth Drive, Suite 207, Raleigh, NC 27609.

—JIM CASE

# J

## JET LAG

Jet lag is a colloquialism which refers to a syndrome associated with air travel across multiple time zones. The syndrome may include both psychological effects and physiological changes. The most obvious symptoms of jet lag are trouble falling asleep or staying asleep throughout the night in the new location and periods of severe drowsiness at inappropriate times during the day. Less obvious effects include gastrointestinal problems, changes in appetite, feelings of being in a daze or fog, and impairment of the ability to think clearly, solve problems effectively, react quickly, and form new memories. The symptoms are most severe one to three days after arrival. The possible adverse effects of changing time zones rapidly were first described in 1931 by pilot Wiley Post, who set a world record for a solo flight around the world.

Jet lag occurs because the body clock is synchronized to the home time zone and takes a while to reset itself to the new local time. Some of the symptoms of jet lag are related to the loss of sleep which occurs because the natural sleep rhythm is altered. The body clock gradually shifts to the new local time because of the influence of "zeitgebers"—time cue givers—which include the rising and setting of the sun, meal times, and other environmental factors. Certain body rhythms adapt more quickly than others, so there is a period of adjustment in which the harmony of the various physiological rhythms is temporarily disrupted.

Jet lag may be a problem even after time changes of only three hours; however, it is most evident when the time shifts are 6 to 9 hours from home time. Research has shown that jet lag is more severe when the flight goes from west to east; it is generally easier to adapt when travel is in the westward direction, due, in part, to the fact that it is easier for the body clock to adjust to a lengthening of the day, which occurs in westward flight.

## Relationship to Work

Frequently, workers are required to travel by air to new work locations and conduct important business soon after arriving. The individual may not be adequately alert to do the job well due to jet lag. The passenger aboard the aircraft has the opportunity to obtain some rest enroute. However, some workers who experience jet lag have the added responsibility of being required to perform their jobs effectively aboard the aircraft. For pilots who fly long haul flights across many time zones, jet lag is an occupational problem. Pilots complain that they are unable to obtain good sleep in hotels on layovers. Because they are constantly changing time zones, pilots and other airline crew members find that they might not adjust to any time zone completely and, consequently, they have many complaints about their sleep and alertness. Jet lag is also a consideration for the military, which may need to move large numbers of troops by air to new locations and have them ready to fight immediately after arrival. In critical combat situations, the degrading effect of jet lag on operational readiness is a major concern to military planners. In many ways, shift workers are in a constant jet lag-type situation, since, on the night shift, they are required to work when their body clock is telling them it is time to sleep. Shift workers also have problems obtaining adequate sleep during the day.

## Application

When planning work after flying across three or more time zones, it is important to realize that jet lag is a performance issue. The worker can avoid or lessen the jet lag effects by following these suggestions:

1.  On short trips, you can remain on home time. Keep your watch set to your home time zone, go to bed, get up, and eat meals according to home time. Most importantly, schedule important meetings or other business according to what time would be best for you, based on your home time clock.

2. On longer trips or when you cannot schedule the work time to your convenience, you may begin to change your body clock before you travel. Set your watch to your destination time two days ahead of travel. Begin to conduct your daily schedule according to the destination time.

3. Obtain adequate sleep prior to travel, since sleep deprivation will magnify the jet lag effect.

4. En route, try to sleep aboard the aircraft. Avoid eating too much and drink plenty of water to avoid dehydration. Do not drink alchoholic and caffeinated beverages which also cause dehydration.

5. You may wish to ask your medical doctor to prescribe a short-acting sleeping pill for use the first few nights after your arrival to help you go to sleep.

*See also* Shift Work; Stress; Work Hazards: Psychosocial.

## Bibliography

Ehret C. F., & Scanlon, L. W. (1983). *Overcoming jet lag.* New York: Berkley Books. This book, one of few on the subject, presents self-help techniques and emphasizes a dietary approach.

Fuller, C. A., Sulzman, F. M., & Moore-Ede, M. C. (1981). Shift work and the jet-lag syndrome: conflicts between environmental and body time. In L. C. Johnson, D. I. Tepas, W. P. Colquhoun, & M. J. Colligan (Eds.), *The twenty-four hour workday: Proceedings of a symposium on variations in work-sleep schedule* (pp. 305–20). Cincinnati: National Institute for Occupational Safety and Health, Pub. No. 81–127. This collection of reports provides an excellent overview of the current knowledge from research in the area of jet lag and circadian rhythms.

Klein, K. E., Wegmann, H. M., Athanassenas, G., Hohlweck, H., & Kuklinski, P. (1976). Air operations and circadian performance rhythms. *Aviation, Space, and Environmental Medicine* 47: 221–30. This paper is one of the important classic papers in the area written by internationally known experts from the West German DFVLR, an organization similar to NASA.

Post, W., & Gatty, H. (1931). *Around the world in eight days.* London, England: John Hamilton, Ltd. This first writing about jet lag is an excellent historical presentation.

Spinweber, C. L., Webb, S. C., & Gillin, L. C. (1986). *Jet lag in military operations; field trial of l-tryptophan in reducing sleep-loss effects.* Naval Health Research Center Report No. 86-15. This research article on a major field study of jet lag in U.S. marines is easily read and provides a good introduction to the research issues in the area. Copies available on request from the Naval Health Research Center, P.O. Box 85122, San Diego, CA 92138-9174.

—CHERYL L. SPINWEBER

## JOB CHANGING

Job changing refers to a voluntary move from one occupation to another in the same or different work environments. This could include moving from one job to a second with a different set of tasks within the same organization, changing from one job to a similar position in a different work environment, shifting to an entirely different kind of work, becoming self-employed, or moving from homemaking to the marketplace or vice versa.

### Relationship to Career Development

There is disagreement regarding the frequency of job changes. For example, the U.S. Bureau of the Census suggests that approximately 10% of employed persons change jobs in one year and that this mobility rate has remained stable over the last 20 years (Markey & Parks, 1989). On the other hand, other researchers (Hoyt, 1987; Kanchier, 1988) report that job changing is increasing due to technological and economic changes and accompanying reorganization, cutbacks, mergers, and acquisitions. The differences in these interpretations seem to be due to the varied definitions given job change.

Most writers agree that 60% of the job moves occur within the same occupational category representing "in-career" rather than "new career" movements. Another 20% of the changes are between closely related fields such as sales and management. The remaining 20% of the moves are to entirely different fields. About 8% of the foregoing changers become self-employed. Most individuals who make shifts, regardless of direction, believe their accumulated experience and training have value.

The majority of changers are under age 45 and have higher levels of education than those who don't move. Unmarried workers have higher mobility rates than married workers but there is no difference in the movement rates of men and women.

Factors which facilitate job change include: (a) the desire to derive more meaning from work and to define success personally; (b) dissatisfaction with authoritarian, impersonal work environments and decreased loyalty to employers; (c) more flexible attitudes toward personal liberation and occupational change, and the perception that job moves are opportunities to develop personally and professionally; (d) adults' awareness that they will continue to grow and develop throughout their long lives, making the concept of one life-long occupation obsolete; and (e) the desire of partners to help one another change by sharing obligations.

Forces which discourage job change include: (a) social institutions which encourage the maintenance of one occupation throughout life; (b) "golden fetters" such as pension plans and seniority which tie many adults to organizations; (c) individual differences in personal characteristics and family obligations; (d) lack of financial resources; and (e) the time and energy involved in decision making which provide stresses on personal, family, and work lives.

Adults change jobs for many reasons. Economic or externally motivated reasons include the desire to increase pay and security or to accumulate marketable skills. Noneconomic or growth-oriented reasons involve the desire to attain more challenge, autonomy, responsibility, and use of skills and ideas. The desire to grow personally and to acquire compatible corporate values are other motives.

Changers are willing to risk, to take charge of their careers, and to be flexible by keeping their options open. Growth-oriented changers, who see their positions as vehicles for self-expression and growth, measure success by internal standards and seek a sense of purpose from their work. Many believe that career advancement means growth of the whole person. In contrast, individuals who stay put prefer extrinsic work rewards such as security, money, status, and prestige. Family responsibilities, the economy, or other situational factors tend to control their choices.

There appears to be a relationship between occupational change and the transition period of changers' life cycles (age-30, midlife, age-50, and age-60). At these times adults tend to evaluate their career and life goals. Their self-appraisals are often intensified by crises such as job dissatisfaction, illness, marriage, or divorce.

These transition periods often parallel the occupational cycles of entry, mastery, and disengagement. Changers tend to move from their jobs after progressing through one occupational cycle (average 7.5 years) when they perceive they are no longer deriving desired growth rewards and can no longer identify with their positions or employers (Kanchier, 1988).

Most changers believe that they gain from their moves. Their attainments include greater autonomy, authority, challenge, and income. Opportunities for growth and innovation, enhanced self-esteem, a healthier life style, and more control over their destinies are other gains.

Nevertheless, the job change process involves tradeoffs. Losses or sacrifices are highly subjective, but changing is stressful and involves hard work. Temporary loss of self-esteem and personal and financial deprivation may be other tradeoffs.

The barriers to change are often fear of failure or success; fear of loss of a secure income, pension, or other benefits; or guilt that one won't meet family or other responsibilities. Not knowing where to start one's job search or how to make decisions are other obstacles.

## Application

Only you can make the decision to change jobs or stay put. You must feel comfortable being yourself and doing what is best for you. Keep in mind, however, that change is a constant today. To prevail in uncertain times requires managing your own career by being flexible, open to change, and keeping your options open.

To determine if you are ready for a job change, work through the first steps of the following decision-making process.

1.  Tune into your feelings and listen to the messages your body and mind may be sending you. "I can hardly wait until Friday!" is a message. If you are unhappy, admit it.
2.  Define the problem. Ask yourself what you like and dislike about your job, and whether your position can help you attain your desired career goal? Determine whether or not you are doing your best work, whether your job is damaging your self-confidence and health, or whether the bad points you listed about your job can be resolved? Also discover whether non-job factors (e.g., relationships, health) are influencing your work performance and attitudes.

    Identify any barriers that may be blocking you from leaving an unsatisfying position. Change means letting go of the familiar and moving to something new and untried. Then admit your problem and decide to either change or not.

    The decision to change can cause mixed feelings of anxiety, depression, and guilt, as well as excitement of trying something new. If you decide to change, work through the remaining decision-making steps. Planning can improve the efficiency and effectiveness of job change as well as reduce risk.
3.  Take charge by setting and recording tentative goals. Ask yourself what you always dreamed of becoming and what your major life purpose is. Fantasize. Reflect on your tentative goals.
4.  Explore by identifying your needs, interests, skills, and other characteristics. A good counselor, career workshop, or book can help you. Next, match your personal qualities to occupational options.

    Investigate at least 10 options. Information about occupations may be obtained from books and directories, job tryouts, interviews, contact networks, and counselors. Restructuring your present job or looking for another position in your company are other alternatives.

5. Prioritize your options mathematically by evaluating each alternative with job criteria that are important to you (e.g., income, challenge). Then, listen to your feelings. If an option with fewer points feels good, go with your feelings. Have a second and third choice.

6. Take action by acquiring appropriate job search or business planning skills. Target your job search by defining three or more targets to sell yourself to different markets. Broaden your contacts by volunteering for committees, soliciting the assistance of colleagues and superiors, reading magazines and newsletters, and attending meetings, workshops, and conferences.

   Prepare one resume to match each job target using guides available at libraries and bookstores. Personally contact business or professional people who are in positions to help you. Send out letters, describing what you can offer, to people who are in positions to hire you. Answer help wanted advertisements. Follow contacts up with phone calls requesting interviews. Accentuate the positive and persevere. Prepare for interviews by researching the organization and knowing how your background and experience can contribute to the company.

7. Thoroughly evaluate each offer using your intellect and intuition. Don't grab the first job that comes along, take a job you dislike, or work for someone you don't respect.

8. Make a commitment by accepting the job that feels best.

9. Evaluate your decision by asking yourself whether your work needs are being met, what you gained from the move, and how you feel about yourself.

A reputable professional career counselor can help you with the transition. Free or inexpensive counseling is available at colleges and universities, state employment agencies, continuing education centers, religious institutions, and private agencies such as job clubs and YWCA and YMHA. Many of these organizations and professionals also offer career planning workshops.

Learning to risk will enable you to develop the courage to be open to new experiences. Look at failure as the beginning of growth and job change as a learning experience. View job change as reversible by building in fail-safe and retreat positions as well as contingency plans. Have positive expectations, investigate all choices, then persevere and act decisively.

*See also* Career Changes at Midlife; Career Counseling; Career Plateauing; Choosing an Occupation; Decision Making; Managing Transitions; Recruitment; Self-Employment; Women: Reentry into the Workplace.

## Bibliography

Bolles, R. N. (1990). *What color is your parachute?: A practical guide for job hunters and career changers.* Berkeley, CA: Ten Speed Press. Updated annually and recommended by many career counselors, it has sound, practical, detailed advice for job changers and offers a wealth of additional sources.

Hoyt, Kenneth. (1987). The impact of technology on occupational change: Implications for career guidance. *The Career Development Quarterly,* 35: 269–78.

Kanchier, Carole (1988). *Questers—Dare to change your job—And your life.* New York: Master Media. Explains emotions involved in decision making and the relationship between job satisfaction and personality development throughout life's transitions by using questionnaires, guidelines, and case studies.

Markey, James, & Parks, William. (1989). Occupational change: Pursuing a different kind of work. *Monthly Labor Review, 112,* 3–12.

Rust, H. L. (1979). *Jobsearch: The complete manual for jobseekers.* New York: AMACOM.

Scher, Barbara, & Gottlieb, Annie (1986). *Wishcraft: How to get what you really want.* New York: Ballantine. Helps readers explore their fantasies and dreams and channel their energy into creating a more fulfilling life/career.

—CAROLE KANCHIER

## JOB CLUBS

Job clubs are multifaceted, group-based job hunting programs designed to train and motivate clients to become proficient job hunters. The job club model incorporates learning, self-help, and support group principles. The effectiveness of job clubs in helping people, particularly hard-to-place populations, find jobs has been demonstrated in a variety of well controlled research studies.

### Relationship to Job Hunting

The job club program is based on the application of applied behavioral methods to the job hunting process. Simply stated, this methodology uses proven behavioral and psychological principles and techniques to understand and control behavior—in this case job hunting behavior.

At one level the job club can be best understood as a set of general principles or beliefs which constitute the job club philosophy. These principles include individual responsibility, group support, positive encouragement, directive counseling, full-time activity, and continued assistance.

**Individual Responsibility.** Similar to self-help programs, the job club emphasizes individual responsibility. This approach seems well suited to the job hunting role because the hidden job market and networking are best tapped by the individual job hunter (see **Networking**).

**Group Support.** While the individual must take responsibility for his or her own job search, the group is considered a valuable source of job finding information, encouragement, and assistance. Attempts are made to activate and capitalize on these effects in the job club.

**Positive Approach.** Positive reinforcement (encouragement of and reward for desired behaviors) is at the heart of any behavioral method. This orientation is central to the job club approach.

**Directive Counseling.** While the job club leaders also provide support and encouragement, they assume very directive roles in guiding and focusing the client's job hunting activities.

**Full-Time Activity.** Job hunting is viewed as an activity which should be pursued as a full-time job. Participants in most job clubs are engaged in training or actual job hunting all day, five days a week.

**Continued Assistance.** Job clubs are ongoing, open-ended programs; participants continue to attend job club meetings until they find a job.

On another level the job club can be best understood as a complex intervention package. Since job hunting performance depends on so many factors, the typical job club program utilizes a variety of behavioral or psychological components and features. Each component or feature is intended to directly or indirectly affect job hunting performance.

**Instruction.**

1. *Job Hunting Knowledge.* Knowledge about what to do and how to carry out one's job search is critical to job hunting success. Job club programs typically provide brief instruction, written materials, including "how to" guides and scripts on a variety of topics, including:

   a. *Sources of Job Leads.* A great deal of time is usually devoted to this topic. Instruction emphasizes the value of informal sources of leads like one's personal network and how to find unpublicized jobs through "cold calls" to employers.

   b. *Labor Market Information.* Every local job market differs in various respects. Job club participants are given information about specific local employers, skills in demand, etc. (see **Occupational Information**).

   c. *Self-Presentation.* Instruction and assistance are given on how to stress and emphasize personal skills and attributes through resumes, applications, interviews,

and during other less formal interactions with employers or sources of job leads.

2. *Job Hunting Skills.* Successful job hunting requires more than information and knowledge, it requires mastery and performance of various skills. A great deal of job club time is spent on practicing and engaging in actual job hunting activity (e.g., identifying leads, calling prospective employers, etc.). Job clubs utilize modeling, role playing, and feedback, and practice to insure participants master and perform various skills including:

   a. *Interviewing.* Instruction emphasizes how to make a favorable impression during an interview (see **Job Interviewing**).

   b. *Phone Contacts.* The telephone, if used skillfully, is viewed as a useful and important vehicle for identifying job leads and securing interviews.

**Motivation.**

Like any learning task, motivation is essential to job hunting competence. However, motivation takes on a particular importance because a job hunt may take weeks or even months. Thus, success often depends upon persistent performance of job hunting activities. Programmatic and group mechanisms are used to motivate clients to pursue and maintain effective job hunting efforts.

1. *Programmatic Mechanisms.* As mentioned above, the job club counselor makes liberal use of behavioral principles like reinforcement, goal setting, etc. These methods motivate and maintain various behaviors. For instance, in many job clubs clients set daily job seeking goals. This helps focus their activities and serves as a means of rewarding clients for active, persistent job hunting.

2. *Group Mechanisms.* The group is a primary source of motivation in the job club. Encouragement and support from fellow job seekers is encouraged and facilitated through various practices and procedures, including a "buddy" system among job club participants. Many job clubs also use the success of job club "graduates" to help motivate their clients. Clients are also given advice and help in mobilizing their personal networks.

**Institutional Support.**

Hard-to-place populations often face additional obstacles to employment because they lack the money or resources to mount an effective job hunt. Job clubs offer concrete assistance in the form of telephone banks, secretarial support, transportation assistance, and referral to other agencies to help overcome these obstacles.

In summary, the job club can be seen as a set of principles which makes up the job club "philosophy" and a complex behavioral intervention package. Each program feature has been designed to enhance job hunting competence and result in placement success.

## Application

The job club model represents an attempt to construct a comprehensive and scientifically grounded program to aid job hunting. Since research has consistently proven the job club to be more effective than traditional job placement strategies, these efforts appear to have been successful (Braddy & Gray, 1987).

Regrettably, implementation of a complex program like the job club is likely to vary considerably from one community to another and from one agency to another. While some variation is to be expected, and may represent necessary adaptation to local circumstances, some so-called job clubs may lack the very features which make the program successful. What feature should you look for if you're considering joining a job club? It is recommended you weigh the following considerations very heavily when you select a program:

- *Skills Orientation.* Many so-called job clubs amount to nothing more than job hunting courses which provide information but no skills. A job club should provide opportunities to both practice and carry out job hunting skills on-site and with counselor and group feedback.

- *Continued Assistance.* Many job hunting programs offer a limited number of classes on various job seeking issues and skills. While this kind of program is useful, when the last class ends participants are usually on their own. Such programs fail to provide the important opportunity to continue to practice and carry out a job hunt and receive guidance and feedback until a job is found.

- *Group Support.* While most job hunting programs use a group format, some fail to capitalize on the group's potential to assist and support fellow members. The support system deliberately fostered through various job club procedures and practices may be the critical ingredient which sets the job club apart from other job search programs.

- *Special Populations.* Many job clubs are open to anyone who wants help in finding a job. While these programs are fine for most people, certain populations face unique problems securing employment.

Some job clubs specialize in the needs of special populations, including the handicapped, older workers, welfare clients, juveniles, etc. These programs are probably better able to tailor their procedures and support systems to the unique circumstances of these individuals.

*See also* Job Interviewing; Job Search; Networking; Occupational/Information.

## Bibliography

Azrin, N.H., & Besalel, B.A. (1981). *Job club counselors manual.* Baltimore: University Park Press. A how-to book, including forms and handouts and charts, designed for use by job club counselors.

Azrin, N.H., & Besalel, B.A. (1982). *Finding a job.* Berkeley, CA: Ten Speed Press. Designed for use by the individual who can't attend or find a job club. Includes information provided in job club meetings.

Braddy, B.A., & Gray, D.O. (1987). Employment services for older job seekers: A comparison of two client centered approaches. *The Gerontologist,* 27: 565–68.

Wegman, R., Chapman R., & Johnson M. (1989). *Work in the new economy.* Indianapolis: JIST Works. Provides a broad coverage of changes which will influence an individual's ability to find a job. Includes a chapter that reviews and compares various job search assistance programs including the job club.

—DENIS O. GRAY

# JOB DESCRIPTION

A written definition of a specific job within an organization is a job description. It places the job in the company hierarchy and delineates the tasks and responsibilities of the position. The information needed to write a job description is usually collected by conducting a job analysis.

Job analysis data may be gathered from questionnaires, interviews, and/or on-site observations. The job analyst collects information about the job context and content (duties, performance criteria, organization level, working conditions, responsibility, etc.); worker characteristics (skills, professional/technical knowledge, experience, etc.); and interpersonal relationships (internal and external).

Once the analysis is completed, the results are documented in a job description. There is no one format for job descriptions, but an organization should choose one format, or, at most, one format for exempt personnel and another for non-exempt. If the format is not consistent, the job descriptions will not be useful to the organization.

No matter what format is used, a job description must clearly identify the job and the properties that differentiate it from others in the organization. The first section of the job description shows the name or title of the job and the department or work site. It may also include the wage level, reporting relationships, or number of people in this position. For example, there would be only one bank president, but there could be five junior tellers all performing the same task.

The second part of a job description summarizes the purpose of the job and the way that it fits into the overall organization. End results (the products or services) expected from the job and the major responsibilities are included in this section.

The actual duties, techniques, guidelines, and controls are described in the third section. This section should give a good idea of what the person holding the job does on a daily or weekly basis.

## Relationship to Work

Job descriptions have several uses. Organizations can not hire qualified individuals for a job if they do not know what the position entails. The personnel/human resources department uses the job description to develop a worker (job) specification for each opening. This document lists the knowledge, skills, abilities, and other human characteristics that a person should possess in order to be successful in that one position. Recruiting sources are chosen and newspaper ads written based on the requirements of the job.

Job descriptions allow companies to evaluate jobs for compensation (pay) purposes. They show managers how one job differs from another and the level of difficulty and responsibility for each job.

Performance appraisal is often based on the job description. The job holder's actual performance is measured against the end results and criteria defined in the job description. Job descriptions usually are provided to new employees upon hire or during the orientation process. This written documentation helps employees understand what is expected of them and where they fit in the organization.

Organizations have also found that well-prepared job descriptions and analyses may reduce their exposure to lawsuits claiming discriminatory or unfair practices. Employers need to have accurate and up-to-date job descriptions, and they need to develop their worker specifications from actual job requirements. Organizations must be able to prove that selection criteria that result in discrimination (intentional or unintentional) are bona fide occupational criteria (BFOQ) or validly related to job performance. Unwritten descriptions or irrelevant criteria will not stand up in court.

## Application

If you are considering applying for a particular job, you can review the job description for it and decide whether you are qualified or interested in it. Many organizations post or publicize job descriptions for open positions. Often, this is done within the firm first so that current employees can be considered before outsiders are interviewed.

You or your employer may also use job descriptions as an educational guide. If you wish to be promoted or transferred to another department, you can read the job description to determine the skills and education that you must acquire to be eligible for consideration. Training programs based on promotional opportunities and organizational needs are offered by some organizations. Employees who want to progress can take advantage of these offerings.

If you are applying for a job, it is important that you understand all of its requirements before accepting an offer of employment. You may want to review the job description and ask if there are any duties not shown.

You should go over your job description with your manager or supervisor so that you both agree on the duties of the job. In this way you will clearly understand what is expected of you, and it will minimize the risk of misunderstanding when a performance appraisal is done.

If your job duties change due to company reorganization, technological innovation, or any other cause, your job description should also change. It is important to keep the job description up-to-date, because changed duties may also mean increased pay and promotional opportunities.

*See also* Performance Appraisal.

## Bibliography

Ghorpade, J. (1988). *Job Analysis: A handbook for the human resources director.* Englewood Cliffs, NJ: Prentice-Hall. See Chapter 4, pp. 93–134.

—NANCY R. RUSSELL

# JOB HUNTING: INTERNATIONAL

International jobs for U.S. citizens generally fall into four categories: working in the U.S. with international clients for U.S. firms; working for U.S. firms outside the U.S.; working for internationally owned firms in the U.S.; working for international firms outside the U.S.

## What Employers Seek

There are similarities in what most internationally oriented firms are seeking in employees:

1. Strong technical skills relevant to their particular industry (e.g., accounting, finance, marketing, operations).
2. Cultural fluency, the ability to work with and deal sensitively with the culture, background, and approaches of clients, suppliers, and in-country colleagues. In some cases cultural fluency extends to language fluency.
3. Acquaintance with the language of countries of economic interest is a strong foundation for the international job search; however, it does not take the place of a sophisticated understanding of industries and job functions.
4. Flexibility and adaptability.

## The Decision to Pursue an International Career

A decision to pursue an international career will have an impact on the type of training, educational background, study, and travel of the serious job seeker. Many people pursue an internationally oriented job after significant experience in a particular industry or function.

Internationally oriented jobs often require expatriation, significant amounts of travel, and multiple rotating assignments. This continuing adaptability and flexibility is required not only on the part of the employee but on the part of the family as well.

In the case of expatriation, the employee often incurs costs of currency translation, loss of contact with headquarters corporate issues, difficulties in making dependent educational arrangements, and frustrations with managing in a local context.

The substantial benefits include a broader view of an organization's operations, typically a new view of world events, significant opportunities to absorb and understand a different culture, and often tremendous opportunities for travel.

## Career Options

International career options are many and varied. *Private Sector* options include banking, consulting, professional services (accounting, advertising, law), media, and manufactured goods (consumer, electronic, commercial, industrial). *Public Sector/Nonprofit* options include the U.S. government through such agencies as the Department of State, AID, USIA, Overseas Private Investment Corporation, Export-Import Bank, International Trade Administration, Department of the Interior, and the Congressional Research Service; development assistance groups such as Bread for the World, Catholic Relief Services, and Lutheran World Relief; and nonprofits such as the Red Cross and CARE. *Supranational* options include the United Nations through such agencies as UNICEF, UNDP (Development Programme), UNFPA (Fund for Population Activities), UNEP (Energy Programme), UNESCO (Scientific, Cultural), UNITAR (Training and Research), WHO (World Health Organization, World Bank, International Monetary Fund, International Bank for Reconstruction and Development, and the World Court. *Research/Think Tanks* such as Brookings, Rand, Hudson, and the Center for Strategic and International Studies also offer options. *Education* options include teaching U.S. dependents and in private schools.

## Application

**Logistics.** As you pursue the international job hunt, you may find the time and distances involved somewhat daunting. The time for turnaround of correspondence, the location of interviews, translation of documents, and the simple logistics of arranging a mutually convenient time to connect for a telephone conversation can strain your patience and resources.

**Expectations.** Realistic expectations are key to a successful hunt. Be prepared to answer questions about the country or countries of interest to you. Do substantive research on the historical, cultural, economic, and political background of the areas of interest. Your preparation should allow you to exhibit your knowledge of countries, regions, the industry, and job functions in both your correspondence and face-to-face connections.

**Skills.** An appropriate skill set is critical to presenting a viable candidacy. Your skills in presentation, negotiation, analysis, and communication are important (see **Managerial Skills; Negotiating; Skills**). So is your understanding of the cultural context, global interconnections, and specifics about your potential employer's products, functions, and markets. The complexity of international operations demands that you display creativity, adaptability, and flexibility in your initial contact with an employer through the final interview.

The people component is critical in the international job search. Networking and maintaining personal correspondence and relationships is an important element in eventual success (see **Networking**). If you are dealing internationally, you are dealing with people of various ethnic, political, economic, and religious backgrounds. Your sensitivity to the varying needs of colleagues, clients, and customers will be a major factor in your job search and future international career success (see **Culturally Different: Working with**).

**Resources.** Several major resources will be helpful in establishing your potential target organizations. Standard and Poor's *Principal International Businesses* is arranged on a country basis and includes general information regarding types of products, employees, and sales. The typical entry also includes key officers of the organization. Use these entries to identify the specific operating officers appropriate for your areas of interest. If you are interested in marketing, write to the marketing, advertising, or market research names listed in the directory.

*The Directory of Corporate Affiliations (Who Owns Whom)* is helpful in identifying the "family tree" of an organization. The foreign country index identifies U.S. participation in international companies and international interests in U.S. companies. The major piece in this directory provides key company officers and brief descriptions of the business. If you have an interest in a particular country or area, this is a very valuable resource in identifying those organizations with a strong interest in the U.S. and most likely in U.S. personnel.

*The International 1000* gives one-page overviews on the largest industrial and financial organizations around the world. Two publications prepared by World Trade Academy Press identify firms of interest to international job seekers: *Directory of American Firms Operating in Foreign Countries* and *Directory of Foreign Firms Operating in the United States.*

These resources are a good place to start. You will want to pursue additional background information through periodical indexes identifying particular articles written about the organizations of interest. You may also want to look at additional financial information on companies. Some companies file financial information for U.S. financial markets; others include it in annual reports or fact sheets.

Working with international chambers of commerce and local consulates or embassies can be useful in identifying organizations involved in particular countries or regions. In many major metropolitan areas, a world affairs council or world trade association sponsors a variety of meetings and symposia providing an excellent opportunity to meet with professionals with similar interests.

*See also* Culturally Different: Working with; Job Interviewing; Job Search; Managerial Skills; Negotiating; Networking; Relocation; Resume; Skills; Women Who Live/Work Overseas.

## Bibliography

Cohen, Majorie A. (1990). *Work your way around the world.* New York: Council on International Educational Exchange. An annually updated source of information on work opportunities around the world. Includes information on seasonal and casual opportunities, appropriate governmental agencies, study options, and travel information.

Kocher, Eric. (1989). *International jobs.* New York: Addison-Wesley. Divides the international job market into major categories, including public and private sector employers. Entries provide significant information on specific employers. Substantial bibliography.

Powers, Linda. (1989). *Careers in international affairs.* Washington, DC: Georgetown University School of Foreign Service. Covers job market, U.S. government, international organizations, commercial banking, business, consulting, trade unions, research organizations, nonprofits, and teaching.

—JONATHAN W. PALMER

# JOB INTERVIEWING

The job interview has been appropriately referred to as "one of the most awkward social interactions." Many interviewees see the interview as an interrogation to be conducted by the interviewer. Viewed in its proper perspective, an interview is an exchange of information between members of the employing organization and the applicant. The individuals involved have goals which they expect to reach. The employer wants to attract, identify, hire, and retain the most qualified and competitive candidate who will "fit" into the work environment. The candidate needs to demonstrate that he or she has the characteristics suitable for the job. Furthermore, the interviewee wants to obtain information in order to decide whether or not this is an appropriate position and organization for which to work.

## Relationship to Work

An organization rarely fills a position without conducting interviews. While a resume may indicate applicant strengths, an employer almost always finds it necessary to meet candidates and discuss pertinent information before making a job offer. For example, a candidate could display excellent credentials on paper, but lack the human relations skills necessary for the position. A less qualified person, on the other hand, could have a more dynamic personality and thus receive the offer. These qualities can not be revealed on a resume alone.

## Application

It is natural for you, whether a first time interviewee or an experienced candidate, to experience anxiety during the interview process. A key to reducing your nervousness and increasing your potential for making a positive impression is *preparation*. (Medley, 1984; Powell, 1990). Knowing what an employer generally expects, being aware of the interview process, gathering related information, and rehearsing typically asked interview questions will not only dispel the mystery associated with the interview process but will increase your levels of confidence and control in the interview.

**Preparation and a Promotional Strategy.** LaFevre (1989), Vice President of Caradco, Inc., states that employers do not hire the best qualified (i.e., years of related experience, strong recommendations, educational background), but rather the "candidates who are the best at getting the job offers" (p. 48). In fact, the author finds that one of the biggest mistakes you can make is to grossly underestimate the competition. Often, candidates will approach the interview in a state of panic or with a casual attitude. Preparation is often the key to outshining others who are being considered for the position, since most candidates do an average to poor job of preparing.

In order to effectively promote yourself, you should apply the most basic marketing techniques: (a) know the characteristics of the product or service (your strengths and weaknesses); (b) know the marketplace needs (the job, the employing organization, and the interviewer); and (c) demonstrate how the product or service can meet the needs of the targeted clientele (develop a promotional strategy).

**Know Yourself.** Prior to entering an interview session, develop a strong sense of what you know and what you can do. Articulating your knowledge, skills, abilities, and preferences related to the position will give the interviewer exactly what he or she needs to know: What can this person do for our company? Employers need to be confident that you will be able to successfully perform the tasks required for the position, fit in with the corporate culture, and work well with other personnel in the office. For these reasons, it is critical to assess various aspects of your background.

Conduct a personal inventory to identify your skills and special knowledge areas developed or demonstrated within the whole realm of your experiences: paid or volunteer jobs (full- or part-time); internships; presentations, papers, or projects for work or a class; leadership positions held; involvement with clubs or professional organizations; participation on athletic teams; military experiences; achievements; and awards. Describe what you accomplished in terms of skills (i.e., calculated, planned, participated, arranged, etc.). In addition, keep in mind quantitative facts such as the number of people for whom you planned

a program, the amount of money in your budget, the increased percentage of yield due to your efforts, and so forth.

**Know the Employer.** Employers are generally impressed by enthusiastic, well-informed candidates. The more you know about the position, the company, its products, research, services, background, and the interviewer, the better you can formulate your answers to typically asked questions. For instance, you can reference facts and information while making inquiries and answering questions during the course of the interview.

Consider the following when conducting your pre-interview research:

1. Ask the company for a complete job description, the interview agenda, annual reports, in-house newsletters, and/or an organizational chart.
2. Refer to employer information in publications found in your local library, such as the Peterson's Guide series, the Dun and Bradstreet reference books, and Standard and Poor's register of corporations directors and executives.
3. Locate employees of the company (perhaps through neighbors, past employers, or friends) and discuss aspects of the organization that are important to you.
4. Read newspaper and journal articles about the organization and significant events, new projects and research findings, recent mergers, and so forth.

**Develop a Strategy.** Now that you know what the position requires; what the employer expects; the company operation; and your skills, abilities and knowledge, ask yourself: What do they need to know about me in order to seriously consider me for the job? Your goal is to make the interviewer's job easy by giving him or her a reason to hire you (Cohen & deOliveira, 1987). This can be effectively accomplished by developing a 10-point promotional message about yourself as it relates to the position.

When constructing this list of 10 strengths, skills, or characteristics, it is best to supply specific examples of how you developed or demonstrated these qualities. Your task will be to communicate each of these points during the course of the interview. Perhaps you can use several points to answer such typically asked questions as:

- Tell me about yourself?
- What are five of your greatest strengths or accomplishments?
- How does your background relate to this position?
- Why should I hire you?

**Develop a List of Questions.** Lynch (1990) states that "nothing excites an interviewer more than a (candidate) who has done his homework and is genuinely interested" (p. 30). An additional way to indicate that you have prepared for the interview is to devise a list of questions to ask the interviewer(s). These questions should serve two purposes: (a) to gather the information necessary for you to make an appropriate decision; and (b) to demonstrate that you have gathered knowledge about the organization. Prior reading and investigation will enable you to formulate questions that will also indicate the level of your knowledge.

**Prior to the Interview.** Consider the following suggestions before entering the interview appointment:

1. Rehearse your answers to typically asked questions. In addition to the issues mentioned above, be prepared to cite your future goals, examples of conflict in past positions, and descriptions of your work ethic, ideal supervisor, and preferred working style. Don't memorize your answers, but be able to offer concise and clear answers, accompanied by concrete examples of past experiences.
2. Plan your wardrobe. Know what the expected and appropriate dress is in a given work environment. For a business setting, the conservative look is generally expected, i.e., a navy or dark gray suit with a light shirt and conservative tie for men and light blouse accessorized by a scarf-bow or pin for women.
3. Take a folder with an ample supply of resumes, pad and pen, writing samples, and exceptional letters of recommendation or work evaluations that may be relevant to the position responsibilities.

**The Interview.** You will have approximately 30 minutes to interact with each interviewer or group of interviewers. During this time the recruiter will be assessing you in terms of your appearance, self-confidence, communication skills, and level of enthusiasm. Interestingly, some employers make hiring decisions within the first 10 seconds of the interview (CPC Spotlight, 1985). A first impression can potentially affect the entire interview. Therefore, what you do or say in the first few seconds needs to create a positive and lasting impression.

1. Arrive 5 to 10 minutes early. If you are unfamiliar with the area, take a practice trip ahead of time to the office so that you know the directions, the traffic patterns, parking facilities, and office location. There is nothing more unnerving than running late for an interview.
2. Shake the interviewer's hand, make direct eye contact, and address the person by name.
3. Experiencing a little anxiety is not only natural, but can be used to your advantage. It can actually energize the interview. "Sit up straight, be animated, and use your nervousness to get your energy and personality across . . ." (Lynch, 1990).
4. Be aware of the the interview process:

*Introduction Stage /Icebreaker.* This is the time that an interviewer will typically develop rapport with the applicant by setting the stage and creating a relaxed atmosphere. Many times superficial conversation will take place, such as weather conditions, similar involvement in civic organizations, or mutual friends. Remember, this is when you are making that first impression!

*Dialogue.* The greatest percentage of time will be spent with the exchange of information. Although employers may control the format of the interview, the interviewee can control the content (Medley, 1984). Questions will be asked about your background, expectations, and goals. This is when you start on your 10-point "promo." Take this opportunity to demonstrate your knowledge about the company by prefacing some of your answers with facts about the organization or position.

*Closing.* In the last stage of the interview you should make any last statements or ask questions. If you truly are interested in the position, say so. There should be no question in the recruiter's mind.

By the end of the interview you should have an idea of their timetable. If the interviewer does not offer this information, feel free to inquire. This will help you plan ahead.

Sometimes a job offer is made at the end of the interview. This is where your prior research will prove useful. If you know what you want (i.e., job responsibilities, location, salary, and benefits) and you have been able to gather the necessary information to make a sound decision, you may be able to respond. It might be wise, however, to ask for a date by which they need to have a decision so that you can take some time to make a decision with which you will be satisfied.

**Follow Up.** After your interview it is advisable to make a follow-up contact with the interviewer(s). Keep in mind that there are probably other candidates being considered for the job. Thus, make the extra efforts to create a favorable impression. Generally, it is appropriate to send a typed thank you letter. Within the body of the letter refer to the position for which you interviewed, the date and time of the interview, and reiterate your strong points as related to the position. Again, mention your enthusiasm about the job and your interest in receiving an offer. You can also add, briefly, information that you forgot to mention during the interview.

If you have interviewed unsuccessfully in the past or are about to launch into your first interview, try these suggestions and see if they work for you. Preparation is the key to reducing anxiety and building your level of confidence. Good luck!

*See also* Abilities; Interests; Job Search; Skills; Work Values.

## Bibliography

Cohen S., & deOliveira P. (1987). *Getting to the right job.* New York: Workman.

CPC Spotlight (1985, January). First impressions affect job interview outcome, 7 (6): 1.

LaFevre, J. L. (1989). Interviewing: The inside story from a college recruiter. In College Placement Manual (pp. 48–50); *1989–90 CPC annual,* Vol. 1. Bethlehem, PA: College Placement Council, Inc.

Lynch, R. W. (1990). Butterflies from hell. In *Managing Your Career.* (pp. 30–31) Chicopee, MA: Wall Street Journal.

Medley, H. A. (1984). *Sweaty palms: The neglected art of being interviewed.* Berkeley, CA: Ten Speed Press. This resource describes aspects and types of interviews, suggests preparation ideas, and deals with approaches to answering difficult questions, interview attire, and other related issues.

Powell, C. R. (1990). *Career planning today.* Dubuque, IA: Kendall/Hunt. The author devotes three chapters to interview preparation, interview management, and interview simulation.

—DONNA E. CASSELL

# JOB OUTLOOK: MAJOR TRENDS

The impact of technological advances, changes in business practices, foreign competition, and shifts in the demand for goods and services will alter tomorrow's job market, making the need for comprehensive, up-to-date, and reliable career information more important than ever before. Every two years, the Bureau of Labor Statistics analyzes changes in these factors and develops projections of the labor force, economic growth, and industry and occupational employment 10 to 15 years into the future. This article presents highlights from the latest set of projections covering the 1988–2000 period.

## Labor Force

The labor force is expected to expand at a much slower pace than in the past. Two factors account for most of the slowdown. First, the baby-bust generation, which is now entering the labor force, is much smaller than the baby-boom generation, which entered the labor force in the 1960s and 1970s. Second, the very rapid growth in the participation rate of women in the labor force is projected to slow, generally because it is already very high. Despite this slowdown, women will continue to increase their share of the labor force as will other minorities—blacks, Hispanics,

Asians, and other races. Young workers, ages 16 to 24, will decline in absolute numbers and constitute a smaller share of the labor force in the year 2000 than currently. The share of older workers, ages 55 and older, will remain relatively constant. Workers in the prime working ages—25 to 54 years old—will be the only group to increase its labor force share.

## Industry Employment

The long-term employment shift to service-producing industries will continue—more than 9 out of 10 of the 18 million new jobs expected by the year 2000 will be in the service-producing sector. Among the service-sector leaders, retail trade is expected to add 3.8 million jobs; private health services, 3.0 million; business services, 2.7 million; government employment—especially in public schools and in state and local safety and general government functions—1.6 million; and finance, insurance, and real estate, 1.1 million.

Within the goods-producing sector, which includes mining, manufacturing, and construction, only construction is expected to increase.

## Occupational Employment

The three fastest growing major occupational groups—executive, administrative, and managerial occupations; professional specialty occupations; and technicians and related support occupations—have the highest proportion of workers with a college degree and the highest earnings. Rapid growth is also expected for service workers, but these workers on average have low educational attainment and low earnings. The two slowest growing major occupational groups—operators, fabricators, and laborers and agricultural, forestry, and fishing workers—have the highest proportion of workers with less than a high school education and the lowest earnings.

Table 1 lists the 30 detailed occupations which are projected to grow fastest through the 1990s. About one-half are health-related occupations. Four occupations are related to the continuing spread of computer technology. In addition to fast growth, large numerical growth also denotes favorable job prospects. Table 2 lists the 30 occupations projected to generate the largest numerical job growth. In most cases, employment size is the major factor in the number of new jobs that will be generated. For example, most occupations on this list provided employment for 500,000 workers in 1988. In contrast, roughly three-quarters of the fastest growing occupations employed 200,000 or fewer workers.

**Table 1. Fastest Growing Occupations, 1988–2000 (numbers in thousands)**

| (Numbers in thousands) Occupation | Employment | | Numerical change | Percent change |
|---|---|---|---|---|
| | 1988 | 2000 | | |
| Paralegals | 83 | 145 | 62 | 75.3 |
| Medical assistants | 149 | 253 | 104 | 70.0 |
| Radiologic technologists and technicians | 132 | 218 | 87 | 66.0 |
| Homemaker-home health aides | 327 | 537 | 207 | 63.3 |
| Data processing equipment repairers | 71 | 115 | 44 | 61.2 |
| Medical record technicians | 47 | 75 | 28 | 59.9 |
| Medical secretaries | 207 | 327 | 120 | 58.0 |
| Physical therapists | 68 | 107 | 39 | 57.0 |
| Surgical technicians | 35 | 55 | 20 | 56.4 |
| Operations research analysts | 55 | 85 | 30 | 55.4 |
| Securities and financial services sales workers | 200 | 309 | 109 | 54.8 |
| Travel agents | 142 | 219 | 77 | 54.1 |
| Actuaries | 16 | 24 | 8 | 53.6 |
| Computer systems analysts | 403 | 617 | 214 | 53.3 |
| Physical and corrective therapy assistants | 39 | 60 | 21 | 52.5 |
| Subway and streetcar operators | 8 | 13 | 4 | 52.0 |
| EEG technologists | 6 | 10 | 3 | 50.4 |
| Occupational therapists | 33 | 48 | 16 | 48.8 |
| Computer programmers | 519 | 769 | 250 | 48.1 |
| Human services workers | 118 | 171 | 53 | 44.9 |
| Occupational therapy assistants and aides | 8 | 13 | 4 | 44.7 |
| Respiratory therapists | 56 | 79 | 23 | 41.3 |
| Correction officers | 186 | 262 | 76 | 40.8 |
| Employment interviewers | 81 | 113 | 33 | 40.1 |
| Electrical and electronics engineers | 439 | 615 | 176 | 40.1 |
| Receptionists | 833 | 1,164 | 331 | 39.8 |
| Registered nurses | 1,577 | 2,190 | 613 | 38.9 |
| Flight attendants | 88 | 123 | 34 | 38.7 |
| Electromedical and biomedical equipment repairers | 7 | 10 | 3 | 37.2 |
| Recreational therapists | 26 | 35 | 10 | 36.9 |

**Source:** Bureau of Labor Statistics.

## College Graduates

Roughly 10% of the college graduates who join the work force in the 1990s probably will not land a college-level job. This prospective job market situation, while very similar to that of recent years, represents a significantly more favorable job market than that experienced by college graduates during the 1970s, when roughly 1 out of 4 ended up underemployed.

## Relationship to Career Choice

Choosing a career is one of the most important decisions that you will face—whether as a student, a worker seeking a career change, or someone entering the labor force after a lengthy absence. A wise choice can lead to rewarding occupational experiences and a job that offers pride in achievement, opportunity for personal growth, and the security of an adequate income.

## Application

Numerous reports in recent years have expressed concern over the prospects of an imbalance between workplace requirements and worker skills. Knowing which occupations are likely to offer the best employment prospects and the education and training required will provide you with a good start on competing for tomorrow's jobs.

Although job outlook is useful to career decision making, it is subject to error because no one can predict the future with certainty. Because of the nature of projections, misunderstandings may arise between users who feel the need for exact numbers, and producers, who recognize their inability to predict with such precision. Because the models used to develop these projections provide numerical answers to non-numerical questions, the probability of such conflict increases.

A particular occupation may not follow the trend projected for the group in which it is found. Always refer to the outlook in a specific occupation by consulting key occupational information references such as those listed below.

**Table 2. Occupations with the Largest Job Growth, 1988–2000 (numbers in thousands)**

| (Numbers in thousands) Occupation | Employment 1988 | Employment 2000 | Numerical change | Percent change |
|---|---|---|---|---|
| Salespersons, retail | 3,834 | 4,564 | 730 | 19.0 |
| Registered nurses | 1,577 | 2,190 | 613 | 38.9 |
| Janitors and cleaners | 2,895 | 3,450 | 556 | 19.2 |
| Waiters and waitresses | 1,786 | 2,338 | 551 | 30.9 |
| General managers and top executives | 3,030 | 3,509 | 479 | 15.8 |
| General office clerks | 2,519 | 2,974 | 455 | 18.1 |
| Secretaries, except legal and medical | 2,903 | 3,289 | 385 | 13.3 |
| Nursing aides, orderlies, and attendants | 1,184 | 1,562 | 378 | 31.9 |
| Truck drivers | 2,399 | 2,768 | 369 | 15.4 |
| Receptionists | 833 | 1,164 | 331 | 39.8 |
| Cashiers | 2,310 | 2,614 | 304 | 13.2 |
| Guards | 795 | 1,050 | 256 | 32.2 |
| Computer programmers | 519 | 769 | 250 | 48.1 |
| Food counter, fountain, and related workers | 1,626 | 1,866 | 240 | 14.7 |
| Food preparation workers | 1,027 | 1,260 | 234 | 22.8 |
| Licensed practical nurses | 626 | 855 | 229 | 36.6 |
| Teachers, secondary school | 1,164 | 1,388 | 224 | 19.3 |
| Computer systems analysts | 403 | 617 | 214 | 53.3 |
| Accountants and auditors | 963 | 1,174 | 211 | 22.1 |
| Kindergarten and elementary teachers | 1,359 | 1,567 | 208 | 15.3 |
| Homemaker-home health aides | 327 | 534 | 207 | 63.3 |
| Maintenance repairers, general utilities | 1,080 | 1,281 | 202 | 18.7 |
| Child care workers | 670 | 856 | 186 | 27.8 |
| Gardeners and groundskeepers | 760 | 943 | 182 | 24.0 |
| Lawyers | 582 | 763 | 180 | 31.0 |
| Electrical and electronics engineers | 439 | 615 | 176 | 40.1 |
| Carpenters | 1,081 | 1,257 | 175 | 16.2 |
| Stock clerks, sales floor | 1,166 | 1,340 | 174 | 14.9 |
| Food service and lodging managers | 560 | 721 | 161 | 28.8 |
| Cooks, restaurant | 572 | 728 | 155 | 27.2 |

**Source:** Bureau of Labor Statistics.

The outlook for any occupation may vary considerably among local job markets. State Job Service offices can provide you with information on local labor market conditions.

Finally, employment prospects should never be the sole reason for choosing a career. Matching your goals and abilities to the work done on the job and the education required is an important part of choosing a career. Where you want to live and how much money you want to earn are also important.

*See also* Choosing an Occupation; Climate for Workers; Job Search; Job Security; Occupational Information.

## Bibliography

U.S. Bureau of Labor Statistics. (1990). *Occupational outlook handbook.* 1990–91 ed. Bulletin 2350. Washington, DC: U.S. Government Printing Office. Published biennially. The 1990–91 edition of the *Handbook* describes in detail 250 occupations comprising about 101 million jobs, or about 7 out of 8 jobs in the economy. For each major job discussed, the *Handbook* offers information on the nature of the work; working conditions; employment; personal qualifications, training, and educational requirements; job prospects to the year 2000; earnings; and sources of additional information.

U.S. Bureau of Labor Statistics. (1990). *Occupational outlook quarterly.* Washington, DC: U.S. Government Printing Office. This magazine includes practical, "how-to-do-it" information on choosing and getting today's and tomorrow's jobs. Articles are written in straightforward, nontechnical language and cover such subjects as new occupations, training opportunities, salary trends, employment projections, and the results of new studies from the Bureau of Labor Statistics.

U.S. Bureau of Labor Statistics. (1990). *Occupational projections and training data.* 1990 ed. Bulletin 2351. Washington, DC: U.S. Government Printing Office. Published biennially. This supplement to the Occupational Outlook Handbook provides the statistical and technical data supporting the information presented in the *Handbook.* Educational and training planners, career counselors, and jobseekers can find valuable information that ranks occupations by employment growth, earnings, susceptibility to unemployment, separation rates, and part-time work.

U.S. Bureau of Labor Statistics. (1990). *Outlook 2000.* Bulletin 2352. Washington, DC: U.S. Government Printing Office. Every two years, the Bureau of Labor Statistics produces detailed projections of the U.S. economy and labor force. This bulletin presents the Bureau's latest analyses of economic and industrial growth, the labor force, and trends in occupational employment through the year 2000. An overview article focuses on important issues raised by these projections.

—MIKE PILOT

## JOB SATISFACTION

*Satisfaction* comes from the Latin, "to make enough," to fulfill requirements. *Job satisfaction*, then, is the feeling people have when they evaluate how well (or how poorly) their jobs fulfill their requirements—what they expect to get out of their jobs. *Overall job satisfaction* (sometimes called global or general job satisfaction) is when they consider the whole job and everything about it all-in-all. *Intrinsic job satisfaction* is when they consider only the kind of work they do, the tasks that make up the job. *Extrinsic job satisfaction* is when they consider the conditions under which they work, such as their pay, their company or work organization, their coworkers, their supervisor. Even though both intrinsic and extrinsic job satisfaction go into and make up overall job satisfaction, they are separate enough so that one can be satisfied with the intrinsic side of the job but not the extrinsic, or vice versa, or be satisfied with both, or with neither.

Different people can have different requirements and may expect to get different things out of their jobs, so that even if they work on the same type of job and under the same conditions, their job satisfaction will be different. Sometimes, even if they have the same requirements, expect the same things from their jobs, and work on the same jobs under the same conditions, they may still feel differently about their jobs because some people are more (or less) easily satisfied than others. The same individual may, of course, be satisfied differently by different jobs, but may also feel differently about the same job at different times.

Surveys since before World War II have shown that 75% to 80% of workers say that they are satisfied with their jobs, but when asked if they would change their line of work (occupation) if they had the chance, 40% to 50% say they would. Thus, although they are similar and at times may coincide, *occupational satisfaction* is different from job satisfaction. Occupational satisfaction is most like intrinsic job satisfaction, but it includes satisfaction with the conditions of work that usually go with the occupation. *Career satisfaction* is similar to job satisfaction and occupational satisfaction, but its most important aspect is satisfaction with career progress—how well one's career goals are being met.

Finally, *satisfaction* and *dissatisfaction* are not merely opposites; they are different experiences. One can be satisfied and dissatisfied at the same time. This happens when we expect many things from a job; we may be satisfied with one thing but dissatisfied with another.

### Relationship to Work

What do people look for (expect from or require from) a job? The following list is representative, and is given in the order people have ranked them over the years:

1. *Type of work:* the kind of work that makes the best use of one's abilities and gives one a feeling of accomplishment.
2. *Security:* having a job that provides steady employment.
3. *Company:* working for a company that has a good reputation, that one can be proud to work for.
4. *Advancement:* being able to progress in one's job and career, having the chance to advance in the company.
5. *Coworkers:* having coworkers who are competent and congenial.
6. *Pay:* being paid at least enough to meet one's needs, and being paid fairly in comparison with others.
7. *Supervision:* having an immediate supervisor who is competent, considerate, and fair.
8. *Hours:* having working hours that allow one enough time with family and/or time to pursue other strong interests and live one's preferred life        style.
9. *Benefits:* having benefits that meet one's needs and compare well with those of others.
10. *Working Conditions:* having physical working conditions that are safe, not injurious to health, not stressful, and even comfortable.

There are other things people look for in jobs, such as autonomy, prestige, and having responsibility, but these 10 are among the most commonly mentioned.

These rankings are average. At any one time, different people may rank these 10 differently, and the same person may rank them differently at different times (although most people keep their rankings more or less the same over several years). Also, not all 10 may be important to every person. What is important may differ from person to person, in the same way that what the job can provide will differ from job to job. Knowing what is important to a person and what a job can provide allows us to predict whether the person will be satisfied in the job.

Do satisfied workers make productive, high performing workers? Yes, but only if (a) the workers are competent (have the requisite skills and knowledge), and (b) the work environment is favorable (e.g., having up-to-date equipment, having enough customers or clients). Conversely, productive, high performing workers are usually more satisfied with their jobs than less productive, low performing workers. These are trends, and not strong trends at that, because one will find satisfied workers who are low performers and not productive enough, as well as productive, high performing workers who are not satisfied enough or even quite dissatisfied.

Satisfied workers are less likely than less satisfied workers to quit their jobs and to absent themselves from their jobs for voluntary, personal reasons. Dissatisfied workers are more likely to have accidents on the job. They are more likely to engage in unsafe behavior (which, combined with unsafe conditions, is what makes for accidents).

Work stress, or stress in the job, is related to job dissatisfaction. Psychosomatic illnesses, depression, anxiety, worry, tension, and impaired interpersonal relationships can result from, or be made worse by, job dissatisfaction. Work has become central to the psychological well-being of most people. Job satisfaction plays an important role in a person's mental health and satisfaction with life. It is worth noting that job satisfaction was found to be the best indicator of longevity, better even than physician's ratings of physical functioning, use of tobacco, or genetic inheritance.

## Application

1. You can start by "knowing yourself." Know what is important to you and what is not, be clear about what you expect from or require of a job or an occupation. Then you will know what to look for when choosing among jobs or among careers.
2. Next, you will have to learn more about what jobs and occupations provide (at least the ones you are considering), in relation to what you expect or require and what is important to you.
3. Sometimes it might help to consult a professional person (a vocational psychologist or a career counselor) to do the above thoroughly.
4. Job satisfactions and dissatisfactions are barometers to your adjustment to work. You should not allow your dissatisfactions to go unresolved for long. They may lead to something worse (loss of productivity, accidents, even mental illness).
5. Overall job satisfaction is a trade-off (like many things in life). You should not expect 100% satisfaction and 0% dissatisfaction. There usually are dissatisfactions even in the best jobs.

6. One way to resolve dissatisfactions is to review what is important to you and what is not. You might find that what is causing your dissatisfaction is not really what is most important to you, or that you are not getting satisfaction in the aspects that are most important to you. Here again, it might help to consult a professional person who will be more objective—and more knowledgeable—than you are.
7. You should look separately at the kind of work you are doing versus the conditions of work (pay, supervisor, coworkers, company, physical working conditions). If you are becoming increasingly dissatisfied with the kind of work you are doing, you should consider a career change. If you are dissatisfied with the conditions of work, you might be able to set matters right by negotiating with your supervisor or your coworkers, or by changing companies.
8. You should look down the road at your possible career progress. Present dissatisfactions might be worth bearing if you see your career progressing.
9. Your values—what is most important to you—are what count in the end. You have to answer this question honestly: How important is your job, your career to you? Only when this question is answered can you put your job satisfaction or dissatisfaction in proper perspective.

*See also* Career Counseling; Choosing an Occupation; Mental Health and Work.

## Bibliography

Dawis, R.V. (1984). Job satisfaction: Worker aspirations, attitudes and behavior. In N.C. Gysbers (Ed.), *Designing careers*. San Francisco: Jossey-Bass. A survey of the research literature on job satisfaction: trends, determiners, correlates, and consequences. Includes a discussion of theories and implications.

Hoppock, R. (1935). *Job satisfaction*. New York: Harper & Row. The "classic" in the field.

Jurgensen, C.E. (1978). Job preferences (What makes a job good or bad?). *Journal of Applied Psychology, 63*: 267–76. Report on responses gathered from 57,000 persons over a 30-year period.

Locke, E.A. (1976). The nature and causes of job satisfaction. In M.D. Dunnette (Ed.), *Handbook of industrial and organizational psychology*. Chicago: Rand McNally. A thoughtful and detailed analysis of the nature of job satisfaction and its causes, supported by evidence drawn from research.

*Work in America: Report of a special task force to the secretary of health, education, and welfare*. (1973). Cambridge, MA: MIT Press.

—RENE V. DAWIS

# JOB SEARCH

Job search is an important career management skill. Learning and using effective job search methods can reduce your job search time and unemployment by half. This may mean several months' worth of additional income. Additionally, effective job search methods provide higher quality information about job opportunities that result in better career decisions, better job offers, and better job fit. Achieving better job fit from the beginning of employment means higher job satisfaction for you, less work-related stress, and higher productivity. In combination, these positive outcomes help to advance your career.

Job search methods can be categorized in a variety of ways. A useful method is to classify job search methods as:

1. Direct approaches whereby you directly and personally initiate contact with prospective employers to uncover job leads and to generate interviews.
2. Indirect methods whereby you work with or through an intermediary as a stepping-stone to locate job leads and interviews.

Generally, direct approaches give you a much higher chance of uncovering job leads than do indirect methods. Although direct methods appear to require more effort, they are more efficient and effective because they reduce your search time and give you better information on job characteristics. Direct methods put the responsibility for the results of your job search exactly where it belongs—on you!

Indirect search methods have appeal because they seem easy to use. However, indirect methods lower your chances of finding a good job more quickly and usually prolong your job search. Any time you allow something or someone to come between you and employers, you lose some control over your job search, add inefficiency, and foster dependence. No one can really conduct a job search for you but yourself.

The job search is essentially a search for information. The information you seek pertains to job leads and the quality of job vacancies. The best source of job leads and vacancy information is people. The more people you contact directly to obtain information, the better your chances of uncovering job vacancies that lead to job interviews that lead to job offers.

People provide the vital communication link that permits job seekers and employers to become informed about each other. Why is the job search such a "people" process? There are several reasons. First, the job market is in a constant state of change. Annually, almost one-third of

the workforce changes jobs. Furthermore, new jobs are created while some jobs get eliminated due to changes in business conditions and technology. The important point is that the job market is always churning. This churning may mean opportunity if you know how to organize and structure your job search to approach people for job leads.

Second, at any given time, only a relatively small percentage of job vacancies are advertised to the public in some way. Approximately two-thirds of known vacancies are unpublicized at any given time. Why? Because lag time exists from when a position becomes available to when it becomes filled. This lag time is due to inefficiencies or "friction" in hiring processes and in the job market. Called frictional unemployment, it may account for 40% of unemployment at any given time. However, being unpublicized doesn't mean that no one knows of these opportunities. On the contrary, people currently employed in organizations know of openings, and they may tell their coworkers, acquaintances, friends, and family about the vacancies. One way to reduce the lag time in your job search is to tap people for job leads.

Third, some employers are reluctant to publicize some vacant jobs. Hiring is risky and expensive. Employers try to reduce hiring risks by accepting referrals and recommendations from employees and business associates, assuming that referrals provide higher quality and more reliable information on applicants than formal mechanisms. Additionally, employers try to reduce hiring costs by recruiting selectively. Open recruiting may be necessary to attract applicants with hard-to-find skills or for lower level, minimal wage positions. However, for better positions, that many people could perform, employers contain hiring costs by limiting the recruitment of applicants through internal posting of positions and word of mouth. A direct job search campaign can help you penetrate internal job markets.

Direct and indirect job search methods are described below. The best approach to finding good jobs in the shortest period of time is to use several job search methods simultaneously, put effort into using them, be consistent, maintain accurate records, and follow up with all job leads.

## Direct Job Search Methods

1. Networking is the common term used for several related job search strategies that put you into direct contact with people who are in a position to know of potential job leads or who know others who may know of job leads. The referral campaign is the primary method in this approach whereby you systematically develop a contact list, approach selected individuals to request a meeting, conduct an information interview, and follow-up appropriately (see **Information Interviewing; Networking**).

Secondary networking methods include attending professional and trade association meetings, hiring conferences, career fairs, and various organizational meetings to meet people and obtain information. Another networking approach is volunteering your time and talents to develop skills, gain experience, make appropriate contacts, and acquire inside information.

Information interviewing and networking are very effective job search methods and account for approximately a third of all job placements. However, just as networking can work for you, it can work against you if you lack social skills, a clear game plan, and common courtesy. Many employers are turned off by unprepared, ill mannered, and unappreciative networkers. As a job seeker, you have a responsibility to make information interviews and other networking activities productive and positive. Networking is not magic; it demands hard work, advanced preparation, good communication skills, and a genuine desire to meet people. Your contacts are doing you a favor; be sure to show your appreciation.

2. Targeted mailing is contacting employers directly with a highly personalized letter to inquire about employment possibilities. Start by identifying employers who do the kind of work you desire. Obtain the name and address of the manager who hires for the job you seek. You may need to call the organization to obtain accurate contact information. Then type a personalized cover letter to the manager expressing your interest in a specific type of work and requesting an appointment to explore possibilities. Close your letter by stating that you will call to see if a meeting can be arranged. Include a copy of your resume. If you are not able to secure an appointment, request that the target person keep your resume on file for the next six months and contact you if an appropriate opening occurs. This job search approach requires that you have a clear work objective in mind and have an up-to-date resume. Targeted mailings are especially appropriate for managers and professionals.

3. A telephone campaign is based on the premise that, at any given time, a certain percentage of employers have job vacancies. The idea is to canvass a large number of employers to uncover any appropriate leads, then follow up accordingly with a letter, resume, or application. When a lead is uncovered, request a meeting to learn more about the job and organization. Use this approach to contact small enterprises. Ask to speak with the owner or manager. Indicate that you are seeking employment and inquiring into possibilities with their firm. One way to organize a telephone campaign is to identify potential employers in the yellow pages of your local telephone directory under the appropriate classification. This also is an efficient approach

when conducting a long-distance job search. As with all job search methods, you are playing the odds or probabilities. Therefore, expect a very high percentage of dead-ends and negative responses. Go for volume and attempt to get through your employer list quickly. The more "no's" you get, the closer you are to getting to a "yes" response!

4. Cold calls are an old sales technique whereby you show up at a prospect's office and request to see the decision maker. Site visits are time consuming, inefficient, and require that you prepare a clear, concise verbal presentation of your interests and qualifications should you obtain face-to-face meetings. Cold calls may be more appropriate for some types of work than others, e.g., retail sales, summer and part-time employment, trade/craft jobs, hospitality (restaurants, hotels, etc.), construction sites, and manufacturing.

## Indirect Approaches Using Intermediaries

1. Want ads in newspapers and trade/professional publications are the most effective of the indirect approaches. Approximately 14% of job seekers find employment through want ads, but the results vary widely depending upon the type of work. Employers are most likely to advertise lower paying and harder to fill vacancies through want ads. Many positions never get advertised. Research indicates that want ads list only a small percentage of available job vacancies in any given city and that perhaps only half the employers in a given metropolitan area use the want ads to recruit during a given year. Actively use the want ads, but don't rely on them solely. Use them in combination with other job search methods.

2. Advertising yourself is an approach in which job seekers attempt to advertise their talents by placing an advertisement in a newspaper or trade publication announcing their availability for a specific kind of work. Usually listed under "positions wanted," it probably benefits the publication most of all. This is an extremely passive approach with little probability of success. Employers discount job seekers who use this method, assuming that people who devote little effort to their job search probably will devote an equal amount of effort to the job. Job seekers who advertise often get responses for commissioned sales and multi-level marketing distributorships.

3. Mass mailing your resume is essentially sending your resume without a cover letter or with only a generic cover letter to large numbers of employers in hopes of uncovering job leads. Unlike the targeted mailing approach based on organizational research and a personalized cover letter, mass mailings are rather indiscriminant. If targeted mailing is similar to using a rifle to sight a target, then mass mailing is the shotgun approach to the job search. Some-

times it gets results; usually, it disperses your energy and falls short of the target—getting a good job. Mass mailing is often viewed as junk mail by employers and often gets discarded. Experienced mail order advertisers may get only a 1% or 2% response to a given mailing, even with their sophisticated market research. Assuming equivalent probabilities, mass mailing of resumes will result in only one or two interviews, at best, for every 100 pieces of mail you send. However, numbers do not tell the whole story. Mass mailing is perceived as a lazy person's approach to job finding. It has little impact with busy employers and is relatively expensive for the job seeker. And, good jobs are seldom found this way.

4. State employment services have been operating since the mid-1930s. At the local level, these agencies vary in how effectively they operate and how many jobs get filled. Often, state employment services are required to support other social programs at the expense of their primary mission. Many suffer from inadequate funding and lack sufficient staff to function effectively. Nationally, on the average, public employment services are credited with filling about 5% of job openings, while only about 5% of employers use this service. Listed jobs tend to be at lower levels of pay, skill, and education, but usually include a wider range of occupations than want ads. While the percentages are relatively low, public employment services may be relatively effective for job seekers in certain occupations. The best way to determine if your local service can help you is to visit, investigate their program, review their job listings, talk with staff members, and give them a try. If you see a fair amount of activity in your area of interest, you may get good results.

5. Commercial employment agencies charge a fee either to the job applicant or the employer whenever someone is hired. Similar to public employment services, commercial agencies function as brokers attempting to link job seekers and employers. Their fees typically run from 10% to 30% of the first year's annual salary, depending on the job. Some agencies cover a broad variety of jobs, while others specialize in an occupation or industry, e.g., secretaries, accountants, computers, health care. Generally, agencies function much like a job seeker. First, they advertise in local newspapers and in the telephone directory to attract applicants, then identify the most marketable applicants. Next, they market these applicants by contacting employers directly until job leads and vacancies are uncovered. Typically, employers list jobs with agencies that are hard to fill, require special skills and experience, or must be filled immediately. Many employers use agencies to supplement their recruiting efforts. While reliable data are hard to find, insiders estimate that agencies assist about 5% of their applicants in finding employment (see **Recruitment**).

6. College and university career services deal primarily with entry-level professional jobs. Many schools provide comprehensive programs which assist graduates to plan their careers, assess their qualifications, write resumes, learn interviewing and job search skills, and link with employers through campus interviews, referral services, and job listings. Like other job and labor market brokers, school services list jobs in high demand requiring specialized skills, e.g., engineering, accounting, nursing, computing. The structured or formal services (campus interviews, referrals, job listings) account for approximately 10% of all placements for graduates. Students who use services such as campus interviews typically have a higher number of offers, more desirable jobs, and wider geographic opportunities compared to those who do not use these services. Unlike other brokers, schools that provide job search counseling can help all graduates organize and implement a direct job search campaign by networking and contacting employers directly. Recall that these job search methods account for approximately two-thirds of the job placements. Students who use a combination of services available to them increase their chances of finding employment.

Career services often have highly specialized resources to help graduates link directly with employers. For example, computerized referral services recently have emerged to give national and regional employers access to graduates from hundreds of schools. The projected shortage of skilled entry-level workers may improve the range and number of openings available to college and university graduates during the 1990s. Like other job search resources, job seekers should investigate college and university career services fully, understand the appropriateness of each program available to them, then take responsibility for using the resource. Career service offices are usually staffed by career counselors who can provide technical assistance to help you prepare for your job search and conduct it effectively; however, they will not do your work for you.

7. Career consulting and marketing firms provide a range of services to job seekers for a fee. The better ones offer career counseling and assessment to help you define career direction; give training in job search methods, interviewing and salary negotiation; and provide guidance in developing your resume. They cater to managerial and professional workers who can afford to pay fees ranging from $3,000 to $10,000 or more. For job seekers who face a major career change and have not been in the job market recently, such services may be worth it. But, the old cliche of "buyer beware" should be kept in mind. Many firms use high pressure sales tactics to get clients to sign contracts, claim that they have special access to top employers, and promise to do the work for you. Before signing any contract, be clear about how the business operates, what you get for

your money, and names of references. One way to evaluate career consultants is to determine how long they've been in business, the credentials of the key staff, and, if counseling is involved, the certification of counselors (see **Recruitment**).

Professionally trained career counselors will hold at least a master's degree and also be certified as a National Certified Career Counselor or be licensed by their state (see **Career Counseling**). The more reputable firms provide counseling and technical assistance and clearly spell out your responsibilities and theirs. Distinguish between the "sizzle" and the "steak" provided by consulting firms; know exactly what your money buys. Ask for references and take your time before signing a contract.

Out of fairness to this industry, it should be mentioned that major advances in career and job search counseling were developed by private consultants in the 1940s. The referral campaign using information interviewing was used initially by private consultants; later this job search innovation became widely diffused and now is recognized as the most effective job search method.

## Other Options

In addition to the direct and indirect job search methods described above, several other options should be understood and perhaps considered.

1. Self-employment may be a viable option depending on your goals, financial situation, skills, experience, and motivation. In the shift from an industrial to service economy and with advances in telecommunications and computing equipment, home-based businesses have proliferated. Additionally, many excellent franchise and distributorship opportunities exist. To investigate what is required to start your own business, check with your local chamber of commerce. Many provide small business consulting through retired executives along with extensive business guides and publications (see **Self-Employment**).

2. Temporary work through agencies may give you an opportunity to gain experience, refine your work skills, investigate various work settings, and develop contacts. Many job seekers stay with temporary agencies for quite a while because of the flexibility and variety such work brings. Additionally, employers have turned increasingly to using "temps" in a wide variety of jobs to respond to shifting business priorities. Most temporary employment agencies require a placement fee if a worker accepts a permanent position with a client organization within a predetermined period of time (see **Temporary Employment**).

3. Volunteer and internship work is a way to gain experience in a job, occupation, or work setting and to reality-test job fit. You may need to present a work plan to various people within a target organization to create a position. However, college and university career services often list internship and volunteer opportunities. Volunteering may be particularly appropriate if you need at least minimal experience to qualify for entry to an occupation (see **Service-Learning; Volunteer Work**).

4. Self-help resources such as job clubs, job search workshops, and job seeker support groups are self-empowering programs you attend to learn effective job search methods, to conduct a more systematic job search, and to obtain support and continuing technical assistance during your search. These programs may be part of special social services for unemployed clients. For example, job clubs are highly structured programs to teach clients specific job search behaviors and to provide a disciplined, rigorous approach to job finding (see **Job Clubs**). Forty Plus Clubs are self-help support groups for mid-career managers and professionals; members typically meet regularly to exchange information on job leads, to trouble-shoot job search problems, and to offer each other encouragement and support. Some public employment services offer similar support groups. Workshops and courses may be offered for a fee by continuing education departments or career services of colleges and universities, by community agencies, and by consultants. The focus usually is on teaching participants a process for conducting a self-directed job search. Although the length, structure, and content of self-help resources may vary considerably, effective ones focus on empowering you to conduct a more disciplined, systematic, and effective job search and emphasize direct job search methods. Assuming that you have access to effective self-help programs, they may be well worth the effort and cost to attend. The very best programs will replicate at reasonable cost in a group setting what top private consultants provide their clients individually at far higher fees.

## Recommended Guidelines

The place to begin your job search is in your head! Your attitude is critical to your success. Assume full responsibility for every aspect of your search. Never delegate your search to someone else, even if you use consultants or brokers. There is no avoiding the obvious: an effective job search is hard work and you are responsible for the results you achieve. Remember, the job search is a process that takes time and effort.

To get good results as quickly as possible, do the following:

1. Use several methods but invest your time according to the probabilities of success each method offers and according to acceptable standards in your type of work.

2. Conduct an intensive search. The more employers you contact directly each week, the greater are your chances for uncovering leads more quickly. Aim for 10 or more direct contacts per week for several weeks to generate interviews.

3. Contact small enterprises. They create a significant number of new jobs each year.

4. Consider service industries since they will account for almost all the new jobs during the 1990s.

5. Get organized, keep good records, be consistent and persistent in your efforts, and show consideration to employers.

6. Know your interests and skills and be able to communicate your value to employers.

7. Be positive toward yourself and others.

Remember that getting hired is a social process that depends upon your ability to deal effectively with others to achieve your goals.

*See also* Career Counseling; Career Planning; Information Interviewing; Job Clubs; Job Interviewing; Job Outlook: Major Trends; Networking; Recruitment; Self-Employment; Service-Learning; Temporary Employment; Volunteer Work.

## Bibliography

Azrin, N. H., & Besalel, V. (1982). *Finding a job.* Berkeley, CA: Ten Speed Press. A very detailed guide based on job club methods appropriate for entry-level and returning workers in service, manufacturing, and trade jobs.

Germann, R., & Arnold, P. (1980). *Bernard Haldane Associates' job and career building.* Berkeley, CA: Ten Speed Press. A classic from pioneers in job search and career counseling. Summarizes over 30 years' worth of experience with thousands of job search clients. Outlines foundational job search skills managers and professionals need to be effective.

Wegman, R., Chapman, R., & Johnson, M. (1989). *Work in the new economy: Careers and job seeking into the 21st century.* Rev. ed. Alexandria, VA: American Association for Counseling and Development. A thorough and readable review of job search research, a discussion of job search methods and their effectiveness, and clear advice on job search approaches.

—WILLIAM J. BANIS

## JOB SECURITY

Job security refers to: (a) an organization's actual employment levels and practices (e.g., staffing, firing, and layoffs); and (b) people's perceptions of how likely they are to retain their jobs. Job security is a basic element of the employment relationship; it reflects what an employer offers to employees in the way of job assurance and stability, and influences people's comfort, commitment, and inclinations to look for other employment.

The past two decades have seen fundamental changes in this aspect of working life. Many companies, for example, have reduced the size of their workforce dramatically through layoffs and job elimination, or what has been called "downsizing." In 1989 alone, an American Management Association study (1990) of 1,241 firms found that some 36% cut their staffing levels by an average of 11%. More broadly, one-in-every-four jobs were eliminated in textiles, steel, automotive, and other manufacturing industries in the 1970s and 1980s (Harrison & Bluestone, 1988). As a result, "cradle-to-grave" job security has vanished for most American workers and managers.

In turn, this era has also witnessed unprecedented mobility on the part of employees. People stay with their companies today an average of less than four years, half as long as in the 1960s. Partly this is accounted for by job instability and the lack of advancement opportunities in many organizations. Another factor is peoples' strong drive toward career- and self-advancement. In any case, company loyalty has declined markedly since the 1960s (Kanter & Mirvis, 1989).

### Perceived Job Security—1990

On the broadest scale, job security is affected by economic trends in the industry and regions in which an organization does business. The AMA study found that 49% of New England companies—a region beset by a slump—reduced staffing in 1989. By contrast, firms in California and Florida—states still enjoying growth—were less apt to have layoffs.

In the current recession, Americans find their jobs to be less secure than six years ago. In one survey designed by myself and Donald Kanter, a representative sample of working people were asked how much they agreed or disagreed that "my organization provides job security for people like myself." Sixty-four percent found their jobs secure in 1984, but in 1990 that number was down to 59%. Importantly, some 22% said that they did not have job security in their companies.

Table 1 reports on levels of job security in the U. S. workforce in selected categories:

- *Type of Employer.* People working for companies in the profit-making sector have less job security today than their counterparts in government or the nonprofit sector. Furthermore, those employed in manufacturing and in retail or wholesale trade feel less secure than those in business services and particularly in health or social services. These findings reflect the economic turbulence in the profit-making sector and the continuing decline in domestic manufacturing and sales.

- *Size of Employer.* Still, there seems to be some "safety in numbers." People working for larger companies feel more secure than those in firms employing between 21 and 500 people. Two factors may account for this. First, smaller firms are particularly vulnerable to economic changes and are more likely to go out of business or be acquired than larger ones. Second, although large companies have laid off more people in recent years, the likelihood of any one person being affected is greater in smaller outfits.

- *Employment Status.* Part-time employees have much less job security than those employed full-time. Part-timers make up a growing segment of the "contingent" workforce whose employment depends directly on business cycles and company performance. They are typically the "first off" in the event of business downturns and layoffs.

Newly hired employees, in turn, have less job security than veterans. Of course, many are on a "probationary" status before they are "vested" in their companies. New hires are also more vulnerable to layoffs. Employees who have been with their companies between one and two years seem also to feel less secure. This is the crucial "shake out" period when employees are expected to have mastered their jobs (c.f., Greenhalgh, 1980). Job security often depends on people achieving acceptable levels of performance.

The national survey also shows union members having more job security than those who are not part of a union. Of course, many union contracts base job security on seniority. Some of the largest unions also have industry-wide contracts with employers that spell out employment levels and provisions for retraining and redeploying members in the event of technological or business changes that eliminate their jobs. Non-union employees, by comparison, typically have no provisions guaranteeing their job security.

**Table 1. Perceived Job Security—1990**

| U.S. Workforce National Probability Sample (N=1115) | |
|---|---|
| The Organization I work for Provides Job Security for people like myself . . . | % Agree |
| **Type of Employer** | |
| Profit-Making | 54% |
| Government | 61 |
| Non-Profit | 63 |
| Manufacturing | 54% |
| Business Trade | 56 |
| Business—Service | 59 |
| Health/Social Service | 68 |
| **Size of Employer** | |
| Less than 20 People | 59% |
| 21 to 100 People | 53 |
| 101 to 500 People | 56 |
| 500 to 5000 People | 68 |
| More than 5000 | 66 |
| **Employment Status** | |
| Part Time | 52% |
| Full Time | 61 |
| Tenure: | |
| Less than 3 Mos. | 46% |
| 3 to 11 Months | 57 |
| 1 to 2 Years | 51 |
| 3 to 10 Years | 60 |
| More than 10 Yrs | 65 |
| Non-Union | 57% |
| Union Member | 68 |
| **Collar Color** | |
| Blue Collar | 56% |
| White Collar | 60 |
| Clerical | 63 |

- *Collar Color.* Certainly blue-collar workers have less job security than those in clerical or white-collar jobs. However, there has been an increase in job insecurity among white-collar workers. The Bureau of Labor Statistics found that 27% of all the unemployed were white-collar in 1983, while in 1990 that number had crept up to 37%.

Finally, our national survey also revealed some differences in the demographics of those who are more and less secure in the jobs:

- Younger (ages 18–24) and older (over age 55) employees report less job security than employees between ages 25 and 54.

- Those having a high school diploma report less security than those who have attended college and especially college graduates.
- Those at the lowest ($20,000 or less in household income) and at the highest ($70,000 or more) ends of the income scale are less secure.
- Women are less secure in their jobs than men.

## Application

Hopefully these data provide a basis for judging how people like you perceive job security today. Some of the following strategies may help you to further assess your own job security and even protect it:

1. *Watch Industry Relevant Trends.* Downturns in employment in heavy manufacturing, for example, can be traced to increased global competition, changing consumer preferences, and export/import practices. Upturns in employment in the service sector, in the same way, reflect on the development of new markets and purchasing patterns. Find out what is (and will) affect employment in your industry.

2. *Study Your Company's Strategies.* Job security within a particular organization is influenced by business strategies. Firms involved in mergers or acquisitions, for example, generally reduce staff more than otherwise. This is because of redundancies between positions in combining companies and efforts to reduce debt. Many companies in recent years have also tried to "de-layer" by reducing the number of levels of management. Outsourcing jobs to foreign countries and closing domestic plants is another way that company strategies impinge on people's job security. Find out what your firm is (and might be) doing and how it could affect you.

3. *Work Hard, Be Honest, and Know What Is Expected of You.* People can be fired for mediocre or poor performance, for illegal or unethical conduct, and for excessive absenteeism and tardiness. These "grounds for dismissal" are usually contained in a company's personnel policies or a union contract. Know the requirements. In addition, make sure you know what criteria are used in performance appraisals. Then meet or exceed the standards. That way there should be no uncertainty as to whether your job security hinges on job performance.

   Of course, petty politics, punitive supervision, and racial, ethnic, or sexual discrimination can also be factors in individual job loss. Some organizations have procedures whereby employees can appeal their dismissal on these grounds. There is always the recourse of a lawsuit.

4. *Be a Star.* There are steps you can take to protect yourself in the event that your department is downsized or your job is eliminated. Be a star! Many companies go out of their way to retain or relocate top performers in the case of cutbacks. Make yourself indispensable to, say, customers or suppliers. They can put in a good word for you.

5. *Stay Mobile.* Still, don't be naive. It could happen to you. It is only sensible to develop broad and marketable skills, cultivate professional networks, and be prepared to "move on" (see **Job Security: The Free Agent Manager**).

6. *You'll Live through It.* It takes an average of 12 to 14 weeks for jobless people to find new employers. However, the interim period can be extremely stressful. Make a budget. Get outplacement help. And, take extra care with your diet, health, and well-being. Also, be prepared for change. A recent *Newsweek* (November 5, 1990) poll found that 62% of those surveyed said that, should they be laid off, they would be willing to change their line of work. Over 40% said they would move to a new location. You may have to.

*See also* Fired/Laid Off; Job Search; Job Security: The Free Agent Manager; Law in the Workplace; Outplacement; Unemployment.

## Bibliography

American Management Association. (1990). *Responsible reductions in force*. New York: Amacom Briefings and Surveys. The AMA's annual survey of employers' staffing practices across the U.S. An excellent source of information on yearly trends in employment.

Greenhalgh, L. (1980). A process model of organizational turnover: The relationship with job security as a case in point. *Academy of Management Review*, 5: 299–303. An academic piece on critical stages of career development in a company when issues of job security arise, including entry, the induction period, a shake-out phase when career paths become clear, and a point of commitment.

Harrison, B., & Bluestone, B. (1988). *The great u-turn*. New York: Basic Books. A well-documented book on trends in corporate downsizing, job creation, and job elimination in the past two decades.

How safe is your job? (1990, November 5). *Newsweek*: 44–55. An article on current worries and how to deal with job loss. Includes national survey data.

Kanter, D. L., & Mirvis, P. H. (1989). *The cynical Americans*. San Francisco: Jossey Bass. A national study of the rise of cynicism in the workforce and the implications for employee loyalty.

—PHILIP H. MIRVIS

## JOB SECURITY: THE FREE AGENT MANAGER

The free agent manager refers to the changing employment relationship and some strategies to cope with it. Where we as managers once expected to find a good job and spend our entire careers with a paternalistic organization, we no longer have that security. Some managers have accepted the loss as an uncontrollable part of changing economic times. Other managers, the free agent managers, have chosen to proactively manage their own careers, scanning opportunities both within their organization and across firms and industries, maintaining knowledge of their own market value while at the same time taking every opportunity to increase that value as they perform the functions of their jobs.

The 1980s saw the elimination of millions of management jobs in corporate America. The reduction crosses industries and management levels; it crosses management styles and historical management cultures; perhaps most important, the trend of downsizing management shows no signs of abating. Companies such as USX and GE have cut employment by over 100,000 people each; both companies anticipate further reductions, albeit at a somewhat slower rate and in a more focused manner. At the same time General Motors and the United Auto Workers negotiate job security clauses for production workers as their top priority, GM announces plans to release more managers (not in the UAW) as well as production employees. Whether driven by intense competition or a redefinition of "good management," the reduction of management at major corporations will continue in the foreseeable future.

When AT & T, Eastman Kodak, DuPont, and Arco stopped providing continuity of employment, many managers concluded that they could only count on themselves from now on. At the same time that we read in the popular business press of the importance of corporate culture, of nurturing relationships, and of an increasing emphasis on the quality of work life, we find the practice of management moving in another, more ominous direction. Instead of the celebration of people and innovation, we find a harsh economic relationship reminiscent of the heyday of scientific management. Companies in the 1980s moved backward in time to a practice of treating people as purchasable assets, to be used, consumed, and replaced.

## Application

As a manager facing this changed relationship, you should take the time to consider your response strategies. Managers who have lived through restructurings summa-

rize their feelings in a simple phrase: "Never again." Yet, you can not assure yourself that another restructuring won't arise tomorrow, next month, or next year; therefore, a proactive strategy seems necessary.

The first and foremost rule for the free agent manager is "Be loyal to yourself." Be aware that anything can happen and probably will. You won't be able to eliminate the possibility of a restructuring, but you can prepare yourself, personally, professionally, and financially. As a free agent manager, you should realize that the time frame of employment in one job is much shorter than it once was. Just as our sports stars have learned that their financial clout increased dramatically with an increase in the mobility of the work force, the middle manager must also know his or her real worth to the organization. The taboo of talking about salaries and benefits with friends and competitors alike no longer applies. Know what other options might be available and push your firm to provide competitive incentives to stay.

A corollary to the first rule is "Protect yourself, financially and emotionally." You enter into an employment relationship but you do not enter into an employment marriage; "till death do us part" need not and should not apply. The free agent manager must keep skills current and transferable, which usually means keeping skills general. You should be very leery of postings that might provide skill development in a specialty only your company uses. If your company later decides that the skill is a luxury, you have no one to turn to for help. Also, limit your emotional involvement with your firm. Remember, you are there primarily for the job.

If the time comes when you must exercise your free agency, and for most of us that time will come at least once in our working careers, exercise as much control over the situation as possible. The motto, "Be prepared," is as appropriate for the free agent manager as it is for the boy scout. But the preparation must start long before you think that you will need to exercise your option.

Some useful guidelines to follow are:

1. Cultivate networks; let the world know where you are and how to find you; if a recruiter calls, return the call even when you don't intend to move in the near future. You may want the help of the recruiter down the line, possibly sooner than you think (see **Networking; Recruitment**).
2. Avoid assignments that detract from your marketability. The guiding rule here is to seek those assignments which will look best on your resume. Also, make sure your resume is current; update it every six months (see **Resume**).
3. Keep your bags packed and be ready to move; having contacts for jobs and skills that others want won't help if you always have "one more thing to

accomplish." In many respects, this is the most important of the guidelines. The free agent manager must look on movement as a challenge and an adventure.

You don't need to take every opportunity if the adventure seems ill-timed or too dangerous—sky diving can be a challenging adventure but it is not advised for those who aren't prepared—but you do need to be ready to grab the chance that is right for you.

*See also* Career Planning; Job Security; Networking; Recruitment; Resume.

## Bibliography

Bennett, A. (1990). *The death of the organization man.* New York: Morrow. Bennett explains how and why the corporate environment changed so dramatically over the last decade. More important, she provides a feeling for the breadth of change and for some of the outcomes—both tragedies and triumphs—associated with the new organizational values forced on middle management.

Hirsch, P. M. (1988). *Pack your own parachute.* Reading, MA: Addison-Wesley. Hirsch offers strategies for the victims and potential victims of downsizing and reorganization. Stepping beyond the economic arguments for and against mergermania, the survival and prosperity of the individual in a cold, economic world is outlined.

Kanter, R. (1989). *When giants learn to dance.* New York: Simon & Schuster. Kanter offers a view of the key, dramatic issues from the perspective of the manager. Accepting change as a competitive necessity, she addresses mechanisms for managing in a new environment and the shared values of management and employee if the transition is successful. A new employment relationship is predicted and prescribed.

—THOMAS H. VONK AND PAUL M. HIRSCH

# JOB SHARING

The innovative concept whereby two employees hold what was formerly one full-time position is called job sharing. Two employees, or even three, can determine with their employer how to restructure existing positions, share responsibilities, divide fringe benefits, and schedule time to meet personal needs and still fulfill job requirements. Salary and fringe benefits are prorated. In some cases, tasks are assigned to each sharer; in others, the effort is collaborative.

## Is Job Sharing for You?

Before making the decision to seek a job shared position, take into consideration your motivation as well as the economic impact that job sharing will have. Your gross income will be halved and while your net income will be a little more than half due to tax considerations you may find yourself paying your own insurance costs as well as having fewer sick and vacation days.

There are two approaches to developing a job shared position. One is to remain with your present employer and share the job you now hold. The second is to approach a potential employer with the concept.

The easier approach is to convince your present employer to allow you to share your existing position. This, of course, rests on your desire to remain with this employer—if you are unhappy, less time will not necessarily make the job more palatable.

## Sharing Your Present Job

Once you have made the decision to approach your employer, you need to carefully plan your strategy. It is essential that you have a clear, well thought out, written proposal. Keep in mind that well-written, well-organized documents are more likely to be read. Include an over-all summary of your proposal, describing briefly what each section covers. Schedule a meeting with your employer and, if possible, bring the candidate for sharing your job to that meeting. You may wish to give your employer a copy of your proposal a day, no more, in advance of your meeting.

Be sure to stress in your proposal how employers benefit from job-sharing programs. Some of the benefits you can point out include greater flexibility in work scheduling, retention of valued employees, reduction of turnover, wider range of skills in one job, recruitment from a broader labor pool, options for older employees, more energy on the job, reduction of absenteeism, and continuity of job performance.

Cost-conscious employers observe a positive result at the bottom line because job sharers, at liberty to schedule medical and personal appointments during their free time, avoid using sick days or company time for these tasks. Job sharers are more inclined to make time up because they have the extra time to do it.

Effective time management cuts the need for extra staff during peak periods. Overtime costs can be significantly reduced, and continued job coverage can diminish the need for temporary personnel during vacations and extended illnesses.

Your employer may question the costs that could be involved in the administration of your job-sharing program, and with the additional paperwork there may be a slight increase. On the other hand, training costs are reduced in many cases when a valued employee remains in a position on a shared basis, training his or her partner. Also, when one team member leaves, the remaining team member takes over the training process, alleviating the need for supervisors to train new employees.

Your job-sharing proposal should contain:

- An up-to-date description of your present job.
- An outline of your skills and your partner's skills (if you have a candidate) and how they correspond to the job description.
- A breakdown of how the job responsibilities, major and minor, will be divided.
- A work-time schedule stating its advantages for the company, peak-time coverage, vacation coverage, holidays, reduced absenteeism, and so on. It may be wise to present alternatives if more than one type of schedule is feasible.
- A suggested division of fringe benefits and what their costs will be.
- The communication tools you and your partner will utilize.
- How you plan to communicate with your supervisor.
- How your job sharing will affect the rest of the organization, including coworkers and unions, and any possible public relations benefits.
- Backup information on job sharing: history, others utilizing the concept, and the like.

When you approach your employer, anticipate questions and have your answers ready. Should a question arise for which you do not have a ready response, offer to do additional research.

If possible, "role play" or rehearse your meeting with your employer with a friend. This can alleviate your nervousness and make your presentation more convincing.

Your commitment to job sharing, your thorough research, your past experience, and your position as a valued employee should convince your employer that this is a program worth pursuing, and chances are good that he or she will work with you in resolving any minor unanswered questions.

## Seeking a Shared Job

While looking for a shared job is more difficult, it may be your only option. There are two ways to apply for a shared job. You can first find a partner and then tackle the job hunt jointly, or you can go it alone, working on the assumption that there may already be someone on the staff of your potential employer who is looking to cut back to less than full-time employment.

Working with a partner to find a shared job is usually preferable. First of all, you present an employer with a solution—not a problem. Secondly, two heads are better

than one, especially in a job hunt. And, thirdly, and perhaps most importantly, the job sharing team can encourage one another.

In either case, you will need a good resume, a covering letter, and a sound foundation in the ways in which you plan to share a job. You must anticipate questions and arm yourself with answers.

Many of the points covered under the heading of "Sharing your Present Job" apply in preparing a proposal for a potential employer. Certainly, all of the benefits to the employer (except the retention of a valued employee) apply.

Keep in mind that the available labor pool will have a major impact on the receptivity of employers. If you and your partner have skills which are in short supply *and* high demand in your area you have a good chance of being hired. On the other hand, if the workplace has a glut of people with your skills it is unlikely that an employer will make the extra effort to design a program for you.

## Summary

Whether you are approaching your present employer or a potential employer always remember that your major selling point is the benefits that job sharing will provide to that employer. While many employers are sympathetic to and supportive of the needs of their employees, the first consideration is the efficient operation of the organization.

*See also* Negotiating; Part-Time Work; Temporary Employment.

## Bibliography

Bahls, J. E. (1990, February). Getting full time work from part-time employees. *Management Review:* 50–52.
Lee, P. (1983). *The complete guide to job sharing.* New York: Walker. A comprehensive step-by-step guide to establishing a job-sharing position.
Managerial job sharing. (1989, October). *Catalyst Perspective:* 1
Olmstead, B., & Smith, S. (1985). *The job sharing handbook.* Berkeley, CA: Ten Speed Press.
One job, two contented workers. (1988, November 14). *U.S. News &World Report:* 74, 76.
Ricci, C. (1988, November). Sell job sharing to your boss. *Working Mother:* 38–42.

—PATRICIA LEE

# L

## LAW IN THE WORKPLACE

## Topics Covered

## Overview

The goal of this article is to provide a brief and practical overview of the many laws and regulations governing the field of labor and employment relations. This article is designed to provide a survey or listing of the rights and prerogatives for employees created by legislation, which come into play on a regular, if not daily, basis. This is not a do-it-yourself guide to resolving labor or employment disputes, but workers should find the information useful in helping to understand many of the issues that can arise. This article is not intended as a definitive restatement of the laws, nor as a substitute for legal advice.

## Employment, an "At-Will" Relationship

### Background

The employment of workers has long been recognized as an at-will relationship, which means that the employee may quit at any time, for any reason, with or without notice, and the employer may terminate an employee at any time, for any reason, with or without notice. In 1884, the Tennessee Supreme Court explained the doctrine in these words: "All may dismiss their employee(s) at-will, be they many or few, for good cause, or no cause, or even for cause morally wrong without being thereby guilty of legal wrong." Over the years, the doctrine has been stated via statutes and/or court decisions in all 50 states plus the District of Columbia.

### Exceptions

There are three exceptions to the at-will doctrine. First, there is the express contract, where the terms and conditions are negotiated and agreed upon prior to employment. The express agreement specifies a fixed duration during which the contract and employment are in effect. This type of contract is usually in writing, but may also be oral. For example, an agreement saying that Employee A will be employed by Company B for three years is an express contract for a specified duration. During this three-year duration, Employee A cannot be discharged unless there is a provision permitting it.

The second exception, a statutory or regulatory limitation, was first implemented in the 1930s as a result of significant changes in social, economic, and institutional conditions. Congress and the state legislatures have enacted laws that have limited and restricted the employers' unfettered right to hire, fire, and set the employees' terms and conditions. For example, some of the statutory labor laws prohibit employers from refusing to hire applicants or discriminate against employees because of their union activities, concerted and protected activities, minority origins, sex, age, safety complaints, and receipt of a garnishment.

The third exception to the at-will doctrine is the court-established wrongful discharge exception. There are two kinds of wrongful discharges: breach of an implied contract and violation of a public policy. An example of an implied contract is where an employer has committed itself to pay wages or provide fringe benefits which the employee has a reasonable expectation of receiving and the employer has a policy or practice of providing the wages or benefit. An example of discharging an employee in violation of public policy would be the firing of an employee who filed a workers' compensation claim or who was required to serve on a jury.

### Reasons for the Exceptions

Why the significant changes? First, economic power has become increasingly concentrated in the hands of large companies and corporations. Modern reality clearly establishes that when the prospective employee is seeking employment, there is little, if any, opportunity to negotiate wages or benefits.

Second, the majority of the workforce is no longer self-employed and, as a result, the individual is dependent on employment-related income. The discharge of an employee without providing justification can impose significant social, psychological, and economic costs on the employee. By the same token, the economically dependent employee has little meaningful ability to resign because of the economic hazards involved.

And, third, as a result of the enactment of numerous laws and the significant number of court decisions, employers have had to redefine their relationships with applicants and employees and to recognize the rights and prerogatives of employees. Employees expect to be given job-related reasons when decisions are made that affect their employment status.

## Recruiting and Hiring

Many of the rights and opportunities accorded employees are also applicable to applicants for employment. There are certain restrictions, as well as requirements, upon employers and recruiting sources in the recruiting process, which involve advertising, screening, and testing.

### Advertising

The simplest and least expensive way for employers to advertise job openings is to let the employees know of the vacancies and permit them to pass the word around among their friends. However, this word-of-mouth recruiting may violate the anti-discrimination rules if it causes or perpetuates an imbalance of minorities and females or has a discriminatory impact upon the protected group(s). The same requirements apply to employers who obtain their applicants from labor unions (through hiring halls or referral systems) or via an employment agency.

Placing an ad with the various forms of communication media also imposes various nondiscriminatory requirements on the employer as well as upon the media. For example, employers advertising for "recent college grads," "trainee," "girl Friday," or "retired person" are using terms that could lead to charges of sex or age discrimination. Similarly, the listing of sex-segregated columns of "Male" or "Female" is an indication of sex discrimination under federal and most state laws.

### Employment Applicant/Interview

What an employer asks during the hiring process, including the interview stages, can also lead to charges of discrimination. Both the hiring forms (e.g., application form, medical survey) and oral interviews must be free from questions or subjective feelings of bias regarding race, religion, national origin, sex, age, and handicap. The information sought must bear a direct relationship to the job and the qualifications of the employee to be hired.

### Testing and Examinations

Employers may administer tests and examinations to applicants. The tests must be substantially related to the requirements of the job, fair and reasonable, fairly administered, properly evaluated or validated, and must not have a discriminatory impact upon minorities or females. The Equal Employment Opportunity Commission (EEOC) has established the Uniform Guidelines on Employee Selection Procedures, which set forth information for public and private employers to follow in order to ensure that their selection procedures are nondiscriminatory and do not adversely affect minority groups or females.

There are other kinds of tests that job applicants or employees may be asked to take. These include drug tests, lie detector tests, and medical examinations (see **Testing; Testing: AIDS; Testing: Genetic**).

**Drug Testing.** In the private sector, employers may require applicants and employees to undergo drug and alcohol tests. Initial or continued employment based upon taking and passing the tests is legal. There are, however, two possible exceptions. First, there may be state laws regarding privacy rights. These laws could limit blood and urine tests because they constitute an illegal search or seizure unless the employee voluntarily agrees to participate.

The second exception applies to employers whose employees are represented by unions. The labor laws require employers and unions to negotiate and agree on terms and conditions of employment. Testing for alcohol or drugs is a condition of employment and, therefore, cannot be required by the employer without permission by the union.

In the public sector, employees are protected by constitutional guarantees of privacy against involuntary testing. Only employees who work in safety-critical or sensitive positions can be required to take drug or alcohol tests. The courts have upheld involuntary testing, for example, to train locomotive engineers, police officers, border patrol agents, and air-traffic controllers (see **Testing: Drugs**).

**Lie Detector Tests.** The Employee Polygraph Protection Act of 1988 (EPPA) prohibits most private-sector employers from using lie detector tests either for pre-employment screening or during the course of employment. The polygraph is one of several lie detector testing devices, but it is the only one permitted for use in three limited areas under the law. First, employees may be tested if they are reasonably suspected of involvement in economic losses in the business or property destruction at the workplace. A second exception allows pre-employment testing for certain security-conscious businesses, such as armored car, security guard, and security alarm companies. Thirdly, applicants and current employees may be tested in firms authorized to manufacture, distribute, or dispense controlled substances. The EPPA has no application to governmental employees, federal contractors who contract with private individuals for counterintelligence services, and Federal Bureau of Investigation contractors. Government employers are exempted on the basis that public-sector employees may invoke constitutional protection and rights of privacy guarantees. Federal contractors are exempted because of the country's compelling interest in national security (see **Testing: Integrity**).

**Medical Examinations.** Pre-employment medical exams are not prohibited. Likewise, employers can require current employees to take medical examinations in order to determine their continued fitness to perform the jobs. However, most state laws require the employer to pay for the examination and the medical information must be confidential.

### Oral and Written Representations

Statements made by recruiters or supervisors to a prospective employee or applicant may give rise to an implied contract of employment and, therefore, a lawsuit if the statements are later disregarded or not fulfilled. For example, promises of job security or wage increases that were not kept have led to lawsuits in the 1980s.

### Alien Employment Controls

It is unlawful for an employer to hire any person knowing that such person is an illegal alien. Under the Immigration Reform and Control Act (IRCA) of 1986, employers are required to verify the identity and authorization to work of employees hired after November 6, 1986 through an examination of documents. IRCA applies to all employers who are subject to sanctions for hiring illegal aliens or failing to comply with the requirements of the law. The sanctions include civil fines and criminal penalties (including jail terms of not more than six months) (see **Immigration**).

IRCA provides an exception for agricultural workers. A new program is authorized for the employment of nonimmigrant persons to perform temporary agricultural work. Agricultural employers must obtain certification from the secretary of labor that there are not sufficient workers available and that the importation of aliens will not adversely affect the wages and working conditions of domestic workers.

## Rights and Responsibilities on the Job

### Equal Employment Opportunity

The major purpose of Title VII of the U.S. Civil Rights Act of 1964 is to provide equal employment opportunity. Title VII prohibits employment practices that discriminate against applicants and employees because of their race, color, religion, sex, or national origin. Other anti-discrimination laws passed by Congress include the Age Discrimination in Employment Act of 1967 (ADEA) (which has been amended to protect workers who are over 40 years old), the Rehabilitation Act of 1973 (protecting qualified handicapped individuals from discrimination), the Americans with Disabilities Act of 1990, and the Veterans' Readjustment Benefits Act of 1972 (which protects disabled veterans and Vietnam-era veterans from job discrimination). Prior to and after enactment of Title VII, there have been a series of executive orders designed to eliminate employment discrimination on the part of federal government contractors by requiring the contractors to initiate affirmative action programs.

### Affirmative Action

Affirmative action obligates employers who are government contractors or who are recipients of certain federal funds to provide preferential treatment for the hiring, upgrading, and promoting of qualified employees who are members of minority or protected groups. Affirmative action is also a measurement of an employer's commitment to equal employment opportunity using a numerical comparison between the proportion of minorities and women in the company's workforce and the availability of those groups in either the population or the appropriate labor force. The basic objective of affirmative action is to eliminate the effects or vestiges of past discrimination by society as well as by employers doing business with, or receiving funds from, the federal government. Equal employment opportunity laws, as well as affirmative action requirements, have also been adopted by most state governments and a significant number of local governments.

The Office of Federal Contract Compliance Programs (OFCCP), which is part of the U.S. Department of Labor, is charged with the responsibility of administering and enforcing affirmative action programs under the executive orders.

### Employee Privacy

Over the past several years, laws have been passed and court decisions have been rendered that give employees protection against the use or disclosure of confidential information. The privacy rights extend to employees before, during, and after employment. However, there is a fine line between what is confidential and nondisclosable and the obligation to use or disclose the information.

The right of privacy is offset by the employer's right to obtain information about the employees he or she is going to hire or continue in employment. This includes medical information that is directly related to determining the employee's qualifications for the job or capability of per-forming the work. It includes the right to information from a previous employer that would help determine the individual's qualifications, competency, reliability, and honesty.

Confidential information is also disclosable when a collective bargaining union requests information about the employees it represents. The disclosure of this information is an obligation under the National Labor Relations Act. Also, employers are required to give information about their employees to governmental agencies.

On the other hand, there are limitations on employers, labor organizations, and governmental agencies. An employee is protected against defamation. Although an employer may provide information about a former employee, the information cannot be false, derogatory, or impugn the former employee's reputation. Also, information regarding an employee or former employee is on a "need to know" basis. Disclosure of information to supervisors, employees, or others who have no necessity for receiving the information may be a violation of the right of privacy. By the same token, an employer who makes a public disclosure of embarrassing private information about an employee, such as revealing medical information or test scores, may violate the employee's privacy rights.

In the public sector, employees have the right of privacy based upon the constitutional guarantee against searches, seizures, and self-incrimination. Some states have enacted laws that give this same protection to private-sector employees. Also, depending upon circumstances, these same rights may be protected by court or arbitration decisions. For example, employers are limited in their ability to search the private property of their employees. It means that arbitrary searches of purses, lunch boxes, automobiles, and lockers cannot be made. Depending upon circumstances, an employee is entitled to have a witness or representative available during an investigatory interview or meeting where the results could lead to discipline or discharge. Also, if an employee's detention during an investigatory meeting is unreasonable, the employer may be liable for false imprisonment.

Under the Fair Credit Reporting Act, if an employer requests credit rating information or investigative reports from consumer reporting agencies, the employee must be notified and provided with a copy of the report. This law also prohibits a creditor from calling an employee at work or from contacting the employer about a debt without first receiving the employee's permission.

Under the Federal Crime Control and Safe Streets Act, an employer cannot intercept an employee's confidential communication. This prohibits eavesdropping and the monitoring of employees' telephone calls.

There has also been a growing number of cases involving the issue of employee life styles, living arrangements, and social relationships. Denying employment benefits or discharging employees because of their association with individuals has been found to violate the rights of privacy. Examples of life styles given protection are the homosexual relationship or the marital or nonmarital status. Employees are also protected in their off-duty activities as long as such activity does not interfere with their job performance or does not cause embarrassment to or undermine the reputation of the employer. Some of the off-duty activities that may be given protection include political activities, moonlighting, and club or organization membership.

### Wages and Hours

The Fair Labor Standards Act of 1938 (FLSA) establishes certain wage and hour standards for employers and employees engaged in or affecting interstate commerce. Specifically, the FLSA establishes the minimum rate of pay and a maximum number of hours for which straight-time wages can be paid. Time worked in excess of 40 hours must be paid at the overtime rate of time-and-one-half. Employers must also comply with state and local laws.

The FLSA's coverage is broad; the U.S. Supreme Court has held that the law is to be liberally applied to an employer-employee relationship. However, most employment practices are not covered or regulated by the FLSA. These include, for example, vacation or holiday pay, severance pay, wage increases, or fringe benefits.

Every employer subject to the minimum wage and overtime provisions of the FLSA is required to make and preserve certain records concerning employees, even those who are exempt from the minimum wage and overtime provisions. Also, employers are required to post, and keep posted, a notice explaining the requirements of the FLSA. The notice must be posted in a conspicuous place and/or made available to all employees and applicants for employment.

### Job Safety

State and federal laws require employers to maintain workplaces free from safety and health hazards. In addition, a growing number of states have enacted right-to-know laws that require the disclosure of information about hazardous chemical substances. Congress has also enacted a broad right-to-know law.

The federal safety and health laws and right-to-know laws are codified under the Occupational Safety & Health Act (OSHA) and Mine Safety & Health Act (MSHA). These laws require employers to provide their employees with safe and healthful working conditions by maintaining a workplace free from hazards that may cause physical harm, illness, or injury. The federal laws are enforced by the U. S. Labor Department's Occupational Safety and Health Administration (OSHA) and the Mine Safety & Health Administration (MSHA). Many states have similar laws that are administered and enforced by state agencies working together with OSHA and MSHA.

In addition to eliminating safety hazards, employers must also comply with federal and state regulations regarding job safety and health standards. These standards include fire protection, construction and maintenance of equipment, safety training, machinery and equipment protective devices, appliances, and apparel. Employers are also obligated to provide employees (and others) with specific information regarding chemicals or compounds that may be dangerous or hazardous. Employees have the right to report unsafe or unhealthful working conditions and under both federal and state laws, they are protected against retaliation because they questioned or reported safety defects or unsafe conditions (see also **Work Hazards** and related articles).

### Labor Relations

Under a series of laws first enacted in 1926, Congress has established protection for workers who wish to organize and bargain collectively, be represented by labor organizations, and/or join unions. These laws include the Railway Labor Act of 1926 (RLA) and the National Labor Relations Act of 1935 (NLRA), as amended.

The NLRA guarantees the rights of workers to organize and bargain collectively with their employers, or to refrain from all such activity. To enable employees to exercise these rights and to prevent labor disputes which may impede interstate commerce, the NLRA places certain limits on activities of employers and labor organizations. The NLRA generally applies to all employers engaged in interstate commerce. It does not apply to railroads and airlines because they are covered by the RLA.

**Administration of the Law.** The NLRA is administered and enforced by the National Labor Relations Board (NLRB) and its General Counsel acting through more than 45 regional and other field offices located throughout the United States. The General Counsel and his or her staff in the regional offices investigate and prosecute unfair labor practice cases and conduct elections to determine employee representatives. The five-member Board decides cases involving charges of unfair labor practices and determines representation election questions that come to it from the General Counsel.

**Employee Rights.** Employees have the right to form a union among the employees of a company, to join a union whether or not the union is recognized by the employer, to assist a union to organize the employees of an employer, to strike for better working conditions or protest an unfair labor practice, to engage in picketing for information purposes, to engage in protected and concerted activities regarding wages, hours, and other terms and conditions of employment, and to refrain from activity on behalf of or for a union.

A labor organization may be recognized by an employer or be certified by the NLRB as the duly-authorized representative of the employees in an appropriate unit for bargaining, following an NLRB-conducted secret-ballot election. If there is a collective bargaining representative, the representative and the employer must engage in good faith collective bargaining. For example, they are expected to meet at reasonable times and confer in good faith with respect to wages, hours, and other terms and conditions of employment. They are not required, however, to agree to a proposal or make concessions.

**State Labor Laws.** Because the NLRA does not apply to all employers, many states have enacted laws similar to the NLRA which provide for many of the same rights and obligations for employees, labor organizations, and employers who are not covered by the NLRA. The NLRA has also authorized states to pass laws which can place limitations on the requirements of whether or not employees need to join labor organizations in order to retain their jobs. There are 21 states that have passed legislation that prohibits union security clauses from being negotiated and/or enforced. These laws are commonly referred to as "right-to-work" laws, and they prohibit any requirements that employees join and/or pay service charges to labor organizations.

**Union Obligations.** Under the RLA, NLRA, and the Labor Management Reporting and Disclosure Act of 1959 (LMRDA), labor organizations are required to represent, in a nondiscriminatory way, all members and/or employees within the collective bargaining unit they represent, i.e., unions must engage in fair representation of all employees and members.

There are approximately 55 nationwide unions, many of which also have operations located in Canada. Generally, unions have a national office and regional, district, and/or local offices and units. Unions are governed by constitutions and by-laws that establish them as democratic organizations and which define the rights and responsibilities of the officers and members.

Most nationwide unions, but not all, are members of the AFL-CIO (American Federation of Labor-Congress of Industrial Organizations), which was formed in 1955 by the merger of the two organizations. The AFL-CIO activities, like those of many business associations, include legislative action to promote laws, provide services, and assist in resolving inter-union or jurisdictional disputes.

In addition to the rights and protections accorded the members under the unions' constitutions and by-laws, many rights of union members are established and regulated by the LMRDA. Unions are required to file copies of their constitutions, by-laws, annual reports, and other financial information with the U. S. Department of Labor and to make records available to their membership for examination. The LMRDA also governs the responsibilities of union officers; establishes procedures for electing, selecting, or removing officials from office; and safeguards the rights of union members.

## Employment Discrimination

### Federal Regulations

As noted earlier, the nation's public policy is to promote equal employment opportunity. The principle federal employment discrimination law is Title VII of the Civil Rights Act of 1964. Other federal anti-discrimination laws include the Age Discrimination in Employment Act of 1967 (ADEA), and the Equal Pay Act of 1963 (EPA), which prohibits wage differentials because of sex. The Vocational Rehabilitation Act of 1973 requires employers who receive federal funds to employ and promote qualified handicapped individuals. The Vietnam Era Veterans' Readjustment Assistance Act of 1972 requires employers having federal contracts to employ disabled veterans and qualified veterans of the Vietnam era. Title VII, the ADEA, and the EPA are administered and enforced by the Equal Employment Opportunity Commission (EEOC). The handicapped and veterans' EEO laws are enforced by the U. S. Department of Labor, Office of Federal Contract Compliance Programs (OFCCP).

### Determining Discrimination

Under Title VII and the ADEA, there can be no discrimination in hiring, firing, or terms and benefits of employment on the basis of an individual's race, color, religion, sex, national origin, or age. This includes, but is not limited to, promotions, transfers, assignments, pay, training opportunities, leaves of absence, fringe benefits, and retirement and welfare plans. Title VII does not require employers to employ or retain employees who are not qualified and, under the EPA, does not prohibit employers from basing pay differentials on factors other than sex.

There are two major theories involving employment discrimination. They are disparate or differential treatment and disparate or differential impact. Most cases of employment discrimination are analyzed under either of these theories.

**Disparate Treatment Theory.** This occurs if the member of the protected category is treated differently than a nonminority employee. For example, if a black employee is discharged for a rule infraction whereas a white employee is not, a prima facie case of disparate treatment is established.

**Disparate Impact Theory.** This involves a neutral rule or impartial standard that has a greater effect upon a protected group. For example, a rule that requires all employees to be over 5'7" tall would have a greater, and thereby discriminatory impact upon females, Hispanics, and orientals.

### State and Other Antidiscrimination Laws

Title VII provides for the establishment of anti-discrimination laws by state and local governments. Referred to as deferral laws, these state and local laws are complimentary with (and not preempted by) the federal law.

In addition to Title VII and the state laws, there are other federal laws that provide a remedy against employment discrimination. These are the civil rights acts of 1866 and 1871. They have been codified as 42 U.S.C. 1981, 1983, and 1985. Under Section 1981, all persons shall have the same right to make and enforce contracts regardless of race or color. Under Section 1983, state and local governmental bodies are prohibited from making or enforcing laws that deprive citizens of their rights, privileges, or immunities secured by the Constitution and other laws. Section 1985 prohibits conspiracies by private individuals that cause racial discrimination. It also prohibits conspiracies by governmental officials that cause discrimination because of race, color, sex, religion, national origin, and age.

### Race Discrimination

Any type of discrimination because of race or color is prohibited by Title VII. There are no exceptions. This includes both employees and qualified applicants. Title VII also prohibits inverse or reverse discrimination (i.e., preferential treatment to racial minorities) unless the preferential program is pursuant to a valid affirmative action plan, pursuant to a court-ordered remedy, or part of a compliance agreement with the EEOC or other federal or state agency (see also **Discrimination: Race**).

### Native Americans

Courts have found Native Americans protected by Title VII on the basis of race, on the basis of national origin, or on the bases of both race and national origin. In addition, Native Americans are protected against discrimination under the civil rights acts of 1866 and 1871. Title VII also provides preferential treatment to Native Americans in certain employment (i.e., preferential treatment given to any individual because he or she is an Indian living on or near a reservation).

### National Origin Discrimination

Although the laws prohibit discrimination because of "national origin," the term is not defined in any statute. Nevertheless, it means discrimination against individuals because of their place of origin, ancestry, heritage, or background. The majority of national origin discrimination cases have involved Spanish-surnamed persons, which includes Mexican-Americans, Puerto Ricans, Cubans, and others whose primary language is Spanish. Other groups included within the meaning of national origin are orientals and American Indians. National origin discrimination has been found where persons are excluded from employment because of a characteristic peculiar to their heritage. For example, a height requirement for employment that would exclude Mexican-Americans or orientals would be discriminatory. Likewise, an employment rule prohibiting the use of foreign languages in certain jobs or the denial of employment opportunity because of an individual's accent or manner of speaking have been considered discrimination based on national origin (see **Discrimination: Language; Nonstandard English**).

### Religious Discrimination

It is a violation of Title VII and state anti-discrimination laws for employers, employment agencies, and labor organizations to discriminate against individuals because of their religious beliefs.

The term "religion" includes all aspects of religious observances and practices and the laws require employers and labor organizations to reasonably accommodate employees and job applicants in observing their religious commitments. Whether an employer has satisfied the duty to accommodate will frequently turn on what efforts the employer has attempted. If the efforts would create an undue hardship on the conduct of the business, the employer has fulfilled the requirements of the law.

### Age Discrimination

Under the ADEA, it is unlawful for an employer to discriminate against persons who are over the age of 40, except for fire fighters and law enforcement officers who are over 70. The ADEA covers most private employers, state and local governments, educational institutions, employment agencies, and labor organizations. Most states retain an upper limit (ages 65 or 70) and also have lower age limits (ages 18 or 21). The most recent amendment to the ADEA, the Older Workers' Benefit Protection Act of 1990, prohibits discrimination because of age in virtually all employee fringe benefit plans. Under the new law, a benefit plan will be legal if it provides equal benefits to, or incurs equal cost for benefits on behalf of older workers (see **Discrimination: Age**).

### Sex Discrimination

Title VII and the state anti-discrimination laws prohibit employment discrimination on the basis of sex. Although the laws did not spell out or define what was meant by "sex discrimination," the ban on sex discrimination has developed over the years to include such areas as differential treatment, sex stereotype treatment, pregnancy protection policies, sexual harassment, equal pay, and comparable worth. Female employees, individually and collectively, must be treated the same as male employees in regard to wages, hours, fringe benefits, retirement benefits, and other terms or conditions of employment. If not, the female may be a victim of sex discrimination. Also, employer policies or rules that have a greater effect or impact upon female employees may cause discrimination. For example, a rule that the employees have to be of a certain height would affect more females than males (see **Discrimination: Sex**).

In the sex stereotype situation, it may constitute discrimination where the female is not hired because of the historical misconceptions that have existed. For years, laws have limited the employment of females in certain occupations, restricting the weight to be lifted, precluding work during certain hours of the night, limiting work hours to a specified number during the day or week, or setting forth periods of time before and after childbirth when the female employee could not work. Discrimination based on stereotyping also applied to the claim that mothers, and not fathers, have an unacceptably high rate of absenteeism; that mothers might be subject to overriding domestic concerns, making them questionable risks in times of crisis; and that mothers returning from pregnancy leaves would require expensive retraining. All of these laws and myths have been struck down by the federal and state laws prohibiting sex discrimination (see **Sex-Role Stereotyping**).

## Pregnancy

Title VII covers most private employers, state and local governments, public or private educational institutions, employment agencies, labor organizations, and apprenticeship programs. Title VII and the EEOC Guidelines provide specific protection against discrimination because of pregnancy and sexual harassment. One of the amendments to Title VII requires employees who are disabled because of pregnancy to be treated the same as all other employees who are temporarily disabled because of medical reasons (see **Parental Leave**). Abortions, however, are not within the coverage of the law. Although the law speaks in terms of equal treatment, the U.S. Supreme Court has ruled that state laws which provide preferential treatment to pregnant employees are not violative of the federal law.

## Sexual Harassment

The U.S. Supreme Court has also upheld the EEOC's stated prohibition against sexual harassment. In this regard, harassment involves any unwelcome sexual advance, request for sexual favors, or other verbal or physical conduct of a sexual nature directed at an employee by an employer or its supervisors or agents. Such conduct constitutes sex discrimination if submission to it is a condition of employment, used as a basis for making employment decisions, has the effect of unreasonably interfering with the employee's work performance, or creates an intimidating, hostile, or offensive work environment (see **Sexual Harassment**).

## Equal Pay

The Equal Pay Act of 1963 (EPA) prohibits sex discrimination in payment of wages to females and males performing substantially equal work in the same establishment. Substantially equal work refers to equal skill, effort, responsibility, and similar working conditions. There are exceptions to the EPA. These include sex differences that result from a seniority system, a merit system, a system which measures earnings by quantity or quality of production, or pursuant to a differential based on a factor other than sex. Generally, a violation of the EPA is also a violation of Title VII.

## Comparable Worth

Closely related to equal pay for equal work is the comparable worth theory. This is a theory for proving sex discrimination in wages that would allow one group or class of employees to compare their wages to those of another group or class of employees (who are performing dissimilar jobs) based on the relative value or worth to the employer. According to the theory, whole classes of jobs may be undervalued because they have been traditionally segregated by sex. For example, in hospitals the maintenance personnel (who are male) may be paid a higher wage than the nurses (who are female) although the nurses may have a greater value to the mission and operation of the hospital. Under the comparable worth theory, the nurses would be permitted to bring Title VII sex discrimination charges against the hospital based on a comparison of the value of their jobs to those of the maintenance men. However, very few courts have accepted or adopted the comparable worth theory. One of the overriding reasons for its non acceptance is the inability to compare jobs in such a way that the wage differential could be made meaningful.

## Handicap Discrimination

Under the Rehabilitation Act of 1973 (Sections 503 and 504) and various state laws, discrimination against individuals who have a physical or mental impairment that substantially limits one or more of the individual's major life activities is prohibited. The term "handicap" has been interpreted to include physical impairments, medical disabilities, contagious diseases, and previous physical or mental disabling impairments (including alcoholism, drug addiction, heart attack). The Rehabilitation Act applies to all employers who are contractors or subcontractors with the federal government or who are the recipients of certain federal assistance.

In 1990, Congress passed the Americans with Disabilities Act (ADA), which prohibits discrimination against disabled individuals in private and governmental employment, public accommodations, public transportation, government services, and telecommunications. The purpose of the ADA is to eliminate discrimination against individuals with disabilities and to bring them into the economic and social mainstream of American life. With regard to employment, the law becomes effective in July 1992 for those employers with 25 or more employees. Effective July 1994, employers with 15 or more employees will be covered. The ADA will be administered and enforced by the EEOC.

A person with a disability is someone who has a physical or mental impairment that substantially limits one or more of his or her major life activities or has a record of or is regarded as having an impairment. Impairments include visual, speech, and hearing impairments; epilepsy; heart disease; learning disabilities; mental retardation; paraplegia; multiple sclerosis; cerebral palsy; muscular dystrophy; schizophrenia; cancer; infection with the HIV virus (AIDS); alcoholism; and drug addiction. However, drug addiction does not cover individuals currently using illegal drugs, but may cover those who are recovering from or are former users of illegal drugs, including those participating in a supervised rehabilitation program, as well as those erroneously regarded as using illegal drugs but who do not in fact use them.

Conditions that are not covered by the ADA include age, prison record, homosexuality, bisexuality, voyeurism, compulsive gambling, kleptomania, current use of illegal drugs, and an alcoholic who either uses alcohol or is under the influence of alcohol at the workplace.

Both the Rehabilitation Act and the ADA require the employer to provide reasonable accommodation to the handicapped/disabled person unless it results in an undue hardship. Reasonable accommodation does not (a) unduly disrupt or interfere with the employer's normal operations; (b) threaten the health or safety of the handicapped individual or others; (c) contradict a business necessity of the employer; or (d) impose undue hardship on the employer based on the size of the employer's business, type of business, financial resources of the employer, and/or the estimated cost and extent of the accommodation. Such accommodation includes architectural accommodations (e.g., doorways, rampways, toilets), equipment accommodations (e.g., headset phones, page turners, pressure-sensitive tape recorders), and job accommodations (e.g., modifications of job duties, shift changes, flexible scheduling).

Almost all states have adopted some form of protection against handicap discrimination. However, the scope of who is considered to be handicapped or disabled differs from state to state. In some states, only the physically handicapped are protected and in other states, the protection includes those with mental and physical handicaps (see **Discrimination: People with Disabilities**).

### Veteran Discrimination

Under the Vietnam Era Veterans Readjustment Assistance Act, employers with federal contracts are prohibited from discriminating against Vietnam era veterans and qualified special disabled veterans. The law also requires affirmative action to employ and advance in employment these qualified veterans.

### AIDS in the Workplace

Acquired Immune Deficiency Syndrome (AIDS) has become one of the most important and perplexing health issues confronting employers. The continued increase in the number of AIDS cases means that employers will have to respond to the needs of employees with a serious and potentially life-threatening disease, as well as the honest, though generally unfounded, health and safety concerns of fellow employees or customers. Despite the seriousness of AIDS, it is a health matter and the law is treating it as such. However, AIDS presents employers with complex legal obligations, both as to employees who have it and to those employees who are concerned about their own safety and welfare in the workplace.

Generally, employees with AIDS or who test positive for the human immunodeficiency virus (HIV), are protected under the handicap laws (including the new ADA), privacy laws, and other laws. Although the various laws contain differences in language, their intent is to prohibit discrimination against employees who, with reasonable accommodation, are capable of performing the job without endangering themselves or others. If, however, the employee with AIDS is no longer able to perform the usual or normal duties and functions of the job, the protection of the law ends.

Many states have laws or court decisions that require confidentiality of medical test results. Disclosure of AIDS or test results for the HIV antibody cannot be made without violating the rights of privacy. Privacy rights also prohibit the use of test results in determining insurability or suitability for employment (see **Testing: AIDS**).

While the rights of employees with AIDS are well-established, employers must also acknowledge and protect the rights of fellow employees who are concerned about their safety in the workplace. Because the consensus in the medical community is that AIDS cannot be spread by casual contact, it seems unlikely that the presence of employees with AIDS could create an unsafe work environment. However, the major concern involves those employees who believe—even wrongly—that their working conditions are unsafe and who demand that the employee with AIDS be transferred to another job. This circumstance has created a dilemma for employers. Courts have ruled that the employer cannot take action against the employee with AIDS under the various handicap laws and, at the same time, cannot take retaliatory action against employees making the demand. As the Supreme Court pronounced in a 1980 case, workers who have a reasonable belief of a workplace hazard and who protest it are protected against retaliation.

The solution is to educate employees so that they know that they are not really at risk. If the employer provides useful AIDS education, the employees will know that AIDS is not transmitted at work. Doing so would show that an employee who protests is doing so without a reasonable belief of a safety hazard.

## Rights of Government Employees

### Constitutional Guarantees

Governmental employees enjoy significantly greater employment protection than their counterparts in the private sector. Public-sector employees initially have the protection of the federal constitution. State and local government workers also have the protection of their respective state constitution. The constitutional guarantees require public-sector employers to provide their employees with substantive and procedural due process. Such employees are also protected, generally, against illegal or unwarranted search and seizure and self-incrimination.

### Civil Service Protection

There is also a scheme of administrative law and regulation that provides for procedural due process and protection to public sector employees. Generally referred to as a civil service system, it establishes wage schedules, competitive service procedures, job descriptions and ratings, and various rules, regulations, and standards for benefits, discipline, and grievances.

### Public Sector Labor Relations

Under various federal and state laws and executive orders, public sector employees are provided with rights of representation by labor organizations, collective bargaining, employment contracts, job tenure, and certain fringe benefits. For example, the U.S. Postal Service is under the NLRB's jurisdiction while other federal employees have certain collective bargaining rights and protection under Executive Order 11491, which permits federal employees to join (or refrain from joining) labor organizations, provides procedures for resolving bargaining unit and majority status determinations, allows grievance procedures to be instituted, and provides a code of fair labor practices and standards of conduct. The Executive Order also establishes a Federal Labor Relations Council to make interpretations and rulings regarding grievances, disputes, discrimination charges, and impasse resolution.

At least 37 states and the District of Columbia have enacted legislation that gives some state and local governmental employees various labor-relations rights, including the right to organize, bargain collectively, and/or engage in union activities.

### Security by Laws

Also, there are federal and state laws that prohibit retaliation or discrimination against a government worker who discloses safety hazards, government illegality, waste, corruption, abuse, and/or unnecessary government expenditures. Commonly referred to as a whistleblower protection law, the rights of federal or state government employees are protected, to prevent reprisals or adverse personnel actions, and to eliminate wrongdoing or safety hazards within government.

Other state laws that afford public sector employees protection include the various teacher tenure laws, laws providing for paid holidays, and laws protecting against discrimination because of political affiliation or membership in various organizations. Also, public sector employees are covered and governed by the Fair Labor Standards Act, Title VII, ADEA, other anti-discrimination laws and safety and health laws.

## Protection Against Termination

The decision to terminate an employee has traditionally been the employer's ultimate tool for maintaining a disciplined, effective workforce. And since employment has been considered an "at-will" relationship, employers have had the right to terminate an employee at any time for any reason. However, there are many exceptions to this doctrine, and they are growing in scope. New laws, regulations, and court decisions have created a complete body of law against arbitrary, capricious, or unreasonable discharge.

### Federal Laws

Since the passage of the National Labor Relations Act in 1935, Congress and state legislatures have enacted numerous laws that protect employees against discrimination, retaliation, and wrongful discharges. Among them are:

1. The National Labor Relations Act (NLRA), which prohibits discharge in retaliation for union activities and for concerted and protected activities.
2. The Civil Service Reform Act, which allows dismissal only for unacceptable performance or "for such cause as will promote the efficiency of the service."

3. Title VII of the Civil Rights Act of 1964, which bars discrimination (and retaliation) on the basis of race, color, religion, sex, or national origin.

4. The Age Discrimination in Employment Act of 1967 (ADEA), which protects older workers (over 40 years of age) from discriminatory treatment.

5. The Consumer Credit Protection Act, which prohibits discharge of those whose wages are garnisheed for indebtedness.

6. The Fair Labor Standards Act, which makes illegal the retaliatory discharge of those exercising rights under the Act.

7. The Vietnam War Veterans' Readjustment Assistance Act, which grants most veterans the right to return to a former job after release from military service and prohibits their discharge except for just cause for one year after re-employment.

8. The Equal Pay Act, which prohibits retaliation against an employee who submits a complaint.

9. The Jury System Improvement Act of 1973, which entitles permanent employees discharged for jury service in Federal District Court to back pay, reinstatement, attorneys' fees, and a penalty of $1,000.

10. The Occupational Safety & Health Act (OSHA) and Mine Safety & Health Act (MSHA), which prohibit discharge of and retaliation against employees who file complaints, institute or participate in proceedings under the laws, or exercise any statutory rights.

11. The Rehabilitation Act of 1973, which protects employees with physical or mental handicaps from discrimination.

12. The Employee Retirement Income Security Act (ERISA), which prohibits discharge of employees to prevent them from receiving vested pensions/retirement benefits.

13. The Employee Polygraph Protection Act, which prohibits discharge and retaliation against private-sector employees who refuse to take lie detector tests, file complaints, or act on behalf of others regarding their rights under the Act.

14. Various other laws, including federal statutes that prohibit discrimination against certain federal employees for disclosure of nonprivileged information which they reasonably believe to evidence a violation of law, mismanagement of public funds, or substantial and specific danger to public health or safety.

### State Laws

Because many of the federal laws are based upon interstate commerce jurisdiction and, therefore, contain minimum limits of coverage, many states have enacted their own laws. In addition to labor-management relations laws and employment discrimination laws, they have enacted a series of anti-retaliation statutes. These include laws prohibiting discharges because a worker takes time off to vote, participates in jury duty, files a workers' compensation claim, serves in the military or national guard, engages in "whistleblowing," refuses to take a lie detector test, files an occupational safety or health complaint, executes a wage assignment or has wages garnisheed, or refuses to take a test for AIDS, drugs, or alcoholism.

### Tenure Laws

Some jobs are protected by statutes commonly referred to as tenure laws. They usually apply to teachers and judges. Generally, tenure occurs after the individual has served a probationary or trial period. After receiving permanency, the individual can not be terminated except according to procedures that are set forth in the statutes or developed by regulations.

### Judicial Limitations on Terminating Workers

Court decisions have also limited the "at will" doctrine, limiting employers' rights to terminate workers. The court-made exceptions to this doctrine fall into three areas: public policy, implied contract, and good-faith/fair-dealing.

**Public Policy.** This exception has emerged quite rapidly throughout the United States. Generally, if an employer fires an employee and that firing is against an important public policy, the termination may be a wrongful discharge for which the employee can sue the employer. The employee may be entitled to compensatory damages and punitive damages. The public policy exception occurs when employees are discharged because they (a) refuse to perform an act that public policy would condemn (e.g., committing an illegal act), (b) performed an act that public policy would encourage (e.g., serving on a jury), (c) exercised a legal right expressly established as a public policy (e.g., discharge for filing a claim under a workers' compensation statute), or (d) reported illegal or unsafe conduct to an appropriate official (e.g., "whistleblowing").

Generally, the public policy exception is available because the law does not provide a remedy. In recognizing the public policy exception, the courts have noted that discharging an employee for "bad cause" violates the rights guaranteed to the employee by law. However, taking action or refusing to take action because it is considered to be morally wrong, against one's religious beliefs, or based upon a purely private right (e.g., statutory rights of a shareholder) are not within the exception.

**Implied Contract.** The second exception to the at-will doctrine is the implied-in-fact contract exception. This involves a discharged employee who claims that some oral or written statement has created a binding contract. The most common claim of a breach has been based upon the statements made in a personnel manual or employee handbook. For example, if the handbook specifies procedures that are to be followed if a person is to be discharged, these procedures are considered a legal contract. If the employer does not follow these procedures, the discharged employee may take the employer to court and claim compensatory damages (back pay and value of lost fringe benefits).

**Good-Faith/Fair-Dealing.** This third exception involves a breach of a so-called implied covenant of good faith and fair dealing. Some courts view this covenant as part of the general law of contracts and, therefore, part of the employment relationship. It is an obligation to refrain from interfering with the right to receive the benefits the employee or the employer bargained for or came to expect and rely upon. For example, it has been used to protect an employee from a discharge motivated by the employer's desire to avoid payment of earned commissions. The difference between an implied contract and the good-faith covenant is based upon the court remedy available to the employee. For breach of an implied contract, the employee may be entitled to back pay and the costs of fringe benefits. For breach of the covenant, in some states, the employee may be eligible for compensatory and punitive damages.

## Whistleblowing

An employee who is discharged for exposing wrongdoing on the part of his or her employer is commonly referred to as a whistleblower. There is a growing public interest in encouraging employees to report violations, especially in areas affecting safety and health. For example, defective products, corruption, safety hazards, and cost overruns are practices that have been exposed by whistleblowers. A number of federal and state laws have been written to protect whistleblowers from retaliation by their employers. Most of these laws either protect a particular class of employee (e.g., government employees) or protect particular disclosures (e.g., matters affecting safety or health). Where there are no laws, the courts have held that whistleblowing protection should be given employees who further the public good by exposing illegal or unsafe conduct or practices. On the other hand, if the employee's action is private or proprietary, then it does not further the public good and does not fall within the meaning of whistleblowing (see also **Whistleblowing**).

## Terminations Due to Plant Closings and Layoffs

Plant closings and layoffs affect employees across a broad range of industries and in all parts of the United States. The economic and employment impact caused by shutdowns and mass reductions in force has led to legislation enacted by Congress and approximately a dozen states.

The federal law, the Worker Adjustment and Retraining Notification Act (WARN) became effective in February 1989. Essentially, WARN requires employers, employing 100 or more employees, to give 60 days' advance written notice if during any 30-day period the employer orders a "plant closing" or a "mass layoff" that would result in an employment loss. The 60 days' advance notice must be given to the affected employees or their collective bargaining representative and to the appropriate local unit of government. An employer who fails to give the required notice is liable to each affected employee for back pay and employment benefits (including medical expenses) for up to 60 days, as well as a civil penalty of up to $500 a day, up to 60 days, for failure to give the required notice to the appropriate local unit of government.

**Closings and Layoffs.** Plant closing means the permanent or temporary shutdown of a single site of employment, or one or more facilities or operating units within a single site of employment, if the shutdown results in an employment loss at the single site of employment during any 30-day period for 50 or more employees, excluding part-time employees. Mass layoff means a reduction in force which is not the result of a plant closing but which results in an employment loss at a single site of employment during any 30-day period for (a) at least 33% of the employees, excluding part-time employees; and (b) at least 50 employees, excluding part-time employees; or (c) at least 500 employees, excluding part-time employees.

**Exceptions to Employee Notification.** There are three exceptions to the requisite notice. The faltering company exception is where the employer fails to receive sought-after capital or business, which had been actively sought and, if obtained, would have enabled the employer to avoid or postpone the shutdown. This exception is applicable only to a plant closing and not a mass layoff. A second exception, the unforeseen business circumstances exception, is where the closing or mass layoff is caused by business circumstances that were not reasonably foreseeable as of the time that notice would have been required. An example would be a fire. Under the third exception, the natural disaster, notice is not required if the plant closing or mass layoff is due to any form of natural disaster, such as flood, earthquake, or drought.

## Drug Testing

In 1988, Congress passed a group of laws known as the Anti-Drug Abuse Act. One part of the law is titled the Drug-Free Workplace Act, which became effective in 1989. This law applies only to employers who are federal contractors or who are recipients of federal grants. The law sets forth the national policy that prohibits the use of illicit or illegal drugs in the workplace. In addition to the federal law, more than 28 states have passed laws or issued executive orders mandating drug-free workplaces for various private-sector and public-sector employers.

The Drug-Free Workplace Act does not impose drug or alcohol testing or screening (hereinafter "drug testing") requirements on the contractors or grantees. However, it is believed that the law cannot be effective unless drug testing occurs. Generally, there are four circumstances in which drug testing occurs: pre-employment testing, routine physical examinations, reasonable suspicion testing, and random testing.

Generally, drug testing prior to employment or as part of a periodic physical examination has become an accepted practice, as long as the applicant or employee is informed that drug testing will occur and the drug test is administered in a medical environment. Reasonable suspicion testing occurs when some act, accident, incident, or other circumstance gives rise to a reasonable suspicion of drug use or there are grounds to believe that further investigation is necessary. It is usually based upon a suspicion that has some factual foundation in light of the surrounding circumstances or is within the observer's knowledge. Depending upon circumstances, reasonable suspicion drug testing has been upheld by the courts. Random testing occurs when an employer informs its employees that they may be required to undergo drug testing at any time during their employment, for any reason or for no reason at all. Although random testing may be the most effective means available to detect and deter drug and alcohol use, their legality is questionable. The usual claim against random testing (as well as other tests) has been that it violates the rights of privacy.

Under the Fourth Amendment of the U.S. Constitution, which protects against unwarranted searches and seizures, an invasion of an individual's legitimate expectations of privacy must be reasonable. To determine the reasonability, courts utilize a balancing test, which balances the government's interest (such as public safety, employment in a sensitive position, the need for supervision, and/or control and efficient operation in the workplace) against an employee's expectations of privacy. If the government's need outweighs the employee's privacy, then it is referred to as a "compelling interest" and it is not barred by the constitutional guarantee.

Although the Fourth Amendment applies only to public-sector or governmental employers, it will also apply to private-sector employers whose operations are closely related to or acting pursuant to government regulations. Nine states have constitutional guarantees of privacy which may cover private-sector employers. Where courts have been called upon to decide drug testing cases in states that have constitutional provisions of privacy, they have used the balancing test to determine whether or not a compelling need was present (see **Testing: Drugs**).

## Employment and Post-Employment Benefits

### Health Insurance Continuation

Under the Consolidated Omnibus Budget Reconciliation Act (COBRA), employers must provide continuation of group health care to employees (and certain beneficiaries) even after an employee is no longer working for the employer. COBRA is an effort by Congress to ensure that employees and their families have access to health care coverage, at least for a limited period of time, even when unemployed. COBRA includes provisions requiring certain employers to continue health plan coverage for employees and other beneficiaries, provided the ex-employee or beneficiary pays the cost of the continued coverage. Noncompliance can result in serious consequences to the employer, including tax penalties and remedies available under the Employee Retirement Income Security Act (ERISA).

COBRA covers employees who are terminated, either voluntarily or involuntarily, employees whose hours of work are reduced so that they are no longer entitled to coverage under the group health plan, and the spouse and dependent children of employees. These individuals become eligible for the continuation of the group health plan coverage upon the happening of a qualified event, which includes (a) termination of employment for reasons other than gross misconduct; (b) reduction in hours that would result in the loss of health plan eligibility (e.g., from full-time to part-time status); (c) death of an employee, in which case coverage must be continued for the surviving spouse and dependents; (d) divorce or legal separation, in which case coverage must be continued for the former spouse and dependents; (e) entitlement of the employee to Medicare benefits where the employee's eligibility would otherwise terminate health insurance for the spouse or dependents; and (f) cessation of a child's dependent status under the terms of the plan (e.g., when a child obtains a certain age or marries).

For the terminated employee or reduced-hours employee, the duration of the coverage is 18 months from the date of the event. For all other beneficiaries, the coverage must be made available for 36 months.

### Unemployment Benefits

Unemployment benefits are funded by employers through payroll taxes. Levels of benefits and tax rates are established by each state. The amount of the tax paid by the employer is usually based upon an experience rating (i.e., an employer with greater unemployment (layoffs, terminations, etc.) pays a higher tax rate than the employee with lesser turnover or attrition). The tax is adjusted annually according to the unemployment experience-rating.

Generally, the laws cover most employers and employees. Depending upon state laws, coverage extends to state and municipal government employees, school district employees, agricultural employees, and charitable institutions.

The primary purpose of unemployment benefits laws is to provide benefits (compensation) for employees who are unemployed by reason of circumstances not their own fault or within their own control. In order to qualify for benefits, certain requirements must be met. One requirement is that during a base period of time, usually a 12-month period prior to his or her unemployment, the individual must have been employed for a minimum number of hours per week and earned a minimum amount of pay. A second requirement is that the individual must be unemployed for a certain waiting time (usually one week). A third requirement that is generally applicable is that the individual must not be disqualified from obtaining unemployment compensation. The amount of weekly benefits depend upon the wages earned while employed. In some states, the number of dependents is also a factor.

The benefits are available on a weekly basis and usually for a maximum of one year. The claimant must go to his or her unemployment compensation office in order to obtain the weekly compensation check. Before the payment is made, the claimants must certify that they are available for work, and actively seeking work. If they are unable to work or have removed themselves from the labor market, then they may lose benefits for any week in which that occurs.

Although each state establishes its own qualifications and disqualifications for benefits, the three most common grounds for disqualification are when a person voluntarily quits without a good reason caused by the employer, is discharged for employment-related misconduct or refuses to seek or accept suitable work. Individuals who are engaged in a strike, lockout, or other labor dispute that causes unemployment are not eligible for unemployment compensation.

### Dislocation Assistance

Under the Economic Dislocation and Worker Adjustment Assistance Act, employment and training assistance is available for dislocated workers. These are employees who (a) have been terminated or laid off and are unlikely to return to their previous industry or occupation; (b) have been terminated as a result of a plant closure or substantial layoff; (c) are long-term unemployed and have limited opportunities for employment or re-employment in the same or similar occupation in the area in which they reside; or (d) were self-employed (including farmers and ranchers) and are unemployed as a result of general economic conditions in the community in which they reside or because of natural disasters. Generally, the individuals who are eligible for the training assistance are those who have exhausted their entitlement to unemployment compensation.

### Social Security Disability Insurance

Individuals who are unable to work because of an injury or illness, regardless of whether or not it is job related, may be eligible for social security benefits. There are two basic requirements for an individual to be eligible for social security disability benefits. First, the individual must be under age 65 and have a physical or mental impairment that prevents him or her from working for at least 12 months. Second, the individual must have worked under social security long enough to earn sufficient credits for eligibility for disability benefits. These credits are earned when monies are deducted from the individual's pay by the employer for social security purposes.

The rules for determining whether an individual is disabled within the coverage of the law are generally more stringent than other federal laws, workers' compensation laws, or private disability insurance programs. In other words, a person may be disabled under workers' compensation or receiving disability insurance, but will not necessarily qualify for social security disability benefits. To be considered disabled under the social security law, an individual must not only be unable to perform past work, but must also be unable to engage in other substantial or gainful work activity (see **Social Security Disability Claim**).

### Workers' Compensation

Workers' compensation laws, which have been passed in all of the states, provide for fixed awards to employees and their dependents in the case of industrial accidents and employment-related diseases and dispense with proof of negligence and legal actions. The laws vary from state to state as to the extent of workers and employment covered, the amount and duration of benefits, and the type of illness or disease within the coverage of the laws. The purpose of the laws is to make the employer strictly liable to an employee for injuries or illnesses sustained, which arose out of and in the course of employment, without regard to the negligence of the employer, the employee, or fellow employees. Prior to the passage of workers' compensation laws, employees injured on the job who sued their employers, usually lost. If the injury occurred because of a fellow worker, or if the injured employee was also negligent, or if the employee assumed the risk, then these defenses precluded the injured employee from winning the suit. Workers' compensation laws have eliminated these suits and defenses. There are, however, some states that permit employees to reject recovery under the compensation law and allow them to file a lawsuit for damages. But, if an employee opts to file a lawsuit, the customary defenses to such action are available to the employer (see **Workers' Compensation**).

Federal employees have their own set of injury-compensation laws. Generally, they are covered by the Federal Employees Compensation Act.

## Retirement Benefits

Individuals enjoy retirement benefits—income after retirement from employment—through both public and private retirement programs or pension plans. The basic retirement program for most individuals is via the Social Security Act, which provides for old age, survivors, and disability insurance benefits. In this regard, it provides assistance for the aged, blind, disabled, family and child welfare, medical aid, and, a cooperative system to the states for unemployment compensation. However, the Social Security Act is not an unemployment compensation law or a part of the federal tax laws. The social security laws are administered and enforced by the Social Security Administration.

### Social Security Act

This law covers employees and self-employed individuals. Monies are deducted from the wages or income of the individual by the employer under the Federal Insurance Contributions Act (FICA), which is the law that authorizes the deduction of social security taxes from the employee's wages. An equal amount of this excise tax deducted from the wages is paid by the employer. To qualify for benefits, an individual must have earned credits for a certain amount of work under the social security system and the amount of social security benefits will depend upon the individual's level of earnings. Full-time benefits are available to individuals after age 65; reduced benefits are available at age 62. In order to receive benefits, the individual must make application through the Social Security Administration.

### Private Retirement Programs

Retired employees may also receive retirement benefits through various retirement programs and/or pension plans. Federal legislation has been enacted to encourage the institution of private or personal retirement programs and plans. For example, through tax laws, individuals are encouraged through tax benefit to establish Individual Retirement Accounts (IRAs) or salary reduction plans commonly referred to as "401(k)" plans and "Keogh" plans, which allow larger tax deductible contributions than IRAs and are available to self-employed persons.

No laws require an employer to establish a retirement or pension program. However, because of tax-benefit opportunities, employers are encouraged to provide pension plans for their employees. Such pension plans are governed by and must meet the requirements established by the Employee Retirement Income Security Act (ERISA). ERISA and its amendatory enactments are a complex set of laws dealing with pension and employee welfare benefit plans. Administration and enforcement are within the jurisdictions of the U.S. Department of Labor, Internal Revenue Service, and the Pension Benefit Guaranty Corporation.

An employee welfare benefit plan means any plan, fund, or program that is established or maintained for providing its participants (or their beneficiaries) medical, surgical, or hospital care or benefits; or benefits in the event of sickness, accident, disability, death, or unemployment; or vacation benefits, apprenticeship or other training programs; or day care centers, scholarship funds, or prepaid legal services. An employee pension or retirement plan means any plan, fund, or program that provides retirement income to employees, which can include benefits for retirees at a normal retirement age (65), early retirement, and for disability.

## Procedures for Remedial Action

What can individuals do if they have been denied equal employment opportunities or been discharged because of union activities or have not been paid overtime? Can the individual file a lawsuit? If so, are there certain procedures that first must be completed? Some laws require the individual to file a charge or complaint with the administrative agency responsible for administering and enforcing the statute. Other laws permit individuals to file a claim with the administrative agency or file a lawsuit.

### National Labor Relations Act

If employees believe themselves to be discriminated against because of their union activities or their protected and concerted activities, they must file an unfair labor practice charge with the National Labor Relations Board (NLRB) regional office where the unfair labor practice occurred or where the employer is located. The charge must be filed within six months from the date of the alleged unfair activity.

The NLRB regional office investigates the charge in order to determine if there is or is not merit to it. If the results of the investigation establish a reasonable belief that a violation of the law has occurred, the regional office initiates an administrative trial. The trial is conducted by an administrative law judge and the rules of evidence that are used in a court of law are also used in the administrative trial.

The individual has no right to file an independent lawsuit. Under the doctrine of federal preemption, the individual is precluded from filing a lawsuit where the claim is (or may be) covered by the National Labor Relations Act.

Where a company and union have a collective bargaining agreement and an employee believes that a violation has occurred, he or she must file a grievance and proceed through the grievance-arbitration procedure. An employee has no right to file a lawsuit claiming a violation of the collective bargaining agreement. Instead, the employee is bound by the doctrine of exhaustion of administrative remedies. This means that the employee must follow the grievance-arbitration procedures in the collective bargaining agreement. If he or she does so, that is the end of the case and the employee has exhausted the contractual procedures. Similar to the doctrine of preemption, the employee is precluded from filing a lawsuit.

### Employment Discrimination

If an individual believes that he or she has been discriminated against because of race, color, religion, sex, national origin, or age, the individual may file an unfair employment practice charge with the EEOC's office where the discrimination took place or where the employer is located. The individual may also file a charge of discrimination with the state agency or local government agency that administers and enforces state and/or local government laws prohibiting employment discrimination. Under the federal laws, the charge must be filed within 180 days after occurrence of the alleged discrimination. If there is a state or local government agency, referred to as a "deferral agency," then the charge may be filed during a period of up to 300 days after the alleged discrimination took place.

Upon investigation by the EEOC, if there is probable cause to believe that a violation occurred, the EEOC may file a lawsuit against the charged party or issue a notice to the employee of his or her right to file a lawsuit. If the notice of right to sue is issued, the employee must file the suit within 90 days. Once the suit is filed, it follows the court procedures that are applicable in any other lawsuit. Even if the EEOC concludes that there was no violation of the law, the same notice of right to sue is issued.

For claims of handicap discrimination, Vietnam era or disabled veterans discrimination, or violations of an affirmative action plan, the individual may file a claim with the Office of Federal Contract Compliance Programs (OFCCP). The claim should be in writing and to the OFCCP office nearest the facility where the alleged discrimination occurred. This OFCCP officer will then conduct an investigation, often referred to as an audit.

### Wage-Hour Claims

Claims relating to minimum wage, overtime pay, child labor, and other requirements of the Fair Labor Standards Act may be filed with the Wage-Hour Division of the Department of Labor. This claim can be made orally or in writing to a Wage-Hour Division office covering the geographic territory where the alleged violation took place or where the employer is located. There is no formality in filing the claim. It is investigated by a compliance officer from the Wage-Hour office. If the investigation reveals that a violation of the law has occurred, and if it can not be settled with the employer, the Wage-Hour office refers the case to the Department of Labor Solicitor General's office for the filing of a lawsuit.

There is no requirement for an individual to file a claim with the Wage-Hour Division. At any time, an individual may file a lawsuit for a violation of the Fair Labor Standards Act.

### Safety and Health Complaints

Any employee who believes that a violation of a safety or health standard exists, or that an imminent danger exists, may request an inspection by giving notice to OSHA, MSHA, or the state office where the safety or health danger exists. The notice must be in writing. If the agency office determines that there are reasonable grounds to believe that a violation or danger exists, a special inspection will take place. If the inspection reveals that dangers or violations exist, the employer may be issued a citation, which orders the employer to fix the problem or be subject to fines and penalties and possible legal action.

If an employee is retaliated against because he or she filed or participated in a claim of an unsafe condition, the employee can file a charge with the agency office which initiates an investigation. If there is reason to believe that retaliation has occurred or if the worker appeals the results of the initial investigation, an administrative trial is held before an administrative law judge in order to determine whether or not retaliation occurred.

### Location of Agency Offices

The U.S. Government agencies have national offices in Washington, D.C. and also have offices located throughout the United States. Most of these agencies also have regional, district, and area offices. The telephone numbers for the offices will be found in telephone directories under "United States."

*See also* Discrimination: Age; Discrimination: Language; Discrimination: People with Disabilities; Discrimination: Race; Discrimination: Sex; Immigration; Nonstandard English; Parental Leave; Sex-Role Stereotyping; Sexual Harrassment; Social Security Disability Claim; Testing; Testing: AIDS; Testing: Drugs; Testing: Genetics; Testing: Integrity; Whistleblowing; Workers' Compensation; Work Hazards.

## Bibliography

American Bar Association (1987). *Law in the workplace.* Chicago: American Bar Association, Public Education Division. Information for employees regarding their employment rights and responsibilities.

Bakaly, C.G., Jr. & Isaacson, W. J. (1983). *Employment at-will and unjust dismissal: The labor issues of the '80s.* New York: Law & Business, Inc./Harcourt Brace Jovanovich. Discussion of the changes in the employment relationship and the exceptions to the at-will doctrine.

Hunt, J.W. (1984). *The law of the workplace: Rights of employers and employees.* Washington, DC: Bureau of National Affairs. Information regarding the workplace laws and how the laws affect employers and employees.

Morris, C.J. (Ed.) (1983). *The developing labor law.* 2nd ed. and 4th Supplement 1982–87 (1988). Washington, DC: Bureau of National Affairs. Comprehensive presentation of the labor laws involving union activity and representation, collective bargaining, unfair labor practices, etc.

Murphy, B.S., & Azoff, E.S. (1987). *Guide to wage & hour regulation.* Washington, DC: Bureau of National Affairs. Information regarding minimum wage, overtime, child labor, recordkeeping, and other features of the wage-hour laws.

*Plant closings: The complete resource guide.* (1988). Washington, DC: Bureau of National Affairs. Discussion of the federal and state laws that are applicable to plant closings and the rights of terminated employees.

Rappoport, S.S. (1989). *Age discrimination: A legal and practical guide.* Washington, DC: Bureau of National Affairs. A detailed analysis of federal and state laws and cases dealing with age discrimination.

Schlei, B.L., & Grossman, P. (1983). *Employment discrimination law.* 2nd ed. and 5-year cumulative supplement (1989). Washington, DC. Bureau of National Affairs. A comprehensive presentation of the statutes and cases regarding equal employment opportunity, employment discrimination, and affirmative action.

West, R.C. (Ed.) (1989). *U.S. labor & employment laws.* Washington, DC: Bureau of National Affairs. Compilation of selected statutes covering labor laws, personnel relations laws, and employment laws.

—CHARLES L. FINE

# LEISURE

*Leisure* is any activity or experience that an individual intends to be leisure and which produces inner satisfaction. *Work* is any activity in which an individual engages to sustain oneself and/or others.

## Relationship to Work

Technological changes have brought about major changes in the work world which have caused people to examine the meaning and importance of work in their lives. Technological changes have a reduced the time devoted to work. Shorter work weeks, earlier retirements, and prolonged unemployment have increased the amount of leisure time people have. Individuals who are not achieving a high degree of satisfaction from their work are increasingly turning to leisure activities as a source of life satisfaction.

Leisure has traditionally been described as:

1. *An Extension of a Person's Occupation.* This occurs when no distinction can be made between work and leisure activities. An example of this pattern is the teacher who enjoys tutoring others after school.
2. *Compensation for a Person's Occupation.* Work, in this pattern, has little intrinsic reward, so individuals must look to leisure for a sense of satisfaction. For example, an accountant who compensates for the lack of physical activity at work by playing softball in his or her leisure time.
3. *Unrelated to a Person's Occupation.* An example of this would be a machinist who enjoys reading mysteries for leisure.

Studies show that people are happiest in their leisure, regardless of the work they do, when they are able to engage in leisure activities that they really enjoy. Regardless of whether your leisure is similar to or different from your work, the important thing is that leisure is a form of self-expression and an outlet for you to do the things you like to do.

## Application

Leisure can combine with work in a variety of ways to enhance an individual's career development. It is important for you to become aware of the many ways in which leisure can enhance your career development. These might include:

1. *Leisure and Job Search.* If you are unemployed, leisure can assist you in a variety of ways. Leisure can serve as a source of marketable skills (see **Job Search**); a method of networking for job leads, e.g., hearing about job openings while bowling with friends; an escape from stress related to the pressures of unemployment; or a motivator to help break the monotony of the job search process, such as going to the beach to "reenergize" before continuing with the job search.
2. *Leisure and Career Exploration.* Leisure can be a valuable tool for exploring occupationally related activities. Leisure can provide you with an opportunity to: (a) experience various vocations; (b) explore the nature of different jobs by observing and talking with workers; (c) expand job-related skills by perfecting vocational skills you already have by returning to school or volunteering for jobs that interest you; and (d) identify alternative career possibilities, such as work-at-home programs, entrepreneurships, or small businesses.
3. *Leisure and Personal Development.* Leisure activities can enhance your mental health and overall life satisfaction by providing you with an opportunity

for self-expression through a variety of intellectual, physical, and creative activities; with autonomy by allowing you to determine the activities you wish to engage in; with satisfaction and self-esteem by engaging in personally meaningful life activities; and with opportunities to develop and maintain interpersonal relationships by engaging in activities organized around common interests.

4. *Leisure and Work Balance.* Many people lead unbalanced lives, engaging in work or leisure to the exclusion of the other. By taking too much time and energy away from the duties of your job, leisure can conflict with your work. Leisure, on the other hand, can also help restore balance to your life by adding interest and zest.

5. *Leisure and Stress.* Leisure can provide relaxation away from the pressures of your job or studies. Leisure activities can help you achieve and maintain good mental health. Leisure can provide you with an opportunity to escape stress through activities which are relaxing and entertaining; it can rid you of negative emotions, fears, anxieties, and frustrations, and can restore energy lost from being in a stressful situation (see **Job Stress**).

Leisure activities play an integral role in your career development. You need to identify, explore, and implement your leisure interests. In order to do this you might talk with and/or observe people who have put their leisure to work. Take advantage of the available educational leisure options, and identify community resources such as clubs and agencies which can provide valuable leisure opportunities. By identifying and implementing your leisure interests, you will enhance your career development and increase your life satisfaction.

*See also* Career Exploration; Career Planning; Job Search; Skills; Stress; Volunteer Work.

## Bibliography

Kimeldorf, M. (1989). *Pathways to leisure.* Bloomington, IL: Meridian Education Corporation. An enthusiastic do-it-yourself workbook for people interested in identifying new leisure interests and job possibilities through leisure search.

McDaniels, C. (1989). *The changing workplace: Career counseling strategies for the 1990s and beyond.* San Francisco: Jossey-Bass. A thorough, scholarly, discussion of where people will be working in the future, the settings in which work will take place, and the relationship between leisure and work in the changing workplace. Practical advice is given to help individuals put their leisure to work.

Super, D.E. (1984). Leisure: What it is and might be. *Journal of Career Development*, 11, (2): 71–80.

Super, D.E. (1986). Life career roles: Self-realization in work and leisure. In D.T. Hall & Associates (Eds.), *Career development in organizations* (pp. 95–119). San Francisco: Jossey-Bass. A thorough review of the concept of career being comprised of

many roles, including work and leisure. Excellent discussion of how leisure combines with work to help both unemployed and employed workers.

—JOHN J. LIPTAK

## LESBIAN WOMEN

A woman is considered lesbian if her sexual, affectional, and emotional needs are met primarily by other women. Because many individuals do not understand the complexity of this life style, there exist negative stereotypes concerning the emotional health and vocational abilities and interests of this group of women. For example, a common misconception is that most lesbian women are skilled in areas more typically masculine in nature (i.e., truck driving, skilled labor) and are, therefore, unqualified to work in areas requiring the traditionally "feminine" characteristics of nurturing or personal care of others (i.e., teaching, nursing, social work). Despite these stereotypes, there is no conclusive research to indicate that as a group lesbian women are more successful in typically male-dominated professions. Lesbian women are a diverse group with great differences in interests, skills, communication styles, and appearances. Because of these stereotypes, however, lesbian women may face discrimination when training for their careers or applying for jobs, but are not protected against discrimination because in many communities they are not recognized as a legitimate social group.

### Relationship to Career Choice

Because of the negative stereotypes about lesbian women, one of the first steps a lesbian woman will need to make in her career decision-making process is how open she will be about her life style. This decision is based on many factors, one of which being the extent to which her identity or "who she sees herself being" is founded in her sexual preference. If this is a large part of her self-concept, she may choose to disclose more about her life style both before she begins her job search and while on the job. This may cause negative reactions from coworkers or employers resulting in increased personal and job-related stress for the lesbian woman (Gillow & Davis, 1987). On the other hand, if sexual preference is a large part of her identity and she chooses not to share this with others on the job, the incongruence she feels may also produce anxiety.

The ideal situation would be for the lesbian woman to be able to disclose the information she wishes about herself and be accepted by coworkers and employers for her skills and talents. This may be the case in career areas more open to this life style. Many times, however, these are difficult to ascertain because lesbian women in particular jobs may not disclose their life style initially, only becoming more open once they feel comfortable in the job situation.

## Application

In considering your sexual preferences as a factor in your career decision-making process:

1. You need to explore the role that your sexual preference plays in your life. If it is a major role, you may need to assess the impact of having a career that may not be supportive of your life style or that may not allow you the opportunity to find a peer group or role models.

2. It is important for you to determine the degree to which you see your career filling your needs. It may be possible that the career you choose does not support the values and attitudes that are part of your life style, but does allow expression of skills, beliefs, and knowledge that are also a part of your identity. Because of this you may choose to pursue this career and look to other means as an outlet for the needs surrounding your sexual preference.

3. It is important for you to be able to separate your occupation (teaching, sales, electrician) from that of a particular "job" (teaching within a specific school system, sales within a particular company, electrician with a specific firm). This is especially true for lesbian women who are currently employed in a job that satisfies their career needs but may not be tolerant of their life style. You cannot assume an entire profession is discriminating based on your experience with your current position. You may need to network with lesbian women in your field in other, more support companies. This may help you find a specific job in your career area to satisfy both personal and career needs (see **Networking**).

4. Another important factor is whether or not you are involved in a relationship at the time of making these decisions and how great a role you are willing to give your partner. It is possible that her values and beliefs concerning openness and identity are different from yours. If this is the case, it will be important to determine if this will have an influence on your decision about a particular career.

5. If you find that the issue of sexual preference is causing stress on the job, it will be essential to develop personal stress management strategies. These may be something you can do by yourself (meditation, exercise, listening to music) or something that involves the support and feedback of others (support group meetings, professional contacts, individual or group counseling). It is vital that you learn what works best for you.

*See also* Career Exploration; Career Planning; Networking; Sex-Role Stereotyping; Stress.

## Bibliography

Bell, A. P., & Weinberg, M. S. (1978). *Homosexualities: A study of diversity among men and women.* New York: Touchstone. A good overview of the issues surrounding the diversity of the homosexual life style of men and women. Attention is paid to specific concerns of sexual preference and work.

Gillow, K. E., & Davis, L. L. (1987). Lesbian stress and coping methods. *Journal of Psychosexual Nursing,* 25(9): 28–32. This discussion of life stressors, including those that are job-related, is based on a survey of 142 lesbian women.

Hetherington, C., & Orzek, A. (1988). Career counseling and life planning with lesbian women. *Journal of Counseling and Development,* 68(1): 52–57. A more thorough review of the issues surrounding career decision making for lesbian women. Includes a list of professional organizations and resources for lesbians, gays, and bisexuals.

## For Further Information

*Directory of Homosexual Organizations and Publications*
Homosexual Information Center
4758 Hollywood Boulevard, Suite 208
Hollywood, CA 90028
(213) 464-8431

**The Gay Employment Protection Project**
P.O. Box 7382 Gaithersburg, MD 20898
(301) 820-1636

—ANN M. ORZEK

# LIBERAL ARTS AND CAREER CHOICE

What does acquiring general knowledge and general intellectual capacities (reason and judgment) have to do with job preparation? with earning a living? with vocational skills? Many of the hundreds of thousands of liberal arts graduates turned out annually need some help in making the connection. What, they ask, do literature and language, mathematics and philosophy, history and psychology have to do with the world of work? Are there really curriculum choices I can make and campus resources I can use to further my career development with a bachelor's degree?

## Relationship to Work

**Liberal Arts Strengths.** Surveys of employers have identified the following job skills as the most useful ones liberal arts students bring to their jobs:

- Oral communication
- Ability to write
- Analytical, problem-solving skills
- Ability to interact effectively with peers, subordinates, and superiors
- Well-rounded, broad background
- Flexibility and adaptability

Perhaps liberal arts graduates' greatest assets are a broad base of knowledge and interests, a tolerance for different life styles and points of view, and an enthusiasm for continuing to learn. Liberal arts graduates should not be defensive or apologetic in approaching the world of work, but they do need to know how to articulate their skills to employers, how to sell their liberal arts degrees.

**Liberal Arts Limitations.** The skills that professional and technical graduates (engineering, business, computer science) have that liberal arts students must make a special effort to acquire are:

- Administrative, management, marketing know-how
- Statistics and accounting knowledge
- Computer programming and information systems proficiency
- Related work experience

**Liberal Arts Employers.** Consider this array of employers who recruit at the University of Washington: Home Savings and Loan, King County, Allstate Insurance, Children's Hospital, Amtrak, Klopfenstein's Department Store, Pizza Haven, YWCA, and Union Oil. This is a mix of for-profit businesses, nonprofit organizations, and government agencies.

**The Liberal Arts Option.** Well, it's graduate school. But the important thing to remember is the different priorities of graduate school admission committees versus employers of B.A. holders. Graduate schools are interested in one's overall GPA, Graduate Record Exam scores, letters of recommendation from faculty, publications, awards, and honors in school. Graduate schools are looking for an academic orientation toward undergraduate life.

## Application

What steps should liberal arts majors take to strengthen their baccalaureate degrees?

1. *Goals.* Like any other job applicant, you must be able to answer the questions, "Where do you see yourself in five years, in ten years?" and "What are your career goals?" College placement centers are one place to find the answers to these questions; they offer career decision-making seminars, job skills workshops, and professional counseling.

2. *Supplementary Courses.* Take at least one business administration course. At best take as many classes as you can in such areas as marketing, management, accounting, and statistics. Liberal arts job applicants must have some business knowledge.

3. *Work Experience.* When you go looking for a job, your resume should show the equivalent of three years full-time, relevant work. That's a lot of work experience and takes a combination of internships, volunteer work, part-time jobs and summer employment. And remember, you've got to make it "relevant" to your career goal or objective, that statement you make at the top of your resume when you go job hunting.

4. *Extracurricular Experiences.* Employers regard clubs and organizations connected with one's college major more important than being involved in sports or sororities and fraternities.

5. *Leadership Roles.* This is what is looked for regardless of whether your extracurricular participation is in student government, athletics, or a special interest group. Employers want you to describe on your resume project completion, coordination, and responsibility. They want you to have been in charge because that shows you are organized, ambitious, and can assume responsibilities.

*See also* Career Choices: Youth; Career Exploration; Choosing an Occupation; Internships; Job Search; Service-Learning; Volunteer Work.

## Bibliography

Baumgardner, S. R. (1989). *College and jobs: Conversations with recent graduates.* New York: Human Sciences Press.
Alumni say the first year is disappointing but it gets better.

Briggs, J. I. (1984). *The Berkeley guide to employment for new college graduates.* Berkeley, CA: Ten Speed Press. Good career planning and goal setting book with a section called "Working in Business with a Liberal Arts Degree."

Carter, C. (1990). *Majoring in the rest of your life: Career secrets for college students.* New York: Noonday Press. Practical strategies from first semester freshman year to post-graduation first job with exercises/assignments for liberal arts majors.

Leape, M. P., & Vacca, S. M. (1987). *The Harvard guide to careers.* Rev. ed. Cambridge, MA: Harvard University Press. This guide discusses career exploration, resumes, interviewing, letter writing, researching employers, and internships for liberal arts majors.

Munschauer, J. L. (1986). *Jobs for English majors and other smart people.* Princeton, NJ: Peterson's Guides. A marketing approach to job hunting for liberal arts majors, generalists, the inexperienced, and career changers.

Nadler, B. J. (1989). *Liberal arts jobs: What they are and how to get them.* 2nd ed. Princeton, NJ: Peterson's Guides. Comprehensive career guidance book with exercises and worksheets. Features top 15 careers for liberal arts majors, which include banking, insurance, merchandising, advertising, and telecommunications.

Nadler, B. J. (1989). *Liberal arts power!* 2nd ed. Princeton, NJ: Peterson's Guides. Success stories of graduates in anthropology, music, economics, etc. illustrate this job search and resume writing guide.

—PATRICIA W. LUNNEBORG

## LOW BACK PAIN

Low back pain afflicts such a large percentage of workers that it is considered a major cause of lost wages as well as a severe economic loss to industry. Exact statistics have not been compiled but studies estimate that 2% of all employees in the United States have back "injuries" requiring financial compensation each year.

What causes these back injuries? A number of factors have been investigated and imputed. These factors include the weight of the object lifted, the size of the object, the frequency of lifts, the heights from which the weight is lifted, the fitness of the individual, the training in proper techniques of lifting, the atmosphere of the workplace, and the psychological influences upon the injured person. An evaluation of these and other factors have failed to find a common denominator.

### The Low Back "Machine": Its Parts and How They Function

The low back can be understood as being a well coordinated machine of moving parts. Each part must be reasonably normal in structure and well conditioned. There must be adequate elasticity and sufficient strength for the intended task. More important, the machine must be operated, or "driven" properly. Individuals who have or wish to avoid trouble with their lower back, need to understand how this "machine" works, how to properly maintain it, how to properly operate it, and how psychological factors can adversely influence its operation.

To better understand why low back pain symptoms occur, the parts of the low back, and how they function, are described here. The spinal column is comprised of numerous functional units. (Figure 1). Within these units exists tissues that, when injured, inflamed, or stressed, become the site of pain and dysfunction. A typical functional unit is portrayed in Figure 2 which shows two adjacent vertebral bodies separated by a hydraulic tissue called the intervertebral disc. Each disc contains water incorporated in a gel

**Figure 1. The Lumbosacral Spine**

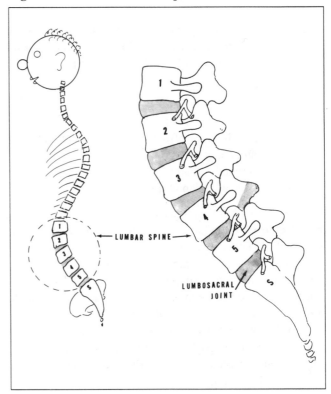

Copyright by Rene Cailliet. Reprinted by permission.

**Figure 2. The Functional Unit**

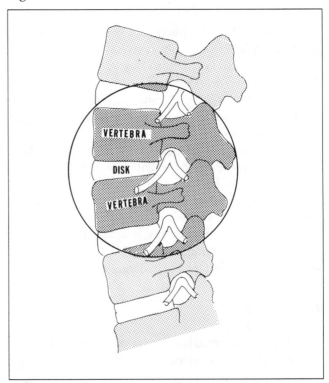

Copyright by Rene Cailliet. Reprinted by permission.

(proteoglycans) that absorbs (imbibes) this fluid, as does a sponge. The fluid contained within the disc acts as a hydraulic system cushioning pressure and allowing bending, twisting, and turning of each "unit."

Ligaments reinforce the disc while restricting excessive motion that could damage the fibers of the disc. The fibers within the disc, called annular fibers, form into sheets to contain the gel fluid. These fibers contain a central ball of fluid called the nucleus. Each annular fiber can elongate (stretch) a specific distance; if this distance is exceeded, the fiber tears. Once the fiber is torn, the enclosed fluid escapes. Injury prevention seeks to avoid incidences that can tear these fibers because treatment of torn fibers is difficult and limited.

Behind the vertebral bodies are bony structures form a tube (spinal canal) containing the nerves that carry sensation from the legs and give motor control to the legs and lower back muscles. These nerves enable the low back and legs to function normally and pain free. When these nerves are irritated, damaged, or inflamed, they fail in their normal function. Pain and impairment result.

Normally the low back has a curve, termed lordosis, that is arched in standing positions and flexed in the sitting posture or in bending forward. Both of these curves are normal. The low back can go from lordosis to a forward flexed position when all of the tissues are adequately flexible. Prolonged or improper sitting or standing causes excessive strain upon the low back tissues. This accounts for many of the painful conditions in the "sedentary" occupations or activities. This strain on the tissues is shown in Figure 3.

Forward bending, such as in lifting, requires flexibility of the tissues involved and muscular strength to resume the erect posture. After being bent forward, the low back must return to the upright posture properly. This implies that there must be minimal and controlled twisting-untwisting in resuming the erect posture, and that the lordosis be resumed slowly and correctly.

## Pain and Impairment

Misuse or abuse of the sensitive tissues of the low back results in pain and impairment. Mechanical "trauma" is the predominant cause of the usual benign low back pain. The tissues that are susceptible are the ligaments, joints, muscles, and tendons. In spite of daily accusations, only rarely is the disc *the* source of pain. When the cause significantly involves the disc, there are often neurological symptoms, such as pain, numbness, or weakness in the buttocks, thighs, lower leg foot, and ankle. The presence of these symptoms requires a thorough medical evaluation to determine their site, degree, and significance.

Pain is usually accompanied by a protective muscular "spasm." This term indicates that a muscle has become contracted to prevent movement of the irritated part. While this is "protective," it also becomes a site and source of pain. Low back pain sufferers may fear the aftereffects of the injury; this anxiety often aggravates the condition and may even prolong recovery.

**Figure 3. Prolonged Sitting Posture. The tissues of the lower functional units (in enlargement) showing the strain upon the muscles (M) and ligaments (L) with posterior bulging of the nucleus (N) of the disc.**

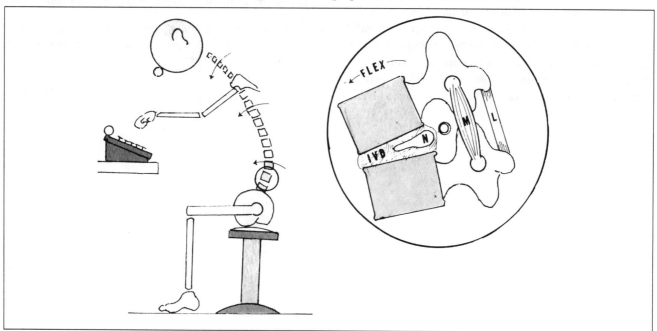

Anxiety invariably accompanies low back pain, as people worry about the symptoms, length of recovery, and curtailment of daily activities. This anxiety intensifies muscular tension, adding to the painful disabling muscle "spasm" already existing. Anxiety and the loss of a normal sleep pattern intensify symptoms and may prolong recovery.

A person's mental state can adversely influence the operation of his or her lower back. These psychological impediments include anger, anxiety, impatience, fatigue, boredom, tension, and even depression. Any or all of these can weaken judgment and impair the operational efficiency of the "driver." When improperly operated the machine can malfunction, literally "break down" (see **Anger; Anxiety; Depression; Self-Talk**).

## Recovery from Low Back Pain

Most benign (mechanical) low back conditions recover in three to four weeks "regardless of what treatment has been instituted." Such individuals should seek appropriate treatment to shorten the duration of pain disability, to prevent unnecessary complications, to prevent recurrence, and to avoid the chronic pain aftereffects.

To start recovery, ice is applied to decrease pain, inflammation, and the abnormal accumulation of fluid in the area. This also allows early mobility. Applying heat later infuses the area with a good blood supply to remove irritating toxins and initiate recovery. Gentle active and passive motion prevents contracture with subsequent limited motion. Early isometric exercises prevent disuse, weakness, and wasting of muscles.

Early *active* treatment prevents disuse, despair, depression, dependency, and drug reliance. A briefer period of immobility and early active exercises, in benign, painful low back conditions not having neurological aftereffects, can hasten recovery and return to work, thus belying the adage of rest and its value. Early return to work has in itself been determined to be beneficial to the person's recovery.

## Prevention of Low Back Pain

The chances of your having low back pain can be significantly reduced by:

1. Exercising to regain flexibility and strength in the trunk and leg muscles.
2. Avoiding potentially harmful exercises.
3. Learning the proper way to bend, lift, and sit (see Posture and Body Mechanics).
4. Learning proper methods of doing work.
5. Recognizing and overcoming emotions that may adversely affect normal back function. Normal control may be negatively affected by anger, impatience, fatigue, anxiety, and depression. These emotional factors are addressed by stress management, counseling biofeedback, and even psychotherapy.
6. Evaluating your work setting. Is it a safe environment that fits your body? Faulty work conditions such as table height, cramped quarters, slippery floors, and inadequate lighting should be identified and made safe.

*See also* Anger; Anxiety; Depression; Posture and Body Mechanics; Self-Talk; Work Hazards: Ergonomic.

## Bibliography

Cailliet, R. (1984). *Understand your backache*. Philadelphia: F. A. Davis. A paperback edition for the lay public with numerous illustrations. Discusses all terms currently used by the medical profession.

Cailliet, R. (1988). *Low back pain syndrome*, 4th ed. Philadelphia: F. A. Davis. A paperback volume originally written for the medical profession but understandable by the lay public. It includes an update of recent studies regarding the lumbosacral spine.

Gross, L., & Cailliet, R. (1987). *The rejuvenation strategy*. New York: Doubleday. A discussion of exercises and proper daily activities for anyone over 35.

—RENE CAILLIET

# M

## MANAGERIAL SKILLS

Managerial skills involve abilities (a) to recognize organizational and environmental needs and changes, (b) to articulate different points of view that reflect these needs and changes, (c) to identify actions that will respond to these needs and changes, and (d) to persuade organizations to act on these insights. Managerial skills include an appreciation of needs and changes as these affect organizations directly, and also as they affect relationships with environments. They include the personal and interpersonal skills which people use to advocate the advantages of particular points of view. Last, but not least, they include "whatever it takes" (McCall & Kaplan, 1990) to ensure that proposed organizational actions are implemented.

In applying managerial skills, the aim is to ensure that organizational actions and environmental demands stay more or less aligned with one another. If an organization faces rapid external change, for example, a manager who is prepared to make quick decisions that commit an organization to particular actions may appear highly skilled. In a more placid environment, however, the same haste is probably unnecessary, may be wasteful, and a more deliberate decision-making style may be more effective. This implies that what is managerially skillful depends on the particular situation—the particular person, the particular tasks, the particular organization, and the external circumstances.

## Relationship to Work

Due to time pressures and performance constraints, managers must often make decisions based on incomplete information. The result is that misunderstandings, differences of opinion, confusion, breakdowns, and conflict are inevitable aspects of managerial jobs. Finding appropriate ways to resolve these issues requires a wide variety of abilities, here encompassed under the notion of managerial skills. In many ways, managerial skills are relied upon to hold an organization together, to resolve its problems, and to direct and coordinate its subunits so that they work effectively, both together and separately (McCall & Kaplan, 1990).

Before managerial skills can be effectively applied, managers must recognize the demands that are imposed on organizations, along with what can be done about them. They must also appreciate the limitations that characterize organizational functioning. For example, organizations are not naturally integrated wholes, but rather loosely connected clusters of specialist subunits, each performing a different and separate function. Managers must often exercise considerable sensitivity and initiative to achieve the cooperation necessary for ongoing organizational functioning. An additional problem is that people can have quite unrealistic expectations as to what organizations are able to accomplish. Organizational goal accomplishment, far from being effortless, usually depends on the continuous application of managerial skills.

Most managers develop their managerial skills on the job (McCall, Lombardo, & Morrison, 1988); their managerial skills reflect the ways things were managed in their organizations. In different organizations, however, different cultures emphasize different ways of doing things. Some cultures place more emphasis on hierarchy, for example; others emphasize meetings, or risk-taking and entrepreneurship, or team-work, or work in isolation. While each emphasis has its advantages, each is also biased and so creates a unique set of typically unanticipated but recurring issues. People with managerial skills are expected to compensate for the costs implicit in these biases and somehow resolve recurring problems (see **Organizational Culture**).

In the process of improving their managerial skills, managers almost always become both more aware and more critical of the limitations they see in the ways things are done in their organization. More positively, they also become aware of the types of managerial initiative upon which their organization rely and the steps they, personally, can take to compensate for organizational limitations. They may also observe that most organizational problems can be broadly described, but can not be resolved in one-shot;

instead, they require the continual application of a broad range of managerial skills. Consequently, managerial skill development usually reflects a broad perspective. Attention is to be directed towards increasing managers' awareness of the variety of behaviors that may prove useful in particular managerial situations (Thornton & Cleveland, 1990). In addition, attention is drawn to different levels of organizational functioning. As well as day-to-day issues, there are also underlying and continuing social processes involving influence, power, control, and conflict that are always playing themselves out in organizations. Managerial skill consists of an awareness of the options available to limit the negative potential implicit in these underlying social processes and to channel the positive aspects in ways that achieve organizational benefits.

## Application

You improve your managerial skills by becoming more aware of the limitations and pathologies that inevitably characterize organizations and of what you can do to compensate and overcome these limitations. One way to do this is by simply being more aware of the style of managing going on around you. By being more aware of what it is you like about this management, and what about it annoys you, you can consciously select those aspects you wish to copy, those you wish to avoid, and those you may wish to change. A second way to improve your managerial skills is by doing some reading about organizing and managing. A third way is for your organization to invest in managerial skills training programs.

**Being More Aware.** One of the best ways for you to improve your managerial skills is to develop your own ability to acknowledge and appreciate the way your work world really is and the way it is managed. This is not easy to do because, like everybody else, you too see your work through your hopes, expectations, dreams, and fears. These different orientations bias your perceptions, assessments, and interpretations. Acknowledging that these different understandings provide alternative perspectives on reality is often crucial in resolving managerial issues. In fact, just talking about your perspective along with the problems it highlights and what you think should be done differently can often bring about some organizational adjustments and quick improvements.

Though not uncommon, extensive efforts to identify a culprit for current organizational problems usually doesn't help or change very much. If you can find ways to act either to change the problem or avoid it, the problem is well on the way to being organizationally solved. Having done something that changed what had been a problem, you are also likely to be in a much better position to assess the various causes of the problem and the issues surrounding it. This will be gratifying for you and for your organization. It is the process by which one not only develops one's own managerial skills but also demonstrates how they have been enhanced.

**Reading about Managerial Skills.** Books that talk about developing managerial skills take a variety of approaches. How-to books, for example, come up with lists of rules concerning what managers should do. At one level, they may present behavioral, prescriptive rules summarizing what seems to have worked well in practice. An example is Peters and Waterman's *In Search of Excellence*. At another level, they may present a list of rules that reflect a quite explicit underlying framework for achieving a particular goal, as in the book on negotiating by Fisher and Ury, *Getting to Yes*. Many *Harvard Business Review* articles also adopt a how-to approach. In each case, the study pulls together insights from practical experience, presents examples from a variety of organizations, and suggests the possibility of general applicability. Some these studies present provocative ideas that persuade you to think about whether their suggestions may have some relevance for you and your managerial skills, they are probably enhancing your managerial skills. They succeed as they increase your awareness of what particular managerial skills may, in fact, be relevant and needed in your organization.

Other books focus more on story-telling. A number of prominent executives, for example, have written reminiscences about the managerial skills they think they used to accomplish what they did. Based on what they think worked for them, they imply advice for you. With this approach, self-serving bias is an obvious risk, and you should be cautious in adopting this sort of advice. Another approach is provided by investigative journalists, who have written some very entertaining histories describing the events leading to various mergers, takeovers, and organizational changes. The intent of these pieces is also to present personal opinions—the assessments of the investigator—and convince you to share them. As opposed to how-to studies that raise questions and make suggestions about methods and approaches that might help you, business stories usually present another person's view about another time and another place. In reading such stories, therefore, you usually have to work harder to find ideas that may be relevant for your situation and managerial skills.

If you decide that what you are reading does relate to your organization, then you should also be very aware of what is analogous between your situation and the situation you are reading about, as well as the limits of this analogy. This is to avoid the frustration and shock that can occur if one over-generalizes based on analogies from one situation to another. On the other hand, when a story describes a situation that parallels your own, you are likely to feel excited at some of the insights and possibilities that become evident. Such parallels are likely to improve your managerial skills by increasing the options that you perceive for managerial action.

**Training Programs.** When is an investment in training to develop and improve managerial skills likely to prove beneficial? In general, the answer is at those times when your organization is facing problems which only managers can solve. Such occasions occur whenever your organization makes changes where some degree of disruption is inevitable and managerial skills are expected to compensate for any reduced effectiveness and efficiency. Examples of such changes might include the adjustments that result from an expansion or a downsizing (see **Job Security: The Free Agent Manager**), from efforts to establish new facilities, from alterations to products or services, and the reorientations that follow from financial restructurings. Potentially disruptive changes might also include the introduction of profit centers, efforts to decentralize or centralize organizational control, the introduction of new reporting systems, and the adjustments that always stem from the introduction of new technology. If managerial skills are expected to cope with these disruptions, then organizational efforts to check out, support, and further develop managerial skills would seem appropriate and in order.

Another time for developing managerial skills may be as new employees are introduced to your organization. New employees have little organizational knowledge and do not know how you expect them to behave. Your organization is also likely to be reluctant to give these new people responsibilities until they are appropriately socialized into organizational ways. As new employees are also usually eager to learn, efforts to explain organizational methods and introduce people to experiences promoting desired managerial skills may be very appropriate during this honeymoon period. A similar logic suggests the appropriateness of additional programs promoting managerial skills for more senior employees who are targeted for higher promotion or are about to be assigned additional organizational responsibilities.

The question arises as to what form developmental efforts to promote managerial skills in organizations should take. It is always important that those paying for such a development effort, those organizing it, and those participating in it all agree on why the effort is being undertaken and what it is expected to accomplish. This means that in any discussions, you must always include an explanation of what the effort to develop managerial skills is attempting to do, how it is attempting to do it, and why (see **Performance Appraisal**).

Conceptions of ideal managerial behavior differ depending on the perspectives, the positions, and the approaches of managers. In training programs, therefore, it usually does not make sense to seek a uniform perspective because organizational problems requiring intervention are not standardized and managers have distinctive styles. Rather, development programs should flexibly build on the unique managerial styles of managers. This is why you may find that training efforts built on experiences derived from behavioral practice (e.g., behavioral simulations) have some important advantages. They preserve individuality and, at the same time, enable trainees to try out, assess, and learn about the effectiveness of those behaviors they believe are the most appropriate to use in their organization. Large-scale behavioral simulations seem to be most effective for this type of managerial skill development. Stumpf and Dunbar (1990) review a variety of possibilities.

For a training development effort to be worthwhile for both participants and the organization paying for it, there should be well-known organizational issues that the training is designed to influence or remedy. Thus, a prerequisite before undertaking a training development program is an organizational diagnosis that has specifically determined how the particular training program is expected to improve organizational functioning (Levinson, 1972). If such a diagnosis has been done, transferring what is learned in the training back to the on-the-job situation becomes easier. For a relatively small investment in time and money, developmental trainings can provide quick improvements in managerial skills.

***See also*** Assertion; Assessment Centers; Career Development System within the Organization; Continuing Education; Decision Making; Job Security; Job Security: The Free Agent Manager; Mentoring; Negotiating; Networking; Organizational Culture; Organizational Politics; Performance Appraisal; Self-Managed Change; Skills; Women's Barriers and Opportunities.

## Bibliography

Fisher, R., & Ury, W. (1981): *Getting to yes: Negotiating agreement without giving in.* Boston: Houghton Mifflin.

Levinson, H. (1972). *Organizational diagnosis.* Cambridge, MA: Harvard. Based on decades of experience and study, this is a classic, exhaustive, step-by-step program for diagnosing broad organizational issues and needs for developing managerial skills. Includes illustrative, provocative "how to" case studies.

McCall, M. W., Jr., & Kaplan, R. E. (1990). *Whatever it takes: The realities of managerial decision making.* Englewood Cliffs, N.J.: Prentice-Hall. An excellent down-to-earth discussion of what managerial skills are about, reflecting what managers have to do.

McCall, M. W. Jr., Lombardo, M. M., & Morrison, A. M. (1988). *The lessons of experience: How successful executives develop on the job.* Lexington, MA: Lexington. Based on surveys and interviews, this is a well-written description of the sorts of things managers learn on the job.

Peters, T.J., & Waterman, R.H., Jr. (1982). *In search of excellence.* New York: Harper & Row.

Stumpf, S. A., & Dunbar, R. L. M. (1990) Using behavioral simulations in teaching strategic management processes. *The Organizational Behavior Teaching Review,* 14(2): 43–62. A comparative description of seven large-scale behavioral simulations suitable for developing a wide variety of managerial skills.

Thornton, G. C., & Cleveland, J. N. (1990). Developing managerial talent through simulation. *American Psychologist,* 45(2): 190–99. A review of the types of programs available and most successful for managerial skill development.

—Roger L. M. Dunbar

# MANAGING TRANSITIONS

Rosalyn and Jimmy Carter, who felt bitter and defeated after leaving the White House, wrote a book about their experiences and toured the country with tales of how they grew from pain. Betty Ford turned her drug addiction into a mission to help others by founding the Betty Ford Center. Lee Iacocca, despite being fired by Ford Motor Company, became a folk hero by saving the Chrysler Corporation from extinction. Stories such as these attract and intrigue all of us. Every disaster can not be turned into an inspirational success, but every person can be helped to master change.

Since change is such a global term, some definitions will provide focus for this article. Transitions are those events (like promotion or retirement) or nonevents (like not getting the promotion or infertility), which alter our lives. The important point is not the particular event or nonevent but the degree to which it changes roles, relationships, routines, and assumptions about oneself and one's world.

This article discusses ways of managing changes or transitions that alter lives. Although all the examples will not be about work, almost every transition, whether or not it originated in the work setting, reverberates on work. One woman's situation illustrates this. She was married, with a good job, a darling baby, and a second child on the way. Her second child was born with multiple handicaps. At first she withdrew from her husband, sent her two-year-old to live temporarily with her parents, left her job, and wrapped herself totally in the new baby's life, problems, and operations. Eventually she brought her other child home and reunited with her husband. Her family situation dramatically changed her life, and her work life was definitely affected. She said: "I lowered my aspirations. I knew I would never run anything and be responsible for too large a project. I had to have work that was limited in scope."

By the same token, a major change at work—a promotion or a demotion—clearly affects one's family.

There is no way, therefore, to separate out work transitions since work, family, and personal development are inextricably intertwined.

The remainder of this article will discuss how to understand transitions and then use this understanding in the management of change.

## Understanding Transitions: Their Relationship to Work

The first step in managing change is understanding the various dimensions of transitions: the type of transition being experienced, the impact of the transition on one's life, and where one is in the transition process.

**Type of Transition.** Transitions can be positive, negative, or neutral; they can be anticipated, unanticipated, nonevents, or "double whammies." (See Figure 1.)

- *Anticipated transitions* are those major life events we usually expect to be part of adult life, such as marrying, becoming a parent, leaving home, starting a first job, retiring, finishing school. Some of these are culturally prescribed, like leaving home, going to work; others are individual, such as divorce, returning to school; others are becoming so common as to be part of cultural expectations, like caring for aging parents, young adult children returning home. People can rehearse for these anticipated transitions.

- *Unanticipated transitions* are those surprises, both positive and negative, that are unexpected. These include a plant closing, getting a big bonus, a car accident, death of a significant other, or winning the lottery. These unanticipated events catch one off guard.

- *Nonevent transitions* are those expected events that fail to occur. These can include not getting married, infertility, or even living longer than expected.

- *Double whammies* refer to the pile up of related transitions which seem to occur during one period of time. For example, a return to school can necessitate a change in one's work role which invariably impacts one's family.

**Impact of Transition.** Transitions such as the birth of a first child or taking early retirement appear to have little in common, but both change a person's life. It is not the transition per se that is critical but how much it alters one's roles, relationships, routines, and assumptions. Thus, similar transitions can result in very different situations. For example, when one woman divorced her husband of 30 years, the decision was mutual and a long time in the making. Her children were grown; she stayed in the same job, the same apartment, the same community. Another woman's divorce stemmed from her husband announcing he was leaving. She had three small children at home; she had to take on a full-time job and move to a less expensive neighborhood. All aspects of her life were undergoing

**Figure 1. Steps in Managing Transitions**

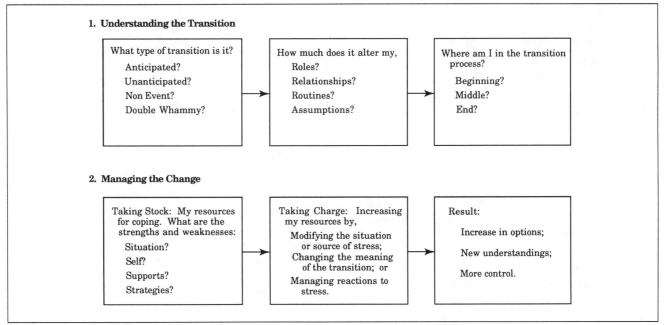

major change. Though both women were divorcing, and for both it was painful, the impact on one was more pervasive than on the other.

**The Transition Process.** Transitions are a process over time and people's reactions to them change. If a transition is major (altering roles, relationships, routines, and assumptions), it pervades one's life. The person thinks only of the new marriage, the new job, the plant closing. Then, in the middle period of a transition, individuals can become confused. "Who am I?" asked one woman whose husband had moved into a nursing home because of Alzheimer's disease. "Am I separated? Married? Committed?" Finally, individuals integrate the transition into their lives, move into new situations, and develop new roles, relationships, routines, and assumptions. In a study of men whose jobs were eliminated, those men able to obtain new jobs felt the transition was completed, while those unable to replace what they had lost felt stuck and still in the midst of the transition (Schlossberg & Leibowitz, 1980).

Transitions come in many shapes; they impact lives differently and they are a process over time. Understanding these dimensions provides the basis for coping.

## Applying the Knowledge of Transitions in the Management of Change

There are two parts to the management of change: "taking stock" of one's resources for coping, and "taking charge" by increasing one's resources for coping.

**Taking Stock of One's Resources for Coping.** Studies of change have shown that people in transition have both strengths and weaknesses. These potential resources

or deficits cluster into four major categories, labeled here the 4 S's: Situation, Self, Supports, and Strategies. Any individual in any transition can take stock of his or her 4 S's (Schlossberg, 1989).

- *Situation.* Does the person see the transition as positive, negative, expected, unexpected, desired, or dreaded? Did the transition come at the worst or best possible time? Is it "on time" or "off time"? Is it surrounded by other stresses? Is it voluntary or imposed? Is this the transition's beginning, middle, or nearly the end? Is this a transition that happened to the person or one that happened to someone else but reverberated and affected the person?

- *Self.* There are many ways to gauge a person's inner self or strengths for coping with the transition. What is the person's previous experience in making a similar transition? Does the person believe there are options? Is the person basically optimistic and able to deal with ambiguity?

- *Supports.* Supports and options include both financial assets and potential emotional support from family, close friends, and coworkers. Is one receiving more support than sabotage?

- *Strategies.* Pearlin and Schooler (1978) point out that there is no "magic bullet" coping strategy. Rather, the creative coper uses a number of strategies flexibly, depending on the situation.

These 4 S's can be scored as to whether each is seen as a positive resource or a deficit.

**Taking Charge.** This step includes strengthening those resources or S's seen as deficits. The individual can then take the low resource and turn it into a more supportive one. For example, one adult learner felt initially supported by her family when she returned to school. After a short time, the support felt like sabotage. Her task was to figure out some new approach to turning this low support system into a high support system. To do this, she examined the many potential coping strategies Pearlin and Schooler (1978) identified from studying the coping strategies of 2,300 people between 18 and 65. They distinguished three major clusters of coping:

- Responses that modify the situation and seek to alter the source of stress (i.e., negotiating, asserting, brainstorming, taking legal action.
- Responses that change the meaning of the transition in order to neutralize the threat (i.e., developing rituals, relabeling or reframing, using denial, humor, faith.
- Responses that help one manage reactions to stress (i.e., playing, relaxing, jogging, swimming, reading, therapy.
- Another strategy that people do not think of is: Doing nothing.

By applying this framework of taking stock and taking charge to the case of Virginia, the steps will become clearer. Virginia returned to school at 50 to study accounting so that she could move out of her low-level office job. She saw returning to school as her last chance to upgrade herself. Although she was in control of the transition—choosing when, where, and how to return to school—it turned out that her situation and supports were low. If Virginia had taken stock of her resources, and then systematically taken charge by turning her liabilities into assets, perhaps she would not have dropped out of school.

Her situation included a chronically ill mother who was living with her. Virginia had expected support from her mother. Although her mother's words were supportive, her actions were negative and included last-minute demands for food and medicine just before Virginia left for classes. Because of the combination of a stressful situation, an unsupportive mother, and the use of very few strategies, Virginia dropped out of school.

The crux is how to Take Charge. Virginia could have looked at any of her low resources—say, low support—and asked herself the following series of questions based on the coping strategies identified by Pearlin and Schooler.

- Should she try to change her Supports? She might have negotiated with her friends or neighbors to come in on the days she had classes in exchange for some favor she could do for them.
- Should she change the meaning of the situation? She could say to herself that she can live with an unsupportive mother; she can set boundaries; she can develop some rituals for each class day.

- Should she change the way she reacts to the demands of her mother? She might do this through relaxation exercises, therapeutic writing or therapy.
- Or, should she do nothing?

People in transition can look at their transition, take stock of their 4 S's, select the ones in need of strengthening, and then look over the various coping strategy mechanisms and see which new ones to apply.

## A Final Word

Transitions that require a change in one's life can sometimes cause havoc. It is possible to take the mystery, if not the misery, out of change by analyzing the type of change one is experiencing, the impact on one's life, and where one is in the transition process. Then one can take stock of one's resources, and finally take charge by identifying new ways to cope.

The end result is an increase in options, new understanding of what is being experienced, and more control of one's reactions to transitions. There is clearly no simple, easy answer. There is merely a system to use, an approach to incorporate, amd new strategies to try.

*See also* Networking.

## Bibliography

Bridges, W. (1980). *Transitions: Making sense of life's changes.* Reading, MA: Addison-Wesley. Bridges describes transitions through the life span by focusing on three factors: "endings," marked by an event or changed state of mind; the "neutral zone," a time to integrate what's happening; and a "new beginning." Simple, easy-to-understand style.

Lazarus, R. S., & Folkman, S. (1984). *Stress, approval, and coping.* New York: Springer Publishing Company.

Pearlin L. I. C., & Schooler, C. (1978). The structure of coping. *Journal of Health and Social Behavior,* 19: 2–21.

Schlossberg, N. K. (1989). *Overwhelmed: Coping with life's ups and downs.* Lexington, MA: Lexington Books. Schlossberg shows how to evaluate each transition or change, to determine how it has affected or is likely to affect one's life, to assess personal strengths and support systems, and to pinpoint the best coping strategies. A positive guide to dealing with the challenges that accompany change.

Schlossberg, N.K., & Leibowitz, Z.B. (1980). Organizational support systems as buffers to job loss. *Journal of vocational Behavior,* 18: 204–17.

Viorst, J. (1986). *Necessary losses.* New York: Simon & Schuster. Viorst views loss as an essential theme throughout the life span. She describes the losses incurred at each stage of life and how we deal with them, for she believes it is only through loss that we are able to grow. Provocative commentary for professionals and others seeking meaning in losses.

—NANCY K. SCHLOSSBERG

# MENTAL HEALTH AND WORK

Work provides more than economic benefits for most people. Work can be and is for many workers the principal source of human relationships and friendships, feelings of competence and mastery, self-esteem, order in one's life, and personal identity. Former U.S. Secretary of Education Bell has referred to work in the U.S. as the means whereby "a person is tested as well as identified. It is the way a youngster becomes an adult. Work shapes the thoughts and life of the worker. A change in atmosphere and life-style can be effected by an individual by simply changing the way he or she makes a living" (Riegle, 1982).

Given its potential to be the source for multiple human satisfactions, work plays a crucial role in the creation and maintenance of mental health. The success of one's choice of and adjustment to work and one's ability to find in work gratifications for the personal purposes to be served by work are related to general life satisfactions, family functioning, and associated phenomena.

## Relationship to Work

A satisfying work life is likely to increase positive mental health; a negative work life will likely reduce mental health. In essence, "success in one life role facilitates success in another, and difficulties in one role are likely to lead to difficulties in another" (Super, 1980).

Relationships between mental health and work are particularly visible where persons are unemployed or underemployed. In such instances, the loss of or distress and dissatisfaction with work have been associated with a range of personal and social problems. For example, job dissatisfaction is consistently found to be related to absenteeism, accidents, job turnover, psychosomatic illnesses, anxiety, worry, tension, impaired interpersonal relationships, coronary heart disease, alcoholism, drug abuse, and suicide. Similar findings are apparent for the underemployed: those who can only work part-time when they want to work full-time; persons only partially using the technical competencies or leadership skills they possess. Such persons frequently need help with stress reduction and anger management, finding ways to obtain needed satisfactions in nonwork roles, and differentiating the constraints in the workplace that cause them underemployment from perceptions of personal inadequacy (Herr, 1989).

The most dramatic relationship of work to mental health issues is seen when persons become unemployed. Researchers in several countries have identified the tenden-cies of unemployed persons to go through a grief process similar to what happens when one loses a loved one (Borgen & Amundson, 1984; Levi, 1984). Unemployed workers are likely to experience stages of mourning and bereavement, including denial, anger, bargaining, depression, and acceptance. They frequently report feelings of victimization—shock, confusion, helplessness, fear, and depression—similar to persons who have experienced rape, disease, or crime. Persons react differently to the stress associated with unemployment. Some persons react in physical terms, cardiovascular disease, cirrhosis, hypertension, and chemical dependency have each been related to abrupt loss of job for some people. Other persons react in behavioral terms. They act out their stress by becoming aggressive or violent, or engaging in spouse or child abuse. Many unemployed persons experience their stress in psychological terms, experiencing depression, anxiety, or panic attacks (see **Underemployment; Unemployment**).

Prolonged work adjustment problems or unemployment are serious threats to physical and mental health and to the quality of life. They typically affect not only the primary person experiencing the difficulty with work, but also other family members and the community. Evidence suggests that children of unemployed parents are also likely to experience stress, including moodiness, digestive problems, irritability, school problems, and strained relationships with other children. Spouses of unemployed persons are also likely to experience depression, anxiety, and other mental health problems. Because of the significant physical, behavioral, and psychological problems associated with unemployment and other work-related difficulties, communities also bear social costs, such as unemployment benefits, mental health and substance abuse services, family welfare, and reduced tax revenue, as well as the less visible costs of lost productivity.

Personal adjustment, or mental health, and work adjustment occur together for many persons. A change in adjustment in one of these areas affects the other. The workplace is the center in which personal and work adjustment converge. The workplace becomes the context in which positive and negative, healthy and unhealthy, good and bad outcomes are stimulated. The workplace allows people to find purpose, affiliations, and economic livelihood; conflicts, thwarted aspirations, and family or personal problems are also brought into the workplace where they filter and shape one's life as a worker. The processes involved are complex, but the importance of viewing work and mental health as related is essential to thinking about how persons can be helped to deal with each of these matters.

## Application

In considering personal status with regard to mental health and work, theory and practice suggest the following:

1. In order to determine the personal relationship between work and mental health, you need to identify what purposes you want work to serve for you in the social, economic, and psychological realms. Are these purposes being served in a relatively balanced and effective way? If not, where are the deficits? Are there ways for you to be more assertive in achieving the purposes in your present job? Does not achieving these purposes cause you to feel job dissatisfaction? Does this job dissatisfaction affect other parts of your life? How? What have you done about any physical, behavioral, or psychological problems you have experienced in relation to job dissatisfactions or frustrations? (see **Career Roles; Job Satisfaction; Leisure**).

2. If there appear to be negative relationships between your job satisfaction and your more general feelings about yourself, others, or your productivity or future opportunities, these feelings may signal a need for you to see a professional counselor trained to help you evaluate such feelings and consider plans of action that might alter your current circumstances. National Certified Career Counselors, counseling psychologists, and other types of professional counselors (school, university, rehabilitation, employment) would be appropriate sources of assistance (see **Career Counseling; Employee Assistance Programs**).

3. If you are experiencing problems of job dissatisfaction, work adjustment, underemployment or unemployment, you need to realize that each of these is likely to stimulate one or more of the following: stress, possibly physical symptoms, exaggerated aggressive behavior, low self-esteem, family discord, abuse of alcohol or other substances. These outcomes are less likely to occur because of mental illness, personal incompetence, or inadequacy; they are more likely to be related to a poor job fit or the lack of specific employability skills that can be identified and acquired.

4. You need to understand that many people experience work-related problems at different times in their life that affect their mental health. If you do, you are not abnormal, unique, or a social isolate. There is a system of community, church, educational, public, and private resources to help you deal with your concerns. You need to seek out such resources rather than accept work-related problems as inevitable, unsolvable, or conditions from which you cannot escape.

5. If you are experiencing work-related problems that are creating mental health issues for you, you will likely profit from some combination of several simultaneous approaches: stress reduction; perhaps anger management; clarification of your marketable and transferable work skills; career planning; job search and presentation skills; identification and assessment of financial, familial, marital, and other types of support; assessment of self, values, and interests; job search support groups; assertiveness training; possibly some form of technical retraining. These are techniques that career counselors and related professionals can help you use to find new direction, purpose, and self-worth as you make more positive your connections between work and mental health.

*See also* Anger; Assertion; Career Counseling; Career Planning; Career Roles; Employee Assistance Programs; Job Satisfaction; Job Search; Leisure; Underemployment; Unemployment; Work Hazards: Psychosocial.

## Bibliography

Borgen, W. A., & Amundson, N. E. (1984). *The experience of unemployment. Implications for counseling the unemployed.* Scarborough, Ontario: Nelson Canada. A study of how different populations of males and females, immigrants and nationals cope with unemployment. Describes the emotional roller coaster, the grieving process, the sense of victimization experienced by these persons, and the techniques that were useful in helping them.

Herr, E. L. (1989). *Counseling in a dynamic society. Opportunities and challenges.* Alexandria, VA: AACD Press. Discusses the impact of advanced technology in the workplace and other shifts in the occupational structure. Describes the worker stresses, underemployment, and unemployment resulting from such shifts and how counselors can respond to such work-related and mental health problems.

Levi, L. (1984). *Stress in industry.* Geneva, Switzerland: International Labor Office.

Loughead, T. A. (Guest Ed.) (1989). *Journal of Career Development,* 16: whole issue. A special thematic issue on the integration of career development and mental health counseling. The articles summarize the research on career development and mental health and discuss ways to facilitate the approaches developed from this research.

Riegle, D. W., Jr. (1982). Psychological and social effects of unemployment. *American Psychologist,* 37: 113–15.

Super, D. E. (1980). A life-span, life space approach to career development. *Journal of Vocational Behavior,* 16: 282–98.

—EDWIN L. HERR

# MENTORING

Mentoring refers to relationships between juniors and seniors (in terms of age or experience) that exist, primarily, to support the personal and career development of the junior person. These relationships provide a wide range of developmental functions (including coaching and counseling), and require both individuals to invest considerable time and emotion. Mentoring relationships last, on average, about two to five years, and necessarily end as individuals' needs or organizational circumstances change.

Mentoring relationships enable both individuals to build new skills, prepare for advancement and other growth opportunities, adapt to changing organizational circumstances, and/or build self-esteem and self-confidence. Recent research suggests that other kinds of relationships with superiors, peers, and subordinates can also aid development, even though they are more limited than a classic mentor relationship in terms of involvement and impact (Kram, 1988; McCall, Lombardo, & Morrison, 1988).

## Relationship to Work

Relationships are now considered to be a critical source of development for individuals at every career stage—as important as the job itself or formal classroom training. Mentoring relationships provide career functions which facilitate advancement up an occupational ladder, and psychosocial functions which help to build self-esteem, self-confidence, and a clear sense of work identity (Kram, 1988). In the long run, both types of mentoring are desirable.

Mentors enable career advancement through the following activities (career functions):

1. *Sponsorship.* Opening doors. Having connections that will support the mentee's career advancement.
2. *Coaching.* Teaching "the ropes." Giving positive and negative feedback to improve performance and potential.
3. *Protection.* Providing support in high risk situations. Acting as a buffer when necessary.
4. *Exposure.* Creating opportunities for the mentee to demonstrate competence where it counts.
5. *Challenging Work.* Giving assignments that stretch the mentee's knowledge and skills and to prepare for advancement.

Mentors help to build self-esteem, self-confidence, and professional identity through the following activities (psychosocial functions):

1. *Role Modeling.* Demonstrating behavior, attitudes, and values that the junior admires and wishes to emulate.
2. *Counseling.* Creating opportunities to explore personal and professional dilemmas in a supportive and confidential context.
3. *Acceptance and Confirmation.* Providing ongoing support, respect, and admiration which strengthen self-confidence.
4. *Friendship.* Mutual caring and sharing that goes beyond what is required at work.

In providing career and psychosocial functions to their juniors, mentors benefit as well. They derive personal satisfaction from contributing to others' development, gain technical and psychological support from loyal subordinates, learn new perspectives from their juniors, and enhance their reputations as effective developers of young talent. Overall, being a mentor is a revitalizing experience.

Mentoring relationships occur more naturally between individuals who are alike than between individuals who are different in terms of gender, race, or ethnicity (Thomas,1989; Morrison, White, & Van Velsor, 1987). Building relationships in a diverse workforce requires good communication skills and the commitment to valuing differences. Some organizations make conscious efforts to create a culture that encourages mentoring for all employees through formal mentoring programs or through education and rewards (Kram & Bragar,1991; Kram, 1988).

## Application

If you want to develop a mentor relationship consider the following guidelines:

1. Know what you want and need in a mentor relationship, as well as what you have to offer. As a young person, you bring enthusiasm and eagerness to learn, as well as a set of skills. As a senior person, you bring a desire to teach others, and wisdom and experience to share. Determine which mentoring functions are relevant to you. Conduct such self-assessment periodically, since your needs are sure to change over time.

2. Seek and recognize opportunities to build developmental relationships. In the context of boss-subordinate relationships, performance appraisal discussions provide a forum for building a mentor relationship. With others, there are a number of forums, including task forces, temporary assignments, social events, and community service activities where you can meet and build rapport with potential mentors and mentees. Very often, asking seniors questions about how they got to where they are, or for feedback on a project you are currently working on, can be the beginning of a mentor relationship.

3. Keep in mind that it takes time to build a mentor relationship. You can encourage a relationship to grow by acknowledging the benefits you are getting from your potential mentor, showing eagerness to learn, taking the initiative, and demonstrating a commitment to helping a prospective mentor and the organization to reach their goals.

4. It is best to build a system of supportive relationships, rather than to limit your search to finding one mentor. It is far too risky, and often disappointing, to rely on one individual to meet all of your needs. Mentor relationships go through four predictable phases: initiation, cultivation, separation, and redefinition. They generally begin with great excitement and positive feelings, and end with feelings of loss, anxiety, or confusion. Not only do mentees have to leave their mentors to grow, but sometimes mentors become less available to lend support when they face difficulties in their own careers. Do not overlook relationships with your peers as valuable sources of coaching, role-modeling, counseling, and friendship.

5. Address the additional complexities you are likely to encounter in mentor relationships that cross gender, racial, or ethnic boundaries. Be willing to discuss your concerns with trusted confidantes who share similar concerns, and with your mentor or mentee when sufficient rapport has been established. Men and women should acknowledge any concerns about sex-role stereotyping, the limitations of an opposite sex role model, increasing intimacy and/or sexual attraction, and/or public scrutiny of the relationship. Similarly, those in interracial relationships should explore how cultural differences may interfere with building trust and empathy. Generally, it is helpful for mentors to invite discussion of these sensitive issues.

6. When you are seeking a new job, consider the extent to which a "mentoring culture" exists. You are most likely to find conditions that encourage mentoring in settings where managers are rewarded for developing subordinates, much of the work occurs in teams and task forces, there is a high level of trust among people at different levels, and relationship building and other developmental activities are considered important rather than extraneous. Be sure to look for these characteristics during your job search, and remember that no organization will achieve them perfectly.

7. Remember that mentoring relationships can become destructive if individuals' needs are out of sync, or if either party enters a crisis of esteem. When you begin to sense that a relationship is no longer supportive, it is time to rely on other alliances and to let this one go. Most important, do not blame yourself for a failed relationship; more often than not, such a dramatic change in a previously supportive relationship has little to do with your behavior, and more to do with personal concerns of the other person, or with organizational politics.

*See also* Career Identity; Networking; Promotion/Raise; Self-Efficacy; Self-Esteem; Sex-Role Stereotyping; Women's Barriers and Opportunities.

## Bibliography

Collins, N. W. (1983). *Professional women and their mentors: A practical guide to mentoring for the woman who wants to get ahead.* Englewood Cliffs, NJ: Prentice-Hall.

Kram, K. E. (1988). *Mentoring at work: Developmental relationships in organizational life.* Lanham, MD: University Press of America. A scholarly and readable review of in-depth studies of mentoring relationships between managers in a corporate setting. Discussions of mentoring functions, relationship phases, cross-gender mentoring, and peer mentoring.

Kram, K. E., & Bragar, M.C. (1991). Development through mentoring: A strategic approach for the 1990s. Forthcoming in D. Montross, & C. Shrinkman (Eds.), *Career development in the 1990s.* New York: Charles C. Thomas Press. Written for human resource practitioners and managers who want to encourage effective mentoring for a wide range of employees in their organizations. The authors critique the benefits and limitations of formal mentoring programs, and offer a broader approach that is linked to strategic business objectives and considers a wide range of human resource practices that shape the mentoring process.

McCall, M., Lombardo, M., & Morrison, A. (1988). *The lessons of experience.* Lexington, MA: Lexington Books. Based on a study of 166 successful managers and executives, the authors illustrate the various ways in which relationships—along with job assignments and hardships—play a critical role in learning and development. Many case examples are presented.

Morrison, A., White, R., & Van Velsor, E. (1987). *Breaking the glass ceiling.* Reading, MA: Addison-Wesley Publishing.

Phillips-Jones, L. (1982). *Mentors and proteges.* New York: Arbor House.

Thomas, D.A. (1989). Mentoring and irrationality: The role of racial taboos. *Human Resource Management,* 28,(2): 279–90. Analysis of the complexities of cross-race/cross-gender mentoring relationships, including vivid illustrations of the forces leading to superficial alliances between blacks and whites.

Zey, M.G. (1984). *The mentor connection.* Homewood, IL: Dow Jones-Irwin. A thorough discussion of mentoring based on interviews with more than 150 executives in large and small firms. Practical advice is given to mentors, mentees, and those who want to set up formal mentoring programs.

—KATHY E. KRAM

# MILITARY CAREER: CHANGING TO A CIVILIAN CAREER

Leaving the military and entering a civilian career is a challenge faced by most persons in the military. In many respects it is more complex than a job change among civilians. Military personnel are faced with several emotional and psychological issues, including a total life-style change that impacts the individual and the family, possible changes in geographic area, and a change in status in the community and in personal identity. This is often accompanied by an awkward struggle to transfer military skills and experience to comparable civilian occupations. But the most difficult hurdle is the cultural difference between military and business organizations.

## Emotional and Psychological Issues

Significant life-style changes are among the first of many transitional issues awaiting the newly separated military person. By merit of hard work and years of dedicated service, military personnel have earned certain benefits and privileges of rank, some of which extend to members of the family. Upon separation, these normal and customary courtesies are no longer available. For example, access to base personnel and services becomes particularly difficult for the spouse and family members. A simple appointment with the base doctor or dentist becomes a major ordeal in negotiation and diplomacy. When affordable on-base housing is no longer available, a temporary relocation until a new permanent home can be established becomes necessary. Even though an effort may have been made to obtain an assignment at or near the desired retirement location, the probability of having to relocate to where the jobs are increases the pressure and stress on all members of the family. The substantial change in take-home pay after retirement and the possible loss of income from a spouse's job, if relocation is necessary, frequently results in difficulty in qualifying for adequate financing for housing at the new location. The change from Col. or Sgt. Smith to plain Mr. or Ms. Smith is possibly the most troublesome of the emotional and psychological issues experienced by the separating individual because the comfortable routine and prescribed duties which defined the person's identity are gone. These abrupt changes in life style, status, geographic location, and personal identity often sow the seeds for transition adjustment problems (see **Managing Transitions; Relocation**).

To minimize the impact of these problems, begin planning for your departure from the military as much as a year or more in advance. Maintaining or re-establishing relationships with other military families who have successfully established themselves in civilian life can prove to be an enormous help. They can be sources of advice on dealing with the stress and provide tips on how to simplify the transition. Sometimes the transition may throw the entire family unit into crisis; if so, the base family support center has experienced counselors available to help you and your family deal with these issues.

Career counseling and transition assistance should be factored into your planning for yourself and your spouse. The military will provide some transition assistance counseling to you, but not for your spouse, and, unfortunately, not to the depth and extent necessary to realistically equip you to land a management or executive position. There are many career counseling services around and care should be taken in selecting a professional service. Professional career counselors will hold an advanced academic degree in counseling or psychology; they may be licensed by the state in which they practice and should have had experience working with military personnel as well as corporate executives.

## Transferability of Skills

It is fairly common for military personnel to struggle with identifying comparable work in the civilian arena as well as isolating existing skills which are transferable and marketable. For example, after many years of military service most enlisted personnel and officers have risen to a level where their work consists largely of management and supervision. Upon leaving the military, their stated career objective is often a "management position" or a job in which "I can work with people." These generalized career objectives are so vague and overused that most organizations do not give serious consideration to such applicants. The problem is further complicated by the dissimilarity of titles for essentially the same jobs, which further contributes to vagueness and leads to totally inappropriate job objectives based on actual skill and experience. Consequently, military personnel must hone their research skills to a keen edge to be sure the civilian who reads their resume can clearly see and understand where they could fit into the organization.

The problem of skill identification and transferability can be remedied in several ways. The first thing you should do is attend the new "Transition Assistance Program" developed jointly by the Department of Labor and the Department of Veterans Affairs. This new program, available to all military personnel who are within 180 days of separation, became operative in May 1990. The program, conducted by representatives of the various state employment services, covers all the essential how-to job search issues, including skill identification, resume development, networking techniques, interviewing, and much more.

Second, if you're the resourceful type, you can go to the library and get the *Dictionary of Occupational Titles (DOT)* and the accompanying *Guide for Occupational Exploration (GOE)* and research the jobs and skills you possess. This will lead you to many civilian career fields that are more or less comparable to your present job.

The third option is to engage the services of a professional career counselor/consultant who has experience working with military personnel. This may be the best option for nontechnical and field grade officers who may experience difficulty in identifying and focusing on the most viable alternatives. In addition, a professional career counselor will have access to databased programs to identify specific civilian occupations which will utilize your exact skills. He or she will also help you market yourself and advise you on the subtle art of positioning in the business world. The fees of a good career counselor/consultant will not be inexpensive, but will certainly be in line with the fees you would pay such other professionals as a C.P.A. or attorney (see **Career Counseling**).

## Cultural Differences between Military and Business Organizations

There are significant and subtle differences in organizational culture and values between military and business institutions of which the newcomer should be aware. For example, in the business world the ultimate concern is bottom line profit or loss, while the military is focused on accomplishment of the mission by whatever means it takes. The difference may appear subtle but the end result is not. The executive would rather abort his mission, withdraw from battle to fight another day rather than risk the loss of profit. They just don't call artillery in on their own position for the sake of the mission. It's not that corporate executives are less committed; often they are nearly fanatical. The difference lies in their values and tactics. Other differences in cultural values involve loyalty, stability, discipline, level of responsibility, and manner of dress.

Military personnel are known and respected for their loyalty and dedication to duty. In the civilian sector these qualities may well work to your disadvantage. If, for example, you become associated with a financially troubled company, your intense loyalty is likely to cause you to stay to the bitter end. Your loyalty will not allow you to leave the field of battle and attempt to reposition for your own survival.

Stability in the military forces is well known, however, work life in the civilian sector is often uncertain and changeable. When changes in mission occur, military forces are transferred and redeployed to accommodate the new circumstances. Changes in profitability and shifts in the economy within the business world result in layoffs and downsizing of work forces. Since the single largest overhead expense is payroll, companies typically respond to economic threats by cutting their personnel head count.

Discipline is another area of cultural difference. Civilians abhor what they perceive to be the rigidity of military discipline. It appears inflexible and raises questions about situations where orders alone won't get the desired results. However, civilian executives and managers can often be very autocratic and punitive in their dealings with subordinates, especially if they hold ultimate authority in the company. In such cases, there is no one to put restraints on their actions. Unlike the military, where forbearance and time will eventually solve the problem of a difficult superior, the private sector frequently offers no alternative but to leave the firm.

Career progression and responsibility are handled quite differently in industry as well. A military person by merit of rank and time in grade is assured a challenging assignment and an orderly progression. From the day one received their commission or was promoted to N.C.O., he or she held as much or more responsibility as the majority of supervisors and managers in civilian jobs. No doubt, your first civilian job will entail significantly less authority, responsibility, and fewer people under your direct supervision.

Appropriate dress in the civilian world is also sometimes problematic for the military person. A civilian could not don your uniform and show up at a military facility without detection as an outsider because of his lack of knowledge about the appropriate conventions of how the uniform should be worn. The military person often experiences some of the same problems concerning what is and is not appropriate attire for business. Although this may seem trivial, it often makes a critical difference in the selection decision.

To minimize the consequences and impact of cultural differences between military and business organizations, you would be wise to conduct some primary research through visits and interviews with former military personnel holding positions in organizations similar to those you might target. An old-fashioned reconnaissance mission to several high profile companies in your immediate area should also prove helpful. Secondary research in such books as *Office Warfare, Office Politics, Skills for Success*, and *The New Dress For Success* (see bibliography below) will also provide valuable insights concerning appropriate dress, work values, and the culture of corporate America.

***See also*** Career Counseling; Career Planning; Climate for Workers; Information Interviewing; Job Search; Job Security; Law in the Workplace; Managing Transitions; Networking; Organizational Culture; Organizational Politics; Relocation; Skills.

## Bibliography

Allen, J. G. (1983). *How to turn an interview into a job.* New York: Simon & Schuster. An excellent reference on interviewing techniques and behind-the-scenes information about what interviewers are really looking for.

Beatty, R. H. (1989). *The perfect cover letter.* New York: John Wiley & Sons. An exceptional source of examples of everything you ever want or need to know about cover letters and related job search letters.

Camden, T. M., & Bishop, N. (1987). *How to get a job in Dallas/ Fort Worth.* Chicago: Surrey Books. This series covers most major cities in the U.S. An insider's guide to thousands of companies, names of key executives, and techniques for job search.

Chapman, J. (1987). *How to make $1000 a minute.* Berkeley, CA: Ten Speed Press. A step-by-step guide to handling salary negotiations. A must for all job changers.

Deal, T. E., & Kennedy, A. A. (1982). *Corporate cultures.* Reading, MA: Addison-Wesley. The rites and rituals of corporate life and how to understand and use this knowledge to gain influence.

Harrington, T. F., & O'Shea, A. J. (1984). *Guide for occupational exploration.* Circle Pines, MN: American Guidance Service. The premiere guide to occupational alternatives and self-exploration for career changes.

Kennedy, M. M. (1980). *Office politics.* New York: Ballantine Books. A survival guide about how to use politics to your advantage.

Kennedy, M. M. (1985). *Office warfare.* New York: Ballantine Books. A companion work to *Office Politics* dealing with success and survival in the political wars within corporations.

Malloy, J. T. (1988). *New dress for success.* New York: Warner Books. A standard in executive fashion and protocol.

Marshall, R., & Green, E. G. (1977). *Directory of occupational titles.* Washington, DC: U.S. Department of Labor. A compendium of occupational descriptive information for over 30,000 jobs in U. S. business and industry.

Nyman, J. T. (1981). *Re-entry—turning military experience into civilian success.* Harrisburg, PA: Stackpole Books. One of the few books available written specifically for the military person who is in the process of transitioning to civilian work.

Scheele, A. (1979). *Skills for success.* New York: Ballantine Books. A strong guide to handling office politics and managing your corporate success.

Wright, J. W. (1987). *The American almanac of jobs and salaries.* New York: Avon Books. A compendium of hard data on hundreds of professional, managerial, and hourly jobs, including job descriptions, salary ranges, and other useful salary information by industry.

—Robert E. Rainey

# MYERS-BRIGGS TYPE INDICATOR

The Myers-Briggs Type Indicator (MBTI) is a self-administering questionnaire designed to identify personality strengths and attributes. These strengths and attributes easily lend themselves to career planning decisions. The MBTI provides information about general patterns of perceiving and deciding about information. Because research has tied particular personality patterns to various careers, the MBTI gives an easy way to understand how your personality relates to the career/work world. Designed to make Carl Jung's theory of psychological types applicable to everyday life, the MBTI provides a handy model to examine how you interact with others and express your general work style.

The MBTI can be used for self-understanding and for exploring the match between interests and behaviors to the work world. With over 3 million individuals having completed the MBTI in various occupations, there are abundant data relating type to careers and occupations. To understand these data, a knowledge of the basic scales on which you are sorted by the MBTI is essential.

## Four Preferences and Sixteen Types

The 4 sets of preferences on the MBTI generate 16 types. The MBTI as an indicator—not a psychological test—sorts your relative preference between the polarities of extraversion or introversion attitudes, sensing or intuitive perception, thinking or feeling judgment, and judging ("Let's decide now") or perception ("Wait, we need more information before we decide").

The four sets of preferences are listed below:

| | | |
|---|---|---|
| Extraversion | _____ | Introversion (Energy) |
| Sensing | _____ | iNtuition (Perceiving) |
| Thinking | _____ | Feeling (Judging) |
| Judging | _____ | Perception (Orientation) |

Depending on how the MBTI sorts you on each set, you will have a 4-letter code (e.g., INTJ, ESFP, ISFJ, ENTP) with up to 16 possibilities. This code is a short-hand way to express preferences and to indicate how you deal with day-to-day situations and choices. The 4-letter code is a "working hypothesis" about your preferences. Each type is assumed to be as valuable and competent as any other type.

As you can see from the following two tables, most of the 16 types can be found in any given career; however, a particular type tends to be more prevalent. For example, in Table 1 you see the percentage of each type found among certified public accountants in a study of 494 individuals. Type theory would suggest that individuals who enjoy details and practical, logical tasks are likely to be drawn to accounting. Table 1 shows that over half of the participants in this study prefer the sensing and thinking functions. In contrast, Table 2 reveals the percentage of types found in studies of those who select counseling as a career. Type theory suggests that individuals who prefer working with possibilities and with individuals are likely to score in the intuitive and feeling categories. In Table 2, 45% of the counselors are intuitive feeling types.

**Figure 1. Table of Sixteen Types for Certified Public Accountants**

|  | ST | SF | NF | NT |
|---|---|---|---|---|
|  | ——— | ——— | ——— | ——— |
|  | ISTJ | ISFJ | INFJ | INTJ |
|  | 26.7% | 5.06% | 2.02% | 5.6% |
|  | ISTP | ISFP | INFP | INTP |
|  | 4.6% | 1.2% | 1.8% | 4.8% |
|  | ESTP | ESFP | ENFP | ENTP |
|  | 3.04% | 1.01% | 3.4% | 5.8% |
|  | ESTJ | ESFJ | ENFJ | ENTJ |
|  | 19.2% | 4.05% | 3.04% | 8.3% |
|  | ——— | ——— | ——— | ——— |
| Totals | 53.6 *** | 11.3% | 10.3% | 24.7% |

N = 494

Each Preference

| E 47.9% | I 52.02% |
|---|---|
| S 64.9% *** | N 35.02% |
| T 78.3% *** | F 21.6% |
| J 74% | P 25.9% |

*** used to highlight the self-selection.

**Source:** G.P. Macdaid, M.H. McCaulley, & R. Kainz, *Myers-Briggs Type Indicator Atlas of Type Tables,* Gainesville, FL: Center for Applications of Psychological Type, 1987. Reprinted by permission.

## Extraversion and Introversion

Individuals with an extraversion attitude seek to engage the environment, to be involved with a variety of tasks, and to problem solve with others. They will often say that the more interactions they have the more energized they become. These persons often like such careers as sales representative, marketing personnel, and office manager.

Individuals with an introverted attitude seek engagement with their inner world, to be involved with a variety of concepts and ideas, and to problem solve alone before seeking interaction. Those who prefer the introverted attitude will often report being energized by reflecting on tasks, interactions, and concepts rather than being actually engaged in them. The introverted attitude often is preferred among those who select positions as engineers, scientists, librarians, and computer programmers.

## Sensing or Intuition: Mental Functions for Perception

The second set of preferences deal with the way we prefer to perceive information. Those with a sensing preference focus on the real, practical, immediate facts of the moment. Those preferring the sensing function, have senses that seem to be finely tuned to the details of day-to-day life. Such individuals tend to like planned and controlled work environments where consistency is rewarded and valued. These individuals often select accounting, police and detective work, and service-oriented professions like dental or radiological technicians.

The intuitive preference functions to direct the individual to patterns, various connections of facts, and possible meanings of facts. Those with an intuitive preference, in contrast to sensing, focus on patterns within a context, future possibilities, and relationships among facts (rather than the facts themselves).

**Figure 2. Table of Sixteen Types for Counselors**

| | ST | SF | NF | NT |
|---|---|---|---|---|
| | ISTJ<br>6.7% | ISFJ<br>6.1% | INFJ<br>6.05% | INTJ<br>3.6% |
| | ISTP<br>1.9% | ISFP<br>2.8% | INFP<br>11.9% | INTP<br>3.4% |
| | ESTP<br>1.5% | ESFP<br>3.9% | ENFP<br>17.6% | ENTP<br>4.5% |
| | ESTJ<br>7.1% | ESFJ<br>7.04% | ENFJ<br>10.1% | ENTJ<br>5.6% |
| Totals | 17% | 20% | 45% *** | 16% |

N = 1803

Each Preference

| | | |
|---|---|---|
| E 52% | I 48% | |
| S 37% | N 63% *** | |
| T 34% | F 66% *** | |
| J 52% | P 48% | |

**** used to highlight the self-selection

**Source:** G.P. Macdaid, M.H. McCaulley, & R. Kainz, *Myers-Briggs Type Indicator Atlas of Type Tables,* Gainesville, FL: Center for Applications of Psychological Type, 1987. Reprinted by permission.

It often appears that intuitives report information that sounds more like a "hunch" and less connected to specific facts. These individuals often seek such careers as college professor, counselor, writer, psychologist, attorney, and entertainer.

## Thinking or Feeling Decision Making: Mental Functions for Decision Making

When we collect information through our preferred perceiving process of sensing or intuition, we make decisions about that information. We judge the usefulness of this information through either a thinking or feeling judgment process.

Those who prefer the thinking process often weigh options by predicting outcomes. In the work world, the preference for the thinking function is often found among those who work in administration, management, consulting, computer programming, and engineering.

In contrast, those with a feeling preference analyze information according to their values and probable outcomes on human relationships. These individuals often select careers as counselors, clergy (all denominations), teachers, health service workers, and curators.

## Judging or Perceiving Orientation

The fourth set of preferences on the MBTI sorts your orientation toward making decisions quickly or being open and curious for more information. Those with a preference for judging are driven to organize, plan, and structure. Those with a preference for perception tend to keep their options open. Both preferences can meet deadlines, but judging types often get a thrill at completing the assignment before the deadline and perceiving types "get a charge" out of just meeting the deadline.

A high occurrence of judging types can be found in chemical engineering, technical teaching, dentistry, bank officers, accountants, and school administrators. Perceptive types are likely to be journalists, entertainers, editors, and social scientists.

## The MBTI Scores

As individuals answer the questions on the MBTI, the responses are like "votes" for each of the preferences. The scale for each pair which receives the most votes is listed as the preference in your four-letter code. Some of the questions are weighed for one or two points (which you will see on all of the self-scorable MBTI forms) simply because some items are stronger predictors of your preference than others. Your points for each preference are counted and put into a formula to give you a preference score for each set of the four polarities ( E or I, S or N, T or F, J or P). The higher the score, the more consistent you are in selecting a preference. Please note that scores are not a reflection of skill, ability, or competence.

## Type Development

Psychological type theory developers Jung (1971) and Myers (1980a, 1980b) suggested that type develops over the life span. Though the theory assumes that each person is born with innate preferences, the environment either supports or impedes the natural expression of these preferences. It is important that each person live and work in an environment which supports the use of an individual's natural preferences.

Jung believed that no one could develop all of the preferences at the same time. You could not, for example, equally develop the thinking and feeling preferences. In fact the theory states that it is better for an individual to have a fully developed set of preferences and to be clear regarding one's specific gifts and needs.

An essential part of the theory is that for each type there is a dominant and auxiliary preference. The dominant and auxiliary preferences always come from the mental functions (i.e., the middle two letters of the type code S, N, T or F). The dominant process is used as the favorite and most developed function. The auxiliary process assists the dominant and provides balance within the type. A close reading of the descriptions from *Introduction to Type* (Myers, 1980b) and *Gifts Differing* (Myers, 1980a) will provide specific information concerning both type development and identification of the dominant and auxiliary functions.

## Uses of the MBTI

The MBTI can effectively be used with individuals and groups. Those individuals in career counseling or career development programs will find abundant information in the *Manual: A Guide to the Development and Use of the Myers-Briggs Type Indicator* (Myers & McCaulley, 1985) and the *Atlas of Types* (1986). In general, those using the MBTI should remember that the indicator does not measure skill, competency, ability, or even satisfaction in given careers. The MBTI gives us an understanding of why certain individuals are attracted to particular careers.

Just as the MBTI identifies preferences which are attracted to specific careers, those preferences also affect the career decision and career development process. For example, if you are an extravert you may need to force yourself to read more information to confirm your expectations before discussing the material with others. If you are an introvert you may need to push yourself for more interactions such as informational interviews in order to confirm your expectations about the work environment.

The other preferences may show themselves in the career development process. Individuals who prefer sensing may need to ask more questions about the work environment. Intuitives need to ask more questions about job specifics in order to prevent a mistake by paying more attention to the work climate than to the job tasks.

Disappointment in career decisions will await you if you have a preference for thinking and fail to connect values to the work—particularly if you are at midlife. Feeling types should explore the consequences of working in a given setting in terms of the congruence between the work and personal values. Finally, judging types need to be careful not to reject options that seem too distant while perceptives should be careful to become focused.

The MBTI took 40 years to develop. It is a complex tool that is helpful for personal and professional development. Knowing your personality type can enrich career choices and add to your knowledge about individuals with similar personalities in terms of career directions. To purchase the MBTI you must either complete a qualifying course or have completed a graduate course in tests and measurement. For information regarding qualification programs, write the Association for Psychological Type at Box 5099, Gainesville, Florida, 32602. To get research information and specialized training for using the MBTI, write the Center for Applications of Psychological Type, Box 13807, Gainesville, Florida, 32604.

*See also* Career Counseling; Career Tests and Inventories; Job Satisfaction; Trait-Factor Approach to Career Choice.

## Bibliography

*Atlas of types.* (1986). Gainesville, FL: Center for Applications of Psychological Type. A thorough collection of type tables by career and occupation.

Jung, C.G. (1971). *Psychological types.* Princeton, NJ: Princeton University Press. Jung's original work is readable but tedious.

Myers, I. B. (1980a). *Gifts differing.* Palo Alto, CA: Consulting Psychologists Press. A thorough introduction to type, type uses, and the MBTI.

Myers, I.B. (1980b) *Introduction to type.* Palo Alto, CA: Consulting Psychologists Press. A very readable and useful 32-page booklet.

Myers, I.B., & McCaulley, M. (1985). *Manual: A guide to the development and use of the Myers-Briggs Type Indicator.* Palo Alto, CA: Consulting Psychologists Press. A complete reference guide for using the MBTI.

—ROGER R. PEARMAN

# N

## NEGOTIATING

Negotiating is the process whereby two or more individuals or organizations whose goals are in apparent conflict attempt to reconcile their differences and achieve an outcome more advantageous than they can realize alone. On any given day, we all engage in innumerable negotiations both within and without the workplace.

### Relationship to Work

In recent years, professionals, managers, and scholars all have realized that negotiating is an interpersonal skill essential both to the successful performance of the individual and the continued viability of the organization itself. Every day the organization, through its key personnel, must negotiate with its customers, its suppliers, governmental agencies, and/or community representatives. In addition, the individuals within the organization negotiate with their superiors, their subordinates, and their organizational peers. Recognition of this fact is the first step in understanding how sharpening one's negotiations skills can lead to increased confidence on the job while at the same time enhancing job performance and effectiveness.

Negotiation does not occur only when two persons from two different organizations with totally opposed views or interests confront one another. This classic "win-lose" bargaining scenario certainly is an important part of the overall dynamic of negotiation. But far more often negotiations prove useful for resolving the differences that arise when units within the same organization compete for scarce resources or when two department heads or supervisors attempt to coordinate and smooth the flow of work between their functional areas of responsibility.

Lax and Sebenius (1986) identify four elements or preconditions that, when present, indicate a need for negotiation. The first element is interdependence of two individuals or organizations. Interdependence is present when two persons (i.e., two individuals, two organizations, or two sub-units within an organization) can achieve more through a joint effort than they can realize acting on their own. The second element is the existence of some perceived conflict. Used in this sense, conflict does not necessarily mean acrimonious discord. Rather, conflict can exist when two persons are of different ethnic backgrounds, age, gender, or socioeconomic backgrounds, or when they disagree as to what constitutes the best solution to a given problem or the optimal allocation of a scarce resource.

The third element of negotiation is the existence of a potential for two persons to engage in "opportunistic interaction." This occurs when neither party to a negotiation is willing, at the outset, to reveal all their "bottom lines" with regard to a given dilemma. Instead, the parties engage in a type of "verbal dance" in an effort to achieve an outcome advantageous to themselves. This process is the grist of negotiations. Finally, negotiation is called for when the true priorities and goals of the parties are such that a negotiated settlement is better than their respective "Best Alternative to a Negotiated Agreement" or "BATNAS" (Fisher & Ury 1983).

When you determine in any given circumstance that negotiation is an appropriate means for seeking an outcome you can live with, the verbal dance of negotiation begins.

### Application

Different types of bargaining situations call for different types of negotiating tactics. Lewicki and Litterer (1985), building upon the work of Walton and McKersie (1965) identify two primary variants of bargaining: *distributive bargaining* and *integrative bargaining*. In distributive bargaining situations, your goals and the goals of the other party are in direct conflict. Resources are fixed and each party seeks to maximize his or her individual gain. The best example of a distributive or "win-lose" bargaining situation is a price-focused negotiation between a buyer and a seller. Gain for you will mean a loss for the other party.

The second primary type of negotiating scenario involves two parties with common, shared, or joint goals; this situation offers the opportunity for a "win-win" outcome.

In *distributive bargaining,* you focus your efforts on influencing the other party's perception of what goals and priorities can be achieved and the costs of delaying or terminating negotiations. This achieved by screening your true priorities at the beginning of the negotiations by bluffing, posturing, using information you possess in strategically productive ways, etc. Of course, the other party is working to influence you in the same way.

One of the keys to success in distributive bargaining situations is knowing when and how to drop the "screen" and communicate to the other party your true bottom lines on the critical matters at issue. This is a skill you will develop over time and the manner in which you approach this process will depend a great deal on your own personal negotiation style, your ethical framework, and the style and ethical character of the other party. Much has been written in this regard. Although you will find it difficult to effect a negotiating style that is alien to your personality, a number of helpful guides can be found in books like *Getting to Yes* (Fisher & Ury, 1983).

Unlike distributive bargaining, the parties to an *integrative bargaining* exercise focus upon the identification of their common, shared, and joint goals and the fashioning of ways to achieve those goals through negotiation. Thus, in integrative bargaining you will expend very little effort in concealing your true outcome utilities structure or withholding information from the other party. The bargaining relationship need not necessarily lose its core adversarial or "conflict" nature in integrative bargaining. You must always make clear the firmness of your positions, but at the same time you must be willing to disclose material information, initiate trusting, cooperative behavior; and make concessions to a greater degree than is typically displayed in distributive bargaining situations.

The point of the dichotomy drawn above is that a skilled negotiator is able to recognize whether a given negotiations venue will be, or should be dominated by distributive bargaining or integrative bargaining and adjust his or her conduct accordingly. In addition, a single negotiation will often present opportunities for both distributive and integrative bargaining.

The actual technique of negotiations focuses upon the processes of communication and persuasion. Critical to the communication process are minimizing the distortions caused by ambiguous messages (spoken or nonverbal), ensuring the maintenance of clear feedback channels between the parties, remaining alert to and acting to reduce errors in perception, and expending the effort necessary to listen carefully and demonstrate to the other party that you are doing so.

The keys to maximizing the persuasive effect of the messages you convey to the other party in negotiations are always remaining attentive to the other party's perceptual frame of reference and framing your communication in ways that complement rather than conflict with the likes, dislikes, and orientation of your counterpart across the table. It is equally important that you act consistently to defuse and minimize the type of dysfunctional defensive reactions of persons with whom you are negotiating when they may perceive that you do not acknowledge the legitimacy of their goals and priorities, do not wish to hear what they have to say, or are concerned only with achieving a total victory without concern for their needs.

*See also* Assertion; Bosses: Managing Relationships with Superiors; Managerial Skills.

## Bibliography

Fisher, R., & Ury, W. (1983). *Getting to yes.* New York: Penguin Books. This is the most widely known of the popular literature books on the negotiation process. Fisher and Ury advocate an approach to negotiations they call "principled negotiations" or "bargaining on the merits." This approach offers the interests that underlay the positions each party takes in negotiations as an alternative to the traditional choice of being a "hard" or "soft" bargainer that positional bargaining often compels one to make.

Lax, D., & Sebenius, J. (1986). *The manager as negotiator.* New York: The Free Press. This text presents a very useful negotiations guidebook for the working manager in all work-related activities. It sets forth a balanced, generalized, and realistic "logic of negotiation" that represents a middle ground approach between the more focused academic treatises on negotiations and the popular literature works that espouse a particular style or strategy for successful negotiating.

Lewicki, R., & Litterer, J. (1985) *Negotiation.* Homewood, Il: Irwin. This scholarly text presents a comprehensive and insightful overview of the negotiations process that is firmly grounded in the relevant social science literature. It thoroughly examines each of the major components of the negotiation process and places each component in its proper place within the overall framework of the topic.

Walton, R.E., McKersie, R.B. (1965). *A behavioral theory of labor negotiations: An analysis of a social interaction system.* New York: McGraw-Hill.

— STEPHEN L. HAYFORD

# NETWORKING

Networking is planning and making contacts and sharing information for professional and personal gain. Key words in that definition are planning and personal. Networking has to be planned; it doesn't just happen. Quality networking happens only; when supportive friendly relationships, as well as business contacts, are built.

## Relationship to Work

In an increasingly competitive and uncertain work world, building a network of contacts is an essential tool for success. It's no longer enough to be good at one's work. Managers and entrepreneurs need to plan a strategy to be known and visible ("it's not what you know, but who you know"), so that when opportunities *do* arise, the "right" people will be thinking of them.

To build an effective network, an individual needs both formal and informal networks in place. *Formal networks* are the type you actually join, usually with dues and regular meetings. These could include an entrepreneurs association, a civic group, or an alumnae association. *Informal networks* consist of individuals more loosely tied together, such as friends you run into at an annual holiday party, colleagues you keep up with from a former job, or the people you met while white-water rafting. A good network contains both types and has a healthy mix of both business and social connections.

Networking is a 24-hour process that's about giving as well as getting. People can't expect to attend one network meeting every six months and get results. Individuals must always be on the lookout for people to include in their network, and whose networks to join. Understand that benefits often are not immediate, that networks aren't built in a day, and that "crisis" networking won't work. It's best to constantly work at building a network, so there will be people in place when someone suddenly faces a job loss or has to take a transfer to a new town. No one wants to scramble for a support system; it needs to be built over time.

## Application

Here are some steps to building your network:
1. *Set Your Goals.* Every individual you meet can be looked at as having access to other individuals. Decide who you want in your network and how you will contact them. Some people prefer making telephone calls to writing letters; others feel just the opposite. Try doing what you're most uncomfortable with. After all, networking is about pushing yourself forward and learning new skills.

How will your "networking rendezvous" take place: over coffee, at lunch, at someone's place of business, or on the telephone? Maybe you'll concentrate on joining organizations and attending meetings. Plan your strategy. Make lists of names. Go through your rolodex and list the people with whom you haven't talked in six months. Perhaps you want to reconnect with people from over a year ago; list them. And don't forget to make cold calls. Maybe you've read articles about "stars" in your profession or friends have told you about wonderful speakers or authors they've heard. Many of these people (sometimes well-known) could be included in your network. List them too.

2. *Organize Your Network.* All your contacts won't do you any good unless you organize them. Think about how all this information will be most helpful to you. Many people use a multiple-rolodex system. The one on top of your desk is for current, frequently used contacts. A second business-card file is for people you want access to, but know you won't be speaking with more often than once or twice a year. An optional third file can be for the "old-timers," people you haven't contacted in a year or more.

You can also organize your network on color-coded or alphabetized index cards, categorizing your contacts and keeping track of the calls you make to each. Give your network a checkup at least once a year. Weed out and reorganize your card files, rolodexes, and address books. Keep your list of current and active contacts close at hand. Don't discard old contacts; you can always reconnect with them.

3. *Take Action.* Set a timetable to achieve your goals; perhaps you can aim for one cold call, one lunch, and two reconnecting calls a week. Create a file or "networking" notebook to record who you've called and what the outcome or response was. Stick to your schedule and, to stay on track, read over your responses from time to time. You'll be surprised and encouraged by how many contacts you are making.

It helps to set aside a special networking time, such as 3 p.m. to 5 p.m. on Thursdays, if your work schedule allows. Quiet Sunday evenings at home can be good times for telephone networking, often the only way to make long-distance contacts. If you put yourself on a mental schedule, you're more likely to really make contacts. When attending meetings, set goals to meet a certain number of new people or leave with a certain number of business cards. Then do it!

4. *Practice Networking Etiquette.* The last, but possibly most important, tool for good networking is to make sure you observe networking etiquette. Here are a few essentials to remember:
   a. Always respect your contacts' names. Get an OK before you use a person's name as a referral to get to someone else.
   b. Make sure you call people at times that are convenient for them. If you're on the East Coast, don't forget about the three-hour time difference and call someone

NONSTANDARD ENGLISH / 197

on the West Coast at 6 a.m. Don't wake someone at midnight just to "touch base."

c. Follow through on your promises. If someone asks for a copy of an article you've mentioned, jot that request on the back of her or his business card and send the article within the week. If you offer to give someone a phone number, make sure you send it. Even if you haven't made specific commitments to your contacts, communicate with them to stay visible. Send them cards at holiday time, ask them to lunch "for no reason at all," clip articles you know they would appreciate and send them with your card. Think of creative ways to keep in touch.

d. Thank everyone who helps you or provides you with leads. At any given meeting, you're bound to come away with at least three ideas or tips. Thank the people who offered them with a one-minute phone call or a brief handwritten note. It's wise to thank people for leads even if their suggestions don't pan out; your contacts will appreciate the follow-up.

e. Finally, the biggest "do" of all is to remember that networking is a challenge. Always push yourself. Approach new people at meetings and start a conversation, even if you're not in the mood. Taking the initiative really pays off. Whether you're a novice or an expert, you get only as much out of networking as you put into it.

*See also* Assertion; Mentoring; Self-Managed Change.

## Bibliography

Boe, A., & Youngs, B. B. (1989). *Is your "net" working?* New York: Wiley. Shows how to master the new rules in using key contacts to get ahead. Serves as a blueprint for increasing personal power, visibility, and career effectiveness.

Roane, S. (1988). *How to work a room.* New York: Warner. Offers key secrets to perfecting social skills: remembering names, planning a personal benefits list, and developing the confidence and know-how to meet new people.

Smith, Leslie. (1987). "Networking." An ongoing column in *Executive Female Magazine.* Published by National Association for Female Executives, 127 W. 24th St., New York, NY 10011.

—LESLIE E. SMITH

# NONSTANDARD ENGLISH

Any variety of English not conforming in pronunciation, grammatical structure, idiomatic usage, or choice of words generally characteristic of educated native speakers of American English is nonstandard English. Standard En-

glish is itself a variant, or dialect, of American English. Specifically, it is that variant generally taught in schools and regarded as the "prestigious" dialect in this society.

Nonstandard English, on the other hand, is spoken by groups of people who have been isolated from the standard dialect, who have not had the opportunity to acquire the dialect of the social elites, or who see value in preserving their own group dialect. Some varieties of nonstandard English include Appalachian Mountain speech, black English vernacular, Hawaiian Creole, Puerto Rican English, and southern white speech. In general, these varieties are closely related to standard English, only following different versions of the same rules that govern all varieties of English (Labov, 1969).

Typically, the differences in the varieties of American English have been recognized on four levels of language organization (Wolfram, 1981). First, there are differences in the vocabulary or *Lexicon* of the languages. The use of words like *"hang ten," "hang loose,"* or *"relax"* to convey the same concept are an example of differences on this level. Another level of differences among nonstandard varieties of English concerns the pronunciation or *Phonology* of the language. A person who notices how a New Englander says *"New York"* or how a Louisiana Creole speaker says *"onion"* is recognizing a difference at this level. A third level of organization on which English varieties differ is at the *syntactic* level—how sentences are structured. Differences in how "time relations" are expressed when a black English vernacular speaker says *"He ben gone"* and a standard English speaker says *"He has been gone for a long time"* reflect differences at this level. Finally, there may be differences in language use, such as politeness forms used by speakers of nonstandard English.

## Relationship to Work

Linguists agree that nonstandard varieties of English are cohesive, logical, highly structured linguistic systems in their own right. However, negative values are often associated with the use of nonstandard English by members of our society at large. In most cases the nonstandard English varieties are seen as inferior to their Standard English counterparts.

In general, two major misconceptions concerning standard and nonstandard English exist. One is that there is a "correct" standard English which is uniform and definite and that it has been reduced to a set of consistent rules. The other is that these "correct" English rules should be followed by all American English speakers. Most Americans believe that language can be used "correctly" or "incorrectly." This notion of "correctness" is a myth. Language is dynamic and ever changing; as a result, there are no permanent or absolute standards. In fact, the notion of "good" or "bad" English is a misguided one. We can better evaluate linguistic systems by whether they are the most appropriate or most effective variety of English for the particular type of communication at hand. From this perspective, nonstandard English can be just as appropriate as standard English depending on the particular communicative situation.

The other major misconception about language is that standard English must be maintained or safeguarded by everyone connected with its use. Indeed, this misconception is held by many employers. Many feel that a particular variety of standard English must be used on and off the job because it lends prestige to the company and an air of competence to the employee. In his research, Anderson (1981) found that although many jobs did not require proficiency in the use of standard English, many employers reported that they would most likely hire standard English speakers regardless of the type of job. Research also confirms that many employers use nonstandard English as a criterion for automatically eliminating certain otherwise good and capable workers simply because they associated its use with low intelligence, low efficiency, and low job skills. Because of these perceptions, job hiring, job continuity, and job promotions are often heavily influenced by one's use of nonstandard English.

## Application

Language and dialect usage can strongly influence a person's earning power and career opportunities. Without question, research findings have confirmed that speakers of nonstandard English have been relegated to marginal positions in society. Although linguists agree that "all varieties of language are equally valid systems of communication and are therefore equally deserving of respect," the problems facing nonstandard English speakers in the workplace are not likely to change until employer attitudes and the attitudes of society at large become more accepting of different cultural groups and their linguistic patterns. Until the celebration of cultural diversity becomes a national priority, the primary responsibility for change remains with the individual nonstandard English speaker.

The frustration of knowing that you are qualified for an advanced position, only to be rejected because you don't speak a standard variety of English may motivate you to seek out alternative programs that can help to modify your speech patterns in job situations. Several speech communication authors have proposed language programs for individuals who do not speak standard English.

Basic courses in speech and rhetoric are also taught at colleges and universities. Their primary goal is to present the communicative conventions and linguistic rules of standard English. Some community colleges also offer programs that enable students to modify their speech patterns. These programs are usually offered in colleges that service communities with racially diverse populations.

*See also* Discrimination: Language; Self-Managed Change.

## Bibliography

Anderson, E. (1981). Language and success. *College English*, 43 (8): 807–12, 817.

Biegeleisen, J. I. (1987). *Make your job interview a success.* New York: Prentice-Hall. This self-help publication contains sections on "Corrective Measures to Improve Your Speech" and "Words, Phrases, and Expressions that Do You In" that might be helpful during the job interview.

Labov, W. (1969). *The study of non-standard English.* Champaign, IL: National Council of Teachers of English. This classic monograph succeeds in dispelling a number of old myths about nonstandard dialects and presents practical suggestions to teachers and students interested in this subject.

Martin, R. (1987). *Oral communication: English language arts teachers' guide.* Salem, OR: Oregon State Department of Education. This guide lists specific communication competency skills needed to compete in this information age, and the characteristics of a strong oral communication program. It also stresses awareness of when standard and nonstandard English are appropriate.

Medley, H. A. (1984). *Sweaty palms: The neglected art of being interviewed.* Berkeley, CA: Ten Speed Press. This publication contains a section on "The Question and the Answer," which may be useful in interpreting and responding to culturally different questions during the job interview.

Strumpf, M., & Douglas, A. (1985). *Painless, perfect grammar.* New York: Prentice-Hall. A simple, direct, and easy-to-use guide that answers all your questions on grammar, usage, and spelling.

Wolfram, W. (1981). Varieties of American English. In C.A. Ferguson & S.B. Heath (Eds.), *Language in the U.S.A.* (pp. 44–68). Cambridge: Cambridge University Press.

—ARNETHA F. BALL

## NONTRADITIONAL JOB FOR ONE'S SEX

For a woman, nontraditional jobs have 75% or more men in them, and for a man, 75% or more women in them. In 1989, the percentages of women in four traditionally female occupations were secretary (99%), child care worker (97%), registered nurse (94%), and telephone operator (90%), and in four traditionally male occupations were engineer (8%), mechanic (3%), dentist (9%), and data processing equipment repairer (9%). Thus, secretarial and child care jobs are nontraditional for men and engineering and mechanical jobs are nontraditional for women. In 1989, nontraditional jobs were held by 9% of all working women and, by the author's calculations, 9% of all working men. These figures, and those below, were taken from two fact sheets published by the National Commission on Working Women (1989, 1990).

## Relationship to Work

Most occupations are segregated by sex. The more male an occupation's workforce is, the higher the average pay. Thus, advocates of equality see integrating women into male-dominated jobs as a key strategy for shrinking the wage gap. In 1988 women working full-time, year-round earned only 65 cents to every $1 earned by men.

Salary thus has a powerful relationship to nontraditional work. Women in nontraditional jobs earn 20% to 30% more than women in traditional occupations. It is even true that men who work in traditionally female occupations earn more than women working in those occupations, just as men earn more than women in the same traditionally male occupations. For example, in 1989 male nurses had a median weekly wage of $629 compared to $564 for women, and male motor vehicle operators made $408 to $307 for women.

Sex role socialization also has a powerful relationship to nontraditional work. Several barriers inhibit people from doing nontraditional work. The first is socialization by families, friends, and classmates to do what is traditional for one's sex. Schools direct students toward traditional classes and away from nontraditional options. On the job there may be discrimination in hiring and firing and sexual harassment.

But discrimination and resistance on the job are primarily experienced by women entering nontraditional jobs because of male workers' worries that the job will lose wages and status if women do it. Men entering nontraditional jobs, in contrast, are welcomed by women coworkers and experience advantages, not disadvantages (Ott, 1989).

Despite men's hostility and objections, the movement of women into every area of nontraditional work continues slowly. For example, a recent issue of *The American Woman* contained articles about women politicians, women orchestra conductors, clergywomen, farm women, women in road construction, and women in law enforcement (Rix, 1988).

## Application

Why would you want to do a job nontraditional for your sex? Well, we've already answered that for women—money. But there are reasons that apply to both sexes, such as your interests, values, abilities, and skills. Why be miserable inside when you'd rather work outdoors? Why work with things when you'd rather work with people? Or perhaps it's a matter of working hours, style of clothing allowed, the pace of your coworkers, or amount of variety in job activities.

Because men who want to be secretaries, child care workers, and dental assistants usually experience no difficulty in simply pursuing these occupations, this application section is primarily for women. How do you explore male-dominated occupations?

1. *Job Description Information.* At the public library you can find out about nontraditional jobs in the *Dictionary of Occupational Titles,* in books about women engineers, blue-collar tradeswomen, and police officers; and in brochures and pamphlets published by civil service job centers (see **Occupational Information**).

2. *Interviews and Visits.* Attend events such as Women in Trades conferences and workshops offered by community colleges for women interested in entering nontraditional jobs. Find a woman in the job you're interested in and interview her. Then, get the name of another woman and keep repeating the process (see **Information Interviewing**).

3. *Role Models.* Make friends with people in the occupation and spend time with them. Are they the kind of people you want to be with and become like?

4. *Prerequisite Courses.* Women typically lack prerequisites, such as math and science. Recognize that you need extra help and extra time and take the classes that will make all subsequent learning so much easier.

5. *Information about Apprenticeships and On-the-Job Training.* Your training might be done through a union apprenticeship, opportunities industrialization center, civil service on-the-job employment, or community college.

6. *Locate Support Groups for Women in Nontraditional Jobs.* Such groups include your local electrical union women's support, San Francisco Women in Trades, and the National Association of Women in Construction (see **Networking**).

Gains by women in nonprofessional, nontraditional jobs have been slight over the past five years. Probably the greatest barriers are the continued channeling of women in secondary school and publicly funded training programs toward low-wage clerical and service jobs, and discrimination in hiring, firing, and promotion for the women who have the requisite education and training for "men's work."

*See also* Discrimination: Sex; Information Interviewing; Networking; Occupational Information; Sex-Role Stereotyping; Sexual Harassment; Women in the Workforce; Women's Barriers and Opportunities.

## Bibliography

Lunneborg, P.W. (1989). *Women police officers: Current career profile.* Springfield, IL: Charles C. Thomas. Review of the professional and popular literature of the 1980s with emphasis on job motivation and job satisfaction.

Lunneborg, P.W. (1990). *Women changing work.* Westport, CT: Greenwood Press. Based on over 200 interviews with women in nontraditional occupations. Discusses how female sex-role socialization and values are altering the very concept of work.

Martin, M. (Ed.) (1988). *Hard-hatted women: Stories of struggle and success in the trades.* Seattle, WA: Seal Press. For women interested in blue-collar life on and off the job.

National Commission on Working Women. (1989, Fall; 1990, Winter). *Women at work fact sheets.* Washington, DC: National Commission on Working Women.

Niemann, L. (1990). *Boomer: Railroad memoirs.* Berkeley, CA: University of California Press. First-hand account of life on the railroad by one of the few women conductors.

Ott, E.M. (1989). Effects of the male-female ratio at work: Policewomen and male nurses. *Psychology of Women Quarterly,* 13: 41–57.

Rix, S.E. (Ed.) (1988). *The American woman 1988–89: A status report.* New York: W. W. Norton.

—PATRICIA W. LUNNEBORG

# O

## OCCUPATIONAL GROUPS

There are more than 20,000 different occupations. How does one think about such a large number without being overwhelmed? To solve this problem, numerous classification systems have been devised. Occupations have been grouped according to categories like occupational prestige, income, and type of industry, depending upon the purpose the system is to serve.

### Relationship to Career Decision

A frequent problem faced by persons making an occupational choice is identifying occupations that fit their abilities and needs: "What possibilities should I consider and investigate? Are there other occupations similar to the one(s) I am thinking about that might be suitable?" Persons with questions like these will find the classification systems that group occupations according to *interests* most useful (see **Interests**).

To help readers who may be faced with this problem, three interest-based systems are briefly described here, along with a table readers will find useful.

### Three Interest-Based Classification Systems

**The USES System.** In his introduction to the *Guide for Occupational Exploration (GOE)*, William B. Lewis noted that: "Many youths and other jobseekers are ill-prepared for effective job search because of lack of knowledge about kinds of jobs to look for. They have difficulty in relating their interests, skills, and potentials to appropriate occupations. A major reason has been the lack of readily understandable and usable information about fields of work with which they can match their own abilities. . . . [the GOE] has been designed by the U.S. Employment Service to help meet this need" (U.S. Department of Labor, 1979b, p. ii). The U.S. Employment Service developed an excellent classification system to achieve this goal.

To create their classification system, the USES job analysts first (Droege & Padgett, 1979) assigned all occupations to one of 12 *interest* areas (e.g., artistic, scientific, and selling). They then went a step further and added another category called "Worker Trait Group," which is simply a group of occupations having workers that share similar traits, such as abilities and educational level.

To illustrate how these worker trait groups were formed, imagine all of the artistic occupations you can think of: artist, dancer, fashion designer, model. Then ask yourself, "How might these occupations be sorted into groups based on the traits of the workers in them?" This is what professional job analysts did. For the artistic interest area, for example, they created eight worker trait groups, like "Literary Arts" and "Visual Arts." This last group contains occupations like fashion artist, art teacher, and painter.

This system is easy to use and is found in several career guidance publications, including the *Guide for Occupational Exploration* (Harrington & O'Shea, 1984) and the *Worker Trait Group Guide* (1988). The USES *Interest Inventory* and *Interest Check List* can be used to link your interests to the occupational groups in the *GOE*. The *GOE* also has a self-assessment section you can photocopy and use, called the *Checklist of Occupational Clues* (covering values, leisure and home activities, and school courses). It also has a section that describes each of the 12 interest areas.

**Holland Typology.** Interests are closely related to what John Holland (1985a) calls *personality type*, and he has developed a system for grouping occupations that is used by many career counselors. It is based on six personality types: Realistic (R), Investigative (I), Artistic (A), Social (S), Enterprising (E), and Conventional (C). The types are briefly described in Figure 1.

Occupations are grouped according to combinations of three personality types. For example, one group of occupations is Social-Artistic-Enterprising, abbreviated SAE. This group includes such occupations as career counselor, high school teacher, and home economist.

There are a number of instruments designed to assess your resemblance to the six types; Holland's (1985b) *Self-Directed Search* (SDS) is the best known. The SDS also contains an extensive list of occupations organized according to their three-letter Holland code. The *Dictionary of Holland Codes* (Gottfredson & Holland, 1989) is the comprehensive source for the codes of all occupations (see also **Vocational Choice: John Holland's Theory**).

**Combined System.** Jones (1980) combined the USES and Holland systems to take advantage of the positive features of both. This system is used in two career guidance instruments that he developed: *Occ-U-Sort* (Jones, 1981) and *The Career Key* (Jones, 1991). In this system, the occupations are first organized according to the six Holland personality types. Then, within each type, the occupations are grouped according to worker trait groups. This can be seen in Table 1, where an abridged version is presented.

To use Table 1, review the occupations listed under the personality types and worker trait groups that you most closely resemble and write their titles down for further investigation. The numbers you see in the Table are to help you get more information. The four-digit numbers after the subheadings, like 04.04, are the worker trait group numbers used in the *Guide for Occupational Exploration*. The nine-digit numbers after each occupation are the *Dictionary of Occupational Title* numbers (U.S. Department of Labor, 1979a).

With the development of these interest-based classification systems, people can now more easily identify occupations that appeal to them. The next step, of course, is to learn more about them. The articles in this book referred to below are highly recommended.

*See also* Career Exploration; Choosing an Occupation; Interests; Occupational Information; Trait-Factor Approach to Career Choice; Vocational Choice: John Holland's Theory.

## Bibliography

Droege, R.C., & Padgett, A. (1979). Development of an interest-oriented occupational classification system. *Vocational Guidance Quarterly,* 27: 302–10.

Gottfredson, G.D., & Holland, J. L. (1989). *Dictionary of Holland codes.* 2nd ed. Odessa, FL: Psychological Assessment Resources.

Harrington, T.F., & O'Shea, A. J. (1984). *Guide for occupational exploration.* 2nd ed. Circle Pines, MN: American Guidance Service.

Holland, J.L. (1985a). *Making vocational choices: A theory of vocational personalities and work environments.* Englewood Cliffs, NJ: Prentice-Hall.

Holland, J.L. (1985b). *The self-directed search: Professional manual—1985 edition.* Odessa, FL: Psychological Assessment Resources.

Jones, L.K. (1980). Holland's typology and the new Guide for Occupational Exploration: Bridging the gap. *Vocational Guidance Quarterly*, 29: 70–75.

Jones, L. K. (1981). *Occ-U-Sort.* 2nd ed. Monterey, CA: CTB/Macmillan/McGraw-Hill.

Jones, L.K. (1991). *The career key.* Largo, FL: Careers, Inc.

U.S. Department of Labor. (1979a). *Dictionary of occupational titles.* 4th ed. Washington, DC: U.S. Government Printing Office.

U.S. Department of Labor. (1979b). *Guide for occupational exploration.* Washington, DC: U.S. Government Printing Office.

*Worker trait group guide.* (1988). Bloomington, IL: Meridian Educational Corporation.

—LAWRENCE K. JONES

**Figure 1. Holland Personality Types**

 Realistic: prefers working with tools, objects, machines, or animals and tends to avoid social activities

 Investigative: prefers observing and studying scientific objects and tends to avoid selling or social activities

 Artistic: prefers working freely and creatively, expressing ideas or feelings through dance, drama, music, writing, craft arts, or other art fields and tends to avoid highly-ordered or repetitive activities

 Social: prefers helping or teaching people and tends to avoid working with tools or machines

 Enterprising: prefers selling or persuading people and tends to avoid activities that require careful observation or study

 Conventional: prefers activities involving numbers, records, or clerical materials and tends to avoid those that are not well ordered or that demand creative abilities

## Table 1. Occupations Grouped Using "Combined System"*

### Realistic Occupations

**Plants and Animals [03.01, 03.02, 03.03, 03.04]**
__ Animal Trainer (159.224-010)
__ Farmer (407.161-010)
__ Forester (040.061-034)
__ Greenskeeper (406.137-010)
__ Livestock Rancher (410.161-018)
__ Logger (454.684-018)
__ Nursery Manager (180.167-042)
__ Teacher, Vocational-Agriculture (091.227-010)
__ Tree Surgeon (408.181-010)

**Safety and Law Enforcement [04.01, 04.02]**
__ Detective (375.267-010)
__ Fire Fighter (373.364-010)
__ Fish and Game Warden (379.167-010)
__ Narcotics Investigator (375.267-018)
__ Park Ranger (169.167-042)
__ Police Officer (375.263-014)
__ State-Highway Police Officer (375.263-018)
__ Wildlife Agent (379.137-018)
See also Regulations Enforcement, under Conventional Occupations.

**Engineering [05.01]**
__ Architect (001.061-010)
__ Chemical Engineer (008.061-018)
__ Civil Engineer (005.061-014)
__ Electrical Engineer (003.061-010)
__ Electronics Engineer (003.061-030)
__ Electronics Technician (003.161-010)
__ Land Surveyor (018.167-018)
__ Landscape Architect (001.061-018)
__ Mechanical Engineer (007.061-014)
__ Nuclear Engineer (015.061-014)
__ Pollution-Control Engineer (019.081-018)
__ Software Technician (020.262-010)
__ Teacher, Industrial Arts (091.221-010)
__ Tool Designer (007.061-026)

**Engineering Technology [05.03]**
__ Air-Traffic-Controller (193.162-018)
__ Building Inspector (168.167-030)
__ Commercial Drafter (017.261-026)
__ Drafter, Architectural (001.261-010)
__ Flight Engineer (621.261-018)
__ Radio/TV Transmitter Operator (193.262-038)
__ Safety Inspector (821.367-014)
__ Technical Illustrator (017.281-034)

**Managerial Work: Mechanical [05.02]**
__ Manager, Food Processing Plant (183.167-026)
__ Manager, Solid-Waste-Disposal (184.167-078)
__ Superintendent, Electric Power (184.167-162)

**Musical Instrument Fabrication and Repair**
__ Electronic-Organ Technician (828.261-010)
__ Piano Tuner (730.361-010)
__ Pipe-Organ Installer (730.381-046)

**Printing**
__ Document Restorer (979.361-010)
__ Job Printer (973.381-018)
__ Offset-Press Operator (651.482-010)

**Gem Cutting and Finishing**
__ Diamond Expert (770.267-010)
__ Gem Cutter (770.281-014)
__ Gemologist (199.281-010)

**Custom Sewing, Tailoring, and Upholstering**
__ Automobile Upholsterer (780.381-010)
__ Bookbinder (977.381-010)
__ Custom Tailor (785.261-014)
__ Dressmaker (785.361-010)
__ Furniture Upholsterer (780.381-018)
__ Shoe Repairer (365.361-014)
__ Shop Tailor (785.361-022)

**Air and Water Vehicle Operation [05.04]**
__ Commercial Air Plane Pilot (196.263-010)
__ Flying Instructor (097.227-010)
__ Tugboat Captain (197.133-030)

**Craft Technology [05.05]**

**Building Construction and Maintenance**
__ Bricklayer (861.381-018)
__ Carpenter (860.381-022)
__ Dry-Wall Applicator (842.381-010)
__ Plumber (862.381-030)
__ Tile Setter (861.381-054)

**Electrical-Electronic Equipment Repair**
__ Avionics Technician (aircraft electronics) (823.281-010)
__ Cable-Television Technician (822.281-030)
__ Electric-Motor Repairer (721.281-018)
__ Electrician (824.261-010)
__ Elevator Repairer (825.281-030)
__ Line Repairer (821.361-026)
__ Telephone Office Repairer (822.281-014)

**Metal Fabrication and Repair**
__ Automobile Body Repairer (807.381-010)
__ Machinist (600.280-022)
__ Millwright (638.281-018)
__ Sheet-Metal Worker (804.281-010)
__ Structural-Steel Worker (801.361-014)
__ Tool-and-Die Maker (601.280-046)
__ Welder, Arc (810.384-014)

**Woodworking**
__ Cabinetmaker (660.280-010)
__ Furniture Finisher (763.381-010)

**Mechanical Work**
__ Aircraft Mechanic (621.281-018)
__ Automobile Mechanic (620.261-010)
__ Diesel Mechanic (625.281-010)
__ Furnace Installer-Repairer (869.281-010)
__ Locksmith (709.281-010)
__ Motorcycle Repairer (620.281-054)
__ Office Machine Servicer (633.281-018)
__ Refrigeration Mechanic (637.261-026)
__ Small-Engine Mechanic (625.281-034)
__ Supervisor, Aircraft Maintenance (621.131-014)

**Scientific, Medical, and Technical Equipment Fabrication and Repair**
__ Camera Repairer (714.281-014)
__ Dental Laboratory Technician (712.381-018)
__ Optician (716.280-008)
__ Orthodontic Technician (712.381-030)

**Crafts [05.10]**
__ Auto Transmission Mechanic (620.281-062)
__ Baker (313.381-010)
__ Cook (315.361-010)
__ Diver (899.261-010)
__ Exterminator or Termite Treater (389.684-010)
__ Farm Equipment Mechanic (624.381-014)
__ Floor Covering Installer (864.481-010)
__ Front-End Mechanic (automobile) (620.281-038)
__ Glazier (glass installer) (863.381-010)
__ Motion Picture Projectionist (960.362-010)
__ Muffler Installer (auto) (807.664-010)
__ Painter (840.381-010)
__ Recording Engineer (194.362-010)
__ Roofer (866.381-010)
__ School Cafeteria Cook (313.381-030)
__ Television-Radio Repairer (720.281-018)

**Equipment Operation [05.11]**
__ Bulldozer Operator (850.683-010)
__ Miner (939.281-010)
__ Motor-Grader Operator (850.663-022)
__ Street-Sweeper Operator (919.683-022)
__ Tower-Crane Operator (921.663-054)
__ Well-Drill Operator (859.362-010)

*Adapted from *The Career Key* by Lawrence K. Jones. Copyright © 1991.

## Table 1. Occupations Grouped Using "Combined System" (continued)

**Food Preparation**
__ Chef (313.131-014)
__ Dietetic Technician (077.121-010)

**Systems Operation** [05.06]
__ Boiler Operator (950.382-010)
__ Engineer, Ship (197.130-010)
__ Electric Power Plant Operator (952.382-018)
__ Refrigerating Engineer (950.362-014)
__ Water-Treatment-Plant Operator (954.382-014)

**Quality Control** [05.07, 06.03]
__ Airplane Inspector (621.261-010)
__ Garment Inspector (789.687-010)
__ Log Grader (455.367-010)
__ Machine Tester (706.387-014)
__ Telephone Equipment Inspector (822.261-014)

**Land Vehicle Operation** [05.08, 09.03]
__ Bus Driver (913.463-010)
__ Route Driver (292.353-010)
__ Taxi Driver (913.463-018)
__ Tractor-Trailer-Truck Driver (904.383-010)
__ Truck Driver, Light (906.683-022)

**Materials Control** [05.09]
__ Linen-Room Attendant (222.387-030)
__ Shipping and Receiving Clerk (222.387-050)
__ Stock Clerk (222.387-058)

**Production Technology and
Production Work** [06.01, 06.02]
__ Chair Upholsterer (780.684-034)
__ Dry Cleaner (362.382-010)
__ Electric-Sign Assembler (729.684-022)
__ Press Operator (690.682-062)
__ Quality-Control Inspector (701.261-010)
__ Supervisor, Engine Assembly (806.130-010)
__ Supervisor, Feed Mill (529.132-054)
__ Weaver (683.682-034)

**Craft Arts** [01.06]
__ Graphic Arts Technician (979.382-018)
__ Jeweler (700.281-010)
__ Photoengraver (971.381-022)
__ Sign Painter (970.381-026)
__ Sound-Effects Technician (962.281-014)
__ Taxidermist (199.261-010)

**Elemental Work: Mechanical-Industrial**
[05.12, 06.04]
__ Assembler, Small Products (739.687-030)
__ Building Custodian (Janitor) (382.664-010)
__ Hotel Housekeeper or Assistant (323.687-014)
__ Hospical Cleaner (323.687.010)
__ Knitting Machine Operator (685.665-014)
__ Machine Cleaner (699.687-014)
__ Punch-Press Operator (615.685-030)
__ Tire-Repairer (915.684-101)
__ Window Cleaner (389.687-014)

### Investigative Occupations

**Physical Sciences** [02.01]
__ Astronomer (021.067-010)
__ Chemist (022.061-010)
__ Geographer (029.067-010)
__ Geologist (024.061-018)
__ Mathematician (020.067-014)
__ Metallurgist, Physical (011.061-022)
__ Meteorologist (025.062-010)
__ Oceanographer (024.061-018)
__ Paleontologist (024.061-042)
__ Physicist (023.067-010)
__ Teacher, Physical Sciences (091.227-010)

**Life Sciences** [02.02]
__ Agronomist (040.061-010)
__ Animal Scientist (040.061-014)
__ Biochemist (041.061-026)
__ Biologist (041.061-030)
__ Botanist (041.061-038)
__ Food Chemist (022.061-014)
__ Geneticist (041.061-050)
__ Horticulturist (040.061-038)
__ Microbiologist (041.061-058)
__ Pharmacologist (041.061-074)
__ Plant Pathologist (041.061-086)
__ Soil Scientist (040.061-058)
__ Teacher, Life Sciences (091.227-010)
__ Zoologist (041.061-090)

**Medical Sciences** [02.03]
__ Anesthesiologist (070.101-010)
__ Chiropractor (079.101-010)
__ Dentist (072.101-010)
__ Dermatologist (070.101-018)
__ General Practicing Physician (070.101-026)
__ Gynecologist (070-101-034)
__ Internist (070.101-042)
__ Neurologist (070.101-050)
__ Opthalmologist (070.101-058)
__ Optometrist (079.101-018)
__ Orthodontist (072.101-022)
__ Pediatrician (070.101-066)
__ Psychiatist (070.107-014)
__ Surgeon (070.101-094)
__ Veterinarian (073.101-010)

**Laboratory Technology** [02.04]
__ Dietetic Technician (077.121-010)
__ Laboratory Technician (019.381-010)
__ Pharmacist (074.161-010)
__ Physical Therapy Technician (076.224-010)
__ Photographic Darkroom Technician
   (976.681-010)
__ Seed Analyst (040.361-014)
__ Ultrasound Medical Technologist (078.364-010)

**Mathematics and Statistics** [11.01]
__ Computer Programmer, Business (020.162-014)
__ Financial Analyst (020.167-014)
__ Statistician (020.167-026)
__ Teacher, Mathematics (091.227-010)

**Social Research** [11.03]
__ Anthropologist (055.067-010)
__ Developmental Psychologist (045.061-010)
__ Historian (052.067-022)
__ Political Scientist (051.067-010)
__ Sociologist (054.067-014)
__ Urban planner (199.167-014)

### Artistic Occupations

**Literary Arts** [01.01]
__ Book Editor (132.067-014)
__ Critic (131.067-018)
__ Playwright (131.067-038)
__ Poet (131.067-042)
__ Writer (131.067-046)

**Visual Arts** [01.02]
__ Architect (001.061-010)
__ Art Teacher (149.021-010)
__ Commercial Designer (141.081-014)
__ Fashion Artist (141.061-014)
__ Illustrator (141.061-022)
__ Industrial Designer (142.061-026)
__ Interior Designer (142.051-014)
__ Painter (144.061-010)
__ Photographer (143.062-030)
__ Sculptor (144.061-018)
See also Craft Arts, under Realistic Occupations.

## Table 1. Occupations Grouped Using "Combined System" (continued)

**Drama and Dance** [01.03, 01.05, 01.07, 01.08]
__ Actor/Actress (150.047-010)
__ Choreographer (151.027-010)
__ Comedian (159.047-014)
__ Dancer (151.047-010)
__ Dance Studio Manager (187.167-086)
__ Dancing Instructor (151.027-014)
__ Disk Jockey (159.147-014)
__ Drama Teacher (150.027-014)
__ Model (297.667-014)
__ Motion Picture Director (159.067-010)
__ Radio and Television Announcer (159.147-010)
__ Stage Director (150.067-010)

**Music** [01.04]
__ Choral Director (152.047-010)
__ Composer (152.067-014)
__ Music Director (152.047-018)
__ Music Teacher (152.021-010)
__ Musician (152.041-010)
__ Orchestra Conductor (152.047-014)
__ Singer (152.047-022)

### Social Occupations

**Social Services** [10.01]
__ Clergy or Religious Workers (120.007-010)
__ Counselor (045.107-010)
__ Counseling Psychologist (045.107-026)
__ Director, College Career Planning and Placement
Center (045.107-018)
__ Dean of Students (091.107-010)
__ Parole Officer (195.167-030)
__ School Psychologist (045.107-034)
__ Social Worker, Psychiatric (195.107-034)

**Nursing, Therapy & Specialized
Teaching** [10.02]
__ Athletic Trainer (153.224-010)
__ Dental Hygienist (078.361-010)
__ General Duty Nurse (075.374-010)
__ Licensed Practical Nurse (079.374-014)
__ Occupational Therapist (076.364-010)
__ Physical Therapist (076.121.-014)
__ Physician Assistant (079.364-018)
__ Radiologic (X-ray) Technologist (078.362-026)
__ Recreational Therapist (076.124-014)
__ Respiratory Therapist (079.361-010)
__ School Nurse (075.124-010)
__ Teacher, Handicapped Students (094.227-018)
__ Teacher, Kindergarten (092.227-014)

**Child and Adult Care** [10.03]
__ Emergency Medical Technician (079.374-010)
__ Hospital Orderly (355.674-014)
__ Nurse Aide (355.674-014)

**Educational and Library Services** [11.02]
__ County-Agricultural Agent (096.127-010)
__ Extension Service Specialist (096.127-010)
__ Librarian (100.127-014)
__ Teacher, College (090.227-010)
__ Teacher, Elementary (092.227-010)
__ Teacher, High School (091.227-010)
__ Teacher, Industrial Arts (091.221-010)

### Enterprising Occupations

**Sales** [08.01, 08.02]
__ Auctioneer (294.257-010)
__ Buyer (162.157-018)
__ Fund Raiser (293.357-014)
__ Pawn Broker (191.157-010)
__ Sales Agent, Real Estate (250.357-018)
__ Salesperson, Automobiles (273.353-010)
__ Salesperson, Office Machines (275.357-034)
__ Sales Representative, Building Equipment
and Supplies (274.357-018)
__ Sales Representative, Jewelry (279.357-018)
__ Travel Agent (252.157-010)

**Hospitality, Beauty, and Customer Services**
[09.01, 09.02, 09.04]
__ Bartender (312.474-010)
__ Cosmetologist (332.271-010)
__ Flight Attendant (352.367-010)
__ Guide, Hunting and Fishing (353.161-010)
__ Hair Stylist (332.271-018)
__ Sales Clerk (290.477-014)

**Attendant Services** [09.05]
__ Bellhop (324.677-010)
__ Counter Attendant, Cafeteria (311.677-014)
__ Gate Agent, Airport (238.367-010)
__ Manicurist (331.674-010)
__ Railroad Conductor (910.667-014)
__ Waiter/Waitress (350.677-030)

**Law** [11.04]
__ Arbitrator (169.107-010)
__ District Attorney (110.117-010)
__ Hearing Officer (119.107-010)
__ Judge (111.107-010)
__ Lawyer (110.107-010)
__ Paralegal Assistant (119.267-026)

**Business Administration** [11.05]
__ Commissioner, Public Works (188.117-030)
__ Manager, Branch (183.117-010)
__ Manager, City (188.117-114)
__ Manager, Department Store (185.117-010)
__ Manager, Office (188.167-058)
__ Manager, Personnel (166.117-018)
__ Manager, Sales (163.167-018)
__ President, Financial Institution (186.117-054)
__ Purchasing Agent (162.157-038)

**Finance** [11.06]
__ Accountant (160.167-010)
__ Appraiser (191.287-010)
__ Credit Analyst (191.267-014)
__ Loan Officer (186.267-018)
__ Revenue Agent (160.167-050)
__ Sales Agent, Securities (251.157-010)
__ Securities Trader (186.167-058)
__ Treasurer (161.117-018)
__ Underwriter (169.167-058)
See also Mathematical Detail, under Conventional
Occupations.

**Administration of Services to the Public** [11.07]
__ Administrator, Hospital (187.117-010)
__ Curator (102.017-010)
__ Director, School of Nursing (075.117-030)
__ President, Educational Institution (090.117-034)
__ School Principal (099.117-018)
__ Superintendent, Schools (099.117-022)
__ Welfare Director (188.117-126)

**Communications** [11.08]
__ Editor, Newspaper (132.017-014)
__ Editor, Technical and Scientific Publications
(132.017-018)
__ Radio/TV Newscaster (131.267-010)
__ Reporter (131.267-018)
__ Translator (137.267-018)

**Promotion** [11.09]
__ Director, Fundraising (165.117-010)
__ Lobbyist (165.017-010)
__ Manager, Advertising (163.167-010)
__ Manager, Promotion (163.117-018)
__ Public-Relations Representative (165.067-010)

**Regulations Enforcement** [11.10]
__ Chief Bank Examiner (160.167-046)
__ Customs Inspector (168.267-022)
__ Inspector, Fraud (376.267-014)
__ Occupational-Safety-and-Health Inspector
(168.167-062)
See also Safety and Law Enforcement, under Realis-
tic Occupations.

**Table 1. Occupations Grouped Using "Combined System" (continued)**

**Business Management** [11.11]
__ Director, Food Services (187.167-026)
__ Director, Funeral (187.167-030)
__ Manager, Apartment House (186.167-018)
__ Manager, Automobile Service Station
__ Manager, Health Club (339.137-010)
__ Manager, Hotel or Motel (187.117-038)
__ Manager, Insurance Office (186.167-034)
__ Manager, Retail Store (185.167-046)

**Contracts and Claims** [11.12]
__ Booking Manager (191.117-014)
__ Claim Adjuster (241.217-010)
__ Claim Examiner (241.267-018)
__ Literary Agent (191.117-034)

**Conventional Occupations**

**Administrative Detail** [07.01]
__ Court Clerk (243.362-010)
__ Credit Analyst (241.267-022)
__ Credit Counselor (160.207-010)
__ Driver's License Examiner (168.267-034)
__ Eligibility Worker (195.267-010)
__ Financial-Aid Counselor, College (169.267-018)
__ Manager, Office (169.167-034)
__ Medical Secretary (201.362-014)
__ Secretary (201.362-030)
__ Title Examiner (119.287-010)
__ Town Clerk (243.367-018)

**Sports** [12.01, 12.02]
__ Head Coach (153.117-010)
__ Professional Athlete (153.341-010)
__ Sports Instructor (153.227-018)
__ Stunt Performer (159.341-014)
__ Umpire (153.267-018)

**Mathematical Detail** [07.02]
__ Account Analyst (214.382-010)
__ Accounting Clerk (216.482-010)
__ Bookkeeper (210.382-014)
__ Collection Clerk (241.357-010)
__ Insurance Claim Examiner (168.267-014)
__ Insurance Clerk (214.362-022)
__ Payroll Clerk (215.482-010)
__ Tax Clerk (219.487-010)
__ Timekeeper (215.367-022)
See also Finance, under Enterprising Occupations.

**Financial Detail** [07.03]
__ Bank Teller (211.362-018)
__ Cashier (211.362-010)
__ Post Office Clerk (243.367-014)
__ Ticket Agent (238.367-026)
__ Toll Collector (211.467-030)

**Oral Communications** [07.04]
__ Dispatcher, Maintenance Service (239.367-014)
__ Hotel Clerk (238.362-010)
__ Information Clerk (237.367-022)
__ Receptionist (237.367-038)
__ Reservation Agent, Airline (238.367-018)
__ Taxicab Dispatcher (913.367-010)
__ Telephone-Answering-Service Operator (235.662-026)
__ Telephone Operator (235.662-022)
__ Train Dispatcher (184.167-262)

**Records Processing** [07.05, 07.07]
__ Clerk, General (209.562-010)
__ File Clerk (206.367-014)
__ Mail Carrier (230.367-010)
__ Mail Clerk (209.587-026)
__ Proofreader (209.387-030)
__ Repair-Order Clerk (221.382-022)
__ Stenographer (202.362-014)
__ Title Searcher (209.367-046)

**Clerical Machine Operation** [07.06]
__ Billing Machine Operation (214.482-010)
__ Computer Terminal Operator (205.582-054)
__ Proof-Machine Operator (217.382-010)
__ Typist (203.582-066)

# OCCUPATIONAL INFORMATION

## Relationship to Career Decisions

Quality career decisions depend upon what you *do*. This includes (a) considering a wide range of alternatives, (b) weighing the possible positive and negative consequences of each, and (c) making plans for implementing your decision. All of these actions require information that is complete, up-to-date, and accurate. To the extent that you do not take these actions or rely on faulty information, the more likely you are to experience setbacks and postdecisional regret (Janis & Mann, 1977)(see **Choosing an Occupation; Decision Making**).

## Application

There are four basic questions that you will want to answer in your search for information.

### What Are Your Alternatives?

Before you make a career decision, you want to be sure you have not overlooked a promising option. This is more likely to occur when a person is inexperienced about the world of work, feels rushed to make a choice, or is emotionally under pressure. If you are already working and considering a career change within your company or organization, there are two articles in this book that you will want to read: **Career Development System within the Organization** and **Career Path Possibilities within the Organization.** If you are considering changing your career, **Job Changing** and **Self-Employment** are recommended. If you are trying to identify an occupation that fits your interests, skills, and needs, the article **Occupational Groups** will help you. **Choosing an Occupation** is recommended to everyone.

### What Do You Need to Know?

While each situation is unique, there are several basic facts that most people will want to know.

1. *Nature of Work*: duties, both unpleasant and pleasant; physical demands; involvement with people, data, and things; and performance expectations (see **Job Description; Realistic Job Preview**).
2. *Work Environment*: physical characteristics (e.g., hot/cold, clean/dirty, indoor/outdoor, noisy, etc.); the kind of involvement that you will have with coworkers; extent and type of human resource development systems (see **Assessment Centers; Career Development System within the Organization; Employee Assistance Programs (EAP); Performance Appraisal**); presence of work hazards (see **Work Hazards**); and desirability of the geographic location (see **Climate for Workers**).
3. *Requirements*: aptitudes, skills, abilities; physical requirements; tools or other equipment, training; testing (see **Testing**).
4. *Opportunities for Advancement and Development*.
5. *Earnings and Benefits* (see **Benefits; Pay**).
6. *Discrimination* (see the discrimination: articles; also **Women in the Workforce; Women's Barriers and Opportunities**).
7. *Employment Outlook* (see **Job Outlook: Major Trends; Job Security**).

### Where Do You Find This Information?

There are two basic sources: original and published media. The articles on **Information Interviewing, Mentoring,** and **Networking** give valuable tips on how to get this information from these various sources.

1. *Original Sources*: workers on the job; employers or supervisors of these workers; government agencies that license or regulate employment; direct observation (see **Cooperative Education; Internships; Realistic Job Preview; Service-Learning; Volunteer Work**); and a mentor or individuals you network with.
2. *Published Media*: audiovisual materials (e.g., videotapes); printed materials; and computer-assisted career guidance (see article by this name).

Since published media are fairly easy to find and use, it is tempting to rely only on them. This is usually a mistake. Original sources often provide invaluable information. Don't overlook them!

### Is the Information Accurate?

There are several critical questions to ask:

1. Is this information up-to-date? If it's an individual, does he or she have current information? If a published source, when was the information collected? For a book, look at the first copyright; that is a good clue. If it is more than five years old, the information is probably worthless.
2. Who is the source? If it is an individual, is it someone you can trust? Do they have a bias? What is their information based on? If published, is it by a reputable publisher? For example, you can rely on the occupational researchers who prepare U.S. government publications.
3. What motivates the information source? Is the information offered for the purpose of recruitment? Some occupational information is distributed, often for free, to recruit you; it is often misleading, omitting disadvantages. Be cautious; conflicts of interest can lead to faulty information.

## Reference

Janis, I. L., & Mann, L. (1977). *Decision making*. New York: The Free Press.

## Bibliography

Many books provide occupational information. Below is an outline showing the types of occupational information available, and an annotated bibliography of several basic career reference books.

### Types of Published Occupational Information

I. *Annotated Bibliographies:* An excellent example is Career Planning Materials by Roberta Riethmiller Egelston (Chicago: American Library Association, 1981). She has identified, categorized, and annotated books, directories, and catalogs providing information on career planning. This outline is adapted from the one used in her book.
II. *Career Reference Books*: These books contain facts about a large number of occupations. An annotated bibliography for the major books of this type is given at the end of this outline.
III. *Career Profiles:* These are books on specific occupations (e.g., Occupational Therapy Careers) or occupations sharing a common trait (e.g., Working with Animals).
IV. *Where Jobs Exist*
A. Directories of Employers: These are directories of organizations and companies that employ people in

different areas (e.g., *Industrial Research Laboratories of the United States*).
  1. White-Collar Employers
      a. Business and Industry
      b. Communications and Arts
      c. Education, Library, and Museum Work
      d. Government and Public Service
      e. Law
      f. Medicine and Health
      g. Social Service
      h. Sales
  2. Blue-Collar Employers
      a. Construction
      b. Processing
      c. Transportation
  3. Employment Abroad
  B. Government Opportunities
    1. Federal Government
        a. Federal Employment in General
        b. Employee Directories
    2. State Government
    3. Local Government
V. *Education and Training*
  A. School Catalogs
  B. Guides to Postsecondary Study
    1. General Guides (e.g., accredited institutions, apprenticeships, trade schools, two-year colleges, colleges, graduate study)
    2. Specific Guides: A Particular Area of Study (e.g., anthropology, geography, medicine).
    3. Other Considerations
        a. Financial Assistance
        b. Internships
        c. Study Abroad

For help in locating specific publications for these different types of information, consult with your local librarian.

### Career Reference Books

These books are primarily designed to give information about occupations, such as the nature of the work, earnings, training required, and job outlook. They will often help identify occupations compatible with the reader's interests, values, and abilities (see **Occupational Groups**). These features make them quite valuable in planning career change. In using them it is important to use the most recent edition and supplement them with other sources of information, particularly original sources. Most libraries and career resource centers have the books listed below:

*Occupational Outlook Handbook.* (U.S. Department of Labor, Washington, DC: U.S. Government Printing Office). Gives detailed descriptions for 225 occupations (approximately 80% of all jobs) and summary information for 125 more. The descriptions include nature of work, working conditions, employment, training requirements, job outlook, earnings, related occupations, and sources of additional information. Related occupations are grouped together, so by browsing the table of contents readers can see which occupations share similar characteristics. It is related to the *Dictionary of Occupational Titles* (DOT) (see below). Each occupation described in the *Handbook* is preceded by a nine-digit *DOT* number so that the occupation can be found in the *DOT*. The *Handbook* also gives an up-to-date forecast regarding economic growth and labor force change. It is published by the Bureau of Labor Statistics and revised every two years. The most recent edition is for 1990–91.

*Occu-Facts.* (1990, Largo, FL: Careers, Inc.). This book is similar to *Occupational Outlook Handbook* in the information it provides. It differs primarily in format and the number (565) of occupations reviewed. It uses a standardized outline format in presenting the "facts" about occupations; there are no paragraphs. This feature makes it easier to compare different occupations and get to the relevant information quickly. It is also related to the *DOT* and *GOE* (see below).

*Encyclopedia of Careers and Vocational Guidance.* 8th ed. 1990, Chicago: Ferguson. This excellent source of information contains four volumes: Volume 1 describes and evaluates 76 major industries, such as advertising, book publishing, insurance, railroad transportation, and religion. Each industry is described in terms of it history, structure, career titles and paths, levels of education and training for the occupations in it, and economic outlook. Volumes 2, 3, and 4 describe more than 2,300 jobs, including nature of work, requirements, employment outlook, conditions of work, methods of entering and advancement, earnings, social and psychological factors, and sources of additional information. At the end of each article, the *DOT* and *GOE* numbers are given.

*Dictionary of Occupational Titles* (DOT). 4th ed., Revised 1991, U.S. Department of Labor, Washington, DC: U.S. Government Printing Office. *DOT* contains descriptions of approximately 20,000 occupations that are based on extensive research conducted by the Department of Labor.

*DOT*'s principle value lies in its comprehensiveness and ability to lead a person to related occupations. Since related occupations are grouped together, looking up one leads to many other similar ones. For example, "Veterinarians" is a cluster of occupations that includes 15 veterinary-related occupations, and this cluster is next to such clusters as "Dentists," "Pharmacists," and "Registered Nurses."

Another useful feature is the section called "Occupational Titles Arranged by Industry Designation." If a person were interested in working in a library, for example, he or she could look under that "industry" and find more than 70 different occupations listed. *DOT* has some entertainment value as well. It is interesting to learn what other people do in their work, such as dinkey operators and pickle pumpers!

*Guide for Occupational Exploration.* (GOE) (2nd ed., 1984, Circle Pines, MN: American Guidance Service). *GOE* is an excellent resource for identifying occupations that might suit a person. The article **"Occupational Groups"** describes how it can be used in this way. *GOE* serves as a bridge connecting seven aspects of an individual—interests, work values, leisure experiences, home activities, school subjects, work settings, and military occupational specialties—to related occupations. Each of these seven areas may by considered separately or the reader may combine them using the "Checklist of Occupational Clues" printed in the book. The Checklist systematically leads individuals through an evaluation of their values, interests, and the other areas so they can identify the most promising occupations. Browsing through the separate areas can also be helpful. For example, readers can see which occupations are related to such work values as adventure, competition, or variety. Similarly, the occupations related to such leisure activities as, "Serving as a volunteer in the town fire department or emergency rescue squad" or "Reading medical or scientific magazines" are given.

Since *GOE* was designed to be used for high school students as well as career changers, some of its questions are elementary, which may discredit it in the eyes of some. This would be unfortunate, because *GOE* is grounded in research and provides a useful bridge for those having difficulty spanning the gap between occupations and aspects of themselves.

—LAWRENCE K. JONES

# OFFICE ROMANCE

An office romance is a workplace relationship between a man and woman that is characterized by mutual sexual attraction and is made known to others through the participants' actions. Office romance is distinguished from sexual harassment by the mutual nature of the attraction; harassment occurs when one party is unwilling to reciprocate unwanted sexual advances. Office romance takes place between willing parties who consciously make the decision to act upon their attraction out of their own free choice.

## Relationship to Work

Incidence rates for office romances are reported to be surprisingly high. In a recent survey of 100 executive women, 76% reported they were aware of or had been personally involved in an office romance in their firms (Mainiero, 1989). Other surveys (Anderson & Hunsaker, 1985; Quinn, 1977) report similar findings.

Several reasons have been advanced to explain the rise in incidence rates for love at work:

1. *Geographic and Spatial Proximity.* Employees become attracted to one another when working closely together (Quinn, 1977).
2. *Demographic Similarity of Coworkers.* Coworkers are hired on the basis of similar values and interests, and are socialized to become more similar over time.
3. *Intensity of Work Relationships.* Intense tasks and work assignments, such as what occurs in mentor-protege relationships, breed attraction among coworkers (Clauson & Kram, 1984).

4. *Societal Trends.* The current focus on workaholism, coupled with a reluctance to date strangers due to fear of sexually transmitted diseases, may lead employees to focus on socializing at work with people with whom they are already well-acquainted (Mainiero, 1989).
5. *Increased Numbers of Women in the Workplace.* More women are present in record numbers at all levels of the corporate hierarchy, influencing the likelihood that heterosexual romances will take place in work settings.

Both risks and benefits should be considered when contemplating an office romance. Some of the risks include threats to career advancement, concern about maintaining professional relationships after a breakup, disrupted morale of coworkers brought about by accusations of favoritism, and termination due to strictly held anti-nepotism policies in some firms. The benefits may include enhanced morale if the department supports the romance; improved motivation and productivity; better teamwork, communication, and cooperation between departments; and greater ability to recruit and retain dual-career couples (Mainiero, 1989).

The degree to which benefits and risks are experienced are primarily a function of two factors: (a) whether the romance involves a direct reporting relationship or any relationship that could be a conflict of interest, and (b) whether the company's culture is conservative or liberal, as this influences attitudes within the firm toward those involved in office romances.

Hierarchial romances, defined as those that occur between a boss and a subordinate or between levels of the corporate hierarchy, have been found to be very disruptive due to accusations of favoritism, and concern about the misuse of power in the relationship and the loss of objectivity in business judgments. Peer romances were more favorably evaluated (Bureau of National Affairs Report, 1988; Mainiero, 1989).

Very conservative firms present greater risks as office romances in such firms were less public. In more liberal, action-oriented firms that recruited a younger demographic population, office romances were more open and there was more discussion of benefits.

## Application

In considering a romantic relationship at work, experience and research suggest these guidelines:

1. *Diagnose Your Corporate Culture.* Be aware of the attitude of management toward those who become involved in office romances. Are office romances

**Figure 1. What Is Organizational Culture?**

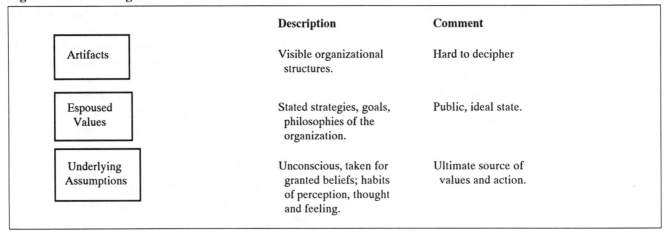

| | Description | Comment |
|---|---|---|
| Artifacts | Visible organizational structures. | Hard to decipher |
| Espoused Values | Stated strategies, goals, philosophies of the organization. | Public, ideal state. |
| Underlying Assumptions | Unconscious, taken for granted beliefs; habits of perception, thought and feeling. | Ultimate source of values and action. |

openly known? Or do most couples who become involved keep their romance secret? Is your firm comprised of younger employees who are at the right age to develop romantic commitments? Or do the members of your firm hold more parochial attitudes toward love at work? Is your firm receptive to women in management? Or is there greater risk for women who become personally involved with coworkers? Answers to these questions can help you determine the climate for love at work in your firm.

2. *Avoid Hierarchial Relationships.* Do not date your boss or anyone above you in the corporate hierarchy. Such relationships disrupt morale and lead to accusations of favoritism and "sleeping your way to the top." Should you become involved with your boss, consider a transfer to another department as soon as possible. Peer relationships, however, present few problems.

3. *Maintain Professionalism at All Times.* Discuss personal issues at home but focus exclusively on work at the office. Do not constantly lunch with your lover or work in his or her office; be certain to maintain professional relationships with other colleagues. Many couples agree that creating a sense of boundary separation at the office is helpful and prefer working for different departments.

4. *Be Aware of the Complexities of Breaking Up in the Office.* Develop a contingency plan should the romance dissolve. Determine whether or not you could continue working with your ex-lover. If not, request a transfer to another department before the breakup occurs.

5. *Don't Be Fooled into Thinking Your Romance Is a Secret.* Most colleagues were aware of attractions between coworkers even before coworkers became involved. Extramarital affairs are especially diffi-

cult to hide. Be aware that others around you will pick up on the signs of attraction and will suspect an involvement.

*See also* Organizational Culture; Organizational Politics; Sexual Harassment.

## Bibliography

Anderson, C., & Hunsaker, P. (1985, February). Why there's romancing at the office and why it's everyone's problem. *Personnel*: 57–63.

The Bureau of National Affairs. (1988). *Corporate affairs: Nepotism, office romance, and sexual harassment.* Washington, DC. A discussion of the risks, benefits, and realities of office romance, harassment, and nepotism, including case studies of several firms and sample corporate policies.

Clauson, J., & Kram, K. (1984, May). Managing cross-gender mentoring. *Business Horizons:* 22–32.

Mainiero, Lisa. (1989). *Office romance: Love, power and sex in the workplace.* New York: Rawson Associates/Macmillan Publishing Co. A review of the issues concerning love at work using illustrative cases. Includes discussion of corporate strategies.

Quinn, R. (1977). Coping with cupid: The formation, impact, and management of romantic relationships in organizations. *Administrative Science Quarterly*, 22: 30–45.

—LISA A. MAINIERO

## ORGANIZATIONAL CULTURE

Organizational culture is the pattern of shared basic assumptions that a group or organization has learned in dealing with its problems of external adaptation and internal integration and that are considered valid enough to be taught to new members as the correct way to perceive, think about, and feel in relation to these problems.

In order to develop a culture, a group or organization must have enough stability of membership and enough shared experiences to have learned common ways of perceiving, thinking, and feeling. The longer the history, the more numerous and intense the shared experience, and the more powerful the initial feelings of the group founders and subsequent leaders, the stronger the culture will be.

Cultural assumptions will develop in any group that has a shared history. Thus a total organization will not only have an overall culture, but its various units—functional groups, geographical units, and hierarchical units such as top management, middle management, first line management, and shop floor work groups—will also develop subcultures.

Subcultures within an organization can be highly congruent or can be in conflict with each other. The total organization is not necessarily uniform in its assumptions, which means that during the course of a career in an organization the career occupant may be exposed to many different subcultures.

## Relationship to Work

Organizational culture relates to all aspects of shared member experiences, and, therefore, impacts how people perceive organizational goals, how they perceive and think about the means by which those goals are to be accomplished, how progress will be measured, and what kinds of remedies will be applied if progress is insufficient. In this sense, culture determines the most basic aspects of how work is defined.

For example, in one company work may be defined in terms of collaborative teamwork because the fundamental technology requires high degrees of interdependence. In another company, the technology may require intense individual effort, leading to an entirely different work system.

Cultural assumptions govern the most fundamental aspects of human relationships in the organization: how status is awarded and measured; what kinds of behavior are heroic or sinful; how rewards are allocated; how formal or informal relationships are to be across hierarchical, functional, or geographic boundaries; how truth is determined; how time and space are viewed; and how human nature and activity are perceived.

To analyze culture it is best to think of it as manifesting itself at three levels (see Figure 1). At the level of visible and feelable artifacts the culture is very palpable but hard to decipher. For example, one might notice that the office layout is very informal with open cubicles, and that people address each other by first name, but one would not know just what this means in terms of how work actually gets done or how authority is really exercised.

At the level of espoused values the culture manifests its ideology and its ideal state. For example, the company may have published a pamphlet stating its basic values, and slogans about these values may be posted on the walls of offices. But these stated values and slogans may not necessarily reflect how people actually behave.

The level of taken-for-granted, shared assumptions is the "essence" of the culture and explains why things happen in the way they do. For example, the company may assume that the only way to solve problems is to maximize communication, hence the open office layout. In order to understand a culture, therefore, one must make an effort to go beyond artifacts and espoused values to try to decipher the underlying assumptions.

## Application

Organizational culture must be deciphered and understood every time you cross an organizational boundary (e.g., when you first enter the company, when you are transferred, when you are promoted, and/or when you are moved geographically). Each new part of the organization that you enter will have potentially a different subculture.

Since culture determines the basic requirements and daily style of how work is done and how relationships among organizational members are structured, it is essential for you, as the career occupant, to determine whether your personal cognitive and interpersonal style fit the culture into which you are moving. This matching is most crucial at the initial entry into the organization, but must be re-assessed at every career choice point in order to avoid getting into a mismatch between the norms, values, and rules of the culture and your own personal style.

**Culture and Organizational Socialization.** The time when culture is most evident is when the new employee enters the organization and is taught not only the technical aspects of the job but "the ropes" or "the way we do things around here." Some of this learning comes directly from the boss, from more senior workers, from training programs, and from literature about the company. These materials will emphasize rules and espoused values, how the company would like to operate. The deeper assumptions of how things really work are usually not articulated in formal materials, but are passed on by colleagues, past members of the organization, and others in various informal briefings, "Dutch Uncle" talks, and by example.

Most organizations have cultures, so the new employee should expect a period of socialization lasting anywhere from weeks to months to years, depending on the complexity of the work role and the degree of consistency among the subcultures that he or she must decipher.

**Culture and "Getting Ahead."** Ability to assimilate the organizational culture is probably one of the most important criteria for getting ahead. As a new employee or when you have been promoted or transferred, you must not only learn to do your job adequately, but must learn to fit in, in the broader sense of adopting the cultural assumptions. For example, in one company the hierarchy may be very important and bosses expect subordinates to follow orders precisely. In another company the emphasis on individual responsibility may be more important and to fit in may mean to think for oneself and argue with the boss when necessary. In either company, you must be comfortable with the assumptions about work and hierarchy in order to get ahead.

**Deciphering Culture.** There is no satisfactory typology of culture that would enable you to easily decipher how a company really works. Furthermore, culture covers all aspects of how things work, and it is not always clear from the outset which assumptions are the most central in any given company. In deciphering a culture, therefore, you must develop a broad strategy of observing what is going on, identifying the things that most puzzle you, and then asking many questions of company members about those aspects.

It is especially important to visit companies or new units to which you may be assigned to get your own feeling for the way things are done there before deciding whether or not to accept an offer to that unit. A mismatch between your own working style and values and those of the company can lead to poor performance and dissatisfaction.

*See also* Organizational Politics.

## Bibliography

Jones, M. J., Moore, M. D., & Snyder, R. C. (1988). *Inside organizations: Understanding the human dimension.* Newbury Park, CA: Sage. A collection of articles that highlights the subtleties and variations in cultures in different kinds of organizations.

Ott, J. J. (1989). *The organizational culture perspective.* Chicago: Dorsey. A good review of the various aspects of organizational culture and how to view it in organizations.

Schein, E. H. (1985). *Organizational culture and leadership.* San Francisco: Jossey-Bass. This book covers all aspects of organizational culture. What it is; what functions it serves; how it arises, evolves, and changes; and what special roles leaders play in the creation and management of culture.

Van Maanen, J., & Barley, J. R. (1984). Occupational communities culture and control in organizations. In B. M. Staw & L. Cummings (Eds.), *Research in organizational behavior, Vol. 6.*

Greenwich, CT.: JAI Press. An account of how culture arises in different kinds of occupations and how culture functions as a control mechanism in organizations.

—EDGAR H. SCHEIN

# ORGANIZATIONAL POLITICS

Organizational politics refers to the use of power or influence to achieve individual or group ends.

## Relationship to Work

The effects of organizational politics may be perceived as positive when desirable organizational or personal goals are achieved in such a way that the people involved are benefitted in one or more ways. For example, a manager may use her or his influence and knowledge of employees' foibles, internal friendships, and outside connections in order to reduce customer complaints and increase repeat sales. The manager does this in a sensitive, ethical manner so that customers, employees, and their friends believe the situation has improved and that they helped contribute to that improvement.

Dirty politics is the playing of power games in order to gain personal advantage at the expense of someone else. Dirty politics leaves a trail of resentment, anger, or embarrassment with those who lost the last game. Winners may gloat for a while, but are often uneasy with the knowledge that the losers are probably plotting to get their revenge via a new political game. The people who initiate such games usually do so out of insecurity and fear, but their behavior often seems arrogant and cruel.

## Application

In order to succeed within an organization—that is, to achieve your job goals and fulfill your job responsibilities and to gain promotions and raises—you must learn the political ropes without getting tangled up in them. You must learn them not to use them against others, but to keep others from using them successfully against you. Using dirty politics against others leads to unnecessary conflict and will come back to haunt you. On the other hand, if you are too naive, you may be drawn unwittingly into others' games, skirmishes, and even all-out wars before you know what is really going on.

Understanding the ins and outs of organizational politics helps you to understand what people are up to, who aligns with whom, what you can probably expect from certain people, and similar crucial knowledge. You need to understand something about the games people play and how to counter the ones that could do you in. Here are some common political games:

1. Creating a crisis to get recognition for saving the day rather than for preventing problems or crises in the first place. Giving special recognition and other rewards for preventing problems and crises may end the game. After the crisis, focusing on what could have been done to prevent it will signal that the organization values prevention even more than problem solving.

2. Making oneself indispensable by hoarding information and not training others to take over in one's absence is another game workers play. Praising those who prepare for the day they will not be around helps to block the game. Insisting on written procedures can help.

3. Withholding key information from people, hoping they will stumble and fall is played at all levels. Often the message is given, but is buried in a long memo, computer printout, vague phone message, or other device. Sometimes the game is to tell you what you want to hear, especially when a worker wants to avoid confrontation or unpleasantness. Doublecheck and verify all important information. Develop and use a support network of many people who will keep you informed and will serve as verifiers.

4. Discrediting rivals through innuendo is most often played by peers who are rivals. The really devious ones try to befriend you in order to get inside information about your weaknesses and problems, past and present, so they can later backstab you by using the information against you. As you enlist trusted work associates into a mutual-support network, they can help you to learn who to trust and will speak up for you when you are attacked. In general, reveal only those current job problems that call for the cooperation of the persons you are discussing them with. Limit your gripe sessions and counseling sessions to trusted off-the-job friends.

5. Excluding people from committees, meetings, or other opportunities may be played by the boss or rivals, if they wish to see you fail. Subtle exclusion is even more difficult to deal with than the overt type. For example, other(s) may listen politely to your ideas and then ignore them. Later the same idea may be presented by another and readily adopted. Do not take the exclusion personally. Keep your goals in mind. Confront the specific exclusion in a professional manner, expressing your desire to participate because you need to achieve job objectives, contribute to company objectives, etc.

6. Another game is setting someone up for a flareup by learning what triggers their anger or fear, then using it in high-stress, high-visibility situations. Do not discuss personal problems, problem emotions, or give out other information that may be turned against you. Read self-help books or attend seminars to learn how to manage your emotional responses. On the job, when you lose your temper, you lose.

7. Setting a person up to fail by not giving them the support and resources they need to carry out their assigned responsibilities is a game most often played by bosses and occasionally by rivals. Do not assume that you will get the cooperation and support you need to do your job. Ask probing questions of the persons you must depend upon, as well as any mentors or supporters you may have.

8. Divide and conquer is a game played by bosses who lack confidence in their power to survive. You and your peers may be set up to be suspicious of each other or to fight among yourselves so you will not form an alliance against the boss. Tactful questioning of peers may uncover this game, and peer solidarity can block it.

9. Giving advice that serves the advice-giver but not the recipient may be played at any level, but you are especially vulnerable when your boss plays it. Think for yourself and get the opinions of respected others.

10. Letting a project or proposal die on the vine from neglect rather than candidly turning it down and explaining why may be played by the boss who does not want to openly oppose your plan but does not want it implemented. You must decide whether to confront the issue or back off.

11. Stealing ideas and credit may be played by weak bosses or rivals. To protect yourself, write tactful but clear memos to your boss—with a copy to the next-level boss—that document your ideas and accomplishments.

12. Getting rid of subordinates by getting their job positions abolished, kicking them up the ladder to a low-power staff job, making life miserable, offering to help them get a job outside the company if they will resign, and threatening to give a bad reference if they don't are games bosses play to get rid of people whom they do not have adequate grounds for firing.

Recognizing the common games helps you to understand what is really going on in the workplace. This in turn helps you to prevent some of the more negative effects from harming you. You need to have specific game-coping strategies, such as those suggested above. You also need some ongoing general strategies, such as the following:

1. Get your own fears and ego problems worked out, so that you will have the inner resources to put negative politics into perspective and respond calmly.
2. Schedule regular quiet times to relax and reflect on such situations. Get in touch with your values and priorities; use your intuition and other inner resources.
3. Avoid knee-jerk reactions, especially when you are feeling angry or fearful.

4. Be as open and honest as the environment allows, but do not talk with associates unnecessarily about your personal problems or past job-related problems.

5. Try to get at the root of persistent game-playing and to determine exactly what the players are trying to accomplish, and how aware they are of the "game" aspects of their behavior.

6. Don't take it personally. Hardcore game players don't bother to get to know people on an authentic, personal basis, only on a manipulative basis.

7. Stay goal-oriented. If you keep your goals in mind, you tend to steer a steady course toward them and to keep politics in perspective.

8. Be as knowledgeable as possible about what's going on, absorb verbal and nonverbal communication from as many people as possible. Just keep your antennae up. Also, know company policies, procedures, and rules and use them.

9. Observe behavior patterns; people tend to repeat the same types of games over and over.

10. Develop a support network and use it. Alliances increase your clout.

*See also* Anger; Bosses: Managing Relationships with Superiors; Mentoring; Networking; Promotion/Raise.

## Bibliography

Blank, R. (1981). *Playing the game.* New York: Morrow. The author describes this book as a psychopolitical strategy for your career.

Carr-Ruffino, N. (1985). *The promotable woman: Becoming a successful manager.* Belmont, CA: Wadsworth, Inc. See especially Chapter 2 on "Surviving the Transition to Manager."

Dubrin, A. J. (1982). *Winning at office politics.* New York: Ballantine Books. This is a hard-hitting, on-the-job guide to political game-playing.

Harrigan, B. (1977). *Games mother never taught you.* New York: Rawson Associates. This book defines the business game and its barriers for women. The chapter on sexual games is especially valuable.

Kennedy, M. M. (1980). *Office politics.* New York: Warner Books. Claiming that 75% of all office firings are political executions, the author discusses seizing power and wielding clout through constructive use of office politics.

—NORMA CARR-RUFFINO

## OUTPLACEMENT

The process of supporting discharged employees in their transition to new career opportunities is called outplacement. Whether performed by external outplacement consultants or internal human resources staff, the first step is to assist the management of an organization in planning and implementing employee terminations so as to reduce the trauma experienced by everyone involved. The discharged employees then receive counseling to help deal with their job loss and are provided career planning, job search training, and job development programs.

### Relationship to Work

When organizations need to restructure due to a merger, acquisition, economic hardship, shift in strategic direction, or some other change agent, a common result is the displacement of employees. Difficult decisions must be made regarding who is retained and who is discharged. Individuals may be terminated for a variety of reasons, most of which relate to their job not being a match with their skills, knowledge, or interests. Regardless of the circumstances, losing one's job can be a very traumatic event. Outplacement services reduce the stress and provide a strong foundation for the effective transition to a new career opportunity. The steps of a comprehensive outplacement program include:

**Pre-Termination Planning.** After consulting with the human resources department of a company on the necessary policies and procedures relating to the employee termination process, the outplacement professional trains line management to properly apply these principles. Issues which are addressed include verification of the reasons for the discharge, timing, logistics, and communications. A great deal of time and effort is spent training management on the dynamics and protocol of the termination interview.

Sensitivity training is employed to ensure that the manager considers the dignity and self-respect of the terminated employee. Stress reduction techniques are presented, especially in major downsizing situations where many managers must each fire a number of employees.

**Post-Termination Counseling.** The outplacement consultant meets with the discharged employee immediately after the termination interview and helps the individual deal with the anger and frustration of losing a job. The individual needs to view the termination in proper perspective and regain self-esteem and confidence as the first step in the career development phase.

**Career Planning.** In one-on-one counseling sessions, workshops, or a combination of both, the consultant assists the individuals in gathering and analyzing relevant information regarding their history and knowledge, skills, and accomplishments. Psychological inventories may be used to determine environmental, behavioral, and vocational preferences of the individual. Based on these assessments, viable career directions are explored and specific short-term objectives and long-term goals are developed.

**Job Search Training.** The next phase is to assist the displaced worker in planning, developing, and implementing an effective job search. Again, through one-on-one sessions, workshops, or a combination of both, the consultant trains the individual in the steps toward locating the best career opportunity available and the skills necessary for a successful job search. These steps include:

1. *Resume and Cover Letter Preparation.* Written communications, including the proper method of completing an employment application, are emphasized.
2. *Interviewing Techniques and Strategies.* Verbal communications are discussed, including telemarketing and salary negotiating.
3. *Development of Job Leads.* All sources of career opportunities are explored, including responding to advertisements, utilizing recruiters, attending job fairs, networking, and researching and directly contacting decision makers in organizations.
4. *Organizing the Job Search.* Effective information management and scheduling of activities are emphasized.
5. *Job Referral Systems.* To supplement the displaced worker's own job development activities, outplacement consultants provide referrals to career opportunities.

**Follow-up Consulting and Administrative Support.** The final phase of the outplacement process is to provide on-going advice to individuals and ensure that they effectively transcend the emotional roller coaster that is indicative of a typical job search. Administrative support can be provided in the form of office space, telephone answering service, use of reference library, and secretarial support.

When a major staff reduction takes place in an organization, the consultant can assist the company in creating a transition center where follow-up counseling, administrative support, and job development activities take place.

**Fees.** All fees and expenses for outplacement services are paid by the organization that is discharging the employees. The cost of outplacement services varies widely depending on the extent of the programs and the number of displaced employees involved. To avoid conflicts of interest, outplacement consultants do not charge a fee to prospective employers for referring individuals for career opportunities. In this way, consultants can be completely objective in providing career advice and in assisting individuals in developing all sources of job leads.

## Application

To get the best results from outplacement services, you must have an open mind and be willing to devote a great amount of time and effort to the process. There is no external source, whether it be a consultant, book, or assessment exercise, which will tell you exactly what career direction to pursue. They can facilitate your decision making and point you in general directions, but the ultimate decision must come from you.

You must also be willing to explore many career alternatives at first and be prepared to work hard at finding a new job. While outplacement services can bring a high level of efficiency to the process, including providing you with specific career opportunities, you must develop the skills and knowledge to effectively represent yourself in the job marketplace and pursue all the appropriate sources of job leads. By researching new opportunities and seeking advice from a lot of people, you are gaining the information necessary to make the right decisions about your career objective. You also are raising your visibility in the job market and are increasing the opportunity for people to refer you to specific jobs.

The skills and knowledge you gain from receiving outplacement services can be useful to you in the future. To facilitate your career development, you must constantly assess your skills, knowledge, and accomplishments and compare your progress to others in your field. You also need to analyze your interests and priorities regarding your career and relate them to family and personal issues.

*See also* Anger; Career Exploration; Career Planning; Fired/Laid Off; Job Search; Job Security; Job Security: The Free Agent Manager; Law in the Workplace; Managing Transitions; Self-Esteem; Unemployment.

## Bibliography

Brammer, L. M., & Humberger, F. E. (1984). *Outplacement & inplacement counseling.* Englewood Cliffs, NJ: Prentice-Hall, Inc.

Bridges, William. (1988). *Surviving corporate transition.* New York: Doubleday.

Ciabattari, Jane. (1988). *Winning moves: How to come out ahead in a corporate shakeup.* New York: Rawson Associates/MacMillan. A comprehensive guide to personally surviving the fast-paced changes in today's corporate world.

Plumez, Jacqueline Hornor. (1985). *Divorcing a corporation.* New York: Villard Books. Sound advice on when to leave a company and, once out, how to effectively hunt for a new job.

Sweet, Donald H. (1989). *A manager's guide to conducting terminations.* Lexington, MA: Lexington Books. An easy-to-read guide to the process of termination and the transition services available to discharged employees. Written from management's perspective.

Taft, Bradford H. (1988). Effective selection and utilization of outplacement services. *Employment Management Association Journal,* 3, (1): 25–26.

Wolfer, Karen S., & Wong, Richard G. (1988). *The outplacement solution.* New York: Wiley.

## For Further Information

**Association of Outplacement Consulting Firms**
364 Parsippany Road
Parsippany, NJ 07054
**Employment Management Association**
4101 Boone Trail, Suite 201
 Raleigh, NC 27607

—BRADFORD H. TAFT

# P

## PARENT INVOLVEMENT IN CAREER PLANNING

Research has shown that parents influence their children's careers in many ways (Schulenberg, Vondracek, & Crouter, 1984). In fact, children are most likely to consult with family members when they have questions about career issues. Many parents find it difficult to advise their children since it is hard to predict job trends or opportunities with the possibility of various economic and social changes. However, parents can assist their children in making effective decisions (Otto, 1984).

### Parents and Their Children's Career

It is important for parents to help their children look at themselves, the world of work, and how the children's characteristics and work world interact. Parents can assist their children in their career planning by helping them identify their personal strengths and limitations. The more individuals know about themselves, the greater the likelihood that they will be able to find a career that is satisfying to them. Parents can also help their children in gaining more knowledge about the multitude of occupations in the world of work (Hummel & McDaniels, 1979).

The activities that parents initiate to assist their children in selecting a career direction will depend on the developmental level of the children. According to some of the research on career development, preadolescent children often go through a stage where they want to enter a fantasy career, such as professional football player or rock star. Adolescents will often be in a stage of exploration, where they will consider many different careers and frequently change their minds, which sometimes results in parents worrying that their child will never make a decision. Often it is in early adulthood when an individual's interests formalize and career choices become more focused. In all of these stages it is important for parents to listen to their children's expressions of dreams and concerns. Good communication between the parents and the child is fundamental to assisting a child in career planning.

### Application

As a parent, the better the communication between you and your children, the more effective you will probably be in assisting them in their career planning. Good communication involves listening closely to what your child is saying and reflecting what you have heard in a nonjudgmental fashion. Parents often feel that they should have all the answers concerning career issues, while children frequently just need someone to listen to their hopes and fears about the future. Career planning involves knowledge of oneself, and parents can be most effective in helping their children learn about themselves when the relationship is open and encouraging.

**Interests.** In helping your children know more about themselves you may want to encourage them to examine their interests. Interests usually have a major impact on career choices and are closely related to job satisfaction. Individuals are more likely to be satisfied with their jobs if they find the work interesting. However, sorting the vast number of careers one can be interested in into manageable categories can expedite the exploration process. You can assist a child in junior high school to identify broad areas or categories of careers that interest him or her. An excellent system for categorizing careers is John Holland's typology which puts jobs into primarily one of six interest areas (see **Vocational Choice: John Holland's Theory**). You could also start the process by having your children identify whether they would rather work with people, data, or things.

When a child is in senior high school or enters college, the exploration of interests needs to become more focused and should be of specific careers or fields. *The Guide for Occupational Exploration (GOE)* by Harrington and O'Shea (1984) is an excellent resource for exploring specific occupations related to an individual's interests. The *GOE* categorizes interests into 12 areas and then provides information on specific job titles, training, and work requirements. Another method for exploring interests is to contact a counselor and have your child take an interest inventory. During this exploration keep in mind that a person's career interests usually do not crystallize until his or her early 20s. You must also examine whether your career interests are influencing your children's career selection or if you are allowing your children to base the decisions on their own interests (see **Career Exploration; Interests**).

**Skills and Abilities.** Parents can also help their children in identifying their skills and abilities. Often children can only list a few skills which they think that they have. You can assist your children in recognizing that they have many skills by having them list all their activities for a week. Common work-related skills that are often overlooked are listening, reading, phone skills, and following instructions. In addition, you may want to help your children determine skills they want to enhance. It is productive to provide opportunities for children to experiment with new skills by encouraging a wide range of activities, such as hobbies, extracurricular organizations, voluntary and part-time work, and traveling (see **Abilities; Skills**).

Parents need to be sensitive to the impact they have on children's perceptions of their abilities. Research indicates that often there are differences between the perception of males and females concerning their abilities to perform certain tasks (Lent & Hackett, 1987). For example, many females perceive that they are weak in mathematics, while in fact some of them are proficient in solving mathematical problems but don't perceive themselves as being capable because of the sex-role stereotyping. This perception of low math ability will often keep female students from taking higher level math courses, which impacts on their ability to enter the higher salaried positions of the technical fields. The early messages that children hear at home have an influence on the careers they will enter and you may want to examine the opportunities you are providing for your child to gain experience and skills in nontraditional areas. Parental comments have an impact, so stress what your children are doing well rather than focusing on their shortcomings (see **Self-Efficacy; Sex-Role Stereotyping; Shyness**).

**Values.** Values are internal beliefs or principles that strongly influence our behavior. People often don't examine their values when they are making career decisions, but such examination is critical to effective career planning. Children need to know what they consider worthwhile, important, or meaningful when selecting a career. However, when you discuss values with your child, be aware of the potential for conflict. Sometimes it is very difficult for parents to accept that their children have different values. If there is the potential for disagreement between you and your children, then you may want them to explore their values with their school counselor or some other helping professional. The important thing is that your children understand what is of value to them and they need to examine their priorities in such areas as achievement, security, income, independence, excitement, family issues, and leisure activities. It is also important for you to examine your own values in these areas and analyze your impact on your children's freedom to consider their career options. For example, some parents place a very high value on achievement and their children feel that they must enter a career with the necessary prestige to please their parents. Children who select a career based on their parents' value systems and not their own will frequently experience difficulties (see **Work Values**).

**Decision Making.** All of us will make many career-related decisions and the effectiveness of those decisions depends on our decision-making skills. Decision-making skills should be learned and practiced before your child is faced with a major life decision. You can help your children to learn the steps of good decision making by having them use these steps with some of their everyday decisions, e.g., whether to buy an outfit, where to go for dinner. The first step in effective decision making is to determine what the difficulty is or what decision needs to be made, which is followed by gathering information on that topic. After gathering the information, the third step is evaluating it. Having your children list the positive and negative aspects of the alternatives they are presently considering will help them use this technique in the future. The fourth step is making and implementing the decision. As parents, we often are afraid our children will make the wrong decision, so we decide for them. However, if children are going to learn to make good career decisions they need to have experience in making decisions (see **Decision Making**).

One of the steps in effective decision making is gathering information, and children need to gather information about the world of work in order to make good career decisions. Your public library is one of the best resources for career information. A librarian can help your child find information on virtually any career that is being considered. A useful book that includes information on a variety of careers is the *Occupational Outlook Handbook* by the U.S. Department of Labor.

Many schools and libraries now have computers which have career exploration and information programs. These computerized career information systems can provide a wealth of information and, if they are available in your community, your children should be encouraged to use them (see **Computer-Assisted Career Guidance Systems**).

Your child can also gain valuable information by interviewing or talking to your friends and acquaintances who are working in areas related to your child's interests. An extraordinary learning experience can occur when your child spends time at a work site observing the actual duties and procedures involved in an occupation (Mangum, Gale, Olsen, Peterson & Thorum, 1977) (see **Information Interviewing**).

In conclusion, most of our children, both male and female, will work for most of their lives, so it's important that we help them in planning their careers. However, this assistance involves communicating with your child about career issues rather than gathering the information yourself and making the decision for your child. We need to provide opportunities for our children to learn about themselves and the world of work, but understand that the ultimate responsibility for their careers rests with them.

*See also* Abilities; Career Choices: Youth; Career Counseling; Career Exploration; Computer-Assisted Career Guidance System; Decision Making; Information Interviewing; Interests; Self-Efficacy; Sex-Role Stereotyping; Shyness; Skills; Vocational Choice: John Holland's Theory; Work Values.

## Bibliography

Harrington, T.F., & O'Shea, A.J. (1984). *Guide for occupational exploration.* Circle Pines, MN: American Guidance Service.

Hummel, D.L., & McDaniels, C. (1979). *How to help your child plan a career.* Washington, DC: Acropolis. A practical and creative manual for parents to use in assisting their children in planning their careers.

Lent, R.W., & Hackett, G. (1987). Career self-efficacy: Empirical status and future directions. *Journal of Vocational Behavior,* 30: 347–82.

Mangum, G.L., Gale, G.D., Olsen, M.L., Peterson, E., & Thorum, A.R. (1977). *Your child's career.* Salt Lake City, UT: Olympus Publishing Co. Provides parents with information concerning their children's career development and methods for helping children learn about the world of work.

Otto, L.B. (1984). *How to help your child choose a career.* New York: M. Evans and Company. Discusses methods for parents to assist their children in career decision making, including sample exercises and worksheets.

Schulenberg, J.E., Vondracek, F.W., & Crouter, A.C. (1984). The influence of the family on vocational development. *Journal of Marriage and the Family,* 10: 129–43.

U.S. Department of Labor (1990). *Occupational outlook handbook.* 1990–1991 ed. Washington DC: U.S. Government Printing Office.

—SUSAN C. WHISTON

## PARENTAL LEAVE

Parental leave is a leave of absence taken by mothers and fathers to care for their newly born or newly adopted child.

Today 58.5% of women with children under six years of age and 53.5% of women with children one and under are in the labor force (Hayghe, March, 1990). Ten years ago just 39.2% of women with children one and under worked. Over 56% of today's families consist of dual-earning couples. Only 18.9% of all families consist of the head of the house as the sole breadwinner.

In light of these changes, issues such as child care and parental leave have received increasing attention; legislators and corporate leaders alike are discussing and beginning to take action in developing programs and policies that help parents balance their responsibilities at home and at work. Employees, especially those in their childbearing years, should be aware of their employers' parental leave policies as well as current legislation.

The objectives of this article are to describe the different components of a parental leave, explain the current state legislation and the most recently proposed federal legislation, and suggest ways for individuals—both managers and leavetakers—to successfully arrange and manage parental leaves.

### Components of a Parental Leave

A typical leave policy usually consists of several types of leave: disability leave, parental leave (or family leave), and sometimes a limited part-time return to work. These first two terms are often used interchangeably, but their distinctions should be clear.

*Disability leave* is a leave taken by women for the period of time that they are medically disabled due to pregnancy. This typically begins up to four weeks before the delivery date, and lasts for six weeks after delivery (eight weeks for a caesarean section). The length of disability is subject to the doctor's discretion, and it will also vary depending upon the nature of the pregnancy and the woman's job. Only a pregnant woman can take a disability leave, since only she can be technically "disabled" by pregnancy.

*Parental leave* is taken by parents to care for their newly born or adopted child. Maternity leave is the same as a parental leave but applies to the mother only. Natural mothers take parental or maternity leave after their disability leave. A family leave may be taken by a male or female employee to care for a newly born or adopted child, or to care for an ill family member or an elderly relative. Both family and parental leaves are usually unpaid.

A *limited part-time return to work* is an interim period during which a new parent works part-time to adjust to the dual responsibilities of home and work.

Ideally, a parental leave policy will include the following options: disability leave with full or partial salary reimbursement; additional unpaid parental, maternity, or family leave for one to six months (in some companies it may be for a full year); a transition period of part-time work for one month to one year for returning leavetakers; and reinstatement to the same or comparable position at the same salary.

## Legislation

The United States is the only industrialized country (besides South Africa) that does not have a federally mandated family leave policy. Bills have been submitted in Congress for the past few years but they have not been passed.

The only federal legislation related to parental leave is the 1978 Pregnancy Discrimination Act. The Act requires that companies with a short-term disability policy (not all companies have one) treat pregnancy like any other disability. This means that if a company has a short-term disability policy, it must consider pregnancy a disability and grant pregnant employees the same rights and benefits given to other employees on short-term disability.

In 1990, the Family and Medical Leave Act (FMLA) was passed by both houses, but was vetoed by President Bush. The FMLA mandated that companies with 50 or more employees provide a minimum of 12 weeks annual leave-of-absence to employees to care for newly born or adopted children or to care for members of their immediate family who become sick. In addition, the Act stated that the jobs of workers who take up to four months of annual sick leave would be guaranteed. Supporters of the FMLA plan to propose similar legislation each year until it is passed.

Because of the lack of responsiveness to this issue on the part of the federal government, much of the progress made has been at the state level. Twenty-seven states and Puerto Rico currently have family or maternity leave legislation, (asterisk denotes that law applies to public employees only): California, Connecticut, Delaware*, Illinois, Iowa, Kansas, Kentucky, Louisiana, Maine, Maryland*, Massachusetts*, Minnesota, Missouri*, Montana, Nevada, New Hampshire, New Jersey, North Dakota*, Oklahoma*, Oregon, Puerto Rico, Rhode Island, South Carolina, Tennessee,Vermont, Washington, West Virginia*, and Wisconsin.

## Application

Managers and leavetakers need to approach parental leave as a business issue and not as a personal problem. The employee taking leave is a valuable business resource. In order to ensure the continued productivity of the employee, both the manager and the leavetaker must work together so that each party understands the leave arrangements, the work will continue smoothly while the employee is on leave, and the transition back into the workplace can be made smoothly. Below are suggested ways managers and leavetakers can best manage a leave.

### Managers

1. When an employee comes to tell you that he or she is planning to take a parental leave, convey a positive attitude. Offer to assist the employee in her or his planning and encourage the employee to plan to return to the company.

2. Make sure you are fully aware of the disability and parental leave policy. Speak with your human resources representative about the latitude of the policy and the arrangements other managers have made with their subordinates.

3. During the first meeting with the employee, discuss the elements of the policy, salary, benefits, and any other ramifications of taking a leave such as the effect on seniority, profit sharing, or performance review. Explore the employee's intentions: On what date do they plan on leaving? Do they know how long a leave they will take? At this time you may want to suggest that the employee return on a part-time basis, which will ease the transition period.

4. At least three months before departure, discuss how ongoing work is to be handled. The employee knows his or her work best and should offer suggestions as to how the responsibilities can best be divided. The manager should assess the workload and set priorities. Work may be managed by hiring a temporary replacement from within or outside of the company, or rerouting work to existing staff. Discuss the sort of training that will be required for those covering the employee's work and arrange to have those individuals begin taking over tasks while the employee is still in the workplace. Such overlap will allow for a smoother transition of the work and will decrease the likelihood that the employee will be interrupted while at home.

5. Before the employee leaves, make sure that all involved parties are aware of their responsibilities. Confirm with the employee the total length of leave that is planned and whether his or her job will be held open. Determine what other arrangements need to be made regarding the employee's return to work.

**Leavetakers**

1. Find out what the disability and parental leave policies are at your company. The policy may be under "maternity leave" or "short-term disability" in the policy manual. Clarify the provisions of the policy as well as your responsibilities and those of the human resources department and your supervisor. At the end of your information-gathering process you should know whether you will be paid during the disability period, how long a leave you can take, whether benefits are continued, how to get your child on your health insurance policy at work, what programs your company offers new parents (such as child-care assistance), and what forms or procedures must be completed at certain points throughout the process.

2. Your supervisor should be the first person to learn that you are planning a parental leave. When arranging your leave with your supervisor, approach the situation as an order of business. If you are a valuable employee, the company should encourage your return and help to facilitate an easy leave. Be straightforward about your expectations of the leave; determine the issues on which you will compromise and those on which you will not. Be open with your supervisor about your intentions regarding return to work, as well as the length of leave you are planning and when leave will begin. If you are unsure of your plans at this time, discuss some ideas and explain that you would like to re-evaluate your decision as your last day comes closer.

3. Write out your job responsibilities and divide them into manageable components. Offer suggestions as to how your work could best be completed, and agree to train any replacements. It may be helpful to write out specific details of each task so that others in the office will not disturb you while you are on leave.

4. Discuss whether you plan on doing any work at home during the leave and whether you want people to call you. You might suggest that you will call in once a week at a predetermined time to answer questions. You are entitled to set parameters. Remember that you are taking this time off to be with your child. Of course you may still be helpful to those in the office, but you should not feel obliged to be spending all of your time on the phone with coworkers and subordinates.

5. Clarify the status of your position when you return. Will it be exactly the same? Will you have to wait and see, and possibly take a comparable job in another area? You may want to offer to come back sooner if you can do so on a part-time schedule for a while. If you foresee that there may be a problem with the nature of your job when you return, discuss possible solutions. For example, if you are a sales representative with a very large territory, you may need to discuss a smaller territory or consider sharing the current territory with a coworker. If you travel a lot on business, you may want to discuss the maximum number of overnight trips you will have to take in a month. It is important to realize that a child brings many things to one's life, including unpredictability. Be ready to be flexible and to evaluate and periodically re-evaluate your priorities.

6. Once you and your supervisor agree on the terms surrounding your leave, put the agreement in writing. This can be especially important if you find yourself with a new, less accommodating supervisor in the future.

## Conclusion

The changing demographics and legislation in this country will continue to make parental leaves common occurrences in companies. In the future more and more men will also take advantage of this benefit. It is in the best interest of employers, parents, and their children that parental leave be seen as a brief and manageable interruption in one's career.

*See also* Child Care; Dual-Career Families; Elder Care; Job Sharing; Part-Time Work; Sequencing: A Career and Traditional Mothering; Working Family Issues.

## Bibliography

Catalyst. (1988). *The corporate guide to parental leaves.* New York: Catalyst. A how-to guide for human resources managers that explains how to put together a comprehensive parental leave policy and offers examples from actual corporate policies.
Hayghe, H.V. (March, 1990). Family members in the work force. *Monthly Labor Review,* 113, 14–19.
Marzollo, Jean. (1989). *Your maternity leave: How to work, have a baby, and go back to work without getting lost, trapped, or sandbagged along the way.* New York: Poseidon Press. This book is organized around the three parts of a parental leave: before the baby comes, during maternity leave, and return to work. The author discusses such topics as negotiating a leave, treasuring your baby, finding child care, and easing the return to work.
McCulloch, K. J. (1990, Summer). State family leave laws and the legal questions they raise. *Employment Relations Today,* 103–9.
Nobile, R. J. (1990). Leaving No Doubt About Employee Leaves. *Personnel,* May, 54–60.
Planning for Parental Leaves. (1988, March/April). *Executive Female:* 9.

—STACEY J. POMERANTZ

## PART-TIME WORK

Since what constitutes a "full time" work schedule varies according to the job or place of work, "part time" is given the precise statistical definition of less than 35 weekly work hours. In fact, about 50% of part-time workers are employed between 15 and 29 hours a week. Part-time workers are further differentiated as voluntary part-timers, who work part time by choice, and involuntary or economic part-timers, who prefer to work full time but only have part-time jobs because of employment conditions beyond their control. Such employment conditions include slack work or inability to find a full-time job.

There were about 20 million part-time workers in 1989. They accounted for about one-fifth of all nonagricultural employment. Three-fourths of these workers work part time by choice, a proportion that has remained fairly constant over time. Although between 1980 and 1988 the number of part-time jobs increased more than the rise in the total labor force (21% v. 14%), the rise was largely due to an increase in involuntary rather than voluntary part-time work.

## Relationship to Work

Part-time work is one of several kinds of flexible work schedules that accommodate employer or employee interests (see **Flextime; Job Sharing**). It can further be described according to the occupations where part-time work is common, in terms of the varieties of part-time work structures and benefits which reflect the conditions surrounding such work, or in terms of the kinds of persons who work part time. In each case, one must think not only about what is, but also what could be, for the potential value of part-time work is far greater than its present structures provide. Moreover, understanding the relationship of reduced hours to the way work is organized provides a context for thinking about whether part-time work would be a feasible work schedule for a specific job.

**Occupations and Part-time Work.** At present, part-time work is concentrated in a few occupations. About three-fifths of part-time workers are located in sales, clerical, or service jobs; many fewer do skilled craft or managerial or professional work. But this need not be so. There are examples of highly successful part-time work arrangements throughout the occupational spectrum, including managerial and executive positions.

**Part-time Work Structures.** Part-time work exists in several forms. *Job sharing* involves two individuals sharing the responsibilities of an equivalent full-time position. *Job pairing* is similar except that each part-time worker is responsible for the whole job. *Work sharing* lessens the impact of a temporary production retrenchment by rotating the number of hours or days worked with periods of nonemployment. In a number of states, legislation combines work sharing with partial unemployment insurance benefits so that income loss is minimized while labor market attachment is retained. These programs provide silent testimony to the broad potential application of part-time work. Lastly, *phased retirement,* provided by national legislation in Sweden, but available in the U.S. only through company programs, gradually reduces hours in a regular job for persons near retirement. Such programs ease this transition for an employee while extending the use of skills which benefit the employer.

**Benefits and Part-time Work.** Old concept part-time jobs are often temporary, low status, and low pay, with few fringe benefits. They do not allow an individual to advance over time in status or pay. New concept part-time work provides permanent attachment to a job and includes a possibility of career advancement. Pro-rated earnings and at least some fringe benefits are included in the income package. Obviously, the new type is a more attractive kind of work for employees. It also results in benefits for employers, such as lower absenteeism and turnover and higher levels of motivation and performance.

**Composition of the Part-time Workforce.** Two-thirds of all part-time workers are women. More than one-fourth of all employed women work reduced hours (10% of men do), and they do so mostly by choice because such a schedule enables them to combine duties of caring for children, home, and frail elders while retaining labor market attachment and work skills in paid work. Although their part-time earnings are usually insufficient to support a family as a single parent, women do help to cover family expenses or maintain a customary standard of living when another family earner is present. For older workers (18% of part-time workers are age 55 and older), part-time work relieves work stress and protects health while providing for an income supplement and a productive contribution to society. For youth, part-time work often helps to pay for education even while young people are in school. Twenty-one percent of part-time workers are ages 16 to 19. Two-thirds of employed teenagers work part time. Most working-age men are employed full time, but some of them also reduce work hours for reasons of family or education or to change career directions or pursue nonwork interests.

## Application

Understanding why people choose to work part time can help in making your own decision about whether voluntarily working reduced hours suits your needs. You must first think through what your goals are. Is a full-time income essential? Is strong attachment to a particular workplace a priority? If so, you may need to work full time. On the other hand, are you interested in acquiring additional training or education? Do you want to minimize stress and lead a tranquil, healthful life? Do you wish to pursue vocational or non work-related interests? If these are immediate rather than long-term goals, then you may prefer part-time to full-time work.

You must also know the customs surrounding the jobs that you seek, including whether part-time work is a regular option and what are its benefits and costs for the particular kind of work you seek. Answers to these questions will tell you what alternatives are realistic ones and how much you sacrifice in earnings and benefits in order to achieve work flexibility. On the basis of your judgment, you may even decide to reject a wage or salaried job and embark on a part-time self-employed venture.

If the part-time hours that you want are not a customary alternative in your work, you may want to negotiate with a potential employer before you accept the job. Alternatively, you may want first to build up a track record as a valuable full-time worker before asking for special consideration. Making this decision will involve assessing your strengths in relation to an employer's needs and evaluating whether an employer is flexible in thinking about ways to maximize job productivity. If the employer agrees to your request for reduced work hours it could involve you in finding your own partner for a job sharing situation or redesigning your job to accommodate the reduced hour schedule you want to work.

Each of the above alternatives could be "the best case" under particular conditions. There is no preconceived standard that works well for all persons or work situations. The goal is to assess well your own needs in relation to the realistic options that might be available to you in the workplace.

My own hope is that employers will be increasingly convinced that new concept part-time work is not only necessary and better for some workers at certain times in their work lives, but that such arrangements could also benefit them by reducing absenteeism, training costs, and labor turnover, and increasing production flexibility, productivity, and work commitment. But this will not happen without the support of social policy and the demands of such groups as women, elders, and others for whom part-time work can be particularly beneficial. We need both research and the cooperation of involved parties in designing good policies. If successful, the hopes embodied in part-time benefits will more than outweigh the costs or possible perils, and individuals, employers, and society will all gain.

*See also* Elder Care; Flextime; Job Sharing; Temporary Employment; Women in the Workforce.

## Bibliography

Belous, R. S. (1989). *The contingent economy: The growth of the temporary, part-time and subcontracted workforce.* Washington, DC: The National Planning Association. A review and analysis of company policy with respect to temporary and contingent workforce, including part-time workers.

Kahne, H. (1985; Paper 1987). *Reconceiving part-time work. New perspectives for older workers and women.* Totowa, N.J.: Rowman and Allanheld. An overview of prevailing attitudes and experience of part-time work, including policy recommendations. Focus on older workers, women, and new concept part-time work.

Lundy, K., & Warme, B. (Eds.) (in press). *Working part-time: Risks and opportunities.* New York: Praeger. A series of papers by a variety of experts describing positive and negative aspects of part-time work.

Tilly, Chris. (Fall, 1990). *Short hours, short shift: Causes and consequences of growing part-time work.* Washington, DC: Economic Policy Institute. An up-to-date study of the experience of part-time work in the U.S.

—HILDA KAHNE

# PAY

Pay consists of the total of direct cash payments received by an employee in exchange for work. Excluded from employee pay are employee benefits (such as income protection, health insurance coverage, and time off with pay) and "psychic pay" (such as positive performance feedback and job satisfaction). Employee pay, employee benefits, and psychic pay (see **Benefits; Job Satisfaction**) make up the total compensation received by the employee, and many companies now develop total compensation packages to attract, retain, and motivate their employees.

## Relationship to Work

Pay levels are set by an organization in accord with the value of the work accomplished by the employee to the organization. Most organizations try to tie some portion of pay directly to the performance level of the employee. The typical organization develops pay programs in accord with four ideas of equity, (comparability or fairness): external equity, internal equity, individual equity, and process equity.

**External Equity.** Organizations compete with each other to attract and keep good employees. Much of this competition is centered on pay levels, since it is the one measure of job attractiveness which can be easily compared across organizations. To assure their pay is competitive, companies buy or conduct surveys of salary levels in equivalent organizations. Most companies try to keep even with the market, while some peg their salary levels above average market levels.

**Internal Equity.** While competitive pay levels are the most important factor for most companies when they set pay levels for a job, the comparison of pay levels of different jobs within the organization is an important factor too. Most companies use a process called job evaluation for this internal comparison. A set of 3 to 30 common job characteristics is chosen (most relate to effort, skill, responsibility, and working conditions) and all jobs are rated on each characteristic. Job evaluation scores are used along with salary survey data to construct a salary structure. This salary structure consists of a number of salary grades, each with a minimum, midpoint, and maximum. The midpoint represents the salary an average job in the grade is worth in the marketplace. Employees typically begin near the minimum and work up to the midpoint as they gain job proficiency (one to three years). Movement beyond the midpoint is typically slower, and depends on performance and seniority.

**Individual Equity.** Most companies want to reward employees with high performance. A whole set of programs has been developed to tie pay levels to performance. The most typical is the merit increase, when an employee receives a raise to base pay; the size of the increase is a function of performance level.

In the last several years most companies (and some public employers) have implemented programs where incentive, or performance-related pay is not added to base pay on a permanent basis, but must be re-earned each year. Typical forms include lump-sum bonuses (any performance-related pay is given to the employee in a single bonus check), profit-sharing (some percentage of company profits are distributed to employees, typically in accord with salary level), and gainsharing (as work groups increase productivity, part of the gain is shared with the groups responsible).

**Process Equity.** Until the recent past most pay-setting process in companies were carried on by compensation specialists and management. Few employees knew much about the pay structure, their own salary potential, or the processes used to determine pay. In some companies, discussion of pay with other employees was grounds for dismissal. (In contrast, pay in government organizations has always been open, frequently by law. Likewise, when pay is set through negotiation with a union, the system is communicated to employees by union officials.)

Many companies now communicate pay information to employees regularly, although individual pay levels are still considered private information. In addition, an increasing number of companies involve employees in all stages of the pay-setting process, including job evaluation and the design of incentive pay programs.

## Application

To maximize your pay, experience and research suggest these guidelines:

1. Widen the choice of occupations open to you. Remember that organizations value jobs partly on the basis of skills required. Education is increasingly a good investment.
2. Choose the right occupation from among those open to you. Many occupations which require very similar qualifications have different pay levels (see **Career Counseling; Choosing an Occupation**). Adult education teachers and corporate trainers have very similar skills; corporate trainers, however, usually get higher salaries.
3. Choose to work for an organization in the right industry. In general, large organizations pay more than smaller ones, companies in some industries pay more than others (oil companies pay more than retailers, even for secretaries), and unionized companies pay more than nonunion companies. For lower level jobs, government pays more, at middle and upper levels private organizations pay more. Companies with higher pay levels tend to have better benefits packages, so you can expect good benefits to go along with good pay.
4. Choose an organization that discusses pay programs with employees. It is legitimate to raise this issue in final employment interviews. If the organization communicates pay programs to employees, and if it involves employees in the development of pay programs, you will have a better idea of actions you can take to increase your pay. In addition, you are likely to be much more satisfied with your pay and your job when you understand how pay is determined.
5. Choose an organization which has performance-related pay *and* a good performance appraisal program. If both of these are present, you should have the opportunity to shape your performance so that you will get the maximum raises possible. Even if your organization does not have a good performance appraisal system it is worthwhile discussing performance expectations with your manager. Many performance problems occur because the employee does not know what the expectations are.
6. Be realistic in your pay expectations. Keep track of pay levels for jobs similar to yours through employment advertising. Most importantly, recognize that pay is not the only reward for a job. For many employees the psychic pay is just as important to job satisfaction as actual cash payments received.

*See also* Benefits; Career Counseling; Choosing a Career; Job Interviewing; Job Satisfaction; Negotiating; Performance Appraisal; Promotion/Raise.

## Bibliography

Berger, L. (ed.) (1991). *Handbook of compensation*. Philadelphia: MLR Publishing Company. One of the standard reference books covering compensation topics. While written for practicing compensation practitioners, most of the articles are readily understandable by nonspecialists.

Fay, C. H., & Beatty, R.W. (1988). *Compensation sourcebook.* Boston: Human Resource Development Press. Consists of readings taken from specialist journals and the popular press which cover all areas of compensation and benefits. There is an emphasis on why organizations set up compensation practices as they do, and several forecasts of future compensation practices.

Gomez-Mejia, L. (ed.) (1988). *Compensation and benefits, Volume III of handbook of human resource management.* Washington, DC: Bureau of National Affairs/American Society for Personnel Administration.

Wallace, M. J., Jr., & Fay, C.H. (1982; 2nd ed., 1988) *Compensation: Theory and practice.* Boston: Kent. This textbook provides a unified approach to the whole subject of compensation, including what organizations attempt to achieve with compensation programs and the practices they use to achieve their aims.

—CHARLES H. FAY

# PERFECTIONISM: OVERCOMING

Perfectionism is a style of thinking about oneself that plays a major role in a wide variety of psychological, physical, and occupation problems. It refers to the tendency to set excessively high standards for oneself which are accompanied by overly critical self-evaluations. Setting very high standards for oneself, although an important component of perfectionism, does not, by itself, constitute perfectionism. In fact, setting high standards can be healthy, reflecting competence and success. When these high standards exist in someone who will tolerate nothing but absolute perfection, however, a host of unfortunate things happens. Minor mistakes in an otherwise adequate performance result in the perception that one's standards have not been met, and by implication, that the performance was a failure. This type of self-evaluation process can result in striving for accomplishment because of a fear of making mistakes (a negative motivation), rather than a striving to produce something of quality (a positive motivation). In addition to an excessive concern over mistakes, there are other aspects of this critical self-evaluation style that are a part of perfectionism. One is a sense of doubt about the quality of one's performance. This is a vague sense (independent of the recognition of mistakes) that one's performance is not good enough and therefore that the job is not satisfactorily completed. This experience has been extensively described in the literature on obsessional experiences.

Perfectionistic self-criticism also reflects beliefs about other peoples' expectations and evaluations. Beliefs about what other people expect contrast an individual's own criteria for success. Perfectionists have a tendency to believe that their behavior must be perfect in order to be valued by others. The consequences of not meeting the perceived standards of others is feeling criticized by or at risk for criticism from others. Most prominent in this form of perfectionism are the beliefs one has about parents. Highly perfectionistic individuals perceive their parents as having very high expectations for them and, at the same time, being very critical of their accomplishments. Theorists believe that perfectionism develops out of interactions with perfectionistic and demanding parents (Frost, Marten, Lahart, & Rosenblate, in press). Perfectionistic thinking also can be expressed in the setting of excessively rigid standards for other people. Setting such excessive standards for others can greatly hamper social/interpersonal relationships.

## Relationship to Work

A perfectionistic thinking style can inhibit performance at work in several ways. Because anything less than perfect performance is interpreted as failure, excessive evaluation anxiety often accompanies perfectionism. This may be especially true among perfectionists, whose goal is avoiding criticism from others. As a result, perfectionists tend to avoid tasks on which they may be evaluated. Unfortunately, avoiding tasks prevents learning from mistakes, and for some skills, learning from mistakes is crucial. For instance, learning to write effectively usually means correcting drafts which have been reviewed and critiqued by others. Avoiding this will hamper development as a writer. Frost & Marten (in press) have found the writing of perfectionists to be lower in quality than that of nonperfectionists. Many other occupational skills are learned from experiences which are evaluated by others. These skills may remain underdeveloped in the perfectionist.

For a perfectionist, every new task is viewed as an opportunity to fail rather than an opportunity for achievement. Such an orientation makes the prospect of starting a new project frightening, and perfectionists become apprehensive and fearful about such an enterprise. One way of coping with this apprehension, albeit a temporary one, is to avoid thinking about (and working on) the project. Procrastination can be an effective way of alleviating these feelings until the torment of not completing the project is greater than the torment of working on a potential failure. The unfortunate result is a frantic working pace and, often, a less than desirable outcome (see **Procrastination: Overcoming**).

Other more subtle working patterns may be affected by perfectionism. Because of their excessive self-criticism, perfectionists are not eager to try new and different things. They may turn down opportunities and challenges which could be rewarding but risky. In some occupations, such behavior can stifle advancement.

To avoid mistakes, perfectionists often focus excessively on details of a project. Often this detailed focus prevents them from developing a broader understanding of the project, its implications, and its relation to other related work. This can severely limit one's occupational horizons.

Finally, individuals who demand perfection from themselves and others around them can be problem employees who experience high levels of distress (see Frost, Marten, Lahart, & Rosenblate, in press). On the other hand, perfectionists can be tyrannical employers whose employees never receive the recognition and respect they deserve.

## Application

One way to begin to overcome perfectionism is to change the way in which you approach each new task. When starting a new project ask yourself the following questions.

1. Are you doing this project because you "want to" or because you feel you "should" or "must"? If you are doing it because you feel you should or must, your behavior is negatively motivated and you are probably focused on avoiding mistakes rather than on producing something of quality. To create a positive motivation, concentrate on the reasons for and benefits of doing the task itself, and not on how you will be evaluated for it (see **Rational Thinking**).

2. Can you do this task in a less than perfect way and still feel good about it? People can sometimes learn to overcome perfectionism by consciously scaling back the expectations they have for themselves. Picking a goal which is less than perfect means changing your definition of success, however. You must be willing to honestly say to yourself, "This was a success," despite the fact that there may be flaws in it.

3. Once the task is complete, can you reward yourself for accomplishing the task satisfactorily? Because perfectionists rarely perceive their performance to meet their standards, they frequently complete a task and admonish themselves to work harder and do better next time. Seldom do they take time to savor a success. By rewarding yourself for a satisfactory job, you can begin to develop the positive motivation necessary for true success.

4. Are you telling yourself things that hamper your efforts to change, such as "I'm so stupid," or "I should have known (done) better"? These self-statements are sometimes used by perfectionists to motivate themselves to try harder. As with other perfectionistic work strategies, these are negative motivators which focus on avoiding failure rather than on the intrinsic value of the task (see **Self-Talk**).

5. Does your self-esteem depend on how well you perform on this task? Perfectionists often equate who they are with how well they do. You must separate how you feel about yourself (e.g., how good a person you are) from your performance on any given task. Only then can you begin to be positively motivated to do good work.

*See also* Procrastination: Overcoming; Rational Thinking; Self-Esteem; Self-Talk; Workaholism.

## Bibliography

Burns, D. (1980). *Feeling good: The new mood therapy.* New York: Morrow & Co. Written for the general public, this book is an extensive introduction to cognitive therapy for depression. Much of its content focuses on perfectionism.

Burns, D. (1980, November). The perfectionists script for self-defeat. *Psychology Today*: 34–51. This highly readable introduction to perfectionism describes perfectionistic thinking in some detail. Examples of treatments make this work beneficial to all who are interested in the topic.

Frost, R., & Marten, P. (1990). Perfectionism and evaluative threat. *Cognitive Therapy & Research* 14, 559–72.

Frost, R., Marten, P., Lahart, C., & Rosenblate, R. (1990). The development of perfectionism. *Cognitive Therapy & Research* 14, 449–68.

Pacht, A. (1984). Reflections on perfection. *American Psychologist,* 39: 386–90. Based on his extensive work as a therapist, Ascher Pacht outlines the nature of perfectionism, its development, and the effect it can have on people's lives.

—RANDY O. FROST

## PERFORMANCE APPRAISAL

A performance appraisal is an assessment by an immediate supervisor of an employee's performance for a specified time period. However, this definition is changing to encompass a broader notion of performance management. Performance management emphasizes clarifying expectations with an employee *before* appraising the employee, as well as providing coaching and counseling to achieve expectations. In addition, more recent approaches have emphasized that the "strategic" contributions of human resources be linked to the strategic objectives of the organization, as shown in Figure 1. To ensure this linkage, new sources of information on employee performance are being considered, as well as an expanded pool of potential assessors of performance. These changing concepts of performance appraisal have been driven by global competitiveness concerns.

**Figure 1. Linking Performance Management Systems to Organizational Strategy**

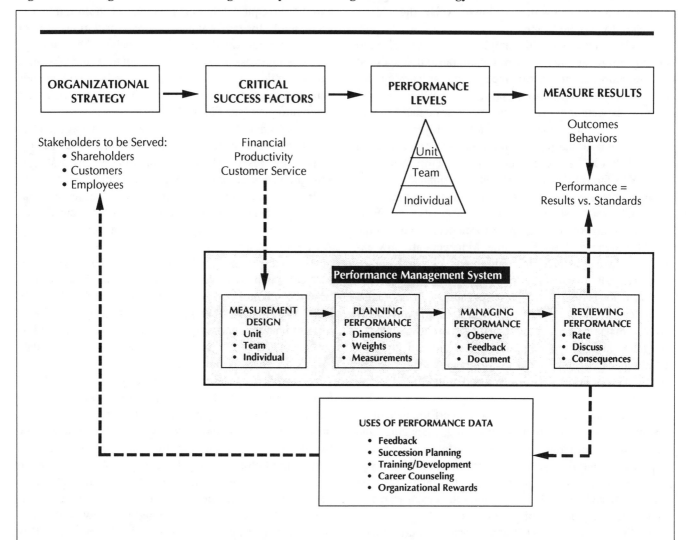

## Relationship to Work

The major components of the human resource function (formerly "personnel") are selection, training and development, and motivation. These components are directed at enhancing an employee's performance. These activities build an organization's human resource capability and are receiving renewed attention because they are designed to enhance employee performance within the context of organizational objectives. Another force driving change in performance appraisals has been litigation, especially allegations of age discrimination. This has led management to redesign performance systems to ensure that the measurement and management of performance are well articulated, and that employees know what is expected in terms of what should be accomplished, how well it should be accomplished, and how important each performance target is relative to others.

## Application

How can you deal more effectively with performance appraisals in your organizational experiences? First, you will find it beneficial to know what is expected of you *before* you are hired, such as the various tasks, duties, and responsibilities, relative importance of each, and, most importantly, how well you are to perform (i.e., the level of performance that meets, exceeds, or falls below expectations). If you have the opportunity to obtain such information before you are hired, use it in making your decision to join the organization. You might also request a copy of the performance appraisal format that will be used in assessing your performance, if not during the interview, at least on your first day at work.

The performance appraisal itself is much like a scorecard. Instructions to rater(s) (usually your boss) are the rules by which the game is played. Make certain you understand how to keep score, who is doing the scoring, and who is to provide you with coaching to explain the rules as you learn to play the game.

Some of the difficulties employees have experienced include not receiving a copy of the appraisal document at the beginning of the performance period, or learning (for the first time) during the appraisal session that they were not meeting expectations. This occurs because managers often "Monday-morning quarterback" an employee's performance, that is, assigning a performance score even though the "rule book" had not been given to the employee.

You should also be aware that performance appraisal is more recently referred to as a "performance management system." The "system" aspect places greater emphasis upon planning and managing performance, so you do the "right things right" the first time. Managers are now expected to work to make every employee succeed by clarifying expectations and providing interim feedback before the appraisal is finalized. The process approximates what a good teacher does: telling students at the beginning of the course what is expected, providing feedback on the student's progress through quizzes, etc., and at the end giving a comprehensive final exam to measure the student's overall performance. Performance appraisal is really not much different.

From the employee's viewpoint, performance management thus has three steps: planning, managing, and reviewing performance. In *planning* performance you and your boss generally discuss the boss's expectations of you during the next performance period. In this phase, the boss tells you what is to be done, how important each aspect is, and the level expected—often referred to as the job dimensions, the dimension weights, and the scale points (or level) of performance expected. The level of performance expected may have numerical (e.g., sales volume, units produced). Or it may have narrative standards; these standards use words to describe expectations, which are often behaviors (e.g., customer service) to articulate what meets, exceeds, or falls below standard. Narratives are also used where expectations are difficult to measure by counting.

*Managing* performance has three steps: observation of performance by someone involved in the final rating, provision of feedback on how well you are doing relative to expectations, and documentation of the observed performance. Observation may consist of an assessment of numbers (e.g., sales made during a performance period) or behaviors (e.g., quality of service a clerk renders guests in a hotel). You should expect feedback to be both positive and negative. Letting you know you are doing well has a very positive motivational force; likewise, learning where you are not doing well can also serve as a motivational force by creating a "positive anxiety" to improve performance. You should not rely on the assumption that "no news is good news." If your boss is not giving you feedback, then perhaps you should request it. It is not reasonable to hold employees accountable for performance where expectations are not clearly communicated, nor is it reasonable where employees do not possess the skills or training to do the job. Once a manager determines that the employee both understands what is expected and can do the job, motivational issues come into play (see Figure 1).

The final step in the performance management is *reviewing* performance. Here someone rates your performance, rewards it, and conducts the final review. Rating is a judgment exercised by a designated individual, generally your supervisor. But rating may also incorporate information from other sources as well (e.g., from peers, customers, or even subordinates if you are in a managerial position). An important question here is who is in the position to observe performance. If your job is rendering customer service, then perhaps your customers should have an input in your evaluation. The word "customer" is defined broadly and may be internal or external to your organization. If you are a manager, perhaps input from those you lead is important. What is critical is the collection of relevant data by those who observe the performance.

*Reviewing* performance generally refers to the formal inspection (your final exam), as opposed to the informal, day-to-day feedback you receive throughout the performance period. You should know that the review is to be based only upon what was done during the designated period, not before or after. Ideally, you should expect no surprises. If the rater has kept you informed throughout the performance period, the process is a review, which means going back over what was planned and how well it was performed. During the review you should receive no new information other than the overall judgment of the rater relative to expectations. At this time career expectations may also be discussed, for instance, future positions for you within the organization.

The reward process can be financial, nonfinancial, or both. Many organizations attempt to differentiate financial incentives based upon how well you have done during the performance period. Currently, organizations are attempting to place more employee compensation "at risk," so that the financial compensation you receive is not simply an entitlement based on longevity but reflects your contributions to the organization. The philosophy is very simple: Those who contribute more should be rewarded more. This issue is often controversial in many organizations because of lack of trust in the accuracy of measurement. Nevertheless, more organizations are moving toward at-risk pay as an incentive to motivate productivity. Don't expect compensation to be discussed during the review; the general practice is that it follows the review by a week to 30 days in a separate discussion.

*See also* Bosses: Managing Relationships with Superiors; Job Description; Job Satisfaction; Pay; Promotion/Raise.

## Bibliography

Beatty, R. W. (1989). Competitive human resource advantage through strategic performance management. *Human Resource Planning Journal,* 12: 3. This article attempts to demonstrate the linkage of performance planning to strategic performance for all levels within the organization. It demonstrates alternative performance appraisal formats and some of the new paradigms for performance management.

Bernardin, H. J., & Beatty, R. W. (1984). *Performance appraisal: Assessing human behavior at work.* Boston: Kent/Wadsworth.

Bernardin, H. J., & Beatty, R. W. (1987, Summer). Can subordinate appraisals enhance managerial productivity? *Sloan Management Review.* This article reviews the many organizations which are using subordinate appraisals and discusses the successes and failures of subordinate appraisals as well as the many purposes for which subordinate appraisals are used.

Carroll, S. J., & Schneier, C. E. (1982). *Performance appraisal and review systems.* Glenview, IL: Scott Foresman.

—RICHARD W. BEATTY

# POST HIGH SCHOOL TRAINING

Post high school training programs help non-college bound students prepare for work. Although there has been a dramatic growth of college graduates during this decade, at least 75% of our students in public schools are unlikely to obtain a baccalaureate degree (Parnell, 1985). This "neglected majority" is neither prepared for college nor the workforce. Now, business and industry, feeling the effects of a shortage of trainable workers, are becoming involved in school systems and legislative processes in an attempt to upgrade the skills of the existing workforce and prepare new workers for a constantly changing economy. Post high school training programs offer excellent options for high school students and are a necessity for business and industry as they continue to compete in world markets.

Five major programs available for high school graduates are described here.

1. Technical Preparatory (Tech Prep)—a program beginning in high school which offers a planned curriculum in an area of interest to the student that will prepare him or her for a two-year community or technical college. The program allows students to enroll in classes in both the local school system and a community/technical college. Tech Prep reduces the amount of remedial work for students as they enter the community/technical college since they have been prepared at the high school level prior to admission. It gives the student with little or no direction focus and guidance. For example, a student would choose during high school an interest in either health/sciences, engineering, or business. Their high school curriculum would offer academic courses to satisfy the prerequisites for admission at the community/technical school and vocational courses in the area of interest to the students. Tech Prep programs make the connection for many students from school to the workforce and are up to date with the type of training business and industry are seeking.

2. The Ford Asset Program (Automotive Student Service Educational Training) is a joint effort of three organizations: a community/technical college, the Ford Motor Company, and the Ford and Lincoln-Mercury dealerships. It is a two year automotive program designed to upgrade the technical competence and professional level of the incoming dealership technician. The curriculum is designed by the automotive company and the community/technical college. The program incorporates classroom studies as well as cooperative work experience at a sponsoring dealership. Instructors at the community/technical college receive training by the automotive company. Since the students are paid for the time they are working at the dealership, it is a cost-effective training program. Job placement at the cooperative education dealership upon the completion of the program is likely.

3. Apprenticeship programs are voluntary systems of employee training combining on the job training with technical instruction. Programs can be either state, local, or privately operated. A person learning a trade, an apprentice, is taught by a skilled worker, a journeyman. Related technical instruction is often provided by the employer or community/technical college. Apprenticeship programs are primarily offered in areas of building and construction trades, industrial trades, service trades, and public employment trades. An apprentice is paid at approximately half the journeyman rate but never below the minimum wage rates, and rates increase as the apprentice progresses through the program.

4. The community/technical college system offers several training programs. Associate degree programs, certificates and diplomas can be obtained depending on the type of program. Focused Industrial Training is offered in some states through the community college system to provide training services to existing industries. It provides employees the opportunity to upgrade their skill level as the particular industry responds to technological changes.

5. The military operates one of the largest programs available anywhere. Among the five Armed Forces branches, 300 technical training schools are offered that include more than 10,000 separate courses of instruction. A necessary requirement for students interested in the military is to take

the *Armed Services Vocational Aptitude Battery* (ASVAB) test. The test is offered annually at many high schools and also through the local military recruitment offices. It is used by the military for placement into specific occupations in the military. High school graduates may qualify to train for occupations such as carpenters, tank drivers, mechanics, air traffic controllers, and electronic technicians. Most training courses take two to four months. Training courses for many technical specialties may take six to twelve months. The *Military Career Guide* (U.S. Department of Defense, 1989) lists all military occupations, which branch it is available in, and the requirements. Besides training, the military offers various educational benefits including college tuition reimbursement. While the military is not for everyone, students may want to consider this path for further training and education.

## Relationship to Work

There is a definite connection between economic development and a trained workforce. New industry moves into areas that have the most educated workforce the jobs of today and tomorrow demand. (Governor's Commission on Workforce Preparedness, 1990). Post high school training programs are designed to link students' skills to jobs and careers.

1. What are these skills? The new basics include skills in interpersonal communications, team building, problem solving, creative thinking, and technical expertise. Preparation in high school that continues in post high school training programs must be relevant to the constantly changing economy and have the flexibility to respond to fluctuating markets.
2. Where will students learn these skills? Complex and high tech machines and equipment require smarter workers, not only to operate them, but to keep them running efficiently and, if necessary, re-tool them for new applications. To be effective, programs need to start in high school by giving students the academics, skill development, work ethics, and career guidance relevant to the labor market. A smooth transition from high school curriculums to various post high school training programs and community/technical colleges is needed that will match the demands of business and industry with the interests and aptitudes of students.

## Application

To determine if a post high school training program is for you and which particular one, consider the following:

1. Think about your interests, skills, abilities, aptitudes, temperament, and values. Discuss these with your school counselor or private career counselor in your community. Interest inventories and aptitude tests may assist you also.
2. Explore occupations in the library or school career center. Reference books such as the *Dictionary of Occupational Titles, Occupational Outlook Handbook,* and the *Encyclopedia of Careers and Vocational Guidance* can help you find information such as salary, job outlook, work description, related careers, advancement opportunities, etc. The *Guide for Occupational Exploration* contains information on apprenticeships (see the article **Occupational Information** for more on these and other reference books.).
3. Consider the amount of education and training required for the occupations which interest you. Compare the costs of training programs with your financial resources. Look for other cost factors such as tools, uniforms, safety equipment, books, and supplies.
4. Ask about the job placement rate of the program completers. Try to contact people who have finished programs of interest to you for further information and their assessment and satisfaction with the training they received.
5. Consider a training program leading to an occupation that is nontraditional for your sex. This is particularly true for women. Women in nontra-ditional fields, like construction and law enforcement, *earn 20 to 30% more* than women in traditional fields. Today, men work as dental assistants, secretaries, and nurses. The point is, choose an occupation that suits your needs, interests, and abilities.

*See also* Career Choices: Youth; Career Counseling; Career Exploration; Choosing an Occupation; Nontraditional Job for One's Sex; Occupational Information.

## Bibliography

Basch, R. (1990). *Technical, trade and business school data handbook*. Concord, MA: Orchard House. A complete and up to date directory of approximately 3,000 schools and community colleges, both public and private. The book is published by region or your can get it with the whole nation listed.

Carlson, C. (1990). Beyond high school: The transition to work. *Focus*, 25, whole issue. Educational Testing Service.

Chronical Guidance Publications (1990a). *Two year college data book*. Moravia, New York: Author Lists 984 occupational-career programs offered at two year colleges. Data on nondegree awards, degrees, accreditation, enrollment, admissions, costs, and financial aid for 2,325 schools.

Chronical Guidance Publications (1990b). *Vocational school manual.* Moravia, New York: Author Lists 4,469 vocational schools, 846 programs of study, admissions, costs, enrollment, government job training aid, financial aid, and student services.

Daggett, W. (1990). How can we help our students cope? *North Carolina Education*, 21, 2–9.

Governors' Commission on Workforce Preparedness. (November, 1990). *The skills crisis in the workplace: A strategic response for economic development.* Raleigh, North Carolina: Author.

Parnell, D. (1985). *The neglected majority.* Washington, DC: Community College Press.

U.S. Department of Defense. (1989). *Military career guide.* Washington, DC: Author. A comprehensive source of information on enlisted and officer military occupations. Descriptions are given for 205 military occupations, including work descriptions, training and environment, and similar civilian occupations.

—BARBARA M. SEEGER

# POSTURE AND BODY MECHANICS

Many work-related activities can contribute to the development of neck and back problems by increasing the pressure on the discs and joints of the spine. These include long periods of sitting or standing, frequent bending and twisting, and repeated heavy lifting. Proper posture involves maintaining the natural, comfortable position of the spine in sitting or standing. Good body mechanics are patterns of movement which likewise reduce the stress on the discs and joints of the spine. This article will discuss ways in which we can protect our spines while performing job-related activities.

## The Neutral Position

Every part in the body has a "range-of-motion" through which it can move. The healthy neck, for example, can bend forward (flex) so that a person can look toward the floor, and extend to a position in which the person is looking straight up. Yet holding the neck in either a fully flexed or fully extended position for more than a few seconds is uncomfortable for nearly everyone. A more comfortable position is one in which the neck is near the middle of its range-of-motion. In a similar way, the neutral position of the low back is one in which the back is neither bent forward (as in touching the floor) or arched backwards to the end of its range, but in a comfortable position in mid-range. Long periods of deviation from the neutral position tend to increase the probability of neck and back problems. To develop a strategy to keep our spines healthy, we need to examine what factors repeatedly bring us out of our neutral positions and thereby increase the stress on our spines.

## Posture and Your Eyes

Your body follows your head and eyes. To preserve proper posture, the target of your vision must be within your line of site and at an appropriate distance. A visual target which is too high or too low forces your spine to compensate. An example of this is the attempt to sit in an erect posture to read or write on a flat desk (see Figure 1).

Each of us experiences our clearest vision at a certain distance. This is called our focal length. For detailed work like reading and writing, this point usually falls between 15 and 25 inches from the eyes or the eye glasses. If your focal length is 16 inches, work that is much farther than that from your eyes will bring your body forward to see it more clearly. As our focal length increases with age, many people use bifocals. This will bring the focal length back into the range of 15 to 25 inches, but will lower the line of vision. When possible, try to position your work so that it falls comfortably in your line of sight and at an appropriate distance. Work benches which are too low may be raised by placing them on a pallet or placing a brick beneath each leg. Work benches which are too high may be accommodated by building a wooden or metal platform for the shorter worker to stand on.

## Chairs

Chairs should fit your body size and weight. If you sit too low your back will tend to bend forward as you do your work. Taller people often sit too low. They need to raise themselves and their work surfaces to achieve good sitting posture. Shorter people are often placed in chairs that are too high. This results in pressure under the thigh and behind the knees, often resulting in discomfort in the legs and feet. If this is the case, lowering the chair and work surface or using a foot stool at a higher desk is advisable. The idea that proper sitting posture always involves a 90 degree angle between the torso and the thigh is a myth. Most people are comfortable with an angle between 115 degrees and 145 degrees between their torso and thigh. This is true in a variety of sitting positions.

There's more than one way to sit right. In fact, there are three fundamentally different types of sitting.

1. *Reclined Sitting.* This is comfortable for conversation, driving, and in some cases, using a computer. In reclined sitting the backrest is available to support a portion of the body weight. Lumbar support and, sometimes, a neck rest are critical to preserve the neutral position of the spine (see Figure 2).
2. *Upright Sitting.* This is used when working with the hands close to the body and the eyes focused straight ahead. Many people sit upright to type, to drive, and to use a computer (see Figure 3).

**Figure 1. Posture and Your Eyes**

Your body follows your eyes. To preserve proper posture, your visual target must be parallel to your face and within your line of sight. Poor visual target position forces your spine to compensate by bending. This often occurs when you sit in an erect posture to write on a flat surface. If you wear bifocals, your line of sight may be lower than usual.

desk too flat for
reading or writing

desk at better angle
for reading, good
angle for writing

desk at best angle
for reading

Each of us experiences our own best visual acuity at a certain distance. For near work like reading and writing, this point normally falls between 15 and 25 inches from the eyes. All of us are a little different. If your visual acuity point is at 16 inches, you will strain your body forward to focus on work that is more than 17 inches away. This is a common problem for computer users. Rather than strain your body forward, move your work closer. Reposition your work materials and equipment with computer arms, copy holders, slant boards, and book stands.

trying to focus on a computer
screen that is too far away

computer screen in good position

**Source**: Back Designs, Inc. Catalog, 614 Grand Ave., Oakland, CA 94610. Reprinted by permission.

**Figure 2. Reclined Sitting Postures**

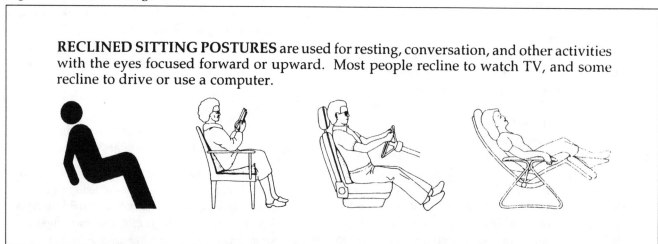

**RECLINED SITTING POSTURES** are used for resting, conversation, and other activities with the eyes focused forward or upward. Most people recline to watch TV, and some recline to drive or use a computer.

**Source**: Back Designs, Inc. Catalog, 614 Grand Avenue, Oakland, CA 94610. Reprinted by permission.

**Figure 3. Upright Sitting Postures**

**UPRIGHT SITTING POSTURES** are used for working with the hands close to the body and the eyes focused straight ahead. Most people sit upright to type and eat, and some sit upright to drive or use a computer.

**Source:** Back Designs, Inc. Catalog, 614 Grand Avenue, Oakland, CA 94610. Reprinted by permission.

3. *Forward Sitting.* This posture is used for active tasks which involve reaching, writing, and similar activities. In addition, many people who begin to work in upright sitting find themselves bending forward to focus the eyes downward. A chair which tilts forward reduces the flexion of the spine and allows for a more neutral posture in forward sitting. If the seatpan does not slope forward, a wedge-shaped cushion may be placed under the buttocks to accomplish the same purpose. In such a situation, a backrest is not important, as it will not be providing any significant amount of support to the spine (see Figure 4).

Please note that in reclined sitting postures, the knees are often higher than the hips, whereas in upright sitting, the knees are at approximately the same height as the hips.

Shorter people may find that they need to use a footrest to put them into a comfortable position in these two sitting postures. In forward sitting, however, the knees are usually lower than the hips. This assists the worker in tilting the torso forward towards the work and allows the hips to bend more than the spine.

## Lifting

Lifting from the floor requires that the worker bend some portions of his or her body to be able to grasp the object. A safe lift is one which utilizes bending of the hips and knees while avoiding bending of the spine. The particular approach will vary according to the size, shape, and location of the object to be lifted. For example, a narrow

**Figure 4. Forward Sitting Postures**

**FORWARD SITTING POSTURES** are used for reaching tasks and tasks with the eyes focused downward. Writing, drafting, dentistry, and using a microscope usually require forward postures.

**Source:** Back Designs, Inc. Catalog, 614 Grand Avenue, Oakland, CA 94610. Reprinted by permission.

object which can fit between the knees can be lifted with a "deep squat." This allows the worker to keep the back both in neutral and in an erect posture. It is often helpful to place one foot in front of the other, so as to straddle the object (see Figure 5).

Objects wider than about 12 inches, however, will be difficult to lift between the knees and will often cause the worker to bend at the waist to supplement hip and knee bending. This results in a high-stress, flexed position of the spine. Even though the knees are bent, the stress on the spine is no different than it would be if the person merely bent at the waist as in Figure 6.

**Figure 5. Safe, Deep Squat Lift**

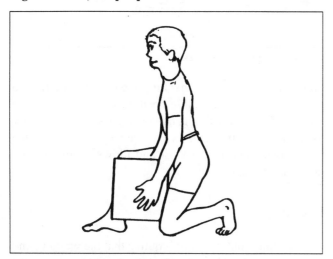

**Source**: Spine Center of the Eastbay, 310 Grand Avenue, Oakland, CA 94610. Reprinted by permission.

In situations such as this it is necessary to tilt the back without actually bending it. This kind of lift is known as the "straight back bend." It involves maintaining the neutral position of the spine while bending the hips and the knees.

**Figure 6. Unsafe, High-Stress Lift**

**Source**: Spine Center of the Eastbay, 310 Grand Avenue, Oakland, CA 94610. Reprinted by permission.

This strategy is especially useful when handling bulky objects or when reaching into an enclosed area such as the trunk of a car (see Figure 7).

Overhead reaching or lifting presents a different problem. In this case the tendency is not for the spine to bend forward but to arch backward. Tightening the abdominal muscles and keeping the knees slightly bent allows the worker to maintain a neutral position of the spine (see Figure 8).

**Figure 7. Safe, Straight Back Bend Lift**

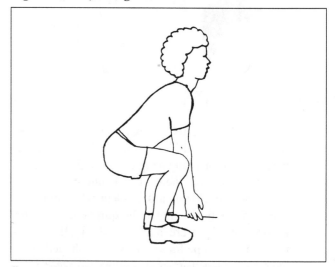

**Source**: Spine Center of the Eastbay, 310 Grand Avenue, Oakland, CA 94610. Reprinted by permission.

**Figure 8. Overhead Reaching**

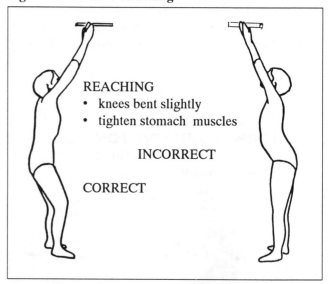

REACHING
• knees bent slightly
• tighten stomach muscles

INCORRECT

CORRECT

**Source**: Spine Center of the Eastbay, 310 Grand Avenue, Oakland, CA 94610. Reprinted by permission.

An additional source of stress on the spine in lifting is the use of rapid motions. Overcoming the inertia of an object to be lifted exerts forces on the spine in excess of the actual weight of the object. When objects are accelerated rapidly, either in lifting or lowering, the additional stress may be more than a worker's back can handle. For this reason it is important to avoid jerking motions as much as possible and to use a smooth lift. Testing or "hefting" the load to assess its weight is a good first step to help avoid jerking the object. If an object is heavier than your comfortable lifting capacity, assistance in the form of a hoist or another worker may convert an unsafe lift to a safe one. In addition, surveying the path in which an object is to be moved can help you plan the lift and carry in a safe manner.

Twisting the spine is another direction in which people lose their neutral posture. The combination of flexion and twisting produces what can be called the "washcloth effect" in which extremely high forces are placed on the spine. This is to be avoided if at all possible. Pivoting on the feet or stepping to the side as one would in throwing a basketball helps reduce this problem.

In summary, lifting can be made more safe by observing the following rules:

1. Plan the lift so as to avoid unexpected loads or motions.
2. Use a broad stance so as to increase your balance. This is especially important when lifting liquids or other unstable loads.
3. Lift as slowly and smoothly as possible.
4. Avoid twisting or bending the spine. Try to maintain your neutral spine while bending the knees and hips. Pivoting will help avoid rotation of the spine.
5. Keep the load as close to your torso as possible. An object held at arms length places a stress on the spine equivalent to 10 times its weight.
6. Avoid lifting from below knee level or above shoulder height. Very low or high lifts place the most stress on the spine and make it most difficult to maintain neutral posture.
7. Get help if needed! However, when two or more people are lifting together, they must set up some means of communication to be sure that they act in concert. Often, they will agree to lift on the count of "three" so that one person is not left with more than his or her share of the load.

## Pushing and Pulling

Many people bend repeatedly at the waist when pushing or pulling. This produces high levels of "wear and tear" on the spine by taking a person in and out of their neutral posture. A safer way to perform pushing activities involves placing one foot well in front of the other and shifting the weight from the rear to the forward foot while keeping the spine in neutral (see Figure 9). For pulling, the weight is shifted from the front foot to the rear foot. A broad stance with the knees slightly bent helps to maintain balance and control. Exerting the force as close to hip height as possible will minimize the stress on the spine. Keep in mind that it requires at least twice as much force to initiate the movement of an object than it does to keep an object moving on a horizontal surface. Prepare for this by tightening the abdominal muscles and using them to "brace" the spine for the increased forces generated by overcoming an object's inertia. Pushing an object around corners will likewise require more force and more control on the part of your muscles. Again, prepare for this by tightening the abdominal muscles and slightly bending the knees.

**Figure 9. Safer Way to Push**

**Source**: Spine Center of the Eastbay, 310 Grand Avenue, Oakland, CA 94610. Reprinted by permission.

## Ergonomics

It is the responsibility of all employers to provide a safe workplace. Although the principles and suggestions outlined above may assist workers in adapting to a variety of situations, there are often jobs which are inherently poorly designed. For example, reaching into a deep bin for materials, spare parts, or laundry is an example of poor workplace design. Such a situation may be addressed by raising and tilting the bin so that its opening is at waist height. A bin can have a bottom which is spring-loaded so that as its contents are removed, the bottom rises toward the worker.

Manual materials handling can be made much less stressful on the spine by the provision of hoists, forklifts, and hand trucks. As pallets are being loaded or unloaded, they can be placed on adjustable pallet stands or scissor lifts which can adjust to a comfortable height. "Lazy Susans" and pallet carrousels can rotate so that their contents can be exposed to the worker without bending and twisting. Such ergonomic improvements reduce the risk of injury and decrease the time needed to perform many of these manual material handling tasks.

*See also* Low Back Pain; Work Hazards: Ergonomic.

## Bibliography

MacLeod, D. (1982). *Strains and sprains: A worker's guide to job design.* Publication #460. Detroit: United Auto Workers. An excellent summary of ergonomics (the study of the effects of work on the human body). This 36-page booklet provides many examples of ways to improve the design and layout of work situations. Available in Spanish and English.

McKenzie, R. (1985). *Treat your own back* and *Trust your own neck.* P.O. Box 93, Waikanae, New Zealand: Spinal Publications Ltd. These easy-to-read books are written by an internationally known physical therapist. He presents a method to evaluate your own neck and back pain and develop a program of exercise and management for your own unique condition. One of his greatest contributions is an explanation of when it is safe and unsafe to push through pain. A good discussion of body mechanics and posture is included. Available in Spanish and English.

Saunders, H.D. (1986). *For your back.* Edina, MN: Educational Opportunities. An excellent survey of the causes of back problems, including examples from work situations as well as activities of daily living. This 48-page book includes suggestions for exercise, as well as comments on the treatment of back problems. Available in Spanish and English.

Vollowitz, E. (1989). *Back designs product selection guide and catalog.* Oakland, CA: Back Designs, Inc. This comprehensive guide to ergonomic chairs and other neck and back-care products explains how to go about choosing and adjusting office and other furniture in ways which are kind to the neck and back. Available in English only.

—Ira L. Janowitz and Eileen Vollowitz

## PRE-RETIREMENT PLANNING

Pre-retirement planning is the process of building the resources essential for defining retirement as independence. The strategy is to anticipate the potential options and changes retirement eligibility may mean to each person; accumulate the resources to exercise the choices that are most important to each situation; and control the impact of changes so that positive effects are maximized and negative effects are minimized or eliminated. The five categories of resources that have been found to be critical for independence are financial, health, social supports, housing, and personal resources (see **Retirement**). The planning skill is a simple three-step process: (a) build awareness of what options and choices are important for future independence, (b) collect relevant information for sound decision making, and (c) take action to follow-up on decisions until goals are reached.

## Relationship to Work

Many people plan independently (self-directed planners) using a variety of materials and resources available to them, while others participate in group meetings designed for pre-retirement planning (PRPPs). Surveys of retirees support the importance of this effort; most wished they had done more planning and started it sooner in their careers when they had time working for them rather than against them (Harris and Associates, 1979). Employers have recognized that advice by increasingly offering formal programs to their employees. However, research has shown that only a small percentage of people take advantage of PRPPs and those who do so are more likely to have higher income and be the higher educated employees of organizations offering the program (Palmore, Burchett, Fillenbaum, George, & Wallman, 1985; Grant, 1985).

Pre-retirement planning programs began in 1949 when an insurance company offered a PRPP as an adjunct to the new consumer product, pension plans. The subtle purpose was to countermand the prevailing work ethic and convince older workers to accept the traditional definition of retirement, removal from the paid work-force to leisure activities. Thus, the objective of the early PRPPs was attitude change rather than helping workers build resources for independence. Even today, many programs still emphasize attitude change rather than planning skills. Consequently, there is a potpourri of programs, varying considerably in length of time, topics covered, and method of presentation, as well as objectives. For example, programs may range anywhere from a token presentation of a gold watch, to one-on-one counseling about benefits, or to a seminar over several days covering typically the following topics:

1. Pension benefits (private, public, and Social Security).
2. Supplemental and personal retirement plans (IRAs, Keogh, 457b, 401k).
3. Savings and investments.
4. Money management.
5. Medicare, Medicaid, and group health insurance plans.
6. Health and wellness.
7. Legal and estate planning.
8. Housing
9. Friends and family relationships.
10. Transitions to retirement.
11. Retirement activities
12. Meaningful use of time.

Topics may be labeled differently, but essentially fall into the four categories of resources, finances, health, social supports, and personal skills and competencies.

Narrow-based programs typically cover only the financial issues, usually just pension and benefit information, while broad-based programs cover most of the above. However, even these comprehensive PRPPs vary considerably in the amount of time dedicated to the program (usually anywhere from 8 to 24 hours). The most common methods are either lecture presentations from resource experts or group discussion where the leader and the group explore topics using their own resources. A growing number of programs combine the expertise of the resource expert followed by the group discussion technique for improved retention of the material. This method has been shown to be an effective method for encouraging the planning of behaviors of pre-retirees (Grant, 1989).

An assortment of materials are available for both self-directed planners or workshop participants. Again, they vary considerably in type, quality, and sophistication. Some are simply textbook discussions of topics, others are workbooks intended to be used to develop a personal plan for independence, and others are sophisticated computer programs for personal planning (see the bibliography and references for a suggested selection).

## Application

Whether you take advantage of existing PRPPs or do it alone using materials and resources available to you through your personnel office, libraries, or bookstores, the process is the same. The essence of planning is to think ahead to the time when you will be eligible to retire, consider what options may exist due to that eligibility, and what effect each option would have on your future life style. For example, a sample of questions you should ask yourself are: When will you be eligible for pension benefits? How much will they be? What factors could change that amount of money? Can you maintain your current life style on that amount? If not, how much can you save today to afford "independence" at that future date? What will your health status be by then? What steps can you take now to improve your chances for an active late life? Who is affected by your retirement decisions beside yourself? Will you have others dependent on you at the time you want to do something different? Where do you want to live? What would you like to do then if you are financially free to do something different? If you decide to retire from your primary career, what will you miss about that work that could be very important to you?

Answers to those questions and many more are generally covered in the specific planning areas for each of the five major account.

1. *Financial Resources:* (a) cash management—determine your net worth, monthly income/expenses, and maintain 3-6 months of living expenses in easily accessible funds; (b) insurance and risk management—create an umbrella against premature demands on your financial resources that includes disability, life, property, liability, and medical insurance products; (c) legal and estate planning—develop a plan to pass your assets to your heirs after your death (a will or trust), but create at the same time a plan to cover the possibility that you may not be able to act on your affairs while alive, whether due to travel, temporary health problems, or incompetency (power of attorney, guardianships, and living wills); (d) retirement planning—project future income from Social Security and/or other private and public pensions, estimate retirement expenses, determine if there is any gap between future income and expenses, develop a systematic method of saving and investing money to fund that gap; and (e) investment management—set goals for investments, determine systematic strategies for spreading risk among various types of investments, and review periodically the results of investment strategies against investment goals.

2. *Health Resources:* (a) health assessment—periodically evaluate physical health in order to catch threats to wellness early and to monitor wellness plan progress; and (b) wellness goals—accept personal responsibility for your own well-being, develop a physical and mental fitness program that you enjoy and practice regularly, get control of stress, substance abuse, and weight management, and develop good safety habits, such as regular use of seat belts.

3. *Social Support Systems:* (a) relationships—assess quality and quantity of important relationships, such as family, spouse, parents, siblings, friends at work, friends at home, social networks, (b) social skills—improve communication skills, develop sensitivity to others' needs, and broaden exposure for relationships so as not to be dependent on only one source of meaningful relationships; and (c) coping with losses—develop good coping skills to accept inevitable changes and losses of important relationships.

4. *Housing Resources:* (a) current housing—assess your current life style, considering the financial and physical condition of your home; (b) future housing needs—determine if current housing has the potential to satisfy needs as you age; and (c) alter housing to satisfy potential future needs—consider other housing options available or creative ways of altering present home to meet future needs.

5. *Personal Resources:* (a) skills and competencies—assess current interests and skills, build new ones, keep existing skills current with technology; (b) attitudes—develop and maintain a positive perspective for living; (c) strategies for success—develop a Type C personality:

a. *Commitment*. Be fully involved in what you are doing and with whom you are doing it. Have a reason to get up in the morning.

b. *Change Is a Challenge*. View change as a natural part of life, as an opportunity to grow and develop, as something to look forward to rather than to avoid.

c. *Control*. Believe that you can influence the world around you and be willing to act accordingly. Be in charge of your feelings, actions, and goals. Control can be achieved through planning. Exercise control over your five valuable resources by planning (be aware, get accurate information, and take action). Define retirement in your terms, not someone else's.

*See also* Benefits; Leisure; Retirement.

## Bibliography

American Association of Retired Persons. (1988). *Think of your future: Retirement planning workbook.* Washington, DC: Worker Equity Department, AARP. A widely available and comprehensive retirement planning workbook that includes a MAP or Master Action Plan for retirement planning. The materials are part of a retirement planning workshop given by employers or AARP volunteers. Check with local AARP chapters for information about workshops in your area.

Chapman, E. N. (1987). *Comfort zones: A practical guide for retirement planning.* Los Altos, CA: Crisp. Elwood Chapman provides step-by-step information for planning a successful retirement. He discusses attitudes, transitions, decision making, and myths and misconceptions about retirement, as well as the more usual topics of financial planning, use of time, wellness, and support systems.

*FRED—Friendly Retirement Education Database.* (undated). Columbia, SC: Employee Benefit Systems, Inc. Computer software package for comprehensive retirement planning that discusses health, life style, living, occupation, legal affairs, records, Social Security, and financial affairs. Package is leased and updated annually. Good tool for self-planners.

Grant, K.A. (1985). *Survey of participant and nonparticipant factors in preretirement planning: A needs assessment.* Master's thesis, North Carolina State University, Raleigh, NC.

Grant, K.A. (1989). *An experimental evaluation of a primary prevention program: PREPARE.* Doctoral dissertation, North Carolina State University, Raleigh, NC.

Harris, L. and Associates. (1979). *American attitudes toward pensions and retirement.* New York: Johnson & Higgins.

Palmore, E.B., Burchett, B.M., Fillenbaum, G.G., George, L.K., & Wallman, L. M. (1985). *Retirement causes and consequences.* New York: Springer.

## For Further Information

**American Association for Retired Persons**
1909 K Street, N.W.
Washington, DC 20049

The Social Security Administration can provide free, detailed financial statements to workers, estimating how large a benefit check they will get each month when they retire. Called the "Personal Earnings and Benefit Estimate Statement," it is available by mail free on written request from anyone who has paid Social Security taxes, is younger than 65 years old, and is not yet drawing benefits. Call toll-free, 1-800-937-2000, to request copies of the disclosure form, SSA-7004. This statement will also disclose how much a worker and family would get each month in disability or survivors' benefits.

—KATHERINE A. GRANT

## PROCRASTINATION: OVERCOMING

Procrastination refers to the act of needlessly delaying tasks to the point of experiencing anxiety. For most people, procrastination while in school or at work is more common and results in more distress than procrastination at home or in the community.

### Relationship to Work

People procrastinate in completing their work for a number of reason.

1. *Fear of Failure*. Procrastination can be a way of avoiding situations that might result in failure. Failing to give a report to a committee avoids possible embarrassment, criticism from the audience, or difficult questions. Not submitting an article to a magazine guarantees that it won't be rejected.

2. *Perfectionism*. Perfectionists feel that they should be perfect in everything they do. They set overly high standards for all tasks, including those that are not important. Procrastinating can excuse an imperfectly done task completed at the last minute.

3. *Task Aversiveness*. Some work-related tasks are simply boring or repetitive. It is difficult to feel motivated by piles of repetitive desk work. However, some people feel guilty about idle time. By procrastinating, they stretch out the empty hours and fill them with timewasters. Or they procrastinate as the result of taking on too much work, which feels overwhelming to complete.

4. *Dependency*. Some people believe that if they put off doing their work, other people will help them complete it. Procrastinators may have learned that as deadlines approach, friends, and coworkers pitch in to help them in their distress.

5. *Lack of Assertion*. Some people have great difficulty asserting their rights or speaking up when they have been wronged. They will procrastinate when they

need to ask a supervisor for a raise, request a letter of recommendation, or criticize an employee for poor performance.

6. *Rebellion Against Control.* When people have little power, they may act in ways that increase their control. They might keep others waiting, come late to meetings that can't start without them, or not return phone calls.

7. *Difficulty Making Decisions.* People who have difficulty making decisions will put off this process as long as possible. Some people procrastinate on decisions so long that eventually enough deadlines pass so that only one last choice remains. However, this is rarely the best or wisest choice.

## Application

In order to overcome procrastination, it is important to know which reasons for procrastination most often apply to you. Each reason for procrastination has different strategies for improvement:

1. *Overcoming Fear of Failure.* Use relaxation exercises to decrease anxiety and tension during anxiety-provoking activities. Imagine positive rather than negative outcomes resulting from completing the task. Try to engage in as many of the anxiety-provoking activities as possible, rather than avoiding them (see **Self-Efficacy**).

2. *Overcoming Perfectionism.* Focus on performing a task adequately rather than perfectly. As long as it meets basic requirements of competency, it does not need to be improved. Prioritize activities according to their importance. Whereas it is important to type a resume or cover letter for a job perfectly, it is unnecessary to worry about the wording of routine memos to coworkers. Don't take on extra work because you feel that others won't do the work according to your standards. Instead, delegate authority and share responsibility for work (see **Perfectionism: Overcoming**).

3. *Overcoming Task Aversiveness.* Accept free time without guilt. Completing a task early does not mean having to begin another. Use leisure time as a reward for engaging in boring or aversive tasks that have to be done. Learn to say no to assignments and requests that are unimportant or overwhelming (see **Self-Managed Change**).

4. *Overcoming Dependency.* If the activity indeed requires outside help, contact the relevant people early on, then complete the task yourself. Use decision-making skills to improve your own ability to complete a task without help (see **Decision Making**). Be assertive about refusing help from overprotective others who may have intervened in the past.

5. *Overcoming Lack of Assertion.* The longer you wait to approach another person with a difficult request, the more anxious you will feel. Procrastination about interpersonal requests or criticism increases your chances of rejection, as the other person becomes irritated by the approaching deadline or has already made other plans. Adhering to deadlines will decrease the possibility of being turned down. Assertion training—learning to increase assertive skills—is helpful (see **Assertion**).

6. *Overcoming Rebellion Against Control.* Be direct about your feelings. Let someone know when you are angry, or when you feel powerless to change a situation (see **Anger**). There are positive ways to be indispensable, such as by providing new ideas at a meeting. Develop alternative solutions to tasks that seem to result in power struggles.

7. *Overcoming Difficulty Making Decisions.* Determine several avenues for gathering information relevant to making a decision. As you cover each source of information, make a list of advantages and disadvantages of each choice. As soon as you have depleted the sources of information, act on them. Procrastinating after you have enough information will not help your decision.

*See also* Anger; Anxiety; Assertion; Decision Making; Perfectionism: Overcoming; Self-Efficacy; Self-Managed Change; Time Management.

## Bibliography

Burka, J.B., & Yuen, L.M. (1983). *Procrastination: Why you do it. What to do about it.* Reading, MA: Addison-Wesley Publishing Company. Examines several reasons why people procrastinate, such as fear of failure, fear of success, control, separation, and attachment. The book is based on the authors' extensive counseling experience, and presents strategies on how to overcome procrastination.

Ellis, A., & Knaus, W.J. (1977). *Overcoming procrastination.* New York: Institute for Rational Living.

Mack, K., & Skjei, E. (1979). Overcoming writing blocks. Boston: Houghton-Mifflin Publishing Company.

Porat, F. (1980). *Creative procrastination: Organizing your own life.* San Francisco: Harper & Row. This book argues that time management strategies are useless without free time for relaxation, thinking, and creating. Dr. Porat presents strategies to achieve a balance between productivity and leisure.

Rothblum, E.D., & Cole, E. (1988). *Treating women's fear of failure: From worry to enlightenment.* New York: Harrington Park Press. Using research, clinical evidence, and personal anecdotes, the authors examine why women (especially successful women) still have feelings of insecurity and rejection.

—ESTHER D. ROTHBLUM

# PROMOTION/RAISE

A promotion to a higher level job normally entails greater job responsibility and a pay raise.

## Relationship to Work

Promotions and raises are the major rewards that motivate most employees. Promotions offer the opportunity for professional growth and development as the employee learns to meet the demands and challenges of the new position.

## Application

Here are some suggestions for winning promotions and raises.

1. Take responsibility for your own career plans and progress. Do not expect that your boss will take care of you, promoting you as a reward for working hard and doing a good job.

2. Identify as best you can what your ultimate career goal is. Try visualizing yourself in various types of positions at various levels. Where do you think you ultimately belong? What is your ultimate niche? Next determine some flexible career paths that you think will get you there. Identify specific jobs that might be next on that path. If possible, ask a more experienced person within the company for advice on career paths. Get all the good input that you can, from your boss, mentor, human resources staff, career assessment center, and similar sources.

3. Determine those jobs that would be a good fit for you, considering your goals, life style, values, interests, skills, willingness and ability to develop new skills, and similar considerations.

4. In mapping your career path, do not rule out lateral moves. If you plan to move into a general management job, you probably need exposure to all major functional areas of the organization. While lateral moves usually carry little or no pay increase, they can pay off handsomely in the long run. Make lateral moves before you become accustomed to a higher pay scale at the general management level and before you reach a ceiling because of your limited range of experience (see **Career Path Possibilities within the Organization**).

5. Set clear, specific job goals. Regularly review and write down your goals, both long-range (where do you want to be in five years?) and short-range (what do you need to achieve next year? next month?). Make goals as measurable as possible and give them a time target: To master the XYZ computer program by June 1; To reduce customer complaints by 20% next year; To be promoted to department head by January; To get a pay raise of 15% by February 1 (see **Self-Managed Change**).

6. Communicate your goals to key people. Your boss is usually in the best position to help you get a promotion. Determine other key people who would probably support your efforts if they understood your goals. Are there competitors who should not have too much information about your plans?

7. Pay your dues. If you are a relative newcomer to the company, you need to learn the ropes and prove your mettle before the people in power will be willing to listen seriously to your suggestions for change or to turn over significant new responsibilities to you.

8. Learn the next-level job(s) you would like to move into. What skills do you need to master? What information or knowledge should you gain? Who could help you? What committee or task force could you join that would help you to make connections with the right people and to position yourself for the job? What projects or tasks could you add or expand upon within your present job that could prepare you? (see **Assessment Centers; Managerial Skills**).

9. Dress and act the part. How do the managers at the next level (and higher) dress and act? How do they interact with various types of people? What do you know about their life styles and work styles? Do you fit in? Do you want to? If you start projecting the appropriate image, key decision makers are likely to consider you a likely candidate.

10. Keep your options open. Connections are the name of the game, and you should know as many movers and shakers as possible—in your own firm and at other, competing firms. You owe your company your loyalty while you are there, but you don't owe them a lifetime guarantee any more than they can guarantee your job. Keep your resume current and your networks active. When you know your services are in demand, you are in a more confident bargaining position (see **Job Security; Job Security: The Free Agent Manager; Networking**).

11. Base promotion requests on specific achievements. If you regularly set measurable work goals and clear them with your boss, then those achievements form a solid basis for granting a promotion. Think in terms of your contributions to the firm—ways you have brought in business, improved productivity, met customer needs, cut costs, and similar achievements. See if you can somehow translate those contributions into resulting profits the firm has made, and use this to justify your pay raise request.

12. Size up your competition, if their existence will be a strong unmentioned presence when you ask your manager for a promotion. During that meeting focus on at least one area in which you are unique or unquestionably stronger. If you must discuss areas where your competition is stronger than you, associate yourself with your competitor. Talk about how you work together in these areas or the similarities you share.

13. Study your boss's position in the raise-getting process within the company. If the boss has the most influence over the size of your raise, then he or she is in an adversarial position to you because the boss's job is to keep salary costs down. Consider company plans for the immediate future, current prosperity of the company and the industry, the budget process, the decision-making process regarding promotions and raises, and similar concerns your boss must consider (see **Bosses: Managing Relationships with Superiors**).

14. Time your request to fit in with the budget process so that the boss cannot legitimately put your request on hold for several weeks or months. On the other hand, if you have just pulled off an outstanding coup, you may want to take advantage of the moment by getting a commitment from the boss that when promotion or raise time does come around, you will be rewarded.

15. Fine-tune your image just before requesting a promotion. Think twice before making unpopular stands, bringing in sticky problems without offering solutions, trying too hard to make a good impression, talking about your intended request with others, or being away from the work scene for an extended period. On the other hand, this is the time to sharpen your image as a problem-preventer and problem-solver, as a confident and positive achiever who also makes the boss look good and who makes his or her life easier by being responsible and supportive.

16. If your boss brings up a weak area in your performance, try to turn the negative into a positive. First, mention your key strong areas and then try to get agreement that the one weak area is the only obstacle to granting your request. Then offer evidence of improvement and a plan for further improvement. Avoid excuses or alibis and focus on solutions and plans. Follow a similar approach if you have botched an assignment. You should be more concerned than your boss about it, communicate specific plans to prevent a recurrence, and focus on the lesson you learned from the situation.

17. Ask for more than you expect to get. Leave yourself some room to bargain. Be realistic about the company's ability to pay, but don't sell yourself short. Try to determine the top raise your boss is probably willing to give you and ask for 10% to 25% more (see **Negotiating; Pay**).

18. If your boss turns down your request, try to get a statement of the main objection. Answer the objection and restate your request. Imply the negative results that may result from not granting your request and the positive results of granting it. If necessary, make one concession on terms or salary. Reassure the boss that he or she will be making the right move by saying "yes."

19. If your boss turns down your promotions request, ask for specifics. Try to get a clear, complete picture of why you were turned down, what your future prospects are, and what you must do in order to move up. See if you can get an agreement that if you achieve certain goals, you will receive a specific promotion and raise. Include a target date. Follow up with a confirming memo (see **Performance Appraisal**).

20. If the answer is yes, do all you can to reassure the boss that the decision was a sound one. But do not establish an artificially high level of performance that you cannot sustain. Write a brief confirming memo summing up the agreements and repeating your thanks.

21. Have a positive attitude, whether the answer is yes or no. If you have an attitude problem, try attending inspiring seminars, listening to self-development tapes, and being around cheerful people. Be a class act by being a considerate team player, looking at the brighter side, and speaking well of others.

*See also* Assessment Center; Bosses: Managing Relationships with Superiors; Career Development System within the Organization; Career Path Possibilities within the Organization; Career Planning; Job Description; Job Security: The Free Agent Manager; Managerial Skills; Mentoring; Negotiating; Networking; Organizational Politics; Pay; Performance Appraisal; Self-Managed Change; Women's Barriers and Opportunities.

## Bibliography

Bolles, Richard N. (1990) *What color is your parachute?* Berkeley, CA: Ten Speed Press. This classic in career planning includes exercises for determining what you really want to do and how to create an ideal job for yourself.

Carr-Ruffino, N. (1985). *The promotable woman: Becoming a successful manager.* Belmont, CA: Wadsworth, Inc. See especially the first two chapters, which discuss gaining power within the organizational hierarchy and developing effective career plans, and the last chapter on getting a promotion and a raise. Chapter 2 includes a series of exercises to help you pinpoint your skills and interests, set goals and priorities, and develop a career action plan.

Fisher, R., & Ury, W. (1983). *Getting to yes: Negotiating agreement without giving in.* New York: Penguin Books. The authors provide practical suggestions based on their experiences directing the Harvard Negotiation Project.

Malloy, J. (1989). *Dress for success.* New York: Follett. This is a basic resource for proper business dress. All suggestions are based on extensive research into actual reactions of business decision-makers.

Tarrant, J. J. (1986). *How to negotiate a raise.* New York: Simon and Schuster.

Wright, J. W. (1989). *The American almanac of jobs and salaries.* New York: Avon. Updated every two years, this almanac offers a wealth of previously unobtainable information about salaries for all types of positions. Covering both profit and nonprofit organizations, it includes detailed job descriptions and salaries by region and metropolitan area.

—NORMA CARR-RUFFINO

# R

## RATIONAL THINKING

Rational thinking supports an individual's (or group's) goals and values, and usually does so by emphasizing thoughts that are realistic, empirically based, logical, and flexible. "One is rational when one justifies one's beliefs by considering the reasons for holding them and forms new beliefs on the basis of reasons" (Moshman & Hoover, 1989, p. 33).

### Relationship to Health, Happiness, and Work

The theory and practice of rational-emotive therapy (RET), originated by Albert Ellis in 1955 (Ellis, 1962, 1972, 1988; Ellis & Dryden, 1987; Ellis & Harper, 1975), specifically applies rational thinking to problems of effective living, including functioning more efficiently and happily at work. RET holds that, when people think irrationally, they often needlessly create their own emotional disturbances (e.g., intense feelings of anxiety, depression, or self-denigration) and they also often construct their own behavioral and work difficulties (e.g., procrastination, compulsions, and addictions).

Rational thinking, therefore, is significantly correlated with, and in some ways it is an integral component of, emotional and physical health. People who think, and especially who forcefully talk to themselves, rationally, tend to (a) make themselves feel only *appropriately* sorry and disappointed, instead of *inappropriately* panicked and depressed, when they fail at work or love; (b) have helpful self-interest *and* considerable social interest; (c) strive to achieve their strong *preferences* without turning them into godlike demands and commands; (d) be long-range, disciplined rather than short-range, undisciplined hedonists; (e) accept themselves (and other people) *unconditionally*, whether or not they accomplish great things and whether or not they are uniquely loved; and (f) be flexible and alternative-seeking, rather than rigid and masturbatory, in their approaches to work, love, and enjoyment.

RET holds that thinking, feeling, and behavior are not pure or separate processes, but that they significantly overlap and include each other. The well-known ABCs of RET (Ellis, 1962, 1988; Ellis & Dryden, 1987) state that when unfortunate Activating Events (A) occur in our lives and *seem* to cause emotional Consequences (C), such as feelings of panic and depression, it is actually our Beliefs (B) about A that mainly make us feel and behave dysfunctionally at C. We have a *choice* in this respect and can make ourselves feel *appropriately* sorry, disappointed, or frustrated at C when we perceive something "bad" happening at A, and we can tell ourselves rational or self-helping Beliefs at B to produce these appropriate Consequences (C) (see Figure 1).

However, we can consciously or unconsciously choose to make ourselves feel *inappropriately* panicked, depressed, and self-hating at C (Consequence) when the same unfortunate Activating Events (A) occur and we tell ourselves irrational or self-defeating Beliefs at B to produce these *inappropriate* Consequences (C) (see Figure 2).

If, then, we recognize and use the ABCs of RET (and of the other kinds of cognitive-behavior therapy that have followed in the steps of RET), we can adopt rational, preferential philosophies that help us feel and act effectively, or we can adopt irrational, masturbatory philosophies that help us to feel and act self-defeatingly.

### Application

In using the principles and practice of rational-emotional therapy (RET) to help yourself function more effectively and happily at work (and at home), here are some suggestions you can consider, experiment with, and carefully check:

1.  Acknowledge that you do not merely *get* disturbed by unpleasant events in your life but that to a considerable degree, you *choose* to needlessly upset yourself. You largely do so by changing your appropriate *desires* and *preferences* for enjoyable work and love relationships into grandiose, absolutist, irrational *musts, shoulds,* and *commands.* For ex-

**Figure 1. Consequences of Rational Thinking**

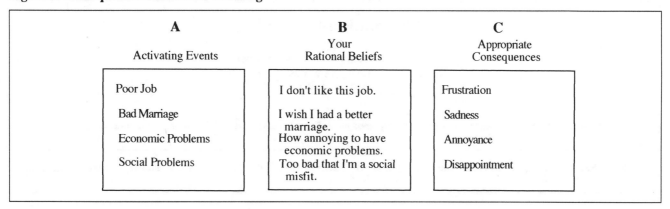

| A<br>Activating Events | B<br>Your<br>Rational Beliefs | C<br>Appropriate<br>Consequences |
| --- | --- | --- |
| Poor Job<br><br>Bad Marriage<br><br>Economic Problems<br><br>Social Problems | I don't like this job.<br><br>I wish I had a better marriage.<br>How annoying to have economic problems.<br>Too bad that I'm a social misfit. | Frustration<br><br>Sadness<br><br>Annoyance<br><br>Disappointment |

**Figure 2. Consequences of Irrational Thinking**

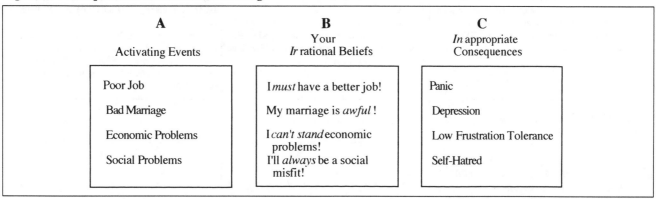

| A<br>Activating Events | B<br>Your<br>*Ir*rational Beliefs | C<br>*In*appropriate<br>Consequences |
| --- | --- | --- |
| Poor Job<br><br>Bad Marriage<br><br>Economic Problems<br><br>Social Problems | I *must* have a better job!<br><br>My marriage is *awful*!<br><br>I *can't stand* economic problems!<br>I'll *always* be a social misfit! | Panic<br><br>Depression<br><br>Low Frustration Tolerance<br><br>Self-Hatred |

ample: "I *must* at all times do well at work and *have to be* approved by my coworkers! If I don't do well, I am a worthless person, and if they don't approve of me, they are rotten bastards!"

2. Look for your rigid musts and irrational thoughts when you observe that your feelings (e.g., anger, panic, or depression) are disturbed. Use the scientific method to actively dispute and challenge them. For example: *Disputing*: "Why *must* I at all times do well at work?" *Answer*: "There is no reason why I *must*, but it would be greatly *preferable* if I did. So let me try to do better. But if I never improve, I am merely a *person who* failed this time, and not a *rotten, worthless* individual." Be persistent. Forcefully reduce these irrational musts, shoulds, and commands.

3. Discover or create some rational philosophies or coping self-statements that you keep vigorously repeating to yourself, and concertedly think about, until you really believe and act upon them. Such as "I definitely do *not* need to make more money, though I will do my best to make more!" "Some people at work *will* treat me unfairly and *will* malign me. Too bad! But I can take their unjust treatment and *not* put myself down nor hate them!" Repeating these positive self-statements until you accept and believe them is the key to success.

4. Reframe some of the unfortunate things that happen to you, such as rejection by someone you favor, by finding their *good* aspects, such as getting rid of rejecting people *fast* saves time and energy that would be wasted with them.

5. Do rational referenting. Make a list of the disadvantages of your harmful addictions (e.g., procrastination) and review and rationally think about them 10 times a day until you motivate yourself to give them up.

6. Use RET to dispute other people's irrational, self-defeating beliefs, and thereby get practice in talking yourself out of your own irrationalities.

7. Use cognitive homework, such as the RET Self-Help Report Form (Sichel & Ellis, 1984; see Figure 3) to monitor and change your main irrational beliefs.

8. Humorously rip up some of your irrational ideas. Use some of my rational humorous songs (Ellis, 1977) to laugh at your irrationalities.

9. Use rational-emotive imagery (Maultsby & Ellis, 1974). Imagine one of the worst things that could happen to you (e.g., a boss criticizing you in front of

**Figure 3. RET Self-Help Form**

# RET SELF-HELP FORM

Institute for Rational-Emotive Therapy
45 East 65th Street, New York, N.Y. 10021
(212) 535-0822

**(A) ACTIVATING EVENTS,** thoughts, or feelings that happened just before I felt emotionally disturbed or acted self-defeatingly: _____

_____

**(C) CONSEQUENCE or CONDITION**—disturbed feeling or self-defeating behavior—that I produced and would like to change: _____

_____

| **(B) BELIEFS—Irrational BELIEFS (IBs)** leading to my CONSEQUENCE (emotional disturbance or self-defeating behavior). Circle all that apply to these ACTIVATING EVENTS (A). | **(D) DISPUTES** for each circled IRRATIONAL BELIEF. Examples: "*Why* MUST I do very well?" "*Where is it written* that I am a BAD PERSON?" "*Where is the evidence* that I MUST be approved or accepted?" | **(E) EFFECTIVE RATIONAL BELIEFS (RBs)** to replace my IRRATIONAL BELIEFS (IBs). *Examples: "I'd PREFER to do very well but I don't HAVE TO." "I am a PERSON WHO acted badly, not a BAD PERSON." "There is no evidence that I HAVE TO be approved, though I would LIKE to be."* |
|---|---|---|
| 1. I MUST do well or very well! | ............................................ | ............................................ |
| 2. I am a BAD OR WORTHLESS PERSON when I act weakly or stupidly. | ............................................ | ............................................ |
| 3. I MUST be approved or accepted by people I find important! | ............................................ | ............................................ |
| 4. I NEED to be loved by someone who matters to me a lot! | ............................................ | ............................................ |
| 5. I am a BAD, UNLOVABLE PERSON if I get rejected. | ............................................ | ............................................ |
| 6. People MUST treat me fairly and give me what I NEED! | ............................................ | ............................................ |

**(OVER)**

**Source:** Institute for Rational-Emotive Therapy, 45 E. 65th Street, New York, NY 10021. Reprinted by permission.

**Figure 3. RET Self-Help Form (continued)**

| | | |
|---|---|---|
| 7. People MUST live up to my expectations or it is TERRIBLE! | | |
| 8. People who act immorally are undeserving, ROTTEN PEOPLE! | | |
| 9. I CAN'T STAND really bad things or very difficult people! | | |
| 10. My life MUST have few major hassles or troubles. | | |
| 11. It's AWFUL or HORRIBLE when major things don't go my way! | | |
| 12. I CAN'T STAND IT when life is really unfair! | | |
| 13. I NEED a good deal of immediate gratification and HAVE to feel miserable when I don't get it! | | |
| Additional Irrational Beliefs: | | |

**(F) FEELINGS and BEHAVIORS** I experienced after arriving at my EFFECTIVE RATIONAL BELIEFS: _____

**I WILL WORK HARD TO REPEAT MY EFFECTIVE RATIONAL BELIEFS FORCEFULLY TO MYSELF ON MANY OCCASIONS SO THAT I CAN MAKE MYSELF LESS DISTURBED NOW AND ACT LESS SELF-DEFEATINGLY IN THE FUTURE.**

Joyce Sichel, Ph.D. and Albert Ellis, Ph.D.

your coworkers) and let yourself feel very furious or depressed, and then work on making yourself feel, instead, appropriately sorry and disappointed. You do this by using rational coping statements.

10. Do some RET shame-attacking exercises (Ellis, 1988; Ellis & Dryden, 1987). Deliberately do something you consider "shameful" or "foolish" in public (e.g., yell out the stations as a train or subway car stops or ask for condoms in a shoe store) and work on your feelings until you don't feel ashamed. Again, you do this by rationally telling yourself that it's too bad but not horrible or shameful to be seen as a fool.

11. Deliberately keep doing acts that you are irrationally afraid to do—like riding on elevators or giving a public speech—while also talking to yourself rationally until you overcome your needless fears. *See also* Self-Talk.

## Bibliography

Ellis, A. (1962). *Reason and emotion in psychotherapy*. Secaucus, NJ: Citadel.
Pioneering book on RET and cognitive-behavior therapy.

Ellis, A. (1972). *Executive leadership: The rational-emotive approach*. New York: Institute for Rational-Emotive Therapy.
Application of RET to business and management problems.

Ellis, A. (Speaker). (1977). *A garland of rational humorous songs*. (Cassette recording and songbook). New York: Institute for Rational-Emotive Therapy.

Ellis, A. (1988). *How to stubbornly refuse to make yourself miserable about anything—yes, anything!* Secaucus, NJ: Lyle Stuart.
Up-to-date self-help book applying RET.

Ellis, A., & Dryden, W. (1987). *The practice of rational-emotive therapy*. New York: Springer.

Ellis, A., & Harper, R.A. (1975). *A new guide to rational living*. North Hollywood, CA: Wilshire Books.

Ellis, A., & Knaus, W. (1977). *Overcoming procrastination*. New York: New American Library.

Maultsby, M.C., Jr., & Ellis, A. (1974). *Techniques for using rational-emotive imagery*. New York: Institute for Rational-Emotive Therapy.

Moshman, D., & Hoover, L.M. (1989). *Rationality as a goal of psychotherapy. Journal of Cognitive Psychotherapy*, 3: 31-t1.

Sichel, J., & Ellis, A. (1984). *RET self-help form*. New York: Institute for Rational-Emotive Therapy.

## For Further Information

More RET cognitive, emotive, and behavioral exercises are found in *How to Stubbornly Refuse to Make Yourself Miserable About Anything—Yes, Anything!* and other RET pamphlets, books, and cassettes. For a free catalogue of RET material, write the Institute for Rational-Emotive Therapy, 45 East 65th Street, New York, NY 10021-6593.

—ALBERT ELLIS

## REALISTIC JOB PREVIEW

Realistic job preview (RJP) is a job orientation technique designed for new or prospective employees. It presents detailed information about both the negative and positive aspects of the job being applied for so that applicants can make more informed decisions about taking or rejecting the job.

### Relationship to Career Choice

The realistic job preview is typically presented to the applicant early in the entry phase of the job, either before the job is offered, or, more often, shortly after the job has been accepted by that person. While this technique is primarily used to orient new employees, it can also be administered to provide a preview of new jobs in new settings for continuing employees. For instance, previews can be given to employees who are being considered for transfer to other locations in the organization.

The information of the preview has been presented in a variety of ways, including written scripts, audiotapes, videotapes, and interviews. No one method has been found to be superior in all situations. However, providing the information during an interview session, especially by someone currently employed in the job, seems to be a particularly promising approach.

The job preview presents detailed information about the job being filled. Quite often the material presented in the RJP has been formulated from analyses of organizational survey data obtained from people already holding the job being previewed. Although it often contains some general background information about the organization, this information is secondary to facts that are presented about the specific job being filled. In other words, relative to more traditional job orientation programs, the focus of the preview is primarily on the job the employee is filling rather than on the organization. It is designed to reveal not only the actual tasks involved in a job, but also some "insider" information that typically gets transmitted informally to new employees over the first few months of work.

Particularly characteristic of the realistic job preview is its disclosure of the negative as well as the positive aspects of the job being considered. The main goal of the RJP is to provide an objectively balanced job description, that is, what makes the RJP "realistic." Through the RJP, the organization is trying to transmit the following message: "This is what the job is really all about. Carefully consider the positive and negative aspects of this job and then decide if you really want it."

There are three objectives an organization using a realistic job preview is trying to achieve. First, employers are attempting to provide the applicants with valid and relevant information about the organization and the job so that they can make a realistic and informed decision of whether or not to take the job.

Second, by describing both the negative and positive aspects of the job, employers are trying to promote a sense of sincerity about their desire to achieve a good match between employee and organization needs and to reduce unnecessary turnover. Proponents of this approach have noted that traditional orientation methods have two possible shortcomings: they may create inflated job expectations among applicants, or they may not provide any information to hold pre-existing unrealistic job expectations in check. So, among other things, by using the RJP the organization is trying to prevent the unnecessary turnover caused by the disappointment resulting from unmet and unrealistic expectations about the job.

Finally, by describing some negative aspects of the job, the employing organization is attempting to "inoculate" applicants against adverse situations that could arise in the job. The assumption is that in the long run this kind of forewarning leads to a more committed workforce, especially when difficulties on the job emerge. Because these employees are less likely to have unrealistic expectations about their jobs, they are less likely to be caught off guard when unfavorable circumstances arise.

## Application

You should be aware of the purpose of the realistic job preview and you should carefully consider the information that is being provided to you. Try to keep the positive and negative information in perspective and then determine whether the job is going to meet your expectations. For instance, be careful not to discount the negative information, but do not be unduly discouraged by it. You should ask for more details about those things mentioned in the preview that cause you concern.

Use the preview information to develop clear ideas about what the job you are applying for entails and what it will be like working in the organization offering it. Information from the realistic job preview is designed to help you establish realistic performance and career expectations relative to the job being previewed, so take full advantage of what is offered.

*See also* Decision Making; Job Description; Job Search.

## Bibliography

Wanous, J.P. (1980). *Organizational entry: Recruitment, selection, and socialization of newcomers.* Reading, MA: Addison-Wesley. This book provides a thorough description of the realistic job preview and how it has been used in organizations. It also presents a good review of some foundational RJP research.

—SAMUEL B. POND, III

## RECRUITMENT

Instead of being a single activity, recruitment is better defined as a process which, if successful, results in satisfying the hiring needs of employers and the employment goals of applicants.

Recruitment firms or employment services provide "third party" assistance to employers whenever a hiring company determines that use of such assistance will expedite the successful completion of their employment requirements. These outside recruiting resources generally enhance and add more qualified job seekers to the applicant flow for the company to select from.

Job seekers are at an advantage in being on file with recruiting firms because these services must have a continuous inventory of applicants to draw from, while the bottom line for both the recruiter and the applicant is job placement.

Three distinct kinds of recruiting categories provide hiring assistance to employers and job applicants.

1. *Contingency Search/Placement Firms.* In terms of satisfying the hiring needs of business and industry, the contingency firms are the most successful. They produce the highest number of placements and have the most cost-effective program of all. Their fees are only earned if a hire takes place, with the employer paying the cost, never the applicant. Many of the contingency firms additionally market the applicants who have been derived from their ongoing recruiting activity. Oftentimes these firms will network or cobroke with one another as is done in the real estate industry. Sharing knowledge of job orders (hiring specifications) and applicant skills enhances their ability to make placements and earn fees. They handle a broad range of salary levels from $25,000 to $150,000. Contingency firms handle all types of professional occupations. Many of these firms also have a discipline/occupation specialty.

2. *Retained Search Firms.* These organizations are very research and industry oriented in the approach they take to carrying out their client's (hiring company) search assignments. Due to the paid retainer they receive to conduct each search, these firms dedicate their resources to

each client on a case-by-case basis. "Executive" search firms do not network and usually handle more confidential professional openings than the contingency category of recruiting. Salary ranges usually begin around $60,000 and could go into the $400,000 area. Interestingly, companies pay them whether they succeed or fail. It is not unusual for these firms to recruit internationally for their hiring clients.

3. *Employment Agencies.* Hourly workers, skilled and semi-skilled, and entry-level workers and new graduates are most often recruited and placed by this kind of employment service. Placed applicants, not the companies, pay the agencies. The fees are predetermined using a sliding scale equal to a percentage of wages.

## Application

When one is ready to consider new employment, it matters not who solicits the first contact with the other. It may be flattering to be "recruited," but the employment opportunity takes priority over all else. Once convinced that a new employment situation is in your best interest, you may decide to selectively engage multiple employment resources to assist you. Employment services only thrive on achieving mutual satisfaction between you and the new employer.

When you present youself and your qualifications you are also presenting your full condition to the fluctuating interpretation of a third party. You must strive to be attractive and of value; you must define yourself so as to be understood while appearing to be a real and reasonable person.

A well-done resume along with a completed application form serve as important tools which you can use to your advantage in gaining serious attention and understanding (see **Resume**).

As most employment services are placement driven, it is important that you prequalify opportunities described to you so as to avoid a mismatch because your interests or qualifications were misunderstood. You will make a decision anytime you are offered employment. Prior to employment decisions, you will find an abundance of advisors on the subject of your future. After gathering and considering your options, your instincts will usually prove to be your best advisor. Keep in mind that while the ability to make a commitment is commendable, having the fortitude to say "no" or changing one's mind later is much wiser than living with a mistake.

Placement services are regulated in most states by the department of labor, are subject to inspection of their operations, and are held accountable for any unlawful conduct. Most firms involved in the employment process belong to regional, state, or national associations which require strict adherence to a sound code of ethics.

While the field of third party recruiting is an honorable and socially redeeming profession, it is incumbent upon the applicant for employment to determine what services are best suited for her or his needs. Calling employment firms in the yellow pages of your local telephone directory will usually result in determining which type of service is best suited to handle one's interests and whether or not there is a financial obligation.

Confidentiality of a job seeker's identity is maintained during the recruiting and placement process by the placing firms as well as by potential employers. It is understood by all parties that when a person is seeking new employment it is privileged information. In fact, recruiting firms treat the identity of their hiring companies the same way.

*See also* Resume.

## Bibliography

Advice to use the same caution you would in selecting a doctor, lawyer, or banker is provided in Roger K. Williams in *How to Evaluate, Select and Work with Executive Recruiters*, (1981, Consultants News, Kennedy and Kennedy, Inc).

*Secrets of a Corporate Headhunter* by John Wareham, (1980, Atheneum) offers insight into search techniques utilized within the recruiting profession.

The Search Research Institute offers an enlightening (1988) encyclopedia-like book *Placement Management* by Paul Hawkinson and Jeffrey G. Allen, J.D., C.P.C. This publication is especially useful in gaining a thorough understanding of the entire third party employment/recruitment/search/placement business.

—BRUCE A. MONTVILLE

## REHABILITATION COUNSELORS AND AGENCIES

## Rehabilitation Counselors

Rehabilitation counselors are counselors with special expertise in disability related issues. They work with individuals who have physical, mental, and/or emotional disabilities. Rehabilitation counselors work with their clients and a wide variety of other professionals (e.g., physicians, allied health professionals) to analyze and synthesize information. They assist their clients in developing plans for rehabilitation leading to employment or independent living (Parker, 1987; Rubin & Roessler, 1987; Wright, 1980).

**As Employment Resources.** Rehabilitation counselors work in a variety of agencies or in private practice to provide counseling, vocational planning, and other services to assist people with disabilities to secure and maintain jobs and careers and to live independently within their communities. Rehabilitation counselors can be found in state vocational rehabilitation agencies, private rehabilitation agencies, hospitals, rehabilitation facilities, schools, employee assistance programs, insurance companies, and a variety of other agencies (Parker, 1987; Rubin & Rubin, 1988).

**Educational Preparation and Credentials.** As in other counseling disciplines, the use of the title "rehabilitation counselor" does not mean that an individual is qualified in rehabilitation counseling. It is therefore important to inquire about the credentials of a potential service provider.

The complexity of disabilities and employment necessitate a wide range of skills and knowledge for rehabilitation counselors. Rehabilitation counselors must have good counseling skills. They must also have knowledge and skills related to the medical and psychological aspects of a broad range of disabilities, consumer and environmental assessment techniques, occupational and labor market information, community resources, and jobs and hiring requirements (Rubin & Rubin, 1988; Wright, 1980).

The preferred level of education for rehabilitation counselor is the master's degree in rehabilitation counseling from a college or university program accredited by the Council on Rehabilitation Education. Persons with master's degrees in rehabilitation counseling and those with related education and experience can be certified as rehabilitation counselors by fulfilling education and experience requirements and passing the national examination of the Commission on Rehabilitation Counselor Certification. These individuals, who are designated as Certified Rehabilitation Counselors (CRC), must adhere to a code of ethical standards for professional practice (Patterson, 1987).

## Rehabilitation Agencies

Rehabilitation counselors work in a variety of agencies to assist people with disabilities to plan for and obtain employment. They also provide services to help individuals to live independently in their communities. The type of services provided often depends on the agency. The agencies described in this section are not the only ones in which rehabilitation counselors provide services, but rather they are a list of the most common ones.

**State Vocational Rehabilitation Agencies.** Every state has one or more vocational rehabilitation agencies that provide services under the jurisdiction of the Rehabilitation Services Administration of the U. S. Department of Education. Some states have separate agencies for persons with visual impairments and persons with other disabilities. Other states have one agency to serve all eligible persons with disabilities.

To be eligible for services from a state vocational rehabilitation agency, an individual must have a disability that interferes with employment, and it must be determined that vocational rehabilitation services will assist them in becoming employed or living independently. Basic eligibility requirements are set forth in federal regulations.

Services provided by vocational rehabilitation agencies include evaluation, vocational counseling, job placement, job modification, vocational training, and a wide range of other services. Eligibility for specific services may vary and some services require determination of financial need (Parker, 1987; Rubin & Roessler, 1987; Wright, 1980).

Vocational rehabilitation services in each state are administered through a central office and provided through district offices throughout the state. A list of central offices for each state can be obtained from the Rehabilitation Services Administration.

**Private Rehabilitation Agencies and Individuals in Private Practice.** Different types of private rehabilitation agencies offer a wide variety of services. Some agencies work with insurance companies to provide assessment, case-management, vocational counseling, and job placement. Their goal is to reduce insurance costs by helping workers return to employment at the same job, a modified job in the same company, or a different job.

Other agencies may provide specific services, for example, vocational assessments for the state vocational rehabilitation agency. Eligibility for services through private rehabilitation agencies may depend on available funding sources (Parker, 1987).

Rehabilitation counselors in private practice and private rehabilitation agencies may also provide vocational expert testimony. They serve as expert witnesses regarding the vocational options for individuals who have sustained either industrial or non industrial injuries. The Social Security Administration also uses vocational experts (Rasch, 1985).

## Rehabilitation Facilities

There are currently 2,785 rehabilitation facilities accredited by the Commission on Accreditation of Rehabilitation Facilities. They provide a wide range of programs, including personal and social adjustment services, work hardening, psychosocial rehabilitation, community mental health, alcohol and other drug abuse rehabilitation, and industry-based rehabilitation (Commission on Accreditation of Rehabilitation Facilities, 1990). Eligibility for services provided by these facilities depends on the type of service, the facilities' mission, and funding sources.

**Medical or Hospital-Based Rehabilitation Programs.** Many large hospitals have rehabilitation units. There are also free-standing rehabilitation hospitals that provide a broad range of rehabilitation services. These programs serve people with a variety of conditions, including degenerative diseases, stroke, head injury, spinal cord injury, burns, chronic pain, amputation, and multiple traumas. Rehabilitation counselors who work in medical/hospital-based programs are part of rehabilitation teams which usually consist of some of the following professionals: physicians, occupational therapists, physical therapists, speech/language pathologists, social workers, orthotists or prosthetists, and recreation therapists (Kaplan, 1986).

**Other Agencies and Programs.** Rehabilitation counselors work in many different agencies and settings in addition to those listed above. Some work in Employee Assistance Programs to assist employees to maintain their jobs. Others work in student services offices of colleges or universities to help students with disabilities gain access to and benefit from educational programs. In addition, some rehabilitation counselors work in school districts to assist students with disabilities in the transition from school to work or to post-secondary education.

In summary, qualified rehabilitation counselors have special training and expertise in disability, employment, and independent living. They are thus important resources for persons with disabilities who are seeking employment or planning careers.

*See also* Disability: Adjustment to; Disability: Student's Transition from School to Work.

## Bibliography

Council on Accreditation of Rehabilitation Facilities. (1990). Total number of accredited programs. Tucson, AZ: Council on Accreditation of Rehabilitation Facilities.

Kaplan, S. P. (1986). Rehabilitation counseling in medical settings: Career Opportunities. *Journal of Applied Rehabilitation Counseling,* 17, (2): 45–46.

Parker, R. M. (Ed.) (1987). *Rehabilitation counseling: Basics and beyond.* Austin, TX: Pro-Ed. Parker's text provides an introduction to rehabilitation counseling in a variety of settings. Topics include history and legislation, state vocational rehabilitation programs, psychosocial counseling, psychosocial impact of disability, placement and career development, rehabilitation research, independent living, private-sector rehabilitation, computer applications, and transition from school to work.

Patterson, J.B. (1987). Certified rehabilitation counselors. *Journal of Applied Rehabilitation Counseling,* 18, (4); 45–47.

Rasch, J.D. (1985). *Rehabilitation of workers' compensation and other insurance claimants.* Springfield, IL: Charles C. Thomas.

Rubin, S. E., & Roessler, R. T. (1987). *Foundations of the vocational rehabilitation process.* 3rd ed. Austin, TX: Pro-Ed. Rubin and Roessler's text also provides an introduction to rehabilitation counseling. Topics covered include history, the current rehabilitation scene, philosophical considerations, sociological aspects of disability, rehabilitation clients, the role of the rehabilitation counselor, the vocational rehabilitation process, utilizing rehabilitation facilities and support services, job placement, independent living rehabilitation, technology, and private sector rehabilitation.

Rubin, S. E., & Rubin, N. M. (Eds.) (1988). *Contemporary challenges to the rehabilitation counseling profession.* Baltimore: Paul Brookes.

Wright, G. N. (1980). *Total rehabilitation.* Boston: Little, Brown. Wright's text provides technical coverage of many aspects of rehabilitation counseling. Major sections are foundations, resources, assessment, counseling, and placement.

## For Further Information

**American Rehabilitation Counseling Association**
5999 Stevenson Avenue
Alexandria, Virginia 22304
1-800-545-ARCA

**Commission on Accreditation of Rehabilitation Facilities**
101 North Wilmot Road; Suite 500
Tucson, Arizona 85711
602-748-1212

**Commission on Rehabilitation Counselor Certification**
1835 Rohlwing Road
Rolling Meadows, Illinois 60008
708-394-2104

**Council on Rehabilitation Education**
P. O. Box 1680
Champaign, Illinois 61824-1680
217-333-6688

**National Council on Rehabilitation Education**
1200 Commercial Hal, Visser Hall 334
Emporia, Kansas 66801
316-343-5795

**National Rehabilitation Counseling Association**
633 South Washington Street
Alexandria, Virginia 22314
703-836-7677

—EDNA MORA SZYMANSKI AND JEANNE BOLAND PATTERSON

## RELAXATION: PROGRESSIVE MUSCLE

Progressive muscle relaxation (PMR), or deep muscle relaxation, is a procedure which involves alternately tensing (contracting) and relaxing major muscle groups in the body. A physician, Edmund Jacobson (1929), introduced PMR as treatment for neuromuscular or nervous hypertension. PMR is one of a number of techniques, including autogenic training, biofeedback-assisted relaxation, cue-controlled relaxation, sensory awareness training, and transcendental or other forms of meditation, which are used to combat anxiety, stress, and tension-related problems or states, such as tension and migraine headaches, essential hypertension (high blood pressure), insomnia, panic attacks, and even the discomfort of childbirth. From a medical perspective, PMR appears to increase responding in the parasympathetic nervous system and decrease responding in the sympathetic nervous systems. The results of these changes include a decrease in blood pressure and heart rate and slower and more regular breathing coupled with reports that the individual feels less anxious or tense and more in control.

### Relationship to Work

The work environment represents a major source of stress for many individuals. PMR, on the other hand, represents one useful, minimal cost intervention for coping with work-related stressors. Moreover, research has indicated that relaxation training produces reductions in blood pressure during the working day which persist for 15 months or longer and may reduce medical costs (see McCann, 1987; Sallis, Hill, Fortmann, & Flora, 1986 for reviews). In addition, PMR holds promise as an anxiety-reduction procedure for enabling job applicants to present themselves more comfortably and effectively during the employment interview, which is often a critical gateway to the world of work.

### Application

You can learn PMR in a variety of ways. Probably the best way is from a trained instructor (i.e., a professional counselor, psychologist, or therapist). Such an individual is best able to tailor and pace PMR to your needs. In addition, although PMR is a benign treatment for most people, a trained professional can help you avoid or cope with the such rare side effects as a muscle spasm from tensing too tightly or the fear of losing control or other negative thoughts which might be experienced by some individuals as they relax their usual levels of control. Self-help books and cassette tapes provide other means for learning PMR, and some examples of these are listed in the bibliography. Tapes include calming verbal instructions, but are unable to adjust the pacing of those instructions.

Prior to beginning PMR training, some initial preparation is needed. Quiet, dimly lit surroundings and a padded reclining chair which supports the body are especially helpful. You should loosen tight clothing and, if possible, remove contact lenses. In addition, you should be careful about tensing muscles too tightly, especially in areas which have been injured in the past.

Current training in PMR has been abbreviated from the original procedures developed by Jacobson, and you will find that there are several different variations. Although a detailed presentation is beyond the scope of this entry, the typical procedure involves approximately 5–7 seconds of tension for a muscle group followed by 20–30 seconds of relaxing or letting go, and this procedure is repeated with each of the major muscle groups of the body. Initially, two tension-relaxation cycles are typically employed before you proceed to the next muscle group. Later in training, only one cycle is used. Of course, the most important part of the cycle is the letting go or unwinding. The idea is for you to try to let go of the tension in that muscle group more and more over the course of the 20–30-second relaxation interval. The tensing portion of the cycle is designed to help you recognize when you are tense and to highlight the difference between tension and relaxation. Later in your training, you will find that experiencing these sensations of tension will serve as a reminder to use your PMR to combat them. Listed below are some common instructions for muscle tension. The entire cycle of two repetitions per group will take about 20–30 minutes and should be completed on a daily basis.

1. Tense the muscles in your right hand by making a fist.
2. Tense the muscles in your right upper arm by bending it at the elbow and making a muscle.
3. Tense the muscles in your left hand by making a fist.
4. Tense the muscles in your left upper arm by bending it at the elbow and making a muscle.
5. Tense the muscles in your forehead by frowning.
6. Tense the muscles in your eyes by closing your eyes tightly.
7. Tense the muscles in your nose and face by wrinkling your nose.
8. Tense the muscles in your lower face by pressing your lips together tightly and forcing your tongue against the top of your mouth.
9. Tense the muscles in your jaw by clenching your teeth together.

10. Tense the muscles in your neck by attempting to look directly above you.
11. Tense the muscles in your shoulders and upper back by shrugging your shoulders.
12. Tense the muscles in your chest by taking a deep breath and holding it.
13. Tense the muscles in the small of your back by arching your back.
14. Tense the muscles in your abdomen by pushing those muscles out.
15. Tense the muscles in your buttocks and thighs by pressing your heels into the floor.
16. Tense the muscles in your ankles and calves by pointing them away from your body.

As you develop skill in PMR, you will find that you relax more quickly and more deeply. For instance, you will probably find that you only need to complete one tension-relaxation cycle for each of the groups and perhaps that you don't need to relax all of the groups in order to feel calm. In addition, you will be able to dispense with the tension portion of the cycle and be better able to focus on the unwinding portion. As your skills with PMR increase, you will find it especially useful to practice differential relaxation.

Differential relaxation involves relaxing muscles that are not being used. For example, if you are standing and talking with someone, you will notice that, although you are using your leg muscles to support yourself, you are not using your arm muscles. You can practice releasing tension that you may be feeling in those muscles, or in your stomach, or in facial or other muscle groups which are not currently in use in order to combat anxiety feelings that you may be experiencing. Once you master it, you can use differential muscle relaxation to cope with anxiety in work and everyday situations in which it is impractical to use the full PMR procedure.

*See also* Anxiety; Stress; Work Hazards: Psychosocial.

## Bibliography

Budzynski, T.H. (Speaker). (1974). *Relaxation training program.* (Cassette Recording). New York: BMA Audio Cassettes. Three audio cassette tapes cover procedures for tense-slo relaxation, differential relaxation, limb heaviness, arms and legs heavy and warm, forehead and facial relaxation, and stress management. Includes an instructional booklet and sample record-keeping forms.

Jacobson, E. (1929). *Progressive relaxation.* Chicago: The University of Chicago Press. The original treatment of the topic.

Jacobson, E., & McGuigan, F.J. (Speakers). (1982). *Principles and practice of progressive relaxation.* (Cassette Recording). New York: BMA Audio Cassettes. Four audio cassette tapes and two instructional booklets, one for the learner and one for a teacher/clinician. Two tapes provide information on origins, critical concepts, and essentials of progressive relaxation for the clinician. A third tape provides a learner's guide to progressive relaxation, including an introduction and step-by-step instructions. The final tape provides timed instructions for localized and generalized tension reduction. The learner's manual has illustrations of how to tense different muscle groups.

McCann, B.S. (1987). *The behavioral management of hypertension.* In M. Hersen, R.M. Eisler, & P.M. Miller (Eds.), Progress in behavior modification (Vol. 21, pp. 191–229). New York: Academic. Critically reviews research on the management of hypertension with sections on relaxation, meditation, and biofeedback interventions.

Rosen, G. M. (1977). *The relaxation book: An illustrated self-help program.* Englewood Cliffs, NJ: Prentice-Hall. Provides detailed instructions for teaching yourself PMR. Also includes clear pictures of how to tense different muscle groups and self-assessment forms.

Sallis, J.F., Hill, R.D., Fortmann, S.P., & Flora, J.A. (1986). Health behavior change at the worksite: Cardiovascular risk reduction. In M. Hersen, R.M. Eisler, & P.M. Miller (Eds.), *Progress in behavior modification.* (Vol. 20, pp. 161–197). New York: Academic. Critically reviews research on cardiovascular risk reduction in the worksite, including research on PMR and other stress-related interventions.

—JOHN P. GALASSI

# RELOCATION

By the year 2000 the workforce in this country will shrink significantly due to changing life styles. At the same time, the high cost of education combined with the high cost of living will create a need for ambitious, experienced people to find a way to advance and increase their earning capacity. Relocation is one way to fulfill both of these needs for the employee who wants to advance, and the company that needs to meet its staffing needs.

Over a half million people are being relocated by corporations annually. That number could easily double because of the anticipated shrinking workforce by the year 2000 and the fierce competition for top quality people. The average cost for a relocation in our country is rising from $35,000 to $40,000 or $50,000 or more because of many economic factors. Major corporations throughout the country feel that in spite of the high cost of relocation it is still more cost-effective than recruiting and training new applicants for key roles.

## Psychological Stages of Relocation

What happens when people are asked to relocate? Years of research have identified five definite stages of relocation that are experienced by almost all relocating families.

**Stage One—Confusion and Denial**. The relocation offer can trigger this stage. It is one of the more stressful stages because all family members are asked to assess their own lives and their futures to determine if this is something they can accept. Frequently, decisions are made without appropriate information about the new area, opportunities for spouse employment, or whether the children will be able to continue their specific activities. Family members may agree to the relocation because logically they understand it may be the best decision for the whole family, but emotionally it often leads to the next stage.

**Stage Two—Anger**. Even though they have agreed to accept the relocation, often the family experiences anger. It's not unusual for family members to be angry because they have to change jobs, schools, leave their friends, give up being cheerleader the year they finally made it, or simply being angry without even understanding why. Eventually this anger may somewhat fade, only to be replaced by the next stage (see **Anger**).

**Stage Three—Depression**. This occurs once the boxes are unpacked and the house is in order and loneliness sets in. The phone doesn't ring and the family realizes they aren't being invited to participate in activities that had been so much a part of their lives that they took them for granted. Once this realization becomes evident it often causes resentment.

**Stage Four—Resentment**. Even though the relocation was agreed upon, the spouse sometimes realizes they were both on almost parallel career tracks, in earning capacity and professionalism. The partner who agreed to put his or her career "on hold" may be unable to find as satisfactory a position and begins to resent the decision. The partner who had an established place in the community may now have to rebuild a whole new network and resents having to do so, even though he or she accepted the relocation. Resentment is often felt by all family members for different reasons. Relocation decisions always have to be made under time constraints and rarely does the whole family have an opportunity to consider all the ramifications before they decide to accept it. Understanding resentment and the other stages of relocation, and what caused these feelings, and seeking alternatives to overcome them will lead to the fifth stage.

**Stage Five—Acceptance**. This occurs after the family has successfully networked into the new community, the job seeking spouse has located a job that offers a measure of fulfillment, the partners have found a way to participate in the activities they enjoy, and the children have adjusted and made new friends. Acceptance normally can take anywhere from a year to two.

## Relocation Issues

The first issue is do you really have a choice? Is this a case of "we either move or I have to find another job"? If you have a choice, many issues should be considered. Some of them are cost-of-living comparisons, such as real estate, food, taxes, and transportation costs. Others are quality of medical and educational facilities, availability of employment opportunities for the spouse and other family members, commute or driving time required, cultural and athletic events, climate differences, leaving family and friends, and whether each family member can actually cope physically, logically, and emotionally (see **Decision Making; Climate for Workers**).

## Preparation

If you decide to relocate after examining all the issues, you and your family should understand that you probably will experience all the stages to some degree; this understanding will allow you to prepare and minimize negative feelings.

Subscribe to a newspaper in the new community and, if possible, plan a visit. At your local library you can get names, addresses, and phone numbers of the places you want to see or call in the new area. Armed with this information and a current street map you will be able to organize your visit so you can physically cover as much ground as possible.

If you are seeking a job, you might want to have a supply of resumes so you could visit possible places of employment and leave your resume. This is an indication to prospective employers that you are a person with initiative, who is organized and will make effective use of time and energy (see **Job Search; Resume**).

Visiting neighborhoods, houses of worship, schools, and recreation areas will enable your family to visualize themselves in their new environment so they can start taking action and networking into the new community.

Families who have prepared themselves, started taking action even before the move, and formed networks will realize that the time needed to adjust and accept the relocation is greatly reduced, and the relocation is usually very positive.

## Effects on the Worker and Family—The Age Group Most Affected

The people who are most often approached to relocate are mature enough to have gained insight into the full scope of the company goals and young enough to want to remain with the company for at least 10 to 15 years. While people of all ages are relocated for various reasons, people between 35 and 49 meet the criteria in both of these areas, and they are the ones who are most often selected to be relocated.

What are the effects of relocation on this particular age group? Latest statistics show that over 60% of them are dual-career families, and this trend is expected to increase to 75% by the year 2000. The issue that impacts dual-career families most is the need for the trailing spouse to replace the second income as rapidly as possible. Rarely does the relocating employee receive a large enough increase to compensate for the loss of the second income.

**The Trailing Spouse**. When people in this age range are asked to relocate, whether dual-career or not, spouses have major adjustments to make. Non-job seeking spouses will not have an immediate network and may lose their identity; therefore, it is essential that they understand they have to take the initiative to develop friendships and a new place in the new community.

**Parents**. Many families in this age group have aging parents who need their assistance, sometimes because they are no longer able to drive and need help marketing or going to the doctor, or who may live with the family because they need constant care. Do they relocate with the family or do they remain in familiar surroundings, perhaps with other relatives or in a place where they get custodial care? All the options need to be considered to make the best decision for all concerned. What do the aging parents want to do, and how practical is it to abide by their wishes? Many of today's decisions become tomorrow's guilt, and this can be magnified when deciding the future of aging people, particularly if the family is unable to abide by their wishes. How comfortable will the relocating employee and spouse be with the decision at the time it is made and in the future? (see **Elder Care**).

**Children**. Although young children may not adjust as rapidly as we would hope, teenagers are generally the ones who need the most help when they are required to relocate. Even though they may have a voice in the process, they will not make the decision. They were taught to think for themselves and learn how to make valued decisions and then find that they really don't have much of a voice. The ramifications of teenage retaliation are something parents must realize, understand, address, and solve so these young people feel that they are part of the family and their feelings are valued. The more positive they can be made to feel, the happier the whole family will be.

## Relocation Assistance

Why should companies be concerned about helping their relocating families? An employee who has a family that is supportive and content is much more likely to be productive and efficient. When the family is in upheaval, the employee cannot devote full attention to the job at hand. Employees may be unable or unwilling to fulfill their obligations to the team effort of the company. Companies find it in their own best interest to make the relocation as comfortable as possible for the entire family.

The best time for companies to expedite the acceptance of relocation is very soon after the offer is made. They can help by providing time and financial assistance to allow the family to visit the new community, and by making provision for the physical aspects of the move, such as real estate, mortgage, moving van, and other arrangements. They can provide relocation assistance programs that have been specifically developed to address all of the emotional and economic concerns of the entire relocating family.

The most effective programs help you initially understand what is involved, prepare a plan of action to systematically enable you to say "goodbye" to the old life and "hello" to the new one, and provide you with a relocation specialist who is available to help when things don't go as planned. The MOMENTUM Program, offered by The Impact Group of St. Louis, is a good example of this type of program. The program's organized approach, its guides prepared for each age group in the family, and resource directories are used in conjunction with a trained, experienced consultant who is assigned to assist the family. The one thing you can be absolutely certain of is that the unexpected will occur. Knowing that help is as close as the nearest phone will give you the confidence and security to make relocation an opportunity and an exciting adventure.

In conclusion, you can achieve a successful, positive relocation when your family has discovered and addressed the issues, made the decision, prepared and carried out a plan of action based on actual, logical, and emotional needs, begins coping with the change in life style, and starts to feel "at home" in the new community.

*See also* Anger; Depression; Elder Care; Job Search; Managing Transitions; Resume.

### Bibliography

Springen, K., & Miller, A. (July 3, 1989). Easing the moving blues. *Newsweek*, 40–41.

—LAURA HERRING AND LUCILLE CUPPLES

## REPETITIVE MOTION ILLNESSES

Repetitive motion illnesses (RMI) are a group of related nerve ailments of the hand, wrist, arm, and shoulder that result from many jobs in which rapid and repetitive hand

and arm motions are repeated thousands of times each day. The forceful, rapid, and repetitive motions strain muscles, tendons, and nerves, causing swelling and numbness, as well as pain, burning, tingling, muscle weakness, and sometimes permanent disability. RMI includes tendonitis, tenosynovitis, and carpal tunnel syndrome. Carpal tunnel syndrome, often the most severe RMI, is caused by inflammation of the tendons in the arm and wrist that puts pressure on the median nerve, the main nerve of the hand. Carpal tunnel syndrome sometimes requires surgery and leads to permanent disablity.

RMI is the leading occupational illness in the United States. Workers in many occupations are at risk for RMI, including computer, postal, poultry, assembly line, grocery, office, telephone, and textile workers. RMI can be prevented by designing workplaces to fit the worker, rather than having workers to adapt to awkward work stations, and by slowing down the rate of work (see **Video Display Terminals; Work Hazards: Ergonomic; Work Hazards: Tool Design, Workspace**). Treatment for RMI usually involves resting the affected joints, wearing a splint to keep the wrists straight and minimize pressure on the median nerve, and taking anti-inflammatory drugs or injections of cortisone to reduce swelling. In severe cases, surgery is required to release the pressure on the median nerve.

## Relationship to Work

While it is possible to get RMI from other health conditions, such as diabetes or pregnancy, the problem is most often found in people whose work requires rapid and repetitive motions. Occupational health experts attribute the dramatic rise in RMI cases to automation and new technologies, which, while increasing productivity, have also fragmented work tasks to only a few manipulations performed thousands of times each day at increasingly rapid speeds. These excessive work rates combined with poor work station, tool, and equipment design result in prolonged periods of muscular strain that lead to RMI.

Today's workers are human beings forced to be extensions of fast-paced machinery. For example, hosiery workers pack 10,000 pairs of pantyhose by hand each shift. Poultry workers pull the guts out of 90 birds each minute. This same grabbing and pulling motion is repeated 40,000 times each shift. Postal workers average 180 keystrokes a minute, or well over 60,000 strokes a day.

In the past, secretaries' tasks involved use of a typewriter and copier, along with trips to the filing cabinet and the mail room. Now, office workers sit at their computer terminals and write, copy, file, and send documents without ever leaving their chairs. Their arms, wrists, and fingers perform the same strained movements on the computer keyboard thousands of times each day.

Pain is usually the main symptom of RMI, although many sufferers also experience swelling, numbness, tingling, and a feeling of heaviness and tiredness in the affected areas. In the case of carpal tunnel syndrome, symptoms include numbness, an inability to sense the difference between hot and cold, and difficulty holding, grasping, or manipulating objects. Everyday tasks like driving a car or lifting a frying pan can become a struggle.

Employees disabled by RMI can turn to the workers' compensation system in their state for possible relief. The law varies in each state, but a worker disabled by RMI may receive part of his or her weekly earnings and medical expenses while unable to work because of the illness. Compensation may also be awarded for irreversible loss of part or all of the ability to use one's hands or arms. This payment is typically only a fraction of the lost earning capacity of workers who must rely on their hands and arms for work.

Frequently, employers contest employees' RMI claims (see **Law in the Workplace; Workers' Compensation**). Success in fighting compensation claims allows companies to avoid accepting responsiblity for correcting workplace hazards and possible increases in workers' compensation premiums.

Under both federal and some state laws, employers have a general duty to provide employees with a safe and healthy workplace. In levying record high fines against Midwestern meatpacking firms, the federal Occupational Safety and Health Administration (OSHA), the government agency responsible for enforcement of safety and health standards, found that these employers had violated their general duty regarding RMI. Settlements have been reached with the companies mandating evaluation of work stations, redesign when appropriate, job rotation, employee education, and increased rest breaks.

To prevent RMI, occupational health experts recommend evaluating work stations and tools, redesigning them when necessary, increasing the frequency of rest breaks, rotating job tasks so that workers' arm and hand movements vary, and slowing the speed of work. They also suggest more rigorous enforcement by OSHA and increased compensation for workers disabled by RMI.

## Application

To prevent RMI at your job, you should conduct an assessment of the work you do. Ask yourself these questions. Do you have to adjust your body to the work? Do you have to bend your wrists to do your work, when a different height of your chair or work surface would let you keep your wrists straight? Do you have to bend and twist your hands and wrists frequently? Do you or your coworkers have pains in your hands or fingers? Do your hands or wrists tingle or hurt at night or after work?

If you answered yes to any of these questions, then you are at risk for RMI. If you have symptoms you should see a health care provider immediately. If you have a union on your job, talk to your shop steward. With RMI, as with most occupational health problems, working together is most effective in trying to correct workplace problems. You and your coworkers face and experience the same risks.

If you are considering an occupation that has a high incidence of RMI, find out about newly designed tools and methods of doing the work that are aimed at reducing RMI. Follow work practices that are designed to reduce RMI, such as frequent rest breaks. Remember, you only have two hands and arms—protect them!

*See also* COSH Groups; Law in the Workplace; Posture and Body Mechanics; Video Display Terminals; Work Hazards: Ergonomic; Work Hazards: Tool Design; Workers' Compensation; Workspace.

## Bibliography

MacLeod, D. (1982). *Strains and sprains: A workers' guide to job design.* Detroit: International Union, UAW.

Putz-Anderson, V. (Ed.) (1990). *Cumulative trauma disorders.* Bristol, PA: Taylor and Francis.

Scoppetuolo, G. (1990). *Repetitive motion illness: It's in your hands!* Durham, NC: North Carolina Occupational Safety and Health Project.

## For Further Information

**New York Committee on Occupational Safety and Health (NYCOSH)**
275 Seventh Avenue, 25th Floor
New York, NY 10001
212-627-3900

— TOBI MAE LIPPIN

## RESUME

A resume is a written summary of your work experience and education that communicates factual information to prospective employers about your qualifications for a specific type of job. It is an advertising and marketing tool used to generate employment interviews. Your resume should be based on provable facts and should convey what you have to offer an employer. It should be positive, concise, easy to read, and honest.

Why should you develop a resume? Most employers expect you to have one. They will request that you submit a resume for review and, if your qualifications seem to match their job requirements, you may be invited for an interview. Besides its primary purpose of generating interviews, the resume is used to:

- Review your experience so you can communicate your value to employers
- Enclose with applications and cover letters to employers
- Give to professional and personal contacts who might be able to help you, e.g., friends, relatives, colleagues, former supervisors, ministers, fellow alumni, club members
- Give to your references as an aid to help them respond to inquiries about you

Although there is no one perfect resume format or style, an effective resume will:

- Focus on the employer's needs
- Positively communicate your abilities and skills for the kind of work you desire
- Stress significant contributions and show how well you performed, and not simply restate job duties
- Show your career direction and interests; create a favorable impression
- Be concise, easy to read, and professional in appearance
- Communicate that you are a responsible person with a sense of purpose in your career who knows how to get a job done

To develop your resume, you go through two major phases: the preparation and the actual writing. The preparation phase is often handled inadequately; not enough effort is invested in generating a solid database to provide the foundation of the resume. Thorough preparation involves a comprehensive self-inventory of your work and educational experiences, plus a clear understanding of your accomplishments and skills. Preparing a good resume should not be a last minute effort. To develop your resume, follow these steps:

1. Inventory your work and educational background and your marketable skills
2. Study different resume formats and select the most appropriate one
3. Write a first draft of your resume using action verbs
4. Critique the first draft
5. Edit the final draft and make your resume look professional

A detailed discussion of each step is presented below. If you follow the instructions carefully, you should have few problems.

## Step 1: Conduct a Self- Inventory

### Part A: Review Your Work and Educational Background

On separate sheets of paper, list each relevant item listed below. Then, write down all pertinent facts for each item. Be thorough and detailed. Go for volume and condense the information later. This step provides the data for your resume.

1. *Contact Information.* List your full name, address, and day and evening telephone number(s).
2. *Job Objective.* This is the focal point of your resume. It may be helpful to organize the remainder of your information first. Look at your experience in terms of which skills and abilities you like to use, then define your objective. If you have difficulty in defining a work objective, you may want to consult a career counselor.
3. *Education*: List degree(s), major(s) and minor(s), date(s), school(s), and location(s). List such school highlights as extracurricular activities, honors, awards, research, publications, or significant projects. Place highest level of education first. If you are a college graduate, omit high school information unless it supports your objective. List special training.
4. *Work Experience.* Include all paid and nonpaid experiences. List job title, organization, location, description of work, significant contributions and achievements, and dates. Indicate items that point toward your effectiveness: raises, promotions, expansion of duties, etc. Identify demonstrated skills and abilities.
5. *Military Experience.* Note rank, service, assignments, dates, significant contributions and achievements, demonstrated skills and abilities, and reserve status.
6. *Community/Civic Involvements.* List office(s) held, organization(s), date(s), significant contributions, projects, and demonstrated skills and abilities.
7. *Professional or Trade Affiliations and Certifications.* List memberships, organizations, offices held, projects, certification, and licenses.
8. *Special Skills.* List foreign languages you read, write, or speak, and any other marketable competencies.
9. *Interests and Activities.* Examine avocations and hobbies to identify any that are work-related and support your objective.
10. *Miscellaneous.* List responses to these items:
    a. Salary requirements. Amount expected? Bare minimum?
    b. Extent of job-related travel acceptable.
    c. Are you willing to relocate? Where?
    d. When can you be available to start work?
    e. References. May present employer be contacted for a reference? Have you identified people who can attest to your past or present performance as a student or employee?
    f. Anything else you think is important.

### Part B: Analyze Your Marketable Skills

This is very important. Your success in generating job interviews and offers depends upon your ability to communicate your skills and qualifications to employers. Start this communication process with your resume.

Identifying and understanding your skills helps you to define or reaffirm your work objective and evaluate job fit. Skill analysis enables you to communicate your value to employers and to determine whether you can effectively perform specific job tasks.

Additionally, understanding your skills gives you greater flexibility and control in your job search. Many candidates seldom look beyond job titles; however, some job titles do not reflect the task's complexities and can be misleading. By knowing your skills, you can determine which ones are transferable among jobs and work environments. With this information, you can then expand your thinking about the kinds of jobs and employers that could use someone with your skills. Thus, you are less likely to get "hung-up" on job titles.

In summary, analyzing your skills will help you to:

- Define or reaffirm your work objective and options
- Develop a more positive and action-oriented resume
- Select the resume format which suits you best
- Interview more effectively because you have positive information about yourself
- Evaluate job openings and achieve a good job fit; not be misled or confused by job titles

Expand employment opportunities by recognizing that many skills are transferable from one work environment to another (see **Skills**).

How can you identify your strongest skills and the ones you most enjoy using? A powerful approach is to follow the directions in *The Truth About You* by Arthur F. Miller and Ralph Mattson (1989) to understand your intrinsic work motivation, abilities, skills, and other performance factors that contribute to career success and job satisfaction. Another approach is to work through "The Quick Job Hunting Map" in the latest edition of *What Color Is Your Parachute?* by Richard Bolles.

## Step 2: Study Different Resume Formats and Select the Most Appropriate One

The format should reflect your experience, plans, and needs. Consider your qualifications, job objective, work history, and the kind of employer you are seeking before you select a style. No one resume style is suitable for everyone; each person is unique and the resume should reflect that uniqueness. The most common formats are described below.

### Chronological Resume

This type of resume is easiest to write and the most commonly used. Jobs are listed in reverse chronological order with the most recent first. Employment dates are usually listed first, but can be listed at the end of each position description to emphasize what you did (see Figure 1).

**Advantages.** Employers are most familiar with this format and prefer it. It is easiest to prepare, highlights a steady employment record, and provides a concise guide for discussing your background during the interview.

**Disadvantages.** It can reveal employment gaps and put undesired emphasis on job experiences you may want to minimize. Skills may be difficult to spot unless they are communicated clearly and reflected in your most recent job. It may not provide the best presentation of your background if you are changing occupations or if you are re-entering the work force after an extended absence.

### Functional Resume

This format emphasizes qualifications, skills, and related accomplishments and de-emphasizes job titles and employment dates. Persons with little paid experience and those who are planning a dramatic career change often use it (see Figure 2).

**Advantages.** It stresses selected skills that are marketable or in demand, and reduces the impact of employment gaps. It de-emphasizes job titles and promotes the concept that skills are transferable from one work environment to another. This format allows you to incorporate nonpaid, relevant experiences for consideration by the employer. Since few applicants use it, the functional resume may gain more attention than other formats.

**Disadvantages.** Employers are not as familiar with this format and will want to see additional work history information. It does not highlight the organizational affili-

ation. It can be difficult to write unless you have thoroughly analyzed your skills and accomplishments. Many employers do not like this format because it makes work history difficult to interpret.

### Combination Resume

This format is similar to the functional resume, but includes employment history in a separate section. It allows the applicant to stress skills, while satisfying the employer's desire to know names and dates (see Figure 3).

**Advantages.** It emphasizes the applicant's most relevant qualifications and can be varied to emphasize both chronology and functional descriptions. It is a unique, but complete resume that may grab the employer's attention while providing all expected information.

**Disadvantages.** This resume takes longer to read; employers may lose interest unless it is concise, well written, and attractively presented. It is difficult to write; the functional and chronological sections must be very well described and should not be redundant. Many employers do not like this format.

## Step 3: Write a First Draft of Your Resume Using Action Verbs

Employers may receive dozens of resumes for a job vacancy. How can you make your resume stand out from the rest? For your resume to have impact, follow these guidelines.

1. Describe your experience in terms of what you accomplished. Use action verbs to strengthen descriptions. Employers are interested in results. Some examples of action verbs are:

| | | |
|---|---|---|
| established | won promotion | implemented |
| demonstrated | designed | improved |
| researched | organized | wrote |
| managed | conducted | contracted |
| supervised | prepared | maintained |
| negotiated | trained | directed |
| developed | invented | edited |
| sold | expanded | presented |
| operated | evaluated | reorganized |

2. Eliminate the personal pronoun "I" and use short, clearly written phrases starting with the past tense of action verbs. Avoid introductory phrases like, "My duties included . . ." or "My responsibilities were to . . ." List accomplishments whenever possible, rather than only describing duties. Use some jargon of your field, if appropriate, e.g., "can program in Fortran and COBOL." If you are a veteran, translate military jargon and experience into civilian language.

**Figure 1. Chronological Resume**

### JAMES WILLIAMSON

4567 Princess Anne Road     Virginia Beach, Virginia 23462     Telephone 804-789-4321

**OBJECTIVE:** Responsible position in accounts receivable and collections management which will use experience and skills in accounting, sales, and office administration.

**EXPERIENCE:**

Tidewater Distribution Company, Norfolk, VA. (1986 to Present)

ASSISTANT MANAGER, Accounts Receivable Department. Managed account collections functions. Designed accounting and computing systems to track and report past due accounts. Implemented a customer reminder system to notify delinquent accounts, including invoices, letters, telephone follow up, personal visits, and legal procedures. Negotiated settlements with personal and commercial accounts by arranging payment schedules to collect revenues and retain customer base. Advised small business accounts on cash flow management practices. Prepared monthly financial reports. Defined key performance standards for department and all positions. Hired, trained and supervised staff. Installed new computer software system. Reduced bad debts by 65% over three year period while business grew by 10-12% annually without increasing staff. Served on credit union board and provided employee financial consulting. (Since 1988.)

COLLECTIONS INVESTIGATOR, Accounts Receivable Department. Investigated past due accounts. Contacted customers to discuss accounts, trouble shoot problems, and identify possible solutions. Negotiated settlement plans. Referred customers for financial consulting. Wrote reports and recommended action. Coordinated accounting and legal information for management. (1986-88)

The Barris Development Corporation, Chesapeake, VA. (1982-86)

COMMERCIAL REAL ESTATE LEASING AGENT. Served as leasing agent for a variety of commercial sites, including office buildings, shopping centers and industrial parks. Generated leads and qualified prospective tenants. Negotiated lease terms with tenants, including site renovations and special requirements. Conducted credit and background investigations. Coordinated transactions with legal department.

Virginia Bank and Trust Company, Virginia Beach, VA. (1980-82)

HEAD CASHIER. Prepared financial reports, loan applications and new accounts. Entered information into data base. Investigated and verified loan information. Trained second cashier. Handled customer transactions and inquiries. Assisted customers with balancing accounts.

**EDUCATION:** A.A. Degree in Business Administration, Major in Accounting, 1982.
Tidewater Community College, Virginia Beach, VA
Maintained Dean's List Honors. Earned 100% of expenses.

3. State your objective clearly by specifying the type of work you desire and what you have to offer. This shows that you have done serious thinking about your career and that you have a sense of purpose and direction. State your objective in terms of your strongest qualifications that are likely to meet an employer's needs. In other words, make your objective statement work-centered, not self-centered. Avoid trite terms that emphasize what you want: opportunity for advancement; position working with people; a challenging position; etc. Objectives may be stated in various styles and levels of sophistication. At the most basic level, an objective may be stated as an occupational designation, e.g., "Automotive Mechanic" or "Elementary Education Teacher" or "Accountant." An objective also may be stated as an occupational designation with a specialty area, e.g., "Automotive Mechanic—Electronic Systems" or "Special Education Teacher—Learning Disabilities" or "Public Accountant—Taxes." The objective for a person with a general background may simply specify a position and then present skill areas he or she would use. Examples of weak and stronger objective statements appear below along with various styles.

*Weak Objective Statements:* "Management trainee position which will utilize business administration degree and provide opportunities for advancement"; "A position in social services which will allow me to work with people in a helping capacity"; "A position which will fully use my skills and experience."

**Figure 2. Functional Resume**

LYNN WILSON

<u>Home Address</u>                                             <u>School Address</u>
850 Washington Avenue                                 1287 Colley Avenue
Braddock, Pennsylvania 15104                    Norfolk, VA 23517
412-432-7865                                               804-640-7045

OBJECTIVE:   Entry-level position in rehabilitation of youth offenders which will use skills in counseling, program design, and training.

EDUCATION:   B.S. Degree in <u>Human Services Counseling</u>, May 1991
Old Dominion University, Norfolk, VA.
Minor: Criminal Justice and Urban Studies
Internships: Suffolk School for Girls and Norfolk Social Services
Earned 50% of expenses as Resident Assistant and Orientation Leader

**SKILLS AND EXPERIENCE**

Counseling   Provided individual counseling for teenage offenders during internships. Built trust and rapport. Conducted comprehensive personal history interviews. Used self assessment exercises and inventories to develop self awareness and issues for discussion. Used behavioral and cognitive interventions to challenge clients' behavior. Assisted in group and family counseling sessions. Led career exploration process for individuals and groups. Administered and interpreted interest inventories, values scales and ability test under supervision of clinical staff. Reviewed taped sessions to evaluate counseling process and own skills. Wrote assessment reports and intervention plans for clients. Classes included counseling skills, testing, group process, counseling theories, career development, and supervised site experience.

Program Design   Assessed needs of client population. Defined learning objectives and designed programs to meet needs. Designed programs and workshops on interpersonal relations, communication skills, managing emotions, self awareness, personal goal setting, career education, and self esteem. Designed evaluation forms to provide feedback. Wrote training materials, produced visual aids, and arranged field trips. As resident assistant, planned annual program schedule for 70 women, including educational, personal growth and social activities. As member of student orientation committee, planned and designed university orientation program for new students and parents.

Training   Personally conducted workshops and programs on above topics. Varied teaching style to maintain interest. Used a variety of training exercises and techniques to fulfill program objectives. Used role playing, demonstrations, modeling, process observation, small group, and feedback techniques to enhance learning. Operated a variety of audiovisual equipment. Led residence hall meetings with students. Conducted information sessions for new students and parents.

*Stronger Objective Statements:* "Outside sales in home improvement which will use experience and training in home construction and ability to initiate sales leads, qualify clients, plan work, and function independently"; "Special Education Teacher. Certified to teach all levels of mental retardation. Special interest in working with students between the ages of 13 to 18"; "A public relations position in developing and implementing programs, organizing people and events, and communicating positive ideas and images. Effective in public speaking and in managing publicity and promotional campaigns."

4. Support your objective with specific documentation in the text of your resume, much like you would support comments in a school paper with references to relevant evidence in the literature.
5. Place the most important information first in your resume. If your education is most supportive of your objective, then it comes first. However, if you have relevant work experience, then that should come first.
6. Be concise. Lengthy, detailed descriptions often are not read and can be a liability rather than an asset. Emphasize specific areas of expertise beneficial to the employer. Keep it neat and organized.
7. Be consistent in your format, i.e., tense of verbs, order of information, layout, etc.

**Figure 3. Combination Resume**

Confidential Resume
**LEE MATTHEWS**

1657 Lynnhaven Road    Virginia Beach, Virginia 23464    (804-923-1735)

### OBJECTIVE

Sales Management.  Willing to relocate and travel.

### AREAS OF EFFECTIVENESS

**Management**  Managed retail operations including buying, merchandising, inventory, payroll, accounting, and staffing.  Planned advertising and sales promotions.  Established incentive programs for sales staff.  Developed business strategy, objectives and action plans.  Monitored business and staff performance through sales reports.

**Sales**  Generated prospects through advertising, mailings, telephone follow up and personal appointments.  Developed and maintained records to provide excellent customer service.  Assessed customer needs and wants by establishing rapport, asking qualifying questions, attentive listening, and offering appropriate options for products or services.  Achieved and exceeded sales objectives through generating new business, high closing rates and repeat business.  Obtained extensive corporate and industry sales training.

**Training**  Analyzed job requirements and work tasks; defined needed skills and performance outcomes.  Developed training objectives, curriculum and training modules.  Prepared and presented lessons.  Demonstrated techniques and methods.  Observed and evaluated students' progress.

### RELATED EXPERIENCE

<u>Sales Representative</u>.  Atlantic Auto Group, Virginia Beach, VA. (1988 to Present)

<u>Vocational Teacher - Automotive</u>. Virginia Beach Public Schools, VA. (1980-1988)

<u>Night Manager, Sales and Service</u>. Sears Automotive Center. Virginia Beach, VA. (1978-80)

<u>Manager</u>. Kempsville Auto Parts, Inc.  (1976-78)

<u>Counter Man</u>. Kempsville Auto Parts, Inc.  (1973-76)

### EDUCATION

B.S. in <u>Vocational Education</u> with emphasis in Automotive Mechanics, May, 1980.
Old Dominion University, Norfolk, VA.

8. Omit personal characteristics unless they support your objective. Height, weight, color of hair, state of health, and other personal characteristics are usually irrelevant and unimportant.

9. Do not use abbreviations. Use full descriptions.

10. Exclude names of references on your resume. Instead, simply say: "References available upon request." Employers assume that you are able to supply references; therefore, if you need the space, omit the reference section altogether. Instead, list the names of your professional references on a separate sheet of paper and carry the list with you to interviews. The list should be typed and should contain the full name, title, business address, and telephone number of each person.

11. Emphasize important aspects of experience through various visual techniques—spacing, margins, centered headlines, underlining, all caps treatment—in an attractive, uncrowded format. Appearance counts.

12. Have your first draft typed, paying particular attention to layout and design.

## Step 4: Critique Your First Draft

After you are satisfied with your first typed draft, ask several people who are familiar with the type of work you seek to evaluate your resume. Be prepared for all kinds of feedback. Some comments will be valid for you and others should be taken, politely, with a grain of salt! You have to determine which comments are relevant to your situation.

However, assess if the overall reactions to your resume are positive. Specifically, the following items should be critiqued:

1. *Overall Appearance.* Do you want to read it? Is it easy to read? Does it look professional? Does it create a favorable impression?
2. *Contact Information.* Is it clearly presented on the top of the first page? Are both permanent and temporary addresses provided? Do you provide both day and evening telephone numbers where you can be reached or where a message can be left? If you have a two-page resume, do your name and contact information appear at the top of the second page?
3. *Objective.* Is it clear? Is it stated in terms of your strongest qualifications that match the employer's needs? Is it reasonably short? Does it convey your career purpose?
4. *Organization.* Are your strongest qualifications presented immediately under your objective? Do your strong points stand out? Is layout consistent?
5. *Content.* Does the content support and substantiate your objective? Do you stress skills, accomplishments, and results, rather than duties? Do phrases begin with action verbs? Do you use short phrases instead of full sentences? Has extraneous material been eliminated?
6. *Length.* Is it brief (one page, not more than two)?
7. *Wording.* Check once more. Be certain that there are no misspellings or punctuation or grammar errors and that technical jargon has been kept to a minimum.

### Step 5: Edit The Final Draft and Make Your Resume Look Professional

Follow these guidelines:
- Incorporate relevant feedback into the final draft.
- Be ruthless in editing your resume. Make every word count!
- Use a staccato writing style—short, impactful phrases beginning with action verbs.
- Emphasize important aspects of your experience through various visual techniques.
- Describe your most qualifying experience first.
- De-emphasize dates by locating them at the ends of paragraphs to which they relate.
- Attractively use all space on each page.
- Don't use language from official job descriptions.

Don't include:
- Reasons for leaving previous employers.
- Official documents as attachments.

- Your Social Security Number.
- Pictures of yourself.
- Salary history.
- Names of references.

Don't state religion, physical characteristics, health or physical problems, race, ethnic origin, etc. Don't state details of employment more than 10 years old, unless particularly relevant to your objective. Don't include a covering sheet. Don't stipulate a narrow geographical preference.

### Producing Your Resume

Communicate your professionalism with a professional looking resume. Use high-quality paper for final copies and print only on one side of the paper. A conservative ivory, light tan, or light gray paper may help your resume have more impact. Supply the printer with a master copy on high resolution laser paper for electronic publishing that will be reproduced exactly as you prepared it. Make sure that the original has dark, clear type and no errors. Your master should not be on erasable bond or onion skin since it is very difficult to reproduce from this type of paper.

Remember, the main purpose of the resume is to pre-sell you to employers so that you will generate job interviews. Your resume will not, in and of itself, get you a job, but it can open or close the first door.

*See also* Job Search.

### Bibliography

Krannich, R., & Banis, W. (1990). *High impact letters and resumes.* Manassas, VA: Impact Publications. Teaches readers how to develop a highly personalized resume and letters within a larger career planning and job search process.

—WILLIAM J. BANIS

# RETIREMENT

Retirement has been traditionally defined as the leisure period of life following completion of the work career (usually beginning around age 65) and supported by government entitlements (i.e., Social Security) and private pensions. More recently, there has been a blurring of this dichotomy of work and retirement as increasing numbers of retirement eligible older workers experiment with a variety of productive and leisure roles concurrently. Thus, individuals develop a personal mosaic of paid, volunteer, and leisure roles which are the most meaningful to their personal situations. A synonym for this modern definition of retirement is independence.

## Relationship to Work

The traditional concept of retirement was age defined (generally at age 65) because of mandatory retirement regulations and the age for eligibility for full Social Security pension benefits. The more flexible definition of a personally determined pattern of work and leisure is the result of the following factors:

1. Mandatory retirement regulations are virtually eliminated due to age discrimination legislation.
2. Increased numbers of workers are covered by private and public pensions where eligibility standards are based on years of service and age, thus providing financial support for independence at much younger ages.
3. Social Security legislation allows for some earned income without losing all Social Security pension benefits.
4. Increased options are available for older workers to develop flexible work schedules. Key transitional roles fostering a continuum of work and retirement are flextime, job-sharing, mentoring, gradual retirement, part-time or temporary employment, and self-employment. This trend is likely to proliferate as employers cope with the aging of the workforce and increasing shortages in key labor pools.
5. Some employers offer early retirement incentives as a more attractive, cost-effective, and less disruptive method of reducing or restructuring their corporate workforces. Many of these employees accept these inducements to support the opportunity for experimenting with the flexible work roles described above.
6. Retirees disenchanted with the loss of self-esteem often associated with the traditionally defined retirement in a work ethic society demonstrate they can successfully move in and out of the workforce (Bureau of National Affairs, 1987).

## Relationship to the Individual and Family Life

The potential effects of retirement focus on five areas of resources important for independence throughout the life span. They are financial resources, mental and physical health, social support systems, housing, and personal skills and competencies.

**Financial Resources.** The three important components in this resource area are often referred to as a three-legged stool for financial security in retirement: Social Security pension benefits, private or public pensions, and personal savings.

1. Social Security is the major financial support for retirees. Currently 98% of workers in the United States are covered by Social Security programs. Benefits are indexed to the annual cost of living so that retirees are protected somewhat from inflation. This factor has been largely responsible for the dramatic improvement in the poverty ratio of people over age 65. Benefits are calculated by age, number of years contributed to the system, and the inflation-adjusted dollar weighting of the amount contributed each year in the system. The earliest a worker can receive reduced benefits is age 62, although widow(er)s of a worker may receive benefits as early as age 60. Full benefits may be earned at age 65, but recent legislation is gradually increasing that to age 67 for those born in 1960 or later. The method for calculating benefits results in lower wage employees earning a larger percentage of their wages in retirement than higher wage employees, with average benefits at approximately 40% of worker income.

An important concept in the Social Security program is the retirement test. This means that the retiree is eligible to earn through paid or self-employment a certain amount of money and still receive full pension benefits. The threshold for the amount that can be earned without penalty is indexed to the cost of living so the dollar figure of the threshold increases annually and is linked to age. For example, in 1990, from age 62 through age 64, retirees may earn $6840, but for every two dollars earned above that test amount, their Social Security benefit is reduced by one dollar. From age 65 through age 69, retirees may earn, in 1990, $9360, but for every three dollars earned above that test amount, their Social Security benefit is reduced by one dollar. Age 70 and older, retirees may earn any amount and still receive full benefits. The retirement test has the effect of encouraging retirees to work part-time beyond the traditional ages of retirement.

2. Private and other public pensions cover approximately 50% of the workforce. The amount of pension benefits, criteria for eligibility and impact of re-employment standards vary considerably. Some generalities are: (a) Most are not covered by cost-of-living indices and therefore are much more vulnerable to inflation than Social Security benefits. (b) All private pensions are legislated by the Retirement Equity Act, 1984, which provides important protection for the investment security and spousal rights of the pension plans. It is important to note that public pensions, such as held by state government workers, are not protected by this act. (c) Most plans are not portable, which means that if employees leave one organization for another,

their earned credit toward future pension benefits ceases. Unless vested in the prior plan (a term describing the length of time required by the plan to protect earned credit already accumulated in the plan), workers may lose whatever credit has already been set aside by the employer. Thus, private pensions are often dramatically reduced by frequent job changes or the pattern of moving in and out of the paid work-force so typical of working women.

3. Personal savings are the third important component of financial security in retirement. The establishment of Individual Retirement Accounts (IRAs) is an excellent example of the legislative emphasis placed on workers taking some personal responsibility for their future security or independence. The critical factors for supplementing major pension benefit programs are the discipline to save, the availability of funds above the normal living expenses, and the availability and access to investment products. As might be expected, lower income workers have less discretionary income and may not know of investment products unless they are promoted by employers.

Studies of the effect of retirement on income and the net effect of the income on retirement satisfaction are enlightening. Although income usually drops after retirement, the relative decrease is small (about 25%) and has little effect on retirement satisfaction. This supports the objective data of the size, importance, and proliferation of Social Security and private pensions. However, some subgroups of retirees are not so fortunate. Typically, people who have retired early due to poor health, minority groups in lower paying occupations with less likelihood of private pensions, and women who have interrupted paid workforce participation or have lowered benefits as survivors of pensioned workers have much larger decreases in retirement income and, therefore, higher rates of financial difficulties in retirement. For some of those people, the negative impact is so great that life-long work is their only option.

**Health Resources.** The importance of good health to satisfaction in retirement is critical and well documented, a prerequisite for independence in late life. For example, the major cause of involuntary retirement is poor health. Statistics show that only 5% of involuntary retirements are due to lingering mandatory retirement legislation, 10% are due to adverse labor market conditions, and 33% of all workers (but 50% of black males) are due to poor health (Parnes, Crowley, Haurin, Less, Morgan, Mott & Nestel, 1985). These facts show that poor health leads to retirement, reversing the popular myth that retirement leads to poor health.

Certain subgroups are more likely to have problems with health than others because good health is the product of life-long factors such as adequate medical care, sound nutrition, and life style health habits. Specifically, males develop debilitating health problems sooner and have shorter life spans than women, minority races (and particularly black males) are more disadvantaged than whites, and poorer people are likely to show the effects of poverty on health earlier than more advantaged population groups.

**Social Support Systems.** Although not as clearly defined as the importance of financial and health resources for successfully and personally defining retirement, there is growing evidence of the importance of social support systems to successful adjustment in retirement (Kobasi, Maddi, & Kahn, 1982; Parnes et al., 1985). Indeed the lack of friends and family outside the workplace may be one of the fundamental reasons for remaining in the workforce long after retirement eligibility.

However, there is also evidence that having dependent children is a factor in continuing employment (Parnes et al., 1985), while being responsible for elder care may be forcing middle age women into retirement earlier than normal (Bureau of National Affairs, 1987).

Research is fragmentary at best on the effects of retirement on women, but clearly marital status has a more important effect on the patterns of work and retirement on women than on men (Palmore, Burchett, Fillenbaum, George, & Wallman, 1985). Studies suggest that single-career women follow some of the same patterns in retirement as men, while married women were more likely to have less predictable patterns of retirement and related adjustment to retirement because of the likelihood of shorter and more erratic work histories. On the other hand, some of these married women also had the benefit of additional pensions based on eligibility on their husbands' work records. Thus, the more complex the social support system, the more complex and potentially enriched the definition of retirement.

**Housing Resources.** Often overlooked in retirement is the importance of the home as a resource for independence. Financially, the equity built up over a long period of home ownership is an important financial resource. The abundance of home equity loans is one way to use that equity; however, debt and resulting interest charges are accrued. The reverse annuity mortgage is a similar program established just for older home owners. A monthly payment based on the equity in the home is paid by the lender to the homeowner, but the interest and debt repayment are not collected until the homeowner moves, sells the home, or passes the home into the estate via death. The flip side of home ownership as a financial asset is the cost of upkeep and maintenance. One of the major reasons older adults choose to sell their home is to eliminate those costs.

Housing has an important influence on health. Location of the home can determine access to adequate medical services. Consequently, there are a growing number of community based health services, where home health aides go to the home, rather than expecting the client or patient to come to the health resource.

Another response to recognizing the importance of housing on health is the growing number of congregate and continuing care retirement communities. The concept is to provide apartment or group living for older adults around a health service center so that access to health care is immediate. Often this health care is free to residents if they have paid initial fees for entry into the community and have Medicare and supplemental health insurance. Research has shown that congregate housing can improve life satisfaction and longevity (Ehrlich, Ehrlich, & Woehlke, 1982).

Although most men over 65 live with family members (usually a spouse), most women over 65 live alone because women on the average live 7–8 years longer than men and typically marry older men, thus spending perhaps a decade or longer living as a widow. However, over 70% of people over age 65 live within one-half hour of their families, illustrating the importance older adults place on the social support system.

**Personal Resources.** The final resource category is the arsenal of personal skills, competences, attitudes, and coping strategies that people have for building independence. Obviously, keeping job skills abreast of technology developments is critical for continued employment and marketability. Thus, practical issues for older workers are job redesign, retraining, and continuing education. In fact, employers have found older workers to be valuable and dependable employees if they were perceived as adaptable to new skills, competitive, and flexible (Bureau of National Affairs, 1987).

More subjective, yet still supported by the body of research in personality and stress, is the importance of personality and coping styles in managing potential stressful events (Whitbourne, 1985). The common ingredient in many of these studies is the concept of control by planning ahead for change (Danish, Galambos, & Laquatra, 1983; George, 1980). Planners can minimize negative effects of stress or even use stress as a motivator for personal growth.

A recent study summarizes much of the research related to personality and coping styles by describing three factors which differentiated successful managers of stress from unsuccessful ones (Kobasi, Maddi, & Kahn, 1982). Specifically, they asked why some Type A personalities thrived on the stress attributed to their life style, while others developed stress-related health problems. They found three traits common to "hardy" people (or Type C personalities since all three characteristics begin with C):

1. *Commitment.* Hardy people are fully involved in what they are doing and with whom they are doing it. They have a reason to get up in the morning.

2. *Change Is Challenge.* They view change as a natural and positive part of life, an opportunity to grow and develop. Change is something to look forward to rather than to avoid.

3. *Control.* They believe that they can influence the world around them and are willing to act accordingly. They are in charge of their feelings, actions, and goals. They are planners.

## Application

Clearly, certain factors are key elements in successful retirement no matter how you want to define it. Preretirement planning for those factors all through your career regardless of age is a strategy that is more likely to assure that you define retirement on your terms rather than on someone else's.

1. Build your five important resource accounts for independence (financial, health, social supports, housing, and personal resources). Think of each as a bank account in which you make deposits, and protect from premature withdrawals, but have at your side to draw upon when needed for achieving and maintaining independence throughout your life span.

2. Do not put "all your eggs in one basket" in any of your accounts. What holds true for sound financial investment also holds true for your other accounts. For example, if you develop many different marketable skills, you are not as likely to be affected by technology changes. Always have a backup (Plan B) to add to your accounts if losses in any occur.

3. Develop realistic expectations of what changes in any of these accounts may mean to you personally. Mark Twain said "I am an old man and have known a great number of troubles, but most of them never happened." The key is to get good information rather than accepting so many myths of retirement and aging as fact.

4. Stay in control of your planning. For example, if forced to retire from active employment because of poor health, at least determine the date and timing of that retirement. Even that little control can make a difference in your adjustment to your new status. In addition, your health status may prevent you from performing your old job, but could allow you to do something else (perhaps teach others to do your job) or learn a new skill that does not require the same physical demands.

*See also* Benefits; Career Roles; Decision Making; Discrimination: Age; Leisure; Managing Transitions; Part-Time Work; Pre-Retirement Planning.

## Bibliography

Bradford, L. (1979 Nov.–Dec.). Can you survive your retirement? *Harvard Business Review:* 103–109. A succinct and entertaining discussion of Leland Bradford's experience with the transition to retirement.

Bureau of National Affairs, Inc. (1987). *Older Americans in the workforce: Challenges & solutions.* Rockville, MD: The Bureau of National Affairs, Inc. A comprehensive discussion of older worker issues and options, including alternative work options, early retirement, and older worker benefit resources.

Danish, S.J., Galambos, N.L., & Laquatra, I. (1983). Life development intervention: Skill training for personal competence. In R. D. Felner, L. A. Jason, J. N. Moritsugu, & S.S. Farber (Eds.),*Preventive psychology: Theory, research and practice.* New York: Pergamon Press.

Ehrlich, P., Ehrlich, I., & Woehlke, P. (1982) Congregate housing for the elderly: Thirteen years later. *The Gerontologist,* 22, 399–403.

George, L.K. (1980). *Role transitions in later life.* Belmont, CA: Wadsworth, Inc.

Kobasi, S.C., Maddi, S.R., & Kahn, S. (1982). Hardiness and health: A prospective study. *Journal of Personality and Social Psychology, 42,* (1): 168–77. New insight into stress management. Written as a research report, but the message is also available to the general public in a 30-minute videotape, "Coping with change: Emotional fitness" (Carlsbad, CA: Spectrum Films, Inc..)

Palmore, E.B., Burchett, B.M., Fillenbaum, G.G., George, L.K., & Wallman, L.M. (1985). *Retirement causes and consequences.* New York: Springer Publishing Company.

Parnes, H.S., Crowley, J.E., Haurin, R.J., Less, L.J., Morgan, W.R., Mott, F.L., & Nestel, G. (1985). *Retirement among American men.* Lexington, MA: D.C. Heath and Company.

Whitbourne, S. K. (1985). The psychological construction of the life span. In J. E. Birren & K. W. Schaie (Eds.), *Handbook of the psychology of aging.* New York: Van Nostrand Reinhold.

—KATHERINE A. GRANT

# S

## SELF-EFFICACY

Self-efficacy was proposed by psychologist Albert Bandura (1977, 1986) to refer to the evaluations people make in their minds about whether or not they can perform certain tasks. People have expectations about their ability to do such things as give a speech at a business meeting, design a new circuit, or assemble a motor on a production line. The term "efficacy" means the power or capacity to produce an effect; the concept of "self-efficacy," therefore, refers to one's judgments or beliefs about one's own power to produce a behavior, successfully accomplish a task, or solve a problem.

The beliefs and judgments people make about their abilities, the "self-efficacy expectations," significantly affect their *actual ability* to do particular tasks. In other words, people may have the capability to perform a task, but their beliefs may keep them from even attempting something, or adversely affect their performance on things they do attempt.

### Relationship to Work

Hackett and Betz (1981) first discussed the usefulness of self-efficacy theory to career development and work behavior, especially women's work behavior. The literature on women and work has consistently pointed out that women often make career and work choices well below their potential, leaving their skills and abilities underutilized. The traditional sex-role socialization of women is often used to explain why women do not achieve according to their potential. However, there are *some* women who achieve in nontraditional areas, so sex-role socialization does not totally explain why women underachieve. Hackett and Betz (1981) suggested that we need to look at how sex-role socialization *and* early experiences affect how women and men judge what they can do well (self-efficacy). For example, when growing up, boys get more opportunities to be exposed to and practice things that allow them to develop a strong sense of confidence (self-efficacy) in their abilities in working with mechanical things, mathematical problem solving, and leadership activities. These are all areas that directly lead to fields of work that have been described as "male dominated" (e.g., scientific/technical, mechanical, and managerial jobs). Women on average do not get exposure to these "traditionally male" activities as they grow up. The result, according to Bandura's self-efficacy concept, is that women therefore do not develop a strong sense of their competence (self-efficacy) in certain areas and tend to avoid these traditionally "male-dominated" fields. However, women who *do* see female role models engaging in nontraditional activities, and who *do* get to engage in these nontraditional behaviors and activities, can and do develop a strong sense of their competence (self-efficacy) in nontraditional fields. Experience and exposure to models, rather than sex-role socialization *per se,* affects career and work choices.

Investigations focusing on Hackett and Betz's proposals have found that career self-efficacy, confidence in one's ability to succeed in work pursuits, is useful in understanding the career behavior of *both* men and women. Research shows that self-efficacy predicts what college majors women and men choose, how persistent people are in following through on their college major choices, career decision-making, and willingness to engage in nontraditional career activities (see Lent & Hackett, 1987). The consensus of opinion seems to be that attention to the development of strong and realistic career-related efficacy expectations is vital to successful career development for all people. In fact, self-efficacy has been found to be more significant in predicting educational and career choices than actual measured ability (see Lent & Hackett, 1987).

### Application

Because efficacy expectations are cognitive judgments of one's performance, self-efficacy judgments can be modified, unlike personality "traits." Hackett & Betz

(1981) suggest that four major sources of efficacy "information" can be used to strengthen unrealistically low work-related efficacy expectations.

First, actual performance is the most powerful source of self-efficacy information. When you are successful in school and work activities, you tend to be more confident of your abilities in related areas, whereas if you have limited experience you are less likely to feel confident and more likely to be anxious. Second, observing successful models engaging in various work-related activities encourages higher and stronger efficacy expectations. Third, higher levels of anxiety can be discouraging, and tend to lower efficacy judgments. And last, verbal encouragement or discouragement has a lesser but still significant impact on self-efficacy.

If you are unsure whether your judgments about your abilities are accurate, you would do well to examine whether you are underestimating what you can do because of lack of experience, lack of exposure to models, interfering anxiety, or discouragement from others. To strengthen self-efficacy, you would want ideally to combine experiences from all four informational sources, e.g., engage in graduated performance experiences, observe others like yourself who are successful in what you want to do, work on anxiety management, and develop support networks. Both men and women need to examine the degree to which their self-appraisals and choices are based on sex-role socialization messages and pressures rather than on realistic self-efficacy judgments.

*See also* Assertion; Career Exploration; Choosing an Occupation; Nontraditional Job for One's Sex; Sex-Role Stereotyping.

## Bibliography

Bandura, A. (1977). Self-efficacy: Toward a unifying theory of behavioral change. *Psychological Review*, 84: 191–215. Extensive overview of self-efficacy theory.

Bandura, A. (1986). *Social foundations of thought and action: A social cognitive theory.* Englewood Cliffs, NJ: Prentice-Hall.

Hackett, G., & Betz, N.E. (1981). A self-efficacy approach to the career development of women. *Journal of Vocational Behavior*, 18: 326–39. The authors discuss how self-efficacy theory can be applied to understanding career behavior, and strongly argue the usefulness of the approach for enhancing the realism of efficacy expectations.

Lent, R.W., & Hackett, G. (1987). Career self-efficacy: Empirical status and future directions. *Journal of Vocational Behavior*, 30: 347–82.

—GAIL HACKETT

# SELF-EMPLOYMENT

For those people who are unhappy in their work, much of the everyday dissatisfaction and frustration experienced in their lives can be directly tied to the job. To many, a job is seen as the only means to earn a living. But, rather than providing an opportunity to realize personal dreams and aspirations (as well as income), the job becomes a pervasive imposition which kills personal incentive and ambition.

The result of a person's growing contempt for the way they are forced to support themselves and their families often leads to a deepening contempt for themselves as a person. Many in this situation then begin to disassociate themselves from their jobs and start seeking satisfaction elsewhere via hobbies and other diversionary pursuits. Rarely does this create contentment over the long haul. In time, job dissatisfaction and associated negative feelings spill over into all aspects of the person's life, leading to additional problems.

This article will challenge the reader who is unhappy with his or her job to consider self-employment as a means of reconciling work and self.

## Relating Your Work to Your SELF!

Over half of our daily waking hours are spent at work. Given this heavy involvement, it stands to reason that our work environment greatly influences our overall perception of ourselves. Consider these 8 questions that relate to this assumption:

1. Do you look forward to going to work most of the time?
2. Do you feel that your work provides ample opportunities for professional and personal growth?
3. Are your talents used to their fullest?
4. Is your work time devoted to something that you believe in?
5. Is the philosophy that underpins your working environment consistent with your personal philosophy?
6. Are your opinions sought to resolve company/department challenges?
7. Do you have control over your working hours, assigned tasks, and future direction?
8. Does your work environment allow for individualization in terms of career paths, the process of completing assigned tasks, etc.?

If you answered "yes" to all 8 questions then you've found the perfect job—congratulations!! If you answered "no" to two or more questions, then, like many people, your work life is inconsistent with *who you are*! To understand more fully what this means, let's look a little closer at each question.

Question 1 reveals your general attitude toward your work. A good work situation, like a good marriage, invites renewal. Each day provides an opportunity for new discovery and accomplishment. Those who appreciate the gift of a good marriage look forward to most days with gratitude and enthusiasm. This applies as well to positive work situations.

Question 2 has to do with personal/professional advancement and maturity. A good work environment provides exposure to new experiences and learning. Recognition is given to the need to achieve greater competency and to assume greater responsibility and authority.

Question 3 is related to question 2. Advancement and personal/professional maturity can only occur if the full range of an individual's personal attributes and talents are utilized. The old adage, "cessation of growth equals stagnation" applies to all aspects of our lives, particularly our employment. Growth is initiated and sustained when there is constant challenge, the opportunity granted to "showcase" our talents.

Questions 4 and 5 speak to the moral/ethical aspects of our work involvement. Many work situations cause us to compromise personal values and standards. The ideal work environment is one in which there is a high degree of compatibility between personal and business moral/ethical considerations.

Questions 6, 7, and 8 inquire into the degree of control you have in your work environment. Are you paid to simply follow instructions and perform assigned, routine tasks? All of us are multi-talented individuals. Being reduced to a mere "functionary" significantly limits our contributory possibility and subsequently undermines our sense of self-worth.

If you are spending a good portion of your work time in an environment that is not enjoyable and fails to stimulate personal growth through learning and creativity, then you have no doubt been forced to separate your "working self" from your deeper and more real personal self.

## Bridging the Gap Between Your Work and Your Self

In order to maximize the possibility of personal, vocational satisfaction, you must have considerable control over your working environment. Having a business of your own provides the best opportunity to mold your working environment to fit your resources, needs, and aspirations. Planning your own business involves a myriad of factors, technical, organizational, and personal. Obviously, the technical and organizational aspects are critical components in business success; however, the first, most significant, step you must take involves evaluating the "fit" between you as a person and your business idea.

Planning a business that offers enjoyment and personal fulfillment on a regular basis is as simple as recognizing what kinds of things you like doing! Recall past jobs and identify aspects of the position you liked and disliked. Consider how you spend your leisure time, then brainstorm some business ideas that involve doing those things you most enjoy. Of course, not all tasks are going to be enjoyable. For example, if you open a sign-painting business, sign painting will be *one* of the things you will do on a daily basis. After you determine that there is a market for your product(s) and/or service(s), then you're ready to put your business into action!

If you plan to succeed as a business owner, you will be required to wear a number of hats. With the many challenges facing a self-employed person, opportunities to learn are endless. Increased proficiency in management, marketing, sales, and planning is only limited by the effort you put forth.

The more competent you become in these areas the more your business will prosper. Future development of personal attributes, such as leadership, decision making, and interpersonal relations, is a natural outcome of successful business ownership. An in-depth, honest look at your strengths and weaknesses is a necessary first step in determining what you need to learn. Next, a conscious decision must be made to correct weaknesses and maximize the potential of your strengths. The final step is to create a working atmosphere as well as a specific plan of action that provides opportunity for learning.

If your sole motivation for becoming self-employed is to make lots of money, then, chances are, you will be just as dissatisfied in owning a business as you are in your job. This is not to suggest that money isn't a critical factor in running a business. Profit is a primary ingredient in the formula for business survival and ultimate success. But money should be viewed as a by-product (albeit an important one). This is born out by the majority of successful business owners we have worked with. The opportunity to promote an idea, product, or service that has personal meaning for the owner and meets the needs of his or her customers is the driving force behind a successful business venture. To set the stage for your entry into the work of business, list your personal causes; those things that you most value. Then, answer a couple of simple questions for yourself: Does the business idea you are evaluating allow for ties to any of the causes you listed? If not, will the number of hours required to succeed in your own business allow for time to participate in these causes after work? If the answer to these questions is "no," go back to the drawing board! Without *intrinsic* rewards, the amount and intensity of work required to succeed as your own boss will defeat even the most determined new business owners.

The goal for most of us is to get beyond the status quo in both our personal and professional lives and be an integral part of solutions to problems when they arise. Unfortunately, in too many companies operations revolve around maintaining the status quo. When problems do arise, there are, typically, two predictable outcomes: the workers resolve the problem and the boss takes credit for the solution, or the workers aren't consulted regarding the problem but have to deal with *additional* problems resulting from inappropriate decisions made by uninformed or in-competent supervisors. Eventually, employees don't feel they are contributing and begin to do just enough to get by.

You will be the main contributing force in your own business. If you fail to give *yourself* to the business, no one else will and your business will die. However, as your business grows and there is the need for employees remember the things you disliked about working for others and take proactive measures to ensure that your employees don't feel stifled working for *you*!

Achieving a good balance between you as a person and your work should be a primary goal. By following the aforementioned advice, you have a good opportunity to assess the fit between yourself and your idea. This initial step is a key in planning a successful business. Of course, once this task has been completed, much more work remains. In conclusion, a summary of next steps follows.

1. *Research Your Market.* Again, there must be a fit between you as a person, the idea you have in mind, and the market you intend to serve. Some specific questions to be answered include: Who are your customers? Where do they reside? What motivates them to buy? Who is your competition? What are the competitor's advantages and disadvantages? How much market share is available? How do you intend to set yourself apart from the competition?

   To answer questions such as these, we suggest you follow a seven-step program:
   a. Decide what information you need
   b. Organize the research
   c. Conduct the research
   d. Analyze the information you have gathered
   e. Supplement with additional information
   f. Draft a synopsis of your market potential
   g. Determine how to reach your market

2. *Plan Your Production Strategies.* How will you produce/deliver your product/service? How long does it take to produce a single unit? How many can you produce in an hour, a day, a week, a month? Does this production schedule allow for completion of all other tasks a business owner must perform, such as sales, customer service, record keeping, and management?

3. *Plan Your Organizational Management Structure.* Who is responsible for what? How will you control your inventory, personnel, financial resources, time, etc? What insurance needs do you have? What professional consultants do you need at your disposal? An attorney? An accountant?

4. *Plan Your Finances.* How much money do you need to get started? How much do you need to operate for the first year? What terms do you require (time-frame, interest rate, collateral, etc.)? How will you keep your financial records up to date? Specific financial statements you must complete include: Projected Income Statement; Business Balance Sheet (Projected); Cash Flow Statement; Projected Start-Up Expenses; Break-Even Analysis; Personal Balance Sheet; Projected Annual Business Budget; and Personal Budget.

You can significantly increase your chances of business success by following the five-step process:

1. Assess the fit between you and your idea
2. Research your market
3. Plan your production strategies
4. Plan your organizational/management structure
5. Plan your finances

The time to succeed is now!!

*See also* Career Exploration; Choosing an Occupation; Work Values.

## Bibliography

Blake, G., & Bly, R. W. (1983). *How to promote your own business.* New York: New American Library. This book offers specific promotional strategies for business as well as a nuts-and-bolts approach to self-promoting *and* learning when and how to have others promote for you.

Engstrom, T. W., & Juroe, D. J. (1979). *The work trap.* New York: Fleming H. Revell. The authors explore the reasons we stay with careers that are less than personally fulfilling. Specific steps are recommended for escaping the traps we build for ourselves in our work.

Gerber, M. E. (1986). *The E myth.* Cambridge, MA: Ballinger. An insightful look at the myths surrounding entrepreneurship, replete with alternatives to these myths.

Heider, J. (1985). *The Tao of leadership.* New York: Bantam. A philosophical treatise that helps close the gap between business and personal commitments.

Mandino, Og. (1988). *The greatest miracle in the world.* New York: Bantam. A short novel that guides the reader to a reconsideration of vocational accomplishment.

Rich, S., & Gumpert, D. (1985). *Business plans that win $$$*. New York: Harper and Row. Based on the M.I.T. Enterprise Forum approach, this book guides entrepreneurs in writing a business plan that will attract investors.

Rosenblatt, P. C., et al. (1985). *The family in business*. San Francisco: Jossey-Bass. The authors provide a realistic look at the tensions, conflicts, and special problems inherent in a family business. Most helpful is the advice offered for overcoming problems stemming from role confusion, power struggles, and conflict between family and nonfamily employees.

Waxler, M., & Wolf, R. (1987). *Goodbye job, hello me!* Glenview, IL: Scott, Foresman. A practical guide to becoming self-employed which emphasizes the psychological aspects of making the transition from job to self-employment.

## For Further Information

Contact your local chamber of commerce office or your local SCORE (Service Corps of Retired Executives) chapter.

—MYER WAXLER AND TERESA PATTY

# SELF-ESTEEM

Self-esteem is a personality trait describing the extent to which people like themselves. Although our self-esteem varies somewhat from one situation or time to the next, most of us have *generalized* tendencies to like or dislike ourselves. Mental health professionals have long recognized the importance of self-esteem to the human condition; people who are maladjusted are more likely to have generally low self-esteem. More recently, industrial, organizational, and vocational psychologists have begun to explore the role of self-esteem in career decisions and work issues.

Self-esteem pertains to career decisions and work behavior in at least two ways. First, research has shown that individuals' career decisions and workplace behavior are an outgrowth or consequence of their self-esteem. Second, organizational and work-related factors have been shown to cause or influence individuals' self-esteem.

## The Consequences of Self-Esteem

Several studies have shown that high self-esteem individuals view themselves as better suited than their low self-esteem counterparts for the occupation that they are about to enter. High self-esteem people believe that they have more of the abilities needed to succeed in the occupation and that the occupation best matches their personal needs and values. The result of these tendencies is likely to perpetuate individuals' existing levels of self-esteem. High self-esteem persons probably will feel good about themselves for choosing a career for which they believe they are well suited, whereas those with poor opinions of themselves are likely to continue feeling bad about themselves for not choosing a career for which they think they are well suited.

Once in the workplace, high and low self-esteem employees behave differently. Partly because they lack self-confidence, and partly because they need to be positively evaluated by others, low self-esteem persons are more likely to be influenced by a variety of work conditions. For example, whereas most people perform better and feel more satisfied with their job when their coworkers are supportive rather than unsupportive and their formal responsibilities are clear rather than ambiguous, these tendencies are stronger among employees who are low rather than high in self-esteem. In a sense, the low self-esteem employees are more influenced by events in the workplace.

Employees' self-esteem also affects their reactions to negative or failure feedback, particularly in areas that are psychologically important to them. In the face of failure, high self-esteem people tend to maintain (or even increase) their subsequent work motivation and performance. In sharp contrast, low self-esteem employees usually become demotivated by negative feedback. Such reactions to failure by low self-esteem people may lead to a "vicious cycle" of failure, in which the negative feedback causes reduced effort, which is likely to lead to impaired performance, more negative feedback, and a repeat of this chain of events.

## Work Factors That Influence Self-Esteem

Both individuals and those who must manage individuals in the work setting stand to learn from the theory and research on self-esteem. Individuals need to be aware that their self-esteem often channels them to act and think in ways that reinforce or perpetuate their existing level of self-esteem. Of course, such tendencies generally paint a rosier picture for high than for low self-esteem persons. High self-esteem people are likely to benefit from the "success cycle" (Hall, 1971) in which they perform well, set higher goals as a consequence, try harder, and continue to perform well. People who do not like themselves may become victims of the vicious cycle of failure discussed above. Therefore, the latter group needs to be vigilant about not falling prey to the behaviors associated with low self-esteem. Rather than giving up in the face of failure, for example, these people may need to redouble their efforts, so as to increase their chances for success (and thereby break the vicious cycle).

Individuals' self-esteem does more than influence their behavior; it also leads them to *perceive and interpret* their worlds in a manner consistent with their self-esteem. People with high self-esteem usually believe that they are more likeable, have performed better, or have exercised greater control in a given situation than their low self-esteem counterparts, even when there is no objective evidence to support such beliefs. Put differently, high self-esteem people sometimes overestimate their likeability, performance, and control, whereas low self-esteem persons sometimes underestimate themselves along these dimensions. Therefore, all individuals—regardless of their self-esteem—need to seek accurate information about themselves, rather than rely simply upon their customary self-esteem in judging how well they have come across or performed in a given situation.

Managers also need to be aware of their subordinates' self-esteem. For example, if low self-esteem subordinates become more demotivated by negative feedback, then managers should try to ensure that jobs laden with negative feedback—such as many sales positions— are occupied by high self-esteem people. One study found that life insurance salespersons—who are usually bombarded with negative feedback—performed better and quit less often if they had high rather than low self-esteem. Moreover, managers may be able to influence their subordinates' customary reactions to situations. For example, if a manager knows that her low self-esteem subordinate has a tendency to react to failure by blaming himself, or by becoming hopeless about the future, then the manager needs to talk with the subordinate to try to minimize such counterproductive reactions to failure. Indeed, managers who are interpersonally skilled may alter not only their subordinates' behavior for the better, but also over time may be able to effect change in the subordinates' self-esteem. More general ways in which the workplace influences employees' self-esteem are discussed below.

## The Causes of Self-Esteem

Due to life experiences (and probably genetic influence), individuals bring to their work a baseline, or customary level of self-esteem. However, the workplace may also influence individuals' self-esteem, both on a temporary, and more permanent basis. For many people, the world of work is their "home away from home"; they spend much time at work, and much of their psychological energy is devoted to succeeding on the job. It therefore stands to reason that the workplace may influence their self-esteem, for better or worse.

**How Do I Compare?** Because we need to understand and evaluate ourselves, people are forever comparing themselves to each other or other targets of comparison (e.g., their past selves, their ideal selves, or some objective yardstick). If they come out second best in that comparison process, their self-esteem is likely to suffer. For example, if your friend performs better than you on an exam, or if a coworker with whom you are close receives a bigger pay

raise than you, your self-esteem may well decrease. Interestingly enough, it may not even be your *absolute* standing on some dimension that affects your feelings of self-worth so much. Rather, it is how you fare *relative to* others that is particularly influential. For instance, it has been shown that middle income black children have lower academic self-concepts than their lower income counterparts, even though the former group significantly *outperforms* the latter group on objective measures of academic performance. One explanation, provided by relative deprivation theory, is that middle income black children, many of whom attend integrated schools, compare themselves to those around them: their mainly white counterparts, who, on average, outperform them. Lower income children also compare themselves to those around them: other kids who also are not likely to be performing well. As a result, lower income children's self-esteem will not suffer as much. A related study in the late 1970s also showed the importance of relative (rather than absolute) outcomes among professional women. Those who compared their salaries to other women made *less* money but were *more* satisfied with their pay, relative to the women who compared themselves to their male counterparts. One explanation of these findings is that the women professionals who compared their pay to that of men generally made less money than the men. Hence, in a relative sense they felt deprived.

**Do I See What You See?** Sociologists and psychologists have suggested that peoples' self-esteem is determined by how they think they are viewed in the eyes of important others. This process begins early in life, when the role of "important others" is played by family members, parents in particular. The process continues throughout the life span, however, and is likely to occur in the workplace. Organizations are always sending messages to their employees about the employees' value or worth. Certain organizations (e.g., IBM) have the reputation of valuing their workforce, which is likely to foster high employee self-esteem (and commitment to the organization). Even within a given organization, however, some people perceive that they are more favorably evaluated than others. Such evaluations can come during a formal performance appraisal, but they can also come in a variety of more intangible ways (e.g., employees given responsibility to perform a task implicitly are being told that they are highly enough thought of to be given the responsibility).

**You Are What You Do.** Some jobs consist of activities that make people feel good about themselves; for other jobs, just the opposite is true. For example, some jobs give people the opportunity to think for themselves and make independent decisions, without strict supervision. Research has shown that employees' self-esteem flourishes in such a work environment. Employees' self-esteem also increases when they work in a cooperative group atmosphere. In contrast, jobs that are highly routinized, and noncooperative work environments have negative effects on employees' self-esteem. In short, the behaviors that people do while performing their jobs "rub off" on them, affecting their self-esteem, for better or worse.

## Application

Two management practices have received much attention in the past 10 years: charismatic leadership and job enrichment. According to House et al. (1988), "charismatic leaders articulate a mission, or vision in ideological terms, demonstrate a high degree of self-confidence and a high degree of involvement in the mission, set a personal example for followers to emulate, create and maintain a positive image in the minds of followers, peers, and superiors, communicate high performance expectations to followers, and confidence in followers' ability to meet such expectation. . . ." (p.104–105).

Job enrichment refers to a process of changing the nature of employees' jobs, so as to make them more intrinsically interesting. Enriched jobs have variety, provide autonomy to employees, and give people the feeling of working on the complete task from beginning to end. In addition, people with enriched jobs believe that they are doing something important, and they get feedback in the process of doing the work.

Both charismatic leadership and job enrichment have generally positive effects on employee performance and job satisfaction. Furthermore, these positive effects may occur *precisely because* charismatic leadership and job enrichment make employees feel better about themselves. Charismatic leadership encourages employees to believe that they can perform better than others, or better than they might have otherwise believed. Charismatic leaders also communicate to employees that they are valued and respected. Job enrichment provides employees with the experience of making their own decisions, which is one activity that promotes high self-esteem. If the positive effects of charismatic leadership and job enrichment occur because both practices heighten employee self-esteem, then managers may wish to rely on these and other managerial behaviors that promote positive self-images among their subordinates.

From the individuals' perspective, if the workplace influences their self-esteem, then it becomes especially important for people to do a "self-esteem audit" when deciding whether to pursue a particular career, join a certain organization, or accept a given job. Try to ensure that you are well-suited for your chosen career. This requires you to learn about various careers, in particular what it takes to succeed and what rewards (material or otherwise) the

career does *and does not* offer. Just as important, you will need to be (or become) *self*-knowledgeable. Remember, being well-suited for a particular career means that you have (or will acquire) the abilities needed to succeed, *and also* that the rewards offered by the career are consistent with what you desire from your career. Therefore, to know whether you are well-suited for a career, you need to know about the career, and about yourself, and then assess the degree of fit between yourself and the career.

Having decided upon a particular career for which you are well-suited, you then need to learn about particular organizations and jobs, so that you can better evaluate their likely effect on your self-esteem. Does a given organization value its people? Do people cooperate with one another in this organization? What is the nature of a given job; are people who do the job likely to feel better, the same, or worse about themselves as a result of working in that job? These are very important questions for you to consider. Indeed, if you make wise career and workplace decisions, your self-esteem stands to benefit. However, if you choose a career, organization, or job that lowers your self-esteem, it could be hazardous to your (mental) health!

*See also* Career Identity; Job Satisfaction; Rational Thinking; Self-Efficacy; Self-Talk.

## Bibliography

Brockner, J. (1988). *Self-esteem at work: Research, theory, and practice.* Lexington, MA: Lexington Books. A thorough treatment of the role of self-esteem in the workplace, useful for both students and managers. It focuses not only on the consequences and causes of self-esteem, but also on how employee behavior is motivated by the desire for self-esteem.

Burns, D. D. (1980). *Feeling good.* New York: NAL Penguin Inc. This overview of the theories and techniques of cognitive therapy that are used to help people overcome depressions is written in nontechnical language and provides many useful ideas relating to career issues and self-esteem.

Hall, D.T. (1971). A theoretical model of career subidentity development in organizational settings. *Organizational Behavior and Human Performance,* 6: 50–76.

House, R.J., Woycke, J., & Fodor, E.M. (1988). Charismatic and noncharismatic leaders: Differences in behavior and effectiveness. In J.A. Conger & R.N. Kanungo (Eds.), *Charismatic leadership.* San Francisco: Jossey-Bass.

McKay, M., & Fanning, P. (1987). *Self-Esteem.* Oakland, CA: New Harbinger Publications. This book is written primarily for persons suffering from low self-esteem. It gives a thorough, in-depth description of its causes and offers proven methods of cognitive behavioral therapy to raise self-esteem by changing the way you interpret your life.

—JOEL BROCKNER

## SELF-MANAGED CHANGE

Self-managed change means taking responsibility for changing one's own behavior and maintaining that change over time. Usually, people decide to change their behavior for one of three reasons: (a) they regard their behavior as a problem, (b) someone else regards their behavior as a problem, or (c) their behavior is not causing any particular problem but they wish to perform better than they are currently doing in some respect. This article briefly presents the principles of successful self-managed change and describes how these principles are applied in work-related situations.

### Principles of Self-Managed Change

Most successful attempts to change one's behaviors involve the completion of six steps or principles of change. First, self-managed change begins with a desire to change. Unless a person wants to change, the odds of successfully changing are low. People can be forced to change by someone else, but seldom is the change lasting; as soon as the influence of the other person diminishes, the individual is likely to return to old styles of behaving, often with a vengeance.

Second, once a person decides that he or she wants to change, it is important to observe in oneself the specific behaviors that need changing. For example, it is important to know how often, where, when, and under what circumstances the behavior occurs. These observations help not only to decide how to change the behavior but also to monitor the success of attempts to change.

Third, after thinking about the behavior and carefully observing it, the next step is to construct a program for change. Usually, this program involves changing very specific behaviors that are themselves small steps toward the overall goal. For example, a person who wants to lose 25 pounds might set up a program to lose one pound per week by skipping dessert after each evening meal and walking one mile a day. The point is that it is usually best to change behavior in small steps, often referred to as change by "successive approximation," because a person is more likely to find modest steps are more manageable and provide more success experiences. There are exceptions. For example, some people find that it is best to quit smoking by going "cold turkey," stopping all at once rather than gradually. But with more complex behaviors, such as becoming more assertive or learning to speak better in public, progress is best attempted through a series of small, realistic steps.

Fourth, it is critical to identify how you will know if your behavior change program is working. It is easy to determine if you are losing weight or drinking less coffee each day; it is more difficult to determine if you are relating better to your employees or doing a better job for your boss. Unless one has honest and clear ways of measuring change, it will not be possible to determine whether your program for change is effective.

Fifth, it is important that there be rewards for changing one's behavior. Often, these rewards occur naturally. For example, one might feel better after cutting down on coffee or get compliments on losing weight. In other cases, it might be important to build in rewards, such as going to a favorite movie after being appropriately assertive with a supervisor who was making unreasonable demands. In the end, it is unlikely that one will continue to work to change a behavior unless there is some perceptible reward for changing.

Finally, an individual should decide how he or she will handle relapse or temporary failure. This is perhaps the most often overlooked step. Most people relapse: from time to time they eat that favorite dessert, they fall back to yelling at an employee, they let their coworkers push them around too much, and so forth. When this happens, it is tempting to throw in the towel, to say to oneself that you cannot change and therefore why keep trying? Instead of taking this approach, it is critical to recognize that relapses will occur and that dealing with them is part of a successful program of self-managed change.

### Self-Managed Change in the Workplace

Because each person is different, and because of the unending variety of work environments, it is impossible to describe all the types of behaviors or behavior changes that are important for a successful and rewarding career. However, researchers have found that some problems are more frequently encountered in the workplace than others. Plas and Hoover-Dempsey (1988), for example, have identified the following as being among the most likely to interfere with job satisfaction and success in the workplace:

1. Inappropriate expression of anger and feelings in general (i.e., over- or underreacting)
2. Miscommunication
3. Treating coworkers with disrespect
4. Lack of caring or commitment on the job and to teamwork
5. Passivity, lack of assertiveness, failure to confront a problem or situation appropriately
6. Dishonesty, lack of credibility
7. Tardiness
8. Procrastination

## Applying the Principles of Self-Managed Change to Common Work Problems

One of the truisms of self-managed change in the workplace is that a small amount of change can lead to significant improvements. One need not attempt to make major behavioral or personality changes; a few simple changes in behavior often are adequate to resolve a problem. It is also important to begin the change process in the right frame of mind. Change should be viewed as a challenge, not a chore. Optimism, enthusiasm, self-pride, patience, and a tolerance for occasional failure are critical to breaking old habits and establishing new ones.

As an example of how one might apply principles of self-managed change, consider being asked by your supervisor to write a budget report, a task you have avoided in the past because of "writer's block" or difficulty in writing reports. First, be sure that you are ready and want to change. You might realize you need to overcome this problem if you wish to advance in the company, or you simply are tired of the stress and embarrassment that report writing is causing you.

Second, you need to assess the problem. Do you have difficulty writing all types of reports, or only those that involve bad news, numbers, or information that is not totally controlled by your unit? What are the characteristics of the problem? Do you have trouble getting started, deciding the report is good enough to hand in, organizing the material, knowing what to conclude, finding enough time to do the report? Let's assume that the main problem is simply one of feeling overwhelmed at writing the report. You have trouble knowing where to start or how to get the job done.

Third, break down the task into small parts that you can handle. Formulate a plan of steps and be flexible. Start out constructing an outline for the report, perhaps simply by copying down the outline from last year's report. Then read over some of the materials and forms you will use in the report. Next, jot down a few notes under each outline heading, making no attempt to be complete. At this point, quit for the day and turn to other things. The next day you might try to write a paragraph or two of one section. The point is to break down the task into small, attainable steps without undue pressure.

The fourth principle is to identify progress. In this case it will be rather easy; accomplishing each step—such as writing down last year's outline, reading over relevant materials, writing a sentence or two under each heading—is a mark of progress.

Fifth, what are the rewards for accomplishing the steps of your program? It is likely that many people will find that the completion of each step will be reward enough to provide satisfaction. Others might find that it is useful to reward oneself by going to a movie or playing an extra round of golf after accomplishing a few steps of the plan. The nature of the reward is not important; it is simply important that there be one, small or large, intrinsic to the task or external to it.

Finally, realize you might fail with one of the steps. For example, perhaps you could write an outline and a few comments, but you cannot then sit down and write a paragraph. You try, but waste an hour and feel stressed again. If you have time, you might quit for the day and try again the next day. Or you might break down that step into smaller steps. For example, try to write one sentence that expresses the theme or main point, or simply write what might be the first sentence of the paragraph. Or outline with sentences the section you are working on. Or take last year's report and try editing it to see if it can serve as a model for this year's report. The point is to recognize that you might fail at something; rather than become discouraged, take a different approach to the task. And if that does not work, try yet another approach.

The above description of self-managed change is necessarily brief and does not consider many questions that are certain to arise when actually trying to change behavior. In order to gain a more complete understanding of the process of self-managed change, the books listed below in the bibliography are particularly recommended.

*See also* Assertion; Procrastination: Overcoming; Self-Talk; Time Management.

## Bibliography

Goldfried, M. R., & Merbaum, M. (1973). *Behavior change through self-control*. New York: Holt, Rinehard, and Winston.

Lakein, A. (1973). *How to get control of your time and your life*. New York: New American Library. A book designed to help people manage their time better and maximize their productive capabilities.

Masters, J.C., Burish, T.G., Hollon, S.D., & Rimm, D.C. (1987). *Behavior therapy*. 3rd ed. San Diego: Harcourt Brace Javanovich. An introduction to techniques used by professionals to help people change their thinking and behavior. See especially Chapter 10 for a detailed description of self-control techniques.

Plas, J.M., & Hoover-Dempsey, K. V. (1988). *Working up a storm: Anger, anxiety, joy, and tension on the job and how to handle them*. New York: W. W. Norton. A practical book about strategies for managing difficulties at work, with an emphasis on dealing with feelings.

Rathus, S.A., & Nevid, J.S. (1977). *Behavior therapy: Strategies for solving problems in living*. New York: New American Library. A self-help book that shows the reader how to solve personal difficulties and achieve goals.

—CAROLYN J. DOBBINS AND THOMAS G. BURISH

# SELF-TALK

Self-talk is any brain activity that takes a verbal form and includes attitudes, beliefs, expectations, plans, decisions, memories, daydreams and dreams, conversations (both actual and imagined), and "rules of living" (e.g., "Always wash your hands before eating"). Some of this internal dialogue sounds like our own voice, some takes the voices of parents, our third grade teachers, or friends. Self-talk is not evidence that we are crazy, merely evidence of a well-functioning brain that never rests.

During our waking state, our constant brain activity produces images and self-talk. Even when we sleep, our brain continues its activities through dreams. The only times this random internal dialogue called self-talk stops are when we are concentrating heavily on a task, such as writing or doing math, or during states produced by drugs or alcohol. Otherwise, the brain makes its own entertainment when none is provided from the outside.

## Relationship to Work

Here are some examples of positive, rational self-talk related to work:

- I can learn this new skill with time and instruction.
- I want to talk to the boss in a way that would maximize my chances of getting the raise that I am asking for.
- Other people tell me I am good at this task. I'll try to listen to their feedback even though I don't feel real confident yet.
- I know I am not good at that task. Maybe I can delegate it to someone who is good at it.
- Even though that interview did not yield a job offer, they did give me some good feedback about myself that I can use in other interviews.

Some examples of negative, irrational self-talk are:
- I'll never get a job. No one will ever want me.
- I'm not good at that task and they will find out and fire me.
- If I fail at these new responsibilities, I will be demoted and viewed as a failure. My career will then be ended.

Since our internal dialogue is continuous, specific kinds of experiences can trigger specific kinds of self-talk. Any everyday experience at work can trigger career-related self-talk. Especially during times of career choice, such as at the start of our careers or during career transitions, we are more likely to experience an increase in self-talk related to our confusion, self-doubt, or even excitement about new possibilities. Here are some other common times of career self-talk:

- Learning a new skill
- Coping with a change
- Relationships with others at work
- Evaluation of performance, either one's own or others (appraisal)

## Nature of Self-Talk

Our self-talk develops as soon as we become verbal. Have you ever observed toddlers tempted to touch something they are not supposed to touch? Their hands extend and then they say, "No," and then reach again. That "No" is obviously a stored prohibition given by a parent. Gradually, kids rehearse and incorporate messages given by adults until these thoughts are very automatic and below the usual awareness levels. Yet as soon as a similar situation triggers that self-talk, it replays, as though a snippet of prerecorded tape, in milliseconds below our own awareness thresholds, like a subliminal message to buy cola inserted between the frames at the movie theatre. Every time we replay the tape, we are practicing the message and our neurons rehearse firing in a certain pattern that can repeat itself over and over again. This is the reason that people who have received negative messages about themselves early in life continue to have stored messages about low self-esteem despite years of success experiences to the contrary.

Jeffrey Young (1987) and other researchers are finding that our self-talk has layers to it depending on how early we learned it and how much we have rehearsed it over the years. Imagine a topographical map like those showing a cross section of the earth's layers. On the surface we have a thought "The boss wants me to start learning word processing"). Beneath thoughts are beliefs ("I've never been very good at technical things"). In the next layer are assumptions ("I can't learn technical things"). Beneath that layer are found schema, which are very early, possibly before three, thoughts usually "given" to us by others ("I'm dumb").

So although we know that self-talk is a normal part of brain activity and not a sign of "craziness," the content of what the brain spends time thinking can have a bearing on mental health. For example, in studying thought logs of people who suffer from depression, psychologists have found a preponderance of pessimistic thoughts about self, the world, and the future. One thing is clear from the research on depression: unless there are clear signs of a serious biochemical disorder correctable only by medication, depression begins to lift when the internal dialogue changes from pessimism to hope. Whether people make this switchover through self-help or whether they take advantage of some of the new cognitive therapies to do so, they can heal from their depression by learning to tune in and self-regulate that internal dialogue or self-talk.

## Rational Self-Talk

The goal of all the cognitive therapies is to help people view their situation in ways that promote realistic assessments of the the situation, rational statements about the meanings of the situations, and good problem solving or acceptance about the situations.

How can you tell if you are thinking rationally or not? Psychologist Maxie Maultsby (1975) has developed these criteria to evaluate whether thoughts are rational or not. With each criterion I include an application to a work-related situation. Maultsby suggests that thoughts are irrational if they violate three or more criteria. Self-talk is rational if it:

1. Is based on objective reality. (What is the evidence to support the conclusion that I am incompetent?)
2. Helps you to protect your life. Am I protecting my life by this thought? (Especially useful for looking at drug and alcohol use and how it affects performance at work.)
3. Helps you to achieve your short- and long-term goals most quickly. (Will telling off my boss in no uncertain terms help my career?)
4. Helps you to avoid significant trouble with other people. (Will this thought help me resolve this conflict with my coworker?)
5. Helps you to feel the emotions you want to feel. (As I review my work at the end of the day, do I choose thoughts that help me feel happy and productive about how the day went or do I see myself as falling short?)

Some people have difficulty tuning in to their self-talk. They are often aware of an activating event like a job change and are aware of an emotion such as guilt or anger that they are feeling, but are not aware of what thoughts intervene between the actual event and the feelings. It takes a while to develop this awareness, but keeping a thought log of the kind designed by Albert Ellis (see Rational Thinking) or Dave Burns (1980) can make people see patterns in the ways that they are thinking so that they can begin to rewrite the scripts from irrational to rational self-talk. On a loose-leaf paper create three vertical columns, the first to record briefly the situation or activating event that happened just before you experienced the strong emotions. The third column is to record the emotions felt or the behaviors engaged in, such as crying or running away, the conse-

quences as Ellis calls them. In the middle or second column record the intervening thoughts, beliefs, and assumptions as best you are aware of them. At first you may not have any awareness of your internal dialogue. Monitor yourself several times a day, such as at mealtime, to catch any thoughts, even if they seem unimportant. Also record your thoughts as soon as you realize you have been having some strong emotions. Gradually you will train yourself to catch the thoughts more immediately. Remember that the deeper the source of the thoughts in your cognitive map, the more instantaneously, unconscious, and elusive they may seem. After a week or two of catching thoughts you may begin to categorize the thoughts and distinguish between rational and irrational ones.

## Application

Career issues can be stressful enough without the added burden of low self-esteem, depression, and excessive anxiety caused by negative self-talk. Applying rational living principles to our work life prevents needless stress which decreases our effectiveness and takes a toil on our health. Rational thinking also leads to positive benefits, such as increased self-esteem, productivity, and appropriate risk-taking behaviors.

Here are just a few of the many techniques that can be helpful to anyone trying to change their self-talk.

1. *Stress Reduction.* Sometimes irrational self-talk can produce so much emotional arousal that it is difficult to use any of these techniques until you reduce some of that strong emotion. One sure-fire technique is to include regular aerobic exercise on your personal health schedule. The benefits of exercise include a reduction of physiological arousal by giving a direction to the body's fight or flight stress arousal and by dissipating the waste products of that arousal. Another set of stress reduction skills are time managment skills. Knowing your top priorities and planning your time accordingly can reduce that frantic feeling.

2. *Behavioral Assignments and Rehearsal.* Changing behavior and acting "as if" can sometimes change self-talk indirectly by giving us the experiential data to build evidence for new self-talk. We can't decide that we are good at something until we see the behavioral evidence. For example, sometimes self-confidence is built best by risk-taking experiments like trying new social skills. Later, a sentence can be formed in our head about "being socially skilled."

3. *Disputations.* Albert Ellis developed this technique to pick apart the faulty logic of the person's self-talk and replace it with more rational talk. He has devised a self-help form to guide a person in disputing irrational thinking (see his article, **Rational Thinking**). In order to grow the neural pathways in the brain to change a belief, you must

practice the disputation 15–20 minutes, two times a day. Concentrated effort will change an assumption in approximately a month, a schema in a year.

4. *Self-Affirmations.* Positive self-talk statements usually beginning with "I am . . ." and affirm the speaker's abilities or personal qualities in some way. An example would be "I am improving my computer skills by practicing with my new software daily." There are two tips to writing helpful affirmations. Keep them accurate. Don't tell yourself you are wonderful at something if you are not because you won't believe it. Second, be specific rather than global; it increases believability. "I am careful with my programing work," is a better statement than "I am good at computers." There are several ways to use self-affirmations. Some people like to make a deck of affirmations by writing them on 3 x 5 cards, one to a card. Some like to record their own voices reading the affirmations out loud. The key element is to practice them two times a day so that they begin to change your habitual self-talk.

5. *Thought Stopping and Thought Substitution.* This technique is used for worries or obsessive thoughts. As soon as you begin to think the worry, you yell (either out loud or quietly depending on where you are) "STOP." Then you substitute a rational thought (that you have written out ahead of time) so that the worry thought does not rush back into the hole in your thought pattern.

6. *Stress Innoculation.* Imagery rehearsal of a stressful situation in which you allow the anxious feeling to be felt while you imagine coping with the anxious feelings and functioning in spite of them rather that trying to reduce them to more comfortable levels. Steps include preparing for a stressor; handling a stressor; coping with the feelings of being overwhelmed; and Reinforcing self with self-affirmations about handling things.

Anticipating a job interview is a good place to practice stress innoculation because no matter how many times we go out on job interviews, they don't get any less anxiety producing. The best way to approach them is to rehearse handling an interview well while still experiencing a fairly high level of anxiety. When using this technique, it is important to imagine not only the stressful situation, but also the "success video" of handling the stress. Try to picture the video with as much detail as possible, the more vivid, the better. This technique is particularly helpful if your job involves highly observable behaviors, such as public speaking or a performance of some kind. The Olympic athletes use this method to improve their performances and the research shows that once you have the skill well learned, practice of the "success video" can improve your performance as much as actual practice of the skill. As you perform the skill in the "success video" flawlessly, you will be able to update your cognitions about your performance to ones that reflect your increased confidence.

7. *Self-Monitoring.* Ask yourself, "What am I telling myself that is upsetting me? What could I think instead? What are some other ways of thinking about the situation? What's the worst . . . . Asking what's the worst that can happen is often a good way to confront our worst fears and calm our thinking. It helps to follow up with two other questions: "How likely is it that the worst will happen? How would I handle it if it did?" Sometimes, the worst we can imagine has almost a zero probability of happening and needn't be taken seriously.

*See also* Rational Thinking.

## Bibliography

Burns, D. (1980). *Feeling good.* New York: New American Library. Burns reviews the theories and techniques of cognitive therapy that help people out of their depressions. Many of the techniques have direct application to changing self-talk as it relates to career issues.

Maultsby, M. (1975). *Help yourself to happiness through rational self-counseling.* New York: Institute for Rational-Emotive Therapy.

Powell, J. (1976). *Fully human, fully alive.* Allen, TX: Argus. This highly readable volume presents a summary of Albert Ellis' brand of cognitive therapy. Includes many practical examples and exercises.

Young, J. (1987). *Schema-Focused: Cognitive therapy for personality disorders.* Unpublished manuscript.

—SUSAN M. ROBISON

## SEQUENCING: A CAREER AND TRADITIONAL MOTHERING

Sequencing is a three-stage life style plan which enables a woman to direct her energies toward her career and her family at different stages in her life. Sequencing is comprised of (a) a full-time career stage in which women complete their educations and gain career experience, a (b) focus on family stage wherein women leave careers entirely or cut down dramatically during the years they are bearing and rearing young children; and (c) a career reintegration stage wherein as their children grow, women innovate ways to re-incorporate career activities into their lives so that their careers and families don't conflict. Sequencing is opposite in concept to the Superwoman paradigm which calls for women working full-time throughout their adult lives, raising families as an addition to already heavily burdened work schedules.

The question of how to finance the focus on family stage of sequencing is crucial to couples contemplating the option. Ideally, the couple plans for the woman to sequence years in advance of the birth of their first child. They (a) live day-to-day on his income alone, (b) use her salary only for large-ticket infrequently purchased items (e.g., the downpayment on a house, a car, or major appliance), (c) invest what portion of her salary they can in safe interest bearing funds or accounts. Then, during their one-income years they are already accustomed to living on one salary, and defer major purchases and further saving until she is once again earning money.

When the couple does not plan in advance, more drastic measures often need to be taken, including scaling down the entire life style, which often means selling one dwelling and moving to a smaller one in a different location, and forgoing expensive vacations, restaurant meals, etc. Usually couples find that the combined tax toll and work-related expenses of the wife's job account for well over 50% of her gross earnings. Therefore, the loss of one income is not so great as first perceived because they also lose the need to pay child care expenses, transportation, meals, clothes, etc., related to her work as well as the expense of convenience food shopping and fast-food eating that often occurs in two-career households. Sequencing is an option elected by those with incomes in the very low, poverty line five figures as well as those with higher incomes.

## Relationship to Work

Because the concept of career interruption conflicts with the traditional vertical career model, every woman who contemplates sequencing asks the question: If I leave my career for a period of years will I be able to resume it again in a comparable way? The answer is yes. Sequencers have helped to spearhead social changes based on more flexible models in which persons can interrupt careers for months or years, work part-time, telecommute, or job-split and yet rise in their professions.

These changes are evidenced by the following facts:

1. Many corporations have successfully rehired female MBAs who took years away from their careers to start their families. Many women who elect to return to corporate settings wish to do so on a part-time basis, gradually reintegrating their careers into their total lives. Others elect to return to work full-time. Both kinds of situations are now possible.
2. Many law firms now give credit for the number of years a woman has worked toward partnership track before she leaves to sequence. Thus, if she works for four years, interrupts her career for three, then returns, she does not start all over again, but rather resumes work in her former firm, or in a new one, at the stage at which she left.

3. Many fields, such as education, nursing and other branches of health care, have policies in place so that women interrupting careers can keep up their credentials and certifications and thus return to comparable positions when they are ready.
4. New strides are being made in all fields so that women who wish to cut down dramatically on time spent on their careers, yet maintain some career involvement, can do so through part-time work options, job-splitting, and flexiplace options, including telecommuting and independent consultancies.
5. Entrepreneurial options abound in most fields today. Thousands of sequencing women each year decide to be their own managers when they reincorporate careers into their lives. This gives them greater control over their own time, and thus their own lives.
6. Sandra Day O'Conner, Geraldine Ferraro, and Governor Kay Orr of Nebraska are well-known examples of women who have interrupted their careers to raise families and later have risen to top leadership positions in American society.

## Application

The application of sequencing falls into three categories which parallel the three stages of the sequencing paradigm. At the close of Stage 1, the full-time career stage, it is important to leave your position with your contacts preserved. You can facilitate this by:

1. A frank discussion with your superior about your present family and career goals.
2. Letting your superior know that you intend to resume your career some months or years hence and that when you do you hope that the door will be open.
3. Suggest a consultancy as an interim measure; you would be available for special projects from time to time, or would work a limited number of hours a month.

In Stage 2, at home with your family, you can enhance future opportunities by:

1. Maintaining professional contacts. This can be as simple as sending holiday greeting cards or pertinent clippings to former colleagues, or as involved as meeting for lunch or extending a dinner invitation (see **Networking**).
2. Keeping up professional certifications and association memberships. It may seem to be money ill spent at the time, but when you want to return to your career you will find it's been an excellent investment.

3. Reading in your field. You may find that you now have the time to keep up on current developments, whereas when you were involved full-time in the field you lacked time and perspective to do so.

4. Using professional skills on a volunteer basis, a limited number of hours per year, as a way of keeping involved in your field and enhancing your resume when you wish to resume career activity.

5. Becoming active in your professional association, especially during the period prior to your return to work. It will help revitalize contacts and keep you up to date in the field.

6. Taking additional coursework, to sharpen your edge, to keep abreast of new advances, or to give yourself a specialty area within your field. For instance, many women who lack computer skills develop computer expertise during the years they are sequencing, a plus for any field today (see **Continuing Education**).

In Stage 3, when you are first ready to reincorporate career activities into your schedule, chances are that like most sequencers you will not wish to return to full-time work, especially if your children are in preschool or early grade school. There are many less than full-time options you can exercise if you take the initiative:

1. Present a new professionally composed resume to all potential employers. Be sure to include all information on course work, and community or professional association activities in which you have engaged during your years away from employment in your field (see **Resume**).

2. Allow plenty of time, at least 6–9 months, to research your employment possibilities (see **Information Interviewing; Job Search**).

3. Target the firms in which you would most like to work. See what kinds of part-time work are already in place at your level and apply for them.

4. Or, assess what full-time positions are available and innovate ways in which you could fill them on a reduced time basis. Sometimes this means job-splitting, other times it means seeing what the total job description consists of, then assessing how you can do it in less time (see **Job Sharing**).

5. Work as a freelancer or an independent contractor. You can then control the amount of time you spend per month on career activity, can work on various projects within a firm getting to know a variety of persons, and can perhaps create a permanent part-time niche for yourself in one of their divisions. Or, you can work for more than one organization while assessing each to see where you might like to spend more career time (see **Self-Employment**).

*See also* Career Planning; Continuing Education; Information Interviewing; Job Search; Job Sharing; Networking; Part-Time Work; Resume; Self-Employment; Temporary Employment; Women: Reentry into the Workplace.

## Bibliography

Cardozo, A.R. (1986/1989). *Sequencing.* New York: Macmillan.
Describes sequencing in detail from decision-making processes to economics, from networking with other at-home mothers to ways to reincorporate work into one's life. Includes information on ways to innovate entrepreneurial, freelance, and consulting opportunities as well as flexible ways to work for others. Based on interviews with 350 women throughout the United States who have combined the best of modern feminism with the best of traditional mothering, this is a guidebook for all women contemplating or currently employing the sequencing option.

Olmstead, B., & Smith, S. (1983). *The job sharing handbook.* Hammondsworth, England: Penguin Books.
Excellent guide to the fundamentals of innovating a job-sharing situation.

Olmstead, B., & Smith, S. (1989). *Creating a flexible workplace: How to select and manage alternative work options.* New York: American Management Association.
Although written primarily to provide managers and owners with models of workplace flexibility, this is an excellent resource for any individual wishing to have a more flexible work situation. The authors are founders of San Francisco's *New Ways to Work* and national authorities on workplace changes

—ARLENE ROSSEN CARDOZO

## SERVICE-LEARNING

Service-learning makes a conscious attempt to have a person providing service develop an ability to critically analyze his or her work through a formal or informal process. In contrast, volunteering often implies providing only a service without thinking about the implications of the service being provided.

Jane Kendall, in the introduction to *Combining Service and Learning* (1990), distinguishes between service-learning as a type of program and service-learning as a philosophy of education. As a type of program, service-learning "emphasize[s] the accomplishment of tasks which meet human needs in combination with conscious educational growth" (p.20).

As a philosophy of education, service-learning is "a philosophy of reciprocal learning, a dynamic and interactive approach which suggests mutuality in learning between the [service providers] and the community with whom he or she is actively engaged" (pp. 22–23). While not necessarily tied to a formal classroom experience, this philosophy of service-learning encourages people to know and understand the issues involving the community and those with whom they work. Rather than imposing a perceived "right" answer, people who are providing a service are encouraged to learn from the community and to allow community members to determine what their needs are (Johnson Foundation, 1989).

## Application

Service learning can be a valuable addition to your life outside of work because it can provide the following opportunities:

1. *Develop Community-Based Knowledge.* Besides paying taxes and voting, one of the obligations of being a citizen involves helping those who are unable to provide for themselves. Working in the community will give you an understanding of the issues facing others in the area where you live.
2. *Explore Career Options.* Have you ever wondered what it would be like to be a fundraiser? Have you ever tried developing policies for an organization? Have you ever wondered what the health profession would be like? Working with a nonprofit organization can open your eyes to new possibilities and directions for your life.
3. *Find Balance in Your Life.* Nothing will give you a better perspective n life than working with a new-born child who has AIDS. On a lighter side, you can develop a whole new circle of friends with whom you are connected through a common cause.
4. *Develop Creativity.* Community service agencies are often in need of people who are willing to implement new ideas that they may not be able to afford otherwise. Creating a brochure, devising a marketing plan, or starting a reading club with children may be a god-send to a struggling organization.
5. *Apply Your Skills for the Common Good.* The skills that you already possess could be just the ones an agency needs. Writing skills, accounting ability, and counseling are but a few that could enhance an agency's effectiveness in the community.
6. *Develop New Skills.* Working on behalf of the community can give you a chance to try new things. You can try writing grants, organizing a fundraiser, teaching English as a second language, or a variety of things which you have never had the opportunity to do.
7. *Enhance Personal Growth.* Working in a community agency can help you understand yourself and others in a new way. As you struggle to teach someone who wants to read the newspaper, as you talk with an elderly rest home patient, or as you serve as a mentor to a junior high student, your life will be enhanced as well. In order to experience service-learning at its fullest, you should arrange to meet with your agency supervisor or develop a group that will talk with you about your common experiences. In order for you to chart your own personal growth, you might want to keep a journal that addresses the work experiences you are having, how you are impacted by the people you meet, and what questions are raised that you wish to explore further.

*See also* Leisure; Volunteer Work.

## Bibliography

Anzalone, J. (Ed.) (1985). *Good works: A guide to careers in social change.* New York, NY: Dembner Books.

Bellah, R., Madsen, R., Sullivan, W., Swindler, A., & Tipton, S. (1985). *Habits of the heart.* New York: Harper & Row. A thought-provoking book that examines America's fierce sense of individualism and simultaneous desire for caring communities.

Delve, C., Mintz, S., & Stewart, G. (Eds.) (1990). *Community service as values education.* New Directions for Students Services, 50. San Francisco: Jossey-Bass. Both a theoretical and practical publication that outlines how people, specifically college students, can develop their moral sensibilities as they engage in community service experiences. Chapters touch on leadership, faith, and community issues.

Johnson Foundation. (1989). *Principles of good practice for combining service and learning.* Racine, WI: Wingspread Conference. These 10 principles were the result of extensive consultation with over 70 organizations. The principles state that an effective program engages people in responsible and challenging actions for the common good; provides structured opportunities for people to reflect critically on their service experience; articulates clear service and learning goals for everyone involved; allows for those with needs to define those needs; clarifies the responsibilities of each person and organization involved; matches service providers and service needs through a process that recognizes changing circumstances; expects genuine, active, and sustained organizational commitment; includes training, supervision, monitoring, support, recognition, and evaluation to meet service and learning goals; ensures that the time commitment for service and learning is flexible, appropriate, and in the best interests of all involved; and is committed to program participation by and with diverse populations.

Kendall, J. and Associates, (1990). *Combining service and learning— A resource book for community and public service—Vol. I.* Raleigh, NC: National Society for Internships and Experiential Education. A three-volume set that includes theories, research, practical applications, and an extensive annotated bibliography.

—Cecilia I. Delve

## SEX-ROLE STEREOTYPING

Sex-role stereotyping is the process by which we generate expectations or assumptions regarding the behavior of a particular individual by using the individual's gender as our exclusive point of departure. Stereotyping is a time-saving, efficient cognitive enterprise, serving to simplify and organize the vast amounts of information with which we are confronted in our daily lives, but stereotyping can pose grave problems. Considerable experimental evidence documents the pervasiveness of counterproductive sex-role stereotyping in the United States. Many studies conducted over the past two decades indicate that we tend to view men and women as being polar opposites with respect to a wide range of personality attributes. For instance, with regard to achievement-oriented traits, men are perceived as being competent, strong, independent, and aggressive. Women, on the other hand, are portrayed as being incompetent, weak, dependent, and passive.

### Relationship to Work

There has been an increasing interest in the potential effects of sex-role stereotyping on the career and employment opportunities available to women (Ruble & Ruble, 1982). In particular, social scientists have hypothesized that sex-role stereotypes might act as a barrier to the occupational attainment of those women interested in nontraditional occupations. In essence, the available evidence suggests that stereotyping might lead to a series of biases which may, in turn, affect a woman's career preference and choice, and her advancement within a career (Ruble, Cohen, & Ruble, 1984).

1. *Occupational Sex-Typing and Career Choice.* Just as we develop stereotypes about men and women, we also develop stereotypes about particular jobs and professions. For instance, certain occupations, such as auto mechanic, airline pilot, and mechanical engineer, seem to conjure more masculine descriptions, while others, such as nurse, school teacher, and secretary, seem to most people to be feminine occupations. According to Ruble, Cohen, and Ruble (1984), occupational sex-typing does not simply serve to define jobs as men's work or women's work, but also seems related to the perception of the characteristics considered necessary for success in that career. A study conducted by Heilman, Block, Martell, and Simon (1989) serves to illustrate this point. Using a 92-item attribute inventory, the researchers asked over 200 male managers to characterize either "women in general," "men in general," or "successful middle managers." There was a significant correspondence between the attributes listed as characteristic of "successful middle managers" and "men

in general" but not between the attributes of "successful middle managers" and "women in general." These findings indicate that women are still not believed to possess the qualities essential for success in managerial positions.

2. *Career Entry.* Perceptions may, in turn, drastically influence people's career paths. The decision to hire one job applicant versus another typically rests on an employers's perception that the credentials and abilities of the chosen applicant are more congruent with the requirements of the position than those of the rejected applicant. A number of studies on sex-role stereotyping have shown that hiring decisions tend to be biased in favor of job candidates applying for "sex-appropriate" positions (Bersoff & Verrilli, 1988). This finding has serious implications for women who try to penetrate traditionally male occupations and, similarly, for those men interested in pursuing traditionally female professions. It should also give pause to any employer who wishes to have access to the full talent pool.

3. *Career Advancement and Performance Evaluation.* According to Bersoff and Verrilli (1988), sex-role stereotyping can bias the manner in which the performances of employees are evaluated after hiring. Sometimes women's achievements are perceived in a manner consistent with stereotypic conceptions, regardless of whether the facts warrant such conclusions. As the research of Deaux (1984) documents, noteworthy accomplishments by a woman tend to be given less weight than exactly the same accomplishments by a man because of a pervasive tendency to attribute the successful performance of a female employee to unstable causal factors such as good luck or hard work rather than to stable dispositional factors such as ability or competence. This attributional bias may result in lower overall performance evaluations given to females, and, ultimately, in reduced pay increases, promotions, and opportunities for further growth.

### Application

Because stereotypic categorization is such a basic feature of human thinking, we cannot provide a magic recipe to avoid thinking in stereotypical terms. However, we can provide some suggestions on how to recognize categorization, how to resist the temptation to evaluate others in stereotypical terms, and how to break the link between categorization of individuals into groups and its judgmental consequences, thus reducing the likelihood of engaging in discriminatory action (see **Discrimination: Sex**). According to Bersoff and Verrilli (1988), three conditions contribute to the reduction of stereotypic thought and discriminatory actions:

1. *The Provision of Additional Information.* Individualizing information about a particular person can help reduce the reliance on stereotypes, particularly

if that information is inconsistent with the stereotype. For instance, one commonly held stereotype about women is that they act emotionally and irrationally. If, however, we are told that during an inflight emergency a particular flight attendant kept her composure and was successful in getting all passengers to put on their life vests, we will be less likely to evaluate her in stereotypical terms.

2. *Paying Increased Attention to that Information.* You should pay close attention to counter-stereotypical information instead of disregarding it.

3. *Provision of Motivational Incentives that Discourage the Use of Stereotypes.* An organization can discourage the use of stereotyping among its employees by stressing the importance of teamwork, by emphasizing accuracy and thoroughness on performance evaluations, and by soliciting the opinion of an impartial third party in the evaluation process. In sum, although sex-role stereotyping is a very pervasive tendency, it is by no means inevitable! Tendencies to evaluate women and men on the basis of their group membership can be overcome by systematic organizational change.

*See also* Discrimination: Sex; Nontraditional Jobs for One's Sex; Women in the Workforce; Women's Barriers and Opportunities.

## Bibliography

Bersoff, D.N., & Verrilli, D.B. (1988). Price Waterhouse, Petitioner, v. Ann B. Hopkins, Respondent. Brief for Amicus Curiae. *American Psychological Association in support of respondent, No. 87-1167.* Washington, DC: American Psychological Association. An up-to-date, comprehensive review of the social psychological research on sex-role stereotyping. In addition, this article illustrates rather nicely how laboratory research can be applied to "real world" situations.

Deaux, K. (1984). From individual differences to social categories: Analysis of a decade's research on gender. *American Psychologist,* 39: 105–16. A scholarly review of the decade's most important research on gender. Worthy of the highest praise is Deaux's discussion of the attributional biases inherent in our judgments of female successes.

Hamilton, D.L. (1979). A cognitive-attributional analysis of stereoyping. In L. Berkowitz (Ed.), *Advances in experimental social psychology,* 12: (pp. 53–84). New York: Academic Press. Better suited for the more advanced reader, this article presents a fairly technical cognitive- attributional analysis of stereotyping.

Heilman, M.E., Block, C.J., Martell, R.F., & Simon, M.C. (1989). Has anything changed? Current characterizations of men, women, and managers. *Journal of Applied Psychology,* 74: 935–42. This article replicates and extends earlier work conducted in the early 1970s by Schein. Interesting to note how little things have changed in nearly two decades. Although a familiarity with statistical methods is helpful in understanding this article, we feel that the general public, especially managers, can benefit enormously from reading it.

Ruble, D.N., & Ruble, T.L. (1982). Sex Stereotypes. In A.G. Miller (Ed.), *In the eye of the beholder: Contemporary issues in stereotyping* (pp. 188–252). New York: Praeger.

Ruble, T.L., Cohen, R., & Ruble, D.N. (1984). Sex stereotypes: Occupational barriers for women. *American Behavioral Scientist,* 27: 339-56. A very readable analysis of the manner in which sex-role stereotyping can be a barrier to women's occupational attainment and career progress.

—DIANA I. CORDOVA AND FAYE J. CROSBY

## SEXUAL HARASSMENT

Sexual harassment covers a wide range of behavior, from the subtle end of the spectrum (unwanted sexual teasing, remarks, jokes, or questions) to the severe (actual or attempted sexual assault). However, all sexual harassment includes at least the following elements:

- Behavior of a sexual nature (verbal, physical, graphic)
- Unwanted behavior
- Deliberate and/or repeated behavior that results in tangible economic harm or creates a hostile work environment.

Sexual harassment is highly *subjective;* the recipient decides if the behavior is unwanted. It is also *context-dependent;* a host of other factors help determine the precise boundary between appropriate and inappropriate: the formal and informal power relationship between the parties (including workplace status, age, personal style); cultural, religious, and personal background attributes; and whether the offended party feels she or he can object without reprisal.

Numerous surveys conducted in the public sector and proprietary studies for large and small private corporations indicate that anywhere from 15% to 21% of female employees experience some form of sexual harassment in any given year. The incidence for male employees is 5% to 7% annually.

Data on the types of sexual harassment reported from two large studies—the Merit Systems Protection Board survey of federal employees in 1987, and a 1988 study of Fortune 500 industrial and service firms—are presented in Table 1. Both males and females are represented. The data reflect only those who report that they have experienced sexual harassment.

### Sexual Harassment and Gender Balance

In studies of both public- and private-sector employees, the gender balance of one's work unit repeatedly emerges as the single greatest predictor of the presence or

**Table 1. Types of Sexual Harassment Complaints, by Percent, within the Past Twelve Months**

|  | 1987 Federal* | 1988 Corporate** |
|---|---|---|
| Sexual remarks, jokes, teasing, questions | 35 | 42 |
| Suggestive looks, gestures | 28 | 11 |
| Pressure for dates | 15 | 12 |
| Deliberate touching, leaning over, cornering | 26 | 26 |
| Pressure for sexual favors | 9 | 17 |
| Letters, phone calls, materials | 12 | 9 |
| Actual or attempted sexual assault | 1 | 1 |

Note: Columns do not total 100% since sexual harassment complaints often involve more than one type of behavior.

* Federal data are the results of a survey conducted by the Merit Systems Protection Board of a random sample of civilian employees across all agencies. The questionnaire was sent to a representative sample of approximately 13,000 federal employees, and 8,523 responded.

** Corporate data are the results of a survey conducted by Klein Associates of sexual harassment in the Fortune 500 manufacturing and service firms. The survey was commissioned by Working Woman magazine; full results appeared in their December 1988 issue.

absence of sexual harassment. Work units that are predominantly male (i.e., at least 75%) have significantly higher rates of sexual harassment than do work units with a gender balance. In addition, the types of harassment reported by women in highly imbalanced work units tend to be more severe and of longer duration when compared to the types and duration of harassment reported by women working in groups with a more even distribution of men and women. Women "pioneers" in both hourly and professional jobs are at far greater risk of victimization.

## The Effects of Sexual Harassment

Individuals who experience sexual harassment report an array of consequences, including deterioration of mental and physical health, loss of confidence in one's ability to perform one's job and/or to fulfill career goals, and diminished productivity.

Negative consequences ensue to the employer as well. Table 2 depicts the diverging views of employees who have and have not experienced sexual harassment; these data are from proprietary surveys of corporate employees conducted by Klein Associates, Inc. Men and women were both represented with a response rate of over 92%.

Employees who feel they have experienced sexual harassment once within the past year are less positive about the following aspects of their employment when compared to employees who have not experienced sexual harassment:

- Less job satisfaction
- Lower rating of their immediate supervisor
- Less favorable view of company communication
- Diminished confidence in their senior management team
- Reduced organizational commitment
- Increased likelihood to leave the company

Employees who feel they have experienced sexual harassment two or more times within the past year report a further decline on each of these dimensions. While one experience of sexual harassment has a measurable impact on employees' views, repeated experiences have a cumulative, more negative impact. Whether the organizational purpose is public service, delivery of health care or other services, or production of goods, sexual harassment undermines its attainment.

## Sexual Harassment and the Law

Sexual harassment has evolved under the law as a specific form of sex discrimination. Every employer in the United States with 15 or more employees is subject to Title VII of the 1964 Civil Rights Act; Title VII prohibits many types of discrimination in employment, including discrimination based on sex. In 1980 the Equal Employment Opportunity Commission (EEOC) issued guidelines to employers outlining when they will be held responsible for sexual harassment by supervisors, coworkers, and sometimes by customers or the public. The EEOC has issued subsequent

**Table 2. Impact of Experiencing Sexual Harassment within the Past Year**

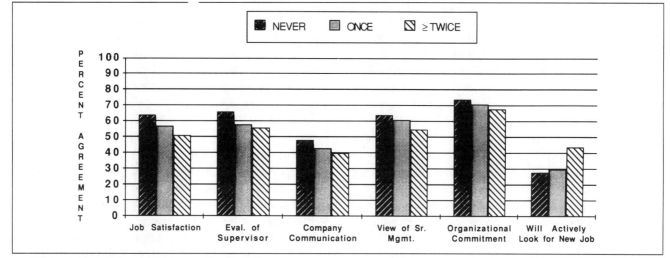

guidelines as the courts have applied Title VII to sexual harassment cases. In addition, most states have statutes prohibiting sex discrimination which also cover sexual harassment.

In 1986 the U.S. Supreme Court issued its first decision on sexual harassment in *Meritor Savings Bank v. Vinson*. The court gave credence to the notion of "hostile environment" claims, i.e., those situations where the sexual harassment created a hostile, intimidating, offensive, or coercive work environment.

## Creating and Maintaining Work Environments Free from Sexual Harassment

A concerted approach to preventing sexual harassment involves: (a) the modification and dissemination of policies prohibiting sexual harassment; (b) establishment of formal and informal complaint procedures; (c) training for all employees, managers, and those who handle complaints; (d) mechanisms to monitor the incidence, types, and resolution of sexual harassment; and (e) unequivocal commitment to prevent sexual harassment from senior managers and other leaders of the organization.

**Policies.** Policies prohibiting sexual harassment need to include definitions and examples of both "quid pro quo" and environmental sexual harassment that are easily understood by all employees. Possible perpetrators need to be spelled out: coworkers, supervisors, the public, and anyone else an employee must come into contact with to perform her or his job duties. In addition, a description of complaint avenues, clear protection from reprisal, and an explanation of different possible resolutions should be included. It is especially important to inform potential complainants of the circumstances under which their complaints will or will not be kept confidential.

Policies should be distributed to all new employees, posted in visible places, contained in accessible handbooks, and periodically disseminated. Given the unique environment of the courts, policies should specify protection and remedies for nonemployees, such as attorneys, litigants, and witnesses.

**Complaint Procedures.** The recent EEOC guidelines on sexual harassment, issued in October 1988, make it clear that employers must establish complaint channels which " ... encourage victims to come forward." Corporate ombuds and others studying the effectiveness of complaint procedures, recommend a multiplicity of options for complainants, both informal and formal. Informal channels should be confidential, and capable of providing an accurate discussion of all available courses of action, assisting the complainant in making an informed choice about how to handle her or his situation. Formal options should be clearly defined, including each step and timetable, investigative methods, decision-makers, and appeal routes. Procedures weighted toward peer review are most likely to gain the confidence of employees.

**Training.** Since gender and educational level both play a part in influencing how an individual defines sexual harassment, training should provide ample opportunity for dialogue. Women and individuals with greater levels of formal education tend to consider a wider range of behaviors as constituting sexual harassment. In addition, women are more likely to see sexual harassment as an abuse of power, while men are more likely to view it as sexual behavior.

Training should be available to all employees. Managers' training should focus on their responsibility to maintain work units free from harassment of any kind.

**Mechanisms to Monitor Sexual Harassment.** Sexual harassment is known to be significantly underreported; therefore, special efforts should be made to discern the frequency and types of unwanted sexual attention that are occurring. Establishing hotlines, conducting employee surveys, and convening women's committees are all methods that employers have found helpful. In addition, raising the topic routinely during exit interviews can also cause problems to surface.

Tracking the outcome of formal complaints is also important. Sexual harassment cases should be handled consistently, based on the seriousness of the complaint, not on whether the accused is considered a "star" within the organization. Discipline should be consistent with that given for the violation of other serious employment policies.

**Commitment from the Top.** As with many other types of organizational behavior, employees take their cue from senior management. When leaders make clear their stand that sexual harassment will not be tolerated, and when this message is backed up by procedures and consistent practice, both the overall rates and the severity of sexual harassment should decline.

Evidence from the private sector suggests that implementing specific steps to prevent sexual harassment does, indeed, bring results. Corporations with training programs, and with special mechanisms to surface sexual harassment complaints are more likely to hear about problems in their early stages when there are greater options for resolving the situation.

## Application

If you are being harassed, the first thing to remember in deciding what to do is that every individual's situation is different. Your reaction and your decisions about a course of action will differ from another person's. The emotional investment and repercussions of filing a complaint can be extremely draining and upsetting and will require that you find support. The amount of control you can exercise over the process, once it is initiated, varies. And if you decide to pursue your case through the courts, it can take many years for the case to be resolved. So taking action is not a decision to be made lightly. But neither is accepting sexual harassment without taking action a viable route to follow.

Ignoring sexual harassment will not make it go away; in fact, the behavior is more than likely to escalate. In addition, your failure to deal with the behavior directly could be used against you should you later decide to file a formal complaint.

In any case, there are many options for dealing with sexual harassment. Generally, they involve *dealing with the company* and/or *dealing with the harasser*. Specific steps you may want to consider, for these two areas, are outlined below.

## Dealing with the Company

1. *Get Information.* The law protects you against discrimination, and sexual harassment is a specific form of sex discrimination. Companies vary with regard to the methods they offer for your protection. Some questions which you should answer are: Does your company have a specific policy against sexual harassment? What is it? Does your company have a grievance procedure? How can you access it? Does your company have an employee relations officer or some other designated complaint handler? What is that person's reputation? Is there anyone else you can approach about this problem? What's involved in filing a formal complaint at your company? Does it have to be written? Will it be handled confidentially? How rapidly will it be investigated? Will you be notified of the outcome of the investigation? In writing? If you are a union member, who is the designated union representative to deal with sexual harassment? What is that person's reputation? What's been the track record of the union in representing employees with complaints of sexual harassment?

2. *File a Formal Complaint.* If you feel that your company's policies and track record for dealing with sexual harassment and other forms of discrimination guarantee you adequate protection, and if your own attempts to stop the harassment fail, consider filing a formal complaint. If the person harassing you is a coworker, a client, or a customer, your company must know about the harassment before it can be held responsible. If you've gotten the answers to the informational questions listed above, you should have a clear idea of the steps involved in filing a formal complaint.

3. *Take Legal Action.* If your employer does not take action to stop the harassment and/or any retaliation, you may want to consider legal action. You can file a sex discrimination complaint with the Equal Employment Opportunity Commission (EEOC). Such complaints must be filed within 180 days of the last incident. Some government employers require complaints to be made within 30 days of the last incident. It's important that you check the specific requirements at your place of employment and in your state.

## Dealing with the Harasser

1. *Talk with the Harasser.* If you think the harasser can be reasoned with, talk to the person. Be firm and professional in requesting that he or she maintain a professional relationship with you.

2. *Write a Letter to the Harasser.* Letters can be a very effective way to confront the harasser with his or her behavior and request that it change. A letter also serves to document the incidents of harassment and action you have taken to stop the harassment should you later decide to pursue legal remedies.

The letter should have three parts. The first should specifically detail the facts as you see them. Include the dates and descriptions of each incident. The second part should describe the feelings and reactions the harasser's behavior has evoked in you. This is where opinions belong. You should mention any costs and damages, transfers requested, or behavioral changes that are outcomes of the harassment.

In the closing, or third part of the letter, make a statement as to what you would like to happen next. For example, "I ask that our relationship from this point forward be on a purely professional basis." In cases where the harasser is someone with whom you have been in a relationship in the past, it is important to acknowledge that and separate it from the current problem: "Although we once were happy dating, it is important to me that we now re-establish a formal and professional relationship, and I ask you to do so." If you believe that some remedy is in order, this is the place to mention it: "Please withdraw my last evaluation until we can work out a fair one," "I will need a written answer as to the reference you will provide from now on."

Deliver the letter in person, if you can, so that you know it has arrived, and when. If necessary, bring a security officer or some other protector and/or witness with you. Keep a copy of the letter. If you prefer not to deliver it in person, you can mail it and request a return receipt. Be sure to mark it "Confidential" to ensure that the harasser is the person who opens it.

3. *Talk with Coworkers, Discreetly.* You may find that others are being harassed by the same individual. If this is the case, a group complaint to your employer may offer more protection than any individual complaint alone. In addition, you may find a coworker who is willing to be a witness for you. You should also be prepared to encounter some resistance from coworkers who fear disruption and don't want to "rock the boat."

## Some Other Measures

Keep a journal or diary to log the incidents themselves and to document actions you took to stop the harassment, including anyone you spoke to about it. Note dates, what was said or done, where it happened and who was present. Should you pursue legal action at some point, these notes will be important.

If you receive any notes, letter, cards, or memos that are suggestive, *keep them.* Note the date you received them and how you got them (left on your desk, mailed to your home, etc.). In writing, acknowledge your receipt of these materials and request that the mailings stop. Keep a copy of whatever you send to the harasser.

*See also* Assertion; Discrimination: Sex; Law in the Workplace; Sex-Role Stereotyping.

## Bibliography

Baxter, R. (1989). *Sexual harassment in the workplace: A guide to the law.* New York: Executive Enterprises Publications. This guide explains the current state of the law, analyzes the principle issues in these court cases, and suggests steps employers can take to limit their exposure to liability suits. The author provides a good explanation of the law in nontechnical language.

Gutek, B. A. (1985). *Sex and the workplace.* San Francisco: Jossey-Bass. A psychologist discusses the impact of sexual behavior and harassment on women, men, and organizations based largely on her ground-breaking research. This book will enrich your understanding of how sexual behavior affects individuals in their work and how this behavior influences, and is influenced by, the organization. Recommendations are offered for management.

Sandroff, R. (1988, December). Sexual harassment in the Fortune 500. *Working Woman Magazine.* This is an excellent source.

Shilling, D. (1985). In *Redress for Success.* New York: Penguin Books, 1985.

— FREADA KLEIN

## SHIFT WORK

Shift work is any regular employment outside the 6 a.m. to 6 p.m. window defining the outer boundaries of the "normal working day." It need not involve night work, but very often does. Shift work prevalence varies between 20% and 25% in the United States, Western Europe, and Japan, affecting scores of millions of people. The trend is toward a greater proportion of shift work, as production machinery becomes ever more costly and rapid in its depreciation, requiring 100% utilization to pay for itself, and as around-the-clock coverage is increasingly required in the service sector.

### Relationship to Work and Family Life

The human being is inherently a diurnal creature designed for sleep at night and activity during the day. Each person has a biological clock that functions to "set the stage" for sleep and for wakefulness, accomplishing this with a set of daily or "circadian" rhythms in physiology, mood, and performance ability. Circadian rhythms are gradual nontrivial fluctuations over the entire 24 hours, which can be observed in almost every physiological measure or vital sign (e.g., body temperature, heart rate, blood pressure). Such rhythms will continue to be expressed, even if the individual has an irregular routine, stays awake, and is unaware of time of day.

Although circadian rhythms can be reset to be appropriate to a new routine (e.g., night work), the process of phase adjustment is a slow one, taking several days to accomplish. While the process of phase adjustment is taking place, sleep will be disrupted and on-job safety and productivity impaired. Besides the effects of sleep disruption, other factors in this impairment are being required to perform at "down phases" of the circadian cycle and the malaise that occurs when the harmony of the circadian system is lost.

Precisely because humans are diurnal creatures, society is organized with the expectation that people will be asleep at night, and available for recreation in the evening. For example, although there is a strong social taboo protecting a day worker's sleep from 2 a.m. phone calls, there is none protecting a night worker's sleep from 2 p.m. ones. Moreover, there is a pervasive view that a night worker's day sleeps are "fair game" for disruptions from domestic commitments (deliveries, shopping, child care) to a much greater extent than would be tolerated at night. This can be especially crucial for female shift workers who are also expected to be homemakers.

Social alienation for shift workers can also become a problem as their schedules prevent evening participation in clubs, sporting activities, classes, or satisfactory interaction with their children. This is particularly true for evening shifts which have the most negative effect on the social and domestic life, while having a minimal impact on sleep and biological rhythms.

The various stresses arising from the biological and social mismatches can lead to strain in the shift worker's life. This strain can become apparent in sleep disorders, stomach disorders, cardiovascular problems, and psychiatric disorders, including substance abuse and a breakdown in interpersonal relationships.

## Application

Unless you are on a very rapidly rotating schedule in which morning, evening, and night shifts are all worked within a single week, your aim should be to acquire the change in timing of your biological clock which is most appropriate to the new work shift as rapidly as possible and to maintain that timing throughout your spell of duty on that shift.

Studies of jet lag and laboratory experiments have found that the human biological clock copes more easily with a *delay* to a later timing than with an *advance* to an earlier one. When doing night work you should therefore take your sleep straight after work, rather than sleeping in the afternoon before work. Since excessive napping can interfere with the quality of the major sleep episode, you should only use afternoon naps as "make-ups" and should limit them to two hours or less.

On night work, the time cues working in your favor will be a regular morning bedtime, three meals per day, with a proper lunch half way through the working night, and physical activity and social interaction through the night. Time cues working against you will be daylight on the journey home from work (perhaps warranting the use of sunglasses), sleep during the night shift, and social or work commitments during the first half of the day (8 a.m. to 4 p.m.).

You should jealously guard the time set aside for your sleep. This time should be regular and predictable, and free from social or other commitments. During that time, telephones, doorbells, and domestic appliances should be silenced. Use heavy curtains and thick carpets to make the bedroom as quiet and as dark as possible. Use the bedroom only for sleep and lovemaking. Avoid caffeine within five hours of bedtime. Do not use alcohol as a sedative since your subsequent sleep will then be light and disrupted. Because of problems of tolerance and withdrawal, use sleeping pills only very occasionally. See your doctor about gradual withdrawal if you are regularly using sleeping pills more than three or four times per week.

To succeed with these coping strategies, you will need the support of your family and friends. Gain your family's understanding of your predicament and rally their support in coping with it. Develop friendships with other shift-work families who are more likely than day-working friends to be supportive and understanding. Set aside specific times when you and your spouse and children can be together. Work hard to keep the family lines of communication open. This is vital if you are to succeed in coping with shift work.

*See also* Work Hazards: Psychosocial.

## Bibliography

Folkard, S., & Monk, T.H. (Eds.) (1985). *Hours of work: Temporal factors in work scheduling.* New York: John Wiley & Sons. This edited book brings together an international team of experts who between them cover many different aspects of work scheduling. It provides an insight not only into shift work, but also into the related areas of flextime, shift lengths, prolonged work, and napping.

Monk, T.H. (1989). *How to make shift work safe and productive.* Des Plaines, IL: American Society of Safety Engineers. This easy-to-read book describes some of the reasons for the problems experienced by shift workers and puts forward possible solutions to them.

Scott, A.J. (Ed.). (1990). *Shiftwork: Occupational medicine: State of the art reviews, 5, No. 2.* Philadelphia: Hanley & Belfus. This edited volume gives a comprehensive picture of many different aspects of shift work; it is written in an academic style by leading experts in the field, and is an authoritative reference resource for current U.S. and international shift-work research.

—TIMOTHY H. MONK

# SHYNESS

Shyness is a condition of behavioral inaction or avoidance in social situations that is out of harmony with a person's conscious wants, needs, and values. The shyness experience is precipitated by a real or imagined social situation that clashes with the victim's low interpersonal anxiety threshold. Informal social situations requiring spontaneous, friendly improvisation are likely to trigger strong anticipatory anxiety feelings in a shy person.

There are basically two types of shyness, and each varies greatly in terms of severity. About 10% of the population is born with the physiological/neurological and biochemical condition that has come to be called *behavioral inhibition*—the scientific name for biologically rooted "shyness." Another 30% of the population have learned their shyness.

This distinction between *inborn* shyness and *learned* shyness (a "trained incapacity") is crucial. People afflicted with learned shyness almost always benefit much faster and far more thoroughly from psychotherapeutic attention than do those whose shyness has a biochemical, neurological basis. Most studies point to an 80% to 90% success rate for the cognitive and systematic desensitization therapies when such therapies are performed by competent professionals, and the shyness is rooted primarily in faulty learning (see Rosenham & Seligman, 1989).

Simply put, people with learned shyness have had their minds unfavorably programmed by such significant others as parents, peers, major relatives, and teachers. The subconscious mind acts like a robot computer. It is the "automatic pilot" of a person's life, and is most effectively "programmed" during the formative, impressionable years.

Those with inborn behavioral inhibition are especially vulnerable to being negatively programmed. This is because the inborn attributes of such people (a) make it easy for them to learn self-defeating patterns of social avoidance, (b) cause them to be perceived as aloof, unfriendly, and a good target for bullying and hazing, (c) make social risk-taking far more painful and difficult than it is for most people, and (d) result in an immaturity of social skills and of social self-confidence. In a highly competitive society a seriously diminished self-esteem is a highly probable consequence of such outcomes.

However, not all research has suggested the necessity of a bleak future for inborn shyness sufferers. Just as important as biology is the power of *mind* and *thought*. Thinking and self-talk are greatly influenced by the socialization process (see **Self-Talk**), which includes a person's full history of feedback from parents, peers, teachers, and psychotherapists. Competent parenting, in particular, can go a long way towards enabling children with inborn shyness to become normally sociable and competent in social situations (see Thomas & Chess, 1987).

Parents who do a competent job in rearing their more naturally outgoing and energetic children are often much less effective in relating with and parenting their shy offspring. As Zimbardo and Radl (1982) showed, such parents fail because they find great difficulty in accepting their shy children *as is*. People who are accepted, respected, and loved *as they are* become free to change in constructive directions (Johnson, 1983).

The neurological and biochemical forces underlying chronic shyness appear to be modifiable through the administration, in some cases, of anti-depressant drugs, involvement of the shy person in a support group, and cultivation of a positive mental attitude. Positive attitudes are normally a direct outgrowth of the knowing the importance of keeping an optimistic outlook, and feeling accepted as is by significant others.

When normal children are led through socialization to a set of negative expectations about themselves and their life chances, the robot computer of their subconscious minds is likely to lead them to the affective, cognitive, and behavioral handicap known as "shyness." When those with *inborn* behavioral inhibition (the least fortunate 10%) are so led by their socializers, we can duly expect a most unpropitious synergy—combining the powers of biology with those of learning. The by-product of this synergy is the kind of intractable shyness that often proves refractory to all therapeutic methods that might be tried.

## Relationship to Work

Shyness may affect a person's career choice and development in a variety of ways. For example, one study (Phillips & Bruch, 1988) showed that, compared to nonshys, shy university students were more indecisive regarding career options, less likely to seek out information about careers, less likely to express interest in interpersonally oriented career fields, and less likely to expect that assertive job interview behaviors would lead to favorable evaluations from employers.

Another study (Caspi, Elder, & Bem, 1988) examined the records of 87 shy boys and 95 shy girls over a 30-year period. Compared to a control group of nonshys, the shy boys were more likely to experience a delayed entry into stable careers. And over the 30 years, the shy boys experienced substantially less occupational achievement, stability, and remuneration. In contrast, shyness had little impact on the futures of the girls. This may be because during the decades covered by the study, few women entered careers requiring assertiveness and social self-confidence.

Of the 300 severely shy men studied by Gilmartin (1987), 88% were very nervous about using the telephone, even in business situations. Only 11% of the nonshys admitted to such nervousness. More importantly, 58% of the shys were unable to use the telephone even in response to an advertised job opening. This was not true for the nonshys. For 100 of the shy men in the 35–50 age category, 25% were unemployed compared to an unemployment rate at the time of only 3.6% for men of the same demographic characteristics. Some 73% of these men had suffered prolonged periods of unemployment or underemployment. And 82% had been fired from one or more jobs because shyness had interfered with their ability to fulfill various job responsibilities (e.g., making telephone calls, entertaining clients, delegating work assignments to subordinates, attending luncheons or evening parties with colleagues, initiating informal conversations with colleagues and customers).

## Application

If you are still in school and not decided on an occupation, you should seek out career information and counseling services. Ask an abundance of questions, and make an active effort to expose yourself to the many career-related materials that are available to you. Try to find out what kind of schooling (including academic major) is recommended for the occupations you are considering. Also, try to find out as much as you can about the typical, day-to-day job responsibilities of each career. And don't neglect to ascertain in as much detail as possible the amount and kind of both informal and formal social assertiveness that each career would require of you.

On the basis of the information you are able to obtain both about yourself and about career options, try to "zero in" on an academic major as early in your studies as possible. If you are shy, continued indecisiveness will only serve to maximize both the number and the noxiousness of the anxiety-provoking situations to which you will be exposed (see **Procrastination: Overcoming**). Simply put, indecisiveness and procrastination will ultimately aggravate (not relieve) your shyness problems!

If you are shy, you should bear in mind that some areas of employment require much greater social self-confidence than others do. Generally speaking, the greater the amount of technical knowledge that is required for entrance into a career field, the less social self-confidence, assertiveness, and social skills that field is likely to require. Contrariwise, the smaller the amount of technical training and knowledge a job opportunity requires, the greater the demands and expectations are likely to be in terms of social assertiveness, interpersonal skills, and social self-confidence. What this means is that academic majors in the liberal arts, social sciences, and humanities are likely to be more risky for shy people than academic majors in such technical areas as engineering, computer studies, accounting, nursing, medicine, architecture, and drafting. Another advantage of technical careers is in job hunting, as these jobs tend to be more specific and more skill-oriented.

Shys who are already employed in their chosen field are likely to benefit from becoming involved in a therapeutic support group. Your local medical group or university counseling center should be contacted for information and suggestions in this regard. Feel free to make such contacts by letter if you feel that you would be too shy to articulate your needs over the telephone. You might also find it helpful to seek out a neurologist who has some additional medical training in psychiatry. Such a physician would be in a position to inform you of the extent to which brain biochemistry and neurology might be playing a role in your shyness. He or she might also be able to prescribe and monitor drugs that could be beneficial.

In addition to (not instead of) such pharmacological treatment, you are also likely to benefit from the services of a competent cognitive-behavior therapist. Your local university counseling service or department of psychology would be able to furnish you with an appropriate referral. Even though drug therapy often proves quite helpful in alleviating anxiety problems, you are likely to make the most rapid progress to the extent that you simultaneously receive some form of cognitive-behavior therapy.

Finally, you should take advantage of some of the excellent self-help books and audio-cassette programs that are available. Audio-cassette programs can prove especially helpful because they allow for repeated listening and enhanced learning. You should find quite helpful the bibliographic and reference listings indicated below under the names Parker, Tracy, Waitley, and Zimbardo.

*See also* Career Indecision; Procrastination: Overcoming; Rational Thinking; Self-Efficacy; Self-Esteem; Self-Talk.

## Bibliography

Asher, J. (1987, April). Born to be shy? *Psychology Today*, 21: 56–64. To date this is the best "written for the layperson" article yet to appear on the biological bases of shyness.

Caspi, A., Elder, Jr., G. H., & Bem, D. J. (1988). Moving away from the world: Life-course patterns of shy children. *Developmental Psychology*, 24: 824–31.

Gilmartin, B. G. (1987). *Shyness and love: Causes, consequences, and treatment*. Lanham, MD: University Press of America. An intensive and richly detailed study which compared and contrasted the lives of 300 severely shy men with those of 200 nonshys. Pages 441–62 focus on the impact of shyness on career effectiveness and on the job search.

Johnson, S. (1983). *The one minute father*. New York: Morrow.

Kagan, J., & Reznick, J. S. (1988). Biological bases of childhood shyness. *Science*, 240: 167–71.

Parker, J. (1986). *Build a winning self-image/The prosperity solution.* Ojai, CA: Gateways Research Institute. This audio-cassette program is likely to prove especially helpful for shy people. It can be obtained from the Gateways Research Institute, P.O. Box 41, Ojai, CA 93023, or from Nightengale-Conant, 7300 North Lehigh Avenue, Chicago, IL 60648.

Phillips, S. D., & Bruch, M. A. (1988). Shyness and dysfunction in career development. *Journal of Counseling Psychology*, 35: 159–65.

Rosenham, D. L., & Seligman, M. E. P. (1989). *Abnormal psychology.* 2nd ed. New York: W. W. Norton.

Thomas, A., & Chess, S. (1987). *Know your child.* New York: Basic Books.

Tracy, B. (1987). *The psychology of achievement.* Chicago: Nightengale-Conant. This audio-cassette program offers many helpful hints for shy people. It can be obtained from Nightengale-Conant, 7300 North Lehigh Avenue, Chicago, IL 60648.

Waitley, D. (1981). *The psychology of winning.* Chicago: Nightengale-Conant.

Zimbardo, P. G., & Radl, S. L. (1982). *The shy child.* New York: Doubleday. This book gives excellent advice to parents and teachers on what they can do to effectively prevent shyness. The suggestions are all research-based and sensible.

—Brian G. Gilmartin

# SKILLS

Skills are specialized abilities to do things well that come from one's knowledge, aptitudes, and experiences. Skills play a vital role in choosing an appropriate career and attaining positive job satisfaction.

## Types of Skills

Sidney Fine's definitions and classifications of worker functions have provided the most definitive guidelines for working with skills. Fine, who was affiliated with the U.S. Bureau of Employment Security for many years, was instrumental in developing the Structure of Worker Functions, which identifies skills relating to Data, People, and Things. Within each of these categories are hierarchical descriptors of up to nine skills, such as supervising people or analyzing data. Fine also divided skills into three different broad categories: Functional, Adaptive, and Specific Content Skills.

1. *Functional Skills.* This type of skills refers to abilities that enable a person to relate to Things, Data, and People in ways that accomplish some desired end. They are probably rooted in natural born talent and refined by education, related experiences, and specific training. Examples of functional skills are coordinating, computing, and negotiating.

2. *Adaptive Skills.* These skills are more like personality traits or characteristic ways of behaving. They have been called self-management skills because they help the person get along with others and meet the demands of the environment. Examples of adaptive skills are dependability, neatness, being good-natured, and seeing things in perspective.

3. *Specific Content Skills.* These kinds of skills refer to those abilities that enable a person to perform at a specific job according to the required standards or specifications. These skills are most often learned on the job or in a specific training program designed to teach that skill. Examples of specific content skills are the operation of a specific data analysis system that is unlike any other system, or knowledge of a bookkeeping practice that has become obsolete.

## Transferable Skills

A skill that is applicable to more than one situation is a transferable skill. For example, a woman who has shown an organizing skill as a volunteer in her church can also transfer that skill to an office. Functional and adaptive skills are often seen as transferable, but specific content skills are seldom transferred. Each person develops skills of all three types while on a job or during other life experiences. The transferable skills are the ones that will enable a person to adapt to changing job markets.

## Motivated Skills

These skills are identified by studying achievements and other valued experiences (Haldane, 1988). Motivated skills are transferable, valued, and enjoyable. Such skills are also likely to be at the core of future activities which will be experienced with a sense of achievement. For example, helping others find jobs may be a motivated skill for Jack, while Mary may find this skill a chore, even though she is proficient at helping others find jobs.

## Skills Identification

Systematic methods for identifying skills are the primary activities of programs designed to facilitate career exploration and planning. In 1974, Haldane (1988) described the System to Identify Motivated Skills (SIMS), a refinement of an earlier process which he called Success Factor Analysis. Since that time, processes similar to SIMS have been called Skills Identification (Bolles, 1990; Figler, 1988). In a skills identification process, individuals identify and organize the skills that they think they possess.

## Relationship to Work

Skills are crucial to functioning in the world of work. Skills should be the primary focus of employers when they seek employees and of people when they seek work that is best suited to their talents and interests.

Transferable skills are especially important in the world of work because they allow workers to move from one job to another with a minimum of retraining or prolonged preparation. Awareness of transferable skills and the ability to convince others of their applicability in new jobs, will enhance a person's career development. Perhaps more important are persons' motivated skills, which are a special variety of transferable skills. Motivated skills are more potent than other varieties of transferable skills because they combine interest and value with ability. Consequently, they lead to higher productivity and job satisfaction. People who primarily use their nonmotivated skills rather than their motivated skills are more likely to become bored and under stress.

## Application

If you want to identify your own skills and use your new understanding of these skills to find work that is compatible with those skills, you have several possibilities. Books that offer guidelines for identifying skills are described in the references listed below. Most communities have workshops and classes that are designed to help you understand yourself, make career decisions, and seek more compatible jobs. You can investigate these offerings and determine their emphasis on identifying skills. In addition, most career counselors are trained to assess skills and assist in decision making. Likewise, books or materials that have extensive listings of well-used skill words will be useful as you seek to identify your skills or strengths. The following listing of 16 groups of skills or functions was described in more detail by Haldane (1988):

1. Design, color, shape things.
2. Calculate, count, keep records.
3. Observe, operate, inspect.
4. Write, read, talk, speak, teach.
5. Hand skills: Fix, build, assemble.
6. Analyze, systematize, research.
7. Invent, develop, create, imagine.
8. Help people, be of service, be kind.
9. Ideas, beauty, foresight.
10. Participate in physical, outdoor, travel activities.
11. Manage or direct others.
12. Perform independent work, own or collect things.
13. Perform: music, acting, demonstrations.
14. Foods, cooking, homemaking.
15. Persuade, sell, influence others.
16. Sciences, engineering.

The suggestions offered below provide a sample of Haldane's process designed to identify and use your motivated skills.

1. The first step is the recalling of past achievements, defined as experiences when you feel you have done something well, that you also enjoyed doing, and of which you are proud. It is helpful if you recall and list about 20 of these achievements.

2. After these have been identified, use them as the focus of your search for skills. First prioritize your achievements before you look into them for skills. The most prized and valued achievements usually lead to the identification of more skills that you enjoy and value. Some of the ways of using these achievements are: (a) Start with a list of skills which can be used to systematically study each of your most valued achievements. Consider each achievement one at a time and record a mark next to each skill that was clearly used during that achievement. When you are done, some of the skills will have several marks. These skills may be the ones you later claim as your top motivated skills. (b) Describe each valued achievement in great detail and look for words that identify what you did to make the experience happen the way it happened. These words are likely to be skill descriptors. (c) Describe these same achievements to a selected group of listeners and ask them to give you their ideas about your skills.

3. After you have identified a number of words or phrases for describing your skills, group those that are similar into about four to ten clusters. Then try to name those clusters, thereby reducing the large number of potential skill words to a manageable number.

4. After you have focused on four to ten words or phrases that may be getting close to identifying your best motivated skills, test them for "reality" by these activities: (a) write a brief description of what you want to be doing in a future job or in a life style where you are using your most valued skills, (b) select about six separate skills you would need to be successful in that future situation and put each one at the top of a blank sheet of paper, and (c) describe on each page several examples of past experiences where you demonstrated skills like those you have described at the top of each page. If you cannot think of several past experiences where you demonstrated the skill required for the future ideal activity, you may not be able to substantiate your claim to that particular skill.

5. Finish off the process by preparing a page where you list your most valued skills and then give several examples of past experiences where you demonstrated those particular skills. From this page you could prepare a functional resume or a presentation that could be used in a job interview.

*See also* Career Exploration; Career Planning; Choosing an Occupation; Resume; Self-Efficacy; Self-Esteem; Self-Managed Change.

## Bibliography

Bolles, R. N. (1990). *What color is your parachute?* Berkeley, CA: Ten Speed Press. This popular book includes a job-hunting map, which is a workbook that helps the user identify functional and transferable skills. The listing of skills is organized in a format using the categories of Data, People, and Things. In addition to identifying skills, the workbook facilitates clarification of values and researching an ideal job.

Figler, H. (1988). *The complete job-search handbook: Revised and expanded*. New York: Henry Holt & Co. This book emphasizes two kinds of skills, those that help the person complete a successful career search and those that are marketable for obtaining a fitting job. Chapter three includes many usable ideas about identifying and using transferable skills.

Haldane, B. (1988). *Career satisfaction and success: How to know and manage your strengths,* Rev. ed. Seattle: Wellness Behavior (Northwest). A revision of a book first published in 1974 by AMACOM, a division of American Management Associations, this book is both a text and a workbook that can help you get the most out of your career. It can help you identify your motivated skills and use them to increase your productivity.

Haldane, B., Haldane, J., & Martin, L. (1980). *Job power now! The young people's job finding guide*, rev. and updated. Washington, DC: Acropolis Books Ltd. This book covers motivated skills and job search methods in easy-to-understand language.

—JERALD R. FORSTER AND BERNARD HALDANE

# SOCIAL SECURITY DISABILITY CLAIM

A social security disability claim is an application by an individual under the age of 65 to the Social Security Administration (SSA) to receive benefits because a medical condition prevents the person from working.

The SSA administers a disability benefits program that includes (a) disability insurance benefits, (b) supplemental security income, (c) disabled adult child's benefits, and (d) disabled widows, widowers, and surviving divorced wives benefits. This article focuses on benefits for workers who have become disabled and are unable to work.

## Eligibility Requirements

First, workers must be insured. In general, workers are insured if they have paid the FICA tax on their earnings, and have worked for five out of the last ten years. If there is a question whether a person is insured or not, a report of his or her earnings records should be requested from the local security office.

And, second, the person must be disabled. Unfortunately, the definition of "disability" is complicated and full of jargon. I will quote it here and then give you a simpler one. Disability is the inability "to engage in any substantial gainful activity by reason of any medically determinable physical or mental impairment which can be expected to result in death or which has lasted or can be expected to last for a continuous period of not less than 12 months." And, an individual "shall be determined to be under a disability only if his physical or mental impairment or impairments are of such severity that he is not only unable to do his previous work but cannot, considering his age, education, and work experience, engage in any other kind of substantial gainful work which exists in the national economy . . . in significant numbers . . . ." The simple definition: virtually any injury or illness that keeps a person from working, and that has lasted, or will last, over a 12-month period will be eligible for benefits. In 1990 the maximum benefit for a worker was $975 per month, $1435 for a family. The average recipient is now receiving around $555 in monthly income. There are automatic cost of living increases each year.

## Application

**When, Where, and How to Apply**. If you believe that you are insured and unable to work, you should apply immediately. Obtaining benefits can be an extremely long process taking sometimes up to two years or more, so it is important to get started right away. You should keep in mind, however, that if you do receive benefits, you will not be paid for the period of five months after the first month that you are no longer able to work. For example, if you become disabled today and are approved a year from now, you would receive a check for the period beginning five months from this month.

Application is made to the local SSA office; they have all the forms and receive the completed application. Where practical, you should personally visit the social security office so that they can be sure to get all of the forms and instructions. Information needed for the application includes your social security number, birth certificate, dates of military service (if appropriate), the date you became unable to work, a description of your physical and/or mental impairment(s), job descriptions for the past 15 years, and the names and addresses of sources for medical information.

**Evaluation Process**. There are four administrative levels through which your claim can go: (a) the initial determination, (b) the reconsideration determination, (c) the hearing before an administrative law judge, and (d) the review by the Appeals Council. At each level a determination is made of whether or not you should receive benefits. If the decision is "Yes," then the process stops and you are awarded benefits (start receiving monthly checks). If the decision is "No," then, of course, you receive nothing. *However*, if you are dissatisfied with the decision, you have 60 days in which to request that it be reconsidered (or "appeal the decision"). The process then moves to the next highest level. For example, if you were denied benefits at the initial level, you could request a reconsideration, and it would move to the "reconsideration determination level."

Regardless of the level at which a claim is being considered, your claim is always reviewed using a five-step sequential evaluation process. For each step, there is a basic issue that is considered. If SSA finds that you are disabled or not disabled as they go through this five-step evaluation, the process stops. Each of the five steps is briefly described below:

1.  Are you prevented from engaging in "substantial gainful activity" by impairment(s) that are supported by the medical evidence? This is another term that is difficult to define. Generally, a claimant is not eligible for benefits if he or she is working. However, whether one's work is considered substantial gainful activity is determined by the amount of pay it generates and by a loose interplay of factors that constitute productivity. Currently, average earnings of more than $500 per month constitute substantial gainful activity. However, pay is only one of many factors that are considered.

2.  Is your impairment severe enough to meet a government defined threshold of severity defined by the inability to perform basic work functions like sitting, standing, or carrying out simple instructions?

3.  Does your impairment meet or equal those listed by the SSA for 13 body systems? For example, you would "meet the listing" for blindness if the central visual acuity of your better eye was 20/200 or less with the use of a correcting lens.

4.  Based on a medical doctor's assessment, does your impairment prevent you from returning to your previous work over the past 15 years? This assessment is called your "residual functional capacity."

5.  Based on your residual functional capacity and vocational factors (your age, education, and previous work experience), are you prevented from doing any other jobs that exist in significant numbers in the national economy? It is irrelevant whether you would actually be hired or not. The SSA expects you to be disabled to the extent that you can no longer perform the most minimal level of exertion called "sedentary" work; this is primarily work that in-

volves lifting no more than 10 pounds and is done mostly in a seated position. Generally speaking, you will not be granted disability benefits just because you cannot continue at your old job.

**Administrative Levels**. In the first two of the four levels through which your claim may progress, the initial and reconsideration levels, your claim is reviewed by the state agency. Unless your impairments are very severe and well-documented by the medical evidence, it is likely that your claim will be denied *even though you are qualified to receive benefits*.

You must be willing to go through a very long and stressful battle with the SSA bureaucracy. It is an experience that may produce extreme anxiety, confusion, and frustration. There are very long delays. You must be prepared to be turned down probably twice before having your claim approved. Most successes come at the third stage, the hearing.

The hearing before an administrative law judge is the third level at which your claim is reviewed if (a) you were denied at the reconsideration level, and (b) you requested a hearing within 60 days of receiving your notice of denial. I have found that this stage is the fairest part of the disability process. Social security hearings are private, rather informal proceedings where testimony is taken under oath or affirmation. They are presided over by an administrative law judge (ALJ). The ALJ is assisted by a hearing assistant who tape records the hearing. This record can be used to make a transcript of the hearing for later appeals, if necessary. The ALJ is wholly independent and separate from the claims processing bureau of the SSA and is not bound by the previous two determinations of the SSA. The ALJ protects both the government's interests and those of the claimant. While these interests appear to be inconsistent, ALJ decisions presently result in a reversal rate of over 50% in favor of the claimant.

At the hearing stage, you should retain the services of an attorney experienced in the field of social security disability claims. This is very important. Unfortunately, the language of the regulations and procedures is complicated and difficult to understand. An attorney will usually not charge a fee unless you win your case. Generally, the fee is one-fourth of the retroactive benefits up to $4,000; amounts above that figure are subject to the approval of the ALJ.

Your case may proceed to the fourth level, the review by the Appeals Council, if the ALJ's decision was unfavorable and you ask for a review within 60 days. If you are not satisfied with the Appeals Council review, you and your attorney may file a complaint in federal district court.

If you are severely disabled, can no longer work, and have paid social security taxes as required, then it is your right to receive these benefits. You are not begging for something that is not yours. Don't give up. You have nothing to lose and much to gain financially by trying to obtain benefits. If you succeed, it is bound to mean a great deal to you and your family.

In summary, pursue your rights; know your rights. Seek legal counsel when you pursue your disability claim after stage two (the reconsideration denial) in the disability evaluation process.

*See also* Disability: Adjustment to; Law in the Workplace; Rehabilitation Counselors and Agencies; Workers' Compensation.

## Bibliography

U.S. Department of Health and Human Services. (1981). *Social Security regulations: Rules for determining disability and blindness* (SSA Publication No. 64-014). Washington, DC: U. S. Government Printing Office. An explanation of the laws that is intended to help persons applying for disability benefits. Unfortunately, it is loaded with technical jargon and difficult to understand.

U. S. Department of Health and Human Services. (1990). *Disability* (SSA Publication No. 05-10029). This 23-page booklet summarizes the social security disability program, covering such areas as who is eligible, how to apply for benefits, and the amount of monthly benefits. You may request it by calling the Social Security Administration on their toll free number, 1-800-234-5772; or write to the Department of Health and Human Services, Social Security Administration, Baltimore, MD 21235.

—SUSAN HATCHER BRADSHAW

# STRESS

Stress is the body's physiological and psychological reaction to job conditions at the workplace. Stress is real; stress is something that happens to your body. Stress is not an attitude or a personal failure. Ignoring it won't make it go away and can be dangerous because it allows the body to operate on permanent overdrive.

The best known stress reaction is the "fight or flight" response. If a person meets a bear in the woods, the body gears up for fight or flight. The adrenal and thyroid glands increase production, more sugar is released into the body to create more energy, the heart beats faster, and the lungs take in more oxygen. Other bodily processes slow down. After the crisis, a relaxation response restores the body to normal functioning. A threat to personal well-being, a physiological reaction that makes it possible to deal with the threat, and a period of relaxation makeup a perfectly natural and healthy cycle.

**Dis-Stress.** Dis-stress, or negative stress, occurs when the body continues to react to stress over long periods of time without the necessary relaxation cycle. The chemical balance of the body is affected and a whole series of symptoms may occur. Stress is sometimes called the "invisible disease" because the same stressors affect each individual differently. Symptoms include increased blood pressure, insomnia, stomach ailments, headaches, neck and back aches, and a greater susceptibility to colds and other illnesses. Beyond the immediate physiological effects of stress, there are psychological symptoms as well. These include nervousness, irritability, apathy, and depression.

## Relationship to Work

Work is a central and defining part of people's lives. It is both a psychological and an economic necessity. Because of its importance, what happens at work has a major impact on people's levels of stress and general life satisfaction.

There are three major sources of stress at work: (a) biochemical exposure; (b) physical conditions; and (c) psychosocial stressors. Exposure to biological and chemical substances can interfere with the body's normal functioning. This creates a stress condition in the body that manifests itself in a wide variety of stress symptoms. The following physical and ergonomic hazards also place the body under stress: noise, heat and ventilation, pace of production, overtime and shift work (see **Shift Work; Work Hazards: Ergonomic; Work Hazards: Physical**). Levels of stress at work also reflect psychosocial stessors. Psychosocial stessors include conflicting job demands, isolation, patterns of communication and supervision, lack of respect and recognition, and attitudes of management toward workers. At the broadest level, psychosocial stressors also include racism, sexism, homophobia, class attitudes, and age discrimination.

In talking about job stress it is important to distinguish between the symptoms of stress and the causes of stress. Many stress management programs are primarily concerned with helping people adapt to stressful conditions and minimize the physiological effects by using relaxation techniques and by eating, sleeping, and exercising properly. All of these things are beneficial and bring short-term results. However, research by the National Institute of Occupational Safety and Health (NIOSH) has shown that the benefits of this kind of stress management last only a few months and leave the causes of the stress untouched.

Dr. Robert Karasek has linked work stress to the relationship between how demanding a job is and the degree of control that the worker has over how the work is organized. If demand is high and the degree of control is low (as in the case of a production worker), the level of stress is high. If the degree of control is high and the demand is low (as in the case of an architect), the stress level is low. See Figure 1. The issue of having a degree of control over the

**Figure 1. High Demand + Low Control = Highest Stress**

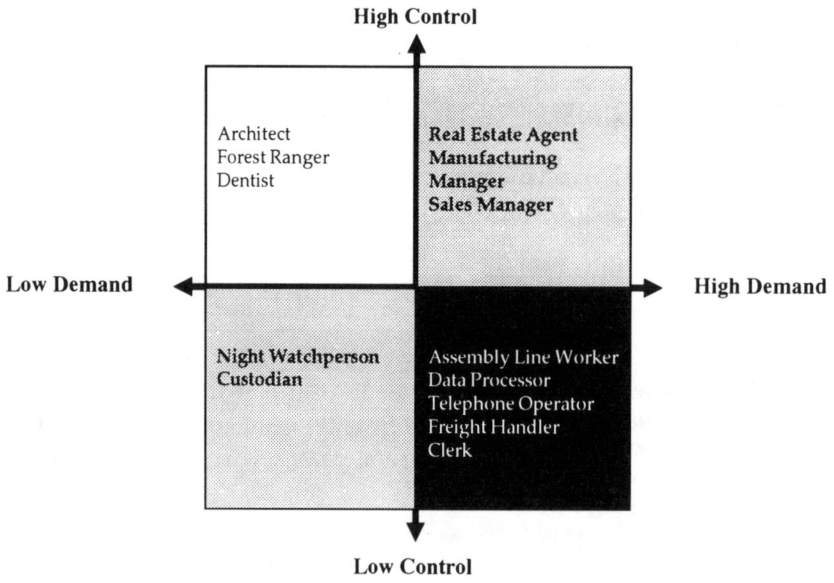

**Figure 1.** Dr. Robert Karasek, of the University of Southern California, found that the jobs with the highest stress were those that combined heavy production demands with a low ability to control how these tasks are done. Not only was the job stress highest for these workers, but they also faced the highest risk of heart disease.

planning and execution of work is an important one in reducing stress. The team approach to manufacturing, which involves workers in the entire production process, has the potential for reducing stress.

**Taking Stress Home.** The effects of work stress do not stop with the end of the work day; they travel home with the worker. Job stress may leave workers with little energy or patience to deal with family and friends. Job stress affects the patterns of interaction between partners and between parents and children. It may result in the increased use of alcohol or drugs, or be reflected in the choice of passively watching television instead of interacting with other family members or friends.

## Application

To understand how work stress affects you, and what you can do about it, there are three basic elements to consider: (a) analyzing the parts of your job that are sources of stress, (b) learning your own stress reactions, and (c) determining what you can do about job stress.

**Analyzing Job Stress.** One of the ways to analyze job stress is to make a stress map of your job. This can be done individually or together with other people. This process involves drawing a "map" of your workplace showing the work you do: the layout of the shop floor or office, the equipment you use, the other people who are there with you, and a sense of the flow of your work (where it comes from, where it goes). Looking at this map you can identify the areas where any of the stressors (biochemical, physical, or psychosocial) we have talked about can be found. In this process you will begin to "get the picture" of the job stress you are experiencing.

**Learning Your Own Reactions.** Once you have identified the areas of job stress, the next step is to identify what happens to you when you experience that stress. People's reactions may vary. For instance, when heavy machinery starts up, many people react to the noise by tensing their muscles. Their bodies are reacting to stress. Other workers know that after a certain period of time at a video display terminal their eyes will begin to squint and their backs will begin to hurt (see **Video Display Terminals**). Adjusting to these physical circumstances is a cause of both physiological and psychological stress. When you become aware of how your body reacts to stress you can use these stress signals to tell you that it's time to take a break, to stretch, to use a relaxation exercise, or to work with your union or other group to establish reasonable work rules or health and safety standards that will limit the causes of stress. The most important stage in the process of dealing with job stress is taking action to protect yourself against the effects of stress and to take a greater degree of control over the conditions that cause stress.

**Determining What You Can Do.** There are many things that you can do to reduce the impact and symptoms of job stress. These include the use of relaxation exercises to create a relaxation response to complete the natural stress cycle. Most relaxation exercises have five basic elements: (a) being in a calm quiet place; (b) being in a comfortable position; (c) having a relaxed mental attitude; (d) having something concrete to think about that takes your mind off the sources of stress; and (e) breathing deeply and regularly (see **Relaxation: Progressive Muscle**).

The effects of stress are also reduced by paying attention to your health. Changing diet can have an important impact. Here are some suggestions: (a) eat *more* fruit, vegetables, whole grain, poultry, and fish; (b) eat *less* meat, dairy products, and eggs; (c) reduce your intake of tobacco, sugar, and alcohol. Getting regular sleep and exercise also makes a difference. Exercising stimulates the body's production of endorphins, chemicals that are natural relaxants and painkillers. For many people, exercising after work leaves them feeling fresh and relaxed. All of these health tips are ways of keeping your body functioning at maximum efficiency, which enables it to better adjust to the demands put on it by job stress.

Social support is a stress buffer. Research in Sweden and the United States has shown that one of the most important buffers to the efforts of job stress is social support. Social support is having friends or groups of friends where you feel accepted and understood. The main sources of social support usually come from people at work and at home, but other groupings (such as unions, churches, or other social and community groups) can also be important sources of this support. Social support breaks down the isolation and self-blame that are often sources of stress (see **Mentoring; Networking**).

One of the simplest and most effective ways to keep job stress from taking its toll is to talk about it. Keeping the stress inside only makes it worse. Talking about stress is more than just complaining. It should help identify the sources of stress and develop individual and collective ways of dealing with it. Collective ways of handling stress may include participating in stress groups that are designed to help you understand the nature of stress and what to do about it, or forming stress committees in the workplace that operate through the union, if there is one, to identify sources of stress on the job and suggest ways to reduce it.

**Long-Range Strategies.** Long-range strategies for dealing with stress involve changes in the workplace and changes in how we view work. NIOSH has suggested the following ways that working conditions could be made less stressful: (a) design work schedules to avoid conflicts with other life responsibilities; (b) allow workers to have meaningful input into decisions affecting their work; (c) avoid excessive workload and allow recovery time after demanding tasks; (d) design jobs to allow workers to use their skills and to provide meaning and stimulation; (e) define work roles and responsibilities clearly; (f) provide opportunities for social support and interaction; and (g) make matters of job security and career development clear.

*See also* Career Burnout; Mentoring; Networking; Relaxation: Progressive Muscle; Self-Esteem; Shift Work; Video Display Terminals; Work Hazards: Ergonomic; Work Hazards: Physical; Work Hazards: Psychosocial.

## Bibliography

Charlesworth, E., & Nathan, R. (1984). *Stress management: A comprehensive guide to wellness.* New York: Ballantine Books. This book emphasizes individual methods of stress reduction, particularly the use of relaxation techniques, but also contains useful sections on planning, time management, and acting assertively.

Karasek, R., & Theorell, T. (1990). *Healthy work: Stress, productivity and the reconstruction of working life.* New York: Basic Books. Based on research in the United States and Sweden, the authors present a comprehensive examination of psychosocial job stressors and their impact on health and well-being. They also discuss how jobs can be redesigned to reduce stress and increase productivity.

Selye, H. (1984). *The stress of life.* Rev. ed. New York: McGraw-Hill. This is the basic medical/theoretical source book that introduced the concept of stress into the popular vocabulary.

Veninga, R.L., & Spradley, J.P. (1981). *The work stress connection: How to cope with job burnout.* New York: Ballantine Books. Relies heavily on interviews with working people.

## For Further Information

**Job Stress Network c/o Center for Social Epidemiology**
75 Livingston Street, Apt. 27A
Brooklyn, NY 11201
The Network produces a newsletter and is a clearinghouse for information on job stress research and practical action programs

—LEE SCHORE

# T

## TEMPORARY EMPLOYMENT

Any kind of work arrangement that is expected to be of short duration and that does not provide for a high degree of attachment to an employer is temporary employment. Paid sick leave, vacations, health coverage, retirement plans, career advancement, promotional opportunities, and the expectation of continuing employment—the hallmarks of permanent jobs—are generally limited or absent.

### Relationship to Work

Employer's needs for workers can fluctuate, from day to day, week to week, or month to month, reflecting vacation schedules, illness, new contracts or orders, or unexpected changes in demand. Having enough full-time, permanent workers to cover all such contingencies is very costly, so many employers make use of one or more types of temporary employment to meet such needs.

Ways of doing temporary work include the following:

1.  Intermittents, or "call-ins," are workers on the payroll of an employer who are available for temporary assignments as needed. They may receive the same fringe benefits as permanent full-time workers, or they may receive less.
2.  Short-term or temporary hires are workers on jobs of limited duration, generally less than six months. These jobs are usually set up to meet very specific needs, such as filling in for someone on leave of absence, or for a special project. Certain benefits, such as health coverage, may be provided, but other benefits usually are not.
3.  Casuals work on jobs of very short duration, often a day or less. They may be referred by an employment office or a union hiring hall. Fringe benefits usually are not provided unless required by union contract.
4.  Temporary help service (THS) employees work on assignments with businesses that have contracted for their services with a third party, the temporary help service. The company where the worker is assigned (called the "customer") supervises the worker, but the THS is the actual employer, holding the full range of employer responsibilities, from withholding taxes and social security contributions to issuing pay checks. The THS bills the "customer" based upon the timesheet submitted by the temporary worker. The THS may provide certain benefits, such as paid vacations or even profit-sharing or retirement plans.
5.  Independent contractors are self-employed workers who provide services to businesses under contracts of fixed duration. Like THS workers, they may work on-site at the business or they may work out of their own homes or offices, but they are not on the payroll of the business. They receive no fringe benefits of any kind and are responsible to appropriate government agencies for taxes and other required contributions.

Fields where temporary work is common include the following:

1.  Office work has the greatest volume of temporary opportunities. Work must go on at insurance companies, banks, and the headquarters of every kind of business, yet absences continually occur. Because office skills are so standardized, there are large numbers of temporary opportunities for secretaries, clerks, word processors, accountants, and other clerical specialties.
2.  Technical workers, such as computer programmers, drafters, technical writers, electronics technicians, and even engineers, frequently work on temporary assignments. Temporary help services that specialize in technical assignments are sometimes called "job shops."
3.  Hospitals balance fluctuating patient loads with nurses, therapists, and lab workers on temporary assignment. Nurses' Registries have evolved into specialized temporary help services for this industry.

4. Blue-collar workers from truck drivers and loaders to assemblers also do temporary work.

## Application

**A Route to a Permanent Job.** Permanent jobs with security, fringe benefits, and chances of advancement are highly sought after and in many fields not so easy to come by. One good way you can improve your chances is through temporary employment. By working as a temp you can learn a great deal about a company and they can look you over. You can overcome such drawbacks as lack of experience, education, or a spotty work history by demonstrating your abilities to an employer through a temporary job.

**Flexibility.** Temporary jobs also provide you with a way of working when you want to, rather than the Monday to Friday, 8 to 5 routine. If you are going to school, are trying to raise a family, or are gradually retiring from the world of paid work, temping is an excellent source of income.

**Finding Temporary Work Assignments.** Temporary help services, in addition to acting as your employer, also find work assignments for you. Based upon your skills, the times you are available, and the approximate number of hours you want, they can usually keep you as busy as you want to be. As you are working on an assignment with one customer, they can be locating the next one for you. You may be able to find casual or limited duration jobs through your local employment service. If you belong to a labor union, the local hiring hall may provide this service. Working as an intermittent generally requires seeking out an employer on your own. Once you have established a relationship with a company, they may call you in whenever temporary help is needed. Independent contractors generally must develop their own leads and promote themselves for each and every new assignment.

*See also* Job Search; Job Sharing; Part-Time Work; Self-Employment.

## Bibliography

Gannon, M. J. (1984). Preferences of temporary workers. *Monthly Labor Review*, 107, (8): 26–28.

Mangum, G. L., Mayall, D., & Nelson, K. (1985). The temporary help industry: A response to the dual internal labor market. *Industrial and Labor Relations Review*, 38, (4): 599–611.

Mayall, D., & Nelson, K. (1982). *The temporary help supply service and the temporary labor market.* Salt Lake City: Olympus Research Centers.

—DONALD MAYALL

## TESTING

Anyone who is in the job market should be aware that many employers require any of a number of pre-employment tests as a condition of hiring and may require also subsequent tests as a condition of continued employment. These tests may include honesty, psychological, polygraph, drug, AIDS, and genetic tests. The choices that you make about taking these tests may be critical to getting or keeping your job. Before you make any decisions about whether you will take a particular test, it is important for you to be knowledgeable in two areas: the test itself and the law relating to testing.

It is important that you educate yourself about the test that you are being asked to take. Questions to which you should have the answers include: What kind of test is it? What is it designed to test? What is involved in actually taking the test? Will the test be evaluated by someone within the organization or someone outside of it? How often is the test wrong? How will the results of the test be used? In some cases, you may want to ask your employer or prospective employer these questions directly. In many cases, it may be wiser to find out this information from other sources.

You should also be familiar with your legal rights. There are four types of rights that may apply to you: constitutional, statutory, contract, and tort. With respect to constitutional rights, it will make a difference if your job is with the government or with a private company. If you are a government employee, provisions of the federal and state constitutions apply to your employer and, for example, may restrict the type of testing that may be done or require that a certain procedure be followed in testing. Private employers are not, except in a few special situations, subject to constitutional restrictions.

Whether you are a government employee or not, there may be federal, state, or local laws (statutes) that protect you or give certain rights to employers. Some of these statutes specifically exempt certain kinds of employers or employees from being covered. You should be familiar with these laws, including the penalties for violating them. State laws may vary from state to state and local laws may vary from location to location, so be sure not to assume that if you move to a new location the same laws will apply.

If you have an employment contract or a collective bargaining agreement, there may be provisions that protect you. If you are in a position to negotiate the terms of your contract, you should consider whether you want your agreement with your employer to cover the issue of testing. In any case, you should be sure that you understand completely all of the provisions of any contract that you sign.

You may also have a remedy through tort law. A tort is a civil wrong, other than breach of contract. Invasion of privacy, wrongful discharge, and defamation of character are examples of torts. If your employer tests you when he or she is not legally permitted to, discloses the results of the tests to someone else, or fires you on the basis of a test that could not legally be given, you may be able to sue your employer to collect money damages or get your job back.

The articles that follow discuss the commonly given tests. They will alert you to important issues involved in particular employment testing. They will also provide you with important information to help you decide what to do when faced with a pre-employment or post-employment decision about testing.

*See also* Biodata; Testing: AIDS; Testing: Drugs; Testing: Genetic; Testing: Integrity.

—SANDRA N. HURD

## TESTING: AIDS

AIDS tests screen applicants or current employees for antibodies to the Human Immunodeficiency Virus (HIV), the virus that causes AIDS. Serologic (blood) tests are the only readily available method to detect evidence of HIV. Currently, there is no direct method for measuring the virus itself.

Testing for HIV involves a two-part process (Centers for Disease Control [CDC], 1988; Nichols, 1989). First, a screening antibody test is utilized. This test is the Enzyme-Linked Immunosorbent Assay (ELISA) test. The ELISA test was designed to be both very sensitive (likely to correctly identify the presence of antibodies) and very specific (likely to fail to react if a specimen is truly negative). In fact, clinical data indicate that ELISA tests currently used in the United States have sensitivity and specificity exceeding 99%. Regardless, false positives still occur, particularly when the test is applied in a low prevalence population. As a result, it is essential that ELISA tests be repeated if initially positive in order to reduce the possibility that technical laboratory error caused the positive result.

If two positive ELISA tests occur, an additional test of high specificity is warranted. The Western Blot test is the favored test. This test is more specific than the ELISA but is also more difficult to perform.

A positive HIV test result requires positives on two ELISA tests as well as the Western Blot test. Such a result is indicative of infection. Test manufacturers and CDC laboratory personnel consider a testing sequence to be negative if the Western Blot is negative in the face of repeatedly positive ELISA tests. At times the test results are "undetermined." This can occur if both ELISA procedures are positive but the Western Blot results are inconclusive. In situations that have been labeled "undetermined," repeat testing is recommended.

Since the ELISA test is considerably less expensive and quicker than the Western Blot test, it may be tempting to rely on a single unconfirmed positive result. However, the medical and social significance of a positive HIV test is such that the use of an unconfirmed result for any purpose is completely inappropriate. Assuring the accuracy of test results requires careful monitoring with respect to both the quality of the test used and the conditions under which it is performed.

## Relationship to Work

The CDC (1985) has determined that AIDS is caused by the blood-borne virus HIV. Accordingly, HIV is not transmitted by casual contact. This means that you cannot catch AIDS from a sneeze, a cough, a handshake, or a hug. Likewise, objects in the workplace, such as public toilets, typewriters, computer keyboards, pens, pencils, papers, and water fountains do not transmit the virus. Thus, AIDS-afflicted applicants or current employees should not, based solely upon their infection, be restricted in or excluded from the workplace. Even so, employers in health care, food service, laboratory, and other public service safety fields should be aware that the CDC has issued specific guidelines for these types of jobs.

The CDC (1985) has also concluded that routine serologic testing to protect the general workforce or the public from the risk of infection is not necessary. In addition, the agency does not recommend routine testing of patients to protect health-care workers or of health-care workers themselves.

Despite these recommendations, many employers are considering adopting AIDS testing policies. In fact, three federal agencies—the Department of Defense, the Foreign Service, and the Job Corps—have already implemented AIDS testing programs. The legality of such testing as well as testing of applicants and employees performing public sector jobs is questionable. Some federal courts have upheld this testing while others have overturned such testing.

Although there is no federal legislation which deals specifically with AIDS testing, recent court rulings have extended victims of AIDS protection under the Vocational Rehabilitation Act of 1973. This Act prohibits discrimination against qualified "handicapped" individuals by government contractors, recipients of federal funds, and government agencies. Thus, covered employers who want to test applicants or current employees for the AIDS virus will have to show that an employee who tests positive for the virus would be limited in his or her ability to perform the job in question. Since individuals who test positive for the AIDS virus often have no other limitations, employers will have a difficult time showing the test to be job related.

Numerous states have adopted statutes prohibiting discrimination in employment against those with AIDS; other states have enacted laws dealing specifically with AIDS testing (Bureau of National Affairs, 1990). For example, Michigan regards AIDS as a handicap and prohibits discrimination in the same manner as for any other handicap. Massachusetts has an AIDS testing statute similar to that of several other states. It prohibits requiring testing as a condition of hiring or continued employment. In addition, the statute prohibits the disclosure of any information related to testing without first obtaining the subject's written consent. Texas prohibits forced testing for AIDS by an employer unless a bona fide occupational qualification can be shown. Since state laws vary considerably, it would be wise to check with the state's human rights commission or applicable agency.

Some local entities have also enacted law regarding AIDS discrimination. Municipal ordinances in San Francisco, California and Austin, Texas ban AIDS discrimination in employment, housing, and city services. A Cincinnati, Ohio, ordinance places restrictions on discrimination and testing for AIDS.

## Application

If you are a job applicant or already employed, you should be aware of your rights concerning AIDS testing in the workplace. While some states and local entities specifically prohibit AIDS testing for employment purposes, others allow such testing. In such states, you may be required to undergo an AIDS test. If such testing is limited to those suspected of having AIDS and you are one of those tested or to be tested, you may be successful with a discrimination claim. Adverse action based on the results of an AIDS test may also violate federal, state, and/or local handicap protection statutes. Thus, you may have recourse under discrimination and/or handicap legislation.

As a job applicant or current employee, you have a right to privacy regarding many aspects of your personal life. Several courts have concluded that AIDS testing may violate a public employee's constitutional right to privacy and to be free from unreasonable search and seizure. This same idea has been somewhat liberally applied to private-sector employees, especially when courts consider that the risk of transmission is practically nonexistent in the particular workplace.

Since test results are extremely sensitive information, unauthorized or improper disclosure of your AIDS test results may subject your employer to substantial liability (Bohl, 1988). You may find, depending upon the specific circumstances, that you have a valid claim for invasion of privacy, defamation/slander if you are wrongly accused of having AIDS, breach of medical confidentiality if the company doctor provides information to supervisors, infliction of intentional or negligent emotional distress, and/or wrongful discharge (Obdyke, 1989).

You may feel that you have a right to know if a coworker has tested positive for the AIDS virus. Since there is little possibility for transmission of AIDS in a normal work environment, you will find little support for this contention from the courts.

If you are a manager, federal, state, and local laws will influence your decision to test as well as the use of the test results for employment purposes. Even more important is the fact that the tests for AIDS only screen the blood for the presence of antibodies to the HIV virus. A positive test result does not necessarily reveal whether a person actually has the disease, will ever develop the disease, or is contagious. It simply indicates that a person has developed antibodies to the virus as a result of exposure to it. Since the tests do not reveal the degree of actual illness, they show little indication of an employee's ability to perform the job.

Since the CDC has determined that there is no need to subject applicants or current employees to routine AIDS testing, it is unlikely that the fear of contagion would justify AIDS testing for employment purposes. After all, the CDC has concluded that the virus cannot be spread by casual contact in the workplace.

Testing your employees or potential employees for AIDS can create unnecessary problems for you as a manager. Thus, refraining from AIDS testing is probably the best course of action.

*See also* Law in the Workplace; Work Hazards; Work Hazards: Biological.

## Bibliography

Bohl, D. L. (1988). *AIDS: The new workplace issues.* New York: American Management Association Publications. Contains detailed information on the medical, legal, and ethical consequences of AIDS in the workplace.

Bureau of National Affairs. (1990). *State fair employment practices manual.* Washington, DC: Bureau of National Affairs, Inc. Chapters 451–457 provide a concise summary of individual state employment laws on various issues, including AIDS.

Centers for Disease Control (CDC). (1985). Recommendations for preventing transmission of injection with HTLV-III/LAV in the Workplace. *Morbidity and Mortality Weekly Report*, 34: 682–94.

Centers for Disease Control (CDC). (1988). Update: Serologic testing for antibody to human immunodeficiency virus. *Morbidity and Mortality Weekly Report*, 37: 833–45. Provides a thorough discussion of the types of HIV tests available as well as the reliability of each.

Nichols, E. K. (1989). *Mobilizing against AIDS*. Cambridge, MA: Harvard University Press. Appendix C contains a detailed discussion of the existing types of tests for HIV.

Obdyke, L.K., IV. (1989). Interpreting AIDS discrimination. *Personnel Administrator*, 34, (6): 83–89.

—GERALYN MCCLURE FRANKLIN

# TESTING: DRUGS

Employers in the public and private sectors have begun to establish drug abuse prevention programs in the workplace that include some form of drug testing, usually in the form of urinalysis. In 1982, less than 5% of the Fortune 500 companies were testing employees for drug abuse. By 1987, nearly half of the Fortune 500 companies conducted some form of drug testing of their applicants or employees.

Drug testing of government employees continues to increase. The military has been using drug testing for many years. In September 1986, President Reagan issued an Executive Order seeking a "drug-free Federal Workplace." The order declared that "[p]ersons who use illegal drugs are not suitable for Federal employment" and ordered agency heads to "establish a program to test for the use of illegal drugs by employees in sensitive positions." The United States Supreme Court ruled in 1989 that two drug testing programs of the federal government did not violate the Constitution's prohibition against unreasonable searches and seizures. The testing programs required blood and urine tests for train workers in the event of certain types of railway accidents, and urinalysis of Customs employees seeking transfer or promotion to positions involving drug interdiction and the carrying of firearms. Local fire fighters, police officers, and operators of buses, trains, and subways are being tested. Prison facilities all over the country are testing correctional officers.

## Testing Methods

Urinalysis methods vary substantially in cost, accuracy, the number of different drugs detected, and the amount of expertise required to perform them.

Three major types of screening methods are currently available: thin layer chromatography (TLC), enzyme immunoassay (EIA), and radioimmunoassay (RIA). The TLC method involves reading a plate on which a drop of urine has been chemically treated to separate its various compounds. Drugs are identified when a dye solution is sprayed onto the plate causing colors to appear. The location of the color spots are then compared to known standards. Although TLC can detect a few prescription drugs that the immunoassay tests do not identify, it is not as sensitive; it will not always detect as minute a quantity of drug as the immunoassay tests.

The EIA and RIA methods are designed to detect the eight major abused drugs or drug classes—amphetamine, barbiturates, benzodiazepine, cannabinoids (marijuana), cocaine, methaqualone, opiates (including heroin), and phencyclidine (PCP)—but will not identify some of the prescription drugs picked up by the TLC test. However, the EIA and RIA methods are slightly more sensitive and give a more definitive test result.

The immunoassays use antibodies to detect drugs. In the test mixture (reagent) designed to detect a certain drug, antibodies attach themselves to that drug if it is present in the urine. In the EIA method the reaction causes a color change which can be measured by a device called a spectrophotometer. In the radioimmunoassay method, a low level of radiation is given off which is measured by a gamma counter.

No matter which method is used to screen applicants or employees for drugs, it is generally agreed that a positive result should be confirmed at the laboratory by a second test, using a different and preferably more sensitive and specific method to achieve accuracy. This is an especially critical step when testing for drugs at the workplace because a person's livelihood and the company's legal liability may be at stake.

Although some laboratories will confirm one type of screening method with another, it is better—and more acceptable legally—to use a more sophisticated technique such as gas chromatography or gas chromatography/mass spectrometry (GC/MS).

Gas chromatography (GC)—sometimes called gas/liquid chromatography or GLC—involves heating and vaporizing a liquid sample while it moves through a column of absorbent material. Individual compounds are separated on this column according to their chemical and physical properties. These separated compounds appear as peaks on a graph and can be identified.

Although GC is sometimes used alone to perform confirmation tests, the best method combines it with a mass spectrometer. The two instruments together are more powerful than either instrument alone. The GC/MS further breaks down the compound molecules into electrically charged ion fragments. Different compounds break down into different fragments and, like fingerprints, no two fragment patterns are alike. Because the GC/MS can match up these patterns to the known patterns of abused drugs, positive identification can be made. Quantification is possible with GC or GC/MS.

Although the GC/MS test is the state-of-the-art drug testing method currently available, it is not practical to use as a screening method because it is too expensive, requires very sophisticated equipment, and must be performed by highly trained technicians. Therefore, a screening method is used first to eliminate the negatives and then the more definitive tests are used only on the positives.

Although it is often used in hospitals, blood analysis currently is not used as frequently as urine for routine screening in an industrial setting because samples are harder to collect. A licensed technician is needed to draw blood. Furthermore, a blood test is a more invasive procedure, making cooperation by employees or applicants more difficult to obtain. According to the weight of scientific evidence, current initial screening tests are more than 90% accurate. With confirmatory tests, the possibility of a false positive result is virtually eliminated. The overwhelming majority of courts that have ruled on the admissibility of drug tests into evidence have found them to meet the stringent legal standards applicable to the admission of scientific evidence.

## Relationship to Work

The available evidence establishes that there is drug abuse among employed individuals. For example, in a survey of drug users who called the 800-COCAINE hotline number, 75% admitted to using illegal drugs on the job, 69% regularly worked under the influence of cocaine, and 25% used cocaine at work every day. The National Institute on Drug Abuse estimates that one in every five workers ages 18 to 25 and one in every eight workers ages 26 to 34 use drugs on the job.

Studies have shown that the drug abusing worker is late for work three times more often than nonabusing workers, has 2.5 times as many absences of eight days or longer, uses three times the normal level of sick benefits, asks for early dismissal or time off 2.2 times more often, is five times more likely to file a worker's compensation claim, and is involved in accidents 3.6 times more often than other employees. The 16 fatalities resulting from the January 1987 crash between an Amtrak passenger train and a Conrail freight train showed the tragic consequences of drug use by workers.

Drug testing allows employers to cull out drug abusers from among job applicants, to deter use by employees, and to identify drug-impaired workers who can then be provided counseling or treatment for their drug problems.

## Legislation

In response to the proliferation of workplace drug testing, several states have enacted laws regulating the practice. Some cities have also done so by enacting ordinances or adopting resolutions. These local laws and ordinances may address drug testing in the private sector, in the public sector, or in both. In addition, agencies of the federal government, and employers in industries pervasively regulated by the federal government (e.g., transportation) must follow certain regulations concerning drug testing of applicants and employees. With the exception of the City of Berkeley, California, neither local governments nor the federal government has prohibited drug testing in the workplace.

The basic provisions of the laws and regulations dealing with workplace drug testing have two underlying principles of constitutional dimensions. The first principle is the protection of privacy, the right to be free from an "unreasonable search." The second principle is fairness, the "due process" requirement. The U.S. Constitution does not regulate the conduct of employers in the private sector. Thus, claiming that drug testing by private employers encroaches upon constitutional rights to privacy, fairness, or due process reflects more individual attitudes than an understanding of the law. Nevertheless, statutes and regulations on drug testing in the workplace generally extend the constitutional constraints imposed on government employers to private employers as well. In addition, even in the absence of such private employer legal constraints, a wise employer will be sensitive to social expectations of reasonableness and discretion.

## Application

If you are applying for a job with a business with a large number of employees, you are much more likely to be screened for substance abuse than if you are applying for a job with a medium to small business. In addition, more firms test applicants than they do employees, and firms that test applicants are likely to test all applicants rather than those applying only for certain jobs. Once you are hired by an employer who tests employees, you are more likely to be tested only under certain circumstances, such as after an accident or for reasonable suspicion. However, random or periodic (e.g., during a yearly physical) testing is not uncommon, particularly in "safety-sensitive" positions such as those in the transportation industry and those that require carrying firearms.

The overwhelming majority of firms will not hire applicants who have tested positive, and will inform the applicants as to the reason they have not been hired. In contrast, when employees test positive, a majority of firms provide the opportunity to participate in a drug abuse treatment program rather than face immediate termination.

Depending on whether you are an applicant or an employee, whether you are dealing with a private or public employer, and your location, your prospective or current employer may be subject to certain constraints if you are asked to undergo drug testing. For example, some laws or regulations may require that your employer have "probable cause," "reasonable suspicion," or "reasonable grounds" to test for the presence of drugs. Of course, this requirement can not be imposed for applicants because the prospective employer has not had the opportunity to observe the applicant. However, there may be other requirements applicable to job applicants, such as that the test be administered as part of a comprehensive physical examination.

All laws and regulations also require at least one confirmatory test before an employee may be discharged or otherwise disciplined for testing positive. This requirement may not apply for testing applicants, however.

Other requirements may include using certified laboratories, keeping test results confidential, collecting samples with due regard to the privacy of the individual, giving an opportunity to explain or contest a positive result, providing written policy on the drug testing program, and establishing employee assistance programs for the treatment and rehabilitation of employees who test positive.

All of these requirements may also be voluntarily adopted by the employer, or negotiated with a labor union and included in a collective bargaining agreement. All successful drug abuse prevention programs that include drug testing also strive to educate employees on the health and safety implications of drug abuse as well as the employer's policies on employees who abuse drugs, and offer rehabilitation opportunities for employees shown to be using drugs.

*See also* Law in the Workplace; Testing.

## Bibliography

Dogoloff, L.I., & Angarola, R.T. (1985). *Urine testing in the workplace*. Rockville, MD: The American Council for Drug Education. Tysse, G.J., &

Gust, S.W., & Walsh, J.M. (Eds.) (1989). *Drugs in the workplace: Research and evaluation data*. Rockville, MD: National Institute on Drug Abuse.

Tysse, G.J., & Dodge, G.E. (1989). *Winning the war on drugs: The role of workplace testing*. Washington, DC: National Foundation for the Study of Employment Policy.

U.S. Department of Labor. (undated). *What works: Work places without drugs*. Washington, DC.

—SAMIA NAHIR RODRIGUEZ AND ROBERT T. ANGAROLA

# TESTING: GENETIC

Genetic screening involves the testing of blood or other body fluids to identify genetic markers which predispose the individual tested to certain genetic-related medical conditions. There are several different techniques used for genetic screening and the test performed may identify either the effects of genes or the genes themselves before they have been expressed. The number of medical conditions for which genetic testing may be performed has increased greatly in just the last few years and it is expected to continue increasing.

## Relationship to Work

Employers have substantial economic interests in maintaining a healthy workforce. Although genetic screening is not used by many employers at the present, many observers think that it may be used more in the coming years in an attempt to avoid employing people who are likely to get sick in the future.

Two important points relative to genetic screening must be kept in mind. First, the predominant form of genetic testing in use today involves biochemical measures of gene expression. Second, the purpose of genetic testing is to identify individuals who are genetically predisposed to occupationally related illness, as well as those individuals with molecular genetic changes caused by workplace exposures (Office of Technology Assessment, 1983, 1990).

Biochemical genetic research remains ongoing, including attempts to determine an increased risk of cancer. Nevertheless, the next phase of genetic testing is likely to be of a different form and is likely to be performed for a different reason. Specifically, recombinant DNA technology may be used to identify individuals with a genetic predisposition to nonoccupational illness. New developments in molecular genetics resulting from the genome projects (efforts by scientists to map and sequence all 100,000 human genes) promise revolutionary changes in our ability to detect and predict genetic-based illness. If these technologies become economically feasible for screening programs, it must be assumed that they would be used. The purpose of such screening would be to exclude from the workforce those individuals who are likely to be a financial drain on employer health benefits.

With the exceptions of government programs for the aged (Medicare) and the indigent (Medicaid), health insurance funding is left to the private sector. Today, 85% to 90% of Americans covered by health insurance are covered by group health insurance and 68% are covered under employer-provided plans (Office of Technology Assessment, 1988). Although in recent years many employers have required their employees to pay a larger percentage of the premiums, employers still pay the bulk of these costs. In 1989 the average per-employee cost of health insurance for employers was over $3,100 per year and costs were increasing at the rate of 20% per year.

Faced with these enormous and growing costs, many companies have adopted non-genetic medical screening programs in an attempt to exclude from employment those individuals who are regarded as health insurance risks (Rothstein, 1989). These programs extend well beyond screening for chronic disease, obesity, hypertension, and hypercholesterolemia. Some companies test for and screen on the basis of HIV status (even though illegal), refuse to employ cigarette smokers (even if they smoke only off-work), and make hiring decisions based on the health status of an applicant's dependents (who also would be covered under employer-provided insurance).

In light of this trend, the future use of genetic screening must be regarded as more than simply a theoretical possibility. Moreover, legislation mandating employers to provide all full-time employees with at least minimum levels of insurance (adopted in Hawaii and Massachusetts and under consideration in Congress) would have the effect of encouraging even more widespread medical screening, including genetic screening.

The workplace application of genetic screening techniques raises a number of important legal issues. Since the late nineteenth century, American employment law has been based on the "at will" rule. In general, employers are free to hire and fire whomever they please for any reason or no reason at all. Employees have the right to quit their jobs at any time and to seek another job. The rule is premised on "freedom of contract" for both parties, although a growing number of critics question whether employees have the equality of bargaining power that the rule presumes. Defenders of the rule assert that it is economically efficient and promotes the unencumbered flow of capital and labor. Even assuming this is true, the price for this freedom of contract, large numbers of arbitrary and unfair hiring and firing decisions, may be too high.

Over the last three decades, several important statutory and judicial modifications of the at will rule have been made. Of particular relevance to genetic testing has been the enactment of civil rights laws prohibiting discrimination in hiring, firing, or any other terms and conditions of employment on the basis of specific proscribed criteria—race, color, religion, sex, national origin, age, or handicap. Indeed, several forms of biochemical genetic screening (e.g., sickle cell, thalassemia) that adversely affect certain racial or ethnic groups might be illegal under these laws.

Four states have passed laws specifically prohibiting discrimination in employment on the basis of one or more genetic traits. Florida and Louisiana prohibit discrimination based on sickle cell trait. North Carolina prohibits discrimination based on sickle cell or hemoglobin C trait. New Jersey prohibits discrimination based on an individual's "atypical hereditary cellular or blood trait," defined to include sickle cell trait, hemoglobin C trait, thalassemia trait, Tay-Sachs trait, or cystic fibrosis trait. The New Jersey law is particularly noteworthy because by prohibiting discrimination against the carriers of traits for diseases affecting newborns and children (Tay-Sachs, cystic fibrosis), the legislature apparently recognized that employers might discriminate against individuals who have or who are likely to have children who suffer from expensive genetic diseases.

The most likely sources of legal protection for applicants and employees against genetic-based discrimination are the federal and state laws prohibiting discrimination in employment on the basis of handicap. The federal Rehabilitation Act of 1973 applies to the federal government, contractors of the federal government, and recipients of federal financial assistance. State handicap discrimination laws, which have been enacted in every state, have less compartmentalized coverage and apply to most public and private employers, with the exception of small companies.

A number of unresolved legal questions are raised by the application of handicap discrimination laws to workplace genetic screening. First, is genetic screening a form of proscribed handicap discrimination? The federal Rehabilitation Act prohibits discrimination against otherwise qualified individuals with handicaps, defined broadly as a person who has "a physical or mental impairment which substantially limits one or more of such person's major life activities, has a record of such an impairment, or is regarded as having such an impairment." Notwithstanding this broad language, it is not clear whether the future risk of an impairment or possession of a certain genotype constitutes a "handicap."

A second unresolved issue concerns the possible defenses employers could raise. Of particular interest is the "cost" defense. Thus far, in handicap discrimination cases courts have rejected the argument that it would be financially burdensome for employers to build wheelchair ramps, widen doors, and make other accommodations to facilitate the employment of otherwise qualified individuals with handicaps. It is not clear to what extent the same thinking would or should apply to the increased health care expenses of an individual who is likely or certain to develop an expensive, genetic disease. Should consideration be given to the nature of the illness, the cost, the size and financial condition of the employer, or other similar factors?

## Application

You should be aware that the uncertainties under current law will be affected by the Americans with Disabilities Act (ADA), which will take effect in July, 1991. The ADA prohibits discrimination in employment based on "disability" (a term increasingly preferred to "handicap") by employers with 25 or more employees (15 or more in 1994). It also explicitly forbids the use of medical tests to detect disabilities in employees, unless the testing provides information about the individual's ability to perform job-related functions.

You should realize that the Americans with Disabilities Act fills some important gaps in coverage and remedies under federal law and proscribes the performing of most genetic tests by employers as well as employer use of information derived from the tests. Nonetheless, even a legal ban on genetic screening and genetic-based discrimination cannot be expected to eliminate the problem any more than other forms of civil rights legislation have eliminated entirely other forms of discrimination, such as race, sex, national origin, or age. Moreover, as long as there are strong economic incentives to engage in genetic screening and it can be performed easily and without the individual's knowledge (e.g., as where a blood sample is taken for some other purpose), then it must be assumed that genetic screening will be used by at least some employers. As you monitor these developments, you should see if labor, management, government, and health care leaders address the legal and social consequences of genetic screening before the technology has been developed.

*See also* Law in the Workplace; Testing.

## Bibliography

Nelkin, D., & Tancredi, L. (1989). *Dangerous diagnostics.* New York: Basic Books. Discusses the social implications of new biological tests involving genetics and the neurosciences in education, employment, health care, and other areas.

Office of Technology Assessment (OTA). (1983). *The role of genetic testing in the prevention of occupational disease* (p.33).

Office of Technology Assessment (OTA., (1988). *Medical testing and health insurance* (p. 3).

Office of Technology Assessment (OTA). (1990). *Genetics in the workplace.*

Rothstein, M. A. (1989). *Medical screening and the employee health cost crisis.* Washington, DC: BNA Books. A thorough discussion of how employers attempt to reduce their health insurance costs by using medical screening involving genetics, AIDS, drug abuse, and other medical criteria.

—MARK A. ROTHSTEIN

## TESTING: INTEGRITY

Integrity testing refers to paper-and-pencil tests which attempt to assess such applicant characteristics as honesty and integrity (e.g., to predict employee theft or other illegal behavior), or more general aspects of personality which might be called productivity vs. counterproductivity or employee deviance (e.g., refusing to take orders, insulting customers, picking fights with coworkers).

### Relationship to Work

Integrity tests are used to screen applicants for work in which the job holders have access to cash or merchandise, such at banks, drug stores, department stores, and grocery stores. Employee theft is a major problem for many of these employers. For example, employees may steal cash or fail to charge their friends for some of the items they purchase. Employees have been found to throw perfectly good merchandise into the dumpster and pick it up later. Counterproductive employee behaviors beyond theft are also of interest to employers. For example, some employees have been found to sell drugs at the workplace, or to hide merchandise until it goes on sale so that they can buy it at a discount.

Paper-and-pencil integrity tests have become popular in retail and financial institutions in part because the polygraph ("lie detector") is now illegal for screening applicants for most jobs. Some of the paper-and-pencil integrity tests were developed by firms that once specialized in polygraph tests.

There are at least 40 different tests which are either devoted to integrity testing or have some honesty or integrity component. These tests can be divided into two major types: "overt" tests and "personality-based" tests. The overt tests directly ask the applicant about his or her views on various illegal activities. (Do most people steal? What should be done to an employee who is caught stealing a candy bar?) The overt test usually has sections which ask about the applicant's behavior as well. (Over the past three years, what is the total dollar amount of cash you stole from your employer?)

The personality-based tests do not ask questions about theft or illegal drug use. Instead, they question the applicant about such attitudes as relations toward authority, risk taking, and social relations. There may also be one or more sections on personal history. (How well did you do in school? How did you get along with your parents?)

How well integrity tests work and how or whether integrity tests should be used by firms is currently controversial. The U.S. Office of Technology Assessment recently prepared an unflattering review of integrity tests. The Society for Industrial and Organizational Psychology, a division of the American Psychological Association, recently prepared a policy statement about integrity tests which was more complimentary. Part of the controversy hinges on conflicting values. Which is more important, to protect the employer from dishonest employees, or to protect the applicant from a false label of dishonesty?

There are serious problems in trying to evaluate integrity tests. One thing such tests try to predict is theft. Very few people are actually caught stealing, however, so the tests cannot predict who will be caught stealing with much accuracy. Because only the test publishers know how the tests are scored, psychologists cannot use and evaluate the tests without the cooperation of the publisher. The Society for Industrial and Organizational Psychology recommended that test publishers give independent psychologists access to all their data so that an unbiased evaluation of integrity tests could be made.

For some integrity tests, there is essentially no evidence to show whether the test is useful to companies. Other publishers have compiled impressive documentation that indicates the usefulness of integrity tests. Studies have shown that integrity test scores (a) predict responses to polygraph examinations, (b) predict admissions of theft by employees, and (c) predict supervisory ratings of employee performance better than chance.

## Application

Overt honesty tests are sometimes jokingly referred to as "dishonesty" tests because the people who honestly admit to theft flunk the test. The "correct" answers to a personality-based test are not obvious to you (which of these three best describes you: (a) cheerful (b) smart (c) reliable.

Pretend that the questions on the test are coming from someone you have known for a long time and feel reasonably friendly toward; you don't have to bare your very soul, but you don't have to pretend to be better than you really are. Although the "correct" responses to some integrity tests may seem very obvious, such tests also contain scales designed to catch someone who "fakes good." For example, you might be asked to agree or disagree with the statement "before voting I thoroughly investigate the qualifications of all the candidates." Anyone who agrees with many such statements will be viewed with suspicion.

You have rights as a test taker. You are allowed to ask how the decision was made about you, how you fared on the test, and what the company policy is for the use of the test. Those hiring you may be reluctant to give you this informa-

tion. If so, call the human resources department, repeat your request, and remind them of the American Psychological Association Standards on testing.

*See also* Law in the Workplace; Testing.

## Bibliography

There are no widely available nontechnical reviews of integrity tests (as of 1990).

Cronbach, L. J. (1990). *Essentials of psychological testing.* 5th ed. New York: Harper & Row. This has a good nontechnical discussion of problems in measuring personality, difficulties of self-report measures, and test takers' rights.

O'Bannon, R. M., Goldinger, L. A., & Appleby, G. S. (1989). *Honesty and integrity testing: A practical guide.* Atlanta: Applied Information Resources. This has a nontechnical review of integrity tests, but is primarily a guide to people who want to buy and use integrity tests. It is hard to find.

Sackett, P. R., Burris, L. R., & Callahan, C. (1989). Integrity testing for personnel selection: An update. *Personnel Psychology*, 42: 491–529. A technical review but you can follow the discussion.

—MICHAEL T. BRANNICK

## TIME MANAGEMENT

Time is all you have, and it's never enough. Pick anyone at random and he or she can tell you what isn't happening, what they don't have time for, what continually goes wrong. You will hear about crises, long hours, stress, and the consequences of poor time management.

Time is a paradox. While we never seem to have enough time, we have all the time there is. There simply isn't any more time to have. The problem is not a shortage of time, but how we use our time. The solution to the paradox is to remember that there is always enough time for the really important things. The problem is, we respond to the urgent things readily and ignore the more important things. Managers respond to personnel crises, but we never have time for proper training. We respond to deadline pressures with hurried last minute efforts, but we never have time for adequate planning. We respond to recurring crises, but we never have time to find out what's wrong and fix it. We always have time to do something over, but we never have time to do it right the first time.

### Wasted Time Is Lost Time

Managing time is a key ingredient to success for anyone. Peter Drucker describes time as your most important resource; he claims that if you can't manage your time, you can't manage anything else. It isn't what you do, it's what you get done that counts most. It isn't your activities that are important, it's your results. Failure to manage your time robs you of the effectiveness that you might otherwise find. It prevents you from making the unique contribution which only you can make.

Most of us waste at least two hours every day. Unfortunately, this is not always intentional time waste. If it were intentional, it would be far easier to solve. Much of this time waste is unintentional and even unconscious. We waste time because of our inappropriate time habits, our sloppy work habits, and inattention to our real objective. We don't clarify our priorities and act decisively.

People frequently ask, "What is a waste of time?" The tendency is to think that a waste of time is what someone else says is a waste of time. The truth is that only you can determine what is a waste of time because wasting time simply means doing something that is relatively less important when you could be doing something more important instead. Important is always determined in relation to your objectives. Just think what you might accomplish if you could only recover those two hours every day!

## Application

To manage and control your time requires that you continually answer the question, "What is the best way to spend my time?" To answer this question, you must know what you are trying to accomplish. You must clarify your objectives, examine your activities, and plan your time.

**Clarifying Your Objectives.** To clarify your goals, or objectives, write down what you are trying to accomplish. Without well-clarified objectives it is impossible to manage your time. Without goals, time management has no meaning. Psychologists have been telling us for years that the reason we are not more successful is because we simply do not have well-defined objectives. Many of us have dreams, hopes, or vague aspirations, but these are not objectives. Objectives are specific statements about desired results toward which you are willing to commit yourself.

Well-clarified objectives meet several criteria. They will be in writing. They will be specific. They will be measurable. They will be realistic and attainable within a given time frame. They will be compatible with each other and each objective will have a time schedule attached to it.

People often question this insistence on written objectives. They claim, "I don't have to *write* my objectives. I have them all in my head." Unfortunately, this isn't good enough. The easiest things in the world to lose sight of are your objectives. Days are hectic and frantic. Dozens of things crowd in upon your consciousness every day of your life. If your goals are not in writing and in front of you, it is very easy to lose track of what you are trying to accomplish.

There is something else important about written objectives. The act of writing an objective actually increases your commitment to work at achieving it. The act of reducing your thoughts to writing is almost magical. Write out your objectives regularly and managing your time will be much easier.

**Analyzing Your Time Use.** Once you have clarified your objectives, examine your activities. You cannot do an objective. You can only do activities. Ideally, your activities should all be consistent with your objectives. The problem, of course, is that often your activities are not consistent with your objectives.

It is easy for activities to become disconnected from objectives. We become accustomed to routines. Much of our time is spent in habitual ways. We fall into patterns of reacting to whatever happens. Yet, activities that are not connected to objectives are the ones that most often lead to wasted time.

An important step in learning to control activities requires focusing on your time habits. Most of us think we know how we spend our time, but we really don't. Countless studies have shown that most of us cannot remember very accurately what we did only yesterday. It is important to know how you spend your time. You can't do better unless you know how you're using your time now. The way you spend your time is largely habitual. Learning to control your time, or use your time better will probably mean changing some of your time habits. You can't change your time habits until you know what those habits are.

For the next week or two keep track of all your time and what you're doing with it. Be very honest with yourself. Record what you are doing, continually, as you are doing it, so you don't forget later. How much of your time is spent in each activity? How much does each activity contribute to the objectives you are trying to accomplish? How many things are you doing that simply don't have to be done? How many things do you do that could be done just as easily by someone else?

Look at each activity and question it closely. What would happen if it weren't done at all? What things could be eliminated? What could be modified? What could be combined with other things? Could you spend less time at some things and still get acceptable results? What things should have more time? How is your time really being wasted each day?

The results of your time log will probably amaze you. You may discover that you are quite different than you thought you were, and that you are using your time in different ways than you imagined.

After you clarify your objectives, and after you have determined exactly where and how your time is being wasted, you must make appropriate changes. This requires that you plan and schedule your time.

**Planning for Better Results.** Most of us are haphazard planners. That doesn't mean that we never plan anything; it only means that most of us don't plan very much unless we are forced to do so. We settle for reacting to whatever happens. Consequently, we often fail to achieve the desired results. Things won't take care of themselves. Things happen because you make them happen. Planned things happen best.

Everyone admits that planning is important. But very few of us are actually spending as much time planning as we should. Finding time to plan involves a very real paradox. On the one hand you don't have enough time to plan; yet, on the other hand, you won't have more time available until you begin to plan better.

In addition to all the other things that might be said, planning is a habit. People who plan consistently develop a habit of planning. Finding time is not the issue. Planning simply becomes a part of the regular routine. People who have not developed this kind of habit will continue to have difficulty finding time to plan.

The Douglass Time Planning System is a simple, but powerful, approach to managing time. It requires minimal time and effort on your part—about 15 minutes each day and an additional 30 minutes once a week. If you will commit yourself to following the system for three to six weeks, it will become a regular habit for you. It will also enable you to get better results than ever before.

Here's how it works. First, write out your objectives for next week on a weekly plan sheet as shown in Figure 1. What do you plan to have accomplished by the end of the week? What results do you expect? Indicate the relative priority of each objective. Be sure to write only significant objectives. Don't be too concerned about routine things. They seem to happen anyway. The routine can fill up so much of your time that the really important things don't happen as often as they should.

Once you've clarified your objectives, complete your weekly plan by asking:

1. What activities must take place if I am going to achieve my objectives?
2. What is the relative priority of each activity?
3. How much of my time will be required for each activity?
4. What day will I do or start each activity?

You cannot do an objective; you do activities. If they're the right ones, you should achieve the objective. In answering the first two questions, you are setting out the action steps in your weekly plan. More importantly, you're focusing your weekly plan around significant events and thinking about what things are most critical.

**Figure 1. Weekly Plan**

**weekly plan** January 21

OBJECTIVES (what I hope to have accomplished by the end of the week)

1. Complete preparation for Personnel Committee meeting 1/30.
2. Finish first draft of year-end Performance Report.
3. Review final plans and cost estimates for West Building.

| ACTIVITIES REQUIRED TO ACCOMPLISH OBJECTIVES | Priority | Time Needed | Which Day |
|---|---|---|---|
| 1. Meet with Personnel Director to plan agenda | 1 | 1 hr. | Mon |
| 2. Review format of YE report with PR staff | 3 | 1 " | Mon |
| 3. Briefing with Acctg. on data display | 2 | 1 " | Mon |
| 4. Complete reviews of all Dept YE reports | 1 | 6 " | Mon |
| 5. Review report and pension plan recommendations | 1 | 2 " | Tue |
| with actuaries for presentation to Per. Comm | | | |
| 6. Review presentation and approve final PC agenda | 3 | 1 " | Wed |
| 7. Brief Chm. Pers. Comm. and Pers. Director | 2 | 2 " | Fri |
| 8. Dictate first draft of YE report | 2 | 2 " | Tue |
| 9. Edit first draft of YE report | 3 | 1 " | Wed |
| 10. Approve draft of YE report for printer | 2 | 1 " | Fri |
| 11. Meeting on remodeling with Controller | 3 | 2 " | Wed |
| 12. Meeting with architect, Controller, Bldg. Comm. | 1 | 8 (all day) | Thu |
| 13. Meeting at bank with Pension Trust officer | 2 | 2 hr. | Tue |
| 14. Walk through and visit with employees | 1 | 2 " | Tue |
| of units to be remodeled | | | |
| 15. Misc. time for problem areas encountered | 1 | 3 " | Wed |
| on walk through | | | |
| | | 35 | |





Once your weekly plan is done, you're ready to translate it into your daily plan, like the one shown in Figure 2. Begin your daily plan by transferring appropriate activities from your weekly plan. Add to that the other routine administrative tasks you must do. Modify your list when necessary to allow for the unexpected things that happen as the week progresses. Only prepare your day list one day at a time. And whatever you do, when you make up your daily list be sure to list activities, priorities, and time estimates!

The weekly plan should be prepared on Friday for the following week. This will take about 30 minutes. The daily plan should be prepared at the end of the day for the next day. This will take about 15 minutes. You should expect to recover at least two or three times as much time each week for important things as you spend planning your time.

To manage your time is to accept responsibility for your own behavior. It means realizing that you can influence things that happen in your life. It means that you can no longer afford the luxury of blaming other people or other things when something goes wrong.

Resolve today to begin developing better time habits. Make the resolution every day and keep it, until you develop a habit of managing time, until you become a different person, in a different world. You will become master of your likes and dislikes, as well as master of your time. You will have formed the habit of doing things that

**Figure 2. Daily Plan**

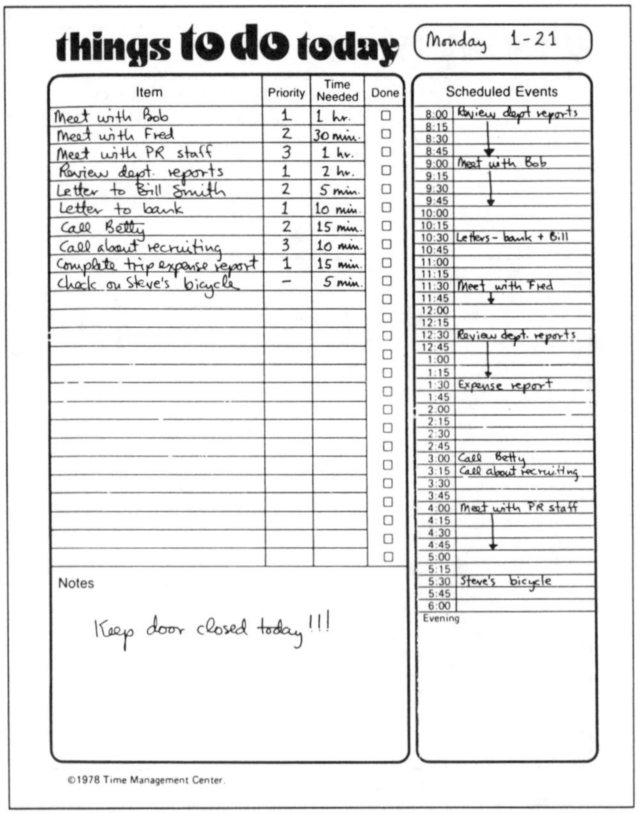

Copyright by Merrill Douglass. Reprinted by permission.

failures don't like to do. You will no longer be bothered with the timewasters that plague most people. And, you will begin achieving the goals that are most important to you. In other words, you will be successful!

*See also* Procrastination: Overcoming; Self-Managed Change; Stress.

## Bibliography

Bliss, E. C. (1983). *Doing it now.* New York: Scribner's. Deals with procrastination as the number one reason for failing to achieve a rich, fulfilling life. Discusses the reasons people procrastinate and shows how it can be conquered.

Douglass, D. N. (1983). *Choice and compromise: A woman's guide to balancing family and career.* New York: AMACOM. Helps women make the difficult choices involved in juggling both a career and a family, and gives practical suggestions for priority setting and focusing on the most important things in order to get it all in. Available from Time Management Center, 1401 Johnson Ferry Rd., Marietta, GA 30062.

Douglass, M. E., & Douglass, D. N. (1980). *Manage your time, manage your work, manage yourself.* New York: AMACOM. This informative and easy-to-read book expresses successful time management techniques that seem to work. Describes characteristics and assumptions about time. The authors emphasize that time management is really self-management.

Mackenzie, R.A. (1972). *The time trap.* New York: AMACOM. Sees time as a unique resource. Discusses what successful time managers know that the rest of us don't. Discusses wastebasketry, closing the open door, and ending telephone tyranny.

Scott, D. (1984). *How to put more time in your life.* New York: New American Library. Emphasis on both information and motivation in a five-step program.

—MERRILL DOUGLASS AND DONNA DOUGLASS

## TRAIT-FACTOR APPROACH TO CAREER CHOICE

The trait-factor approach to choosing a career is based on the idea that a wise career choice is one in which the occupation suits the person and the person suits the occupation. To find such a suitable occupation, the trait-factor approach relies on a technology founded on the following demonstrable facts:

1. People differ with respect to psychological traits, defined as long-lasting dispositions of people to behave in particular ways. These dispositions can be identified through a procedure called factor analysis, hence the "factor" in "trait-factor."
2. Occupations differ with respect to the traits of those people in the occupation who are successful, that is, both satisfactory (successful as viewed from the outside) and satisfied (successful as viewed from the inside).

If both people and occupations can be described in the same way (in terms of psychological traits), one should be able to judge how well or how poorly a given person matches up with a given occupation and how suitable the occupation is for the person.

What traits should be used to describe people and occupations? Two kinds of traits are most useful:

1. *Abilities*: the traits that tell what a person can do (see **Abilities**).
2. *Preferences*: the traits that tell what activities a person likes or dislikes (interests) or what conditions are important or not important to the person (values) (see **Interests; Work Values**).

Occupations can be described in terms of the patterns of abilities (especially the high abilities) that characterize satisfactory workers in the occupation, and in terms of the patterns of preferences (interests, values) that characterize satisfied workers in the occupation. By comparing a person's pattern of abilities with an occupation's pattern of abilities, we can forecast how likely that person will be a satisfactory worker in that occupation. Likewise, by comparing a person's pattern of preferences with an occupation's pattern of preferences, we can forecast how likely it is that person will be satisfied in that occupation. In this manner, we can identify the occupations for which the person is likely to be both satisfactory and satisfied. The person can then choose a career from this list of occupations, taking into account other important considerations, such as family responsibilities, financial circumstances, length and cost of training required, and availability of jobs. Figure 1 depicts the trait-factor approach to choosing a career.

## Relationship to Work

Abilities are the traits that are used to tell if a person has the aptitude for an occupation ("aptitude" being how likely it is that a person can learn the skills required to perform the occupation's tasks, or how easily those skills can be acquired). Preferences (interests, values) can tell how motivated the person will be to perform the occupation's tasks. Ability times motivation, it is said, equals performance. But only if the environment is "right."

The "right" person for the "right" job, then, is the goal of the trait-factor approach. It strives for the best use of a person's capabilities, thus engendering self-confidence and building up self-esteem. At the same time, it seeks the most satisfying arrangement in work, thereby contributing greatly to the person's "pursuit of happiness."

## Application

With the aid of a professional trained in vocational assessment, you could:

1. Learn more about your abilities by taking a multiple-ability test battery, such as the General Aptitude Test Battery. Before looking at your scores, you could try to guess how you would score to see how well you know your own abilities.
2. Find out the occupations for which you meet the minimum ability requirements. Then look them up in the *Occupational Outlook Handbook* to get a better idea of the tasks the occupation requires, how much training is involved, and what the employment outlook is.
3. Find out what your vocational interests and vocational values are by taking such instruments as the Strong Interest Inventory and the Minnesota Importance Questionnaire. Such instruments will identify the occupations whose members have preferences (interests or values) like your own, the ones for which you have the best chance of being satisfied.

**Figure 1. Trait-Factor Approach to Choosing a Career**

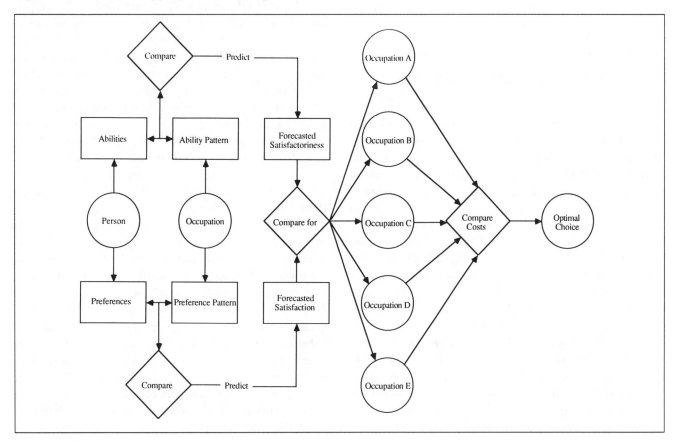

4. Narrow down your list to the occupations for which you have *both* the appropriate abilities and the appropriate preferences. These are the ones for which you have the best chance of being *both* satisfactory and satisfied.

*See also* Abilities; Career Development: Donald Super's Theory; Choosing an Occupation; Interests; Occupational Groups; Skills; Vocational Choice: John Holland's Theory; Work Values.

## Bibliography

Dawis, R.V., & Lofquist, L.H. (1984). *A psychological theory of work adjustment*. Minneapolis: University of Minnesota Press. The trait-factor approach presented in the context of individual differences and person-environment interaction.

Holland, J.L. (1985). *Making vocational choices*. 2nd ed. Englewood Cliffs, NJ: Prentice-Hall. The best-known example of the trait-factor approach to career choice.

Williamson, E.G. (1939). *How to counsel students*. New York: McGraw-Hill. The original "classic" that introduced the trait-factor approach to counseling.

Williamson, E.G., & Biggs, D.A. (1979). Trait-and-factor theory and individual differences. In H.M. Burks, Jr. & B. Stefflre (Eds.), *Theories of counseling*. 3rd ed. New York: McGraw-Hill. Williamson's (with Biggs' help) last statement of his trait-factor approach to counseling, particularly vocational counseling.

—RENE V. DAWIS

## TYPE A BEHAVIOR PATTERN

TABP was first described in the 1950s by cardiologists Meyer Friedman and Ray Rosenman based on their observations of hundreds of coronary heart disease (CHD) patients. The TABP consists of (a) a generalized sense of time urgency and impatience, (b) easily aroused anger and hostility, and (c) extreme striving for achievement and excessive competitiveness. In a number of research studies, a relationship between the TABP and CHD has been demonstrated, especially for middle-aged men (Matthews, 1988). It is not yet clear, however, if all of the components of the TABP carry risk for CHD; some researchers believe that the anger and hostility component is primarily responsible for the increased risk for CHD.

The TABP is assessed most reliably by a structured interview which is either audiotaped or videotaped. While the content of a person's answers may suggest the presence of the TABP, *how* a person answers the questions is even more important. Speech stylistics (e.g., loud volume, rapid speech, explosive emphasis on words), posture and behav-

ior (e.g., knee jiggling, hand gestures, tense facial features), and interaction with the interviewer (e.g., interrupting or talking at the same time as the interviewer, trying to control the interview) provide evidence of the TABP.

### Relationship to Work

The workplace is the main setting in which Type A men and women struggle to prove themselves through their visible achievements. The demands, values, and relationships in the workplace create an environment that strongly elicits and perhaps encourages the TABP. Specific aspects of the workplace can reinforce the attitudes and beliefs that underlie the TABP as well as threaten the precarious self-esteem that characterizes Type A individuals.

An organization that emphasizes how much work can be accomplished and how quickly may encourage the pervasive time urgency and impatience of the TABP. Such an environment could reinforce the typical Type A belief that personal worth depends exclusively on the *quantity* of tasks accomplished. Consequently, Type A individuals struggle to complete more work in less time. Typically, Type A men and women will: (a) set and try to meet extremely high work performance standards (trying to ensure positive self-evaluation), (b) commit to an excessive number of projects or tasks (trying to convey an unquestionable commitment to work to supervisors and peers), (c) take on an ever-increasing number of responsibilities or tasks (in pursuit of advancement), (d) underestimate the length of time a task will actually take (thereby increasing time pressure), (e) have difficulty setting limits and "saying no" even when feeling exhausted or overwhelmed, (f) engage in polyphasic behavior or performing a number of tasks *simultaneously* (usually compromising the quality of performance) (g) accelerate the pace of tasks, (h) set unrealistic deadlines, and (i) forego opportunities for rest and relaxation (e.g., lunch, coffee breaks, personal conversations with coworkers, and vacations) and instead work in the evenings or weekends and/or take work home.

The work environment that encourages competition and social comparison can promote the excessive competitiveness and hostility that characterize the TABP in at least three ways. First, anger and hostility may be activated by time pressure because Type A's become frustrated when they are slowed down by other people or events causing delays in their work. Other people may become viewed as "obstacles to be eliminated." Second, since Type A's are usually very sensitive to actual or perceived criticism (due to their precarious sense of self-esteem), feedback from supervisors or peers will often be viewed as criticism and be met with a hostile counterattack. Finally, organizations that value individual performance more than cooperative efforts will encourage competition, reinforce the Type A belief that "your win is my loss," and promote suspiciousness, distrust of other people's motivations, and cynicism.

## Application

Clinicians who work with individuals who wish to modify their Type A behavior see a continuum of the TABP from very extreme to a veritable absence of Type A characteristics (sometimes called Type B behavior). Goals of an intervention to reduce Type A behavior would typically include:

1. *Increase Awareness of the TABP.* Observation of the characteristics in others and in yourself is a necessary first step in changing the behavior pattern. You can record the behaviors that you see in family members, friends, and coworkers and also keep track of how often you display specific behaviors (e.g., talking fast, walking quickly, interrupting, getting impatient and angry). The development of a "self monitor," the internal voice of a "friendly coach," can help remind you when you are behaving in a time urgent, impatient, or hostile manner.

2. *Change Specific Behaviors.* You may want to select specific behaviors that are part of the TABP and target them for change. Speech characteristics (e.g., loud, rapid, explosive speech) can be changed by having reminders at home and at work to speak more softly and slowly. Psychomotor behaviors (e.g., walking fast, eating quickly, rapid hand gestures) can be altered by practicing slower movements (see Friedman & Ulmer, 1984 for a description of behavioral drills) and by learning an effective relaxation procedure (see **Relaxation: Progressive Muscle; Self-Managed Change**). Time urgency can be impacted by learning to set priorities, by reducing competing demands, and by delegating work to others (see **Time Management**).

   Reducing anger and hostility is a complex task. One useful way for thinking about the experience of becoming angry is the metaphor of becoming "hooked." Each day you encounter unexpected events and difficult situations that you might respond to with anger or hostility. You are like a fish swimming along in a stream and a hook drops into the water with attractive "bait." You make the decision to bite at and swallow the hook (that is, to get angry or irritated) or to swim past the hook. Throughout the day you may encounter numerous hooks at home, at work, and in the community (e.g., driving on the freeway). You can observe how many hooks you avoid, how many you swallow but quickly spit out, and how many still seem to remain in your mouth at the end of the day (see **Anger**).

3. *Change Basic Beliefs that Underlie the TABP.* A common belief is that "successful people are Type A's." An interesting exercise is to list your greatest successes in life thus far. Then ask yourself: "Is my sense of time urgency responsible for these successes? Are my successes due to my anger and hostility?" Most likely, the answer to these questions is a resounding "NO." You do not have to be Type A to be hard-working or successful. In fact, many people realize that they are successful *in spite* of their Type A behavior, since the TABP can create significant problems in their social relationships both at home and at work.

   There are a number of popular expressions for the beliefs and attitudes that are typical of Type A people: "It's quantity, not quality, that counts"; "Every man for himself"; "It's a dog-eat-dog world"; "Your win is my loss"; and "There is no such thing as a good loser." Each belief about the value of excessive competition, the importance of time urgency, and the appropriateness of anger and hostility can be challenged through a process of self-examination. In addition, two basic cognitive skills are useful as you try to change typical Type A beliefs: changing self-talk and reappraising situations (see **Rational Thinking; Self-Talk**).

4. *Increase Self-Esteem.* Changing the basis of your self-esteem—from accomplishments that others observe and acknowledge to an inner, subjective evaluation in which *you* view yourself as a good person, not just the sum of your achievements—may be the most complex task. You can start this process by: (a) reflecting on your past accomplishments, (b) focusing on enjoying the process of an activity instead of valuing only the outcome or end-product, (c) acknowledging your efforts as well as your observable accomplishments, (d) engaging in activities that you enjoy and for which only you know how well you have done, (e) setting realistic goals for what you will be able to accomplish at work (see **Time Management**), (f) making positive statements to yourself about yourself daily, (g) communicating and interacting with others in positive, warm, and caring ways, (h) helping others, and (i) asking for and accepting help from others.

*See also* Anger; Career Burnout; Rational Thinking; Relaxation: Progressive Muscle; Self-Esteem; Self-Managed Change; Self-Talk; Stress; Time Management.

## Bibliography

Friedman, M., & Rosenman, R. H. (1974). *Type A behavior and your heart*. New York: Alfred A. Knopf. The original description of the Type A behavior pattern.

Friedman, M., & Ulmer, D. K. (1984). *Treating Type A behavior and your heart*. New York: Alfred A. Knopf. A description of the most comprehensive treatment program that has been used to help people modify their Type A behavior.

Houston, B. K., & Snyder, C. R. (Eds.) (1988). *Type A behavior pattern: Research, theory, and intervention*. New York: Wiley. An edited book with chapters that thoroughly review current research on the TABP, describe the pattern in women and children, and discuss implications for intervention.

Matthews, K.A. (1988). Coronary heart disease and Type A behaviors: Update on an alternative to Booth-Kewley and Friedman (1987) quantitative review. *Psychological Bulletin*, 104: 373–80.

Price, V.A. (1982). *Type A behavior pattern: A model for research and practice*. New York: Academic.

—JEAN R. EAGLESTON AND PAUL E. BRACKE

# U

## UNDEREMPLOYMENT

People working at jobs which do not fully utilize their whole range of skills and training are underemployed. Perhaps most jobs include some elements of underemployment. When referring to underemployment, most social scientists are referring to those situations in which the difference between the level of skills and training is considerable.

### Relationship to Work

Underemployment is growing according to Rumberger (1984). Workers are becoming more educated, and for many the level of educational attainment exceeds that of many jobs in the economy. One of the reasons for this development is the restructuring of the labor market (Wegmann, Chapman, & Johnson, 1989). The new jobs being created either demand high levels of education (professional, managerial) or fall within a low-level, low-paying sphere (service, clerical). Many people are unable to access the higher level jobs, but find themselves over-qualified for the jobs at the lower levels. If they accept a lower level job, they face underemployment.

The reactions to underemployment are influenced by the perspective one holds on the job. If a person views the lower level position as a stepping-stone to getting something better, the job will be evaluated in a more positive light and job satisfaction will not be a problem. If, however, the job is viewed as a "dead end" and there are few other options, job satisfaction will generally decrease rapidly (Richards, 1984).

The emotional reactions associated with underemployment for college educated males has been studied by Borgen, Amundson, & Harder (1988). In this research, college graduates who were underemployed described their experiences following college graduation. Five phases of development were outlined and are described below:

1. *Disappointment After Graduation*. In this first phase the graduate became disillusioned with the available job prospects. They were hopeful of accessing a good entry level position, but were unsuccessful in their attempts.
2. *Obtaining Employment*. Following the initial frustration, they became desperate and often took the first job that came along, regardless of educational level. Upon obtaining employment, there was some relief from the stress of job search and the fear of prolonged unemployment.
3. *Initial Underemployment Experience*. The satisfaction with finding employment was generally short lived (two to three months) and was followed by feelings of frustration, disillusionment, and anger. Relationships with coworkers, family, and friends were negatively affected. There was also a tendency to withdraw and blame others.
4. *Despair and Resignation*. A prolonged period of underemployment led to an eroding sense of confidence, despair about the future, and a sense of hopelessness.
5. *New Determination to Create Change*. After a period of decline, many people begin a process of renewal.

The phases of underemployment that have been described refer specifically to a group of college educated males. There will undoubtedly be some overlaps with the experiences of females and various other cultural groups. Further research, however, will need to be done to determine the exact nature of the experience for other groups.

### Application

If you are underemployed in your present job, you may be experiencing a sense of job dissatisfaction. The obvious way out is to seek a more fulfilling job, but this is often easier said than done. Your training may need to be updated and you may need to accept a lower wage in order to make the job change. Career counseling may be able to help you identify various career pathways. Your transition will also be smoother if you maintain a positive attitude and obtain support from family and friends.

For a variety of reasons, you may decide to stay with your present position. Under these circumstances, you might want to consider ways of deriving greater fulfillment while working, e.g., getting involved in special projects. You may also want to find additional satisfaction through involvement in extra-curricular and volunteer activities. Many people regard their work simply as a means of getting the necessary money to live, and that real meaning and fulfillment comes from family, friends, and involvement in other activities

*See also* Career Development System within Organization; Job Satisfaction; Job Search; Promotion/Raise.

## Bibliography

Borgen, W.A., Amundson, N.E. & Harder, H.G. (1988). The experience of underemployment. *Journal of Employment Counseling*, 25: 149–59. This research is based on an in-depth study of the experiences of underemployment of 15 college educated men. Their ages ranged from 25 to 48 years and they all had graduated from college within the last 10 years.

Richards, E. (1984). Undergraduate preparation and early career outcomes: A study of recent college graduates. *Journal of Vocational Behavior*. 24: 279–304.

Rumberger, R.W. (1984). The growing inbalance between education and work. *Phi Delta Kappan*, 65: 342–46.

Wegmann, R., Chapman, R., & Johnson, M. (1989). *Work in the new economy*. Alexandria, VA: American Association of Counseling and Development. This book is very readable and it provides a comprehensive overview of the changing labor market.

—NORMAN E. AMUNDSON AND WILLIAM A. BORGEN

# UNEMPLOYMENT

At its most basic level, unemployment is when a person wants to work, but is unable to find a paid job. In determining whether a person is unemployed, the desire to work is a key variable. For statistical purposes, the desire to work generally depends on whether a person is engaged in active job search. If a person has given up, he or she is no longer engaged in active job search and, therefore, would not be counted as unemployed. In view of this, unemployment figures do not provide a complete picture of the numbers of people without work.

## Relationship to Work

The main job for people who are unemployed is looking for work. This can be incredibly difficult because of the uncertainty and emotionally charged nature of the task. Some of the emotional reactions associated with looking for work vary according to the situation in which a person may find him or herself. Some of the factors which will influence the emotional reactions to unemployment are:

1. *Attachment to Previous Job.* People who have a high level of attachment to their previous job will experience greater loss when they have to look for other work.
2. *Social Status.* When people experience a high level of status in their work, the loss of the job will often lead to additional strain.
3. *Financial Situation.* People without some form of financial security will experience increased stress.
4. *Social Support System.* The lack of support from family and friends will make it more difficult to cope with the isolation associated with unemployment.
5. *Future Expectations.* When people have to lower their expectations about their job future they face increased frustration.
6. *Cultural and Individual Personality Variables.* Factors such as internal or external locus of control are heavily influenced by cultural and individual differences and play an important role in determining reactions to unemployment (Borgen & Amundson, 1984).

In general, people have to cope with loss as they consider the job they are leaving behind, and additional stress as they engage in active job search. The interplay of loss and stress often leads to an emotional roller coaster which reduces self-confidence and interferes with interpersonal relationships during the period of job search (Borgen & Amundson, 1987).

## Application

Coping with unemployment is something which requires you to attend to your basic human needs and work toward an increased sense of self-empowerment. It is natural when you are unemployed to feel the "weight of the world" on your shoulders and lose sight of your accomplishments. This acts like a self-fulfilling prophecy. If you don't believe in yourself, you will likely not be able to maintain the necessary positive attitude when contacting employers.

One way to break through the negative feelings and thoughts that might be dragging you down is to get involved in some type of job search support or career reassessment group. Research on the effectiveness of groups indicates that groups can help you learn job search skills, develop new friends, and increase your level of self-esteem (Amundson & Borgen, 1988; Caplan, Vinoku, Price, and Van Ryn, 1989). By contacting and working with others you have the opportunity to share information, compare experiences, and support one another.

Other coping activities which might prove useful include:

1. Staying involved with your family and friends.
2. Setting goals that you can meet each day.
3. Giving yourself positive messages.
4. Considering other career options, including retraining and part-time work.
5. Developing a systematic approach to job search.
6. Becoming involved with extra-curricular activities.
7. Developing an exercise program for yourself.
8. Learning how to get the most from your contacts with agencies.
9. Sticking to a regular routine.
10. Maintaining your spiritual strength (Amundson & Borgen, 1987)

*See also* Fired/Laid Off; Job Clubs; Job Search; Managing Transitions; Temporary Employment.

## Bibliography

Amundson, N.E., & Borgen, W.A. (1987). *At the controls: Charting your course through unemployment*. Toronto: Nelson Canada.

Amundson, N.E., & Borgen, W.A. (1988). Factors that help and hinder in group employment counseling. *Journal of Employment Counseling*, 25: 104–14.

Borgen, W.A., & Amundson, N.E. (1984). *The experience of unemployment*. Toronto: Nelson Canada. This book outlines the experience of unemployment as described by people from a variety of educational, cultural, and work backgrounds. Six patterns of experience are described.

Borgen, W. A., & Amundson, N.E. (1987). The dynamics of unemployment. *Journal of Counseling and Development*, 66: 180–84.

Caplan, R.D., Vinoku, A.D., Price, R.H., & Van Ryn, M. (1989). Job seeking, reemployment, and mental health: A randomized field experiment in coping with job loss. *Journal of Applied Psychology*, 74: 759–69.

—NORMAN E. AMUNDSON AND WILLIAM A. BORGEN

# VIDEO DISPLAY TERMINALS

Video display terminals (VDTs) are the television-type screens that show the information stored in computers. Attached to each screen is a typewriter-like keyboard which is used to enter information into the computer's data bank.

This seemingly innocuous equipment can have profound adverse health effects when used improperly. Vision problems, including blurriness, fatigue, itching, and focussing difficulties can result from inappropriate lighting or too much glare on the screen. Disabling wrist injuries, often called repetitive stress injuries (RSIs), can occur when operators spend a lot of time typing on the keyboards. Poorly designed work stations with keyboards placed at the wrong height increase the chance of injury. General musculoskeletal fatigue and pain and extremely high levels of stress and stress-related illnesses are also common among certain groups of VDT users. Perhaps most frightening is a growing body of evidence which suggests that the low level of radiation emitted from VDTs may contribute to increased risk of miscarriage among VDT users or birth defects among their offspring.

## Relationship to Worker Health and Safety

There are currently over 15 million workers using VDTs on the job. The number of injuries reported by VDT workers has grown steadily over the past 10 years. These injuries are preventable if proper work stations are designed and if proper work rules are enforced.

## Application

1. *Visual Problems*. Inability to focus, fatigue, itching, burning, dryness, and blurriness are among the symptoms experienced by many VDT users. These problems frequently occur because the same lighting is used for VDT work stations that was used for traditional offices.

Because the images on a VDT are created by a source of light, the lighting requirements for the office are different. First, the general level of lighting in the room should be lower, to create better contrast. Second, glare is a significant factor in VDT-related eyestrain. Standard glare reduction measures include the use of anti-glare screens fitted over the front of the terminals, blinds placed over windows to reduce sunlight shining directly onto the screens, and proper placement of VDTs to avoid glare "hot spots."

You should get an annual eye exam by a provider familiar with VDT-related ailments. Uncorrected vision problems can add to discomfort in jobs with high visual demands. Also, some VDT users need special glasses to correct vision for the distance appropriate for VDT use.

2. *Musculoskeletal Problems/Repetitive Stress Injuries*. Sitting in one position for eight hours and repeating the same small hand movements can damage your body. The injuries can be relatively minor: back and neck pain, headaches, fatigue. Other injuries sustained from VDT use, however, can be disabling. Carpal tunnel syndrome and tenosynovitis are two of several repetitive stress injuries that are associated with VDT work. These ailments cause numbness, tingling, and often severe pain in the hands and wrists. Caught early, RSIs can be treated with physical therapy. Severe cases may require surgery. Sometimes, particularly where the worker returns to the same environment that caused the injury, multiple surgeries are required.

Many of these injuries can be prevented by the use of proper VDT furniture. Chairs should be easily adjustable for seat height, backrest height, and back tension. Tables should be bi-level, with each part separately and easily adjustable. Keyboard height should enable you to keep your wrists flat. Monitors should be adjusted to a height that allows you to look straight at the screen without straining your neck.

3. *Radiation/Reproductive Hazards*. There have been several dozen "clusters" of miscarriages and birth defects found among groups of VDT users and their offspring.

While there is still no conclusive proof that these clusters are caused by VDT use, there are several theories concerning this alarming potential hazard.

Stress, both physical and psychosocial, may play a key role in these fetal injuries. It is widely recognized that excessive stress is harmful to a fetus. Certain VDT jobs have proven to have some of the highest work-related stress levels recorded.

The second theory concerning possible adverse reproductive outcomes is that the radiation emitted from VDTs is at fault. VDTs emit a low energy form of radiation called electro-magnetic fields. Again, there are no conclusive studies outlining the risks associated with EMF exposure. However, recent research indicates that it is more harmful than was once assumed.

At this time there is no shielding available to block EMF. It is possible to prevent exposure, however, by putting distance between yourself and the source of the radiation. Much of the energy dissipates at a distance of 3 to 4 feet. In the case of VDTs, the source of the radiation is at the back or sides of the monitor, so it is important to keep a safe distance from neighboring VDTs.

4. *Stress.* A less quantifiable but equally serious hazard posed by VDTs is stress. In study after study, stress has been shown to weaken the immune system, contribute to cardio-vascular disease, and generally make life less pleasant.

VDT-related injuries are preventable. Any job designed to keep you on a VDT for your entire workday will almost certainly cause injury. The best furniture and lighting available will not succeed in preventing damage if you use your VDT for long hours.

*See also* COSH Groups; Repetitive Motion Illnesses; Work Hazards: Ergonomic; Posture and Body Mechanics; Work Hazards: Physical.

## Bibliography

DeMatteo, Bob. (1986). *Terminal shock: The health hazards of video display terminals.* Toronto: NC Press Limited. A readable explanation of the radiation hazards of VDT use.

Frank, Stanley. (1988). *How to prevent office chair backache . . . and sitting fatigue.* New York: Frank Eastern Co. A complete guide to selecting a chair appropriate for VDT use.

National Lighting Bureau. (1987). *Solving the puzzle of VDT viewing problems.* New York: National Lighting Bureau. A complete, easy-to-understand guide on designing a lighting system for use with VDTs.

Pinsky, Mark. (1987). *The VDT book: A computer user's guide to health and safety.* New York: New York Committee for Occupational Safety and Health. A user-friendly guide to identifying VDT-related health problems. The book also contains collective bargaining language, international guidelines, and U.S. government recommendations for safe VDT use.

—Diane Stein

# VOCATIONAL CHOICE: JOHN HOLLAND'S THEORY

Holland's theory of vocation choice explains how personal and work environment characteristics influence career choices and achievements. People are shaped by their parents and other cultural forces, learning to prefer some activities over others. These interests represent a person's basic personality. When choosing an occupation, people search for a work environment that allows them to exercise their skills, and interests, and to express their personal attitudes and values. As people with like personalities and developmental histories band together, they create an interpersonal environment conducive to their own kind. This environment takes on the qualities of the people working within it.

Both people and work environments are described by Holland according to their resemblance to six types: Realistic, Investigative, Artistic, Social, Enterprising, and Conventional. Each of these is described in Table 1.

People and environments are rarely one type; most are a combination of types. A person's resemblance to the types is commonly expressed by a three-letter code, such as SAE or RIC. These sample codes stand for Social-Artistic-Enterprising and Realistic-Investigative-Conventional. The first type listed is most characteristic of the person, followed by the other two types. These codes provide a brief and efficient way to profile an individual's personality.

Occupational interest inventories have been constructed to give such codes. Holland has developed the *Vocational Preference Inventory* and *The Self-Directed Search* for these purposes. Other interest inventories also generate Holland Codes, including the popular *Strong Interest Inventory*. There is also a *Dictionary of Holland Codes* (see the bibliography) that assigns a three-letter code to over 12,000 occupations.

In Holland's theory an equal-sided hexagon is a model for representing the relationship among the types. As Figure 1 shows, each type is placed at a point where the lines in the hexagon intersect. Measuring the relative distance between these points provides a way for determining which types are most like and different from one another. For example, Realistic and Conventional types are more alike than are Conventional and Artistic types. Measure the line between each of these points on the hexagon to see this. The longer the line, the less similar are the types.

Other important concepts in John Holland's theory include:

1. *Consistency.* The relatedness of the types in a code used to describe a person or an environment. Types close to one another along the hexagon are consis-

**Table 1. Holland Types**

| TYPE | PERSONALITY | ENVIRONMENT |
|---|---|---|
| Realistic | Practical, thrifty, frank, hard-headed, uninvolved. | Use mechanical ability; keep things simple. |
| Investigative | Analytical, precise, intellectual, reserved cautious, introspective. | Use scientific skills; be abstract. |
| Artistic | Emotional, expressive, open, original, sensitive. | Expressive of emotions and imagination. |
| Social | Friendly, helpful, warm, empathic, tactful. | Humanitarian, social, and/or religious. |
| Enterprising | Ambitious, extroverted, flirtatious, self-confident. | Use of money, leadership, and power. |
| Conventional | Careful, conforming, orderly, obedient. | Recording and filing data. |

Adapted from John L. Holland, *Making Vocational Choices,* by permission of Prentice-Hall, Inc. Copyright © 1985, 1973.

**Figure 1. A Hexagonal Model for Defining the Psychological Resemblances Among Types and Environments and Their Interactions**

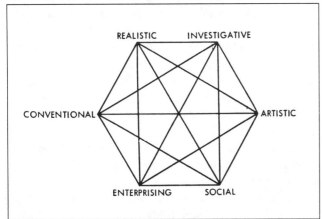

Adapted from John L. Holland, *Making Vocational Choices,* by permission of Prentice-Hall, Inc. Copyright © 1985, 1973.

tent (e.g., IAS); types separated from one another are inconsistent (e.g., RAE).

2. *Differentiation.* The degree of resemblance shown to one or to many types. Undifferentiation is shown by an average (neither high nor low) resemblance to all six types. Differentiation would be shown by a very strong resemblance to only one or two types with very low resemblance to the other types.

3. *Congruence.* The match according to Holland type codes between any of the following: personality, occupation, occupational choice, occupational daydream. If three-letter codes match perfectly, this is extremely high congruence. Congruence of a lesser degree would be a match between only the first letters in two three-letter codes. For example, a person with a code of CRS would have high congru-

ence with the occupation of accountant, because that occupation is also coded CRS. This individual would have a much lower congruence with the occupation of Travel Agent, because that occupation has a code of ECS.

The theory has generated over 500 research studies with its predictions more often than not supported. The main concepts have considerable empirical justification (see Holland, 1985a). However, the secondary concepts (consistency, differentiation, and congruence) have received uneven support.

## The Relationship to Career Choice

People commonly use Holland's theory to make career choices by trying to match their personal Holland codes to codes assigned to occupations. The closer the match between the codes, the more likely the choice will lead to personal satisfaction, achievement at work, and a lower probability of changing occupations. This congruence between personal and occupational code need not be perfect, since there are a variety of personalities within any given occupation.

Holland's theory also explains some of the difficulties people have in making career choices. For example, a high school student might be very uncertain about a future career and undecided regarding a college major. The results from an interest inventory, such as *The Self-Directed Search,* may show that person's Holland code to be both undifferentiated (no strong likes or types) and inconsistent (combines types with conflicting characteristics). Several years later, after much more life experience, the same student solidifies a choice of major and graduates, entering an occupation related to the college major. Resurveying the person's interests shows that the student has changed to become more defined or differentiated, with the resulting Holland code being more consistent. Because of this, the student was able to make a congruent career choice more confidently.

## Application

Holland's theory, with its easy-to-use coding system, is capable of helping you organize a vast amount of information that could help you in any of the following ways: 1) understand dissatisfaction with a job; 2) help you hire personnel that will work well together; 3) select a college major or occupation; 4) if you teach, design learning activities that work well with different college majors; 5) confirm a career choice already made; 6) organize occupational information; and, most importantly, 7) guide exploration of career alternatives.

To accomplish many of these ends, you should first determine your own Holland code by completing an inventory, such as the *Self-Directed Search* (SDS), under the guidance of a counselor. By doing so, you will use *The Occupations Finder* (part of the SDS) to identify occupations that have the same or similar (same letters, but in a different order) codes to you. *The College Majors Finder* (an optional part of the SDS) can identify college majors with similar codes to your own.

With a list of occupations or programs of study congruent with your own code, a counselor can show you how to use the *Dictionary of Occupational Titles*, or some other source for more information about occupations. Some centers even file occupational information according to Holland codes to simplify getting this additional information. It is possible to use your code to match you with a college roommate with a similar code in hopes of increasing compatibility.

The information you have gathered about yourself and career alternatives should give you greater confidence in choosing available alternatives. Your counselor also may give you a booklet called *You and Your Career* when you complete *The Self-Directed Search*. It provides more information about the personality types in Holland's theory.

*See also* Choosing an Occupation; Job Satisfaction; Trait-Factor Approach to Career Choice.

## Bibliography

Gottfredson, G. D., & Holland, J. L.(1989). *Dictionary of Holland codes*. 2nd ed. Odessa, FL: Psychological Assessment Resources.

Holland, J.L. (1985a). *Making vocational choices: A theory of vocational personalities and work environments*. Englewood Cliffs, NJ: Prentice-Hall, Inc. John Holland's most recent statement of his theory included an extensive review of research on the theory. Lay people should be able to understand this book.

Holland, J.L. (1985b). *The self-directed search: Professional manual—1985 edition*. Odessa, FL: Psychological Assessment Resources, Inc. Besides including material on the interest inventory, this manual has many useful ideas on how counselors might use Holland's theory. There is also a 1987 supplement to this manual from the same publisher.

Holland, J.L. (1985c). *Vocational preference inventory (VPI)—1985 edition*. Odessa, FL: Psychological Assessment Resources, Inc.

—DAVID J. SREBALUS

# VOLUNTEER WORK

Volunteer work is a principal way to develop interests and skills for future employment in any area—business administration, sales, science, technology—not just traditional social service. The same practical outcomes to a paid job exist for an unpaid, volunteer job: experience necessary to land another position, important entry on one's resume, job references.

## Relationship to Work

If already performed, no matter how long ago, volunteer work must be written up on one's resume in business language, emphasizing projects and experiences related to the career objective. If volunteer work is sought for career exploration/development, the following aspects are especially important:

1. *Intentional Learning Goals.* Volunteers should actively reflect on what they are learning throughout the experience.
2. *Person-Job Fit.* Sufficient self-knowledge about work values and interests are needed to ensure the assignment is a good match.
3. *Training.* Volunteer workers should be constantly monitored, get valuable training, and learn new skills transferable to paid employment.
4. *Supervision.* Likewise, volunteers should expect good supervision and job performance feedback.
5. *Job Satisfaction.* An important goal is to learn if the activities give personal job satisfaction.

## Application

You can volunteer through college fieldwork or internship courses or set up your own experience. If you are working full-time for a large organization, why not arrange your internship in another part of that organization?

And what do you get out of volunteering? On your resume and in interviews you can describe general work skills gained, such as ability to get along well with staff and clientele and to follow through, and specific, technical work skills, such as word processing and marketing. Learn to express transferable skills from your volunteer work for any career objective.

*See also* Career Exploration; Cooperative Education; Internships; Service-Learning.

## Bibliography

Barbeau, J. E., & Stull, W. A. (1990). *Learning from working: A guide for cooperative education/internship students.* Cincinnati: South-Western Publishing Co. Even though designed for students in official programs, this guide is invaluable for do-it-yourselfers.

Butterworth, A. S., & Migliore, S. A. (Eds.) (1989). *The national directory of internships.* Raleigh, NC: National Society for Internships and Experiential Learning. Descriptions of 28,000 internships for students from high school through graduate school.

The Career Press (P. O. Box 34, Hawthorne, NJ 07507). Has several volumes of *Internships,* edited by Ronald W. Fry, in such areas as advertising, marketing, banking, insurance, brokerage, and the hospitality industry, for organizing your own internship.

## For Further Information

To find a volunteer referral center look in the white pages under Volunteer Center or Volunteer Bureau. For specific groups look in the yellow pages under Social Service Organizations. For the name of a volunteer referral agency in your area write: VOLUNTEER, The National Center, 111 N 19th St., Suite 500, Arlington, VA 22209.

—PATRICIA W. LUNNEBORG

# WHISTLEBLOWING

A whistleblower is an employee who discloses to those in authority an employer's illegal or unsafe practices or policies that threaten public health or safety. The traditional notion of a whistleblower is an employee who discloses conspicuous illegality such as "midnight dumping," the release of pollutants into a public waterway or the atmosphere. The definition of whistleblowing has been expanding in recent years as legislatures and courts strain to find legal protection for employee actions which enhance public health and safety. Included under the rubric of whistleblowing is what has been called the "passive" whistleblower, an employee who does not disclose the employer's practices or policies but refuses to perform acts he or she feels are unlawful or unsafe. A third type of whistleblower has been established as the result of recent federal legislation; the bounty-hunting whistleblower, blows the whistle on government contractor fraud in the hope of recovering a percentage of what the government would recover.

## Relationship to Work

Whistleblowing is a most dramatic example of the intersection of work issues with career decisions. Whistleblowers are generally viewed as conscious-ridden do-gooders who choose the public good over private gain. Whistleblowers are often personally and professionally ostracized and their careers with their employers are often ended. On occasion, a whistleblower may be reinstated by or recover damages from a court; more often, the whistleblower has nothing to show for his or her actions except unemployment, a damaged career, and an uncertain future.

Employees who are contemplating blowing the whistle are well-advised to know their legal rights, if any, before taking any action.

## Legal Summary

Employers in the United States have traditionally had almost unbridled authority to terminate their employees for any reason not expressly prohibited by law. In recent decades, the category of prohibited reasons has grown. Race, sex, age, religion, national origin, citizenship, disability, and sexual orientation are some notable protected categories recognized in some or all states. An employee may also derive substantial rights based on a contract. If the employee is a member of a union, those rights are group rights and are embodied in a collective bargaining agreement. Further, an employee with significant bargaining power may be able to negotiate the individual terms of his or her contract. Finally, company policy or practice— whether or not embodied in a written contract—may be enforceable and offer legal protection for the whistleblower.

A number of states, including New York, Maine, Connecticut, and Michigan, have enacted legislation specifically designed to protect whistleblowers in the private and public sectors. In addition, federal legislation protects federal employee whistleblowers.

The most significant recent legislation in this area is the 1986 revision of the Civil War era law known as the False Claims Act. The Act has made whistleblowing, at least in the government contractor area, an officially sanctioned act. Under the Act, private citizens as well as the United States can recover damages and penalties against government contractors who submit false or fraudulent claims to the government. A whistleblowing employee who brings a successful claim under the Act will be awarded at least 15% and as much as 30% of the monies recovered. Legal support for whistleblowers had previously been merely defensive with the aim of recouping losses and restoring whistleblowers to their former position. Under the Act, the whistleblower, rather than being a Cassandra, has been deputized to act on behalf of the government with the prospect of a substantial financial reward.

## Application

If you are an employee considering blowing the whistle on your employer, you should consider the following:

1. Make sure your facts are complete and accurate. The information you offer will be carefully scrutinized. You may not have all the relevant information or may be misinterpreting the facts. There is no room for error when blowing the whistle.
2. Exhaust all remedies within the organization before choosing to go public unless you are convinced that to do so would be futile. Give your employer a chance to clean up its own mess.
3. Carefully map out your strategy before making your disclosure. How far are you willing to take the issue?
4. Decide whether you can survive a dismissal and a possible blackballing in your industry or profession. Do not start what you cannot finish.
5. Consult a lawyer. Know your legal rights before you may have to exercise them.

If you are an employer, you should consider the following:

1. Do you have a means within your organization for an employee with a potential whistleblower or personnel-related complaint to raise and perhaps resolve such a complaint? If not, the likelihood of a whistleblower claim being made against your organization and the potential damage that goes with it is enhanced.
2. Investigate every whistleblower complaint diligently and document your efforts. If you do not do so, a third party may be asked to.
3. Guarantee that there will be no retaliation taken against a whistleblower.

*See also* Ethical Dilemmas; Law in the Workplace; Work Hazards.

## Bibliography

Elliston, F. (1985). *Managing dissent in the workplace.* New York: Praeger.

Glazer, M.P., & Glazer, P.M. (1989). *Whistleblowers: Exposing corruption in government and industry.* New York: Basic.

Westin, A. (1981). *Whistleblowing: Loyalty and dissent in the corporation.* New York: McGraw-Hill.

—ALFRED G. FELIU

# WOMEN IN THE WORKFORCE

One of the most important decisions facing a young woman is whether and how she should prepare for spending most of her life in the workforce. Paid work used to be something a woman did until she was married, or at most until the first child was born. After that she devoted the rest of her life to caring for her family. Those days are long gone. Today, a substantial minority of women do not leave the labor market even when their children are born, and most of those re-enter when their children grow older.

## Changes in the Labor Market and in the Home

In 1890, the earliest year for which data are available, 19% of all women, and slightly less than 5% of married women worked for pay. The rate of labor force participation has been rising ever since. The increase was slow at first. Over the next 50 years the figures rose to 26% and 14%, respectively. By 1990, however, over 60% of all women, and only a slightly smaller proportion of married women were employed, including more than half the mothers of children under 3 years of age. Meanwhile, other changes have not kept pace, either in the family or in the workplace.

Adjustments in the amount of time women and men spend on homemaking have lagged substantially behind the rapid increases in the amount of time women spend in the labor market. For many years the wife's employment status had little effect on the amount of housework the husband did; this was consistent with the perception that the woman is responsible for the household, whether or not she is employed, while the man merely helps. As late as the 1980s, women were devoting about 30 hours per week to housework, compared to 14 hours for men (Juster & Stafford, 1990) (see **Dual-Career Families; Working Family Issues**).

Similarly, while young women now expect to work outside the home after leaving school, they continue to view husbands as the primary wage earners. Until recently they tended to seriously underestimate the number of years they were likely to spend in the labor force (Shaw & Shapiro, 1987), and even today they are likely to do so to some extent. It appears that the notion of traditional husband/wife roles lingers on, even though the reality is that full-time homemakers are becoming an endangered species. Among workers who live in families, about 60% of men, and over 70% of women have employed spouses. An additional 5% of these men and 20% of these women do not live with a spouse.

## Reasons for Women's Higher Labor Force Participation

There are many reasons why a large majority of women are now employed. With increasing education and expanding opportunities in the labor market, the amount women can earn has risen considerably. At the same time, increasingly more goods and services can be more conveniently purchased than produced at home, so housekeeping has ceased to be a full-time job, except when there are young children or other dependents to be taken care of. Because life expectancy has increased substantially while fertility has declined, caring for young children takes a smaller portion of a woman's adult years. Further, the demand for money income has risen because of the growing number of desirable commodities available only in the market, from air conditioners, cars, and home computers to sophisticated medical care and a college education.

Women have other reasons for entering the labor market as well. As compared to "housewives," employed women tend to have more influence on family decision making, generally live longer, enjoy better health, and are more self-confident (Blau & Ferber, 1986). Children tend to hold them in higher esteem. Most important, they maintain their labor market skills, and gain valuable experience, so that they are in a far better position to support themselves, and their children, should the need arise. This may happen not only in case of divorce, but if the husband becomes unemployed, incapacitated, or dies prematurely. The proportion of families maintained by women has been increasing rapidly in recent years, and reached 16% by the 1980s. Less than 60% of these mothers were awarded child support, and only about 35% received any payments, on average slightly less than $2,500 (U.S. Bureau of the Census, Current Population Reports, Series P-23, No.154, Child Support and Alimony, 1985).

## Equity Issues

Women's labor force participation has increased rapidly. Substantial occupational segregation and a large earnings gap, however, continue to persist. There is now growing concern about achieving greater equality in the labor market. During the first half of this century women were particularly underrepresented among executives and managers, in the prestigious professions, and in skilled blue-collar jobs. About two-thirds of women would have had to change jobs to duplicate the occupational distribution of men. Segregation has declined somewhat since then, to less than 60% (Blau & Ferber, 1986), mainly because women began moving into previously male managerial positions and professions. Nonetheless, it is still very unusual for women and men to do the same work and hold the same job title in the same enterprise (Bielby & Baron, 1984), and there is the possibility that recently integrated occupations may become predominantly female, as men move out, or enter in smaller numbers (Reskin, 1989).

The earnings gap between women and men has declined even more slowly. Women working full-time, year-round earned 64% as much as comparable men both in 1955, the first year for which data are available, and in 1984. Since then the differential appears to be have been narrowing by about one percentage point annually, but women now still earn only about two-thirds as much as men. Many experts ascribe at least part of this remaining gap to discrimination. Much can be done, however, to improve the situation.

There is no question that women in part earn less because, on average, they work fewer hours per week and fewer weeks per year even when they work full-time, and because they gain less valuable on-the-job experience when they temporarily drop out of the labor force or work part-time. They also earn less because they are still overrepresented in the relatively few traditionally female occupations, and underrepresented in the far more numerous male occupations, many of them among the most challenging, powerful, and well paid (see **Pay**).

## Applications to Career Planning

This information can help you in making rational career plans and decisions, so that you will be able to find a job that is both interesting and satisfying, and that enables you to earn an adequate income. Whatever your personal priorities are, it would clearly be a mistake not to prepare for the occupation you think would be most rewarding because of the outdated notions that you should enter a traditionally female field or that marriage and a career are substitutes rather than complements. Similarly, it would be a mistake to drop out of the labor force for a long period of time because of concerns for child and elder care, because successful re-entry becomes increasingly difficult as the interruption becomes longer. Not only do many skills deteriorate and become obsolete, but contacts in and knowledge of the labor market will be lost.

A far better strategy is to reconsider the allocation of household responsibilities, so that both spouses share in "the double burden," just as both enjoy the higher standard of living made possible by the two incomes. Though women are the ones who bear children, this is not an activity that is very time consuming. It is child rearing and care of the elderly that takes time, in addition to the routine household chores. There is no convincing evidence that men can not perform any of these other homemaking tasks equally well. Such an approach will alleviate the burden of the woman in the household, and enable her to do better in the labor market. She will be able to opt for more challenging, better paying jobs, now predominantly male. Further, if enough women do this, fewer of them will crowd into traditionally female fields, so that wages there are likely to increase.

As long as only women permit family resposibilities to encroach on their job, there will inevitably be a preference for hiring and promoting men. When, on the other hand, men as well as women are ocasionally late because the baby sitter did not come on time, get occasional phone calls when children come home from school and need to consult with a parent, and take time off to care for a sick family member, employers will have little choice but to accept this as the inevitable cost of a human labor force.

*See also* Discrimination: Sex; Dual-Career Families; Non-Traditional Job for One's Sex; Pay; Sequencing: A Career and Traditional Mothering; Sex-Role Stereotyping; Women's Barriers and Opportunities; Working Family Issues.

## Bibliography

Betz, N., & Fitzgerald, L. (1987). *The career psychology of women*, New York: Academic Press.

Bielby, W. T., & Baron, J. N. (1984). A woman's place is with other women: Sex segregation in the workplace. In Barbara F. Reskin (Ed.), *Sex segregation in the workplace: Trends, explanations, remedies*. Washington, DC: National Academy Press. This study, relying on data for almost 400 California firms with more than 60,000 workers, shows a far larger degree of occupational segregation than that found by other researchers using broader categories.

Blau, F. D., & Ferber, M. A. (1986). *The economics of women, men, and work*, Englewood Cliffs, NJ: Prentice-Hall. This text explores in considerable depth the history and present situation of women in the labor market and in the household. Much of it is accessible to a reader without economics training.

Bolles, R. (1985). *What color is your parachute*? Berkeley, CA: Ten Speed Press.

Gray, B., Loeffler, D., & Cooper, R. K. (1982). *Every woman works*. Belmont, CA: Lifetime Learning.

Hanson, L. S., & Raposa, R. S. (1978). *Career development and counseling of women*. Springfield, IL: Charles Thomas.

Juster, F. T. & Stafford, F. P. (1990). The allocation of time: Empirical findings, behavioral models, and problems of measurement. Unpublished paper.

Reskin, B. F. (1989). Job queues, gender queues: Explaining women's movement into male dominated occupations. In B. F. Reskin & P. Roos (Eds.), *Job queues, gender queues: Explaining women's movement into male dominated occupations*, Philadelphia: Temple University Press. This chapter discusses the evidence that the rapid influx of women into previously male occupations was often the result of jobs becoming deskilled and hence abandoned by men. Hence they are in danger of "tipping" and becoming female.

Shaw, L. B., & Shapiro, David S. (1987). Women's work plans: Contrasting expectations and actual work experience, *Monthly Labor Review*, 110: 7-13.

—MARIANNE A. FERBER

## WOMEN: REENTRY INTO THE WORKPLACE

Millions of American women are seeking reentry into the workplace. Some are displaced homemakers whose paid employment is often very limited because they went directly from school into homemaking. Other women left jobs or interrupted careers to raise a family. The problems for both groups are the same; they just differ in magnitude.

Why do women reenter the workplace? For the same reason men don't leave it—to make money. For single, divorced, and widowed women with children to raise, the question is gratuitous. And for many married women, as well, finances are the primary motivation. But women also return to work to be with interesting coworkers, to be more independent, and to produce, accomplish, and achieve outside the home. Reentry is historically a female phenomenon, but this chapter also applies to the growing number of househusbands.

### Relationship to Work

Reenterers have the same career-decision making tasks that first-time job enterers have, the principal ones being to "know yourself" and "know the world of work." Just like everybody else, returnees must choose an occupation by consulting person-job fit and must come up with a "career objective" for their resumes. However, reentry has its special problems:

1. *Resume*. The secret is having transferable skills from homemaking and community activities.
2. *Interview*. Returnees should focus on their skills and forget their age.
3. *Low Self-Confidence*. Cited often as a major impediment.
4. *Entry-Level Jobs and Starting Salaries*. Opportunities for advancement are the important thing as returnees settle for less rank and money than they expected.
5. *Quantitative Deficit*. Remedial math and basic accounting are often a must.
6. *Sense of Urgency*. Reenters must fight it because it's self-defeating.
7. *Family Resistance*. As one book put it, families tend to applaud first and pout later. Households have to be completely reorganized. The most important

decision is undoubtedly day care, and outside social obligations will probably dwindle.

8. *Age Discrimination.* A list of advantages to one's age gives returnees ammunition if they get an opportunity to use it.

9. *References.* Must be recent and relevant, and who says volunteer work isn't relevant?

## Application

How to reenter the workplace? Here are 10 first steps. They are not sequential; each is a different starting point. Which is best for you? Rank them in terms of appropriateness for your situation and then write lists of advantages and disadvantages for your rop-ranked choices.

1. *Visit a Career Guidance Center.* If you are very confused about who you are, and need help in assessing your abilities, skills, interests, and values, consult the yellow pages and get expert help to "know yourself" (see **Career Counseling; Career Exploration**).

2. *Visit a Women's Center to Find a Support Group.* If you know yourself, the world of work, and even how to proceed, but lack moral support, get it and advice from others going through similar occupational transitions (see **Networking**).

3. *Explore Nontraditional Work.* Attend Women in Trades fairs, community college apprenticeship programs, and state and city trades projects. Male-dominated technical, mechanical, and outdoor jobs pay far better than traditional women's jobs (see **Nontraditional Job for One's Sex**).

4. *Volunteer for the Express Purpose of Getting Job Experience.* Think of this volunteer work as a professional internship for which you already have the requisite college or vocational training but simply lack experience (see **Volunteer Work**).

5. *Explore Self-Employment.* Contact the American Woman's Economic Development Corporation, 1270 Avenue of the Americas, New York, NY 10020 as a start (see **Self-Employment**).

6. *Take a Full-Time, Low-Level Job.* This will help you adjust to the stresses of working a 40-hour week and to figure out how to manage employment with other aspects of your life. This is a first step for those who truly need to spend a year building self-confidence (see **Self-Efficacy**).

7. *Go Back to School.* Get the job-related skills and knowledge you need to do what you want. Community college, business school, university, vocational/ technical school, and high school night classes provide the classes, AA, BA, or MA required for your career objective (see **Continuing Education**).

8. *Start Your Job Search.* Update your resume, start interviewing, and build up your network of friends, relatives, neighbors, past coworkers, and past supervisors, all of whom have your resume and know you are looking for work (see **Information Interviewing; Job Search; Resume**).

9. *Search Specifically for Part-Time Work in Your Chosen Career.* Maybe you can do it through job sharing where two people share one permanent, full-time position (see **Job Sharing; Part-Time Work**).

10. *Search Specifically for Temporary Work.* This can be done either through a service or through a regular company (see **Temporary Employment**). Like first step 6 (low-level job), this is for people who need to build self-confidence, but it also lets you job shop.

*See also* Career Changes at Midlife; Career Counseling; Career Exploration; Continuing Education; Discrimination: Age; Discrimination: Sex; Information Interviewing; Job Search; Job Sharing; Networking; Nontraditional Jobs for One's Sex; Part-Time Work; Resume; Self-Efficacy; Self-Employment; Temporary Employment; Volunteer Work; Women's Barriers and Opportunities.

## Bibliography

Banning, K. B., & Friday, A. F. (1989). *Planning your career change.* Lincolnwood, IL: VGM Career Horizons. Organized approach for analyzing present skills and potential, resume/ interview preparation, and confidence raising.

Doss, M. M. (Ed.) (1981). *The directory of special opportunities for women: A national guide of educational opportunities, career information, networks, and peer counseling assistance for entry or reentry into the work force.* Garrett Park, MD: Garrett Park Press. Sections on national organizations and government agencies, city and state women's centers, women's colleges, and publications for women in careers and education.

Mendelsohn, P. (1980). *Happier by degrees: A college reentry guide for women.* New York: Dutton. A resource and support book for women returning to school, includes chapters on choosing a career and finding a job.

Schuman, N., & Lewis, W. (1985). *Back to work: How to re-enter the working world.* Woodbury, NY: Barron's Educational Series. Twenty practical steps to a good job.

## For Further Information

**Displaced Homemakers Network, Inc.**
101 Vermont Avenue, N.W., Suite 817
Washington, DC 20005
(202) 628-6767
Regional offices across the country offer counseling, job skills training

—PATRICIA W. LUNNEBORG

# WOMEN'S BARRIERS AND OPPORTUNITIES

*Women's barriers* refers to the specific types of organizational barriers to upward mobility that tend to be unique to women because of their lack of power in the top echelons of business organizations. *Women's opportunities* refers to specific advantages women may have in the workplace due to their newness or uniqueness in jobs or positions that were formerly held by males only, or due to skills that tend to be more highly developed in females than in males.

## Relationship to Work

In the 1950s only 12% of all managers were women, and virtually all top managers were men. By 1989 about 40% of all managers were women, but 97% to 98% of top managers were still men. The affirmative action laws that were fairly well enforced during the 1970s opened the doors for women at the lower management levels, and by the 1990s significant numbers seemed to have moved into middle management jobs. These women have reported some specific advantages and disadvantages of being a woman in formerly male-only roles. In addition, women have moved into technical, professional, and blue-collar jobs in unprecedented numbers, and much of this discussion applies to their situations.

## Application

Women managers see at least five major barriers to equality in the workplace, barriers that they believe must be resolved in the 1990s (Carr-Ruffino, 1988):

1. Becoming adequately represented at the top. The executive team at the top of an organization has the most influence on corporate culture, the climate that fosters or inhibits the motivation and upward mobility of specific types or groups of people within the company, such as women, ethnic minorities, and the handicapped. Nearly half of all workers are women and 40% of all managers are women; when around 40% of top managers are women, parity will be achieved. This critical mass would have a significant impact in changing corporate cultures.

2. Gaining pay equity, possibly through the comparable worth approach. Women on average earned 64 cents for every dollar men earned in 1989. At the vice presidential level women still received only 68% of the salary men received, which indicates that the rationales normally given for women's lower earnings are not valid (see **Pay; Women in the Workforce**).

3. Being able to obtain quality, affordable child care is critical for those women who want little or no interruption of their careers during the child-rearing years. Many women claim that such child care is not readily available to them and this lack creates a formidable barrier to career success (see **Benefits; Child Care**).

4. Finding companies that give adequate maternity leaves (as well as related leaves for medical or family care purposes). Since women bear primary responsibility for child care and eldercare in most families, such leaves are especially important for their careers (see **Parental Leave**).

5. Finding companies that are flexible in their approach to job responsibilities, work schedules, personnel benefits, and related matters; for example, encouraging job sharing, flextime, and cafeteria-style benefit packages that would allow a worker to receive more for child care and less for a pension fund during the child-rearing years.

The specific types of barriers to promotion that women managers report include the following:

1. *Men's Discomfort.* The men at the top do not readily welcome women into their ranks. A typical comment is: "Men only is what they're used to, and that's what they like."

2. *Sexual Stereotyping of Women.* The most damaging stereotypes include the belief that:
   a. Most people in the organization will not accept women in top-level roles because they are accustomed to seeing men there, they doubt women are able to function well at that level, and they prefer to see men there.
   b. Women do not have the single-minded career commitment that is required for the top jobs.
   c. Women are not as capable of making sound, reasoned decisions as men are.
   d. Women are not able to control their emotions, as business leaders must do.
   e. Women are not assertive enough to function well at higher levels; they cannot make the tough decisions and hold the line against pressure from others to back down (see **Sex-Role Stereotyping**).

3. *Exclusion of Women.* Women are often excluded from key informal gatherings where information and opinions are exchanged, deals are made, and the preliminary, background steps are taken toward making important decisions.

4. *Discounting of Women's Achievements.* Women's contributions to the organization's success, their level of productivity, and their abilities are generally not given full credence. Women are not taken as seriously as men are.

5. *Difficulty Finding Mentors.* The idea that people must have one or more mentors within an organization in order to make it to the top is generally

accepted. For a number of reasons, women tend to have fewer mentors and have more difficulty forming mentor relationships (see **Mentoring**).

6. *Lack of Equal Opportunity.* Women report they have more difficulty finding opportunities to serve on important committees, project teams, task forces, and similar groups. They also report fewer opportunities to attend high-level internal and external meetings, key business trips, and similar functions. Many also report that they are excluded from opportunities to attend the highest-level training programs, although they receive ample opportunity to attend lower-level ones (see **Discrimination: Sex**).

The advantages and opportunities of being a woman include the following:

1. *Communication Skills.* Women tend to excel in verbal expression, both written and oral. They also are adept at expressing feelings, which can be an asset on the job if handled in a business-like way.

2. *People Skills.* Women tend to be good listeners and to experience a relatively high level of empathy with others. They often are highly skilled at nurturing and supporting others, which can be applied effectively in work situations; (e.g., in fostering a motivating environment).

3. *Affiliation Need.* More women than men have a high need for affiliation. This translates into establishing an environment in which workers are empowered, allowed to participate more in the decision-making processes, and are less caught up in organizational politics. The culture tends to become more cooperative with less destructive internal competition.

4. *Intuitive Skills.* Women are often encouraged, or at least not discouraged, in developing and applying their intuitive skills, which are especially valuable for understanding people and predicting what they might do next. Such skills become more important as you move up the corporate ladder and are called upon to make decisions for which few hard data are available.

5. *Less Ego-Involvement.* Women tend to have less stake in success on the job. Most do not equate job success with their value or success as a person. Because their ego is not on the line, they may be better able to resolve interpersonal conflict, lead team efforts, empower others, and engage in similar participative-management endeavors.

6. *Visibility.* Being the only woman, or one of a handful of women, in a male-dominated field can be a double-edged sword. The unique candidate comes to mind when decision makers are thinking about who will get the appointment, assignment, sales

contract, promotion, etc. Women who have made a favorable impression, or who have a successful track record, may be given opportunities because of their visibility. On the other hand, women are more visible when they botch an assignment, or when they are unable to succeed in a job position. Unfortunately, their failure may reinforce the stereotype that women are not really cut out for the more responsible positions.

*See also* Assertion; Benefits; Child Care; Discrimination: Sex; Dual-Career Families; Law in the Workplace; Mentoring; Networking; Nontraditional Job for One's Sex; Parental Leave; Pay; Promotion/Raise; Sex-Role Stereotyping; Sexual Harassment; Women in the Workforce; Working Family Issues.

## Bibliography

Carr-Ruffino, N. (1985). *The promotable woman: Becoming a successful manager.* Belmont, CA: Wadsworth, Inc. This entire book is devoted to recognizing and overcoming barriers to women's success in business, and to building on the skills and potential that females tend to develop more fully than males.

Carr-Ruffino, N. (1988). Women in top management— Why so few? How to break through. *San Francisco State University School of Business Journal*, 1: 31–38. This journal article discusses the results of a survey of women in middle- and top-level management positions regarding barriers and facilitators to upward mobility.

Dowling, C. (1981). *The cinderella complex.* New York: Simon & Schuster.

Kanter, R. M. (1977). *Men and women of the corporation.* New York: Basic Books.

—NORMA CARR-RUFFINO

## WOMEN WHO LIVE/WORK OVERSEAS

Women who choose to live overseas can be divided into two broad categories: those who pursue their own careers and those who are the dependents of a primary wage earner employed by an organization with an overseas program. The first group includes women who are single; women who are half of a "tandem couple" (a term commonly used by the U.S. government and its overseas branches and defined as a couple who both work for the same U.S. government organization); and women who move overseas with dependents, whether husband, children, or both. The second category includes women who are housewives by choice or those who have careers but chose to move and find work wherever the primary wage earner is employed.

As was true for U.S.-based professional women, traditional careers overseas have been in education, missionary work, clerical services, and health care. However, this is changing. While it is still unusual to see expatriate women in blue-collar jobs (e.g., riggers at oil field sites or telephone repair persons), they are present in ever-increasing numbers in development agencies, the diplomatic corps, and the white-collar levels of all types of American and multinational businesses.

## Relationship to Career Choice

Professionals can choose careers which demand an expatriate life. The foremost among these is the diplomatic service or government development agencies which work either bilaterally (e.g., the U.S. Agency for International Development) or multilaterally (e.g., any of the United Nations agencies). There are also private organizations, including foundations of all sizes (e.g., The Asia Foundation or The Ford Foundation) or relief-type agencies which have international programs (e.g., CARE, Save the Children). Teachers can find international work either in international schools which cater to expatriate children or Department of Defense schools (DOD) which are located on U.S. military installations in many countries. Religious missions continue to attract women in all professions, particularly teachers and medical personnel.

Women who are seeking a short exposure to overseas work to enhance their career in the U.S. should explore fellowship programs, usually offered through universities, or voluntary service in their career stream (e.g., the U.S. Peace Corps).

Women in business who would like an overseas tour can apply through their company if it is a multinational one. If not, there can be opportunities through affiliate companies, though this may mean the woman will lose her position on the career ladder with the parent company, even if she leaves for only a short time. U.S. corporations usually send young managers overseas for a "learning" experience and expect them to return to the home company after a brief sojourn abroad. European companies, by contrast, train overseas specialists and expect them to continue in that career stream for their career.

Women who move overseas as dependents can find work, though their success depends on many factors. Unfortunately, some of these factors (e.g., the length of the husband's contract; work permit regulations) are beyond their control. Bastress (1986) writes that the most portable careers are counseling, health care, social work, secretarial work, teaching and training, and writing and editing. Women who are dependents of U.S. government personnel may find employment within the U.S. diplomatic or development community.

It is essential that any woman who would like to pursue her own career, even though she is going overseas as a dependent, fact-find on the work situation in her host country *prior* to departure. The U.S. government currently has bilateral work agreements for any U.S. passport holder with only 23 countries (see Table 1).

The Community Liaison Office of the U.S. State Department (1989) offers this information on work agreements. A bilateral agreement ". . . provides an expeditious procedure in which permission to work is granted almost automatically. There is no restriction on the type of employment that may be undertaken." In 88 other countries, there are "de facto" arrangements. This is ". . . only an informal arrangement whereby a country allows US dependents to work and the United States reciprocates. As there is nothing in writing, such an arrangement is subject to unpredictable change, due to economic or political pressures, or even changes in personnel within a foreign ministry. It can be established or withdrawn at any time." It may be legally impossible for a dependent to apply for a work permit in her country of residence. This is a severe limitation and one which the woman should be aware of prior to her departure.

**Table 1. Countries with Bilateral Work Agreements with the United States**

| | | |
|---|---|---|
| Argentina | El Salvador | New Zealand |
| Australia | France* | Norway |
| Bolivia | Grenada | Peru |
| Botswana* | Guatemala | Philippines |
| Brazil | Honduras | Spain* |
| Canada | Israel | Sweden |
| Colombia | Jamaica | United Kingdom |
| Denmark | Liberia | Venezuela |
| Ecuador | Netherlands | Zambia |

*Limited number of dependents permitted to work.

**Source:** U.S. Department of State, *Family Liaison Office Quarterly* Vol. 1, No. 2 (April 1989).

If a work permit is possible, a woman goes about seeking a job overseas much as she would in a new situation in the United States. She should make contacts through her present U.S.-based employer or through her husband's employer; up-date her resume (emphasizing those elements which would make her marketable abroad, e.g., language ability or technical training); and ensure that the references are recent and reflect her unique value in an overseas setting.

A woman who is planning to be overseas for a short time while her husband completes a limited assignment may use her time to volunteer in an area of interest. Though volunteers are welcome in most capacities, particularly in developing countries, a woman should choose carefully to ensure that her time is well spent. Some women on short-term overseas assignments develop other skills which they intend to apply after their return home. These can include language skills or further study either through correspondence or at a local university.

## Application

Working overseas is not for everyone. Though millions of Americans choose the expatriate life, Harris and Moran (1979) write that: "Participants in these intercultural experiences have learned that there are many problems when working and living in a foreign environment. Communication across cultural boundaries is difficult. Differences in customs, behavior, and values result in problems that can be only managed through effective cross-cultural communication and interaction. Persons of dissimilar backgrounds usually require a longer period of time than those of the same culture to become familiar with each other, to be willing to speak openly, to share sufficiently in common ideas, and to understand one another" (p. 12). Several personality traits are helpful in an overseas setting. When considering whether to make an overseas move, it is important for you to analyze whether these characteristics are yours. For example, Guither and Thompson (1969) remind us that "Persons who go abroad must have a personal adaptability and flexibility to perform effectively in addition to being professionally qualified." Harris and Moran (1979) name these characteristics as essential for selecting successful candidates for overseas service: "empathy, openness, persistence, sensitivity to intercultural factors, respect for others, role flexibility, tolerance for ambiguity, and two-way communication skill." Piet-Pelon and Hornby (1985), who are particularly concerned with women overseas as dependents, emphasize the importance of being flexible; a willingness to start over in each new country; an enjoyment of living with new ways; and, when all else fails, the acceptance of the need for the family to live separately so both the woman and her spouse can pursue their careers.

If you have these characteristics, a short time or a lifetime spent in an overseas working environment can be right for you. Most women who have overseas experience agree that the effort made to find work or career enchancements, the challenge involved in doing the job well and overcoming the hurdles encountered, can combine to create in them personal growth of a magnitude they would not likely have achieved staying in the United States.

*See also* Career Exploration; Culturally Different: Working with; Job Hunting: International; Job Search; Networking; Relocation; Volunteer Work.

## Bibliography

Bastress, F. (1986). *The relocating spouse's guide to employment: Options and strategies in the U.S. and abroad.* Chevy Chase, MD: Woodley Publications. This is a concise guide for any relocating spouse, though the author's bias is toward the wife. It has a positive outlook on relocation and includes practical advice on portable careers, as well as first-hand accounts from spouses who successfully relocated. The appendices are particularly rich with networking information.

Geneva Women's Cooperative. (1983). *With our consent?* Federal Republic of Germany: Geneva Women's Cooperative. Based on a survey of expatriate women living in Geneva, this book presents a compelling, though negative, picture of the role of career women in Switzerland.

Guither, H.D., & Thompson, W.N. (1969). *Mission overseas: A handbook for U.S. families in developing countries.* Urbana, IL: The University of Illinois Press. Though this guide for American families is dated, it offers excellent practical and philosophical advice for families contemplating an overseas move.

Harris, P.R., and Moran, R.T. (1979). *Managing cultural differences.* Houston, TX: Gulf Publishing Company. This useful book is "must reading" for anyone contemplating a move overseas with an American business enterprise. It is a factual presentation of the difficulties faced by the American corporate manager in an overseas setting, who is often caught between the demands of the home office and those of the host country.

Kepler, J.Z., Kepler, P.J., Gaither, O.D., & Gaither, M.L. (1983). *Americans abroad: A handbook for living and working overseas.* New York: Praeger Publishers. Based on the authors' personal experiences working for multinationals, this book includes both general advice and specific city sections on London, Brussels, Paris, Rome, Milan, Hong Kong, Tokyo, and Manila.

Kohls, L. R. (1979). *Survival kit for overseas living: For Americans planning to live and work abroad.* Chicago: Intercultural Press. This general book includes self-guided workbook exercises designed to assist the reader when making a decision to live overseas.

McKay, V. (1982). *Moving abroad: A guide to international living.* Hong Kong: Truetone.

Meltzer, G., & Grandjean, E. (1989). *The moving experience: A practical guide to psychological survival.* Clevedon, England: Multilingual Matters Ltd.

Piet-Pelon, N. J., & Hornby, B. (1985). *In another dimension: A guide for women who live overseas.* Yarmouth, ME: Intercultural Press. This is the only current book written about the special issues for women who choose to live overseas or who move overseas as a dependent spouse. The chapter on "Women Who

Work" offers guidelines for women who seek careers wherever they find themselves. The second edition will be published in 1991 and will contain an expanded section on working women.

United States Department of State. (April, 1989). *Family Liaison Office Quarterly*, Volume 1, No. 2.

—Nancy J. Piet-Pelon

## WORK HAZARDS

One aspect of nearly every type of work is the associated risk of injury or illness. For some types of work, this risk may be quite high and has long been understood as an element to be considered in entering that profession (e.g., fire fighting, underground mining). For other jobs, the risks may not be well understood or recognized and therefore difficult to evaluate in making a career decision (e.g., reproductive hazards from working with video display terminals). Past research in occupational safety and health has mainly focused on hazards from exposures to toxic substances and physical agents in manufacturing jobs. However, researchers have recently been focusing more attention on hazards in the office environment and service industries. This effort has provided a more comprehensive understanding of potential workplace hazards.

Workplace hazards arise from many different aspects of a job. Toxic substances may be used or produced in the work environment. Some of these substances may have immediate health consequences, while exposure to others may not lead to health problems for many years. Almost every organ system may be affected by toxic exposures, and the disease outcomes usually are the same as those developing from "natural" causes. This similarity as well as the meager training most health professionals receive in occupational health often impedes or delays the recognition of these illnesses as "work-related." Physical agents in the workplace also may be difficult to detect and can have long-range consequences. In some settings, people may be exposed to viruses and other microorganisms which may occasionally lead to serious infections.

Injuries may occur on the job from work equipment or other aspects of the work environment. Other injuries may occur from repeated physical stress and strain over a period of time. For example, chronic back problems are a major work-related cause of disability. More recently, carpal tunnel syndrome and other wrist and arm disorders have been found in many people doing repeated arm and wrist motions at work (e.g., meat cutters). Psychological stresses at work may also cause major difficulties for many individuals.

There are many different approaches to controlling workplace safety and health hazards. Less toxic alternatives may be substituted for toxic substances used in the workplace. Ventilation systems may be installed to remove contaminants, or machines redesigned to reduce the risk of injury. Personal protective equipment such as hard hats and respirators may be utilized. The work environment may be tested for the presence of a toxic substance, or the worker may be tested for the amount of substance absorbed in the body. These different approaches have advantages and disadvantages depending on the type of work environment and the nature of the hazard.

Responsibility for regulating this wide range of occupational safety and health problems falls on the federal Occupational Safety and Health Administration (OSHA), which develops and enforces workplace regulations, and its sister agency, the National Institute for Occupational Safety and Health (NIOSH), which is responsible for occupational safety and health research. State agencies also may play a role, and some industries (such as mining) are regulated by other agencies. Workers' compensation is largely a state responsibility.

OSHA regulates exposure to most toxic substances by determining a Permissible Exposure Limit (PEL) and then requiring that exposures in the workplace be kept below that level. This PEL may be supplemented with requirements for testing the work environment, labeling containers with the material, and medical monitoring. For safety hazards, OSHA may require certain machinery design, protective equipment, specific work procedures, or some combination of these approaches.

OSHA considers occupational safety and health programs to be a responsibility of the employer, who is held accountable for ensuring that all appropriate regulations are being followed. The responsibilities of the employee are not well-defined and may vary depending on their relationship with the employer (i.e., union contract). Recent OSHA regulations have mandated more access for employees to information on workplace hazards. This "Right to Know" approach has greatly increased employees' understanding of workplace hazards and has increased pressure to better control these hazards. This has been accompanied by a desire for more participation by employees in decisions regarding occupational safety and health in the workplace.

Our base of knowledge in occupational safety and health is rapidly changing. This together with the increasing interest in both the work and general environments will lead to many changes in our approach to occupational safety and health for all types of jobs.

*See also* Appendix I: OSHA Regional Offices; Law in the Workplace.

—James M. Melius

# WORK HAZARDS: BIOLOGICAL

Biological work hazards refer to exposures to bacteria, viruses, or other infectious microorganisms which may be transmitted to people in the workplace. In the broad sense, the common cold transmitted from one worker to another at work may be considered the most common example of this type of hazard. However, the definition of biological hazard is usually restricted to the transmission of infections due to some specific aspect of the work environment and/ or to work situations where employees have been found to be at greater risk of developing that disorder. For example, the transmission of an infectious disease from a patient to a health care worker during a medical procedure would be categorized as a biological hazard. The health care and related industries are probably the major areas where biological hazards are a problem. However, biological hazards may also be found in certain other types of work.

## Health Care

Prevention of the transmission of infections from patients to health care workers and health care workers to patients has long been a focus of infection control practices in health care settings. This control has been achieved through sterilization and disinfection procedures and work practices often specific to the mode of transmission of the infectious agent (e.g., masks to prevent transmission of respiratory infections). These practices have been so well institutionalized in health care settings that they are often difficult to recognize as active occupational safety and health measures.

Despite these practices, some infectious disease continue to be a risk for health care workers. Tuberculosis has long been a problem for health care workers and may be increasing due to the rising incidence of the disease in this country. Rubella, cytomegalovirus, toxoplasmosis, and certain other infectious organisms are a risk for pregnant workers because these organisms may damage the developing fetus.

More recently, attention has focused on hepatitis (particularly Hepatitis B Virus or HBV) and AIDS (Human Immunodeficiency Virus or HIV). The primary risk of exposure to both of these viruses is through blood (i.e., blood borne infections). Needlestick injuries are the most common cause of transmission. However, other procedures where the blood of an infected patient may enter the employee's blood stream may also spread these viruses. Both viruses may also be found in other bodily fluids,

raising the potential for other modes of transmission, although the occupational risk from these other routes appears to be very small, especially for HIV.

Approximately 12,000 health care workers develop HBV from workplace exposures in the United States each year. Dentists, renal dialysis staff, laboratory workers, and surgeons appear to have the highest risks, but nearly all health care workers may be at risk. Although most recover from the illness, many are seriously ill, and a few (1.4%) die. Around 8% become chronic carriers of the virus and may develop later health problems. Women who are HBV carriers may pass it to their infants during pregnancy. Preventive steps have focused on the use of personal protective equipment (e.g., gloves) and careful work practices for everyone in health care settings (i.e., use of universal precautions assuming all patients may be infected). There is clearly a need for better designed medical equipment to reduce the risks of needlestick injuries. For documented exposures to HBV, a special immune globulin may be given to reduce the later risk of developing HBV. More importantly, there is a vaccine which provides active immunization against HBV infection and should greatly reduce the incidence of occupational HBV infections.

The documented number of health care workers with HIV infection due to workplace exposures is small but can be expected to increase with the increased number of people with HIV infection in our health care settings. The long time from initial exposure until clinical symptoms develop makes recognition difficult. HIV is more fragile than HBV and hence appears to be less viable outside the body, which reduces its potential for spread on contaminated surfaces, etc. However, there have been a number of cases of documented spread almost all from needlestick or other medical equipment injuries. Prevention of HIV transmission is similar to that for HBV. However, there is currently no immune globulin or vaccine for HIV. Follow-up after potential workplace exposure is very important. Although clear evidence of efficacy is lacking, drug therapy to prevent infection is being tried. People in these situations also need supportive counseling.

Recently, the Occupational Safety and Health Administration in conjunction with the Centers for Disease Control developed guidelines and regulations to prevent the spread of HBV and HIV in the workplace. With our rapidly increasing knowledge of HIV and the increasing research on methods to prevent workplace transmission, preventive guidance in this area will continue to rapidly change (see also **Testing: AIDS**).

One other area of risk for biological hazards concerns exposures to microorganisms used during biomedical research. Such research may involve direct work with highly infectious organisms (e.g., rabies) or work with animals infected with such organisms. Special procedures are required.

## Work with Animals

People who work with animals may develop infectious diseases transmitted from the animals. This risk may apply only in certain regions or from exposure to certain animals. For example, shepherds, farmers, and hunters in the Southwest may be exposed to plague. Farmers, meatpackers, and veterinarians may develop brucellosis from exposure to infected livestock. Tuleremia and leptospirosis may be transmitted from infected wild animals and anthrax from infected sheep. Usually, individual risks of infection are quite low and may be prevented through common precautions (e.g., protective clothing when handling potentially infectious meat). More recently, Lyme Disease has been recognized as a problem for outdoor workers who may be exposed to infected ticks in areas where the disease is endemic.

## Other Biological Hazards

There are a few other notable biological hazards. Histoplasma is a fungus commonly found in moist soils or in areas with bird and bat droppings. Disturbance of the soil by bulldozing or other activity may transmit the illness. Occasionally, epidemics occur among construction crews. Sporothrix is a mold found on various plants which may infect gardeners and other workers handling the plants. Legonella is a bacteria commonly found in soil and water. Water-filled cooling systems containing the bacteria occasionally lead to occupational transmission. Occasional large outbreaks may occur in a workplace when the legonella is spread through the building by a ventilation system or some other means.

*See also* Appendix I: OSHA Regional Offices; Law in the Workplace; Testing: AIDS.

## Bibliography

Centers for Disease Control. (1990). Protection against viral hepatitis. *Morbidity and Mortality Weekly Report*, 39:1–25.

Department of Health and Human Services. (1989, February) Guidelines for prevention of transmission of human immunodeficiency virus and Hepatitis B Virus to health care and public safety workers.

Department of Labor and Department of Health and Human Services. (1987, October 19). Joint advisory notice: Protection against occupational exposure to Hepatitis B Virus (HBV) and Human Immunodeficiency Virus (HIV).

Rutstein, D., Mullan, R., Frazier, T., Halperin, W., Melius, J., & Sestito, J. (1983), Sentinel health events (occupational): A basis for physician recognition and public health surveillance. *American Journal of Public Health*, 73:1054–62.

—JAMES M. MELIUS

# WORK HAZARDS: CHEMICAL

Chemical work hazards affect almost all U.S. workers, from those employed at oil refineries and gas stations, who may be exposed to gasoline vapors containing the cancer-causing agent benzene, to office workers, who may be exposed to asbestos dust and solvent vapors from many different writing, correcting, and cleaning products. Virtually all U.S. industrial workers, from professional and technical to custodial employees, are exposed to the chemical hazards of their industry. Farm workers are exposed to hazardous pesticides, while firefighters, hazardous waste workers, and other emergency response personnel are exposed to a chemical stew of toxic, often unknown or poorly defined materials.

In response to public awareness of these health and safety hazards, federal, state, and local legislatures have passed a variety of laws and regulations to protect our workplaces and communities. As a result, many Americans are now finding employment and choosing careers as occupational and environmental health and safety specialists, both in private companies and public agencies. Over 700,000 persons were employed in these specialties in the U.S. in 1987, with an estimated need for 121,000 more professional persons (U.S. Department of Health and Human Services, 1988).

## Relationship to Work

Below are brief summaries of the health and safety effects of a number of chemical hazards commonly experienced on jobs in the U.S. as well as some of the industries in which they may be encountered (see Figure 1).

**Acids and Caustics.** These widely used industrial chemicals include sulfuric, hydrochloric, hydrofluoric, nitric, chromic, and various organic acids, and the two major caustics (also called alkalis): sodium hydroxide and potassium hydroxide. Commonly these are liquids, although the two alkalis may be encountered in solid, pellet form. Human exposure occurs through breathing in acid or alkaline vapors and mists, and direct contact with the liquids or solids.

# Figure 1. Selected Chemical Hazards in the Workplace

| Hazard | Substance | Industrial Sources | Health Effects | Control Measures |
|---|---|---|---|---|
| Acids | Sulfuric, hydrochloric, nitric, chromic, organic acids. | Manufacturing of fertilizers, textiles, leathers, paints and pigments, electroplating and metallizing processes. | Short term: irritation of skin, eyes, nose and throat; coughing, shortness of breath, chest tightness, fluid in lungs, and even death. Splashes may cause severe eye damage and blindness. Long term: skin and respiratory sensitization, skin ulcers, erosion of tooth enamel, chronic lung disease. | Substitution of weaker acids; enclosed operations; properly selected protective clothing, safety goggles, respirators; proper storage in chemically resistant containers, and safe transfer methods. |
| Caustics | Sodium and potassium hydroxides. | Production of soaps, detergents, dyes, pulp and paper, pharmaceuticals, mercerized cotton, as well as food processing and printing processes. | Similar to acids; in contrast to acids, however, caustics are often not felt immediately and cause more severe damage. | Similar to acids, above. |
| Dust and Fibers | From asbestos, coal, sugar cane, wood, talc, cotton, grain, moldy hay, vermiculite, bird and animal dander, silica, and detergent enzymes. | Agriculture, livestock, coal mining, home and building construction, textiles, woodworking, clothes laundering, and granite cutting. | Respiratory diseases like occupational asthma, hypersensitivity pneumonitis, and pneumoconiosis depending on type of dust or fiber. These diseases may take 5-15 years to develop and often result in disability and death. | Lowering or eliminating dust exposure by such protective measures as local exhaust ventilation with collection filter to prevent discharge into the atmosphere, use of vacuum machines with special HEPA filters, proper protective clothing and fit-tested respirators with proper cartridges. |
| Gases: Simple Asphyxiants | Nitrogen, methane, carbon dioxide, helium. | Confined spaces such as silos, sewers, storage tanks; frequently affects farm utility, refinery and chemical workers. | Mild overexposure: headaches, dizziness, nausea, weakness. Severe overexposure: rapid onset of symptoms for mild overexposure followed by sudden weakness, unconsciousness and frequently death. | All enclosed and confined space entry OSHA-mandated safety procedures must be followed, such as: persons with proper rescue training stationed outside, use of respirators, safety harnesses with lines attached to outside person, permit entry system be instituted, all affected personnel trained in hazards of work. |
| Chemical | Carbon monoxide. | Work near internal combustion engines, gas or oil-fired heating processes. | | |
| | Hydrogen cyanide. | Electroplating operations, plastic production and metallurgy; fumigants in agricultural operations. | | |
| Irritant | Chlorine: chemical and paper industries and for waterpurification; sulfur dioxide: bleaching of paper, by-product of coal and oil burning and smelter processes. Nitrogen oxides: welding, chemical and fertilizer industries. Ozone: welding, common disinfectant and industrial bleach. | | Cause irritation and burns of lining that may eventually result in bronchitis and emphysema. In more severe cases, it may cause a fatal condition called pulmonary edema. | Exhaust ventilation systems designed to the particular source of the gas; individually fit respirators; appropriate protective clothing and eye protection. |
| Metals | Lead: metallic lead, and lead compounds. | Manufacture of lead storage batteries, paints, pottery glaze; foundries; gun firing ranges. | Gastrointestinal disorders, anemia, nerve and muscle weakness, kidney disease, and birth defects. Early symptoms: fatigue, irritability, constipation, and slight muscle weakness of wrists and fingers. Later: insomnia, impaired concentration, and memory problems. | Plant ventilation and hygiene, including regular removal of lead dust, clean eating areas, shower and washing facilities, protective clothing and respirators. OSHA mandates that exposed workers receive blood tests at least every six months, and annual medical exams if blood lead levels exceed prescribed values. |
| | Chromium compounds. | Chrome plating, stainless steel alloys, leather tanning, photography, paints, dyes, textiles, rubber and inks. | Irritation to the eyes, nose and throat. Chronic exposure: frequent nosebleeds, nasal ulceration, occupational asthma, dermatitis and ulceration of the skin. | Good local exhaust vetilation, protective clothing, respirators, and work designed to limit skin contact. |

* Other hazards are discussed in the article including solvents, pesticides, and "tight building syndrome."

Acids are used in the manufacturing of fertilizers, textiles, leathers, paints and pigments, and in a variety of electroplating and metallizing processes. Caustics are used in the production of soaps, detergents, bleaches, dyes, pulp and paper, pharmaceuticals, and mercerized cotton, as well as in food processing and various printing processes.

The main health effects of short-term exposures to acids are irritation of the skin and the moist tissues of the eyes, nose, and throat, as well as respiratory effects, including coughing, shortness of breath, chest tightness, fluid in the lungs (pulmonary edema), and, at very high concentrations, death. Splashes of acids such as nitric and sulfuric can cause severe eye damage, permanent impairment, and blindness.

Alkalis cause similar types of short-term effects. But unlike acids, caustics on the skin are often not felt immediately and cause more severe damage. Caustics on the skin can cause severe, painful destruction of skin tissue, and in the eyes can cause disintegration of the tissue lining the eyes and opacities of the cornea.

The long-term effects of acids include skin and respiratory sensitization, skin ulcers, erosion of tooth enamel, and, in the case of nitric acid, a serious chronic lung disease. Chronic exposures to caustics do not appear to affect mortality, but can cause vision impairment (Harrison, 1990).

Most of the acids and caustics listed above have limits of exposure in air over an eight-hour day, called Permissible Exposure Levels, set by the federal Occupational Safety and Health Administration (OSHA) (U.S. Department of Labor, 1989a). Control measures for acid and alkaline vapors or mists include substitution of weaker for stronger acids and caustics when possible, fully or partially enclosed operations, nonreactive plastic or other chips floating on liquid surfaces to reduce splashes, foaming and vapor levels, properly selected protective clothing and safety goggles, and individually fit-tested respirators. Proper storage in chemically resistant containers and use of safe transfer procedures to other containers are important as well.

**Dusts and Fibers.** Dust diseases such as silicosis, asbestosis, and coal miner's black lung are among the oldest known occupational diseases. Toxic workplace dusts and fibers include asbestos dust, bird and animal dander, coal dust, cotton dust, detergent enzyme dust, fiberglass, grain dusts, moldy hay and sugar cane, crystalline silica dust, talc, vermiculite, several wood dusts (including California redwood and western red cedar), as well as many metal fumes (Sheppard, Hughson, & Shellito, 1990; Wegman & Christiani, 1988). Affected industries include agriculture, livestock, home and building construction, coal mining, granite cutting, textiles, and woodworking and clothes laundering. Also large numbers of clerical, professional, and managerial employees are exposed to asbestos dust in office buildings.

Depending on the particular dusts and/or fibers they inhale, exposed workers may develop one or more of the following major types of respiratory disease: occupational asthma, hypersensitivity pneumonitis, or a chronic dust disease called a pneumoconiosis.

Occupational asthma is a narrowing and partial obstruction of the airways leading to the lungs, causing wheezing, chest tightness, and/or severe coughing. Clinically occupational asthma is identical to asthma not of occupational origin. It can be caused by animal dander and excreta, graindust, dusts from redwood and western red cedar, as well as by gases and vapors from soldering flux and tolvene di-ioscyanate (TDI, used in making polyurethane foam). Diagnosis of the disease usually involves comparison of lung function tests before and after a workshift, and a detailed occupational history. Bronchodilators are customarily used for treatment of asthma attacks, whatever their origin. But over the long-term, prevention requires a dramatic decrease in worker exposure levels. In some cases of allergic response, job transfer may be necessary.

In contrast to occupational asthma, which affects the airways to the lungs, hypersensitivity pneumonitis is an immunological response involving the air sacs and the small airways of the lungs, i.e., the lower rather than mid-respiratory system. Symptoms include shortness of breath and a dry cough, but not wheezing (Wegman & Christiani, 1988). They are caused by bacterial and fungal growths on dusts and fibers of bird, animal, and agricultural origin, and give rise to diseases with such unusual names as Mushroom Worker's Lung, Bird Breeder's Lung, Paprika Splitter's Lung, Furrier's Lung, and Fishmeal Worker's Lung. While reduction in dust and fiber levels is desirable, effective prevention depends primarily on eliminating or modifying the conditions which give rise to the bacterial and fungal growth. Pneumoconioses are chronic lung diseases usually caused by long-term exposure to certain dusts and fibers, such as asbestos dust, crystalline silica dust, coal dust, fiberglass, talc, and vermiculite. These diseases are slow to develop, taking 5 to 15 years before symptoms appear and resulting often in disability and death.

X-rays, lung function tests, and clinical symptoms follow patterns particular to the type of dust exposure. Asbestosis, caused by asbestos dust, is the most widespread of the pneumoconioses, affecting not only asbestos manufacturing and construction workers, but office and maintenance workers in the many buildings containing asbestos. Shortness of breath and dry, nonproductive cough are early symptoms of the disease. There is no effective treatment for asbestosis. Continued exposure can and has resulted in disability and death among asbestos workers. If exposure ceases or is sharply reduced, the progress of the disease may be halted, or the disease may progress more slowly

(Sheppard, Hughson, & Shellito, 1990). Asbestos dust can also cause lung cancer and mesothelioma, a cancer of the lining of the chest or abdominal cavities.

In part due to the gravity of the above diseases and the widespread population exposure, the Environmental Protection Agency has decided to phase out most uses of asbestos by 1993 (U.S. Environmental Protection Agency, l989). Other protective measures include local exhaust ventilation with collection filter to prevent discharge into the atmosphere, wet working of asbestos to reduce release of fibers, regular inspection and maintenance of areas containing asbestos, use of vacuum machines with special HEPA (high efficiency particulate air) filters, and selection of proper protective clothing and individually fit-tested respirators with cartridges specifically designated and color-coded (magenta or purple) for asbestos use.

**Gases**. There are two major classes of toxic gases: asphyxiant gases, which can cause suffocation, and irritant gases, which can irritate and damage the respiratory tract as well as the skin and eyes (Frumkin & Melius, l988).

*Asphyxiant gases* can cause harm either by simply displacing the oxygen in the air (called simple asphyxiants) or by chemical reactions in the body which interfere with the uptake of oxygen by the blood or by cells (called chemical asphyxiants). Nitrogen gas, carbon dioxide, methane, and helium gas are all examples of simple asphyxiants; carbon monoxide and hydrogen cyanide gas are the two most common examples of chemical asphyxiants.

Simple asphyxiants are often encountered in entering enclosed or confined spaces, such as silos, storage tanks, sewers, and utility manholes, and thus frequently affect farm, utility, refinery, and chemical workers. The chemical asphyxicant carbon monoxide, which blocks oxygen uptake in the blood by combining with hemogloblin in the blood cells, is frequently encountered by those who work with or near internal combustion engines or gas or oil-fired heating processes. Truck drivers, bridge and tunnel operations workers, metal foundry workers, steel mill and coke oven workers, and clay and pottery workers are all subject to carbon monoxide toxicity. Cyanide solutions are commonly used in electroplating operations, usually in the less dangerous form of potassium ferricyanide solutions, but if the acids commonly used in other electroplating operations accidently become mixed with the ferricyanides, toxic hydrogen cyanide gas (also called prussic acid) is released. Cyanides are also used in plastic production and metallurgy and as fumigants in agricultural and horticultural operations.

Early symptoms of mild carbon monoxide and hydrogen cyanide overexposure are headaches, dizziness, nausea, and weakness, and symptoms of severe overexposure can have a sudden onset and prevent safe exit. A specific antidote exists for cyanide poisoning. In cases of carbon monoxide poisoning, oxygen therapy is used.

For simple asphyxiant gases, rapid onset of symptoms followed by sudden weakness and unconsciousness frequently cause fatalities. All enclosed and confined space entry OSHA-mandated safety procedures must be followed: a person or persons with proper rescue training and equipment be stationed outside the space, supplied air respirators be provided and used, safety harnesses or belts be provided and attached to lines going to the outside person, a permit entry system be instituted, and all affected personnel be trained in the hazards of such work (U.S. Department of Labor, 1989b).

*Irritant gases* are primarily respiratory tract hazards. They dissolve in the moist lining of the respiratory system, and the site of action and severity of their effects depends on the extent of their solubility in water, the main constituent of the respiratory fluids. Widely used gases with high water solubility, such as ammonia and hydrogen chloride, dissolve mainly in the upper respiratory system, forming alkaline acid solutions. These solutions can irritate and burn the lining of the nasal passage and throat, as well as irritate the eyes. Moderately soluble gases such as chlorine and sulfur dioxide cause both upper respiratory tract irritation and burns, as well as narrowing of the bronchial airways. Irritation from short-term, lower levels of exposure can cause greater harm and result eventually in cases of bronchitis and emphysema. Chlorine is widely used in the chemical and paper industries and for water purification; sulfur dioxide is used as a fumigant and disinfectant in the bleaching of paper, and is a by-product of coal and oil burning and smelter processes.

Irritants of low solubility are the most dangerous, since they can penetrate deep into the respiratory tract before dissolving and damaging delicate air sacs and bronchioles. Often symptoms of chest tightness and wheezing don't develop until 6 to 24 hours after exposure. The irritation and burns cause fluid to ooze into this region, causing the dangerous, often fatal condition call pulmonary edema (also known as dry land drowning). Later in these cases, pneumonia can also develop. Both ozone and nitrogen oxides are generated in welding fumes, and thus exposures in industrial environments are common. Ozone is a common disinfectant and industrial bleach; nitrogen oxides are used in fertilizer and other chemical industries.

Controls for all types of irritant gases involve use of exhaust ventilation systems designed and adapted specifically to the particular source of the gas. Also, use of individually fit respirators with proper cartridge types and properly selected protective clothing and eye protection is appropriate for occasional or temporary exposure situations.

**Metals**. Except for elemental mercury, all pure metals are solids at room temperatures and atmospheric pressures. Metals are often used commercially in alloys with other metals, and in organic compounds which alter their physical and chemical characteristics and hence their toxicity.

Metals served as an important technological basis of modern industry, although in recent decades their costs of production, their limited reserves, and their environmental toxicities have seen them replaced in part by plastics and other materials. Nevertheless, metals are still widely used in building construction, airplane and automobile production, electrical parts and machinery, the machine tool industry, and the semiconductor industry, as well as in paints and pigments. Metal mining, smelting, and production also contribute significantly to workplace injuries and illness in the U.S.

In industrial situations, metals usually enter the body through inhalation, thus processes involving heat, such as metal smelting and welding, present greater worker exposure risks. Metals also can cause irritation and sensitization upon skin contact.

Metals cause a wide range of human health effects, including neurological disorders (manganese, mercury), kidney disorders (cadmium, inorganic lead), cancers of the respiratory system (arsenic, chromium), other lung diseases (beryllium, cadmium), birth defects (lead, organic mercury), and dermatitis (chromium, nickel). In most cases, the health effects of metals are chronic, due to long-term exposures, with the exceptions of pulmonary edema from cadmium welding and metal fume fever from zinc and galvanized metal welding, a flu-like disease with onset 8 to 12 hours after exposure.

Because of the complex individual toxicities of the various metals, further discussion about their health effects must focus on specific metals, such as lead and chromium, discussed below. For further information about these and other metals, see Hammond & Beliles (1982) and Lewis (1988).

*Lead* exposure is widespread in the workplace and general environment. It is used in lead storage batteries, metal pipe and electrical connections, paints, and pottery glaze, and is still emitted into the general environment, albeit at lower levels, through automobile exhaust fumes. Automobile polishers and grinders, foundry workers, and employees at gun firing ranges can also receive heavy exposures.

Metallic lead or inorganic lead compounds (i.e., compounds not containing carbon) can cause gastro-intestinal disorders, anemia, nerve and muscle weakness, kidney disease, and birth defects. Early symptoms of chronic lead overexposure are deceptively mild and nonspecific, including fatigue, irritability, constipation, and slight muscle weakness of the wrists and fingers. If exposure continues, insomnia, impaired concentration, and memory problems may develop. In cases of lead poisoning, best detected by blood lead measurements, medical chelation therapy is available.

The key to prevention of lead exposure is plant ventilation and hygiene, including regular cleanup and removal of lead dust, clean eating areas, proper shower and washing facilities, and appropriate protective clothing and respirators. Also, under the OSHA lead standard, exposed workers must receive blood tests at least once every six months, and annual medical exams if blood lead levels exceed prescribed values (U.S. Department of Labor, 1978).

*Chromium* compounds are used in chrome plating, stainless steel alloys, leather tanning, and photography, and as pigments and preservatives in paints, dyes, textiles, rubber, and inks. Chromium compounds are quite irritating to the eyes, nose, and throat, and chronic exposure can result in dermatitis and ulceration of the skin, especially on the hands and forearms. Chronic exposure and consequent irritation of the moist lining of the nostrils can result in frequent nosebleeds, nasal ulceration, and eventually perforation of the nasal septum, i.e., a hole in the cartilage separating the two nostrils. Also irritation of the respiratory tract can give rise to occupational asthma.

Chromium in its hexavalent state can cause lung cancer in humans. Chromic acid and the various types of chromates are in this hexavalent state, and thus are carcinogenic. These more hazardous chromium compounds are used in electroplating (chromic acid mists), leather tanning, and the photographic industry. Also some chromates are used as pigments in paints and inks, and thus cause hazardous exposures in the paint, textile, glass, and rubber industries and in printing and lithography.

Control measures for chromium compounds include good local exhaust ventilation, protective clothing, and full-face respiratory and process design to limit skin contact. While all exposures must meet mandated OSHA levels, the goal when dealing with potentially carcinogenic hexavalent chromium compounds is to eliminate all unnecessary exposures.

**Solvents.** Solvents are found in virtually every industrial plant in the U.S., large or small, as well as in most small businesses, stores, and homes. There are several tens of thousands of commercial solvent preparations available, and almost all of them are liquids at room temperatures and atmospheric pressures. Their main route of entry into the body is by inhalation of the solvent vapors, and to a lesser extent through skin contact.

In industry, solvents are used to clean grease and films off metals, often in large vapor degreasing units. They are used in the extraction of fats and oils in the food processing industry. They are a major constituent of paints, inks, lacquers, glues, and epoxies, where they are used to transfer thin layers of pigments or chemicals onto various surfaces. They are used as constituents in chemical reactions by the chemical industry, and to dissolve grease spots and other stains in the dry cleaning industry and in home spot removers.

Solvents cause a wide variety of acute and chronic health effects. Virtually all solvents cause central nervous system depression and dermatitis. The former is a generalized nonspecific depression of the central nervous system, with characteristic early symptoms of headache, dizziness, and nausea, and later symptoms of slurred speech, drowsiness, unconsciousness, and, eventually, death, if heavy exposure continues. The dermatitis is caused by defatting of the surface layer of the skin by action of the solvent and subsequent skin irritation. In view of these universal hazards, there can be no such thing as a "safety solvent." There are only relatively more or less hazardous solvents, chosen to minimize the risks for a particular workplace operation.

In addition to these hazards, the vast majority of solvents present fire and explosion hazards. The only exceptions are two classes of solvents, the chlorinated hydrocarbons and the chlorofluorocarbons (CFC's). The former are chlorine-containing solvents such as carbon tetrachloride, trichlorethylene (TCE), and methylene chloride; the latter solvents contain both chlorine and fluorine and are commonly called Freons. The chlorinated hydrocarbons were developed in part to prevent many of the disastrous fires which had long plagued U.S. businesses and industries.

Various particular solvents present a wide variety of other health and safety hazards (Rosenberg, 1990a). These include eye, nose, and throat irritation (acetone and phenol); liver disorders (carbon tetrachloride); kidney disorders (toluene); muscle weakness in the limbs (n-hexane); and neurotoxicity (acrylamide and carbon di- sulfide). The only solvent which has been proven to cause cancer is benzene, which causes leukemia, but several chlorinated hydrocarbons, such as TCE and perchlorethylene have been found to cause cancers in animals and hence must be treated as suspect human carcinogens (Frumkin & Levy, 1988). Finally, several solvents such as various Freons, toluene, and trichlorethane have been shown to cause cardiac sensitization in some individuals, which can give rise to irregular heat rhythms and occasionally to heart failure and sudden death.

A variety of engineering controls can eliminate or greatly reduce solvent exposures: enclosure of hazardous processes, good local exhaust ventilation near the source of the solvent vapors, substitution of water-based for solvent-based paints, and other such substitutions of less toxic for more toxic solvents. Special attention should be paid to eliminating sources of ignition when using flammable solvents, such as elimination of flame-heated stoves, no welding or smoking near solvents, and electrical grounding of metal containers when pouring solvents to prevent sparking from static electricity.

**Pesticides.** Over 1,200 chemical compounds, marketed in over 30,000 formulations, are used as pesticides in the U.S. Vast quantities are used, representing 35%–45% of the total world supply of pesticides (Rosenberg, 1988b). Farm workers and pesticide manufacturing workers have the greatest exposures to these chemicals, but transportation workers, pesticide applicators, horticulturists, and gardeners have high workplace exposures as well.

Most acute cases of pesticide poisoning are due to organophosphate (such as Parathion) and carbonate overexposures (such as Carbaryl). Symptoms include fatigue, headache, dizziness, nausea, blurred vision, stomach cramps, and diarrhea, and, in severe cases, unconsciousness and death.

Long-term effects of such overexposure include dermatitis, anxiety, mood swings, and impaired memory and concentration. Because many of the long-term effects of overexposure present as nonspecific neurological symptoms, clinical measurements are necessary to confirm these pesticide poisonings, namely plasma or red blood cell cholinesterase levels. Control measures include observation of recommended field re-entry times after spraying, protective clothing where appropriate to reduce skin contact, and routine medical surveillance (Coye & Fenske, 1988).

**"Tight Building Syndrome."** This is a relatively new health and safety problem which first appeared in the U.S. during the late 1970s and the 1980s. It arises in sealed or poorly ventilated offices and other public buildings in which a large percentage of the indoor air is recirculated (to reduce heating costs in the winter and cooling costs in the summer) while only a small quantity of outdoor air is let in.

The symptoms are often those of other common, everyday ailments: eye irritation, sinus congestion, headaches, drowsiness, unpleasant odors, and, occasionally, chest tightness, sneezing, dermatitis, and difficulty in wearing contact lenses. Some of the characteristics which may be indicators of tight building syndrome are the symptoms get worse during the course of workdays, they tend to go away when people leave the building, and/or they persist when pollen counts get low. In trying to determine whether the syndrome is present, health and safety professionals and concerned office employees often distribute questionnaires to find out if the above characteristics are present and/or if the outbreak is localized or widespread.

The National Institute for Occupational Safety and Health, in studying over 400 reports of tight building syndrome in the U.S., found that over half (52%) were caused by inadequate ventilation, 17% by contamination from inside the building, 11% by contamination from outside the building, 5% by microbiological contamination, 3% by contamination from building fabrics such as rugs and furniture, and 12% were of unknown origin (NIOSH, 1987).

Inadequate ventilation could be due to too little outside air (the current recommended building standard by ASHRAE, the American Society of Heating, Refrigeration and Air-Conditioning Engineers, is 20 cubic feet of fresh air per minute per person), poor unbalanced air circulation within the building (must be adjusted by building staff), inadequate or no maintenance of building air circulation systems (air ducts clogged with dirt, air filters not regularly changed), and/or blocking of air intake or exhaust ducts or poor air circulation due to office partitions and furniture. Indoor sources of air contamination include methyl alcohol and ammonia for various copying machines, improperly applied pesticides, improperly diluted rug and floor cleaners, and, of course, cigarette smoke. Outside sources of contamination include motor vehicle exhaust from bus stops or indoor parking garages, near construction or renovation work, and placement of air exhaust vents physically near air intake vents.

Indoor air problems due to bacteria, viruses, and fungi may cause hypersensitivity pneumonitis and diseases such as Legionnaire's Disease. Common sources of contamination are microbial contamination in ventilation systems, such as that due to standing pools of water in these systems, and water damage to carpets and furnishings which can breed such contamination. Finally, formaldehyde gas emitted from plastic rugs, curtains, and office furniture, especially new ones, often causes eye, nose, and throat irritation. Also urea-formaldehyde insulation, plywood, and some common glues and adhesives can cause such problems.

Judicious use of questionnaires and building surveys, especially with the assistance of an experienced industrial hygienist, can reduce or eliminate many indoor air quality problems. Also, if other remedies fail or are inadequate, increased intake of fresh outdoor air will generally reduce most indoor air problems, although at the cost of increased fuel bills in the winter and electricity bills for air conditioning in the summer.

## Applications

Try to become better informed about the potential hazards you face on the job. If you are concerned that you may be working with a dangerous chemical, ask your employer for the Material Safety Data Sheet (MSDS) on that chemical. You are entitled by law to such information under the Hazard Communication Standard of the federal Occupational Safety and Health Act (OSHA). If you live in

a state or territory with its own approved state OSHA plan and you are covered by that plan—e.g., if you are a state or local public employee—you are also protected by the Hazard Communication Standard. Finally, many states and localities have their own Right-to-Know laws, which may give you added protection or information.

If you believe that you or other employees are working in an unsafe work situation, or being unnecessarily exposed to a hazardous material, or are not receiving proper protective equipment, contact members of the workplace health and safety committee, if there is one. Depending on your place of employment, this might be a union health and safety committee, a joint labor-management committee, or a management health and safety committee. If there is no committee in your place of work, speak to your supervisor or employer about the problem.

If the problem continues or if you face imminent danger of serious injury, you may wish to request an inspection by a representative of the Occupational Safety and Health Administration or the agency which administers your state OSHA plan. The location and telephone number of your nearest OSHA office is written on the OSHA placard which must be posted in every covered workplace. If you wish, you may request that your name be withheld during the inspection; OSHA will honor such a request. Also remember that it is a violation of the OSHA law for anyone to be punished by their employer for exercising their rights under this law.

You may also wish to consult local public health organizations about your health and safety concerns and ask for their advice and assistance. For example, in many parts of the U.S., there are local Committees for Occupational Safety and Health (often called COSH groups), and they assist employees with health and safety problems at no cost to the individuals.

Finally, if you believe you are suffering possible symptoms of occupational illness consult your personal physician or, better yet, an occupational safety and health clinic. Such clinics, which currently exist in only 26 states, are experienced in dealing with health and safety problems, often far more so than many local physicians.

*See also* Appendix I: OSHA Regional Offices; COSH Groups; Law in the Workplace; Whistleblowing.

## Bibliography

Coye, M.J., & Fenske, R. (1988). Agricultural workers. In Levy, B.S., & Wegman, D.H. (Eds.), *Occupational health: Recognizing and preventing work-related diseases* (pp. 517-19). Boston: Little, Brown.
Frumkin, H., & Melius, J. (1988). Toxins and their effects. In Levy, B.S., & Wegman, D.H. (Eds.), *Occupational health: Recognizing and preventing work-related diseases* (pp. 194–96, 580–84). Boston: Little, Brown.

Frumkin, W., & Levy, B.S. (1988) Carcinogens. In Levy, B.S., & Wegman, D.H. (Eds.), *Occupational health: Recognizing and preventing work-related diseases* (pp. 22–23). Boston: Little, Brown.

Hammond, P.B., & Beliles, R.P. (1982). Metals. In Doull, J., Klaassen, C.D., &Amdur, M.O. *Toxicology: The basic science of poisons.* 2nd ed. (pp. 409–67). New York: Macmillan Co.

Harrison, R.J. (1990). Chemicals. In LaDou, J. (Ed.) *Occupational medicine* (pp. 327–31). Norwalk, CT: Appleton and Lange.

LaDou, J. (Ed.) (1990). *Occupational medicine.* Norwalk, CT: Appleton and Lange.
A useful reference and text on occupational injuries, illnesses, and exposures. Illnesses are discussed by body system, and exposures by types of chemical hazard.

Levy, B.S., & Wegman, D.H. (Eds.) (1988). *Occupational health: Recognizing and preventing work-related diseases.* 2nd ed. Boston: Little, Brown and Co. An excellent textbook on recognizing and preventing occupational diseases, which does a good job of placing these tasks in their social context. Sections on labor unions, ethics, and problems of women, minority, and Third World workers.

Lewis, R. (1988). Metals. In LaDou, J. (Ed.) (1990). *Occupational medicine* (pp. 297–326). Norwalk, CT: Appleton and Lange.

National Institute for Occupational Safety and Health (NIOSH), Hazard Evaluations and Technical Assistance Branch. (1987). *Guidance for indoor air quality investigations.* Cincinnati: NIOSH, pp. 4–7.

Proctor, N.H., Hughes, J.P., & Fischman, M.L. (1988). *Chemical hazards in the workplace.* 2nd ed. Philadelphia: J.B. Lippincott. An excellent survey of hundreds of chemicals, with emphases on toxicology, diagnoses of work-relatedness, and medical treatments.

Rosenberg, J. (1990a). Solvents. In LaDou, J. (Ed.), *Occupational medicine* (pp. 363–70). Norwalk, CT: Appleton and Lange.

Rosenberg, J. (1990b). Pesticides. In LaDou, J. (Ed.), *Occupational medicine.* (p. 401). Norwalk, CT: Appleton and Lange.

Sheppard, D., Hughson, W.G., & Shellito, J. (1990). Occupational lung diseases. In LaDou, J. (Ed.), *Occupational medicine* (pp. 221–36). Norwalk, CT: Appleton and Lange.

U.S. Department of Health and Human Services. Bureau of Health Professions. (1988). *Evaluating the environmental health workforce* (pp. 21–22). Washington, DC: U.S. Department of Health and Human Services.

U.S. Department of Labor, Occupational Safety and Health Administration. (1978). *Federal register,* 29, November 14, pp. 52952–53014.

U.S. Department of Labor, Occupational Safety and Health Administration. (1989a). *Air contaminants - permissible exposure limits* (Title 29 CFR Part 1910.1000), Publication NO. OSHA 3112. Washington, DC: U.S. Department of Labor.

U.S. Department of Labor, Occupational Safety and Health Administration. (1989b). *Permit required confined spaces* (Title 29 CFR Part l910.146) (proposed).

U.S. Environmental Protection Agency. (1989). *Federal register,* 54, July 12, p. 29460.

Wegman, D.H., & Christiani, D.C. (1988). Respiratory Disorders. In Levy, B.S., & Wegman, D.H. (Eds.), *Occupational health: Recognizing and preventing work-related diseases* (pp. 319–44). Boston: Little, Brown.

—DAVID KOTELCHUCK

## WORK HAZARDS: ERGONOMIC

Ergonomics can be operationally defined as the science of designing jobs to match the capabilities and expectations of workers. It is concerned with studying work in order to understand and explain the relationships that exist among people, their work environment, jobs demands (physical and mental), and work methods. A fundamental principle of ergonomics is that all types of work produce stress. As long as stresses are kept within reasonable limits, work performance will be satisfactory and the worker's health and well-being will be maintained. However, if work stresses are excessive, undesirable outcomes may occur in the form of errors, accidents, injuries, or a decrement in physical or mental health.

### Relationship to Work

The mission of an ergonomics program is to establish a safe work environment by designing facilities, furniture, machines, tools, and job demands to be compatible with such workers attributes as size, physical fitness and strength, sensory capabilities (e.g., sight, touch, hearing), and information processing capacity. This is a challenge because these attributes vary considerably among the working population. A successful ergonomics program should design jobs to accommodate human variability, thus simultaneously improving worker health while enhancing productivity.

Because it is an interdisciplinary science, people who pursue careers in ergonomics can have formal training in a number of areas, including psychology, physiology, biomechanics, engineering, and health sciences. Ergonomists frequently work in teams to assure that all the disciplines needed to solve a problem are available.

### Application

Ergonomic principles can be applied to a broad spectrum of occupational safety and health problems. A few examples are presented below.

**Prevention of Accidents**. The purpose of machine guarding is to prevent a worker from accidentally making contact with moving parts which can cause serious injuries (e.g., lacerations, amputations, crushed bones) or death. Machine guards must be designed so that workers can perform their jobs using smooth, non-awkward, and time-efficient motions. This eliminates the likelihood that the guard will be removed or bypassed. This is particularly important when workers are paid under incentive wage plans. Ergonomic guard design may also reduce the likelihood of disorders such as tendinitis and carpal tunnel syndrome.

**Prevention of Human Error.** People who operate complex systems (e.g., airplane pilots, power plant operators, chemical plant operators) must monitor a large number of displays and gauges and quickly respond to both aural and visual alarms. Errors in reading displays or interpreting alarm signals can contribute to incorrect decisions and cause costly and sometimes life-threatening accidents. Control panels and alarm signals must be designed according to sound ergonomic principles to reduce the likelihood of human error.

People who work unusual shifts (e.g., nurses, firefighters, police officers, airline pilots and flight attendants, factory workers) can experience chronic fatigue that may contribute to errors and accidents. Work schedules may conflict with family demands, further increasing stress and fatigue. Ergonomists and scientists from other disciplines study the effects of shift work and develop schedules and coping mechanisms to reduce stress and fatigue (see **Jet Lag; Shift Work**).

**Prevention of Postural Fatigue.** Workers who sit for extended periods (e.g., truck drivers, garment workers, video display terminal [VDT] operators) can experience postural fatigue and back pain. The equipment and furniture used at seated work stations should be designed to minimize postural fatigue. Chairs must be adjustable in order to accommodate the size and posture preferences of different users.

Workers who must bend their backs while reaching to low or far locations (e.g., farm workers, custodial workers, automobile mechanics) are at increased risk of back pain while workers who must raise their shoulders to reach to high locations such as elevated or overhead assembly lines are at increased risk of shoulder and neck pain. Awkward postures like these can sometimes be eliminated through changes in work station layout or improvements in the design of equipment and tools (see **Posture and Body Mechanics**).

**Prevention of Heat Stress.** People who work in hot, humid environments can experience heat cramps, heat exhaustion, and other disorders (see **Work Hazards: Physical**). Ergonomists who specialize in physiology are called on to evaluate the physical demands of jobs that are performed in hot environments and to design work-rest schedules with sufficient recovery time to avoid excessive fatigue.

**Prevention of Musculoskeletal Injuries and Disorders.** Back injuries are frequently associated with jobs that require heavy lifting. Ergonomists who specialize in biomechanics analyze lifting tasks to determine stresses acting on the lower back and design lifting tasks to assure that these stresses are within safe limits (see **Low Back Pain**).

Specialists in biomechanics also evaluate repetitive, hand-intensive jobs (e.g., assembly work, keyboard work, beef and poultry jobs) to develop improved tools and work methods to reduce the risk of upper extremity repetitive trauma disorders such as bursitis, tenosynovitis, and carpal tunnel syndrome (see **Repetitive Motion Illnesses; Work Hazards: Tool Design**).

*See also* Appendix I: OSHA Regional Offices; COSH Groups; Jet Lag; Low Back Pain; Posture and Body Mechanics; Repetitive Motion Illnesses; Shift Work; Video Display Terminals; Work Hazards: Physical; Work Hazards: Tool Design.

## Bibliography

Chaffin, D.B., & Andersson, G.B.J. (1984). *Occupational biomechanics.* New York: Wiley-Interscience. A detailed presentation of the biomechanical basis of many occupational injuries and disorders. Job analysis methodologies are discussed with numerous applications of ergonomic principles to job design.

Grandjean, E. (1980). *Fitting the task to the man: An ergonomic approach.* London: Taylor and Francis, Ltd. A well-written survey text that covers all aspects of ergonomics. Chapters on work physiology and fatigue provide an excellent introduction to these topics.

Konz, S. (1990). *Work design: Industrial ergonomics.* 3rd. ed. Worthington, OH: Publishing Horizons, Inc. A comprehensive survey of industrial ergonomics, including brief coverage of industrial engineering and occupational safety and health topics.

Sanders, M., & McCormick, E. (1987). *Human factors in engineering and design.* 6th ed. New York: McGraw-Hill, Inc. This ergonomics survey text places special emphasis on the psychological aspects of human performance in work situations.

—W. MONROE KEYSERLING

# WORK HAZARDS: PHYSICAL

Physical hazards in the workplace that may cause injury or illness to workers include noise, radiation, excessive heat or cold, and vibration. These physical hazards may cause the health problem immediately (an acute health hazard) or over a longer period of days, weeks, or years (a chronic health hazard).

## Noise

Noise is unwanted sound. It is a widespread problem throughout industry and can affect the body in a number of ways. The main effect of overexposure to noise is hearing loss. Other effects of noise in the workplace include interference with communications (which may present a safety hazard), annoyance, and effects on performance. High levels of noise have also been implicated in cardiovascular diseases.

Noise-induced or sensorineural hearing loss usually takes place gradually over a period of time; the worker may not notice the hearing loss until she or he has already lost some degree of their hearing. The pattern of noise-induced hearing loss is very distinctive. Hearing is lost first in the higher frequencies (e.g., a siren or a bird singing). However, not all hearing loss is caused by noise; some hearing loss is caused by medically treatable conditions.

Noise-induced hearing loss actually damages a part of the inner ear and can not presently be treated medically. Therefore, it is important to prevent the hearing loss from occurring in the first place. This can be accomplished by:

1. Reducing the noise by either using quieter machinery, by soundproofing the machinery or the noisy area, or by building a soundproof control room or work room.
2. Working fewer hours in noisy areas so that part of the day is spent in areas with noise levels that do not produce hearing loss.
3. By using hearing protection (ear plugs or ear muffs or both). The amount of noise to which a worker can be exposed is regulated by the Occupational Safety and Health Administration (OSHA), the governmental agency that writes and enforces health and safety regulations in most workplaces.

OSHA regulations state that when workers are exposed to noise above a certain level, the employer must institute a hearing conservation program in the workplace. That noise level is 85 dBA (decibels) measured over an eight-hour workday. The hearing conservation program must include regular noise measurements to determine how high the noise level is; yearly hearing tests for workers to determine the state of their hearing; education and training about the effects of noise and how to protect the hearing; and, for workers whose hearing tests show problems, the employer must provide ear plugs or ear muffs and enforce their use. When the noise level is 90 dBA or over, all workers must be provided with ear plugs or ear muffs but the employer is first responsible for reducing the noise by using other methods of control such as quieter machinery or enclosures or soundproofing, if feasible.

In order to accurately know the level of noise present, a health and safety professional must measure the noise with a sound level meter and/or a noise dosimeter. However, there are some "rules of thumb" for judging noise level:

1. If it is necessary to speak very loudly or shout directly into the ear of a person who is standing within arm's reach, then it is possible that the legal noise limit is being exceeded.

2. If workers hear ringing or noises in their ears after a workday, it is possible that they are being overexposed to noise.
3. If workers complain that their hearing seems muffled or softer after work but then seems normal by the next morning, they may be experiencing a temporary loss of hearing that could eventually become permanent upon repeated exposure.

## Excessive Heat or Cold

Temperature extremes are common in some jobs, particularly extremes of heat. The human body is able to function well only within a very narrow temperature range which keeps the body temperature around 98.6 degrees Fahrenheit. If body temperature exceeds 2 degrees below or 3 degrees above normal, a health hazard exists.

The body cools itself by increasing the heart rate, bringing more blood to the capillaries in the surface of the skin for the air to cool, and by sweating (so that the sweat can evaporate on the skin and achieve cooling).

**Heat Stress Illnesses.** It is especially important for workers who work in the heat to know the signs of heat stress and to react promptly in an emergency.

1. *Heatstroke or Sunstroke.* This is the most serious heat illness and can kill or cripple very quickly. It usually happens when the worker is working very hard or even working at a moderate level but in extreme heat. The body cannot cool itself any longer and sweating may stop. The person may have hot dry flushed skin, confusion, fainting, high fever, or convulsions. This is an extreme medical emergency and the person must be immediately cooled down while waiting for the ambulance. This can be done by placing cool wet cloths on the body (remove clothing) or pouring some safe liquid such as water, milk, or soda over the body and then fanning so that the liquid evaporates. The higher the body temperature, the higher the death rate.
2. *Heat Cramps.* These usually occur in whatever muscles have been used to do work. Usually the person has been working in the heat for a while and has been sweating profusely. Too much salt has been lost from the body. The person with heat cramps must receive medical attention and should not just be treated indiscriminately with salt tablets.
3. *Heat Exhaustion.* The person is sweating profusely, may have pale, moist skin, and a slightly elevated temperature. While not as serious as heat stroke, heat exhaustion may be difficult to distinguish from other heat illnesses and several days of heat exhaustion may make the person more likely to get heat stroke. Medical advice should be sought.

4. *Other Heat Illnesses.* Other conditions that may occur in hot environments are heat syncope (fainting) and heat rash. As with the other heat illnesses, it is important to seek medical attention.

**Prevention of Heat Illnesses.** Heat stress illnesses can be prevented by a variety of measures that include changing the work environment to reduce the various sources of heat, by worker orientation and training, and by instituting various work practices. Work practices may include a "break-in" or acclimatization period before a worker is given a full workload in heat; a medical control program; drinking of enough cool water throughout the day to prevent losing any "water weight"; a prescribed number of rest breaks in cool areas; doing hot work in coolest parts of the day; moving hot work out of the sun into cooled spaces; working only part of the workday in hot conditions; wearing reflective aprons or clothing or ice vests; wearing less clothing; and cooling workers with fans, etc. It is not possible to list all the measures that can be used but the employer should put in place a comprehensive heat stress control program that includes measuring the heat conditions and following published standards and guidelines (see Alpaugh & Hogan, 1988).

**Cold Temperature Extremes.** The human body can take very little exposure to cold without protection. The body reacts to cold by reducing the blood flow to the skin, hands, and feet, and by shivering. Both reactions are the body's attempt to conserve body heat.

Possible cold injuries include:

1. *Frostbite.* This occurs when the hands or feet actually freeze with crystals of ice forming in the tissues and damaging them. If the affected part is not too severely damaged, it may heal but may have continuing pain, numbness, or pallor for years. The symptoms may include skin color changing to white/grayish-yellow, to reddish, and finally to black as tissue dies; pain at first and then numbness; and blistering. If the injury is severe, gangrene may set in and amputation may be necessary. *Frostnip* occurs when the face or extremities are exposed to a cold wind and causes the skin to turn white. *Trenchfoot* or *chilblains* is caused by exposure to cold and dampness. Swelling, tingling, itching, and severe pains may be followed by blistering, ulcers, and death of skin tissue.

2. *Hypothermia.* This occurs when the body loses heat faster than it can produce heat. First the temperature drops in the hands and feet. Then shivers and severe shaking begin. If heat loss continues, the person will become confused and disoriented, and coma and death can occur.

A cold stress prevention program should include medical supervision of workers; employee orientation and training; work-rest schedules with heated rest areas and enforced breaks with drinking of recommended fluids; environmental cold measurements to determine the risk and adjust work schedules accordingly; engineering controls of cold such as general and spot heating, protective padding for metal surfaces, hand warming shelters, and powered aids to reduce workload; protective clothing and equipment; and special work practice controls.

## Ionizing Radiation

Ionizing radiation includes X-rays; gamma, alpha, and beta radiation; and neutrons. Ionizing radiation is a highly penetrating radiation that can produce serious damage in any tissues of the human body. Workers may encounter ionizing radiation in the health care environment from X-ray machines and radioactive drugs; in industry where radioactive sources are used to x-ray welds and joints or to check the levels of liquids in closed tanks; in research laboratories; in nuclear power facilities; and in any manufacturing processes using radioactive materials.

This damage can range from acute effects such as skin burns, birth defects, severe radiation illness, and death to chronic, long term effects such as leukemia, cancer, and sterility. The effect of exposure to ionizing radiation depends upon the type of ionizing radiation, the amount or the dose received, and the length of time over which the person receives the dose. In addition, radioactive materials can be either an internal hazard or an external hazard. External hazards are those radioactive materials that can be hazardous even some distance away from the body, such as neutrons, gamma radiation, and X radiation (X-rays). Internal hazards are only hazardous when they get inside the body by inhalation, eating, or through broken skin, such as alpha and beta radiation. (However, beta radiation may also be an external hazard.)

The three basic principles used by radiation specialists to control exposure to the external hazards in ionizing radiation are:

1. *Distance.* The farther away from the radioactive source, the lower the exposure.

2. *Shielding.* Putting a barrier between the radioactive source and the worker. For X radiation and gamma radiation, the shielding material must be lead or concrete of various thicknesses. A quarter inch of aluminum will stop the most energetic beta particles.

3. *Time.* The less time in the radiation field, the less the exposure. Ionizing radiation can be measured with a number of different specialized meters. This is

usually done by a specially trained health and safety professional, such as a health physicist or radiation physicist. There are also personal monitoring devices called film badges that measure the ionizing radiation that a single worker receives. Film badges do nothing to protect a worker, they only measure the worker's exposure. Once the radiation hazard is measured and evaluated, the three control principles listed above can be applied to keep a worker's dose as low as possible. In any case, the exposure may not exceed federal standards.

## Non-Ionizing Radiation

Non-ionizing radiation includes infrared and ultraviolet radiation, microwaves, lasers, radiofrequency radiation, and visible radiation or lighting. Non-ionizing radiation exposures are much more common in the workplace.

Infrared radiation can cause cataracts and eyelid and skin burns. It is given off during melting and pouring of molten metals and during welding.

Ultraviolet radiation can cause eye problems, severe sunburn, and an eye injury called welder's flash. It is given off during melting and pouring of molten metals and during welding.

Microwaves can cause an intolerable rise in body temperature, burns, and cataracts, and can ignite flammable gases and vapors inside metallic containers. Microwaves are found in radar, communications systems, diathermy machines, and microwave ovens.

Radiofrequency (RF) radiation hazards are similar to those for microwaves except that RF can heat metal objects to a temperature that can cause skin burns. RF is usually used for heat sealing of plastic parts.

Lasers are potential eye hazards and potential electric shock hazards. Proper eye protection is necessary; other precautions are also needed, depending upon the use of the laser. Lasers are becoming very common in all types of applications in industry and medicine. They are used for welding parts and heat resistant metals, for communications, for surgical procedures, in chemistry, in laser scanners, and in many other places. Lasers may be visible or invisible.

Visible radiation or lighting affects quality of work and safety at work. Illumination must be bright enough for easy viewing and should be well balanced to avoid glare.

There are safety and health standards for the different categories of non-ionizing radiation and hazard control programs should be in place in workplaces where both non-ionizing and ionizing radiation occurs.

## Vibration

Vibration is transmitted into the body through the feet, the seat, or the fingers when using a mechanical hand tool or riding powered trucks or machinery. Too much vibration can do damage to the joints, bones, muscles, nerves, connective tissues, or the circulation.

A common condition caused by excessive vibration (as found during the use of pneumatic tools such as jackhammers, compressed air chisels and drills, and riveting guns) is called vibration white finger. The fingers become numb and white from loss of circulation. The condition is usually aggravated by cold on the fingers. Usually the numbness disappears but sometimes occurs in both hands and becomes so extreme that the worker must seek other types of work. Solutions include keeping the hands warm, reducing the vibration by damping or well-designed and balanced tools, aiming the air exhaust away from the hands, and medical attention to the condition when it occurs.

## Application

The worker is the best detective in finding physical hazards on her or his job. If a physical hazard is present, you can inform your supervisor or safety and health department, your union health and safety representative or business agent, or the OSHA office which covers your workplace. In some cases, a state OSHA program is in charge of health and safety in your workplace; in other cases it is the federal OSHA program.

OSHA regulations guarantee you a safe and healthy workplace; access to your own medical records; access to any air monitoring results in your workplace; protection against reprisals for complaining about health and safety issues; and the right to training and education on working with any hazards on your job.

*See also* Appendix I: OSHA Regional Offices; COSH Groups; Law in the Workplace.

## Bibliography

Alpaugh, E.L., & Hogan, T.J. (1988). Temperature extremes. In B.A. Plog (Ed.), *Fundamentals of industrial hygiene*, 3rd ed. (pp. 259–81). Chicago: National Safety Council.

Anderson, L.E. (1988). Nonionizing radiation. In B.A. Plog (Ed.), *Fundamentals of industrial hygiene*, 3rd ed. (pp. 227–57). Chicago: National Safety Council.

Cheever, C.L. (1988). Ionizing radiation. In B.A. Plog (Ed.), *Fundamentals of industrial hygiene*, 3rd ed. (pp. 205–26). Chicago: National Safety Council.

National Institute for Occupational Safety and Health (NIOSH). (1986). *Occupational exposure to hot environments, revised criteria*. Pub. No. 86–113. Washington, DC: U.S. Government Printing Office

National Safety Council. (1982). *Pocket guide to occupational health*. Chicago: National Safety Council.

National Safety Council. (1985). *Pocket guide to heat stress*. Chicago: National Safety Council.

National Safety Council. (1986). *Pocket guide to cold stress*. Chicago: National Safety Council.

Plog, B.A. (1988). Overview of industrial hygiene. In B.A. Plog (Ed.), *Fundamentals of industrial hygiene*, 3rd ed. (pp. 1–28). Chicago: National Safety Council.

Standard, J.J. (1988) Industrial noise. In B.A. Plog (Ed.), *Fundamentals of industrial hygiene*, 3rd ed. (pp. 163–203). Chicago: National Safety Council.

Suter, A.H. (1986). Hearing conservation. In E.H. Berger, J.C. Morrill, L.H. Royster, & W.D. Ward (Eds.), *Noise and hearing conservation manual* (pp. 1–18). Akron, OH: American Industrial Hygiene Association.

—BARBARA A. PLOG

# WORK HAZARDS: PSYCHOSOCIAL

Psychosocial stressors are those aspects of the organization of work and work environments that are not directly physical or biochemical, but have a direct impact on the health and well-being of workers. Most psychosocial stressors result from the workers' lack of control over work conditions and how work tasks are accomplished. This lack of control may cause workers to experience anger, frustration, powerlessness, and self-blame. These same work conditions may also under-use, under-value people's skill and training. Working under these psychosocial conditions creates a stressful work environment.

To understand the importance of psychosocial hazards, it is necessary to understand the role that work plays in people's lives. The kind of work a person does, and whether work is available at all, has an obvious economic effect on individuals and their families. Work in this society also determines social status, where people live, what resources are available to them, and the amount and quality of time available for personal life and family responsibilities. Work also occupies a central psychological role in determining people's sense of self-worth and identity. Work represents much more than a source of income and economic survival, it is a central and defining aspect of people's lives. For this reason, the importance of work and the work environment are critical to physical and emotional well-being. Psychosocial hazards that threaten the general well-being of workers and can have far-reaching consequences beyond the hours of work.

## Psychosocial Hazards

The significance of any psychosocial hazard or stressor, seen in isolation, may seem negligible. However, like exposure to chemical hazards, the impact of psychosocial hazards is cumulative and, combined with other work stressors (see **Stress**), may pose a serious health threat to workers.

**Lack of Control**. One of the main psychosocial stressors is the lack of control over the work process and the work environment. The effect of conflicting job demands is one example. Workers are expected to provide high quality, whether in production or in service, and high-quantitative productivity. These demands are often in conflict, and can prevent the worker from performing his or her work well. Being in a work situation where arbitrary orders must be carried out has a similar effect. In these situations, workers are not allowed to use their own intelligence and initiative to make the necessary changes so that appropriate levels of quality and production can be achieved. The stress created by these situations is a psychosocial hazard.

Workers must also deal with the stress caused by under-employment or a level of income that is inadequate to meet their needs, when there is no hope for advancement or when job security is in doubt. All of these factors are beyond the direct control of the individual worker and create a level of stress that represents a serious psychosocial hazard.

**Shift Work and Overtime**. The impact of shift work, especially rotating shifts, and overtime are also psychosocial hazards. Not only does shift work have a major biological impact on the body's natural circadian rhythms (see **Jet Lag; Shift Work**), it also affects people's ability to have a family or social life. Rotating shifts allow no regularly scheduled nonwork activities. Overtime, in addition to the physical stresses involved, affects the amount of time and energy available for nonwork activities, including family.

**Divisions at the Workplace**. The things that divide people in our society (racism, sexism, sexual harassment, class divisions, age discrimination) are also present in the workplace. Other divisions in the workplace include young workers and older workers, skilled and unskilled workers, and workers on different shifts. All of these divisions isolate and separate people and increase the level of stress that they experience.

**Impact of Work on Self-Esteem**. Another major psychosocial hazard results from the impact of work and work conditions on the individual's sense of self-worth. If the social norms define particular kinds of work as less important or "inferior," the people who perform this work take on negative self-images. In conversation people will say, "I'm only a secretary" or "I'm only an autoworker." These statements reflect the internalization of social stereotypes about what kinds of work, and what personal skills and values, are important (see **Self-Esteem**).

**Self-Blame**. The way that workers are treated in the workplace also has a major impact on their sense of self-worth. Being treated in a demeaning or oppressive way, has a negative impact on self-esteem and self-image. While they may complain openly about working conditions and how they are treated, psychologically many workers internalize this experience as what they really deserve and blame themselves. This self-blame is reinforced through the myth of meritocracy.

The myth of meritocracy, in its simplest form, suggests that anyone in this society can be successful if they work hard enough. Therefore, if they work hard and don't succeed, it is because of a personal failing. This myth ignores the objective reality of the conditions of people's lives, but it has a major impact on people's sense of self-blame for the negative things that happen in their lives. Diminishment of self-worth, at work and in the society, results in apathy and a sense of powerlessness.

**Impact of Work on Family Life**. One of the hidden psychosocial hazards of work is the impact it has on families. This is particularly true with the increase in the number of single-parent families, or families where both parents work. Beyond the obvious economic and status considerations, work defines the day-to-day schedules of the entire family. Getting children ready for school, or for child care, must be arranged around work schedules. If one of the family members is not working on a normal day shift, it may mean that he or she is not available to be part of normal family life. Shift work and overtime may have the same effect. Similarly, if work conditions are stressful, that stress is brought home as impatience, irritability, or anger and may also mean a greater reliance on drugs or alcohol as a way of coping with job stress.

The quality of work and the work environment and its psychosocial hazards has a major impact on every member of the family. This is particularly true when someone in the family is laid off and the family must adjust to a lower income, different family roles, disrupted schedules, and the impact of job loss on the worker directly involved.

One of the goals of a democratic society is to provide safe, satisfying employment to all workers so that they will be able to care for themselves and their families and develop their talents and abilities fully. In order to make this dream a reality, the psychosocial hazards of work must be addressed.

*See also* Appendix I: OSHA Regional Offices; COSH Groups; Jet Lag; Self-Esteem; Shift Work; Stress; Working Family Issues.

## Bibliography

Karasek, R., & Theorell, T. (1990). *Healthy work: Stress, productivity and the reconstruction of working life*. New York: Basic Books. Based on research in the United States and Sweden, the authors present a comprehensive examination of psychosocial job stressors and their impact on health and well-being. The authors also discuss how jobs can be redesigned to reduce stress and increase productivity.

Lerner, M. (1986). *Surplus powerless*. Oakland, CA: Institute for Labor and Mental Health. This book discusses the relationship between psychosocial stressors and the individual and collective experience of powerlessness and how it can be transformed.

Sennett, R., & Cobb, J. (1973). *The hidden injuries of class*. New York: Vintage Press. Sennet and Cobb examine the impact of the psychosocial hazards of work and class on the sense of worth and well-being of workers and their families.

—LEE SCHORE

## WORK HAZARDS: ROLES OF UNIONS

Union representatives, primarily elected officers, work with both their members and the employer to recognize, evaluate, and control occupational hazards. Through collective bargaining and participation on safety committees, union representatives attempt to protect their members from work hazards.

### Relationship to Work

As part of their advocacy role, unions promote legislation favorable to workplace safety. Examples of laws passed with union support include the Occupational Safety and Health Act (OSHA), Asbestos Hazard Emergency Response Act, and various state "Right to Know Laws" dealing with labeling of toxic substances. Union representatives should be familiar with these laws and standards.

Research on safety issues may be required in order to provide testimony at government hearings. For example, the Occupational Safety and Health Administration may propose lowering the permissible exposure limit for a toxic substance, such as asbestos (see **Work Hazards: Chemical**). Union representatives could give testimony as to why they agree or disagree with the proposal.

Furthermore, unions represent members' interests through collective bargaining. Specific health and safety language should be written into the labor contract. An example would read: "The Company shall provide a safe and healthful place of employment. The Company and the Union will cooperate in the continuing objective to eliminate safety and health hazards. A joint Union and Company safety and health committee shall be established to accomplish this objective."

Collaboration, not conflict, is essential. Hazard prevention should be a noncontroversial matter. Neither labor nor management should direct efforts at discovering a single, simple cause for occupational accidents or illnesses (such as poor management or employee carelessness). An adversarial approach, or one that continuously lays blame on one side, normally will not succeed in solving health and safety problems.

## Application

If you are a union member, you should expect your union representatives to implement a union health and safety policy. Their responsibility would include bargaining over safety and health conditions with your employer, providing educational classes and materials to the union members, such as fact sheets, articles, newsletters, and library resources, and participating on a committee which provides for continual interaction on safety and health issues.

Your union representative has a responsibility to ensure the company provides a safe and healthy work environment for you and your coworkers. A safety and health committee responsible for preventing, detecting, and controlling workplace hazards is one way to meet this goal.

Duties and responsibilities of the committee should be formally written into your collective bargaining agreement or the company's health and safety policy. Two committees should be established: one comprised only of union members selected or appointed by your union leadership, and a second committee comprised of company representatives and select members of the union committee.

Your union committee should include a top union officer as chair and representatives from each department, similar to the "territory" covered by local union stewards. Safety representatives should be distinct from shop stewards, since they have different training requirements and representation functions.

Union committees should:

1. Investigate all accidents.
2. Keep records on members' injuries or illnesses (computerized if possible).
3. Meet monthly to determine priorities and strategies for joint labor-management meetings (take minutes).
4. Distribute an agenda prior to the meeting.
5. Track your company's OSHA citations, safety-related lawsuits, and workers' compensation claims.
6. File grievances against the company or formal complaints with OSHA when necessary.
7. Keep up to date on workplace hazards through formal training and education programs.

Since labor and management cooperation is essential for job safety and health, your union representative should participate on a joint health and safety committee. This joint committee should be comprised of an equal number of union and management representatives with the position of chairperson rotating between management and labor.

Joint committees should:

1. Have monthly meetings and workplace inspections.
2. Compile information on job-related injuries and illnesses by department, and identify substances and conditions which may be hazardous.
3. Investigate safety violations and accidents.

Your union representatives must work with management to develop training programs on hazard prevention. Preferably, training should be provided by experts in the field and should occur on work time, at the workplace. Under certain OSHA standards, the company is required to provide training.

However, workshops and classes can also be held during nonworking hours at local union halls or nearby facilities. Utilizing instructors from the union or using the services of a university labor education program, membership education can be implemented.

Educational topics include:
1. Accident causes/hazard recognition
2. Using legal rights, emphasizing:
   a. Employer's responsibility to prevent job hazards
   b. Access to results of workplace monitoring and employee medical exams
   c. Hazard communication standard requirements to disclose identity of toxic substances
   d. Right to refuse dangerous work
3. Providing a framework for classifying hazards and developing evaluation methods for risk assessment
4. Basic toxicology: effects of various chemicals and their impact upon the body
5. Understanding technical data: such as monitoring results, material safety data sheets, and various employees' medical exams
6. Functions of a safety & health committee
7. Using the National Labor Relations Act to obtain company information related to safety and health
8. Safety and health resources: written materials, films, videos, professional organizations, and speakers
9. Evaluate educational programs by follow-up surveys

Serving on a health and safety committee is an excellent way for you to work with your union to ensure that you and your coworkers work in a safe environment. If you are a union member, you can also make suggestions to your union for improving contract language relating to safety conditions.

As a union member, you have a right to expect that your union representatives represent your interests and ensure that the company provides a safe workplace. If you are dissatisfied with the type of service your union provides, you can run for union office or vote for different union members to hold leadership positions.

*See also* Law in the Workplace; Work Hazards; Work Hazards: Chemical.

## Bibliography

Bacow, L.S. (1980). *Bargaining for job safety and health.* Cambridge, MA: MIT Press.

DeClercq, N. (1990). *Joint safety and health committees: A union member's guide.* University Park, PA: Pennsylvania State University, Department of Labor Studies and Industrial Relations.

*Labor Studies Journal.* (1981, Spring). 6: 82–94. Various articles discuss job hazards from the point of view of union members. Topics covered include job stress, impact of job hazards on women and minority workers, and regulatory policies. A resource guide is included.

Mintz, B. W. (1984). *OSHA: history, law, and policy.* Washington, DC: Bureau of National Affairs.

*Occupational health & safety.* (all issues). Waco, TX: Stevens Publishing Corp. Articles deal with a variety of job hazards. Each issue contains updates on current legal and technical issues plus information on new health and safety products.

Stellman, J. M., & Daum, S. M. (1983). *Work is dangerous to your health.* New York: Vintage Books. A handbook detailing the many health hazards in the workplace and what workers can do to protect themselves.

—HELEN ELKISS

# WORK HAZARDS: TOOL DESIGN

To avoid being hazardous, tools and jobs should be designed to lower the risk of fatigue and repetitive trauma disorders and to minimize repeated and sustained exertions, forceful exertions, localized mechanical stresses, posture stresses, exposure to low temperatures, and vibration.

## Relationship to Work

Most jobs require the use of hand tools, anything from pencils to wrenches. Technological advances have resulted in replacement of the pencil by the keyboard and of manual wrenches by powered wrenches; these advancements, along with specialization of labor, have resulted in benefits of increased production and quality. In some cases, increased stresses for tool users have occurred also. Workers may spend eight or more hours per day with the same tool in hand performing the same job again and again. Such work patterns have been associated with worker health complaints ranging from localized fatigue to chronic muscle, tendon and nerve disorders, often referred to as "repetitive trauma disorders" or "repetitive motion illness." The symptoms of these disorders include persistent and recurring aching, burning, tingling, and numbness. Persons experiencing these disorders often complain of pain, clumsiness, and dropping things, or they may have trouble sleeping due to pain and numbness.

Work-related causes of repetitive trauma disorders include:

- Repeated or sustained exertions
- Forceful exertions
- Localized mechanical stresses
- Certain postures
- Low temperatures
- Vibration

These factors may act individually or collectively to create a problem. Unfortunately, there are not yet standards for these factors, either individually or in combination with one another, for the prevention of cumulative trauma disorders. It suffices to say that combinations and extremes of these factors should be avoided and that each should be systematically evaluated when problems develop.

## Hand Tool and Work Design

It is often possible to reduce the risk of cumulative trauma disorders by redesigning the tools used, the way in which they are used, or the work station at which they are used. Some of the major factors that should be considered include:

**Repeated and Sustained Exertions.** The durations and frequency of exertions are related to the capacity of the tool. The capacity of electric and air powered tools usually can be determined from manufacturer's power and speed ratings.

**Forceful Exertions.** The forces required to hold and use a tool are related to the tool weight; handle size and shape; attachment of tools to power lines; handle composition; tool torque settings; and glove use.

**Weight.** The weight of the tool affects the force required to hold and use it. The ideal weight varies from tool to tool. Armstrong, Punnett and Ketner (1989) found that workers preferred tools less than three and one-half pounds for work in automobile trim assembly work.

**Handle Composition.** The handle composition of the tool affects friction, which in turn affects how much force is required to hold and use the tool. Workers once spit on the handles of tools to enhance friction, but the same result can now be achieved by using certain kinds of plastic and rubber handle coverings.

**Handle Size and Shape.** The size and shape of a tool's handle affect the posture of the hand, which in turn affects hand strength. The least effort is required when tools are held in a power grip, which is how a baseball bat or tennis racquet is held. The greatest effort is required when a tool is held in a pinch grip posture. That's how most of us hold a pencil. Forceful exertions can be reduced by selecting tools that are held with a power grip rather than with a pinch grip (see Figure 1.). Although less effort is required to hold a tool with power grip, greater manipulation is possible with a pinch grip.

**Attachment of Tools.** Most industrial grade power tools are attached to an air line, power cord, or flexible shaft to provide power. Some tools are connected to flexible ducts to collect dusts and fumes generated by the tool. Forceful exertions can be reduced by attaching these devices in ways that do not interfere with moving and positioning the tool at all work locations and orientations (see Figure 2).

**Tool Torque.** Power tools that are used to tighten fasteners produce reaction forces as they start and stop. These reaction forces depend on the size of the fastener, the materials into which they are being inserted, and the torque settings of the tools. Forceful exertions can be reduced by using tools with reaction bars or by mounting tools on articulating arms (see Figure 3).

**Figure 1. Forceful exertions can be reduced by avoiding tools that are held with the fingers, a, and selecting tools that can be held with a power grip posture, b.**

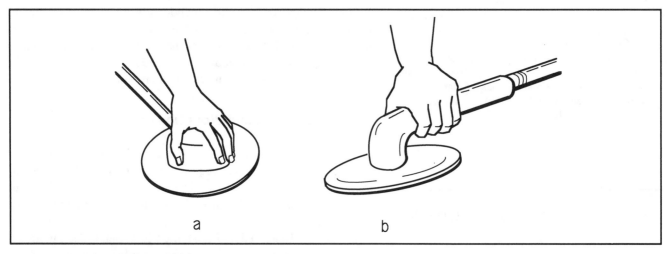

a                                        b

**Figure 2. Forceful exertions due to attachments of air lines, cords, and drive shafts, a, can be reduced by attaching them so that they do not interfere with moving and positioning tool, b.**

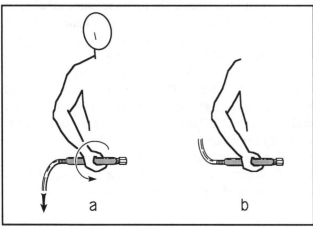

a                    b

**Orientation of Work Surface.** Forceful exertions are affected by the orientation of a work surface. A worker using a tool on a vertical surface will have to support the full weight of the tool, while a horizontal surface would support the weight of the tool. Forceful exertions can be reduced by positioning the work under the tool (see Figure 4).

**Glove Use.** The use of gloves may increase or decrease the strength required to hold and use a tool. Some gloves provide increased friction and reduce the force required to hold and use a tool. The bulk and stiffness of other gloves may interfere with grasping the tool and thus increase the force required to use the tool. Forceful exertions can be reduced by selecting the best fitting gloves for each person and each task. In some cases the fingers should be removed from the gloves, while in other cases just wrapping bare fingers with a medically approved safety tape will improve the grip.

**Figure 3. Forceful exertions required to use power screw drivers and wrenches, a, can be reduced by using tools with reaction bars, b, or mounting tools on articulating arms, c.**

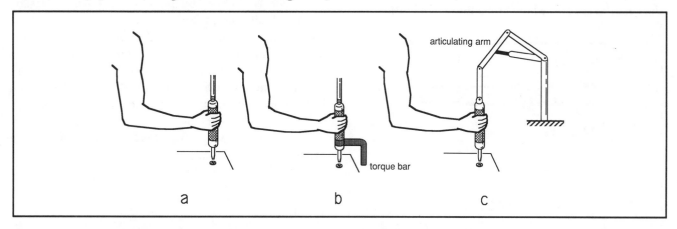

**Figure 4. Forceful exertions to support tools, a, can be reduced by positioning the work under the tool, b.**

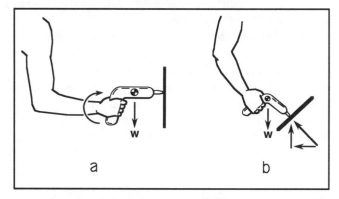

**Figure 5. Localized mechanical stresses can be minimized by selecting tools that do not have hard sharp edges.**

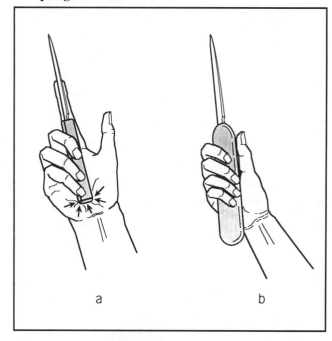

## Localized Mechanical Stresses

These are caused by contact with hard or sharp edges of tools. Examples can be found in the handles of scissors and knives and the throttles of power tools such as screwdrivers and sanders. These stresses can be minimized by selecting tools that do not have hard sharp edges (see Figure 5) or by selecting tools with handles long enough to cross the fleshy areas at the base of the thumb and little fingers (see Figure 6). In some cases these edges can be covered with adhesive or tennis racquet tape and in other cases gloves can be used to protect the hand.

## Posture

The ideal work position of the body is one in which the arm is hanging relaxed at the side of the body. The elbow is close to the torso, the forearm is not rotated to one extreme or the other, the wrist is not deviated side to side, or bent toward the palm, or bent fully backward. While some work postures are more comfortable than others, even the best will eventually become uncomfortable, while even the worst postures can feel good for a short time. For example, most people will be most comfortable working with their arms at the sides of their body rather than above their head. Eventually, however, people working with their arms at the

sides of their body will become uncomfortable and change position. They may even place their arms over the head and stretch. This type of discomfort can be thought of as the body's way of telling us to take a break. The posture required to use a hand tool is related to the location of the work, to the orientation of the work, to the shape of the tool, and to the size of the worker (see Figure 7).

## Low Temperature

These exposures can be reduced by covering the hand, insulating the tool handle, warming parts, and directing exhaust air from tools away from the worker. The effects of cold environments can be diminished by dressing in warm clothes.

**Figure 6. Localized mechanical stresses can be minimized when the handles are long enough to cross the fleshy areas at the base of the thumb and little fingers.**

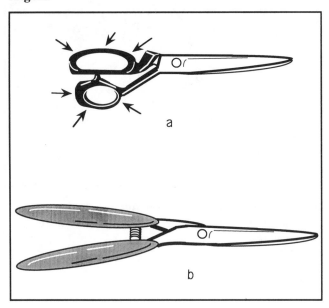

*Tool Vibration*

This is produced by the action of tool abrasives, by worn and unbalanced drive trains, and by certain torque regulators. Beyond recommending regular tool maintenance, control of vibration goes beyond the scope of this article. Vibration measurements require sophisticated instrumentation. Also, how much a tool vibrates depends on how it is used. At this time, manufacturers do not routinely report how much their tools vibrate under given conditions. While many tools are marketed as "low vibration," it often is hard to get supporting data.

## Application

Not all aches or pains indicate that a worker has a chronic muscle, tendon, or nerve disorder. A certain amount of discomfort can be a natural part of any human activity. Short-term discomfort and performance changes caused by exertion of the body are referred to as localized fatigue. Localized fatigue develops and recovers in seconds, minutes, or hours. As a general rule, experienced workers should not be experiencing aches and pains at the beginning of a work shift resulting from the previous shift. If they do, and if this occurs for more than a few days, they should seek

**Figure 7. Stressful postures required to hold and use tools, a and d, can be reduced by reorienting the work, b and e, or by relocating the work, c and f.**

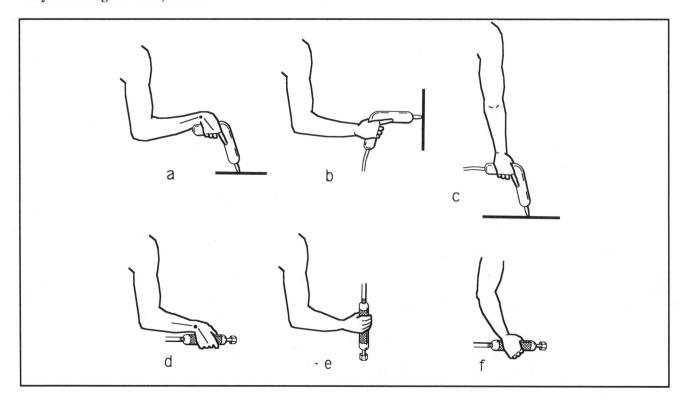

medical attention to determine if the symptoms are due to fatigue or to cumulative trauma disorders. In either case, tools and jobs should be designed to minimize repeated and sustained exertions, forceful exertions, localized mechanical stresses, posture stresses, exposure to low temperatures, and vibration. In this way, it should be possible to design jobs to achieve the highest level of productivity, while minimizing risk of fatigue and cumulative trauma disorders.

*See also* Law in the Workplace; Repetitive Motion Illnesses; Work Hazards: Ergonomic; Work Hazards: Physical.

## Bibliography

Armstrong, T. (1983). *An ergonomics guide to carpal tunnel syndrome.* Akron, OH: American Industrial Hygiene Association.

Armstrong, T., Punnett, L., & Ketner, P. (1989). Subjective worker assessments of hand tools used in automobile assembly. *American Industrial Hygiene Association Journal*, 50: 639–45.

Putz-Anderson, V. (1988). *Cumulative trauma disorders, a manual for musculoskeletal diseases of the upper limbs.* New York: Taylor and Francis.

## For Further Information

**National Institute for Occupational Safety and Health (NIOSH)**
Technical Information Branch
4676 Columbia Parkway
Cincinnati, OH 45226-1998
(513) 533-8328

—Thomas J. Armstrong

# WORK VALUES

Work values are deep and underlying beliefs that influence an individual's occupational choices. These beliefs indicate what an individual feels is important, and are fairly stable throughout the life span. Work values are a more basic dimension of work needs. Work needs are the requirements for rewards that individuals have of their work. If those requirements are met, those individuals will be satisfied.

Work values are a smaller subset of life values, which are those beliefs that are freely chosen, prized, publicly affirmed, chosen from alternatives, acted upon, and acted upon consistently (Sukiennik, Bendat, & Raufman, 1989). Thus, an individual's values are those beliefs that have been actively chosen, about which the individual feels strongly, and which the individual is willing to support in public.

## Relationship to Career Choice/Work

Clarification of work values and needs is extremely important to the career choice process. Values are often the basis for decisions, yet many individuals do not have a clear idea of what exactly their work values are. In making a career choice, individuals often place emphasis on assessing their skills and abilities. This is appropriate in making an initial entry into the job or career. However, knowledge and assessment of work values is important in staying in the job. Working in an environment in which work values are matched and work needs are met is an important part of job satisfaction.

Work values and needs fall into several different areas (Dawis & Lofquist, 1984):

1. *Achievement.* A strong value placed on accomplishment and achievement by the individual.
2. *Autonomy.* A strong value placed on being left free to create on one's own, and making decisions without influence or interference from others.
3. *Comfort.* A strong value placed on job security, pay, good working conditions, being busy, and having a lot of variety in the work.
4. *Safety.* A strong value placed on fair practices, and appropriate supervision, from a technical perspective as well as a human relations perspective (being trained well for a position as well as the boss supporting workers with management).
5. *Status.* A strong value placed on opportunity for advancement, recognition from others, authority over others, and feeling social status in the community.
6. *Altruism.* A strong value placed on helping others, being friendly with coworkers, and feeling the work is morally correct.

Work values may be assessed using values inventories, exercises (examples given below), or through counseling interviews (Yost & Corbishley, 1987). Examples of values inventories are the *Minnesota Importance Questionnaire* (Weiss, Dawis, & Lofquist, 1981), the *Work Values Inventory* (Super, 1970), and the *Values Scale (Super & Neville, 1986)*. These inventories are reviewed in Kapes and Mastie (1988).

The work environment will provide individuals with rewards as a part of their job. Those rewards may be environmental rewards, social rewards, or self rewards. Environmental rewards may be good working conditions, secure position or job, good lighting, good temperature control, variety of tasks to do in a day, and fair compensation. Social rewards (or rewards that come from interactions with people) may be the opportunity for recognition and advancement, managing one or more people, helping others, or having close social relationships with coworkers. Self rewards may come from giving an individual the opportunity to achieve, to accomplish a task, to be creative, and to make decisions autonomously.

Once individuals have clarified their work values (i.e., what they need in a job), then they must find an occupation, career, or job that will meet their needs and provide them with the rewards they find most satisfying. If, for example, an individual finds he or she places a strong value on having good close relationships with coworkers, the person would not be satisfied working as the sole worker in a laboratory.

## Application

In clarifying your work values and needs, it is important that you spend some time analyzing what is important to you. Some ways to do this are:

1. Make a list of all your work experiences. List what you liked and did not like (particularly did not like) about that job or work experience. If you do not have a work history, make a list of activities or volunteer activities and write down what you liked about the activity or experience. For example, did you like the camaraderie with coworkers, the feeling of being useful, the pay? Maybe you didn't like punching a time clock, having to wait on people, or having a boss looking over your shoulder.

   Once you have a list of "likes" and "don't likes," look them over to determine if any pattern begins to emerge. Are there specific needs that you have that have never been met in a job? Or that you thought were not important, but suddenly you find they are?

2. Make a list of the needs and values given above, each on a separate notecard. Sort the cards into at least three piles: Very Important, Important, and Not Important. If you wish, you may resort and make more than three piles. Make a list of those needs and values that are most important to you, and whether you have ever had any of those met in a job or activity. Begin to search for occupations that provide those rewards that you need or value.

3. Values can often become clearer if you imagine yourself free of day-to-day decisions. For example, imagine you are 85 years old. What would you like to be able to say about yourself as you look back on your life?

4. The last exercise often leads individuals to carefully examine the relationship between work and life values. As you think about your life values, think about how you want them to influence your work values. Are they the same? Do you have some values that differ?

5. Another exercise is to ask yourself what role you want work to play in your life. Often, individuals get caught in the rush of routine, and make decisions that are not consonant with their values. Stop to ask yourself if work is playing the role you want it to play in your life? Are you working more than you want to work? Less? Is it demanding enough? Too much? Does your work allow you to live the way you want to live?

*See also* Career Roles; Choosing an Occupation; Job Satisfaction; Trait-Factor Approach to Career Choice.

## Bibliography

Carney, C. G., & Wells, C. F. (1987). *Career planning: Skills to build your future.* 2nd ed. Monterey, CA: Brooks/Cole. A good book with many useful exercises for those making career decisions.

Dawis, R. D., & Lofquist, L. H. (1984). *A psychological theory of work adjustment: An individual differences model and its applications.* Minneapolis, MN: University of Minnesota. An authoritative explanation of the interrelationship between an individual's work values and needs and those rewards or reinforcers provided by the work environment. Discusses how individuals adjust to their environment. Excellent discussion for the practitioner.

Kapes, J. T., & Mastie, M. M. (Eds.) (1988). *A counselor's guide to career assessment instruments.* 2nd. ed. Alexandria, VA: National Career Development Association.

Sukiennik, D., Bendat, W., & Raufman, L. (1989). *The career fitness program: Exercising your options.* 2nd. ed. Scottsdale, AZ: Gorsuch Scarisbrick. Excellent source of exercises and thought-provoking activities. Useful for the practitioner as well as the do-it-yourselfer.

Super, D.E., (1970). *Work Values Inventory.* Boston: Houghton Mifflin.

Super, D.E. & Neville, D.D. (1986). *Values Scale.* Palo Alto, CA: Consulting Psychologists Press.

Weiss, D.J., Dawis, R.V., & Lofquist, L.H. (1981). *Minnesota Importance Questionnaire.* Minneapolis: Vocational Psychology Research.

Yost, E.B., & Corbishley, M.A. (1987). *Career counseling: A psychological approach.* San Francisco: Jossey-Bass. A wonderful source for career counselors, this book summarizes and presents an integrative, balanced model for career counseling.

—NADYA A. FOUAD

## WORKAHOLISM

As recently as 30 years ago, "work" was something of a dirty word, as in "*My* wife will never have to go out and work, thank God!" Even 20 years ago, the term workaholic was used to describe a weirdo—usually male—who voluntarily kept his nose to the grindstone when his colleagues were well into their second martinis. All in all, it was abundantly clear to most folks that one worked because one had to—to put food on the table and a roof over the heads of one's dependents—and worked only as long as was absolutely necessary to achieve those objectives. The family was the indisputable core of life, and work was something undertaken primarily by men to bring home the bacon, buy the wife a mink, and get the kids' teeth straightened.

In the 1940s, however, through their participation in the war effort, women began to discover the enormous personal, as well as financial satisfaction to be derived from work outside the home. In ever-growing numbers over the next two decades, housewives abandoned their kitchens to discover that not only was working in law, finance, or marketing a whole lot more interesting than cooking and cleaning, but employers were actually willing to pay them to do these things. Also, the recognition afforded in the workplace was beguiling. Women who went out to work were perceived as "doing something" with their lives. They were in the mainstream, involved, with it, while those who remained voluntarily unemployed became objects of thinly veiled scorn.

Thus, the trend was launched. Work evolved—not insidiously, not stealthily, but openly and with the enthusiastic support of both sexes—into the central defining element of our identities: At work, we are somebody. People notice what we wear, how we do our hair, a new scent or attache case. At home, they mostly don't. At work, people listen to our opinions, react, agree or disagree with gusto. At home, we may be largely ignored by equally job-involved spouses. When we do something well on the job, it seems as if the whole world knows it. The fact that they also know when we do something badly and get chewed out by our superiors only adds spice to the adventure. Work is challenging, difficult, and on bad days, the frustrations can seem endless. But on good days, when the adrenaline surges and the ideas click, there's no excitement to beat it.

Today, as never before, work has become the focus of adult life. We are struggling as a society and as individuals to accommodate the high priority now given to career issues by spouses, other family members, friends, colleagues, and ourselves. Sheer numbers and the consequent narrowing of opportunity at every upward rung of the organizational ladder, have compelled the baby boom generation to do more, to move faster, to compete harder. The signs of increased stress are legion and have been intensified by an economic climate which mandates that if we marry at all, we marry a working spouse.

To an extraordinary extent, "what we do" has become "who we are," with an undeniable ripple effect on the rest of our lives. The emotional and demographic repercussions have been dramatic. Job-involved adults of both sexes find it difficult to establish and maintain friendships, marriages, and families. Child rearing has become a primarily commercial endeavor conducted by daycare professionals.

Communities suffer as voluntarism and grass-roots political activities reach all-time lows. Clearly, the time has come to put work in its place—to stop seeking self-fulfillment almost exclusively within the workplace.

"The trouble with the rat race," says comedienne Lily Tomlin, tersely summarizing the conclusion to which millions of her contemporaries have also come, "is that even if you win, you're still a rat." We are finally beginning to rethink earlier choices, to recognize the wealth of options now available, and to remember that the point of having options is to exercise them now and again.

## Application

The first step is usually a personal redefinition of "success" to include satisfactions and rewards outside of one's paid work. Instead of choosing a rigid, linear path to career success, it is possible to combine a variety of rewarding endeavors, both paid and unpaid, that reflect the individual's personal values instead of an all-consuming drive to accumulate wealth. A satisfying career is definitely on the agenda for most, but when to work, at what, and for how long are individual choices. It's a matter of re-evaluating priorities periodically.

While work choices can be made and remade throughout one's adult life as priorities change, such compromises involve some measure of personal or financial sacrifice. Conventional wisdom has it that you can't have it all; but I believe that you *can* have it all, but not simultaneously. When raising a family and participating in community life are tops on one's list, the sacrifices are financial and choices include:

- Working only part-time (see **Job Sharing; Part-Time Work**).
- Working not at all until small children enter school (see **Sequencing: A Career and Traditional Mothering**).
- Dividing child-rearing responsibilities with a spouse or significant other (see **Dual-Career Families; Work Family Issues**).
- Changing to a job with predictable hours, more vacation and personal leave time, and benefits more suited to the person juggling home and job responsibilities.
- Declining transfers and relocations that uproot families.

When career interests take precedence, the sacrifices are primarily personal and choices include:

- Working/studying longer hours for a stated duration to achieve a specific career objective.
- Delegating more domestic responsibility to paid help, thus swapping money for time.

- Investing time/energy in a concentrated search for more stimulating, better-paid work.
- Putting nonessential family/social commitments on the back burner temporarily.

The quest to achieve more balance between work and home life is leading many into entrepreneurial pursuits. In growing numbers, men and women are choosing to manage small businesses that offer more control over, and flexibility within, their lives as a whole. This option is daily more viable thanks to the advent of telecommunication, which has given rise to thousands of small businesses that are conducted almost entirely by computer. Working for oneself has become the job of choice for millions of Americans who have put together the precise elements of schedule, compensation, challenge, self-esteem, creativity, and whatever else adds up to exactly the right combination for them. In fact, the many baby boomers who have already abandoned corporate careers and established their own businesses are largely responsible for the new job opportunities now open to their former peers in the corporate trenches (see **Self-Employment**).

Workaholism is most often, after all, a self-imposed way of life. The true workaholic is generally enamored of the idea of work itself, loves work, and resents being dragged away from it. Increasingly, though, even dedicated workaholics are acknowledging the severe limitations of their life styles and are consciously choosing to change their ways. We are beginning to see a backlash as more and more workaholics wake up to the negative effects of such single-minded existences.

The work ethic of the past two decades is thus being supplanted by one that puts work in its place—and keeps it there—encouraging people at all stages of life to plan for a more balanced and personally rewarding future.

*See also* Burnout; Dual-Career Families; Job Sharing; Part-Time Work; Perfectionism: Overcoming; Rational Thinking; Relocation; Self-Esteem; Sequencing: A Career and Traditional Mothering; Time Management; Type A Behavior Pattern; Working Family Issues.

## Bibliography

Aronson, E., & Pines, A. (1988). *Career burnout*. New York: Macmillan and Co. Insights into the causes of career burnout and ideas for its prevention and cure.

Cole, D. W. (1981). *Professional suicide*. New York: McGraw-Hill Book Co. How talented, hard-driving middle managers can avoid burnout, ennui, and other career destroyers for super achievers.

Ebel, H., & Sprankle, J. K. (1987). *The workaholic syndrome*. New York: Walker and Company. Practical advice on how to keep work in proper perspective as you go through the various stages of your life.

Levinson, J. C. (1979). *Earning money without a job*. New York: Holt Rinehart Winston. How to piece together manageable, achievable components of an independent working life.

Lieberoff, A. (1982). *Climb your own ladder*. New York: Simon & Schuster. A practical guide to starting and building one of a dozen suggested self-owned businesses as a profitable and rewarding alternative to salaried employment for self-starters.

Machlowitz, M. (1980). *Workaholics*. Reading, MA: Addison-Wesley. What's wrong, and what's right, with being a workaholic; how workaholics get that way; making the tendency work for you, not against you.

—JUDITH K. SPRANKLE

# WORKERS' COMPENSATION

Workers' compensation is the legal system governing the liability of employers for the work injuries and diseases of their employees. It is the original "no-fault" liability system in that employers are liable for medical care and cash benefits to injured workers without regard to who was at fault in causing the injury. In exchange for this automatic employer liability for work injuries, employees are limited to a statutorily defined benefit that is usually less than a worker would have gotten in a successful lawsuit against a negligent employer.

While primarily a mechanism through which employees are indemnified *after* their work injuries occur, the system also has important implications for how many injuries occur. By penalizing employers for work injuries (through the benefit requirement), the system may create incentives to invest in accident and disease prevention, and thus reduce the number of injuries and diseases that occur.

## Relationship to Work

As with any of life's activities, work inevitably involves a substantial degree of danger. In exchange for such work rewards as pay and fulfillment, individuals tolerate such negative features as danger and reduced control of one's time. Of course any worker seeks employment situations where the various rewards outweigh its negative attributes by the greatest possible amount. The chances of being involved in an accident are to a substantial degree determined by the inherent nature of the work; building bridges or playing professional football are fundamentally more dangerous than teaching classes or writing novels. However, employers and employees typically have a substantial degree of control over the danger of a particular work situation. Employers can influence the degree of danger through means such as purchasing safety equipment, slowing down the pace of work, and providing effective safety training to supervisors and employees. Employees can also influence the degree of danger by using careful work practices, availing themselves of available safety equipment, and voicing their concerns about safety to management or their union.

One of the two key goals of workers' compensation is to provide a degree of financial security to injured workers or their survivors. If an individual is injured in the course of his or her employment, the employer is obligated to provide all medical care costs associated with the injury and cash payments for the length of the disability. The knowledge that such benefits must be paid in the event of an injury is the key to the second goal of workers' compensation—injury prevention. Since an employer must pay these benefits, it is hoped that the desire to avoid such payments will give employers an incentive to invest in prevention, thereby creating a safer workplace. Because the direct regulation of safety through the use of safety standards, inspectors, and penalties (OSHA) has not appeared to be very effective, the incentive approach of workers' compensation potentially plays a very important role in creating safer work environments (see **Work Hazards**).

Every state has its own workers' compensation system, with each operating under the same basic no-fault principles. There is no federal legislation (other than for its own employees, longshore workers, and seamen) or guidelines. The various state laws vary substantially in their operational details, including the procedures for processing cases and resolving disputes, as well as the level of benefits paid to injured workers (see **Climate for Workers**). Many employers choose to supplement the state-mandated benefit, but they are not required to do so.

## Application

The nature of the system is best understood by examining what happens if you incur a work injury such as back pain resulting from lifting. If such an incident occurs, you will be sent to a physician for evaluation (states vary as to whether the employee can choose the doctor). The doctor might advise some treatment and rest, and perhaps two weeks off from work. You may be asked to come back to the doctor after the two weeks for evaluation by the physician. The company will pay all of the medical expenses associated by this incident and, in turn, will be reimbursed by its insurance company. (In every state, employers are required to insure their workers' compensation liability—this is typically done through a private insurance carrier, although larger companies may self-insure. Some states have a state-owned insurance carrier that has a monopoly or competes with private carriers.)

For the period you are out of work, the first three to seven days (depending on the state law) will be without pay. After this "waiting period," you will receive a cash benefit of, typically, $66^2/_3\%$ of lost wages, up to a specified maximum. After you have been out for a period of time (5 to 28 days), the cash benefit will be paid retroactively to the first day of lost work. If you are unable to return to work, these temporary benefits will continue until the point of maximum medical improvement, at which point benefits for a permanent disability (either partial or total) are available.

States assess eligibility for permanent disability in a variety of ways based on either the actual wage loss, the degree of physical impairment, or the loss of earning capacity. These assessments are the most controversial aspect of the workers' compensation system. Permanent total cases are fortunately quite rare, accounting for only .15 of all cases that involve cash benefits. Twenty-four percent of cases are for a permanent-partial disability, but these incidents account for about 69% of benefits paid.

*See also* Climate for Workers; Disability: Adjustment to; Law in the Workplace; Social Security Disability Claim; Work Hazards.

## Bibliography

Berkowitz, M., & Burton, J.F. (1987). *Permanent partial benefits in workers' compensation*. Kalamazoo, MI: Upjohn Institute for Employment Research. This is an analysis of permanent partial disabilities in 10 states. The book ends with substantive suggestions for how this controversial aspect of workers' compensation might be reformed.

Chelius, J. (Ed.) (1986). *Current issues in workers' compensation*. Kalamazoo, MI: Upjohn Institute for Employment Research. This is a collection of essays by many of the leading experts in workers' compensation. The focus is on the states' responses to the substantial increases in workers' compensation costs that have occurred since 1973.

Chelius, J., & Smith, R. (1987). *Small business and the financing of workers' compensation: Issues, evidence, and options*. Washington, DC: NFIB Foundation. This is an examination of three key issues of workers' compensation: competition among workers' compensation insurance companies, self-insurance by groups of small businesses, and the effects of using experience-rated insurance premiums on workplace safety.

U.S. Chamber of Commerce (1990). *1990 analysis of workers compensation laws*. Washington, DC: Chamber of Commerce of the United States. An annual summary of the provisions of workers' compensation laws in the United States and Canada.

—JAMES CHELIUS

# WORKING FAMILY ISSUES

Today's families are revising traditional expectations about work and family life. Currently, more than half of all couples in the United States are employed. This means that the new "typical" American family is a "working family" where both parents are employed and where choices about jobs, work schedules, and other work issues will affect all members of the family. Moreover, work continuity and success will depend on the adult's abilities to balance his or her role as spouse, parent, and employee.

Five family and personal issues can significantly impact on career choices and career continuity in working families: (a) couple's attitudes toward wife's employment, (b) sharing housework responsibilities, (c) perception of self, (d) financial considerations, and (e) impact of children on career. Each of these issues can be discussed between partners or between clients and career counselors.

## Couple's Attitudes to Wife's Employment

When employed women marry, they often choose to change career paths from full-time to part-time work, from high-status to low-status jobs and from nontraditional careers to traditional "female" careers. What attitudes of the husband or wife might lead to this status change? Whether a husband views his wife's employment as competitive with his own career achievement or enhancing the family's occupational prestige may affect his wife's choices about employment. The wife's attitudes of dependence, her perception that her career is secondary to his, or her desire to be home with young children also may affect her work-related choices. In fact, when husbands are supportive of their wives' careers, couples are happier with both their careers and their marriages, and wives work for higher wages and greater status.

*Application*

Your attitude can affect your partner's performance, achievement, and continuity. In addressing issues related to attitudes about wife's employment, you may want to focus on three important concerns.

1. *Clarify goals.* Discussions between spouses may focus on benefits which accrue to the family because of each spouse's employment. To do this, it is essential that you get to know yourself. Are you working for money? Achievement? Prestige? Adult companionship? Do you view your work as a long-term career or a temporary job? (See **Career Roles**).
2. *Spousal Support.* Once you have defined your goals, both husband and wife can begin to develop a support system. This can mean discussing practical

and psychological reasons for working and defining the demands and benefits achieved by career choices. When both spouses work, financial responsibilities may be shared, and, ideally, other family demands may also be jointly pursued.

3. *Recognize gender stereotypes which hamper employment.* You may want to examine and redefine traditional definitions of "masculine" and "feminine." This may require great innovation since most employed parents know of no role models who balanced or shared roles as coparents and coproviders (see **Sex-Role Stereotyping**).

## Sharing Household Responsibilities

An overwhelming majority of men are supportive of the idea of helping their employed wives with household chores. Practically, however, employed wives still do the lion's share of the housework, performing about 20 hours of housework per week as compared to the 5 to 10 hours of housework performed by husbands. This greater involvement at home may place employed wives at a career disadvantage, interfering with their career involvement and ultimate success. Husbands and wives differ in their perceptions of "his" involvement at home and may have different housekeeping standards, suggesting that wives and husbands may also differ in their beliefs about the equitability of the division of household responsibilities.

*Application*

In discussing the issue of shared housework, you may want to focus on three issues.

1. *Communicating Household Needs.* This is particu larly relevant to women. Generally wives assume primary responsibility for the household. If you wish to establish a more equitable arrangement, you may need to supportively explain why your husband's household assistance is insufficient, since husbands may be unaware that their household contribution is not equitable.
2. *Workplace expectations.* For mutual understanding, both spouses should attempt clear discussions of personal needs for career success, of conflicts between housework and career advancement, and of sharing financial responsibilities at work and household responsibilities at home. While wives may need more household help to advance in their careers, husbands may find that helping at home can significantly impact on their career success. Discussing the various advantages and disadvantages of equitable sharing is essential for the working family.

3. *Recognizing personal patterns.* Ideally, couples should try to jointly establish standards for household responsibilities and then let the spouse perform responsibilities according to his or her patterns. Standards for your household and for equitable sharing is what feels right to you. Flexibility and appreciation are the hallmarks of equitable sharing of household chores (see **Time Management**).

## Perception of Self

A positive self-image can significantly impact on employment success. Among workers, self-confidence and self-reliance are related to positive achievements in the workforce. Interestingly, employed women and women who are at home see themselves differently. Women who are employed full-time view themselves as more self-reliant, self-confident, and self-sufficient; whereas full-time homemakers view themselves as more nurturant, dependent, nervous, and emotional (see **Career Identity; Self-Esteem**).

### Application

Achieving positive self-regard can be critical to how others perceive you and can affect achievement within the workplace. Three techniques can be particularly helpful for viewing yourself more positively.

1. *Cognitive Restructuring.* This involves altering the way that you think about your goals and expectations. Instead of saying, "I can't do anything," take a more positive approach. For example, you can say, "Last time, I couldn't do it, but I'll try again, and perhaps next time, I will do better" (see **Rational Thinking; Self-Talk**).
2. *Listing Positive Personal Achievements.* Take time to jot down some of your recent activities. You may want to include volunteer or business achievements and at-home successes. Your spouse can help you identify your positive achievements.
3. *Re-evaluate Past Failures.* Review past problems. Think about what went wrong and how you might do it better next time. Then your poorer performance can be construed as another learning experience, not a failure.

## Financial Considerations

At some point in their worklives, many couples consider the possibility of the wife's work slowdown to accommodate the needs of the household and/or young children. The slowdowns can have serious lifetime financial impact on working families. Continuously employed wives have the highest wages and most prominent positions

at midlife as compared to their peers who are not employed continuously. Women who marry late, however, and take relatively short breaks from the workforce may suffer relatively little compared to their continuously employed peers.

### Application

Essential financial considerations for working families may include the following:

1 *Long-Term Financial Consequences of Different Employment Choices.* If you choose to pursue less demanding positions, calculate the long-term financial implications of your decisions and collect information on skills and experience which would be necessary to eventually get back on track. Alternatively, if you choose to pursue full-time dual-employment, calculate the financial and personal costs of related services like day care or home care, after-school babysitting, additional household help, and so on. Comprehensive information allows you to make more realistic financial choices.
2. *Timing and Length of Time Off for Children.* If you would like to be home with young children, careful planning can minimize the impact of time off on lifetime financial and career achievements. Where possible, keeping in touch with colleagues, attending professional conferences during your leave, and limiting time away from work can minimize long-term financial losses (see **Sequencing: A Career and Traditional Mothering**).
3. *Mediating Factors.* Education and volunteer experiences can affect workforce earnings. You can master a variety of skills necessary to advance in your career through volunteer experiences.
4. *Balance of Family Finances.* If you choose to work less than full-time, then the balance of financial responsibility as well as other responsibilities within the family may change. Your spouse may feel greater financial burdens and may no longer be able or willing to participate in household chores with a partner who is not working full-time.

## Impact of Children on Careers

Parents are often concerned about the impact of their employment schedules on children's cognitive, social, and emotional development. Moreover, both fathers and mothers are concerned with building a closer relationship with their children. Among mothers of young children, factors like women's positive attitudes toward employment of married women, women's sense that their children do not need exclusive parenting by the mother, and women's positive career commitment are all associated with continued labor force participation. Contemporary financial realities will make it difficult, if not impossible, for many women to remain at home with their babies or young children, meaning that effectively balancing the needs of children and work will be a critical issue for many working families (see **Child Care**).

### Application

Parents of older children may find they have limited time with their children, leading to feelings of stress and guilt.

1. *Plan Special Time*. Reserve time to be with your children according to your schedule. This may be one evening a week or one evening a month, but make it regular.
2. *Talk and Listen to Your Children*. Tell them about your work and why it's important to you and to the family. Let them talk to you about things that are important to them.

Two particularly important resources for employed mothers of young children are:

1. *Support Groups*. Organizing support groups at home or at work can help new mothers express and deal with feelings like their babies' exclusive need for them. Sharing views with other parents can be a tremendous source of strength and creative ideas.
2. *Family Support*. Both verbal and physical support from husbands can help new mothers feel a shared burden of responsibility and modulate misgivings about work and family choices. Additionally, having extra help and support from grandparents and other family members can relieve the stress and guilt of employed mothers.

### How Career Counselors Can Help You

Career counselors can offer information and help you develop personal insight and master skills associated with career success.

1. *Negotiation and Communication*. These skills are important if you want to effectively express your opinion and have others consider altering their perspectives. Negotiation and communication are essential for discussions with spouses, children, and employers (see **Career Counseling; Negotiation**).
2. *Perception of Work World*. Recognizing job limitations and career goals can foster personal satisfaction and help you make informed career or family choices.
3. *Feelings about Leaving Children*. To work effectively, it is important to develop positive ways to deal with both guilt over leaving young children and

conflict about the often mutually exclusive demands of work and family. Counselors can help you master time management skills and organizational skills so you can plan more balanced lives.
4. *Work Slowdowns*. Discussions in counseling can focus on expressing feelings about work and family roles, and achieving congruence, where possible, between attitudes and work or family choices. Additionally, career counselors can offer information about options like flextime, job sharing, or part-time work, or strategies for negotiating work options.

### Conclusions

Couples who are part of working families need creative new approaches to balance their many roles. These approaches may be developed between the spouses, in consultation with a career counselor or in group discussions with other working families. The important issue is for you to view your working family as a system where the actions of each person affect the decisions and successes of every other member of the family. Remember, your choices can affect the standards, perspectives, and expectations of the "American Family" as we move into the twenty-first Century.

*See also* Career Counseling; Career Identity; Career Roles; Dual-Career Families; Negotiation; Rational Thinking; Self-Esteem; Self-Talk; Sequencing: A Career and Traditional Mothering; Sex-Role Stereotyping; Time Management.

### Bibliography

Brooks, A.A. (1989). *Children of fast-track parents*. New York: Viking Penguin, Inc. Based on interviews with parents, children, and professionals, this book offers insights into the relationships between parents and children in dual-professional couples. Although the focus of the book is on "fast-track" couples, Brooks' perspectives on parenting, building self-esteem in children, and finding a balance between family and career demands will be significant for all working families.

Hochschild, A. (1989). *The second shift*. Penguin. Hochschild interviewed a series of two-career couples to investigate the balance of participation by husbands and wives in household and family-related chores. A case study method is used to discuss issues like couple interactions, gender stereotypes, and equitability of family sharing.

Sekaran, U. (1986). *Dual-career families: Contemporary organizational and counseling issues*. Sekaran provides creative ideas for addressing family and career issues. Particularly directed to corporate managers.

—MARIAN STOLTZ-LOIKE

# WORKSPACE

Workspace is the physical setting in which individuals, groups, and organizations carry out work-related activities. Typically, workspace refers to office rather than manufacturing settings, and involves knowledge work more than the actual production of goods. It can, however, be applied to any kind of work setting.

## Relationship to Work

How workspace is planned, designed, and managed can affect productivity, employee satisfaction, communication processes, innovation, and employee health and comfort (Becker, 1990; Brill, 1984; Vischer,1989). Aspects of the workspace that research has shown to be especially important for effective communication processes and innovation are the distances between offices (Allen, 1977) and the nature and the location of support spaces such as conference rooms, copy machines, mail, and coffee lounges (Becker, 1990). The design of lighting, temperature, ventilation systems, and good seating has been shown to significantly affect employee comfort and health (Vischer, 1989). Workspace can, therefore, contribute to the effectiveness of an individual and group and to one's own job satisfaction.

**Planning Processes.** While the physical design of the workspace is important, the processes through which it is planned and managed over time also affect employee effectiveness and environmental satisfaction (Becker, 1990; Steele, 1986). A key issue in today's workplace is the manner and extent to which all employees are involved in decisions about the design of the workspace and how it is used over time. There are a number of ways in which greater employee involvement in workspace decisions contributes to an organization's success:

1. *Environment-Behavior Fit.* Increases the likelihood that the workspace design supports actual work patterns and work requirements.
2. *Employee Commitment.* Strengthens employee commitment to whatever decisions are made; creates "buy-in" to decisions.
3. *Cost Reduction.* Minimizes the potential for spending money on furniture, equipment, and design features that are only weakly linked to effectiveness, satisfaction, or health.

Well-designed workspace and planning processes benefit both the individual and the organization.

## Application

Although many workspace decisions are made by senior management, and prior to your taking a job, you can still influence the nature of your workspace by:

1. Asking to get involved in any committee or task force that the organization has created to help plan a new building or redesign existing space. If no such groups exist, you might suggest starting one. It is important to focus on how such groups can help everyone "win." Keep in mind that you want to preserve aspects of the current design that work well, as well as change some things that are making it difficult for you and others to work effectively. Pay close attention to how specific aspects of your workspace (e.g., lighting, storage, or the layout of the furniture) make doing your job difficult. Justify your proposals in terms of how proposed changes will enhance effectiveness. Don't just complain!
2. Do an assessment of your own personal work area. What could you rearrange, eliminate, or add that would improve your effectiveness?
3. Do an assessment of the workplace as a whole. Are you taking advantage of all the possibilities available to you?
4. Think about not only how you use your workspace, but when you do. Could you become more effective by changing your time patterns (e.g., coming in a little earlier, or staying a little later, or concentrating on making telephone calls in the afternoon, and doing work requiring more concentration earlier in the morning)?
5. Try working with your colleagues in adjoining or shared space to develop more effective and satisfying work patterns. Initiate discussions to find out if others are experiencing the same problems as you are. Try to develop mutually acceptable solutions that take into consideration different workstyles, different priorities, and different kinds of work.
6. Guerilla warfare rarely works! Talk with your manager and coworkers before making changes that might negatively affect them. Work together to identify what kinds of workspace decisions you can control yourself, and which kind may require higher management approval or professional expertise to implement.
7. Think about your organization's culture. What are its stated values? If it stresses concern for the employee, or empowerment, or driving decisions down to the level where they will be implemented, try relating proposals about changing the workspace to these organizational values.

*See also* Job Satisfaction; Organizational Culture.

# Bibliography

Allen, T. J. (1977). *Managing the flow of technology*. Cambridge, MA: MIT Press. This is a detailed summary of many research studies investigating the relationship between communication processes, physical distance, and innovation in R&D firms.

Becker, F. (1990). *The total workplace: Facilities management and the elastic organization*. New York: Van Nostrand Reinhold. Becker shows how facilities management practices, processes, and designs used in leading-edge companies around the world can help an organization achieve its business objectives.

Brill, M., with S. Margulis and E. Konar. (1984). *Using office design to increase productivity*. Buffalo, NY: Workplace Design and Productivity. This book is essentially a research monograph based on a national survey of American office workers. It relates individual aspects of the workplace, like lighting, seating, and layout of offices to "bottomline" measures of performance and job satisfaction.

Steele, F. (1986). *Making and managing high quality workplaces*. New York: Teachers College Press. Noted organizational consultant Fritz Steele describes ways in which organizations can improve the planning, design, and use of the workplace by creating processes that are more open, more clearly considered, and involve employees to a larger extent.

Vischer, J. (1989). *Environmental quality in offices*. New York: Van Nostrand Reinhold. This book looks at environmental quality issues in offices, and how employee response to them can be measured.

—FRANKLIN BECKER

# Appendix:
# OSHA Regional Offices

**Region I: Connecticut, Maine, Massachusetts, New Hampshire, Rhode Island, and Vermont**
U.S. Department of Labor - OSHA
133 Portland Street, 1st Floor
Boston, MA 02114
617/565-7164

**Region II: New Jersey, New York, and Puerto Rico**
U.S. Department of Labor - OSHA
201 Varrick Street, Room 670
New York, NY 10014
212/337-2325

**Region III: Delaware, District of Columbia, Maryland, Pennsylvania, Virginia, and West Virginia**
U.S. Department of Labor - OSHA
Gateway Building, Suite 2100
3535 Market Street
Philadelphia, PA 19104
215/596-1201

**Region IV: Alabama, Florida, Georgia, Kentucky, Mississippi, North Carolina, South Carolina, and Tennessee**
U.S. Department of Labor - OSHA
1375 Peachtree Street, N.E., Suite 587
Atlanta, GA 30367
404/347-3573

**Region V: Illinois, Indiana, Michigan, Minnesota, Ohio, and Wisconsin**
U.S. Department of Labor - OSHA
230 South Dearborn Street
32nd Floor, Room 3244
Chicago, IL 60604
312/353-2220

**Region VI: Arkansas, Louisiana, New Mexico, Oklahoma, and Texas**
U.S. Department of Labor - OSHA
525 Griffin Street, Room 602
Dallas, TX 75202
241/767-4731

**Region VII: Iowa, Kansas, Missouri, and Nebraska**
U.S. Department of Labor - OSHA
911 Walnut Street, Room 64106
Kansas City, MO 64106
816/426-5861

**Region VIII: Colorado, Montana, North Dakota, South Dakota, Utah, and Wyoming**
U.S. Department of Labor - OSHA
Federal Building, Room 1576
1961 Stout Street
Denver, CO 80204
303/844-3061

**Region IX: American Samoa, Arizona, California, Guam, Hawaii, Nevada, and Trust Territory of the Pacific Islands**
U.S. Department of Labor - OSHA
71 Stevenson Street, Suite 415
San Francisco, CA 94105
415/744-6670

**Region X: Alaska, Idaho, Oregon, and Washington**
U.S. Department of Labor - OSHA
1111 3rd Ave., Suite 715
Seattle, WA 98101-3212
206/442-5930

# Index

*by Linda Webster*

System to Identify Motivated Skills
(SIMS), 291

TABP. *See* Type A behavior pattern
(TABP)
Tandem couple, 329
Targeted mailing, in the job search, 145
TCE. *See* Trichlorethylene (TCE)
Team building, burnout and, 26
Technical preparatory, 229
Technical training, 229-30. *See also*
Apprenticeships
Telephone campaign, in the job search,
145
Temporary employment, 113, 147, 298-
99, 327
Temporary help service (THS), 298
Tenosynovitis, 318
Tension. *See* Stress
Tenure laws, 164
Termination
career planning and, 214
drug testing and, 165-66
due to plant closings and layoffs, 165
federal legislation on, 163-64
fired/laid off, 111-13
good-faith/fair-dealing exception to,
165
implied contract and, 164-65
job search training and, 215
judicial limitations on, 164-65
outplacement and, 214-15
pre-termination planning, 214
protection against, 163-66
public policy exception to, 164
state laws on, 164
tenure laws and, 164
whistleblowing protection from, 165,
323
*Test Critiques,* 59
Testing. *See also* Career tests and
inventories; and names of specific
tests and inventories
AIDS testing, 162, 300-01
card sorts, 60
career counseling and, 59-60
career tests and inventories, 2, 16, 33,
35, 36, 44, 59-60, 66, 125
for disabled individuals, 60
for disadvantaged, 60
drug testing, 156, 165-66, 302-04
genetic testing, 304-06
during hiring process, 156
integrity testing, 306-07
for interests, 59
legal rights regarding, 156, 299
lie detector tests, 156
medical examinations, 156
Myers-Briggs Type Indicator, 189-92
preemployment testing, 156, 299-300
Thinking decision making, in Myers-
Briggs Type Indicator (MBTI), 191

Thomas, L.R., 30
Thompson, W.N., 331
Thought stopping and thought
substitution, 278
THS. *See* Temporary help service (THS)
"Tight building syndrome," 339-40
Time management
analysis of time use, 308
clarification of objectives and, 308
planning for better results, 309-10
techniques for, 308-10
wasted time as lost time, 306-07
TIPS, 74
Tool design
attachment of tools, 350
factors in, 349-52
glove use and, 351
handle size and shape, 350
health difficulties due to, 349, 352-53
localized mechanical stresses and,
351, 352
low temperature and, 351
orientation of work surface, 350, 351
posture and, 351, 352
tool torque, 350, 351
tool vibration and, 352
weight of tool, 349
Toxic substances. *See* Work hazards
Toxoplasmosis, 333
Traditional dual-career family, 101
Training. *See also* Continuing education;
Education
apprenticeships, 199, 229
burnout and professional training, 26
internships, 126-27, 147
in managerial skills, 179
post high school training, 229-30
relationship with work, 35
retraining and career plateauing, 55
sexual harassment prevention, 285
technical training, 229-30
Trait-factor approach
to career choice, 310-12
to occupation choice, 67-68
Transferable skills, 291, 292
Transitions
coping strategies for, 181-82
impact of, 180-81
management of, 180-82
from military to civilian career, 187
process of, 181
from school to work, for students with
disabilities, 91
taking charge, 181-82
taking stock of one's resources for
coping, 181
types of, 180
Travel
fear of flying, 109-11
flextime and, 114
jet lag, 128-29
Trenchfoot, 344

Trichlorethylene (TCE), 339
Triple A/BM, 110-11
Tuberculosis, 333
Twain, Mark, 265
Type A behavior pattern (TABP), 312-13
Type A personality, 265
Type C personality, 265

Ultraviolet radiation, 345
Underemployment, 316-17
Undocumented workers, 122-23
Unemployment
of African Americans, 3
coping activities for, 316-17
definition of, 316
of Hispanic Americans, 118
mental health issues of, 183, 316
of racial groups, 97
of women, 98
Unemployment benefits, 20, 166-67
Unions, 158-59, 163, 168-69, 347-49
United States Department of Defense,
330
United States Department of Economic
Security, 38
United States Department of Education,
249
United States Department of Labor, 36,
38, 157, 158, 159, 168, 169, 218
United States Employment Service, 202
United States State Department, 330
United Way, 38
Universities. *See* Colleges and
universities
Upright sitting, 231, 233
Ury, W., 178
USES *Interest Check List,* 202
USES *Interest Inventory,* 202
USES System, 202
Utility, in decision making, 84

*Valpar Component Work Sample System,*
60
Value Dimensions (Hofstede), 82-83
Values. *See* Work values
*Values Scale,* 353
VALUESEARCH, 74
VDTs. *See* Video display terminals
(VDTs)
Verilli, D.B., 282
Vertical mobility, 50
Veterans, 157, 159, 162, 169
Veterans Administration, 38
Veterans' Readjustment Benefits Act, 157
Vibration, as work hazard, 345
Video display terminals (VDTs), 318-19
Vietnam-era veterans, 157, 159, 162, 169
Vietnam War Veterans' Readjustment
Assistance Act, 159, 162, 164
Vision. *See* Eyes
Vocational choice, Holland's theory of,
319-21. *See also* Career choices;
Occupation, choice of